Present in the Past

SOURCE PROBLEMS IN
AMERICAN HISTORY

CONTRIBUTORS

GEORGE H. DAVIS

JOHN C. RAINBOLT

GERARD H. CLARFIELD

REBECCA BROOKS GRUVER

RICHARD E. ELLIS

JAMES ROGER SHARP

ROBERT D. ACCINELLI

EDWARD PESSEN

CARROLL PURSELL

RALPH E. MANN, II

WILLIAM HANCHETT

EDWARD A. PURCELL, JR.

ROY LUBOVE

ZANE L. MILLER

KEITH L. NELSON

MICHAEL E. PARRISH

JAMES T. PATTERSON

RICHARD P. TRAINA

JOSEPH T. TAYLOR

PETER J. FREDERICK

Present in the Past

SOURCE PROBLEMS IN AMERICAN HISTORY

EDITED BY

Armin Rappaport

UNIVERSITY OF CALIFORNIA, SAN DIEGO

Richard P. Traina

WABASH COLLEGE

The Macmillan Company

NEW YORK

Copyright © 1972, The Macmillan Company

Printed in the United States of America

The Macmillan Company
866 Third Avenue, New York, New York 10022

Library of Congress catalog card number: 77–163611

First Printing

Printing: 1 2 3 4 5 6 7 8   Year: 2 3 4 5 6 7 8

Note to the Reader

The title, *Present in the Past,* is purposefully ambiguous. In one sense it suggests that to some degree you can be "there" through reading about the controversies of an earlier day as expressed in the words of those who were immediately involved. In another sense it suggests that the American present is somehow contained in its past—as effect to cause, by analogy, or by simple continuation. This book should enlarge your understanding of both past and present by helping you to gain a feeling for historical events as they were happening, and by enabling you to see how your views of the past and present interact.

Present in the Past contains twenty chapters, all of which include several closely related historical documents or source materials, along with an introductory original essay that provides an account of the historical setting. The selections in each chapter were designed by practicing teacher-scholars to present a microcosm of an enduring or recurring issue in American history. The particular incidents and developments in which you will become involved are out of the ordinary for a book of readings.

Themes that will be familiar to you are: the quest for personal wealth and social status; the striving for democratization of political processes; the desire to avoid involvement in war; the resort to violence to effect social change; the effort to determine the "proper role" of women; the impact of technology upon human relationships; and the search by black men and women for a full and rewarding life. The similarity of these issues with those in our own time is apparent; in that fact lies the reason for this volume. We hope it leads you to a deeper appreciation of the uses of history and to a richer educational experience.

A. R.
R. P. T.

Contents

Contents

Chapter

1 : The Puritan Idea of Success

⊂⊃ **GEORGE H. DAVIS**

During the seventeenth century the concept of an American was non-existent. There were native savages; but the colonials were considered, by themselves and their old countrymen, as Europeans living abroad. The new continents were given place names reflective of the old continent's attitudes and hopes for the land. New England, New Spain, New Sweden, New France, and New Holland were examples. The land was new but the expectation was that the civilization erected upon it would be that of the old country.

This hope of those who had the power to give names to the North and South American continents was also the hope of the more humble settlers. In Boston, Plymouth, York, Cambridge, and other new towns with comforting old names, colonials labored to build houses of sawed timbers with gambrel roofs, not log cabins. Along with their cultural tastes, the Puritans brought their social attitudes. A private club, the Honorable Artillery Company of London, whose membership was limited to those of "good means," was recreated in Boston. At the cost of maintaining expensive cannons for the public defense this private company of militia preserved social status. The settlers, in short, refused to surrender their heritage by yielding to what they called the "howling wilderness." Differences from European standards were feared, and what might be called American ideas and opinions were considered corruptions to be rectified.

How successfully did these early settlers reproduce the old country? Certainly the first generation, whose members had spent many of their years in the mother country, largely perpetuated their image of proper English opinions and life styles. They were equally at home on either side of the ocean. Six of the nine members of the first graduating class at Harvard College (1642) returned to England to pursue their careers. Late in his life one of the most famous of these graduates, Admiral

1

George Downing, did some dabbling in London real estate. Downing Street, on which the British Prime Minister lives, is a symbol of his efforts and of the early Americans who returned unnoticed to their native country. Later generations were less successful at preserving their English inheritance and, because of their increasing differences, became known as provincials—a term which distinguished Anglo-Americans from Englishmen.

The explanation for the increasing differences between England and the colonies lay not only in the course of their separate developments during the seventeenth century but also, in the case of New England, in the Puritans' strongly held religious views. While the Puritans' name stemmed from their desire to purify the Anglican church of traits they felt were "non-Biblical" (read Roman Catholic), much of the sect's impact resulted from its views on and its remedies for society's ills. In the seventeenth century, religion pervaded all aspects of life. To be an English Puritan during the period from 1620 through 1660 meant more than holding certain religious beliefs; it also entailed opinions as to the role and purpose of government, concepts of economic theory, commitments to an ideal society, and, more importantly, to a particularly ordered society. At the end of the 1630's these religiously oriented citizens rose in rebellion against the English monarchy, cut off the King's head, and, until their collapse in 1660, strove to establish—amid ceaseless disagreements—a commonwealth based on their ideas. The founders of the Massachusetts Bay Colony in early 1630 came to their New England with the hope that the new world would serve as a model for the correction of the old. Men who refused flight to New England fought in the English Civil War for the same cause.

What lay behind the Puritans' dissension in England? Religious beliefs, as the source of their name would indicate, were paramount. But they were also convinced that, because of the lack of proper religion in the state, evil men, ideas and institutions had emerged to dominate their England. Among these evils were the rise of an increasingly centralized government under a king of questionable virtue, the rise of London's unjustified and too often corrupting domination over the countryside, the demise of many small farmers into shiftless vagabonds, and the prominence of many court favorites who were interested in their own good before that of the nation. These examples of change, which to the Puritans were symptoms of a nation ignoring God's wishes, are now recognized by historians as part of the transition of a medieval into an early modern country. It was in vain that a contemporary ballad urged the Puritans to accept and appreciate this emerging new society:

> Then talk you no more of New England!
> New England is where old England did stand,
> New furnished, new fashioned, new woman'd, new man'd.
>   And is not old England grown new!

This "old England grown new," along with religious persecution and political unrest, motivated at least 20,000 people to cross the ocean during the decade of the 1630's.

The migration stopped as abruptly as it began when the Civil War between the Puritans and the monarchy started in 1640. American colonials did not directly experience the twenty bloody years of discord that followed in the home country, and the lack of such experience created innumerable differences between the two populations. If the colonials did not experience the Civil War, those who stayed in England did not endure the rigors of the wilderness, an equally prolific source of differences. With large numbers of unemployed, England appeared overpopulated. America was underpopulated, indeed seemingly destitute of the manpower needed to construct a European type of society. Land was scarce and expensive in the old country, bountiful and cheap in the new. Under these conditions the leaders of Massachusetts diverged from their English Puritan compatriots in interpreting their mutual heritage.

In the colonials' growing dissimilarity from the mother country modern Americans find signs of the settlers' success. The colonials were gradually becoming Americans as distinct from Englishmen living abroad. Their steady divergence from England disquieted the settlers. That their descendants would proclaim these deviations success would have been more upsetting to them. For success or failure in the Puritan mind hinged on man's relationship to God and not on national characteristics or pecularities. For a man salvation was success; for a society success was conformity to God's laws which provided conditions conducive to individual salvation. The nationality of a man was unimportant in his relationship to God.

As the first Puritan settlers were crossing the ocean, John Winthrop, their first governor, lectured them:

But if we shall neglect the observation of these articles which are the ends we have propounded, and dissembling with our God, shall fall to embrace this present world and prosecute our carnal intentions, seeking great things for ourselves and our posterity, the Lord will surely break out in wrath against us, be revenged of such a perjured people, and make us know the price of the breach. . . . For we must consider that we shall be as a city upon a hill, the eyes of all people are upon us. So that if we shall deal falsely with our God in this work we have undertaken, and so cause Him to withdraw His present help from us . . . we shall shame the faces of many of God's worthy servants, and cause their prayers to be turned into curses upon us, till we be consumed out of the good land whither we are going.

But, if the settlers followed God's ordinances, Winthrop predicted,

We shall find that the God of Israel is among us, when ten of us shall be able to resist a thousand of our enemies, when He shall make us a praise and glory, that men shall say of succeeding plantations: "The Lord make it like New England."

Not having seen the shores of the American continent did not prevent the Governor from describing the conduct necessary to reap such a reward: "Whatsoever we did or ought to have done when we lived in England, the same must we do, and more also where we go."

Winthrop's speech, which shows how the Puritans believed God guided men through His personal interventions in the world, sets forth different standards for the judgment of community and individual success. The society prospers if it acts according to God's laws, and the prosperity is proof of this obedience. But the individual's longing for prosperity is "dissembling with our God" and endangering not only his soul but also his society. In another passage of the same speech Winthrop says, "God Almighty in His most Holy and wise providence hath so disposed of the condition of mankind as in all times some must be rich, some poor; some high and eminent in power and dignity, others mean and in subjection." Why did Winthrop believe God demanded this? "That every man might have need of others and from hence they might be all knit more nearly together." The common good was the aim of a godly society. Those who sought personal gain at the cost of the common good were evil. As another Puritan stated, "And that common saying, 'Every man for himself, and God for us all,' is wicked and indirectly against the end of every calling or honest kind of life."

To the Puritans, life on earth was merely preparation for life after death. God had chosen only an elect few to be saved. How was a person discovered to be saved? God "called" a person—somehow notifying him of His choice in a manner to which the person could testify. If such testimony was convincing to other Puritans, the individual then gained admission to a church and was referred to as a "saint." This calling was also known as *justification*. Men could not save themselves by their acts; they had to be called by God.

While all men hoped for it, few actually achieved justification. Yet they tried to conduct their lives in a "saintly" manner either in preparation for the call or out of hypocrisy. The Puritans could judge only the man's testimony and actions, not the fact of whether God had acted. Of course the Puritans believed that one who had been called would be given the will power and insight to follow God's laws rigorously. As Robert Keayne, a Boston merchant and author of one of the following documents, stated, ". . . all my ways of holiness are of no use to me in point of justification, yet . . . [t]hey are good fruits and evidence of justification." Obeying the laws of God was called *sanctification*.

To act in a manner worthy to establish sanctification entailed the practice of a strict and rigorous social code. Today's popular pejorative sense of the word puritan—that is, a prudish, oppressive moralist—stems from this code. Since the church could never be absolutely sure of the justification of any man, it preached continually the importance of close observation of the actions of its members in regard to sanctification. When a member of a church broke a civil law, it threw his justification into doubt. Thus for the church member there were two trials—one by the civil courts and one by the church. The church explored the possible inferences to be drawn about the member's calling from his lack of sanctification.

Not everyone was called to salvation according to Puritan belief, but everyone was "called" to an occupation. In the words of Winthrop, "God . . . hath so disposed of the condition of mankind as in all times some must be rich, some poor"; or in modern words, God ordains a hierarchical society. The breakup of the traditional pattern of the Middle Ages, wherein men were expected to do whatever work their fathers did, is evident in this second Puritan sense of calling. Whether or not men actually chose an occupation different from their father's, all men nevertheless had to go through the process of choice. This choice was a consequential matter, since the Puritans believed that God required everyone to labor. Each man whose work was productive of the common good, from the lowest servant to the ruler of the state, had a calling as respectable as that of a cleric, for each was doing what God had planned for him if his was the correct calling. A vocational choice was referred to as a man's "particular calling."

Work thus became not a curse but a religous duty—a way of glorifying God. Furthermore, one's particular calling was parallel to one's sacred calling. Just as salvation, justification, and sanctification were the religious components of the Puritan formula, so material prosperity, a vocation, and following God's laws in one's trade were temporal counterparts. Robert Keayne, a poor boy who made good through hard work, wrote:

> I have now traded for myself about 40 or 50 years and through the favor of God, though I had very little at first to begin with, yet I had good credit and good esteem and respect in the place where I lived so that I did ever drive a great trade not only since I came hither but especially in England.

Keayne's words emphasize his belief that God had rewarded him as He could have been expected to reward His servants and punish His enemies. Thus worldly riches, like sanctification, were not absolute proof of the truth of a man's particular calling, but could be considered "good fruits and evidences" of the same. Keayne wrote the above words in answer to a charge that his riches had been the result of illegal and unchristian practices in his trade. If his profits were made in violation of civil law or through conscious violation of God's laws of trade, then Keayne's prosperity proved he had been unable to act with sanctification in his life. Instead of being a sign of his salvation, his riches could prove his damnation.

Until mid-1639, Massachusetts and Boston enjoyed a prosperity which befitted a "city upon a hill." Settlers raised crops which were sold to new immigrants. The English currency of the new immigrants bought English imports from the merchants of Boston. These merchants in turn bought additional imports from the mother country with the cash. Export goods were not important in the trade balance of the colony, and the price of imports was inflated because of their scarcity. The high prices of the English goods caused widespread discontent which, in the case of Robert Keayne, exploded when a slackening of immigration caused an economic slowdown in the fall of 1639. A depression began in 1640 as immigration all but ceased because of the outbreak of the English Civil War. During the 1640's the merchants began an export trade built on the products of the soil and the sea. By the 1650's prosperity had returned. The merchants' exports, not the immigrants' capital, were the sources of the wealth.

By 1660 Boston was a busy seaport often compared to London, though the comparison displeased many of the Puritans. The settlers began to find Boston's domination of New England reminiscent of London's domination of old England. It was of that England that Governor Winthrop had written, "I am verily persuaded, God will bring some heavy affliction upon this land, and that speedily." Under the leadership of their wealthy merchants, the citizens of Boston had imitated their London brethren successfully. Citizens of the country towns and the farms developed hostility to the capital of their colony. Not only did the Boston merchants set the prices of imported goods but they also purchased the produce of the countryside for export. Buyers and sellers always disagree over prices, and the country folk of Massachusetts felt the city's prices and business methods left much to be desired. As the merchants and their city grew more prosperous and more populous, they prompted increasing doubts about their ability to serve God's ordinances in society. Was Boston securing its own prosperity at the cost of the countryside? Was it putting itself before the common good? These doubts were magnified by the presence of vices indigenous to any large seaport in the seventeenth century. The social cost of this new prosperity, if it subverted the colony from God's ways, might be too high.

The following four documents deal with the problem of the Puritan idea of success. The first two deal with an individual, Robert Keayne, and the meaning of his wealth as it related to his individual salvation. Both relate to the period before 1640 and to an economy based on the flow of immigrants, who brought capital to the new world. The second two relate to the later economic period which was dominated by the exportation of goods by Boston merchants. These last two question the economic system used by the merchants while trading with the countryside, and how this system fitted into the Puritan ideal of a society guided by the principle of the common good. Both pairs of documents also contain illustrations of the Puritan's belief in God's direct intervention in the affairs of man and of the constant consciousness of the colony as an extension of the mother country.

John Winthrop (1588–1649) was the dominant figure in the founding and early history of the Massachusetts Bay Colony. The son of a gentleman farmer in Suffolk County, England, the Governor went to Trinity College at Cambridge University and studied law at Gray's Inn in London. Giving up his London legal practice and his family estates, he moved to America in 1630. He served either as governor or deputy governor for the colony most of his remaining years. His *Journal* from which this selection is taken is sometimes published under the title *The History of New England*. The Reverend John Cotton (1584–1652), whose sermon is quoted herein, was also a graduate of Trinity College, Cambridge. He had served at St. Botolph's church in Boston, England, for twenty years before he fled to Massachusetts in 1633. Until his death, he was the leading preacher in New England, and as such had a great influence on all aspects of the colony's life. Was Keayne convicted and fined for a crime which was not in the statutes of the colony? Would Keayne have a right to claim that he was a scapegoat, a victim of public hysteria? On what grounds did the church membership find Keayne's actions insufficient to deny his justification? The selection is taken from the James Hosmer edition of *Winthrop's Journal, 1630–1649*, Vol. I, pp. 315–18, and is reprinted by permission of Barnes & Noble, Inc., N. Y.

⇔ Robert Keayne: Winthrop's View

JOHN WINTHROP

At a general court held at Boston, great complaint was made of the oppression used in the country in sale of foreign commodities; and Mr. Robert Keayne, who kept a shop in Boston, was notoriously above others observed and complained of; and, being convented,[1] he was charged with many particulars; in some, for taking above six-pence in the shilling profit; in some above eight-pence; and, in some small things, above two for one;[2] and being hereof convicted, (as appears by the records,) he was fined £200, which came thus to pass: The deputies considered, apart, of his fine, and set it at £200; the magistrates agreed but to £100. So, the court being divided, at length it was agreed, that his fine should be £200, but he should pay but £100, and the other should be respited to the further consideration of the next general court. By this means the magistrates and deputies were brought to an accord, which otherwise had not been likely, and so much trouble might have grown, and the

[1] A church member.
[2] In the English coinage system there are 12 pence (d.) in a shilling (s.), and 20 shillings in a pound (£). Keayne is charged with profits of 50 to 100 percent.

offender escaped censure. For the cry of the country was so great against oppression, and some of the elders and magistrates had declared such detestation of the corrupt practice of this man (which was the more observable, because he was wealthy and sold dearer than most other tradesmen, and for that he was of ill report for the like covetous practice in England, that incensed the deputies very much against him). And sure the course was very evil, especial circumstances considered: 1. He being an ancient professor of the gospel: 2. A man of eminent parts: 3. Wealthy, and having but one child: 4. Having come over for conscience' sake, and for the advancement of the gospel here: 5. Having been formerly dealt with and admonished, both by private friends and also by some of the magistrates and elders, and having promised reformation; being a member of a church and commonwealth now in their infancy, and under the curious observation of all churches and civil states in the world. These added much aggravation to his sin in the judgment of all men of understanding. Yet most of the magistrates (though they discerned of the offence clothed with all these circumstances) would have been more moderate in their censure: 1. Because there was no law in force to limit or direct men in point of profit in their trade. 2. Because it is the common practice, in all countries, for men to make use of advantages for raising the prices of their commodities. 3. Because (though he were chiefly aimed at, yet) he was not alone in this fault. 4. Because all men through the country, in sale of cattle, corn, labor, etc., were guilty of the like excess in prices. 5. Because a certain rule could not be found out for an equal rate between buyer and seller, though much labor had been bestowed in it, and divers laws had been made, which, upon experience, were repealed, as being neither safe nor equal. Lastly, and especially, because the law of God appoints no other punishment but double restitution; and, in some cases, as where the offender freely confesseth, and brings his offering, only half added to the principal. After the court had censured him, the church of Boston called him also in question, where (as before he had done in the court) he did, with tears, acknowledge and bewail his covetous and corrupt heart, yet making some excuse for many of the particulars, which were charged upon him, as partly by pretence of ignorance of the true price of some wares, and chiefly by being misled by some false principles, as 1. That, if a man lost in one commodity, he might help himself in the price of another. 2. That if, through want of skill or other occasion, his commodity cost him more than the price of the market in England, he might then sell it for more than the price of the market in New England, etc. These things gave occasion to Mr. Cotton, in his public exercise the next lecture day, to lay open the error of such false principles, and to give some rules of direction in the case.

Some false principles were these:—

1. That a man might sell as dear as he can, and buy as cheap as he can.

2. If a man lose by casualty of sea, etc., in some of his commodities, he may raise the price of the rest.

3. That he may sell as he bought, though he paid too dear, etc., and though the commodity be fallen, etc.

4. That, as a man may take the advantage of his own skill or ability, so he may of another's ignorance or necessity.

5. Where one gives time for payment, he is to take like recompense of one as of another.

The rules for trading were these:—

1. A man may not sell above the current price, i.e., such a price as is usual in the time and place, and as another (who knows the worth of the commodity) would give for it, if he had occasion to use it; as that is called current money, which every man will take, etc.

2. When a man loseth in his commodity for want of skill, etc., he must look at it as his own fault or cross, and therefore must not lay it upon another.

3. Where a man loseth by casualty of sea, or, etc., it is a loss cast upon himself by providence, and he may not ease himself of it by casting it upon another; for so a man should seem to provide against all providences, etc., that he should never lose; but where there is a scarcity of the commodity, there men may raise their price; for now it is a hand of God upon the commodity, and not the person.

4. A man may not ask any more for his commodity than his selling price, as Ephron to Abraham, the land is worth thus much.

The cause being debated by the church, some were earnest to have him excommunicated; but the most thought an admonition would be sufficient.

Mr. Cotton opened the causes, which required excommunication, out of that in 1 Corinthians 5:11.[3] The point now in question was, whether these actions did declare him to be such a covetous person, etc. Upon which he showed, that it is neither the habit of covetousness, (which is in every man in some degree,) nor simply the act, that declares a man to be such, but when it appears, that a man sins against his conscience, or the very light of nature, and when it appears in a man's whole conversation. But Mr. Keayne did not appear to be such, but rather upon an error in his judgment, being led by false principles; and, beside, he is otherwise liberal, as in his hospitality, and in church communion, etc. So, in the end, the church consented to an admonition.

---

[3] "But now I have written unto you not to keep company, if any man that is called a brother be a fornicator, or covetous, or an idolater, or a railer, or a drunkard, or an extortioner; with such a one, no, not to eat." King James Version.

Robert Keayne (1595–1656) wrote his will during 1653 in order to leave a public record of his side of the case. He pleaded with his readers to "judge indifferently and without prejudice whether I have justly deserved what here I have undergone. . . ." Professor Bernard Bailyn has edited a modern English version of the will entitled "The Apologia of Robert Keayne," which appears in Vol XLII of the *Publications* of the Colonial Society of Massachusetts, *Transactions 1952–1956* (Boston, Mass., 1964). The excerpts following may be found on pp. 249–250, 254–255, 300–302, 306–308. Keayne played an important role in the early history of the colony and is the first major philanthropist of Boston. Less than a century earlier, a great London merchant had given his city a townhouse which he decorated with his business seal, the grasshopper. When Boston built its townhouse from Keayne's bequest, it was decorated with a weathervane in the design of a grasshopper in imitation of the London building where Keayne had traded as a young man. Does Keayne convince you that he is innocent of the civil crime of usury? What light does he shed on the trading practices of merchants of the city? Why did Keayne confess?

⊂≋ Keayne's Own Case

ROBERT KEAYNE

I, Robert Keayne, citizen and merchant tailor of London by freedom and by the good providence of God now dwelling at Boston in New England in America, being at this time through the great goodness of my God both in health of body and of able and sufficient memory, yet considering that all flesh is as grass that must wither and will return to the dust and that my life may be taken away in a moment, therefore that I may be in the better readiness—freed from the distracting cares of the disposing of my outward estate . . . [at] the time of sickness or day of death when the mind should be taken up with more serious and weighty considerations—I do therefore now in my health make, ordain, and declare this to be my last will and testament and to stand and to be as effectual as if I had made it in my sickness or in the day or hour of my death, which is in manner and form following.

[*Thanks to a Merciful God: His Declaration of Faith*]

First and before all things, I commend and commit my precious soul into the hands of Almighty God. . . .

I do further desire from my heart to renounce all confidence or expectation of merit or desert in any of the best duties or services that

10

ever I have, shall, or can be able to perform, acknowledging that all my righteousness, sanctification, and close walking with God, if it were or had been a thousand times more exact than ever yet I attained to, is all polluted and corrupt and falls short of commending me to God in point of my justification or helping forward my redemption or salvation. They deserve nothing at God's hand but hell and condemnation if He should enter into judgment with me for them. And though I believe that all my ways of holiness are of no use to me in point of justification, yet I believe they may not be neglected by me without great sin, but are ordained of God for me to walk in them carefully, in love to Him, in obedience to His commandments, as well as for many other good ends. They are good fruits and evidences of justification. Therefore, renouncing though not the acts yet all confidence in those acts of holiness and works of sanctification performed by me, I look for my acceptance with God and the salvation of my soul only from the merits or righteousness of the Lord Jesus Christ, and from the free, bountiful, and undeserved grace and love of God in Him. . . .

This faith in the Lord Jesus Christ hath been most plainly and sweetly taught in these churches of New England, in which place, though I met with many and deep sorrows and variety of exercises of spirit and hard measures offered to me, yet with unrepentant thoughts I desire to acknowledge it for a great blessing and undeserved favor of God that He hath brought me hither to enjoy His presence in the beauties of holiness, and to see His walkings in His holy sanctuary. And though there may be failings both in our civil government and churches (for all men have their weaknesses and the best societies of men have their imperfections, so that still there will be some things to be amended and reformed as God shall be pleased to discover new light and means to do it), yet I do unfeignedly approve of the way of the churches of Jesus Christ and the civil government that God hath here set up amongst us, and rejoice therein, as a way that both I pray for and doubt not but God will bless. According to that light that I have received or that which I ever read or heard of, it is one of the best and happiest governments that is this day in the world.

[*Gifts to the Public: A Conduit and a Town House Comprising a Market Place, Court Room, Gallery, Library, Granary, and an Armory*]

I have long thought and considered of the want of [two] necessary things of public concernment which may not be only commodious but very profitable and useful for the town of Boston: a market place and a conduit. The one [would be] a good help in danger of fire, the want of which we have found by sad and costly experience not only in other parts of the town where possibly they have better supply for water but in the heart of the town about the market place. The other [would be] useful for the country people that come with their provisions for the supply of the town, that they may have a place to sit dry in and warm both in cold, rain, and dirty weather, and may have a place to leave their corn or any other things that they cannot sell safe till they come again. This would be both an encouragement to the country to come in and a great means to increase trading in the town. [I have also thought] to have [in the same building] some convenient room or two for the courts to meet in, both in winter and summer, and also for the townsmen and commissioners of the town. In the same building or the like there may also be a convenient room for a library and a gallery or some other handsome room for the elders to meet in and confer together when they have occasion to come to the town for any such end, as I perceive they have many. Then in the same building there may be also a room for an armory to keep the arms of the Artillery Company and for the soldiers to meet in when they have occasion.

[He Is Innocent of the Heinous Sin of Usury: The Entire Truth of the Matter]

I did not then nor dare not now go about to justify all my actions. I know God is righteous and doth all upon just grounds, though men may mistake in their grounds and proceedings, counsel have erred and courts may err and a faction may be too hard and outvote the better or more discerning part. I know the errors of my life. The failings in my trade and otherwise have been many. Therefore from God (the censure) was most just. Though it had been much more severe I dare not so open my mouth against it, nor never did as I remember, [except to] justify Him. Yet I dare not say nor did I ever think (as far as I can call to mind) that the censure was just and righteous from men. Was the price of a bridle, not for taking but only asking, 2 s. for [what] cost here 20 d. such a heinous sin? [Such bridles] have since been commonly sold and still are for 2 s. 6 d. and 3 s. or more, though worse in kind. Was it such a heinous sin to sell 2 or 3 dozen of great gold buttons for 2 s. 10 d. per dozen that cost 2 s. 2 d. ready money in London, bought at the best hand, as I showed to many by my invoice (though I could not find it at the instant when the Court desired to see it) and since was confirmed by special testimony from London? The buttons [were not even] paid for when the complaint was made, nor I think not yet; neither did the complaint come from him that bought and owed them nor with his knowledge or consent, as he hath since affirmed, but merely from the spleen and envy of another, whom it did nothing concern. Was this so great an offense? Indeed, that it might be made so, some out of their ignorance would needs say they were copper and not worth 9 d. per dozen. But these were weak grounds to pass heavy censures upon.

Was the selling of 6 d. nails for 8 d. per lb. and 8 d. nails for 10 d. per lb. such a crying and oppressing sin? And as I remember it was above two years before he that bought them paid me for them (and not paid for if I forgot not) when he made that quarreling exception and unrighteous complaint in the Court against me, (he then being of the Court himself) that I had altered and corrupted my book in adding more to the price than I had set down for them at first delivery. If I had set down 8 d. after 2 years' forbearance for what I would have sold for 7 d. if he had paid me presently, I think it had been a more honest act in me than it was in him that promised or at least pretended to pay me presently that he might get them at a lower price than a man could well live upon, and when he had got my goods into his hands to keep me 2 or 3 years without my money. All that while there was no fault found at the prices, but when he could for shame keep the money no longer, yet he will requite it with a censure in the Court. For my own part, as I did ever think it an ungodly act in him, so do I think in my conscience that it had been more just in the Court to have censured him than me for this thing, though this was the chiefest crime alleged and most powerfully carried against me. Other things, as some farthing skeins of thread, etc., were drawn in to make this the more probable and to help to make up a censure. But the truth of the thing was this:

This man sent unto me for two or three thousand of 6 d. nails. I sent to him a bag full of that sort just as they came to me from Mr. Foote's in London, never opened nor altered by me. These I entered into my book at 8 d. per lb. thinking he would have paid me in a very short time. It fell out that these nails proved somewhat too little for his work. He sent them [back] again and desired me to let him have bigger [ones] for them. I took them and sent him a bag of 8 d. nails of the same quantity at 10 d. per lb. Now because I was loath to alter my book and to make a new charge I only altered the figures in my book and made the figure of "6" a figure of "8" for 8 d. nails and the figure of "8" that before stood for 8 d. a lb. I made "10 d." Now though he knew of the change of these 6 d. nails for 8 d. (which I had quite forgot through my many other occasions and the length of time that they had stood in the book unpaid) yet this he concealed from me and from the Court also. To make the matter more odious he challenged me and my book of falsehood, supposing that because he had kept me so long from my money therefore by altering the figures I had made the price higher than at first I had charged them down, and that I required 10 d. per lb. for 6 d. nails. And so it carried it in the Court (where he was the more easily believed because he was a magistrate and of esteem therein, though it was a most unjust and untrue charge, and only from his own imagination), till I cleared it by good testimony from an honest man in his own town whom he sent for the first nails and [who] brought them back and received the bigger nails for them. [This man] came to me of his own accord and told me he heard there was a difference between such a man and I, which he said he could clear, and related the matter fully to me which I was very glad to hear. [His words] brought all things to my mind, [especially] what was the ground of altering the figures in the book, which before I had forgot though I saw it was done with my own hand. And this was the very truth of the thing. I presently acquainted our honored governor Mr. John Winthrop and some others who were very glad that the truth of that reproach was so unexpectedly discovered and cleared. Many if not most of the Court was satisfied with it, and saw the thing to be very plain in my debt book. But the party himself would not be satisfied, [insisting that] they were 6 d. nails set down at 10 d. per lb., though [he] himself saw the figure of "8" as plain as the figure of "10."

Now I leave it to the world or to any impartial man or any that hath understanding in trade to judge whether this was a just offense or so crying a sin for which I had such cause to be so penitent (this being the chief [accusation] and pressed on with so great aggravation by my opposers) [or whether] my actions, innocent in themselves, were misconstrued. I knew not how to help myself, especially considering it was no oppressing price but usual with others at that time to sell the like so and since [then] frequently for almost half as much more, as I think all know, and yet both given and taken without exception, or at least without public complaint. Yea, the same gentleman himself, since he hath turned merchant and trader, seems to have lost his former tenderness of conscience that he had when he was a buyer and is not so scrupulous in his own gains. . . .

I was much grieved and astonished to be complained of in Court and brought publicly to answer as a grievous malefactor only upon the displeasure of some that stirred in it more than properly did concern them and to be prosecuted so violently for such things as seemed to myself and others so trivial, and upon great outcries, as if the oppression had been unparalleled. And when all things were searched to the bottom nothing of moment was proved against me worthy of mention in a court but what I have here expressed. Yet no other way [was] left me for help, things being carried so highly against me by one party, as I had it by good informations, but by casting myself upon the favor or mercy of the Court, as some had counseled me. Since, though, I think they have had cause to be grieved for as well as I because it had an effect contrary to expectation. The means which should have procured the more clemency was by some made an argument of my greater guilt. If this should convince me of the equity and honesty of such men's moderation who delight to turn things not to the best but worst sense, the Lord help me to see that which yet I have not done. This was not the way to bow and melt my heart, but rather to provoke it to cry more earnestly to God to do me right in such a case.

I confess still as I did then and as I have said before, that the newness and strangeness of the thing, to be brought forth into an open court as a public malefactor, was both a shame and an amazement to me. It was the grief of my soul (and I desire it may ever so be in a greater measure) that any act of mine (though not justly but by misconstruction) should be an occasion of scandal to the Gospel and profession of the Lord Jesus, or that myself should be looked at as one that had brought any just dishonor to God (which I have endeavored long and according to my weak ability desired to prevent), though God hath been pleased for causes best known to Himself to deny me such a blessing. And if it had been in my own power I should rather have chosen to have perished in my cradle than to have lived to such a time. But the good pleasure of God is to keep me low in my own eyes as well as in the eyes of others, and also to make me humble and penitent, lest such mercies should have lifted me up above what is meet. Yet I do say still as I have often done before, that those things for which I was questioned (in the best apprehension, guided by God's word, that I had then or have since attained to) did deserve no such proceedings as was carved out to me, though some blew up those sparks into a great flame. And I am not alone herein, though it was my own case, but many wise and godly servants of the Lord, as well as divers others were and still are of the same mind. Yea, some that were then much against me have confessed since to me that things were carried in a hurry.

[*Action of the Church After an Exquisite Search*]

Yea, and our own church, when they called all those complaints over again that was laid to my charge (as it was meet they should) to see how far there was equity in them and how far I was guilty of all those clamors and rumors that when I lay under, they heard my defense equally and patiently, and after all their exquisite search into them and attention to what others could allege or prove against me, they found no cause but only to give me an admonition. Less they could not do without some offense, considering what had passed in Court before against me. Now if the church had seen or apprehended or could have proved that I had been so justly guilty as others imagined, they could have done no less than to have excommunicated and cast me out of their society and fellowship as an unworthy member.

Of John Josselyn (d. circa 1690) little is known. His brother, Henry Josselyn, was an important early settler in Maine. John visited his brother twice, once during 1638–39, and once from 1669–71. After the second trip, he wrote two books about America which deal mainly with botanical studies but also include other aspects of life in New England. Reflecting in 1675 on the Boston he had surveyed at the end of his first ocean crossing in 1638, Josselyn wrote that it was "rather a village than a town, there being not above twenty or thirty houses." The following description of Boston in 1669 shows rapid development of the town. What geographic and architectural features dominate this larger city? Josselyn's description of the economic relationship of Boston's merchants to the population of Maine is from a Maine perspective and probably reflects the view of his brother and his neighbors. What percentage of profit are the merchants making and how does this compare to the profits allegedly made by Keayne? What effects are the merchants having on the occupations of men? Are the merchants creating conditions which encourage a godly life? These excerpts from Josselyn's *An Account of Two Voyages to New England* (London, 1675) are taken from the edition in the *Collections* of the Massachusetts Historical Society, Third Series, Vol. III, pp. 318–20, 349–52, published in Cambridge, Mass., in 1833.

⊂⊇ A View of Boston and the Maine Economy

JOHN JOSSELYN

OF BOSTON

Two miles northeast from *Roxbury,* and forty miles from *New-Plymouth,* in the latitude of 42 or 43 deg. and 10 min., in the bottom of *Massachusetts-Bay* is *Boston* (whose longitude is 315 deg., or as others will 322 deg. and 30 sec.). So called from a town in *Lincolnshire,* which in the *Saxons* time bore the name of St. *Botolph,* and is the metropolis of this colony, or rather of the whole country, situated upon a *Peninsula,* about four miles in compass, almost square, and invironed with the sea, saving one small *Isthmus* which gives access to other towns by land on the south-side. The town hath two hills of equal height on the frontier part thereof next the sea, the one well fortified on the superficies with some artillery mounted, commanding any ship as she sails into the harbour within the still *Bay;* the other hill hath a very strong battery built of whole timber and filled with earth, at the descent of the hill in the extremist part thereof, betwixt these two strong arms, lies a large *Cove* or *Bay,* on which the chiefest part of the town is built, to the northwest is a high mountain that out-tops all, with its three little rising hills on the summit called *Tramount,* this is furnished with a beacon and great guns, from hence you may overlook all the islands in the *Bay,* and descry such ships as are upon the coast; the houses are for the most part raised on the seabanks and wharfed out with great industry and cost, many of them standing upon piles, close together on each side [of] the streets as in *London,* and furnished with many fair shops, their materials are brick, stone, lime, handsomely contrived, with three meeting houses or churches, and a town-house built upon pillars where the merchants may confer, in the chambers above they keep their monthly courts. Their streets are many and large, paved with pebble stone, and the south-side adorned with gardens and orchards. The town is rich and very populous, much frequented by strangers, here is the dwelling of their Governor. On the northwest and northeast two constant fairs are kept for daily traffic [1] thereunto. On the south there is a small but pleasant Common where the gallants a little before sunset walk with their *Marmalet-Madams,*[2] as we do in *Morefields,*[3] &c. till the nine a clock bell rings them home to their respective habitations, when presently the constables walk their rounds to see good orders kept, and to take up loose people. Two miles from the town, at a place called *Muddy-River,* the inhabitants have farms, to which belong rich arable grounds and meadows where they keep their cattle in the summer, and bring them to *Boston* in the winter; the harbour before the town is filled with ships and other vessels for most part of the year.

ON MAINE'S ECONOMY

Handicrafts-men there are but few, the tumelor or cooper,[4] smiths and carpenters are best welcome amongst them, shop-keepers there are none, being supplied by the *Massachusetts* merchant with all things they stand in need of, keeping here and there fair magazines stored with *English* goods, but they set excessive prices on them, if they do not gain *Cent per Cent,* they cry out that they are losers, hence *English* shoes are sold for eight and nine shillings a pair, worsted stockings of three shillings six pence a pair, for seven and eight shillings a pair, Douglass [5] that is sold in *England* for one or two and twenty pence an ell,[6] for four shillings a yard Serges of two shillings or three shillings

[1] Trade or commerce.
[2] Prostitutes.
[3] A large public park in London.
[4] Barrel maker.
[5] A type of cloth.
[6] A measurement of cloth, twenty percent larger than a yard.

a yard, for six and seven shillings a yard, and so all sorts of commodities both for planters and fishermen. . . .

The planters are or should be restless painstakers, providing for their cattle, planting and sowing of corn, fencing their grounds, cutting and bringing home fuel, cleaving of claw-board and pipe-staves, fishing for fresh water fish and fowling takes up most of their time, if not all; the diligent hand maketh rich, but if they be of a droanish disposition as some are, they become wretchedly poor and miserable, scarce able to free themselves and family from importunate famine, especially in the winter for want of bread. . . .

The fishermen take yearly upon the coasts many hundred kentals of cod, hake, haddock, polluck &c. which they split, salt and dry at their stages,[7] making three voyages in a year. When they share their fish (which is at the end of every voyage) they separate the best from the worst, the first they call merchantable fish, being sound, full grown fish and well make up, which is known when it is clear like a Lanthorn horn and without spots; the second sort they call refuse fish, that is such as is salt burnt, spotted, rotten, and carelessly ordered: these they put off to the *Massachusetts* merchants; the merchantable for thirty and two and thirty ryals a kental, (a kental is an hundred and twelve pound weight) the refuse for nine shillings and ten shillings a kental, the merchant sends the merchantable fish to *Lisbonne, Bilbo, Burdeaux, Marsiles, Taloon, Rochel, Roan,* and other cities of *France,* to the *Canaries* with claw-board and pipe-staves which is there and at the *Charibs* a prime commodity: the refuse fish they put off at the *Charib-Islands, Barbadoes, Jamaica,* &c. who feed their *Negroes* with it.

To every shallop belong four fishermen, a master or steersman, a midshipman, and a foremastman, and a shore man who washes it out of the salt, and dries it upon hurdles pitched upon stakes breast high and tends their cookery; these often get in one voyage eight or nine pound a man for their shares, but it doth some of them little good, for the merchant to increase his gains by putting off his commodity in the midst of their voyages, and at the end thereof comes in with a walking tavern, a bark laden with the legitimate bloud of the rich grape, which they bring from *Phial, Madera, Canaries,* with *Brandy, Rhum,* the *Barbadoes strong-water,* and *Tobacco,* coming ashore he gives them a taster or two, which so charms them, that for no persuasions that their employers can use will they go out to sea, although fair and seasonable weather, for two or three days, nay sometimes a whole week till they are wearied with drinking, taking ashore two or three hogsheads of *Wine* and *Rhum* to drink off when the merchant is gone. If a man of quality chance to come where they are roystering and gulling [8] in *Wine* with a dear felicity,

[7] Work areas on shore.
[8] Drinking or guzzling.

he must be sociable and *Rolypoly* with them, taking off their liberal cups as freely, or else be gone, which is best for him, for when *Wine* in their guts is at full tide, they quarrel, fight and do one another mischief, which is the conclusion of their drunken compotations. When the day of payment comes, they may justly complain of their costly sin of drunkenness, for their shares will do no more than pay the reckoning; if they save a kental or two to buy shoes and stockings, shirts and waistcoats with, 'tis well, other-ways they must enter into the merchants books for such things as they stand in need of, becoming thereby the merchants slaves, & when it riseth to a big sum are constrained to mortgage their plantation if they have any, the merchant when the time is expired is sure to seize upon their plantation and stock of cattle, turning them out of house and home, poor creatures, to look out for a new habitation in some remote place where they begin the world again. The lavish planters have the same fate, partaking with them in the like bad husbandry, of these the merchant buys beef, pork, pease, wheat and *Indian* corn, and sells it again many times to the fisherman.

William Bradford (1590–1657) was the dominant figure in the founding and early history of the Plymouth Colony. Governor Bradford led the colony from its settlement in 1620 (by a sect of the Puritans called Pilgrims) until his death. His *History of Plymouth Plantation* is the most famous work on that settlement and is the equal to *Winthrop's Journal* in importance for colonial historians. Plymouth, soon surpassed by Boston in population and power, became part of Massachusetts in 1691. In the following poem, written by Bradford in the 1650's, what use does he make of the wilderness? Why does the author invest the city with characteristics of human beings? What fears does Bradford express about the fate of the city? The poem was first published in 1838 in the *Collections* of the Massachusetts Historical Society, Third Series, Vol. VII, pp. 27–28, published in Cambridge.

◖ Of Boston in New England

WILLIAM BRADFORD

> O Boston, though thou now art grown
> To be a great and wealthy town,
> Yet I have seen thee a void place,
> Shrubs and bushes covering thy face;

And house then in thee none were there,
Nor such as gold and silk did wear;
No drunkenness were then in thee,
Nor such excess as now we see.
We then drunk freely of thy spring
Without paying of any thing;
We lodged freely where we would,
All things were free and nothing sold.
And they that did thee first begin
Had hearts as free and as willing
Their poor friends for to entertain,
And never looked at sordid gaine.

Some thou hast had whom I did know,
That spent theirselves to make thee grow,
And thy foundations they did lay
Which do remain unto this day.
When thou wast weak they did thee nurse,
Or else with thee it had been worse;
They left thee not, but did defend
And succour thee unto their end.

Thou now hast grown in wealth and store,
Do not forget that thou wast poor,
And lift not up thyself in pride,
From truth and justice turn not aside.
Remember thou a Cotton had,
Which made the hearts of many glad;
What he thee taught bear thou in mind,
It's hard another such to find.
A Winthrop once in thee was known
Who unto thee was as a crown.
Such ornaments are very rare
Yet thou enjoyed this blessed pair.
But these are gone, their work is done,
Their day is past, set is their sun:
Yet faithful Wilson [1] still remains,
And learned Norton [2] doth take pains.

Live ye in peace. I could say more.
Oppress ye not the weak and poor.
The trade is all in your own hand,

---

[1] Rev. John Wilson (d. 1667) was the brother-in-law of Robert Keayne and Assistant Minister (teacher) of the First Church of Boston under both Cotton and Norton.

[2] Rev. John Norton (1606–63) successor of Rev. John Cotton at the First Church of Boston.

Take heed ye do not wrong the land,
Lest he that hath lift you on high,
When, as the poor to him do cry
Do throw you down from your high state,
And make you low and desolate.

Chapter

2: Political Leadership in Eighteenth-Century Virginia

⊂⊒ JOHN C. RAINBOLT

In American politics the personal qualities and social background of aspirants to office have often seemed more important to voters than the candidates' positions on specific issues. Throughout our history we have frequently acted as if we concurred with William Penn's statement, "Let men be good and the government cannot be bad." What constitutes "good" men, however, has often been a subject of controversy. Certain qualities have always found a place on lists of desirable traits for statesmen, but the relative importance of these persistent criteria has not been constant and in each period dissent against the dominant view has occurred. The debate offers the student of American history one index to American values.

At no other time did the question of the ideal credentials for candidates seem more relevant and seldom has the problem sparked a greater variety of responses than in Virginia at the end of the colonial period. The conflicting standards asserted by eighteenth-century Virginians in the documents composing this chapter offer an early instance of a continuous debate in American history.

Although they addressed themselves to a problem which has existed throughout American history, articulate Virginians pondered the issue within a unique political and ideological setting which shaped their specific responses. In contrast to the modern citizen who may vote often and regularly for a bewildering array of candidates, the colonial Virginia freeman, or voter, had an opportunity to evaluate only a few candidates at irregular intervals. With the rare exception of special elections for vestrymen of newly created parishes, representatives to the lower house or the House of Burgesses were the only elected political officials in the province. Most voters selected two burgesses to represent their county. Since royal governors alone could dissolve an old assembly and order new elections, the colonists went to the polls only occasionally. Between

1726 and 1747 only three general elections were held. The infrequency and limited scope of elections did not appear unusual or oppressive to colonial Virginians. Not until during the American Revolution would widespread demand emerge for more elections of more officials with fixed terms.

When an election did occur, the Virginia planters made the most of it. "An election causes a hubbub for a week or so, and then we are dead a while," observed one colonist. The event was social as well as political. From their isolated plantations the planters gathered at the county courthouse. The liquor flowed freely and refreshments were plentiful at barbecues. Candidates were expected to entertain and lived up to expectation. The law restricted such activity but rarely were the restrictions enforced. In the 1758 election George Washington provided 160 gallons of liquor of various sorts for less than four hundred voters. In this festive atmosphere the election became an occasion for wagers among the freemen and occasionally a combination of strong drink, betting, and a close contest produced brawls. In 1736 the sheriff of Hanover County had to cancel the election because "the Candidates had distributed too much strong Liquor amongst the People. . . ." In 1769 a candidate precipitated a riot which closed the election when he assaulted the sheriff for opening the polling earlier than usual.

In these lively and occasionally disorderly elections the voters were in theory to concern themselves with a candidate's background and character rather than his views on specific issues. The effort to promulgate a standard stressing the personal traits of men rather than their positions on political issues accorded with the prevailing concept of representation. The idea that a representative's role was to ascertain and then promote in the assembly the specific desires of his constituents was not the predominant concept. Rather, in theory, a planter secured election to the House of Burgesses to legislate for the good of society, as he, not his constituents, defined that welfare. A leader ideally was an individual with the ability to understand the needs of society better than the mass of men who elected him. He was not a servant of the people so much as an architect of the common good. Voters might indicate their desires to representatives by means of petitions and "instructions" on specific issues, but in theory the voter was to keep separate his role as a voter and as petitioner. His views on issues were not to affect his preference among candidates, and burgesses were to regard instructions as advisory rather than binding.

The view that burgesses were trustees of the society's general interest rather than servants of the people's immediate will encountered opposition especially in the years preceding the American Revolution, when the constitutional debates sparked by the mother country's effort to tax the colonies caused Americans to scrutinize many political concepts which had previously been taken for granted. Beginning with an attack on the idea that Americans could not be represented in or taxed by Parliament, some colonists advanced to the general proposition that true representation existed only when assemblymen understood and acted in accord with the sentiments of their constituents. The newer view endorsed the right of voters to place binding instructions on representatives. The earlier theory, however, remained strong and was reasserted later as part of the rhetoric urging ratification of the federal constitution. Since the ability of a burgess to discover the good of the community and not his willingness to register the will of the community was the criteria for leadership, it followed that voters should look for traits which would maximize the probability that an individual would have such skill. The assumption in this concept of representation was that the mass of men qualified to vote had enough capacity to recognize virtuous and able individuals but not enough to decide upon specific, complex issues. The concept of representation which occasioned concern with personality and background rather than candidates' policies rested ultimately, then, on the view that men were not equal and that the inequality in ability arose from different experiences, in education and in social and economic status.

The recurring effort in the late colonial period to promulgate a certain standard for judging candidates reflected not only a distinct concept of representation but social and political circumstances as well. The conditions of colonial society conspired to weaken the authority of institutions such as government and the church whose traditional role was to create and maintain order. Institutional forms transplanted from England to provide stability could not always thrive in a new environment, and the vast space over which infant institutions had to rule further weakened authority. Greater economic opportunity for all classes produced a highly mobile society and blurred traditional class lines. Society was mobile geographically as well. Especially in the eighteenth century the population increases and expansion far outstripped the growth of institutions. Compounding the difficulty of assimilating the population into institutional structures was its diversity. About one-third of the total population were black slaves. Perhaps a third of the white settlers were by 1776 non-English, including Scots, Irish, and Germans.

A consequence of these conditions was a decrease in habits of deference ordinary colonists exhibited toward the upper classes and the sources of authority. To be sure, the society was deferential when contrasted with America after the American Revolution, but judged in comparison with the mother country—the standard of reference by which eighteenth-century Americans evaluated their society—traditional authority underwent considerable erosion in the colony. The common planter in Virginia simply did not regard the sources of authority with the same automatic feelings of awe and respect which often prevailed in his counterpart in the social order of England.

An increase in the autonomy of individuals resulted from the weakness of the authority of institutions. This development may seem to us today salutary, but at the time articulate Virginians often deplored the society which appeared disorderly rather than free. Leaders of church and state worried that in the absence of strong institutions individuals were in danger of becoming slaves to their base and corrupt passions. Those who sought to establish and enforce values clung to a definition of secular "freedom" or "true liberty" which mirrored Christianity's traditional and paradoxical assertion that a man's spiritual freedom consisted of his enslavement to Christ. Men were free when they were obedient to the values God had ordained for society. Comprehending what the colonial mind meant by "freedom," the student can then understand how it was that those who deplored the autonomy of individuals in the new world could call for greater freedom for individuals. Since weak institutions could not impose "freedom" on individuals, articulate colonists turned increasingly to the task of inculcating values into the people in order that they would, as it were, control themselves.

In no area did it seem more important to internalize values than in the criteria voters used to select representatives. The choice of candidates could not be effectively controlled directly; men could not be coerced into voting for "good" men. The size of the electorate, for one thing, was simply too large. It is true that a substantial portion of the population was excluded from the franchise: blacks, Indians, women, persons who dissented from the Anglican Church, and men who did not possess at least twenty-five acres of developed or one hundred acres of undeveloped land, or a house and lot in a town. But the religious and land qualifications were frequently ignored. Even where sheriffs enforced the land requirements for suffrage, voting was still widespread. Modern scholars disagree on the precise proportion of adult white males who could meet the requirements, but even the more conservative estimates range from thirty to fifty percent, in contrast to perhaps ten percent in the mother country. The electorate was not only large but spread out in relative isolation in the Chesapeake plantation economy. Contact between the common planters and institutions of authority was thus relatively infrequent and short-lived.

The Virginia electorate also lacked attachment to organized political parties. In America, since the early national period, the two-party system has served as a way of narrowing and thus regulating the choices available to voters. Parties additionally have made the electorate more predictable or consistent in their behavior by creating loyalties that transcend considerations of both personality and policy. Political parties did not emerge, however, until the 1790's. "Factions" did exist especially in early eighteenth-century Virginia, but these were distinct from parties in that membership was transitory and limited to a few prominent like-minded political leaders. Moreover in the absence of aggressive royal governors after 1720, political disputes were less frequent and even factions tended to disappear. By the mature colonial period Virginia lacked even the most rudimentary kind of political organizations.

Election procedures did contain practices which worked to limit the voters' freedom of choice. Voting was public. The planters milled around in an open courtroom listening to each individual voter as he approached the sheriff and announced his choice. Usually the candidates along with the leading justices of the peace sat with the sheriff. In the majority of elections the freemen seem to have voted whenever they arrived on the scene or could tear themselves away from the candidate's refreshments, but in some social and economic status roughly determined the order of voting. Members of the county establishment consisting of the largest planters and the clergy voted first in order to provide an example.

At times, public officials also bent or ignored legal procedures in an effort to control the electorate. In 1774 the freeholders of Berkeley County complained that "the time fixed . . . for the Election succeeded so quickly to the Notification and the Notification was given in so partial and private a manner that a great number of Freeholders did not hear of the Election until it was over and many of those who did attend were not acquainted with it till the very day of the Election." Discontented voters in an election in Augusta County in 1755 alleged "That the Sheriff whispered to several Freeholders as they came to vote to know who they were for, and then refused to take their Votes" if they intended to oppose his candidate.

From the standpoint of today, the legal procedures and the actual practices would seem to disqualify Virginia elections as unfettered expressions of the people's will. Virginia's leaders, however, did not have the advantage of history's hindsight to see that they actually presided over one of the more stable social orders in American history. They imagined that their colony stood on the brink of social anarchy owing to the weakness of institutions of authority and the concomitant decline in the people's ability to perceive "The Marks of a Person, worthy to serve his Country."

In the decade preceding the American Revolution, anxiety over the electorate's capability deepened. The correct choice of leadership seemed all the more important if Virginia were to respond properly to the apparent threat to provincial liberty posed by Great Britain's attempts, after the Seven Years' War, to raise a revenue in the colonies and to increase London's control over the empire. Innovations in British colonial policy occasioned not only protests aimed at Parliament but intense scrutiny of the political habits and values of the colonists. The assumption was that only a "free" electorate, that is, one subservient to virtuous standards, could produce a leadership capable of preserving colonial liberty in time of crisis. The first postwar attempt to tax the colonies was the Stamp Act in 1765. Economic boycott of British imports in America and protests from British merchants brought repeal in 1766, but the following year Parliament levied the Townsend Duties. By 1769 a new non-importation movement had swept over the colonies. In 1770 Parliament repealed all the duties except on tea, and the partial retreat produced sharp division in the colonies as Americans disputed whether to continue non-importation until the mother country surrendered completely. By 1771 proponents of ending non-importation (except in the case of tea) had prevailed, but for some colonists the collapse of economic coercion symbolized a weakening of colonial leadership's zeal for preserving American liberty. It was no coincidence that the Virginia authors represented in this chapter turned their attention to the question of the true traits for leadership during the peak of the crisis over the Townsend Duties in 1769–71.

The documents below stress the ideal standards for leadership, and articulated values may either defend or protest the practices of a society. In evaluating the role of each writing, one should keep in mind the type of men who actually acquired seats in the House of Burgesses. In fact Virginians usually selected burgesses from families with large and long-established wealth, English ancestry, and membership in the Church of England.

Four factors, then, occasioned and shaped the debate over the desirable qualities for leadership: the fact that Virginians actually tended to choose members of an economic and social elite, the concept of representation which denied the responsibility of burgesses to follow the desires of their constituents, the need for internalizing values as a means of controlling a seemingly autonomous electorate, and the impact of the tension with the mother country which gave a special urgency to the problem of political leadership. Writing at the end of the colonial period, the authors of the documents which appear below marked out the basic positions which found endorsement or drew criticism in subsequent eras when Americans addressed themselves to the same problem. Careful readers will discover, however, not only points of view that persisted but also attitudes peculiar to an earlier America.

In seeking criteria for leadership, some Virginians looked to the standards of the mother country. The initial two documents of this chapter are examples of these borrowed standards. In the first document a writer styling himself *An Independent Freeholder* recommends to his fellow colonists the advice of James I, King of England from 1603 to 1625. Prefacing his quotation of James is the *Independent Freeholder's* view of why Virginia's electorate may soon lose all ability to make a free and "virtuous" choice of representatives. His readers immediately comprehended what he meant by the "undue influence in elections" which prevailed in the mother country and which threatened Virginia as well. Virginians believed bribery and other forms of corruption permeated political practices, especially elections in Great Britain. In the view of the author, at what point in a society's history did this condition always prevail?

The second document is *The Freeholder's Political Catechism* written in 1733 by the English statesman and philosopher, Henry St. John, Viscount Bolingbroke. James I and Bolingbroke's ideas upon the relationship of the monarch and the House of Commons differed greatly. James endorsed the concept of divine-right-of kings. A century later Bolingbroke developed the concept of Patriot Kings who ruled disinterestedly for the general welfare, but he also emphasized the importance of the House of Commons' autonomy. Do the writings of James and Bolingbroke suggest that Virginians derived conflicting standards from their inheritance of British political thought? The first document appeared in Rind's *Virginia Gazette* on October 31, 1771. The extracts from Bolingbroke's *Catechism* are from the July 12, 1770 edition of the same paper.

☞ Letter from "An Independent Freeholder"

ANONYMOUS

Mr. RIND,

A GENERAL election approaches. The occasion is always important, but at present peculiarly so. I am therefore more than usually anxious that my countrymen should make a prudent and virtuous choice. The mischiefs arising from undue influence in elections threaten to demolish the boasted constitution of Great Britain. The same causes will ever produce the same effects here. Our infant state, indeed, has hitherto preserved us from the maladies engendered in the maturity of every rich and flourishing empire. But this security cannot last always: A period is advancing upon us, at which, unless our early prudence prevent it, we shall experience the same miseries from this source that are so much complained of in our Mother country. Let us guard then in time against this worst of political evils. Let us cherish, as carefully as the vestals did their sacred fire, the spirit of freedom in the choice of our representatives. The open invasions of power are dangerous; but infinitely more so the secret machinations of corruption. As a direction for their conduct upon the approaching important occasion, I beg leave to recommend to the serious consideration of my countrymen the advice of King James the First to his subjects in a like case, which I send you herewith, and beg you to publish. I am

AN INDEPENDENT FREEHOLDER

"BECAUSE the true and antient institution of Parliament do require the Lower House, *at this time,* if ever, to be compounded of the gravest, ablest, and worthiest, members that may be found; we do thereby out of the care of the common good, wherein themselves are participant, without all prejudice to the freedom of elections, admonish all our loving subjects, that have votes in the election of Knights and Burgesses, of these few points following:

"That they cast their eyes upon the worthiest men of all sorts, Knights and Gentlemen, that are lights and guides in their counties, experienced Parliament men, wise and discret Statesmen, that have been practiced in public affairs, whether at home or abroad, grave and eminent lawyers, substantial citizens and burgesses, and generally such as are interested and have portion in the estate.

"Secondly, That they make choice of such as are well affected in religion, without declining either, on the one hand, to Blindness and superstition, or, on the other hand, to schism, or turbulent disposition.

"Thirdly, and lastly, That they be timely sensible not to disvalue or disparage the House with bankrupts and necessitous persons, that may desire long Parliaments only for protection; lawyers of mean account and estimation; young men that are not ripe for grave consultations; mean dependents upon great persons, that may be thought to have their voices under command, and such like obscure and inferior persons: So that, to conclude, we may have the comfort to see before us the very face of a sufficient and well composed House, such as may be worthy to be representative of a third estate of our kingdom, fit to nourish a loving and comfortable meeting between us and our people, and fit to be a noble instrument under the blessing of Almighty God, and our princely care and power, with the loving conjunction of our Prelates and Peers, for settling so great affairs as the proper objects of Parliament."

⊂⊒ The Freeholder's Political Catechism

Viscount Bolingbroke

Who are you?

Answer: I am T. M. a Freeholder of Great Britain.

Q.: *What Privilege enjoyest thou by being a Freeholder?*

A.: By being a Freeholder . . . I am a greater Man in my civil Capacity than the greatest Subject of an arbitrary Prince; because I am governed by Law, to which I give my Consent; and my Life, Liberty, and Goods cannot be taken from me, but according to those Laws. I am a Free-man. . . .

Q.: *Wherein does this* Liberty, *which thou enjoyest consist?*

A.: In *Laws* made by Consent of the People . . . I am free not *from the Law, but by the Law.* . . .

Q.: *What wouldst thou do for thy Country?*

A.: I would die to procure its Prosperity . . . , but as Providence at present requires none of these Sacrifices, I content myself to discharge the ordinary Duties of my Station, and to exhort my Neighbours to do the same.

Q.: *What are the Duties of your Station?*

A.: To endeavour, as far as I am able to preserve the publick Tranquility; and, as I am a *Freeholder,* to give my vote for the Candidate, whom I judge most worthy to serve his Country: for if from any partial Motive I should give my Vote for one unworthy, I should think myself justly chargeable with his Guilt.

Q.: *Thou hast perhaps one Vote of five hundred, and the Member perhaps one of five hundred more; then your Share of the Guilt is but small?*

A.: As he, who assists at a *Murder,* is guilty of *Murder,* so he, who acts the lowest Part in the *enslaving his Country,* is guilty of a much greater Crime than *Murder.*

Q.: *What are the Marks of a Person, worthy to serve his Country in Parliament?*

A.: The Marks of a *good Ruler* given in Scripture will serve for a *Parliament-man; Such as rule over you shall be Men of Truth, hating Covetousness; they shall not take a Gift; they shall not be afraid of the Face of a Man,* Deut. XVI. Therefore I conclude, that the Marks of a *good Parliament-man* are Riches with Frugality; Integrity; Courage; being well-affected to the Constitution; Knowledge of the State of the Country; being prudently frugal of the Money, careful of Trade, and jealous for the Liberties of the People; having stuck to the Interests of his Country in perilous Times, and being assiduous in attendance.

Robert Mumford, author of *The Candidates or the Humours of a Virginia Election* (1770), was a burgess and a member of the planter elite; and in this comedy, he reflected the sentiments of his class. Of particular concern to Mumford in judging the merit of a candidate are his attitudes toward public service and the voters. What are the attitudes sanctioned and condemned by Mumford? The play begins with the decision of an incumbent, Mr. Worthy, not to run again. The other experienced representative, Mr. Wou'dbe, is again a candidate but is joined in the race for the two seats by three disreputable characters: Sir John Toddy, whose name suggests his favorite pastime; Mr. Strutabout; and Mr. Smallhopes. Does Mumford satirize all of the candidates, including Wou'dbe? The better-known younger contemporary of Mumford, Thomas Jefferson, professed his confidence that the people would usually "elect the real good and wise" to office without substantial guidance or influence. Does Mumford share this optimistic view of the Virginia yeomanry? A modern edition, the source of the extract below, appeared in the *William and Mary Quarterly*, 3rd Ser., III (1948), 217–39, edited by Jay B. Hubbell and Douglass Adair.

The Candidates or the Humours of a Virginia Election

ROBERT MUMFORD

ACT I / SCENE I

[Mr. Wou'dbe's house.]

[Enter Wou'dbe with a news-paper in his hand.]

Wou'dbe: I am very sorry our good old governor Botetourt has left us. He well deserved our friendship, when alive, and that we should for years to come, with gratitude, remember his mild and affable deportment. Well, our little world will soon be up, and very busy towards our next election. Must I again be subject to the humours of a fickle croud? Must I again resign my reason, and be nought but what each voter pleases? Must I cajole, fawn, and wheedle, for a place that brings so little profit? . . .

[*Sir John Toddy enters seeking support in the election from Wou'dbe.*]

Wou'dbe: It would be ungenerous indeed, Sir John, to tell you what the people could never be induced to believe. But I'll be ingenuous enough to tell you, Sir John, if you expect any assistance from me, you'll be disappointed, for I can't think you the *fittenest* man I know.

Sir John: Pray, sir, who do you know besides: Perhaps I may be thought as fit as your honour. But, sir, if you are for that, the hardest fend off: damn me, if I care a farthing for you: and so, your servant, sir.

[*Exit Sir John.*]

Wou'dbe: So, I have got the old knight, and his friend Guzzle, I suppose, against me, by speaking so freely; but their interest, I believe, has not weight enough among the people, for me to lose any thing, by making them my enemies. Indeed, the being intimate with such a fool as Sir John, might tend more to my discredit with them, for the people of Virginia have too much sense not to perceive how weak the head must be that is always filled with liquor. . . .

[*Some time later Smallhopes, to discredit Wou'dbe, spreads rumors that Sir John and Wou'dbe have formed an alliance. The Freeholders' reaction is described.*]

1st Freeholder: I don't believe it. Mr. Wou'dbe's a cleverer man than that, and people ought to be ashamed to vent such slanders.

2d Freeholder: So I say: and as we are of one mind, let's go strait, and let Mr. Wou'dbe know it.

[*Exeunt two Freeholders.*]

3d Freeholder: If Mr. Wou'dbe did say it, I won't vote for him, that's sartain.

4th Freeholder: Are you sure of it, neighbour? (To Ned.)

Ned [*another Freeholder*]: Yes, I am sure of it: d'ye think I'd speak such a thing without having good authority?

4th Freeholder: I'm sorry for't; come neighbour, (*to the 3d Freeholder*) this is the worst news that I've heard for a long time.

[*Exeunt 3d & 4th Freeholder.*]

5th Freeholder: I'm glad to hear it. Sir John Toddy is a clever open hearted gentleman as I ever knew, one that won't turn his back upon a poor man, but will take a chearful cup with one as well as another, and it does honour to Mr. Wou'dbe to prefer such a one, to any of your whifflers who han't the heart to be generous, and yet despise poor folks. Huzza! for Mr. Wou'dbe and for Sir John Toddy.

6th Freeholder: I think so too, neighbour. Mr. Wou'dbe, I always thought, was a man of sense, and had larning, as they call it, but he did not love diversion enough, I like him the better for't. Huzza for Mr. Wou'dbe and Sir John Toddy. . . .

[*As the rumors grow, a third candidate, Strutabout, seeks to turn the situation to his favor and approaches Wou'dbe.*]

Strutabout: So far, sir, that I have had overtures from Mr. Smallhopes and his friends, to join my interest with theirs, against you. This, I rejected with disdain, being conscious that you were the properest person to serve the county; but when Smallhopes told me, he intended to prejudice your interest by scattering a few stories among the people to your disadvantage, it raised my blood to such a pitch, that had he not promised me to be silent, I believe I should have chastised him for you myself.

Wou'dbe: If, sir, you were so far my friend, I am obliged to you: though whatever report he is the author of, will, I am certain, gain little credit with the people.

Strutabout: I believe so; and therefore, if you are willing, we'll join our interests together, and soon convince the fellow, that by attacking you he has injured himself.

Wou'dbe: So far from joining with you, or any body else, or endeavouring to procure a vote for you, I am determined never to ask a vote for myself, or receive one that is unduly obtained. . . .

[*Strutabout exits and Act I ends later with the following soliloquy by Wou'dbe.*]

Wou'dbe (pulling out his watch): 'Tis now the time a friend of mine has appointed for me to meet the freeholders at a barbecue; well, I find, in order to secure a seat in our august senate, 'tis necessary a man should either be a slave or a fool; a slave to the people, for the privilege of serving them, and a fool himself, for thus begging a troublesome and expensive employment.

To sigh, while toddy-toping sots rejoice,
To see you paying for their empty voice,
From morn to night your humble head decline,
To gain an honour that is justly thine,
Intreat a fool, who's yours at this day's treat,
And next another's, if another's meat,
Is all the bliss a candidate acquires,
In all his wishes, or his vain desires.

(Exit.

End of the First Act.

[*Rejected by Wou'dbe, Strutabout joins forces with Smallhopes. Act II opens with several freeholders and their wives discussing the candidates.*]

Twist: Well, gentlemen, what do you think of Mr. Strutabout and Mr. Smallhopes? it seems one of the old ones declines, and t'other, I believe, might as well, if what neighbour Sly says, is true.

Stern: Pray, gentlemen, what plausible objection have you against Mr. Wou'dbe? he's a clever civil gentleman as any, and as far as my poor weak capacity can go, he's a man of as good learning, and knows the punctilios of behaving himself, with the best of them.

Prize: Wou'dbe, for sartin, is a civil gentleman, but he can't speak his mind so boldly as Mr. Strutabout, and commend me to a man that will speak his mind freely;—I say.

Lucy: Well, commend me to Mr. Wou'dbe, I say,—I nately like the man; he's mighty good to all his poor neighbours, and when he comes into a poor body's house, he's so free and so funny, isn't he, old man? (*speaking to Twist*). . . .

Prize: Mr. Wou'dbe's a man well enough in his neighbourhood, and he may have learning, as they say he has, but he don't shew it like Mr. Strutabout. . . .

[*Enter Sir John Toddy.*]

Sir John: Gentlemen and ladies, your servant, hah! my old friend Prize, how goes it? how does your wife and children do?

Sarah: At your service, sir. (*making a low curtsey.*)

Prize: How the devil come he to know me so well, and never spoke to me before in his life? (*aside.*)

Guzzle (*whispering to Sir John*): Dick Stern.

Sir John: Hah! Mr. Stern, I'm proud to see you; I hope your family are well; how many children? does the good woman keep to the old stroke?

Catharine: Yes, an't please your honour, I hope my lady's well, with your honour.

Sir John: At your service, madam.

Guzzle (*whispering to Sir John*): Roger Twist.

Sir John: Hah! Mr. Roger Twist! your servant, sir. I hope your wife and children are well.

Twist: There's my wife. I have no children, at your service.

Sir John: A pretty girl: why, Roger, if you don't do better, you must call an old fellow to your assistance.

Twist: I have enough to assist me, without applying to you, sir.

Sir John: No offence, I hope, sir; excuse my freedom. . . .

[*Wou'dbe enters and publicly repudiates the rumour that he seeks votes by allying himself with any other candidate, especially Sir John.*

The scenes then shift from one group of freeholders to another as they converse with the candidates. First Wou'dbe responds to the freeholders.]

Guzzle: Suppose, Mr. Wou'dbe, we were to want you to get the price of rum lower'd—wou'd you do it?

Wou'dbe: I cou'd not.

Guzzle: Huzza for Sir John! he has promised to do it, huzza for Sir John!

Twist: Suppose, Mr. Wou'dbe, we should want this tax taken off—cou'd you do it?

Wou'dbe: I could not.

Twist: Huzza for Mr. Strutabout! he's damn'd, if he don't. Huzza for Mr. Strutabout! . . .

[*The scene then shifts to another part of the field.*]

Strutabout: Gentlemen—I'm much obliged to you for your good intentions; I make no doubt but (with the assistance of my friend Mr. Smallhopes) I shall be able to do every thing you have requested. Your grievances shall be redress'd; and all your petitions heard.

Freeholders: Huzza for Mr. Strutabout and Mr. Smallhopes! . . .

[*When later the freeholders and all candidates gather, tempers flare. Smallhopes and Strutabout challenge Wou'dbe to fight, both boast that they can "lick" Wou'dbe but he calls their bluff by threatening to "explain the opinion I have of them, with the end of my cane." A letter then arrives for Wou'dbe.*]

Wou'dbe: Silence, gentlemen, and I'll read a letter to you, that (I don't doubt) will give you great pleasure. (*He reads*) Sir, *I have been informed that the scoundrels who opposed us last election (not content with my resignation) are endeavouring to undermine you in the good opinion of the people: It has warmed my blood, and again call'd my thoughts from retirement; speak this to the people, and let them know I intend to stand a poll, &c. Yours affectionately.* WORTHY.

Freeholders: Huzza for Mr. Wou'dbe and Mr. Worthy!

Sir John: Huzza for Mr. Worthy and Mr. Wou'dbe! (*hickups*) I'm not so fitten as they, and therefore, gentlemen, I recline. (*hickups*) Yes, gentlemen (*staggering about*) I will; for I am not (*hickups*) so fitten as they. (*falls*) . . .

[*All exit, again allowing Wou'dbe to end the act with a soliloquy.*]

Wou'dbe: Well, I've felt the pulse of all the leading men, and find they beat still for Worthy, and myself. Strutabout and Smallhopes fawn and cringe in so abject a manner, for the few votes they get, that I'm hopes they'll soon be heartily despised.

The prudent candidate who hopes to rise,
Ne'er deigns to hide it, in a mean disguise,
Will, to his place, with moderation slide,
And win his way, or not resist the tide.
The fool, aspiring to bright honour's post,
In noise, in shouts, and tumults oft, is lost.

(*Exit.*

End of the Second Act.

[*Act III opens with Worthy and Wou'dbe in conversation.*]

Wou'dbe: Nothing could have afforded me more pleasure than your letter; I read it to the people, and can with pleasure assure you, it gave them infinite satisfaction.

Worthy: My whole motive in declaring myself was to serve you, and if I am the means of your gaining your election with honour, I shall be satisfied.

Wou'dbe: You have always been extremely kind, sir, but I could not enjoy the success I promised myself, without your participation.

Worthy: I have little inclination to the service; you know my aversion to public life, Wou'dbe, and how little I have ever courted the people for the troublesome office they have hitherto imposed upon me.

Wou'dbe: I believe you enjoy as much domestic happiness as any person, and that your aversion to a public life proceeds from the pleasure you find at home. But, sir, it surely is the duty of every man who has abilities to serve his country, to take up the burden, and bear it with patience.

Worthy: I know it is needless to argue with you upon this head: you are determined I shall serve with you, I find.

Wou'dbe: I am; and therefore let's take the properest methods to insure success.

Worthy: What would you propose?

Wou'dbe: Nothing more than for you to shew yourself to the people. . . .

[*Worthy and Wou'dbe on election day entertain the "principal free-holders" at a decorous breakfast and the play closes with the election itself.*]

1st Freeholder: How do votes go, neighbour? for Wou'dbe and Worthy?

2d Freeholder: Aye, aye, they're just come, and sit upon the bench, and yet all the votes are for them. 'Tis quite a hollow thing. The poll will be soon over. The People croud so much, and vote so fast, you can hardly turn around.

1st Freeholder: How do Strutabout and Smallhopes look? very doleful, I reckon.

2d Freeholder: Like a thief under the gallows. . . .

[*The Sheriff comes to the door, and says,*]

Gentlemen freeholders, come into court, and give your votes, or the poll will be closed.

Freeholders: We've all voted.

Sheriff: The poll's closed. Mr. Wou'dbe and Mr. Worthy are elected.

Freeholders without and within: Huzza—huzza! . . .

Capt. Paunch [*a justice of the peace*]: So we have Mr. Wou'dbe, we have done as we ought, we have elected the ablest, according to the writ.

Henceforth, let those who pray for wholesome laws,
And all well-wishers to their country's cause,
Like us refuse a coxcomb—choose a man—
Then let our senate blunder if it can.

(*Exit omnes.*

End of The Candidates

Accomac County, Virginia, is located on the "Eastern Shore," or the peninsula projecting south from Maryland and separating the Chesapeake Bay from the Atlantic Ocean. The planter aristocracy did not develop there to the extent that it did elsewhere. The following address to the freeholders is a product of Accomac society. Was the standard for leadership strikingly different from the criteria endorsed by Mumford in his comedy? What differences exist between the Accomac Address and the "borrowed standards"? Compared to Mumford's play, does this address contain more or less confidence that voters will spurn treating and bribery and adhere to an ideal standard in their election decisions? The Accomac Address appeared in Purdie and Dixon's *Virginia Gazette* on April 14, 1771.

⋐ The Accomac Address

PURDIE AND DIXON's *Virginia Gazette*

MY DEAR COUNTRYMEN,

The ever to be lamented Loss which has happened to this Province, by the Death of our late worthy Governour, [Lord Botetourt] will probably, in a short Time, give you another Opportunity of exercising one of your most valuable Privileges, I mean that of choosing your Representatives. As this Power, which is vested in you, is one of the principal Hinges on which your Liberties turn, you cannot be too cautious in jealously watching over it; you cannot be too solicitious to make a prudent Use of it, in electing such Gentlemen as shall be most likely to preserve inviolate the sacred Deposit with which you intrust them; and perhaps it may be attended with some Advantage if we here examine what are the Qualifications which ought principally to be sought for in those who may reasonably expect your Favour.

A good Understanding, and penetrating Judgment, are Qualities the Necessity of which must strike the most superficial Inquirer, else may the best Heart be the constant Dupe of ill designing Craft and Deceit. Without these your true Interest cannot be known, and consequently, however zealous he may be to serve you, the proper Steps to procure it cannot be taken; without these he will be unable to scan each Proposal, to view it in every Light surrounded by all the attendant Circumstances, and, piercing into Futurity, behold even how remote Posterity may be thereby affected; and without these will he be unable to strip every Measure of that Disguise under Covert of which it may be artfully obtruded on his Mind, and penetrate through all the sinister Designs and secret Machinations of the Enemies of Freedom, the Slaves of Interest.

But, the greater his Abilities, should he be inclined to prejudice his Constituents, the better will he be enabled to attempt it with Success. To guard against this, it is absolutely necessary that he be a Man of Probity and Integrity; One whose Conduct shall be upright, through Principle; One who regards *Measures*, not *Men;* who will be ready to second any Proposal for the Advantage of his Country, even should its Execution reflect Honour on an Enemy; ready to oppose the contrary, though initiated by a Friend. To the Qualifications above mentioned should be added another, without which even those cannot be exerted to Advantage, I mean that Fortitude, or Strength of Mind, which enables a man, in a good Cause, to bear up against all Opposition, and meet the Frowns of Power unmoved.

These, my Friends, are some of the chief Traits for which you ought to seek. There are some smaller Ones, which render the Character still more finished; but if you find those already mentioned, you may esteem yourselves sufficiently happy. It may be said that the Possession of a large Estate is in some Degree necessary, but it is too commonly seen that the more a Man has the more he desires; and should you find One whose Fortune equalled his Wishes, some other Appetite remains still unsatisfied, his Thirst for Honour is yet unallayed. And what differs it to you (if you are sold) whether it be in Gratification of Avarice, Ambition, or some other Passion. That a Man ought to be independent I grant; but it is Independence of Mind, not of Fortune, that is requisite.

In what I have wrote, I protest to you I have no Design of profiting this Man nor injuring that; I have only just endeavoured to hint at some of the most essential Requisites of those Persons who may be rationally expected to serve you faithfully. The Candidates are those of your old Acquaintance; how well they agree with the Character recommended you are capable to judge; you ought to judge, to judge freely, impartially, unbiassed by Fear or Favour. It is to this that I would, with all my Power, persuade you. It is your greatest Glory, as well as your highest Privilege, that you give Being to your Legislature, that from you they receive their political Existence. This renders an American Planter Superior to the first Minister of an arbitrary Monarch, whose glittering Robes serve but to veil from vulgar Eyes the Chains of Slavery. Guard it then, as the most precious Pledge committed to you by the Deity. Let every Gentleman's true Merit determine his Place in the Scale of your Interest. Say not he is my Neighbour; Can that Circumstance add the Weight of one Straw to his real Value? Say not I am too much in his Power; I shall experience his Resentment unless I give him my Vote: Either you have mistaken his Character, and fear without just Reason; or you are right, and for that very Cause ought to oppose him. . . . Say not he is my Friend: A Gentleman may have Qualities to gain our good Will united with those which would render him an improper Person for a Representative. Say not I am under Obligations to him: you are under still greater to your Country; and though you are bound to compensate the Favours you receive, you are more strongly bound not to compensate them in such a Manner as to injure yourself and Thousands besides. Finally, say not I am but one; my single Vote can be but of little Consequence, let me give it to whom I will. Should each One follow your Example, pray tell me what Sort of a Representative would you send? Should each County do the same, what Sort of a House would you have? I shall only observe, that they who were the Children of Whim, Caprice, or private Interest, would most probably be influenced in their Conduct by Motives much the same. It is a Truth deserves to be well considered, that the publick Virtue of each County consists of that of Individuals, the publick Virtue of the whole Province of that of each County. Perhaps another might caution you to beware of those who seek your Favour at their no small Expense, and that few purchase a Thing without desiring, if possible, to make some Profit thereby; but I think it ought to be considered that gracious Salutations, kind Squeezes by the Hand, Bowls and Glasses, have been so long the high Road to a Seat, that, should any Gentleman, excited by the most disinterested Views, attempt to strike out a new Path, he must meet with so many Rubs by the Way, so many Difficulties, that it is a Thousand to one, after being sadly scratched and torn, and dirted not a little, but he finds himself unable to arrive at the Journey's End. That this is the Case is not so much the Fault of the Candidates, my Countrymen (forgive me the Charge), as it is yours. Had you never given sufficient Intimations that your Interest was to be procured by indirect Methods, the most consummate Impudence would never have thought of it. Had you treated the first Man who endeavoured to seduce your Inclinations by a Bribe with that Contempt he deserved, you would scarcely have found a second so hardy as to attempt it. It would be unjust should any Candidate now suffer for proceeding in a Course you have been so instrumental in establishing; but, my Countrymen, while I declare this, I entreat you, as you value your Liberties, let no such Practices be of any Avail to procure your Interest. Let your Votes be given agreeable to Reason, and not Prejudice. Bribery will, of Course, soon decay. Believe me, few Persons will treat when they find you are not to be influenced thereby. Act then, my Friends, the Parts of Men, of Freemen; strike at the Root of this growing Evil; be influenced by Merit alone. Let your Representatives be Gentlemen, who are sensible and judicious, of incorruptible Integrity, firm and unshaken. Such will serve faithfully, such will be an Honour to your Choice.

NO PARTY MAN.

A form of nativism existed in the colonial period as the following extracts from *The Defense of Injur'd Merit Unmasked . . . (n.p., 1771)* indicate. The anonymous author wrote it to refute a campaign tract by "Philander" (whose candidate in an Accomac election was neither an Englishman nor a member of the Church of England, the colony's established religion). What assumptions about the level of Virginia's development undergird the author's confidence that Anglican Englishmen ought to monopolize public office? What traits does the author associate with "foreigners"?

⊂⋶ The Defense of Injur'd Merit Unmasked

ANONYMOUS

France . . . is mentioned [by you, Philander, as a nation] having foreigners advanced to the highest departments both of the state and army: Wouldst thou set up French policy as a standard to rule a *British Freeholder in his choosing his Representative in Parliament?* Dost thou not know that the government of France is arbitrary, and that the whole nation are slaves to their King and his Ministers? and that the King and people have separate interests in view? How ready are the most exalted Ministers (as well as the most abject vassal) to watch the temper and eye of their Sovereign, and submit to the most servile conditions to flatter his vanity, lust, or any other ruling passion? And if a Minister becomes obnoxious to his master, there are some always ready to use the vilest means (even murder if requisite) to remove the wretched object of their hate.

But these foreigners, ministers, and officers of their armies are not chosen the Representatives of the people to make laws for their government, but are only mere tools to the humour and caprice of their Prince, or to some favourite mistress. If thou, Philander, wert conversant with the history of that nation, thou must soon have found that these foreigners have grievously distressed the miserable subjects of that kingdom. The bravest officers (as Philander calls them) in the French service, both Irish and Scotch . . . I hope are not to be set as patterns for his Majesty's subjects to follow [in Virginia]; because they are traitors to their King and have fled from justice, or voluntarily abdicated their country and rejected her government, and have always endeavoured to destroy that constitution [of Great Britain] which should be so much admired by every loyal subject.

Blockhead, thy [further] comparisons [with Peter the Great of Russia] are odious: Are we in Accomack [County] in the state of that great empire, when Peter undertook the reins of government, the greatest part absorbed in a general ignorance not only of the polite arts, but also of the knowledge of the true religion—Pagans and Idolaters, even the best of them were still attached to their most barbarous customs, and devoid of all human literature. . . . Is it to be wondered at that Peter should invite foreigners to settle in his kingdom, though they were only as secondaries to his grand design of polishing the rusticity of his subjects, but not to represent his people, or to make laws for their government and protection. Their King was an absolute Sovereign, from whose sole will and pleasure all his subjects received their laws; but I hope the witless understrapper would not pretend to insinuate that our situation likewise is equally dreadful, and if any inference can be drawn, it is this, that *his Idol is set up and offers you his service,* to bring you out of that ignorance and barbarism you are now immersed in, enlighten your minds with the true religion of the gospel, inculcate those polite arts and sciences which will make, nay create you a new and polished people. . . .

We are next told that this idol's religion is the same as the established religion of the country, and that the difference consists only in mere idle insignificant forms, as whether we shall stand up like statues, or dirty our breeches in kneeling? . . . To this I shall answer, that in public assemblies for God's worship, the most humble and respectful posture must surely be the most decent . . . , especially as we are commanded to fall low on our knees before his footstool. . . . Judge then, whether standing like statues, or kneeling (though we dirty our breeches knees) be most respectful. I fancy this *Idol* of thine would not scruple to dirty his breeches knees in a dozen puddles, to procure a dozen votes from the freeholders. . . .

The piece which follows, though not aimed directly at the problem of whom Virginians should elect, nonetheless called into question the entire notion of rule by gentlemen. The alternative here proposed anticipated the rhetoric of nineteenth-century Jacksonian Democracy. Written before December, 1769, its author, James Reid, was a religious dissenter, undoubtedly either Baptist or Presbyterian, and probably began his career in Virginia as an indentured servant from Scotland. Reid was a "marginal man" who as an immigrant had severed ties with one culture but had not yet established an identity with his adopted colony. The King Williamite of the satire is the large planter of the tidewater county of King William. The author leaves little doubt as to why the planter gentlemen deserve little respect. What class does he regard as superior and how does he explain their superiority? His satirical humor thinly veils a bitter hostility toward the values and practices of Virginia society. The author leaves little doubt as to why King Williamite, the symbol of the large planters of a tidewater county, deserves little respect and no positions of public trust. How does his portrayal of the planter elite differ from Mumford's or other descriptions in the earlier documents? What type of individual should merit respect, according to Reid, and how does he explain the superiority? Students should also note the attitude toward the Negro which existed side by side with Reid's general social and political view. The combination, tragically, has appeared frequently in American history. The satire appears in *The Colonial Virginia Satirist: Mid-eighteenth-century Commentaries on Politics, Religion, and Society*, ed. with introduction and notes by Richard Beale Davis, American Philosophical Society, *Transactions*, new series, LXVII, Part I (1967), pp. 43–71.

The Gentlemen Condemned

JAMES REID

Among Philosophers and Divines it is a maxim that Virtue is the sole and only Nobility . . . , but in King William County it is quite the reverse, for there one may be a Gentleman without having any Virtue at all. If a King Williamite has Money, Negroes and Land enough he is a compleat

Gentleman. These are screens which supply the place of wit, hide all his deffects, usher him into (what they call) the best of company, and draws upon him the smiles of the fair Sex. His madness then passes for wit, his extravagance for flow of spirit, his isolence for bravery, and his cowardice for wisdom. His money gilds over all his stupidities, and although an Ass covered over with gold is still an Ass, yet in King William County a fool covered over with the same metal, changes his nature, and commences a GENTLEMAN. . . .

Now tell me, for God's sake, O ye Sons of King William County! how money, which in itself is only a piece of mere insignificant dust, can add any real worth to the person who possesses it? How Negroes, in themselves, ignorant, stupid, thoughtless, wicked, profane and of base principles, can add any intrinsic honour to the soul of their Master? Or how a quantity of dirty Acres, the unfeeling, motionless clods of the field, can add any wisdom, any knowledge or any understanding to a Clod Pate? . . .

The son being made a Gentleman by the Negroes & Land given him by his father, who perhaps sprung from a race of Ignoramuses, and who still continued one himself, thinking money bestowed on the education of his Heir apparent would be only thrown away, only imbibed into him this noble Lesson; "by all fair means endeavour to get money, and if you cannot get it that way, get money by any means." This son, full of his own merit, and elevated with the figure he cuts in the world, and with his own importance, immediately assumes the swaggering air and looks big. He drinks, fights, bullies, curses, swears, whores, games, sings, whistles, dances, jumps, capers, runs, talks baudy, visits Gentlemen he never saw, has the rendez-vous with Ladies he never spoke to, . . . eats voraciously, sleeps, snores, & takes snuff. This comprehends his whole life, and renders him a Polite Gentleman, or to use the modern elegant phrase—a damn'd honest Fellow.

Nevertheless of all this he must not forget to augment his Estate, for if that go to ruin his Gentlemanship, his Wit, his Politeness, & Wisdom all go to the Pot together. To prevent this therefore he, at his leisure hours, & when the time sits heavy upon his hand for want of Polite company, impregnates his own Negro wenches, as a very easy way of augmenting his wealth. Solomon tells us that he had seen Servants upon horses and Princes walking upon foot. The meaning of which passage is, that fornication & adultery break down all distinction; for if a King should have a Son by a poor Girl, that son is a Prince although he should all his life reign betwixt the horns of the Plough; and if a Princess should accept the embrace of a Clown, the child is but of the same rank with his father even though he should ascend the throne: So that Solomon might very readily see Servants upon horses and Princes walking beside them on foot, and no doubt he did see it. But were he alive now he would

behold Slave SON running before his Gentleman Father; Slave Brother
driving the Oxen of Brother Gentleman; Slave Sister wiping the shoes of
Lady Sister, and washing the dirty Posteriors of the MASTERS their
young Brothers. . . .

I have a rational aversion at Barbecues . . . and need not go to
church to hear the news of any. They are given from a view to self
interest, and no man ought to eat of them but what can be of service
to the liberal donor. Now I have no vote, no interest in this world, and
why should I consume the victuals and drink of a Gentleman for nothing,
when the same victuals and drink might have procured a good Vote.
May I die the day that I commit so flagrant a piece of injustice. A man's
hogs, sheep, cattle, corn, Rum, wine, oil, salt, pepper, beer, cyder, &c.
(if he has payed for them) are his own; and if his own dumb cattle,
when dead, are able, by being put into the bellies of the living, to make
them speak & chuse him for a Burgess, happy the man, say I, who has a
plentiful stock of dumb Animals. If I was at the helm of affairs, and God
knows I would make but a miserable bad pilot, I would thus consult for
the good of the poor; viz. I would have the general Assembly of the
Colony dissolved every month, and called together every other month
that the poor Planters might live by Barbecues. . . .

As the first step towards the cure of a bodily distemper is to be well
acquainted with the cause of the disease, so in moral distempers the
knowing from what causes they proceed contributes not a little to their
cure. It is highly necessary then that we search into the original spring
of all this degeneracy in morals which is so conspicuous around us. . . .
The iniquities of Sodom were pride, fulness of bread, and abundance of
Idleness, which I think I may venture to affirm have been the sources
from whence have issued all the vice and immorality which abound in
this County. Idleness has been always held in so great disesteem by
learned men, that some Philosophers have ventured to affirm that it is
better to do ill than to sit idle, just as if idleness was not absolutely an
evil. An idle man, say the Arabians, is the devil's companion; and they
have another Apothegm which says, that he who bringeth up his son to
no employment, bringeth him up a Thief. . . .

Before a boy knows his right hand from his left, can discern black
from white, good from evil, or knows who made him, or how he exists,
he is a Gentleman. Before he is capable to be his own master, he is told
that he is Master of others; and he begins to command without ever
having learned to obey. As a Gentleman therefore it would derogate
greatly from his character, to learn his trade; or to put his hand to any
servile employment. His dog & horse are his most favourite companions,
and a negro about his own age, stature & mental qualifications, whom he
abuses & kicks for every trifle, is his satelite. He learns to dance a
minuet, that is, to walk slowly up and down a room with his hat on,

and look wondrous grave, which is an affectation of the body to hide the defects of the mind. He is taught too how to skip and caper when ever he hears a few horse hairs rubbed with rozin, scrapped across the gutts of a Cat, and he procures a competent skill in racing and cock-fighting. With these accomplishments, and a small knowledge in cards and dice, he becomes a gentleman of finished education, of consummate politeness, that is, impudence & ignorance, consequently he is fit to enter into gay company, and to be a companion, humble admirer, & favourite of the fair-Sex. There is no matter whether he can read or not, such a thing has nothing to do in the composition. He has money, land and negroes, that's enough. These things procure him every honour, every favour, every title of respect. He is dubbed an Esquire and hugs himself upon the glorious appellation. . . .

It is observed by Naturalists that little Birds are the best singers, whereas your birds of fine plumage, the Peacock for instance, have a harsh and disagreeable sound. Just so it is with men; the poor have much more gratitude than the rich, and thank God sincerely for benefits which the other would either overlook, reject, or despise. Thus I have heard a rich Deist swear by G—d that it was unbecoming the dignity of a Gentleman to repeate the Lord's prayer: "How sneaking & beggarly is it, said he, for a Gentleman of fortune to be petitioning for his daily bread? If there had been a bottle of wine annexed to it, it would have been something to the purpose, and no Gentleman need have been ashamed to ask the boon, but as it is, by G—d it's scandalous."

Riches may very aptly be compared to Groves; for as Groves, when adorned in all the ornaments of folliage, shut out the beams of the Sun which gave them existence: So Riches banish from the mind of their Possessor all tho'ts of him who bestowed them, and leave him no other deity but themselves; they render a man either a miser or a libertine, and which of these two is worst I shall not at present ascertain.

The supreme Being seems to have a peculiar care of the poor, which he does not bestow upon the rich, & which ought to make a man chuse poverty rather than wealth. I know that this will appear strange doctrine to a King Williamite, . . . but I care not what they think, since I can prove my assertion. We read in Scripture that God went down to the prison with Joseph, but I defy any man to read there that he went up to the throne with him; and indeed it is more than probable that he did not go up, for if he had Joseph would not so soon have learnt to swear the polite court Oaths as we find he did, for when talking to his bretheren, . . . he swears twice by the life of Pharaoh, wch at that time was a genteel way of swearing.

However the middle way of life is by far the best, & therefore Agur . . . prays that God would neither give him poverty nor riches, but only feed him with convenient food; Not riches, says he, lest I be full and deny thee, and say, Who is the Lord? . . . Riches are nevertheless worse to be born than poverty, as they make men forget themselves, whilst poverty, keeps them humble and wise and docible. A man under affliction listens willingly to advice which in prosperity he would have rejected; and for this reason it was that God gave his Laws to the Jews when in the wilderness & oppressed with wants, because he knew that stif-necked and rebellious people at any other time would have lent but a deaf ear to his precepts. "Would to God, said Abdalonymous, that I may bear royalty with as much composure of mind, and enjoy as much felicity as in my state of Poverty."

Poverty is the school of wisdom. It knits, if I may be allowed the expression, the joints of the soul, and teaches us to reason more justly. The man who has never tasted the cup of adversity is a very bad member of society. He thinks he knows much, but he knows nothing. He sees all things with equal apathy. Pleasures to a man who never knew sorrow, must be insipid. His heart is hardened against the miseries of the unhappy. The tear of pity never moistened his plump cheek, nor did the sigh of compassion ever flow from his obdurate breast. Such a man is fit for nothing. . . .

It is a common received opinion that things which are rare and uncommon attract our attention, raise our curiosity, and afford us pleasure and delight; but I find that from this general rule there is an exception; for nothing is more rare and uncommon than Virtue, and yet in this County it is taken no notice of: Though I do not wonder at it, for the virtuous man is often poor, despised and solitary, whilst vice rides in a chariot, lives splendidly, and commands respect. I do not envy those grand Personages, who are only constant in Inconstancy; and though I am sometimes grieved that my lot is cast among them, yet I usually comfort myself with this suggestion, viz. that a man's being in a stable does not make him a horse.

Chapter
3: Revolutionary Diplomacy and American Values

☞ GERARD H. CLARFIELD

During the latter half of the eighteenth century international politics was characterized by a remarkably frank and open struggle for power among the states of Europe. Weak states generally survived only at the sufference of greater ones, and few among the frail managed to preserve a genuine independence. In one extreme case, the large but internally fragmented Poland was simply devoured by the stronger states surrounding her. Seldom, either before or after, has there been a time in which the brutal fact of power has been so frankly and singularly accepted as the sole consideration in determining the course of international affairs.

Paradoxically, Europe's political conflicts, which generally threatened small states with extinction, actually encouraged the birth of the United States. In a very real sense the English colonies might never have secured their independence had it not been for the economic and military aid afforded them by monarchical France. Yet the government of Louis XVI had little sympathy for America's republican experiment. Only her rivalry with England bound France to the American cause. It was France's desire to redress in her favor the balance of power in Europe, to strip the British of their empire and thus of power, which moved her to encourage American independence. But if the French hoped to separate the American colonies from Britain, they were hardly anxious to encourage the growth of a new and potentially powerful rival on the western shore of the Atlantic. The Americans then, who could count on the French to aid them in their struggle against Britain, also faced the potential menace of France. To a point the two countries were natural allies. But after independence, what? How would America avoid becoming another satellite, another pawn in the continuing European game called "power politics"?

Even before independence, Americans made a beginning at solving this problem. As a result of their unusual geographic situation colonial

Americans were granted unique advantages. They were, of course, never isolated from the intellectual or political cross currents of Europe, for America was part of a vast political and commercial community. On the other hand, although the ocean was no barrier, it did offer insulation. From their side of the Atlantic American diplomatists were given an unusual opportunity to fashion a foreign policy reflective of an independent economic, social, and political order. This policy was designed to serve three purposes. First it would fulfill the needs of a practical commercial people. Next it would offer an alternative to the prospect of becoming a satellite of France or of any other great power. Finally it would live up to the vision of a revolutionary people who offered to Europe not only an alternative to absolutism but to the existing amoral system of international politics as well. The components of this policy were the twin themes of commercial expansionism and nonentanglement in Europe's politics.

It was clear to those who witnessed the birth pangs of the republic that the new nation, enmeshed as she was in an international network of trade, would inexorably be drawn into international predicaments. European politics could hardly be ignored. On the contrary, European affairs had to be attended to, and very carefully. But the purpose of that attention was the preservation of both neutrality and sovereignty. American diplomatists relied on one fundamental principle to guide them in their quest. This was to eschew all alliances with European powers. Only then could the United States reserve for itself that independence of action necessary for neutrality.

Nonentanglement was a sensible foreign policy objective. Experience had brought home to the colonials a clear perception of the dangers of becoming involved as a weak state in Europe's continuing conflicts. As colonials the Americans had on more than one occasion during Britain's eighteenth-century wars for empire been pressed into the service of British national interest. That interest, determined in London, seldom took into consideration the needs of a growing colonial population. The colonies had survived and even prospered. But their counsel had too seldom been sought and their interests had not often enough been considered. From experience Americans had learned what it meant to be involuntarily involved in Europe's continuing power struggle. It was a natural and practical political response, then, for early American foreign policy to stress nonentanglement.

Political nonalignment seemed best calculated to serve America's economic interests as well. As republicans, Americans believed they had little at stake in the dynastic squabbles of Europe. As citizens of a nation whose prosperity was dependent upon trade, they sought a foreign policy which would allow a maximum of trade and commerce whether or not Europe happened to be at war. Since they were convinced that

Europeans would continue in a state of international strife and intermittent warfare, Americans believed nonentanglement and neutrality to be the only policy which would allow them the opportunity to trade widely with all nations regardless of the political conditions prevalent in the rest of the Atlantic trading community.

Beyond any practical considerations, however, this approach to foreign policy was a strong affirmation of certain American Revolutionary convictions. If experience had demonstrated the real dangers of playing the pawn in European politics, it had also provided a continuing panorama of the moral degeneracy of European leadership. Europe's system of power politics seemed depraved. The abandonment of ethics in the quest for power, and the emphasis which Europeans placed upon the use of force in the conduct of international relations, disturbed Americans who wanted no part in such a system.

The American choice of republicanism as a system of government is in its own way the clearest indication we have of America's sense of uniqueness and her instinctive rejection of Europe's political system. Republics, Americans believed, were by their very nature "free" governments whose policies reflected the best interests of the inhabitants. Monarchies too often followed policies designed to suit only the pride, passions, or prejudices of their kings. Just as Americans felt that the relative virtue of a government could be judged in terms of the degree to which it assumed a republican character, so they believed that in the field of foreign relations republics would follow policies in the general interest while monarchies would not. To put it simply, true republican foreign policy was peace-loving, concerned only with encouraging moral and economic progress. Monarchical diplomacy, as amply demonstrated by Europe over centuries past, was concerned with the narrow interests of the monarch—the augmentation of princely power. The United States' policy of nonentanglement was the means by which the nation might keep clear of the contagion of monarchical corruption.

What kind of revolutionaries were they, however, who, adopting a defensive foreign policy, remained content to play the passive role of moral exemplars to Europe? Why were so few of America's early leaders willing to make any serious effort to export the movement to Europe? The best answer seems to be that the Revolution was in part characterized by an interesting mixture of hope and doubt. America's revolutionaries were sure of the justice, promise, and morality of their cause. They were equally sure that it represented a vast improvement over a degenerate European political system. They hoped that Europe would catch the contagion of liberty and follow the American lead. There was, however, a feeling that Europeans, as victims of an unjust yet deeply rooted social system, were less capable than Americans of achieving the high plateau of political and social morality represented by the Revolution. Thus, at least until 1789, few really believed Europe capable of following the revolutionary example.

If Americans had their doubts about Europe's potential as a home for liberty, they had no doubts that they were surrounded by hostile despotisms. Political realism, too, dictated caution. The eradication of absolutism would, if it ever happened, take place only as a result of a long and tortuous process. Under the circumstances, working to keep politically isolated from Europe seemed one way, possibly the only way, to preserve the flame of liberty as an example of what Europeans at some future time might accomplish.

Isolationism from European politics did not imply economic isolation. Indeed, a nation whose ships sailed all over the world could hardly adopt anything less than an expansive economic foreign policy. Independence meant tearing loose from the British imperial system, giving up the many old and habitual patterns of trade, and enduring widespread economic dislocation. After the Continental Congress declared America independent, new trading partners were cultivated; new markets for the raw materials and agricultural products of America were sought. American shippers looked to new customers to pick up the slack created by the loss of British cargoes and the West Indies trade. The task was difficult, for other powers were not easily coaxed into allowing American vessels to compete for trade in their ports; foreign competition was viewed by most powers as damaging to the balance of trade upon which the wealth and power of the state depended.

As in the political realm, economically the new American republic was ready with a program which combined her practical needs with a certain degree of revolutionary vision. The Congressional Treaty Plan of 1776 proposed the negotiation on a bilateral basis of commercial treaties between the United States and other nations. The major economic purpose of the plan was to do away with all barriers to trade between signatory powers. The effect of a network of such treaties between the nations of the world would have been the establishment of a world-wide trading community founded upon the principle of totally free trade and complete economic reciprocity. Obviously this plan, designed as an alternative to the existing closed economic system, would have maximized America's commercial opportunities the world over. It was clearly designed to serve America's practical needs first.

But the idea of reciprocity which was basic to the treaty plan reflected something else as well. It was an alternative to mercantilism, the economic philosophy fundamental to the whole system of eighteenth-century international politics. Mercantilism, a philosophy of economic conflict, emphasized differences rather than similarities in the interests of the powers. It taught Europe's leadership that national strength depended upon the continuing influx of wealth; that, therefore, a favorable balance of trade was the principal economic object of the state, and that dependence upon other nations for goods or services was injurious to the national interest. The Treaty Plan of 1776, which called for the eradication of trade barriers and imperial monopolies on trade, suggested that conflict need not be the rule, and that if only the nations would put aside the idea of conflict and replace it with one of cooperation, the bonds of a common humanity might gradually create a community of nations.

Although the vision of a real international revolution was present in early American foreign policy formulations, it would be an error to overestimate its significance. In the last quarter of the eighteenth century a cooperative commonwealth of trading nations seemed a universe away, and American diplomatists realized this. Therefore, during the struggle for independence and in the years which followed, they struggled to work out commercial arrangements with various powers that came as nearly as possible to attaining the ideal. In every negotiation the result was a far cry from the object. In the long run practical Americans settled for what they could get.

How revolutionary was America's early diplomacy? It was an ingeniously flexible blend of the practical and the idealistic, with an emphasis on the practical. And the combination held together fairly well from the outbreak of the War for Independence until the eruption of the French Revolution. At that point ideological issues predominated.

During the American Revolution and the years immediately following, expediency ruled the nation's councils. Again and again the visionary aspects of American diplomacy were moderated in the service of national interest. But in the 1790's, with the expansion of the French Revolution, radical ideas could not be set aside so easily. The war being fought in Europe between France on the one hand and England and her continental allies on the other assumed major ideological proportions in the minds of Americans. The result was that the foreign policy consensus that had more or less been preserved since 1776 came apart. One segment of the populace, those who became known as Federalists, adhered fiercely to the diplomacy of practicality, denounced the Revolution in France, and became strident defenders of a foreign policy which emphasized the expediency of nonentanglement; and they thereby sacrificed the idealistic qualities found in the formulations of 1776. Another group, those who came eventually to be known as Republicans, denounced Britain and her allies as despots anxious to destroy liberty, warned Americans that if France fell they might well be the next victims, and urged a foreign policy benevolent to America's sister republic. Each side, of course, believed the other represented a repudiation of real American foreign policy. Neither side was completely correct.

At the outbreak of the American war for independence, diplomatists faced a real dilemma: a policy of political nonentanglement was already considered axiomatic, yet foreign aid seemed essential to victory. France for her own reasons wanted America to win, and some thought she might be tempted to intervene. But to invite French forces to participate in the war was to invite a potentially new master to land an army and oust the old one. Once the French had driven England from the colonies, could they be convinced to leave? At the very least, was there not the danger that through a military alliance the United States might become a satellite of France, little more than a pawn in Europe's continuing struggle for power?

None gave this question more serious consideration than John Adams, in 1775 and 1776 a delegate from Massachusetts to the Continental Congress. In his *Autobiography*, Adams recalls the debate in Congress over the issue of a French alliance and how he tried to strike a balance between the need for military help and the practical political dangers involved in entanglement. What did John Adams believe to be the principal purpose of foreign policy as Europeans practiced it? Did he seek a political connection with France? To what extent did ideology enter into Adams' calculations? This selection is from *The Works of John Adams*, Charles Francis Adams, ed. (Boston: Little, Brown, 1850), II, pp. 503–506.

ᏟᎬ A Practical View

JOHN ADAMS

At the appointed time, we returned to Philadelphia, and Congress were reassembled. Mr. Richard Penn had sailed for England, and carried the petition, from which Mr. Dickinson and his party expected relief. I expected none, and was wholly occupied in measures to support the army and the expedition into Canada. Every important step was opposed, and carried by bare majorities, which obliged me to be almost constantly engaged in debate; but I was not content with all that was done, and almost every day I had something to say about advising the States to institute governments, to express my total despair of any good from the petition or any of those things which were called conciliatory measures. I constantly insisted that all such measures, instead of having any tendency to produce a reconciliation, would only be considered as proofs of our timidity and want of confidence in the ground we stood on, and would only encourage our enemies to greater exertions against us; that we should be driven to the necessity of declaring ourselves independent States, and that we ought now to be employed in preparing a plan of confederation for the Colonies, and treaties to be proposed to foreign powers, particularly to France and Spain; that all these measures ought to be maturely considered and carefully prepared, together with a declaration of independence; that these three measures, independence, confederation, and negotiations with foreign powers, particularly France, ought to go hand in hand, and be adopted all together; that foreign powers could not be expected to acknowledge us till we had acknowledged ourselves, and taken our station among them as a sovereign power and independent nation; that now we were distressed for want of artillery, arms, ammunition, clothing, and even for flints; that the people had no markets for their produce, wanted clothing and many other things, which foreign commerce alone could fully supply, and we could not expect commerce till we were independent; that the people were wonderfully well united, and extremely ardent. There was no danger of our wanting support from them, if we did not discourage them by checking and quenching their zeal; that there was no doubt of our ability to defend the country, to support the war, and maintain our independence. We had men enough, our people were brave, and every day improving in all the exercises and discipline of war; that we ought immediately to give permission to our merchants to fit out privateers and make reprisals on the enemy; that Congress ought to arm ships, and commission officers, and lay the foundation of a navy; that immense advantages might be derived from this resource; that not only West India articles, in great abundance, and British manufactures, of all kinds, might be obtained, but artillery ammunitions and all kinds of supplies for the army; that a system of measures, taken with unanimity and pursued with resolution, would insure us the friendship and assistance of France.

Some gentlemen doubted of the sentiments of France; thought she would frown upon us as rebels, and be afraid to countenance the example. I replied to those gentlemen, that I apprehended they had not attended to the relative situation of France and England; that it was the unquestionable interest of France that the British Continental Colonies should be independent; that Britain, by the conquest of Canada and her naval triumphs during the last war, and by her vast possessions in America and the East Indies, was exalted to a height of power and preeminence that France must envy and could not endure. But there was much more than pride and jealousy in the case. Her rank, her consideration in Europe, and even her safety and independence, were at stake. The navy of Great Britain was now mistress of the seas, all over the globe. The navy of France almost annihilated. Its inferiority was so great and obvious, that all the dominions of France, in the West Indies and in the East Indies, lay at the mercy of Great Britain, and must remain so as long as North America belonged to Great Britain, and afforded them so many harbors abounding with naval stores and resources of all kinds, and so many men and seamen ready to assist them and man their ships; that interest could not lie; that the interest of France was so obvious, and her motives so cogent, that nothing but a judicial infatuation of her councils could restrain her from embracing us; that our negotiations with France ought, however, to be conducted with great caution, and with all the foresight we could possibly obtain; that we ought not to enter into any alliance with her, which should entangle us in any future wars in Europe; that we ought to lay it down, as a first principle and a maxim never to be forgotten, to maintain an entire neutrality in all future European wars; that it never could be our interest to unite with France in the destruction of England, or in any measures to break her spirit, or reduce her to a situation in which she could not support her independence. On the other hand, it could never be our duty to unite with Britain in too great a humiliation of France; that our real, if not our nominal, independence, would consist in our neutrality. If we united with either nation, in any future war, we must become too subordinate and dependent on that nation, and should be involved in all European wars, as we had been hitherto; that foreign powers would find means to corrupt our people, to influence our councils, and, in fine, we should be little better than puppets, danced on the wires of the cabinets of Europe. We should be the sport of European intrigues and politics; that, therefore, in preparing treaties to be proposed to foreign powers, and in the instructions to be given to our ministers, we ought to confine ourselves strictly to a treaty of commerce; that such a treaty would be an ample compensation to France for all the aid we should want from her. The opening of American trade to her, would be a vast resource for her commerce and naval power, and a great assistance to her in protecting her East and West India possessions, as well as her fisheries; but that the bare dismemberment of the British empire would be to her an incalculable security and benefit, worth more than all the exertions we should require of her, even if it should draw her into another eight or ten years' war.

Adams had been concerned with the problem of preserving America's freedom of action and had approached the problem in a hard-headed way. There is almost nothing in what he wrote to indicate that American diplomacy in this early period had anything of the ideological about it. But it did. Even before independence, colonial writers had taken note of the moral superiority of American society to that of Europe. During the revolutionary crisis, one propagandist, Thomas Paine, related this to foreign policy considerations. From the selection which follows can you see the differences Paine perceived between the conduct of foreign policy in a monarchy as opposed to a republic. Can you explain the ideological foundations for a policy of political isolation? A complete edition of Paine's *Common Sense* may be found in Merrill Jensen, ed., *Tracts of the American Revolution, 1763–1776* (Bobbs-Merrill Co., Kansas City, 1967).

⤂ An Ideological View

THOMAS PAINE

In the early ages of the world according to the scripture chronology there were no kings, the consequence of which was there were no wars, it is the pride of kings which throws mankind into confusion. Holland without a king hath enjoyed more peace for this last century, than any of the monarchical governments in Europe. Antiquity favors the same remark; for the quiet and rural lives of the first patriarchs hath a happy something in them, which vanishes away when we come to the history of Jewish royalty. . . . Where there are no distinctions, there can be no superiority; perfect equality affords no temptation. The Republics of Europe are all (and we may say always) in peace. Holland and Swisserland are without wars foreign or domestic. Monarchical governments, it is true, are never long at rest; the crown itself is a temptation to enterprising ruffians at home; and that degree of pride and insolence ever attendant on regal authority, swells into a rupture with foreign powers in instances where a republican government by being formed on more natural principles, would negotiate the mistake. . . .

Much hath been said of the united strength of Britain and the colonies, that in conjunction they might bid defiance to the world: But this is mere presumption, the fate of war is uncertain, neither do the expressions mean any thing, for this Continent would never suffer itself to be drained of inhabitants, to support the British Arms in either Asia, Africa, or Europe.

Besides, what have we to do with setting the world at defiance? Our plan is commerce, and that well attended to, will secure us the peace and friendship of all Europe, because it is the interest of all Europe to have America a free port. Her trade will always be a protection, and her barrenness of gold and silver will secure her from invaders.

I challenge the warmest advocate for reconciliation, to shew, a single advantage that this Continent can reap, by being connected with Great Britain. I repeat the challenge, not a single advantage is derived. Our corn will fetch its price in any market in Europe and our imported goods must be paid for buy them where we will.

But the injuries and disadvantages we sustain by that connection, are without number, and our duty to mankind at large, as well as to ourselves, instruct us to renounce the alliance: because any submission to, or dependence on Great Britain, tends directly to involve this continent in European wars and quarrels. As Europe is our market for trade, we ought to form no political connection with any part of it. 'Tis the true interest of America, to steer clear of European contentions, which she never can do, while by her dependence on Britain, she is made the make-weight in the scale of British politics.

Europe is too thickly planted with Kingdoms, to be long at peace, and whenever a war breaks out between England and any foreign power, the trade of America goes to ruin, *because of her connection with Britain.* The next war may not turn out like the last, and should it not, the advocates for reconciliation now, will be wishing for separation then, because neutrality in that case, would be a safer convoy than a man of war. Every thing that is right or reasonable pleads for separation. . . . The blood of the slain, the weeping voice of nature cries, 'TIS TIME TO PART.

John Jay had been a successful diplomatist during the American Revolution. It was he who was probably primarily responsible for the success of the negotiations in Paris which closed the war. In the two selections which follow, Jay writes on foreign affairs. Both were written during his tenure as Secretary for Foreign Affairs for the Confederation Congress. The first is an extract from a private letter written in 1786. The second, "The Federalist No. 4," came two years later while he was working in New York for the ratification of the Constitution. What are the idealistic elements in Jay's analyses? What sorts of considerations moderate that idealism? And with what consequences?

Jay's letter to Lord Lansdowne appears in Henry P. Johnson, ed., *The Correspondence and Public Papers of John Jay* (G. P. Putnam's Sons, New York, 4 vols., 1891), III, pp. 191–94. "The Federalist No. 4," is taken from Jacob E. Cooke, ed., *The Federalist* (World Publishing Company, 1961, 1965), pp. 18–20.

Moderated Idealism
John Jay to Lord Lansdowne

JOHN JAY

New York, 20th April, 1786

My Lord:

My Lord, I write thus freely from a persuasion that your ideas of policy are drawn from those large and liberal views and principles, which apply to the future as well as the present, and which embrace the interests of the nation and of mankind, rather than the local and transitory advantages of partial systems and individual ambition; for your lordship's plans on the peace were certainly calculated to make the revolution produce only an exchange of dependence for friendship, and of sound and feathers for substance and permanent benefits. How greatly would it redound to the happiness as well as honour of all civilized people, were they to consider and treat each other like fellow-citizens; each nation governing itself as it pleases, but each admitting others to a perfect freedom of commerce. The blessings resulting from the climate and local advantages of one country would then become common to all, and the bounties of nature and conveniences of art pass from nation to nation without being impeded by the selfish monopolies and restrictions with which narrow policy opposes the extension of Divine benevolence. It is pleasant, my Lord, to dream of these things, and I often enjoy that pleasure; but though, like some of our other dreams, we may wish to see them realized, yet the passions and prejudices of mankind forbid us to expect it.

FEDERALIST NO. 4 [AN EXTRACT]

It is too true, however disgraceful it may be to human nature, that nations in general will make war whenever they have a prospect of getting any thing by it; nay, absolute monarchs will often make war when their nations are to get nothing by it, but for purposes and objects merely personal, such as a thirst for military glory, revenge for personal affronts, ambition, or private compacts to aggrandize or support their particular families or partisans. These and a variety of other motives, which affect only the mind of the sovereign, often lead him to engage in wars not sanctified by justice or the voice and interests of his people. But, independent of these inducements to war, which are more prevalent in absolute monarchies, but which well deserve our attention, there are others which affect nations as often as kings; and some of them will on examination be found to grow out of our relative situation and circumstances.

With France and with Britain we are rivals in the fisheries, and can supply their markets cheaper than they can themselves, notwithstanding any efforts to prevent it by bounties on their own or duties on foreign fish.

With them and with most other European nations we are rivals in navigation and the carrying trade; and we shall deceive ourselves if we suppose that any of them will rejoice to see it flourish; for, as our carrying trade cannot increase without in some degree diminishing theirs, it is more their interest, and will be more their policy, to restrain than to promote it.

In the trade to China and India, we interfere with more than one nation, inasmuch as it enables us to partake in advantages which they had in a manner monopolized, and as we thereby supply ourselves with commodities which we used to purchase from them.

The extension of our own commerce in our own vessels cannot give pleasure to any nations who possess territories on or near this continent, because the cheapness and excellence of our productions, added to the circumstance of vicinity, and the enterprise and address of our merchants and navigators, will give us a greater share in the advantages which those territories afford, than consists with the wishes or policy of their respective sovereigns.

Spain thinks it convenient to shut the Mississippi against us on the one side, and Britain excludes us from the Saint Lawrence on the other; nor will either of them permit the other waters which are between them and us to become the means of mutual intercourse and traffic.

From these and such like considerations, which might, if consistent with prudence, be more amplified and detailed, it is easy to see that jealousies and uneasinesses may gradually slide into the minds and cabinets of other nations, and that we are not to expect that they should regard our advancement in union, in power and consequence by land and by sea, with an eye of indifference and composure.

The people of America are aware that inducements to war may arise out of these circumstances, as well as from others not so obvious at present, and that whenever such inducements may find fit time and opportunity for operation, pretences to color and justify them will not be wanting. Wisely, therefore, do they consider union and a good national government as necessary to put and keep them in *such a* situation as, instead of *inviting* war, will tend to repress and discourage it. That situation consists in the best possible state of defence, and necessarily depends on the government, the arms, and the resources of the country. . . .

For the better part of seventeen years, the uneasy blend of ideology and practicality survived within the context of American diplomacy. But after 1793, when England became involved in the Wars of the French Revolution, the situation changed. The economic and ideological implications of this new European crisis challenged America's previous foreign policy consensus. Public opinion divided into pro-French and anti-French factions. In effect the issues raised by the revolution in France forced Americans to choose between the practical and the idealistic aspects of the old policy. The result was angry political antagonism at home.

In the following selection, "An Old Soldier" pleads for a pro-French policy and warns against adhering to President Washington's proclamation of neutrality which had been issued only a few days before. To what extent is the author concerned with questions of national interest? What similarities do you see beween his position and that taken earlier by Thomas Paine? What importance do you attach to the author's conclusion? The article, signed "An Old Soldier," appears in the *National Gazette*, a newspaper published in Philadelphia. It is dated May 3, 1793.

⊂Ξ An Ideological Response to the French Revolution

"AN OLD SOLDIER"

To the FREEMEN of AMERICA

Fellow Citizens,

This is an awful crisis, the present period is pregnant with the most important events. Freedom and tyranny, dreadful as contending elements, are struggling for pre-eminence, and the issue seems doubtful; amid this scene of desolation, carnage, and horror, we are as yet permitted to solace ourselves under our own vine and our own fig tree; but how long this indulgence will be granted is not within the compass of our calculation to determine. France is fighting the cause of mankind, and the political happiness or misery of the world depends upon the issue; perhaps I would not be wrong in asserting that even our political existence is involved in her fate. What security have we that the same combination of tyrants would not confederate against us to exterminate liberty from the face of the earth; should France relapse into her antient despotism, should Great Britain, after having contributed to the destruction of her liberty, and after having secured her neutrality, renew her claim to the United States (and many more improbable things have happened) with the forces and treasures of conspiring tyrants, to whom are we to look up for assistance? America kindled the flame of liberty in France, and tho' it should be smothered for the present, if not extinguished here, the sparks may again fall upon tyranny, and tyrants well know this and may take means to prevent it; the same reasons that would justify an interference in the government of Poland, and of France, the same motives that would induce such interference there would operate with equal effect here. The argument of force can only be answered by force, and in such a contest we should be found *unequal.* That power & not right is the logic of monarchs; that the interests of monarchs and the people are distinct; that it is their wish to suppress every opposition to their will, no one conversant in the affairs of men will deny: if then they have the power to interfere in our government, will it not be the same right which they had to interfere in Poland, and partition that devoted country? I repeat, my fellow citizens, that France is armed in the cause of mankind and that her revolution is the pivot on which your liberty turns. I will not take into view the indirect means which may be used by European tyrants to sap the foundation of the edifice of liberty; tho' corruption is a worm as certain and as deadly as the Austrian and Prussian legions. *Corruption* renders the king of Great Britain as absolute as the emperor of Morocco or the grand Signior! Can you then in a cause which is yours, which is the world's be indifferent spectators of the struggles of France? Can you censure the unavoidable excesses of a gallant nation, heated by the conspiracies of tyrants, and urged by their robberies to the commission of acts which it would deprecate in the absence of convulsion? Can you tamely bear the rejoicings of *Britons* among us, the rejoicings of some of our own citizens, at the defeats of our gallic brethren? Shake off your insensibility, arouse from your lethargy, and tho' you cannot march armies to the assistance of your brethren, at least convince them that you feel an interest in their cause by your conduct to their enemies among us, and by your affectionate conduct to the representatives here, and by the expressions of joy or sorrow on their victories or defeats.

AN OLD SOLDIER

May 3d, 1793

It was President Washington himself who made the most eloquent statement in defense of neutrality and nonentanglement. In September, 1796, on the eve of his retirement from office, he issued his Farewell Address to the nation. Cool and dispassionate throughout, it was a reminder to the American people of where national interest lay. It stands today as one of the most complete expressions of isolationist thinking in the period. How does Washington define the national interest? What role does he assign to ideology as a factor in determining the course of American foreign policy? Do you find in Washington's statement any themes consistent with those expressed earlier by John Adams? A complete edition of the Farewell Address may be found in Worthington Chauncey Ford, ed., *The Writings of George Washington*, XIII (G. P. Putnam's Sons, New York, 13 vols., 1892).

⊂⊒ Isolationism and National Interest

GEORGE WASHINGTON

Observe good faith and justice towards all Nations. Cultivate peace and harmony with all.—Religion and Morality enjoin this conduct; and can it be that good policy does not equally enjoin it?—It will be worthy of a free, enlightened, and, at no distant period, a great nation, to give to mankind the magnanimous and too novel example of a People always guided by an exalted justice and benevolence.—Who can doubt that in the course of time and things, the fruits of such a plan would richly repay any temporary advantages, which might be lost by a steady adherence to it? Can it be that Providence has not connected the permanent felicity of a Nation with its virtue? The experiment, at least, is recommended by every sentiment which ennobles human nature.—Alas! is it rendered impossible by its vices?

In the execution of such a plan nothing is more essential than that permanent, inveterate antipathies against particular nations and passionate attachments for others should be excluded; and that in place of them just and amicable feelings towards all should be cultivated.—The Nation, which indulges towards another an habitual hatred or an habitual fondness, is in some degree a slave. It is a slave to its animosity or to its affection, either of which is sufficient to lead it astray from its duty and its interest.—Antipathy in one nation against another disposes each more readily to offer insult and injury, to lay hold of slight causes of umbrage, and to be haughty and intractable, when accidental or trifling occasions or dispute occur.—Hence frequent collisions, obstinate, envenomed and bloody contests.—The Nation prompted by ill-will and resentment sometimes impels to War the Governmnet, contrary to the best calculations of policy.—The Government sometimes participates in the national propensity, and adopts through passion what reason would reject;—at other times, it makes the animosity of the Nation subservient to projects of hostility instigated by pride, ambition, and other sinister and pernicious motives.—The peace often, sometimes perhaps the Liberty, of Nations has been the victim.—

So likewise a passionate attachment of one Nation for another produces a variety of evils.—Sympathy for the favourite nation, facilitating the illusion of an imaginary common interest in cases where no real common interest exists, and infusing into one the enmities of the other, betrays the former into a participation in the quarrels and wars of the latter, without adequate inducement or justification. It leads also to concessions to the favourite Nation of privileges denied to others, which is apt doubly to injure the Nation making the concessions; by unnecessarily parting with what ought to have been retained, and by exciting jealousy, ill-will, and a disposition to retaliate, in the parties from whom equal privileges are withheld; and it gives to ambitious, corrupted, or deluded citizens, (who devote themselves to the favourite Nation) facility to betray, or sacrifice the interests of their own country, without odium, sometimes even with popularity:—gilding with the appearances of a virtuous sense of obligation, a commendable deference for public opinion, or a laudable zeal for public good, the base or foolish compliances of ambition, corruption or infatuation.—

As avenues to foreign influence in innumerable ways, such attachments are particularly alarming to the truly enlightened and independent Patriot.—How many opportunities do they afford to tamper with domestic factions, to practice the arts of seduction, to mislead public opinion, to influence or awe the public councils! Such an attachment of a small or weak, towards a great and powerful nation, dooms the former to be the satellite of the latter.

Against the insidious wiles of foreign influence, I conjure you to believe me, fellow-citizens, the jealousy of a free people ought to be *constantly* awake, since history and experience prove that foreign influence is one of the most baneful foes of republican Government.—But that jealousy, to be useful, must be impartial; else it becomes the instrument of the very influence to be avoided, instead of a defence against it. —Excessive partiality for one foreign nation and excessive dislike of another, cause those whom they actuate to see danger only on one side, and serve to veil and even second the arts of influence on the other.— Real Patriots, who may resist the intrigues of the favourite, are liable to become suspected and odious; while its tools and dupes usurp the applause and confidence of the people, to surrender their interests.—

The great rule of conduct for us, in regard to foreign Nations, is, in extending our commercial relations, to have with them as little *Political* connection as possible.—So far as we have already formed engagements, let them be fulfilled with perfect good faith.—Here let us stop.—

Europe has a set of primary interests, which to us have none, or a very remote relation.—Hence she must be engaged in frequent controversies, the causes of which are essentially foreign to our concerns.—Hence therefore it must be unwise in us to implicate ourselves, by artificial ties in the ordinary vicissitudes of her politics, or the ordinary combinations and collisions of her friendships, or enmities.

Our detached and distant situation invites and enables us to pursue a different course.—If we remain one People, under an efficient government, the period is not far off, when we may defy material injury from external annoyance; when we may take such an attitude as will cause the neutrality we may at any time resolve upon to be scrupulously respected. When belligerent nations, under the impossibility of making acquisitions upon us, will not lightly hazard the giving us provocation; when we may choose peace or war, as our interest guided by our justice shall counsel.

Why forego the advantages of so peculiar a situation?—Why quit our own to stand upon foreign ground?—Why, by interweaving our destiny with that of any part of Europe, entangle our peace and prosperity in the toils of European ambition, rivalship, interest, humour, or caprice?—

'Tis our true policy to steer clear of permanent alliances, with any portion of the foreign world;—so far, I mean, as we are now at liberty to do it—for let me not be understood as capable of patronizing infidelity to existing engagements, (I hold the maxim no less applicable to public than to private affairs, that honesty is always the best policy).—I repeat it therefore let those engagements be observed in their genuine sense.— But in my opinion it is unnecessary and would be unwise to extend them.—

Taking care always to keep ourselves, by suitable establishments, on a respectively defensive posture, we may safely trust to temporary alliances for extraordinary emergencies.—

Harmony, liberal intercourse with all nations, are recommended by policy, humanity, and interest. But even our commercial policy should hold an equal and impartial hand:—neither seeking nor granting exclusive favours or preferences;—consulting the natural course of things;— diffusing and diversifying by gentle means the streams of commerce, but forcing nothing;—establishing with Powers so disposed—in order to give trade a stable course, to define the rights of our Merchants, and to enable the Government to support them—conventional rules of intercourse, the best that present circumstances and mutual opinion will permit; but temporary, and liable to be from time to time abandoned or varied, as experience and circumstances shall dictate; constantly keeping in view that 'tis folly in one nation to look for disinterested favours from another,—that it must pay with a portion of its independence for whatever it may accept under that character—that by such acceptance, it may place itself in the condition of having given equivalents for nominal favours and yet of being reproached with ingratitude for not giving more.—There can be no greater error than to expect, or calculate upon real favours from Nation to Nation.—'Tis an illusion which experience must cure, which a just pride ought to discard.

Chapter

4: Federalist Victory in Pennsylvania

ᴄᴈ REBECCA BROOKS GRUVER

The events leading to the ratification of the Constitution in Pennsylvania in 1787, unique as they were, reveal much about the issues being contested throughout the new American nation. The debates in the Pennsylvania ratifying convention covered the same basic points, using much the same arguments for and against the document, as were voiced in the conventions of such states as Virginia, New York, and Massachusetts. Unlike the close results in these last three states, however, the vote in Pennsylvania was decisively pro-Constitution. This is the more surprising since the bitter warfare of Pennsylvania politics was exceeded nowhere in the nation. In other words, the supporters of the Constitution in Pennsylvania won a deceptively easy victory. The state was the second to ratify the document, doing so on December 15, 1787, by a vote of 46 to 23. Behind this apparently smooth surface of support stood a decade of dispute over constitutional theory which had led to the evolution of two well-organized political parties, the Radicals and the Republicans.

The central issue between the two parties was this: what form of government could provide the greatest degree of political participation *and* protection for the civil liberties of the people of Pennsylvania and the United States as a whole? The conflict over this question understandably reached a high point at the time of the ratifying convention. It was also debated at various times on the federal level after the Constitution went into effect.

The circumstances surrounding the calling of the Pennsylvania convention, and the debates on constitutional theory that took place during its sessions, are more easily understood with some knowledge of the economic and political conditions in the state during the 1780's.

Pennsylvania was much more economically prosperous than some of its smaller neighbors. As a colony it had always been attractive to immigrants because of its rich soil and political and religious freedom, and during the Confederation period it continued to attract large numbers of settlers. The state, which had a population increase of almost 155,000 between 1778 and 1790, was a polyglot of English, German, Scotch-Irish, Dutch, French, Irish, and Swedish settlers. Philadelphia was the nation's largest city, and the state teemed with artisans, manufacturers, and farmers who were producing goods for export to other states and foreign countries.

It was in this atmosphere of economic well being that party organizations began to emerge soon after the Declaration of Independence. The Radical party began in 1777 as an outgrowth of the Whig Society of Philadelphia. It soon created a committee of correspondence to keep in touch with similar organizations developing in the interior counties. At the same time an opposition Republican Society evolved using the same tactics. These two groups were at first loosely organized but gained cohesion during the 1780's. In each of the wards and townships of the state, the parties devised the procedure of holding a caucus at which political leaders presented candidates for office and attempted to gain the support of those at the meeting. In the struggle for control of the state which ensued, the Radical party dominated during the late 1770's; but the opposition Republicans triumphed in the late 1780's and controlled state politics at the time of the calling of the ratifying convention.

Although there were no deep economic divisions in Pennsylvania which would have caused the development of opposing political parties, there were social distinctions between the leadership of the two groups. These differences may have created subtle antagonisms which found their outlet in party politics. The leaders of both organizations appear to have had about the same amounts of the same kinds of property and to have engaged in similar occupations. Of the two parties, the Republicans did, however, encompass more men with college educations, Revolutionary Army officers, merchants, large manufacturers, lawyers, judges, and those with the most extensive land holdings. The Republican leadership was thus of a slightly higher social position than that of the Radicals.

Of more obvious importance in the evolution of Pennsylvania's party structure was a deep-seated dispute over political theory. The continual debate over constitutional questions in state politics during the 1780's and in the ratifying convention may have cloaked subtle economic and social conflicts between the leadership of the two parties. However, the history of Pennsylvania during the Confederation period suggests that constitutional issues had a life of their own which transcended the motivation of personal economic advancement.

The Republican party wanted a stronger national government and specifically favored the governmental structure outlined in the Constitution. Its leaders supported the concept of balanced government; they believed that the weaknesses of human nature could best be controlled by a legislature of two houses, each one checking the other, and separate executive and judicial departments with specific powers to restrain each other as well as the legislature. They were particularly unhappy with the much simpler form of organization of the Pennsylvania Constitution of 1776, produced by the Radicals (the "leather aprons," as the Republicans disparagingly called them). It was not until 1790 that the Republicans had enough political strength to put into effect a new instrument of government modeled after the federal Constitution.

The emphasis in the Pennsylvania Constitution of 1776 was on simplicity of structure and an end to special privilege in government. It provided for a one-house legislature with equal representation from each of the state's nineteen counties. (During the colonial period the western counties had been given fewer representatives than the older eastern counties.) There was no qualification for voting except payment of a poll tax, and no assemblyman could serve more than four years in seven. It also instituted a plural executive, a Supreme Executive Council, with a member from Philadelphia and one from each county for a three-year term. One third of the Council was replaced every year to avert "the danger of establishing an inconvenient Aristocracy." The Council elected its own President and Vice President, chose the state judges for seven-year terms, but had no veto over legislation. Another innovation was a Council of Censors with two elected members from each county. It met every seven years to review the legislation of the period, censure officials if need be, and propose amendments to the Constitution.

From a practical standpoint, the continuing constitutional conflict between the parties is well illustrated by the fiscal policy of the Bank of North America, chartered in 1781 by the state of Pennsylvania. The Republican party was a strong supporter of this bank which was authorized by the Continental Congress to help finance, through loans, both the Revolutionary War and federal government operations. It also provided a profitable investment opportunity for several well-to-do merchants (mostly members of the Republican party) and issued a sound and uniform paper currency. Investors in the Bank supported the idea of a national government which would have enough power to collect taxes and pay its debts.

There were also many merchants in the Radical party, but they were opposed to the Bank of North America. Since its investment facilities were under the control of Republican politicians, these merchants felt they were being excluded from adequate participation in the state's economic development. By 1787, they were also aware that its investors were the chief sponsors of the new Federal Constitution, a document which they argued would weaken state power, and as a consequence endanger the liberties of the individual citizenry protected by the states.

These merchants, and even many artisans who wanted to enlarge their businesses, found it difficult to finance their projects, and they called for a state bank which would have the power to expand the amount of paper money in circulation. It was not strange, therefore, that when the Radicals were in control of the legislature in 1785 they revoked the state charter of the Bank of North America; and it was not rechartered again until 1787, when the Republicans were again in power. In the 1785 session of the legislature, the Radicals also incorporated a state bank, issued more paper money, and provided a long-term plan to pay the state debt and Pennsylvania's percentage of the federal debt. Radical party members who held large amounts of the state and federal debt were jubiliant (available statistics indicate that the leaders of that party held more of the federal debt than the leaders of the Republican opposition), and many farmers were also happy at the prospect of paying their debts with the new issue of paper money. However, many of the citizenry did resent the increased taxes needed to meet the state's financial obligations; and the artisans of Philadelphia, who were removed from the tax lists in order that they would not have to help pay the state and federal debts, were disgruntled at thereby inadvertently being removed from the list of those eligible to vote. When the Republicans returned to power, they re-enfranchised this group, which in turn supported the party's call for ratification of the Constitution in 1787.

A number of Republican party leaders, being holders of public securities in large amounts, stood to gain financially by state payment of the national debt. However, they opposed the whole Radical program because the fiscal issue, as Radical leaders correctly had seen, was not as much economic as it was political in implication. Most of the Republicans wanted a sound fiscal policy administered by a strong federal government, because in their opinion such a government not only could gradually pay the domestic debt, but also unify the country and create respect for the United States abroad by paying the foreign debt.

The consistent conflict between the Radical and Republican parties during the Confederation period is the background for understanding the series of events precedent to the acceptance of the Constitution. When the Confederation Congress submitted the document to the states for ratification on September 27, 1787, the Republicans, in firm control of the Pennsylvania state legislature, moved swiftly to secure its approval. They were able to obtain the call for a ratifying convention by an easy 43–19 margin, but 19 Radicals in the legislature then absented themselves in order to prevent a vote on setting a date for the meeting. Two of their number were necessary to constitute a quorum in the assembly. On both September 28 and 29 the Sergeant-at-Arms was sent to their lodgings to request their presence, but in vain. Finally, on September 29 a number of the Philadelphia populace who were supporters of the Republican party took matters into their own hands. They dragged two of the Radicals,

James McCalmont and Jacob Miley, from their lodgings to the State House where they were made to stay, disheveled and angry, until a vote could be taken for a special election and for setting the opening of the Convention for November 21.

Both parties campaigned vigorously for delegates. The Republicans, led by James Wilson, Tench Coxe, and Noah Webster, immediately launched a barrage of pro-Constitution speeches, meetings, and newspaper articles. Special effort was made to ensure Republican victories in the city of Philadelphia, Philadelphia county, and the other eastern counties, from which the most delegates would be chosen and where Republican support was centered. The Radical party, although at a disadvantage in numbers, also appealed to popular opinion with speeches and through the press. Its advocates dramatized for the public the highhanded, hasty, and violent Republican action in calling for the convention.

As could have been expected with the Republican dominance of the assembly and its effective campaign for votes, the party easily won control of the ratifying convention. Its meetings provided the forum for an extension of the debate over the constitutional issues which had dominated Pennsylvania politics for a decade. The Radicals, while knowing they had little chance of preventing ratification, called for several amendments to the Constitution which were very similar in substance to the Bill of Rights added to the document after the new government went into effect. One Radical politician unsuccessfully suggested an adjournment to give time for debate among the populace and to see what the other states decided to do. The Republicans merely defended the proposed constitution and then voted its acceptance overwhelmingly.

The historical background for the ratification of the Constitution in Pennsylvania illustrates important trends in American political evolution. The political parties which emerged there in the 1780's can be seen as the precursors of those which developed on a national scale in the 1790's (and in part for the same reasons). The Republican party, with its emphasis on strong national government under a system of checks and balances and on fiscal responsibility under a privately controlled bank, was similar to the Federalist party of the 1790's. The Radical party, with its fear of strong centralized government and defense of the final authority of the states, and its attack on the Bank of North America as a monopoly of the few to the detriment of equality of opportunity for the many, had overtones of the Jeffersonian and later Jacksonian coalitions.

The following documents, drawn from the debate over ratification of the Constitution, deal with various aspects of the question of what is the best form of government to provide the most popular control and freedom of expression within a state. They are concerned specifically with these problems: the protection of civil liberties, the relationship of state to federal power, the type of government best suited to a true expression of the will of the people, and the most desirable form of political organization to govern a large and varied geographical area. The documents reveal some of the long-range implications of the debate over the ratification of the Constitution.

The Pennsylvania ratifying convention met in Philadelphia from November 21 to December 15, 1787. It provided the opportunity for a full-scale debate of the questions its opponents saw as the crucial ones to be answered before the Constitution should be ratified. One of the most important of these questions was whether a written statement of the basic civil liberties of the American people should have been included in the document. On November 28, a defense of the Constitution without such a bill of rights was undertaken by James Wilson of Philadelphia, the chief spokesman at the Convention for the new document. Wilson had been active in both Pennsylvania and continental politics since the revolutionary period and had also been a delegate to the Constitutional Convention. He was a member of the Republican party. His two Radical opponents in the debate were James Smilie of Fayette County and Robert Whitehill of Cumberland. Why does Wilson say a written bill of rights is not necessary and would, in fact, be restrictive? On what grounds do Smilie and Whitehill challenge this position? Do the comments on the lack of a bill of rights by these two anti-federalists reveal a broader concern about the Constitution as a whole? An account of this debate is to be found in J. B. McMaster and F. D. Stone, eds., *Pennsylvania and the Federal Constitution* (Lancaster, Pennsylvania, 1888), pp. 253–56.

⊂⊃ Protecting the Liberties of the People

JAMES WILSON, JAMES SMILIE,
AND ROBERT WHITEHILL

Mr. Wilson.   Sir, it appears from the example of other states, as well as from principle, that a bill of rights is neither an essential nor a necessary instrument in framing a system of government, since liberty may exist and be as well secured without it. But it was not only unnecessary, but on this occasion it was found impracticable—for who will be bold enough to undertake to enumerate all the rights of the people?—and when the attempt to enumerate them is made, it must be remembered that if the enumeration is not complete, everything not expressly mentioned will be presumed to be purposely omitted. So it must be with a bill of rights, and an omission in stating the powers granted to the government, is not so dangerous as an omission in recapitulating the rights reserved by the people. We have already seen the origin of magna charta, and tracing the subject still further we find the petition of rights claiming the liberties of the people, according to the laws and statutes of the realm, of which the great charter was the most material, so that here again recourse is had to the old source from which their liberties are derived, the grant of the king. It was not till the revolution that the subject was placed upon a different footing, and even then the people did not claim their liberties as an inherent right, but as the result of an original contract between them and the sovereign. Thus, Mr. President, an attention to the situation of England will show that the conduct of that country in respect to bills of rights, cannot furnish an example to the inhabitants of the United States, who by the revolution have regained all their natural rights, and possess their liberty neither by grant nor contract. In short, Sir, I have said that a bill of rights would have been improperly annexed to the federal plan, and for this plain reason that it would imply that whatever is not expressed was given, which is not the principle of the proposed constitution.

Mr. Smilie. The arguments which have been urged, Mr. President, have not, in my opinion, satisfactorily shown that a bill of rights would have been an improper, nay, that it is not a necessary appendage to the proposed system. As it has been denied that Virginia possesses a bill of rights, I shall on that subject only observe that Mr. Mason,[1] a gentleman certainly of great information and integrity, has assured me that such a thing does exist, and I am persuaded I shall be able at a future period to lay it before the convention. But, Sir, the state of Delaware has a bill of rights, and I believe one of the honorable members (Mr. M'Kean [2]) who now contests the necessity and propriety of that instrument, took a very conspicuous part in the formation of the Delaware government. It seems, however, that the members of the federal convention were themselves convinced, in some degree, of the expediency and propriety of a bill of rights, for we find them expressly declaring that the writ of habeas corpus and the trial by jury in criminal cases shall not be suspended or infringed. How does this indeed agree with the maxim that whatever is not given is reserved? Does it not rather appear from the reservation of these two articles that everything else, which is not specified, is included in the powers delegated to the government? This, Sir, must prove the necessity of a full and explicit declaration of rights; and when we further consider the extensive, the undefined powers vested in the administrators of this system, when we consider the system itself as a great political compact between the governors and the governed, a plain, strong, and accurate criterion by which the people might at once determine when, and in what instance their rights were violated, is a preliminary, without which, this plan ought not to be adopted. So loosely, so inaccurately are the powers which are enumerated in this constitution defined, that it will be impossible, without a test of that kind, to ascertain

[1] George Mason was a member of the Virginia ratifying convention.
[2] Thomas McKean was a Republican delegate from Philadelphia.

the limits of authority, and to declare when government has degenerated into oppression. In that event the contest will arise between the people and the rulers: "You have exceeded the powers of your office, you have oppressed us," will be the language of the suffering citizen. The answer of the government will be short—"We have not exceeded our power; you have no test by which you can prove it." Hence, Sir, it will be impracticable to stop the progress of tyranny, for there will be no check but the people, and their exertions must be futile and uncertain; since it will be difficult, indeed, to communicate to them the violation that has been committed, and their proceedings will be neither systematical nor unanimous. It is said, however, that the difficulty of framing a bill of rights was insurmountable; but, Mr. President, I cannot agree in this opinion. Our experience, and the numerous precedents before us, would have furnished a very sufficient guide. At present there is no security even for the rights of conscience, and under the sweeping force of the sixth article, every principle of a bill of rights, every stipulation for the most sacred and invaluable privileges of man, are left at the mercy of government.

Mr. Whitehill. I differ, Sir, from the honorable member from the city [Wilson], as to the impropriety or necessity of a bill of rights. If, indeed, the constitution itself so well defined the powers of the government that no mistake could arise, and we were well assured that our governors would always act right, then we might be satisfied without an explicit reservation of those rights with which the people ought not, and mean not to part. But, Sir, we know that it is the nature of power to seek its own augmentation, and thus the loss of liberty is the necessary consequence of a loose or extravagant delegation of authority. National freedom has been, and will be the sacrifice of ambition and power, and it is our duty to employ the present opportunity in stipulating such restrictions as are best calculated to protect us from oppression and slavery. . . .

On the same day as the debate on a bill of rights, Wilson and White-hill engaged in another discussion over what effect the new government (under the proposed Constitution) would have on the power and importance of the state governments. Why is Whitehill so concerned to protect the independence of the state governments? Is his concern related to the general anti-federalist position on the need for a written bill of rights? How does Wilson defend the Constitution against the charge that it is designed to annihilate the state governments? The debate can be found in McMaster and Stone, *Pennsylvania and the Federal Constitution*, pp. 258–66.

A Confederation of States Versus a Consolidated Nation

JAMES WILSON AND ROBERT WHITEHILL

Mr. Whitehill. True it is, Mr. President, that if the people intended to engage in one comprehensive system of continental government, the power to frame that system must have been conferred by them; for the legislatures of the states are sworn to preserve the independence of their respective constitutions, and therefore they could not, consistently with their most sacred obligations, authorize an act which sacrificed the individual to the aggregate sovereignty of the states. But it appears from the origin and nature of the commission under which the late convention assembled, that a more perfect confederation was the only object submitted to their wisdom, and not, as it is attempted by this plan, the total destruction of the government of Pennsylvania, and of every other state. So far, Sir, the interference of the legislatures was proper and efficient; but the moment the convention went beyond that object, they ceased to act under any legitimate authority, for the assemblies could give them none, and it cannot be pretended that they were called together by the people; for, till the preamble was produced, it never was understood that the people at large had been consulted upon the occasion, or that otherwise than through their representatives in the several states, they had given a sanction to the proceedings of that body. If, indeed, the federal convention, finding that the old system was incapable of repair, had represented the incurable defects to Congress, and advised that the original and inherent power of the people might be called into exercise for the institution of a new government, then, Sir, the subject would have come fairly into view, and we should have known upon what principles we proceeded. At present we find a convention appointed by one authority, but acting under the arbitrary assumption of another; and instead of transacting the business which was assigned to them, behold! they have produced a work of supererogation, after a mysterious labor of three months. Let us, however, Sir, attend for a moment to the constitution. And here we shall find, in a single line, sufficient matter for weeks of debate, and which it will puzzle any one member to investigate and define. But, besides the powers enumerated, we find in this constitution an authority is given to make all laws that are necessary to carry it effectually into operation, and what laws are necessary is a consideration left for Congress to decide. . . . It is strange to mark, however, what a sudden and striking revolution has taken place in the political sentiments of America; for, Sir, in the opening of our struggle with Great Britain, it was often insisted that annual parliaments were necessary to secure the liberties of the people, and yet it is here proposed to establish a house of representatives which shall continue for two, a senate for six, and a president for four years! What is there in this plan indeed, which can even assure us that the several departments shall continue no longer in office? Do we not know that an English parliament elected for three years, by a vote of their own body, extended their existence to seven, and with this example, Congress possessing a competent share of power may easily be tempted to exercise it. The advantages of annual elections are not at this day to be taught, and when every other security was withheld, I should still have thought there was some safety in the government, had this been left. The seats of Congress being held for so short a period, and by a tenure so precarious as popular elections, there could be no inducement to invade the liberties of the people, nor time enough to accomplish the schemes of ambition and tyranny. But when the the period is protracted, an object is presented worthy of contention, and the duration of the office affords an opportunity for perpetuating the influence by which it was originally obtained. Another power designed to be vested in the new government, is the superlative power of taxation, which may be carried to an inconceivable excess, swallowing up every object of taxation, and consequently plundering the several states of every means to support their governments, and to administer their laws. Then, Sir, can it longer be doubted that this is a system of consolidation? That government which possesses all the powers of raising and maintaining armies, of regulating and commanding the militia, and of laying imposts and taxes of every kind, must be supreme, and will (whether in twenty or in one year, it signifies little to the event) naturally absorb every subordinate jurisdiction. It is in vain, Sir, to flatter ourselves that the forms of popular elections will be the means of self-preservation, and that the officers of the proposed government will uniformly act for the happiness of the people—for why should we run a risk which we may easily avoid? The giving such extensive and undefined power is a radical wrong that cannot be justified by any subsequent merit in the exercise; for in framing a new system, it is our duty rather to indulge a jealousy of the human character, than an expectation of unprecedented perfection. Let us, however, suppose what will be allowed to be at least possible, that the powers of this government should be abused, and the liberties of the people infringed; do any means of redress remain with the states or with the people at large, to oppose and counteract the influence and oppression of the general government? Secret combinations, partial insurrections, sudden tumults may arise; but these being easily defeated and subdued, will furnish a pretence for strengthening that power which they were intended to overthrow. A bill of rights, Mr. President, it has been said, would not only be unnecessary, but it would be dangerous, and for this special reason, that because it is not practicable to enumerate all the rights of the people, therefore it would be hazardous to secure such of the rights as we can enumerate! Truly, Sir, I will agree that a bill of rights may be a dangerous instrument, but it is to the views and projects of the aspiring ruler, and not the liberties of the citizen. Grant but this explicit criterion, and our governors will not venture to encroach; refuse it, and the people cannot venture to complain. . . . Will it still be said, that the state governments would be adequate to the task of correcting the usurpations of Congress? Let us not, however, give the weight of proof to the boldness of assertion; for, if the opposition is to succeed by force, we find both the purse and the sword are almost exclusively transferred to the general government; and if it is to succeed by legislative remonstrance, we shall find that expedient rendered nugatory by the law of Congress, which is to be the supreme law of the land. Thus, Mr. President, must the powers and sovereignty of the several states be eventually destroyed, and when, at last, it may be found expedient to abolish that connection which, we are told essentially exists between the federal and individual legislatures, the proposed constitution is amply provided with the means in that clause which assumes the authority to alter or prescribe the place and manner of elections. I feel, Mr. President, the magnitude of the subject in which I am engaged, and although I am exhausted with what I have already advanced, I am conscious that the investigation is infinitely far from being complete. Upon the whole, therefore, I wish it to be seriously considered, whether we have a right to leave the liberties of the people to such future constructions and expositions as may possibly be made upon this system; particularly when its advocates, even at this day, confess that it would be dangerous to omit anything in the enumeration of a bill of rights, and according to their principle, the reservation of the habeas corpus and trial by jury in criminal cases, may hereafter be construed to be the only privileges reserved by the people. I am not anxious, Mr. President, about forms—it is the substance which I wish to obtain; and therefore

I acknowledge, if our liberties are secured by the frame of government itself, the supplementary instrument of a declaration of rights may well be dispensed with. But, Sir, we find no security there, except in the two instances referred to, and it will not, I hope, any longer be alleged that no security is requisite, since those exceptions prove a contrary sentiment to have been entertained by the very framers of the proposed constitution. The question at present, Sir, is, however, of a preliminary kind— does the plan now in discussion propose a consolidation of the states? and will a consolidated government be most likely to promote the interests and happiness of America? If it is satisfactorily demonstrated, that in its principles or in its operation, the dissolution of the state sovereignties is not a necessary consequence, I shall then be willing to accompany the gentlemen on the other side in weighing more particularly its merits and demerits. But my judgment, according to the information I now possess, leads me to anticipate the annihilation of the several state governments—an event never expected by the people, and which would, I fervently believe, destroy the civil liberties of America.

Mr. Wilson. I am willing, Mr. President, to agree with the honorable member who has just spoken, that if this system is not calculated to secure the liberties and happiness of the United States, it should not be adopted; but, on the contrary, if it provides an adequate security for the general liberties and happiness of the people, I presume it ought not to be rejected. Before I comment upon the principles which have brought us to this issue, I beg leave to make one general remark. Liberty and happiness have, Sir, a powerful enemy on each hand;—on the one hand there is tyranny, on the other there is licentiousness. To guard against the latter, it is necessary that adequate powers should be given to the government, and to protect us from the former, it is requisite that those powers should be properly distributed. Under this consideration, let us now regard the proposed system; and I freely confess that if its adoption will necessarily be followed by the annihilation of the state governments, the objection is of very great force, and ought to be seriously weighed. The inference, however, appears rather unnatural that a government should be expressly calculated to produce the destruction of other governments, upon which its own existence must entirely depend; for, Mr. President, it is capable of demonstration, that if the state governments fall, the general government must likewise be involved in one common ruin. Is it not evident, Sir, when we particularly examine the structure of the proposed system, that the operation of the federal legislature necessarily presupposes the existence of the legislatures of the several States? Can the Congress, the president, or even the judiciary department, survive the dissolution of those powers in the separate governments, from which they essentially derive their origin, and on which they must forever depend for their renovation? No, sir! For, we find that the House of Representatives is to be composed of persons returned by the suffrage of freemen who are qualified to vote for the members of the most numerous branch of the state legislature, which legislature must necessarily exist, or the only criterion for supplying the popular department of the federal government will be extinct. The senate, which is to be chosen by the several legislatures, cannot consequently be appointed unless those legislatures exist; which is likewise the case in respect to the president, as this office is to be filled by electors nominated by the respective state legislatures; and, lastly, the judges are to be commissioned by the president and senate, who cannot appoint, unless they are themselves first appointed, and that, it appears, must depend upon the existence of the state legislatures. Thus, Mr. President, by a clear deduction, it is evident that the existence and efficiency of the general government presupposes the existence and full operation of the separate governments. For you can never prove a person to have been chosen, till you have proved that he was the choice of persons qualified to vote; you cannot prove any man to be entitled to elect a member of the house of representatives, till you have proved that he is qualified to elect a member of the most numerous branch of the state legislature. But, Sir, it has been intimated that the design of the federal convention was to absorb the state governments. This would introduce a strange doctrine indeed, that one body should seek the destruction of another, upon which its own preservation depends, or that the creature should eat up and consume the creator. The truth is, Sir, that the framers of this system were particularly anxious, and their work demonstrates their anxiety, to preserve the state governments unimpaired—it was their favorite object; and, perhaps, however proper it might be in itself, it is more difficult to defend the plan on account of the excessive caution used in that respect than from any other objection that has been offered here or elsewhere. Hence, we have seen each state, without regard to their comparative importance, entitled to an equal representation in the senate, and a clause has been introduced which enables two-thirds of the state legislature at any time to propose and effectuate alterations in the general system. But, Mr. President, though in the very structure of the plan the concomitant duration of the state governments is always pre-supposed, yet their power is not the only one intended to be recognized and established. The power of the people, Sir, is the great foundation of the proposed system, a power totally unknown in the present confederation, but here it mediately pervades every department and is immediately exercised in the house of representatives. I trust it is unnecessary to dwell longer upon this subject; for, when gentlemen assert that it was the intention of the federal convention to destroy the sovereignty of the states, they must conceive themselves better qualified to judge of the intention of that body than its own members, of whom not one, I believe, entertained so improper an idea.

The following documents deal with conflicting views over whether the structure of the government as outlined in the Constitution was conducive to popular rule and whether representative government was really possible in a country of the geographic extent of the United States. The anti-federalist position on these questions was effectively advanced by "Centinel" in a series of newspaper columns. They are thought to have been written by Samuel Bryan, the son of the Radical party leader, George Bryan. The anti-federalist minority also published its reasons for voting against the Constitution in the *Pennsylvania Packet and Daily Advertiser* after the Convention ended. The best counterarguments to anti-federalist objections to the Constitution are again to be found in the speeches of James Wilson in the Convention. What form of government does "Centinel" advocate as being the most representative of the people? Why do both "Centinel" and the anti-federalist minority fear the creation of a strong general government over an extensive geographic area? On what grounds does Wilson defend the form of government outlined in the Constitution? What does Wilson see as the advantage of a "Federal Republic"? Finally, are the federalists or the anti-federalists more devoted to popular sovereignty, the "will of the people"?

The documents used in this section can be found in McMaster and Stone, *Pennsylvania and the Federal Constitution*, pp. 218–30, 300–307, 464–65, 567–73.

Faith in Popular Government

"CENTINEL," "THE ANTI-FEDERALIST MINORITY," AND JAMES WILSON

Centinel:[1]

The late revolution having effaced in a great measure all former habits, and the present institutions are so recent, that there exists not that great reluctance to innovation, so remarkable in old communities, and which accords with reason, for the most comprehensive mind cannot foresee the full operation of material changes on civil polity; it is the genius of the common law to resist innovation.

The wealthy and ambitious, who in every community think they have a right to lord it over their fellow creatures, have availed themselves very successfully of this favorable disposition; for the people thus

[1] This "Centinel" column was first printed in the *Independent Gazetteer*, Oct. 5, 1787.

unsettled in their sentiments, have been prepared to accede to any extreme of government. All the distresses and difficulties they experience, proceeding from various causes, have been ascribed to the impotency of the present confederation, and thence they have been led to expect full relief from the adoption of the proposed system of government; and in the other event, immediately ruin and annihilation as a nation. . . . I am fearful that the principles of government inculcated in Mr. Adams' treatise,[2] and enforced in the numerous essays and paragraphs in the newspapers, have misled some well designing members of the late Convention. . . . Mr. Adams' *sine qua non* of a good government is three balancing powers; whose repelling qualities are to produce an equilibrium of interests, and thereby promote the happiness of the whole community. He asserts that the administrators of every government, will ever be actuated by views of private interest and ambition, to the prejudice of the public good; that therefore the only effectual method to secure the rights of the people and promote their welfare, is to create an opposition of interests between the members of two distinct bodies, in the exercise of the powers of government, and balanced by those of a third. This hypothesis supposes human wisdom competent to the task of instituting three co-equal orders in government, and a corresponding weight in the community to enable them respectively to exercise their several parts, and whose views and interests should be so distinct as to prevent a coalition of any two of them for the destruction of the third. Mr. Adams, although he has traced the constitution of every form of government that ever existed, as far as history affords materials, has not been able to adduce a single instance of such a government; he indeed says that the British constitution is such in theory, but this is rather a confirmation that his principles are chimerical and not to be reduced to practice. If such an organization of power were practicable, how long would it continue? Not a day—for there is so great a disparity in the talents, wisdom and industry of mankind, that the scale would presently preponderate to one or the other body, and with every accession of power the means of further increase would be greatly extended. . . .

Therefore, as different orders in government will not produce the good of the whole, we must recur to other principles. I believe it will be found that the form of government, which holds those entrusted with power in the greatest responsibility to their constituents, the best calculated for freemen. A republican, or free government, can only exist where the body of the people are virtuous, and where property is pretty equally divided. In such a government the people are the sovereign and their sense or opinion is the criterion of every public measure; for

[2] John Adams, *A Defense of the Constitutions of the United States of America* (3 vols., published between October, 1786, and December, 1787).

when this ceases to be the case, the nature of the government is changed, and an aristocracy, monarchy or despotism will rise on its ruin. The highest responsibility is to be attained in a simple structure of government, for the great body of the people never steadily attend to the operations of government, and for want of due information are liable to be imposed on. If you complicate the plan by various orders, the people will be perplexed and divided in their sentiment about the source of abuses or misconduct; some will impute it to the senate, others to the house of representatives, and so on, that the interposition of the people may be rendered imperfect or perhaps wholly abortive. But if, imitating the constitution of Pennsylvania, you vest all the legislative power in one body of men (separating the executive and judicial) elected for a short period, and necessarily excluded by rotation from permanency, and guarded from precipitancy and surprise by delays imposed on its proceedings, you will create the most perfect responsibility; for then, whenever the people feel a grievance, they cannot mistake the authors, and will apply the remedy with certainty and effect, discarding them at the next election. This tie of responsibility will obviate all the dangers apprehended from a single legislature, and will the best secure the rights of the people. . . . It is the opinion of the greatest writers, that a very extensive country cannot be governed on democratical principles, on any other plan than a confederation of a number of small republics, possessing all the powers of internal government, but united in the management of their foreign and general concerns.

It would not be difficult to prove, that anything short of despotism could not bind so great a country under one government; and that whatever plan you might, at the first setting out, establish, it would issue in a despotism.

If one general government could be instituted and maintained on principles of freedom, it would not be so competent to attend to the various local concerns and wants, of every particular district, as well as the peculiar governments, who are nearer the scene, and possessed of superior means of information; besides, if the business of the *whole* union is to be managed by one government, there would not be time.

The Anti-Federalist Minority: [1]

We dissent, first, because it is the opinion of the most celebrated writers on government, and confirmed by uniform experience, that a very extensive territory cannot be governed on the principles of freedom, otherwise than by a confederation of republics, possessing all the powers of internal

---

[1] First printed in *The Pennsylvania Packet and Daily Advertiser*, Dec. 18, 1787.

government, but united in the management of their general and foreign concerns.

If any doubt could have been entertained of the truth of the foregoing principle, it has been fully removed by the concession of *Mr. Wilson,* one of the majority on this question, and who was one of the deputies in the late general convention. In justice to him, we will give his own words; they are as follows, viz.: "The extent of country for which the new constitution was required, produced another difficulty in the business of the federal convention. It is the opinion of some celebrated writers, that to a small territory, the democratical; to a middling territory (as Montesquieu has termed it), the monarchical; and to an extensive territory, the despotic form of government is best adapted. Regarding then the wide and almost unbounded jurisdiction of the United States, at first view, the hand of despotism seemed necessary to control, connect and protect it; and hence the chief embarrassment rose. For we know that although our constituents would cheerfully submit to the legislative restraints of a free government, they would spurn at every attempt to shackle them with despotic power." And again, in another part of his speech, he continues: "Is it probable that the dissolution of the State governments, and the establishment of one *consolidated empire* would be eligible in its nature, and satisfactory to the people in its administration? I think not, as I have given reasons to show that so extensive a territory could not be governed, connected and preserved, but by the *supremacy of despotic power.* All the exertions of the most potent emperors of Rome were not capable of keeping that empire together, which in extent was far inferior to the dominion of America."

We dissent, secondly, because the powers vested in Congress by this constitution, must necessarily annihilate and absorb the legislative, executive, and judicial powers of the several States, and produce from their ruins one consolidated government, which from the nature of things will be *an iron handed despotism,* as nothing short of the supremacy of despotic sway could connect and govern these United States under one government.

James Wilson:

[Delivered December 1, 1787]

In order, Sir, to give permanency, stability and security to any government, I conceive it of essential importance that its legislature should be restrained; that there should not only be what we call a *passive,* but an *active* power over it; for of all kinds of despotism, this is the most dreadful and the most difficult to be corrected. With how much contempt have we seen the authority of the people treated by the legislature of this State—and how often have we seen it making laws in one session that have been repealed the next, either on account of the fluctuation of party or their own impropriety!

This could not have been the case in a compound legislature; it is therefore proper to have efficient restraints upon the legislative body. These restraints arise from different sources: I will mention some of them. In this constitution they will be produced in a very considerable degree by a division of the power in the legislative body itself. Under this system they may arise likewise from the interference of those officers, who will be introduced into the executive and judicial departments. They may spring also from another source, the election by the people, and finally, under this constitution, they may proceed from the great and last resort—from the PEOPLE themselves. I say, under this constitution, the legislature may be restrained and kept within its prescribed bounds by the interposition of the judicial department. This I hope, Sir, to explain clearly and satisfactorily. I had occasion on a former day to state that the power of the constitution was paramount to the power of the legislature acting under that constitution. For it is possible that the legislature, when acting in that capacity, may transgress the bounds assigned to it, and an act may pass in the usual *mode* notwithstanding that transgression; but when it comes to be discussed before the judges, when they consider its principles, and find it to be incompatible with the superior powers of the constitution, it is their duty to pronounce it void; and judges independent, and not obliged to look to every session for a continuance of their salaries, will behave with intrepidity and refuse to the act the sanction of judicial authority. In the same manner the President of the United States could shield himself and refuse to carry into effect an act that violates the constitution. . . . The Congress may be restrained by the election of its constituent parts. If a legislature shall make a law contrary to the constitution or oppressive to the people, they have it in their power, every second year in one branch, and every sixth year in the other, to displace the men who act thus inconsistent with their duty; and if this is not sufficient, they have still a further power; they may assume into their own hands the alteration of the constitution itself—they may revoke the lease, when the conditions are broken by the tenant. But the most useful restraint upon the legislature, because it operates constantly, arises from the division of its power among two branches, and from the qualified negative of the president upon both. As this government is formed, there are two sources from which the representation is drawn, though they both ultimately flow from the people. *States* now exist and others will come into existence; it was thought proper that they should be represented in the general government. But gentlemen will please to remember, this constitution was not framed merely for the States; it was framed for the PEOPLE also; and the popular branch of the Congress will be the objects of their immediate choice.

The two branches will serve as checks upon each other; they have the same legislative authorities, except in one instance. Money bills must originate in the house of representatives. The senate can pass no law without the concurrence of the house of representatives; nor can the house of representatives without the concurrence of the senate.

[Delivered November 24, 1787]

To frame a government for a single city or State, is a business both in its importance and facility, widely different from the task entrusted to the Federal Convention, whose prospects were extended not only to thirteen independent and sovereign States, some of which in territorial jurisdiction, population, and resource, equal the most respectable nations of Europe, but likewise to innumerable States yet unformed, and to myriads of citizens who in future ages shall inhabit the vast uncultivated regions of the continent. The duties of that body therefore, were not limited to local or partial considerations, but to the formation of a plan commensurate with a great and valuable portion of the globe. . . .

The extent of country for which the New Constitution was required, produced another difficulty in the business of the Federal Convention. It is the opinion of some celebrated writers, that to a small territory the democratical, to a middling territory (as Montesquieu has termed it) the monarchical, and to an extensive territory the despotic form of government, is best adapted. Regarding then, the wide and almost unbounded jurisdiction of the United States, at first view the hand of despotism seemed necessary to control, connect and protect it; and hence the chief embarrassment arose. For we knew that, although our constituents would cheerfully submit to the legislative restraints of a free government, they would spurn at every attempt to shackle them with despotic power.

In this dilemma, a Federal Republic naturally presented itself to our observation, as a species of government which secured all the internal advantages of a republic, at the same time that it maintained the external dignity and force of a monarchy. The definition of this form of government may be found in Montesquieu, who says, I believe, that it consists in assembling distinct societies which are consolidated into a new body, capable of being increased by the addition of other members—an expanding quality peculiarly fitted to the circumstances of America. . . .

Our wants, imperfections, and weakness, Mr. President, naturally incline us to society; but it is certain, society cannot exist without some restraints. In a state of nature each individual has a right, uncontrolled, to act as his pleasure or his interest may prevail, but it must be observed that this license extends to every individual, and hence the state of nature is rendered insupportable, by the interfering claims and the consequent animosities of men, who are independent of every power and influence but their passions and their will. On the other hand, in entering into the social compact, though the individual parts with a portion of his natural rights, yet it is evident that he gains more by the limitation of the liberty of others, than he loses by the limitation of his own,—so that in truth, the aggregate of liberty is more in society, than it is in a state of nature. . . .

At this period, America has it in her power to adopt either of the following modes of government: She may dissolve the individual sovereignty of the States, and become one consolidated empire; she may be divided into thirteen separate, independent and unconnected commonwealths; she may be erected into two or more confederacies; or, lastly, she may become one comprehensive Federal Republic. . . . The general sentiment in that body, and, I believe, the general sentiment of the citizens of America, is expressed in the motto which some of them have chosen, UNITE OR DIE; and while we consider the extent of the country, so intersected and almost surrounded with navigable rivers, so separated and detached from the rest of the world, it is natural to presume that Providence has designed us for an united people, under one great political compact. If this is a just and reasonable conclusion, supported by the wishes of the people, the Convention did right in proposing a single confederated Republic. But in proposing it they were necessarily led, not only to consider the situation, circumstances, and interests of one, two, or three States, but of the collective body; and as it is essential to society, that the welfare of the whole should be preferred to the accommodation of a part, they followed the same rule in promoting the national advantages of the Union, in preference to the separate advantages of the States. A principle of candor, as well as duty, led to this conduct; for, as I have said before, no government, either single or confederated, can exist, unless private and individual rights are subservient to the public and general happiness of the nation. It was not alone the State of Pennsylvania, however important she may be as a constituent part of the union, that could influence the deliberations of a convention formed by a delegation from all the United States to devise a government adequate to their common exigencies and impartial in its influence and operation. In the spirit of union, inculcated by the nature of their commission, they framed the constitution before us, and in the same spirit they submit it to the candid consideration of their constituents. . . .

Then let us examine, Mr. President, the three species of simple government, which as I have already mentioned, are the monarchical, aristocratical and democratical. In a monarchy, the supreme power is vested in a single person; in an aristocracy, it is possessed by a body not formed upon the principle of representation, but enjoying their station by descent, by election among themselves, or in right of some personal or territorial qualification; and lastly, in a democracy, it is inherent in the people, and is either exercised by themselves or by their representatives. Each of these systems has its advantages and its disadvantages. The advantages of a monarchy are strength, dispatch, and unity; its disadvantages are expense, tyranny, and war. The advantages of an aristocracy are experience, and the wisdom resulting from education; its disadvantages are the dissension of the governors, and the oppression of the people. The advantages of a democracy are liberty, caution, industry, fidelity, and an opportunity of bringing forward the talents and abilities of the citizens, without regard to birth or fortune; its disadvantages are dissension and imbecility, for the assent of many being required, their exertions will be feeble, and their counsels too soon discovered.

To obtain all the advantages, and to avoid all the inconveniences of these governments, was the leading object of the late convention. Having therefore considered the formation and principles of other systems, it is natural to enquire, of what description is the constitution before us? In its principles, Sir, it is purely democratical; varying indeed, in its form, in order to admit all the advantages, and to exclude all the disadvantages which are incidental to the known and established constitutions of government. But when we take an extensive and accurate view of the streams of power that appear through this great and comprehensive plan, when we contemplate the variety of their directions, the force and dignity of their currents, when we behold them intersecting, embracing, and surrounding the vast possessions and interests of the continent, and when we see them distributing on all hands beauty, energy and riches, still, however numerous and wide their courses, however diversified and remote the blessings they diffuse, we shall be able to trace them all to one great and noble source, THE PEOPLE.

Chapter

5: The Election of 1800 and the Development of Political Parties

⊂⊋ RICHARD E. ELLIS

Thomas Jefferson's accession to the presidency in 1801 was the first time under the United States Constitution that the reins of power were transferred from one political party to another. This is a critical juncture in the life of any newly emergent constitutional republic, for two main dangers exist. First, the defeated administration, taking advantage of the great powers still at its disposal, may use force or other extra-legal means to prevent its victorious opponents from assuming the positions of authority to which they are now rightly entitled. Second, the newly victorious group, having gained power, may persecute its enemies or alter the rules of government (usually both) in order to prevent its control of the government from ever being effectively challenged by an opposition group. Despite very intense differences over what the personnel and policies of the government should be, the minority has a legal right (as long as it observes a predetermined set of rules) to become a majority and to take over control of the government—or at least it is the recognition of that principle which is at the heart of the establishment of a viable party system of politics and which allows for changes in the government to take place in a peaceful manner.

For all their wisdom in other matters the Founding Fathers did not understand the crucial function which political parties play in legitimizing and channeling political opposition in a democratic society. They viewed political parties in very unflattering terms. Party or "faction," which was the term used for party in the eighteenth century, meant any group of men who organized themselves to further their own selfish interests at the expense of the rest of the community. Worse than that, it was generally believed that factions were the kind of organizations that revolutionaries formed before trying to overthrow the government —a point of view perhaps natural for a generation that had seen and participated in the overthrow of English rule in America and the downfall of the Articles of Confederation. Sensitive to the ease with which governments could be made to collapse, the Founding Fathers strongly desired to see the heritage of the American Revolution consolidated under a stable national government. The great fear of the Founding Fathers was that their experiment in liberty would prove a failure, a victim of the discord and anarchy that foreign critics claimed was the inevitable result of a government whose authority rested in the people it governed. But if this point of view made sense in light of past experience, it failed to take into account the fact that in any government where final authority rested in the people there had to be institutions through which the people could organize and articulate their feelings. The 1790's saw the development of such an institution in the two-party system of politics; and with it came a whole host of problems that the framers of the Constitution had not anticipated.

The unanimous election of George Washington as first President of the United States in 1788 and the election to the First Congress almost exclusively of men who had favored the adoption of the Constitution seemed to indicate that the consensus type of politics which the Founding Fathers believed in was being established. But it soon became clear that Thomas Jefferson and James Madison and their followers, on the one hand, and Alexander Hamilton and his followers, on the other, had sharply divergent views as to what the proper domestic and foreign policies of America should be. As a consequence, Washington's first administration proved to be a stormy one during which bitter political battles were fought within the administration until Jefferson resigned as Secretary of State, and between the administration and Congress, where Madison was leading the nascent Republican interest. On the whole it was Hamilton who succeeded in making policy for the government, although he did have to make some compromises along the way.

It is difficult to date exactly when political parties first began to appear on the national scene, but an early sign of their existence came in the election of 1792. Washington was standing for reelection and while many Republicans were critical of his policies, they almost all supported him; there did, however, develop widespread opposition among Republicans to the reelection of John Adams as Vice-President. In the resulting election Washington again received unanimous support, while Adams polled 77 electoral votes to 50 for George Clinton, the Republican candidate. Washington's enormous popularity had prevented a nationwide conflict for the presidency from taking place; but from the results of the election of 1792, one could predict the demise of the Founding Fathers' consensus type of politics.

Partisan politics became increasingly tense during Washington's second administration. In particular, differences over foreign policy questions arising out of the wars of the French Revolution heightened the conflict between the Federalists and Republicans. And when Washington announced his retirement from public life in 1796, it assured the fact that the election of 1796 would be the first contested election for the presidency in American history. The Republicans immediately nominated Jefferson as their standard-bearer, and Aaron Burr as his running mate. The Federalists, under the leadership of Hamilton, reluctantly nominated Adams, mainly because he had Washington's backing and because his role in the Revolution and his eight years as Vice-President gave him a strong claim to the first office of the land. As his running mate the Federalists nominated Thomas Pinckney, a diplomat from South Carolina who had just negotiated a highly satisfactory and popular treaty with Spain.

In the ensuing election neither the Federalists nor the Republicans recognized the legitimacy of the other group's position. The Federalists denounced their opponents as power-hungry subversives who were intent upon overthrowing the government established by the Constitution in 1788, while the Republicans justified their opposition on the grounds that it was the Federalists who by their loose interpretation had subverted the meaning of the Constitution, thereby making the Republican election effort necessary to save the government and protect the rights of the people.

The results of the election of 1796 clearly indicated that the framers of the Constitution had not anticipated the rise of political parties. The Constitution as ratified in 1788 provided that each elector cast two ballots and the man with the most votes be elected President and the man with the next number of votes be elected Vice-President. The basic assumption being that the men would be chosen because of their talent and not because of their party affiliation. Hamilton, who did not like Adams and who had great reservations about some of the policies the Vice-President stood for, decided to take advantage of this provision in the Constitution to work out a scheme to make sure that Adams would not be elected President. But at the same time he wanted to make sure that the office went to a Federalist. It was expected that all the Federalist electors would vote for Adams, and that all but a few would vote for Pinckney; but Hamilton plotted to have all the Federalist electors cast their votes for Pinckney while throwing away some of their votes for Adams, which meant that if the Federalists were victorious, it would be Pinckney who would be President. Unfortunately for Hamilton, Adams' friends got wind of the scheme and made sure that a number of the electors who were partial to Adams did not vote for Pinckney. Meanwhile support for Jefferson was growing and the election proved to be very close. The significance of it all became clear when the electoral votes were tallied: Adams received 71 votes; Jefferson, 68; Pinckney, 59; Burr,

30; and the various other candidates, 48. It meant that Adams the Federalist would be President and Jefferson the Republican would be Vice-President.

For a while, in an attempt to return to the earlier type of consensus politics, Adams and Jefferson did their best to get along with each other. But the differences that separated them soon came to the surface. When Adams led the country into an undeclared naval war with France in 1798, Republican criticism of the government reached a new level of intensity. Because they could not recognize that Republican criticism was directed at the policies of the government and not at the existence of the government, the Federalists passed and began to enforce the Alien and Sedition Acts as a way of shutting off the opposition. Refusing to be intimidated, the Republicans issued the Kentucky and Virginia Resolutions and launched their campaign to capture control of the presidency in 1800. The debate that followed was one of the most—perhaps *the* most—vituperative in the history of American elections. The Federalists denounced the Republicans as Jacobins, atheists, anarchists and revolutionaries intent upon overthrowing the very foundations of society, while the Republicans asserted that the Federalists were Tories, and monarchists who were intent upon reversing the principles of the Revolution and establishing a military dictatorship.

The election results once again revealed that the Constitution as adopted in 1788 was not equipped to handle the problems raised by the development of political parties. This time Jefferson and Burr were victorious. However, as the party was determined to prevent a Federalist from slipping in as Vice-President, it had instructed all of its electors to cast each of their ballots for Jefferson and Burr. The result was that each received 73 electoral votes. Under the provisions of the Constitution this meant that the election would be decided in the House of Representatives. A number of the more extreme Federalists viewed this as an opportunity to deny the Republicans the full fruits of their victory by making Burr the Chief Executive instead of Jefferson. Several anxious weeks passed before the tie was broken, and during this time plots and counterplots, some seriously considering the use of force, embroiled the country. Finally, on the thirty-sixth ballot the deadlock was broken in Jefferson's favor.

One of the important results of the election of 1800 was that the Federalists agreed to a peaceful transfer of the government to Republican control. It was a very important precedent to have established. There remained, however, a whole host of other important questions raised by the development of parties, and some of these proved more easily solvable than others. For example, the confusion that resulted in 1796 and especially in 1800 by the failure of the Constitution to distinguish between the election of the President and Vice-President was corrected by the adoption of the twelfth amendment in 1804, which provided that electors cast separate ballots for each office. Less easily resolved and more enduring was the question of what exactly was the significance of the fact that a new party was coming to power. Did it simply mean a change of administrations? Or did it mean actual changes in the government itself? Did the victorious party have a mandate from the people to do whatever it wanted as long as it was legal, or was it obliged, especially after a bitter election contest, to take the feelings and interests of the defeated minority under consideration and try to heal the wounds of the country? Also how was the President to reconcile his position as representative of all the people with the fact that he was also a party leader? Not all Americans in 1801 (or even in much more recent years, for that matter) would have answered these questions in the same way, but some of the precedents established in 1800–1801 were nonetheless crucial for the future development of all of America's political life. The selections that follow illustrate the different ways these questions have been and can be answered, and the kinds of problems that have been indelibly stamped on American political life by the development of political parties.

Official indication of what the course of the victorious Republican party would be came in Jefferson's inaugural address. Jefferson had written the speech with care because he recognized that the policies he adopted as President would affect all future changes of administrations. What does Jefferson describe as the aims of the government? Do you think they are such that a Federalist could not subscribe to them? Do you think they represent a betrayal of the principles that the Republicans stood for in the election of 1800? Given the intensity of the debate in the election, do you think that Jefferson was following the right course? What benefits, if any, could come from conciliation? The address, here given in its entirety, may be found in Adrienne Koch and William Peden, eds., *The Life and Selected Writings of Thomas Jefferson* (New York, 1944), pp. 321–25.

⊂⊋ Inaugural Address

THOMAS JEFFERSON

March 4, 1801

Friends and Fellow Citizens:—

Called upon to undertake the duties of the first executive office of our country, I avail myself of the presence of that portion of my fellow citizens which is here assembled, to express my grateful thanks for the favor with which they have been pleased to look toward me, to declare a sincere consciousness that the task is above my talents, and that I approach it with those anxious and awful presentiments which the greatness of the charge and the weakness of my powers so justly inspire. A rising nation, spread over a wise and fruitful land, traversing all the seas with the rich productions of their industry, engaged in commerce with nations who feel power and forget right, advancing rapidly to destinies beyond the reach of mortal eye—when I contemplate these transcendent objects, and see the honor, the happiness, and the hopes of this beloved country committed to the issue and the auspices of this day, I shrink from the contemplation, and humble myself before the magnitude of the undertaking. Utterly indeed, should I despair, did not the presence of many whom I here see remind me, that in the other high authorities provided by our constitution, I shall find resources of wisdom, of virtue, and of zeal, on which to rely under all difficulties. To you, then, gentlemen, who are charged with the sovereign functions of legislation, and to those associated with you, I look with encouragement for that guidance and support which may enable us to steer with safety the vessel in which we are all embarked amid the conflicting elements of a troubled world.

During the contest of opinion through which we have passed, the animation of discussion and of exertions has sometimes worn an aspect which might impose on strangers unused to think freely and to speak and to write what they think; but this being now decided by the voice of the nation, announced according to the rules of the constitution, all will, of course, arrange themselves under the will of the law, and unite in common efforts for the common good. All, too, will bear in mind this sacred principle, that though the will of the majority is in all cases to prevail, that will, to be rightful, must be reasonable; that the minority possess their equal rights, which equal laws must protect, and to violate which would be oppression. Let us, then, fellow citizens, unite with one heart and one mind. Let us restore to social intercourse that harmony and affection without which liberty and even life itself are but dreary things. And let us reflect that having banished from our land that religious intolerance under which mankind so long bled and suffered, we have yet gained little if we countenance a political intolerance as despotic, as wicked, and capable of as bitter and bloody persecutions. During the throes and convulsions of the ancient world, during the agonizing spasms of infuriated man, seeking through blood and slaughter his long-lost liberty, it was not wonderful that the agitations of the billows should reach even this distant and peaceful shore; that this should be more felt and feared by some and less by others; that this should divide opinions as to measures of safety. But every difference of opinion is not a difference of principle. We have called by different names brethren of the same principle. We are all republicans—we are all federalists. If there be any among us who would wish to dissolve this Union or to change its republican form, let them stand undisturbed as monuments of the safety with which error of opinion may be tolerated where reason is left free to combat it. I know, indeed, that some honest men fear that a republican government cannot be strong; that this government is not strong enough. But would the honest patriot, in the full tide of successful experiment, abandon a government which has so far kept us free and firm, on the theoretic and visionary fear that this government, the world's best hope, may by possibility want energy to preserve itself? I trust not. I believe this, on the contrary, the strongest government on earth. I believe it is the only one where every man, at the call of the laws, would fly to the standard of the law, and would meet invasions of the public order as his own personal concern. Sometimes it is said that man cannot be trusted with the government of himself. Can he, then, be trusted with the government of others? Or have we found angels in the forms of kings to govern him? Let history answer this question.

Let us, then, with courage and confidence pursue our own federal and republican principles, our attachment to our union and representative government. Kindly separated by nature and a wide ocean from the exterminating havoc of one quarter of the globe; too high-minded to endure the degradations of the others; possessing a chosen country, with room enough for our descendants to the hundredth and thousandth generation; entertaining a due sense of our equal right to the use of our own faculties, to the acquisitions of our industry, to honor and confidence from our fellow citizens, resulting not from birth but from our actions and their sense of them; enlightened by a benign religion, professed, indeed, and practiced in various forms, yet all of them including honesty, truth, temperance, gratitude, and the love of man; acknowledging and adoring an overruling Providence, which by all its dispensations proves that it delights in the happiness of man here and his greater happiness hereafter; with all these blessings, what more is necessary to make us a happy and prosperous people? Still one thing more, fellow citizens—a wise and frugal government, which shall restrain men from injuring one another, which shall leave them otherwise free to regulate their own pursuits of industry and improvement, and shall not take from the mouth of labor the bread it has earned. This is the sum of good government, and this is necessary to close the circle of our felicities.

About to enter, fellow citizens, on the exercise of duties which comprehend everything dear and valuable to you, it is proper that you should understand what I deem the essential principles of our government, and consequently those which ought to shape its administration. I will compress them within the narrowest compass they will bear, stating the general principle, but not all its limitations. Equal and exact justice to all men, of whatever state or persuasion, religious or political; peace, commerce, and honest friendship, with all nations—entangling alliances with none; the support of the state governments in all their rights, as the most competent administrations for our domestic concerns and the surest bulwarks against anti-republican tendencies; the preservation of the general government in its whole constitutional vigor, as the sheet anchor of our peace at home and safety abroad; a jealous care of the right of election by the people—a mild and safe corrective of abuses which are lopped by the sword of the revolution where peaceable remedies are unprovided; absolute acquiescence in the decisions of the majority—the vital principle of republics, from which there is no appeal but to force, the vital principle and immediate parent of despotism; a well-disciplined militia—our best reliance in peace and for the first moments of war, till regulars may relieve them; the supremacy of the civil over the military authority; economy in the public expense, that labor may be lightly burdened; the honest payment of our debts and sacred preservation of the public faith; encouragement of agriculture, and of commerce as its handmaid; the diffusion of information and the arraignment of all abuses at the bar of public reason; freedom of religion; freedom of the press; freedom of person under the protection of the habeas corpus; and trial by juries impartially selected—these principles form the bright constellation which has gone before us, and guided our steps through an age of revolution and reformation. The wisdom of our sages and the blood of our heroes have been devoted to their attainment. They should be the creed of our political faith—the text of civil instruction—the touchstone by which to try the services of those we trust; and should we wander from them in moments of error or alarm, let us hasten to retrace our steps and to regain the road which alone leads to peace, liberty, and safety.

I repair, then, fellow citizens, to the post you have assigned me. With experience enough in subordinate offices to have seen the difficulties of this, the greatest of all, I have learned to expect that it will rarely fall to the lot of imperfect man to retire from this station with the reputation and the favor which bring him into it. Without pretensions to that high confidence reposed in our first and great revolutionary character, whose preeminent services had entitled him to the first place in his country's love, and destined for him the fairest page in the volume of faithful history, I ask so much confidence only as may give firmness and effect to the legal administration of your affairs. I shall often go wrong through defect of judgment. When right, I shall often be thought wrong by those whose positions will not command a view of the whole ground. I ask your indulgence for my own errors, which will never be intentional; and your support against the errors of others, who may condemn what they would not if seen in all its parts. The approbation implied by your suffrage is a consolation to me for the past; and my future solicitude will be to retain the good opinion of those who have bestowed it in advance, to conciliate that of others by doing them all the good in my power, and to be instrumental to the happiness and freedom of all.

Relying, then, on the patronage of your good will, I advance with obedience to the work, ready to retire from it whenever you become sensible how much better choice it is in your power to make. And may that Infinite Power which rules the destinies of the universe, lead our councils to what is best, and give them a favorable issue for your peace and prosperity.

Jefferson's inaugural address tended to be very vague on what the specific policies of the new government would be. In the letter below, written to a close friend who had just informed him that his inaugural address had been warmly received by many Federalists, Jefferson more fully elaborated on what his attitude was toward the defeated party and what his administration's policy would be on the sticky question of political removals from office. Given Jefferson's description of the differences between the Federalists and the Republicans, how fundamental would you say the divisions of the 1790's were? Do you think it wise for an incoming President to leave his predecessor's appointees in office? What is to be gained from it? The letter is Thomas Jefferson to Henry Knox, March 27, 1801, Paul L. Ford, ed., *The Writings of Thomas Jefferson* (12 vols., New York, 1899), IX, pp. 236–38.

⊂⊐ Letter to Henry Knox

THOMAS JEFFERSON

Washington, Mar. 27, 1801.

Dear Sir,—

I received with great pleasure your favor of the 16. & it is with the greatest satisfaction I learn from all quarters that my inaugural address is considered as holding out a ground for conciliation & union. I am the more pleased with this, because the opinion therein stated as to the real ground of difference among us (to wit, the measures rendered most expedient by French enormities) is that which I have long entertained. I was always satisfied that the great body of those called Federalists were real republicans as well as Federalists. I know indeed that there are monarchists among us. One character of these is in theory only, & perfectly acquiescent in our form of government as it is, and not entertaining a thought of disturbing it merely on their theoretic opinions. A second class, at the head of which is our quondam colleague, are ardent for the introduction of monarchy, eager for armies, making more noise for a great naval establishment than better patriots who wish it on a national scale only, commensurate to our wants and to our means. This last class ought to be tolerated but not trusted. Believing that (excepting the ardent monarchists) all our citizens agreed in antient Whig principles, I thought it advisable to define & declare them, and let them see the ground on which we could rally: and the fact proving to be so that they agree in these principles I shall pursue them with more encouragement. I am aware that the necessity of a few removals for legal oppressions, delinquencies & other official malversations, may be misconstrued as done for political opinions, & produce hesitation in the coalition so much to be desired; but the extent of these will be too limited to make permanent impressions. In the class of removals however I do not rank the new appointments which Mr. A crowded in with whip & spur from the 12th of Dec. when the event of the election was known, (and consequently that he was making appointments, not for himself but his successor) untill 9. o'clock of the night at 12. o'clock of which he was to go out of office. This outrage on decency should not have its effect, except in the life appointments which are irremovable. But as to the others I consider the nominations as nullities and will not view the persons appointed as even candidates for their office, much less as possessing it by any title meriting respect. I mention these things that the grounds and extent of the removals may be understood, & may not disturb the tendency to union. Indeed that union is already affected from N. York southwardly almost completely. In the N. England states it will be slower than elsewhere from peculiar circumstances better known to yourself than me. But we will go on attending with the utmost solicitude to their interests, & doing them impartial justice, and I have no doubt they will in time do justice to us. I have opened myself frankly because I wish to be understood by those who mean well, and are disposed to be just towards me, as you are. I know you will use it for good purposes only and for none unfriendly to me. . . .

Jefferson's policy of conciliation was sharply criticized by many Republicans. Among those who strongly opposed it were the various party managers, especially from states where the Federalist party remained strong. The letter below written by two editors from New York (which the Republicans had just barely carried in 1800) raises a number of important questions about Jefferson's responsibilities as his party's leader. Do you think it makes sense to dismiss the authors simply as selfish office-seekers? What do you think they mean when they warn that Republican efforts will decline in New York if more appointments are not given to party members? Is this merely a threat or could it be a realistic appraisal of the political situation? Do you think this is an argument that a President should have to listen to? The letter is David Denniston and John Cheetham to Thomas Jefferson, June 1, 1801, Jefferson Papers, Library of Congress.

⊂⊇ Letter to Thomas Jefferson

DAVID DENNISTON AND JOHN CHEETHAM

We take the liberty of addressing you upon a subject highly interesting to our Country. We are placed in an important section of the United States as the guardians, in some degree, of the republican welfare of the country.

As republicans faithfully attatched to the Constitution and the rights of the people, we feel considerable responsibility attatched to our efforts; but while we are sensible of this, we are not less so that there are different grounds on which we may be placed by the measures of government, which will extend or curtail the power of rendering service to the cause in which we are engaged.

There are no citizens who more highly value your talents, your virtues and the republican services which you have rendered your country than ourselves—there are none who are more willing at the present moment to bestow confidence and just applause—none whose affections more anxiously include the idea of a successful issue to the administration which the people and the Constitution have committed to your charge.—We wish to observe however that the people of this city and state look to the new administration with full confidence for a thorough change in the different offices so as to exclude obnoxious characters, those who were inimical to the revolution or have since become hostile to the Constitution and to the principles and progress of republican government. We wish respectfully to express to you our firm opinion that a measure of this sort is absolutely necessary to preserve that republican majority in this state which has contributed so essentially towards placing you in that elevated situation you now hold and which has diffused unusual joy among the friends of liberty in every part of the Union. We have reason to be assured that changes of a similar nature would be extremely useful in the eastern states, whatever may be the situation of the southern part of the country in this respect.

Republican exertions will certainly be relaxed in this quarter if unhappily the people ever be convinced that all their efforts to change the Chief Magistrate, have produced no consequent effects in renovating the subordinate stations of our government. These changes are equally necessary to the preservation of that public spirit which has caused the country to once more return to republican measures and to republican men.

If our anxiety upon this subject should ultimately appear premature, the moment of its discovery would be a moment of satisfaction and pleasure to ourselves and our citizens. But we have reason to apprehend from the sources of information we possess that the idea of a thorough change is not at present contemplated by the executive. In this business, however, sir, we speak not from considerations of personal expectation. Our first wish is the preservation of liberty and our Country, and in no shape whatever is this letter dictated by views including appointments to any office in the power of the executive to bestow.

We have spoken with the freedom which we believe best comports with our duty and which we also believe fully accords with your views concerning the rights of free citizens, which the labours of your life have so eminently contributed to establish.

Our solicitude for the preservation of the Constitution, which we conceive happily confided to your care, for the welfare and liberty of your administration to which we will generously contribute our support, and for the continuation of that affection which our republican citizens have long, and we think justly, placed in you, must be our apology for this letter.

The most basic kind of criticism of Jefferson's policy of conciliation came from those Republicans who viewed his election primarily as a means to substantial change in the structure of the government. The point of view of these Republicans is cogently expressed in a newspaper article, entitled "The Danger Not Over" and written by Edmund Pendleton (1734–1803), that was widely reprinted and endorsed by the Virginia legislature. What do you think the government of the United States would have been like if Pendleton's proposed changes had been adopted? Do you think they might have established a dangerous precedent? What value, if any, is there to constitutional stability? The article, here reprinted in its entirety, was first published in the *Examiner* (Richmond, Va.), October 20, 1801.

⊆ The Danger Not Over

EDMUND PENDLETON

Caroline County, Virginia, October 5, 1801

Although one of my age can have little to hope, and less to fear, from forms of government, as rather belonging to the next world than the present; and possibly may be charged with intermedling where he has no interest, when ever he utters opinions concerning social regulations; yet I feel impelled by an anxious desire to promote the happiness of my country, to submit to the public consideration, some reflections on our present political state.

It is far from my intention to damp the public joy, occasioned by the late changes of our public agents, or to disturb the calm which already presages the most beneficial consequences; on the contrary, I consider this event as having arrested a train of measures which were gradually conducting us towards ruin.

These changes will be matter of tenfold congratulation, if we make the proper use of them: If instead of negligently reposing upon that wisdom and integrity, which have already softened even political malice, we seize the opportunity to erect new barriers against folly, fraud and ambition; and to explain such parts of the constitution, as have been already, or may be interpreted contrary to the intention of those who adopted it.

This proposition does not argue a want of proper confidence in our present Chief Magistrate, but the contrary. It can be no censure to believe that he has a nobler destiny to fulfill, than that of making his contemporary country-men happy for a few years; and that the rare event

101

of such a character at the head of a nation, imposes on Us the sacred duty of seizing the propitious opportunity, to do all in our power to perpetuate that happiness: as to that species of confidence, which would extinguish free enquiry and popular watchfulness, it is never desired by *patriotism,* nor ought to be yielded by *freeman.*

In pursuit of our purpose, we ought to keep in mind certain principles which are believed to be sound; to enquire whether they have been violated under the constitution? and then consider how a repetition of those violations may be prevented—As thus,

I. Government is instituted for the good of the community, and not to gratify avarice or ambition; therefore unnecessary increase of debt— appointment of useless officers, such as stationary ministers to foreign courts, with which we have little connexion, and sixteen additional judges at a time when the business of the Federal Courts had greatly diminished—and engaging us in a war abroad, for the sake of advancing party projects at home, are abuses in government.

II. The chief good derivable from government, is *civil liberty;* and if government is so constructed, as to enable its administrators to assail that liberty with the several weapons heretofore most fatal to it, the structure is defective: of this sort, standing Armies—Fleets—severe penal Laws—War—and a multitude of civil Officers, are universally admitted to be; and if our government can, with ease and impunity, array these forces against social liberty, the constitution is defective.

III. Peace is undoubtedly that state which proposes to society the best chance for the continuance of freedom and happiness; and the situation of America is such, as to expose her to fewer occasions for war, than any other nation; whilst it also disables her from gaining any thing by war. But if, by indirect means, the executive can involve us in war, not declared by the legislature; if a treaty may be made which will incidentally produce a war, and the legislature are bound to pass all laws necessary to give it full effect; or if the judiciary may determine a war to exist, although the legislature hath refused to declare it; then the constitution is defective, since it admits constructions which pawn our freedom and happiness upon the security of executive patriotism, which is inconsistent with Republican Principles.

IV. Union is certainly the bases of our political prosperity, and this can only be preserved by confining, with precision, the federal government to the exercise of powers clearly required by the general interest, or respecting foreign nations, and the state governments to objects of a local nature; because the states exhibit such varieties of character and interests, that a consolidated general government would be in a perpetual conflict with state interests, from its want of local knowledge, or from a prevalence of local prejudice or interest, so as certainly to produce civil war and disunion. If then the distinct provinces of the general and state governments are not clearly defined; If the former may assail the latter by penalties, and by absorbing all subjects of taxation—If a system leading to consolidation, may be formed and pursued,—and if, instead of leaving it to the respective states to encourage their agriculture or manufactures, as their local interest may dictate, the general government may by bountys or protective duties, tax the one to promote the other; then the constitution has not sufficiently provided for the continuance of the union, by securing the rights of the state governments and local interests.

V. It is necessary for the preservation of Republican government, that the legislative, executive, and judiciary powers should be kept separate and distinct from each other, so that no man, or body of men, shall be authorized to exercise more than one of them at the same time: The Constitution, therefore, in consigning to the Federal Senate, a participation in the powers of each department, violates this important principle, and tends to create in that body, a dangerous aristocracy. And

VI. An essential principle of representative government is that it be influenced by the will of the people; which will can never be expressed, if their representatives are corrupted, or influenced by hopes of office. If this hope may multiply offices and extend patronage—If the president may nominate to valuable offices, members of the legislature, who shall please him, and displease the people, by increasing his power and patronage—If he may be tempted to use his power and patronage for securing his re-election—and if he may even bestow lucrative diplomas upon judges, whilst they are receiving liberal salaries, paid as the price of their independence and purity; then a risk exists, lest the legislatures should legislate—the judges decide—and the Senate concur in nominations, with an eye to those offices—and lest the president may appoint with a view to his re-election; and thus may at length appear the phoenomenon, of a government, republican in form, without possessing a single chaste organ for expressing the public will.

Many of these objections were foreseen, when the constitution was ratified, by those who voted for its adoption; but waved then, because of the vast importance of the union, which a rejection might have placed in hazard—Of the provision made for amendments, as trial should discover defects—and the hope that in the mean time, the instrument with all its defects, might produce social happiness, if a proper tone was given to the government, by the several agents, in it's operation: But since experience has evinced, that much mischief may be done under an unwise administration; and that even the most valuable parts of the constitution, may be evaded or violated, we ought no longer to rest our security upon the vain hope which depends on the rectitude of fallible men in successive administrations; But now that the union is as firmly established by the general opinion of the citizen, as we can ever hope it to be, it behoves Us to bring forward amendments, which may fix it upon *principles* capable of restraining human frailties.

Having, I trust, shewn the utility and necessity of such efforts at this time, I will adventure to submit to the consideration of my fellow citizens, with great humility and deference, whether it would not be adviseable to have the constitution amended,

1st. By rendering a president ineligible for the next Turn, and transferring from him to the legislature, the appointment of the judges, and stationary foreign ministers; making the stipends of the latter to be no longer discretionary in the president.

2. By depriving the Senate of all executive power; and shortening their term of service, or subjecting its members to removal by their constituents.

3. By rendering members of the legislature and the judges, whilst in office and for a limited time thereafter, incapable of taking any other office whatsover, (the offices of President and Vice-President excepted;) and subjecting the judges to removal by the concurring vote of both houses of Congress.

4. By forming some check upon the abuse of *public credit*, which, tho' in some instances useful, like Fleets and Armies, may, like those, be carried to extremes dangerous to liberty, and inconsistent with economical government.

5. By instituting a fair mode of impanelling juries.

6. By declaring that no treaty with a foreign nation, so far as it may relate to Peace or War,—to the expenditure of public money—or to commercial regulations, shall be law, until ratified by the legislature; the interval between such treaty and the next meeting of Congress, excepted, so far as it may not relate to the grant of money.

7. By defining prohibited powers so explicitly, as to defy the wiles of construction. If nothing more should be gained, it will be a great acquisition, clearly to interdict laws relating to the freedom of speech, —of the Press—and of religion: To declare that the Common Law of England, or of any other foreign country, in criminal cases, shall not be considered as a law of the United States,—and that treason shall be confined to the cases stated in the constitution, so as not to be extended further, by law, or construction, or by using other terms, such as sedition, &c.; and

8. By marking out with more precision, the distinct powers of the *General* and *State* Governments.

In the Virginia Bill of Rights is expressed this inestimable sentiment "That no free Government, or the blessing [of] liberty, can be preserved to any people, but by a firm adherence to justice, moderation, temperance, frugality, and virtue; and by frequent recurrence to fundamental principles." A sentiment produced, no doubt, by the experience of this melancholy truth, "That of men advanced to power, more are inclined to destroy *liberty*, than to defend it, ["] there is of course a continual effort for its *destruction*, which ought to be met by corresponding efforts for its *preservation*.

These principles and propositions are most respectfully submitted to my fellow Citizens, with this observation: "That it is only when great and good men are at the head of a nation, that the people can expect to succeed, in forming new barriers to counteract recent encroachments on their rights: and when ever a nation is so supine as to suffer such an opportunity to be lost, they will soon feel that "THE DANGER WAS NOT OVER."

Edmond [*sic*] Pendleton

Having been defeated in the election of 1800 the Federalists found themselves in a quandary. They had denounced the concept of an opposition party throughout the 1790's only now to find themselves out of power. The party was not sure what it should do. In the following letter one of the party's elder statesmen proposes a plan of action. Do you think it contains a realistic appraisal of what the Republicans stood for? Do you think it appreciates the value of an opposition group in politics? Why do you think the Federalists never regained power? For the letter, see: Fisher Ames to Theodore Dwight, March 19, 1801, Seth Ames, ed., *Works of Fisher Ames* (2 vols., Boston, 1854), I, pp. 292–95.

⊂⊒ Letter to Theodore Dwight

FISHER AMES

Dedham, March 19, 1801.

Sir,—

There are many federalists who think that nothing can be done, and others who think it is *too soon* to do any thing, to prevent the subversion of property and right of every kind. Some even say that Mr. Jefferson will be a federalist, and, of course, there is no need that any thing should be done. As I happen to entertain a very different opinion on all these three points, I ask leave to state, as briefly as I must in a letter, my sentiments to you. I will crowd the paper that I may do it the more fully. I conceive that the Virginia politics are violent, according to the temper of her Taylors, Monroes, and Gileses, and I may add Jeffersons. They are vindictive, because that State owes much, and the commercial States have gained, and now possess, much; and this newly accumulated moneyed interest, so corrupt and corrupting, is considered a rival interest, that baffles Virginia in her claim of ruling the public counsels. The *great* State has the ambition to be the *great nation.* Philosophism and Jacobinism add vigor to the passions that spring from the sources before mentioned. As political power is to be wholly in their hands; as even the senate will apparently be jacobin; and as the popular current is setting in favor of the extremest use of this power,—it seems strange that any federalist of good sense can see matter of consolation in the prospect before us.

Party is an association of honest men for honest purposes, and, when the State falls into bad hands, is the only efficient defence; a champion who never flinches, a watchman who never sleeps. But the federalists are scarcely associated. Their confidence is so blind, and they are yet acted upon so little by their fears, their trust in the *sinless* perfection of a democracy is so entire, that perhaps suffering severely is the only mode for teaching. Others, who foresee and foretell the danger, must suffer with them. Is it not, therefore, proper, and indispensably necessary, to be active, in order to prevent the dissolution of the feeble ties by which the federal party is held together? Is it not practicable to rouse a part of the good men, and to stay the contagion of Jacobinism within, at least, its present ample limits? It would be wrong to assail the new administration with invective. Even when bad measures occur, much temperance will be requisite. To encourage Mr. Jefferson to act right, and to aid him against his violent jacobin adherents, we must make it manifest that we act on principle, and that we are deeply alarmed for the public good; that we are identified with the public. We must speak in the name and with the voice of the good and the wise, the lovers of liberty and the owners of property. By early impressing the preciousness, if I may use the word, of certain principles, and of the credit, commerce, and arts, that depend on adhering to them, and by pointing out the utter ruin of the commercial States by a Virginia or democratic system, may we not consolidate the federalists, and check the licentiousness of the jacobin administration? I do not believe that the eastern States, if roused effectually, would be assailed in their great interests; I believe as little that if they are suffered to sleep supinely, confiding, instead of watching, they will escape ruin. Smooth promises, and a tinsel called conciliation, are to be used to break their coherence, to invite deserters from their corps, and, after thinning their ranks, the breach of those promises would be safe. Violence would enjoy impunity. It will be too late to alarm after the contagious principles of Jacobinism have made New England as rotten as Pennsylvania.

The newspapers are an overmatch for any government. They will first overawe and then usurp it. This has been done; and the Jacobins owe their triumph to the unceasing use of this engine; not so much to skill in the use of it, as by repetition. . . . We must use, but honestly, and without lying, an engine that wit and good sense would make powerful and safe. To this end, the talents of Connecticut must be put in requisition. The Palladium might be made a great auxiliary to true liberty, and the endangered cause of good order. Its circulation, however, must be greatly increased. Any paper, to be useful at this crisis, must spread ten times as much as any will or can, unless the federal party, by a common concert, join to make it, like the London Gazette, *the* Gazette of the party. Could not your clergy, your legislators, your good men, be impressed with the zeal to diffuse it at once through your State? The attempt is making here; but, I confess, many think it a folly to be alarmed. Many others are alarmed. An active spirit must be roused in every town to check the incessant proselytizing arts of the Jacobins, who will soon or late subvert Connecticut, as surely as other States, unless resisted with a spirit as ardent as their own. If such a spirit could be roused, we should certainly preserve all that we have not yet lost. We should save property, credit, and commerce. We should, I am sanguine enough to believe, throw upon our antagonists the burdens of supporting and vindicating government, and enjoy their late advantages of finding fault, which popular prejudice is ever prone to listen to. We should soon stand on high ground, and be ready to resume the reins of government with advantage. You will suppose that I still bear in mind, that we are not to revile or abuse magistrates, or lie even for a good cause. We must act as good citizens, using only truth, and argument, and zeal to impress them.

The success of this design depends on the diffusion of like ideas among all the federalists, and the exertion of the first talents of the party. I think myself entitled to call upon you, and to ask you to call upon the mighty Trumbull, who must not slumber, like Achilles in his tent, while the camp is in danger of being forced. Mr. Wolcott must be summoned to give his counsels, as well as to mend his excellent pen. Connecticut is the lifeguard of liberty and federalism. I am trying to sound the tocsin. Mr. Dutton, the editor of the Palladium, has talents, learning, and taste; what is no less essential, he has discretion. It is intended that every clergyman in Massachusetts, New Hampshire, and Vermont shall have a paper one year by a subscription.

I write as much, in confidence, to you as the nature of the subject requires. I am, sir, with great respect, &c.

Yours.

Chapter

6: The Panic of 1819

JAMES ROGER SHARP

The period following the conclusion of the War of 1812 was an era of great national pride and optimism for most Americans. The war itself had been less than successful for the United States, but Andrew Jackson's spectacular victory over the British at New Orleans at the close of the conflict and the favorable peace treaty ending the hostilities did much to erase the memory of the dreary war years. Furthermore, the vast virgin territory of the interior was waiting to be exploited by the farmer's ax and plough. In rapid succession the states of Indiana, Illinois, Alabama, and Mississippi were added to the Union. Thousands of Americans moved west to the rich soil, encouraged by liberal land laws which provided credit to prospective farmers and planters. From 1815 to 1819 the debt for public lands rose from $3 million to $22 million.

A major problem affecting America's ability to develop her natural resources was the lack of capital. Like all businessmen in underdeveloped countries with rich natural resources and little capital to exploit them, American entrepreneurs needed money to buy land, to buy (as in the Southern slave states) or hire labor, to make capital improvements, and to build canals and roads so as to open up the interior to the market economy.

In the United States the task of capital creation was undertaken by the banks. Thus, the number of banks and the amount of capital dramatically increased after the War of 1812. For example, in a single year, 1818, the Kentucky legislature chartered forty banks. In 1816 the Second Bank of the United States (BUS) was chartered by Congress. By far the largest corporation in the country, the BUS was capitalized with both public and private funds but with private investors retaining operating control. Besides being the depository of all federal funds, the BUS was supposed to act as a great central bank, using its superior financial resources to regulate the numerous state banks throughout the country.

The banks were enormously influential economic institutions. Since the federal government issued no paper money, the country was heavily reliant upon the BUS as well as the many private banks throughout the country to provide the circulating medium. With this power, bankers could expand or contract the monetary supply in their local communities which, in turn, could influence prices. And through their loan policy they would literally create capital, thereby allowing those businessmen in the community who were favored by loans to expand their operations.

In order to open its doors, each bank (with the exception of the BUS) had to be granted a charter from the state legislature. There were then no general incorporation laws, and each bank charter was granted individually. This meant that any rules and regulations governing banks varied considerably, not only from state to state but also from charter to charter within an individual state. Despite the fact that the banks were such important economic institutions, state regulations were inadequate, and many restrictions were unenforced. One reason for this was that few understood banking operations, and fewer still knew what kind of restrictions would ensure safe and responsible banking. One regulation, however, that was normally found in most charters was some limit on the amount of paper money a bank could issue, usually by some sort of capital-note ratio. In other words, if a bank were capitalized at $100,000, it might be restricted from issuing more than two, three, or five times that amount in notes. Charters also generally forbade the banks from suspending specie payment; that is, refusing to pay gold and silver to the bearers of their notes.

In the years after 1815 the increase in banks had a multiplier effect upon credit. This, in turn, stimulated an inflationary rise in prices and property values. And the entire economy seemed to be built upon a paper foundation. The speculative boom raged out of control, and the prosperity which was built upon such fragile foundations was not to last. The postwar decline of European demand for American agricultural goods, and the contraction policy of the BUS combined to brake sharply the inflationary spiral. The BUS and the banks it was supposed to regulate were hopelessly overextended. The capital-note ratio restriction, found in many of the charters, had been entirely inadequate as a basis for sound banking. Later, bank reformers would argue that specie-liability ratios rather than capital-note ratios should be adopted, and that a bank's notes and liabilities should never exceed more than three times the amount of specie (gold and silver) held in the vaults. The BUS, in 1818, had more thn $22.3 million in demand liabilities (notes as well as other liabilities) covered by only $2.3 million in specie. This meant it had an extremely vulnerable 1 to 10 specie-liability ratio. Because the BUS was so overextended, it began to call in its debts, causing severe contraction of credit, especially in the West. By exercising this rather drastic measure, the BUS escaped bankruptcy, but as one contemporary economist said: "The Bank was saved, and the people were ruined."

What began as a financial squeeze became a general depression. Prices plunged, land values dropped, and the numbers of unemployed swelled. In New Orleans at one point during the year 1818, cotton prices fell from 32 to less than 15 cents a pound. In 1821, the sheriff of St. Louis County in Missouri put up for sale for delinquent taxes over 14,000 acres of land and 105 town lots. Debtors found themselves in the painful predicament of having inflated liabilities and being in danger of losing their property to their creditors. Borrowers in the West, who were most overextended, suffered the greatest hardship. One Western newspaper reported that "Such is the depreciation of the value of property, that the accumulated labor of years is not now sufficient to pay a trifling debt, and property some years since which could have sold for eight to ten thousand dollars, will scarcely, at this time, pay a debt of five hundred. . . ."

The Panic of 1819 dashed the optimistic dreams of prosperity. It brought an end to postwar nationalism by encouraging latent sectional tensions. And it brought to an end the Jeffersonian era of good feelings— an end to one party rule. By the time of the Panic the Jeffersonian party had virtually destroyed the Federalist opposition. But by so doing it had sown the seeds of its own destruction. The Jeffersonian Republicans had become so bloated with success that their party had little shape or form. Men professing adherence to widely varying credos all claimed loyalty to the party, and more vaguely subscribed to Jeffersonian principles. The Panic ended Virginia's domination of the White House and it ended political rule by gentlemen. Furthermore it marked the emergence of dilemmas which bitterly divided the country for the better part of the century. The twin problems of slavery and sectionalism, exacerbated by the depression, were only solved by the Civil War. And economic issues such as the tariff, banking, and the currency—with their enormous political implications— were to remain divisive until the turn of the century.

The postwar panic and depression caused Americans to raise basic questions about their society, questions that were to be echoed and reechoed throughout the remainder of the century. During the prosperous pre-Panic times, latent fears and suspicions of financial institutions had been largely suppressed, and the banks accepted as creative engines of progress. But afterward in the midst of personal financial crisis and general depression, many citizens came to regard banks as agents of the devil.

Ante-bellum Americans seem to have had a dual nature that made them immensely responsive to speculative enterprise but not without some feeling of guilt. And indeed, during the period of economic collapse after 1819, many felt that it was God's method of punishing a people who had sinned—who had expected riches without work. This duality can be seen earlier in the preachings of Benjamin Franklin in his

Poor Richard's Almanack. On the one hand Franklin recommends frugality, thrift, and hard work, and promises as a result both moral and material rewards. But, on the other hand, he puts such an emphasis upon materialistic values, equating wealth with moral rectitude, that a follower of Poor Richard's axioms in his pursuit of wealth could easily forget the necessary relationship between hard work and riches. And the pursuit of riches without hard work—wealth based on speculation—was considered by most Americans as sinful.

The banks represented speculative wealth. Through what seemed to be a kind of alchemy, they created credit and money from paper. But when hard times struck and the banks to save themselves called in loans and thereby brought ruin to their debtors, the fascination of the public with banking wizardry turned to angry bewilderment and frustration. The BUS particularly was regarded with bitter animosity. It was denounced by Senator Thomas Hart Benton of Missouri, among others, who charged: "I know towns, yea, cities . . . where this bank already appears as an engrossing proprietor. All the flourishing cities of the West are mortgaged to this money power. . . . They are in the jaws of the monster! A lump of butter in the mouth of a dog! One gulp, one swallow, and all is gone!"

The new nation's first major nationwide panic and depression, then, was the catalyst for a fundamental crisis in American values. The creation of wealth by printing press, as the banks seemed to do, clashed with fundamental values of thrift and hard work. Agents and symbols of a new commercialized and industrialized society, the banks challenged the conventional wisdom of rural America, and their boom-to-bust cycle seemed to reveal a deep-seated corruption of American society.

Reaction to the crisis took several forms. Some argued that nothing could be done. The delicate balance of God's natural laws had been upset by the tinkering of man, and further tinkering would only aggravate matters. Society's sufferings were retribution, levied by God in punishment for the orgy of speculation. Others maintained that the government had an obligation to help alleviate the distress. The federal government passed a law relieving those who were in debt as a result of their purchases of public land. Many states passed stay laws or minimum appraisal laws that protected the debtor from having his property sold for his debt at greatly deflated prices. Several states established state banks or loan offices in order to expand the money supply. The paper money they issued by law had to be accepted by creditors for debts.

The following documents illustrate the various reactions to this major financial crisis, and they show the anxieties it raised in the country. Americans began to reevaluate the relationships among politics, economics and public morality. In the process, fundamental issues, not to be immediately resolved, were raised. And, indeed, variations of the same questions still confront us.

Even before the Panic of 1819 struck, a number of Americans were sounding warnings about the extravagant inflationary boom the country was experiencing. In the following document the anonymous letter writer employs a much-used nineteenth-century propaganda device of personalizing an issue. Bank reformers felt that their attacks upon the banks would be much more effective if they could illustrate how banking abuses ruined one man's life. The letter was written to Hezekiah Niles and published in his influential *Niles Weekly Register*, which had long been warning about bank abuses. (There is more about Niles in the introduction to the fifth document of this chapter.) What was the main source of the problem, according to the author of the letter? Was it political, economic or moral? Who was at fault for the farmer's dilemma—the banks or the farmer himself? Why does the author refer to his opponents as "aristocracy," "gentry" and "rag barons"? The letter was printed in the *Niles Weekly Register* on August 22, 1818.

⊂϶ The Farmer and the Broker: A True Story

ANONYMOUS

In riding through a neighboring state, in a stage coach, the slowness of which enabled me and my fellow travellers to take a leisurely view of the country through which we were passing, my attention was caught by a house beautifully situated on the projection of a hill at no great distance. There was something particularly charming in its situation, and an air of independent comfort about it, that seemed to bear testimony to the happiness of the inmates.

I enquired of the driver . . . to whom this fine place belonged. He told me the owner's name, but this was all he knew about him. A fellow passenger, however, who was both communicative and intelligent, now took up the affair of answering my questions, and related the following story, to which every landholder ought to pay particular attention.

"The person," said he, "who at present occupies that house, was about three or four years ago the owner of it, and an estate of two thousand acres of rich land extending all around. He was considered, and truly so, one of the best farmers, and one of the most worthy men in the county; but about four or it may be five years ago, in one of his trips to the town of——, like the unfortunate man who was in his way from Jerusalem to Jericho, he fell among thieves, who eventually picked his pocket of all he was worth in the world. This little town had three banks, without capitals, but like all poor d—ls, exceedingly anxious to procure them, in the usual way, by exchanging rags for real property.

For this purpose, in imitation of the great banks who set the fashions to the small fry, they employed brokers and other caterpillars of the community, to hunt game for them—to find out gentlemen who had more land than prudence, and might be seduced into a persuasion that they had occasion for more money than they actually wanted. In short, to put into their heads some foolish speculation, by pointing out the means of obtaining the money to carry it into effect.

"Four of these worthy, useful and honorable caitiffs, accordingly selected out our worthy Farmer, who unluckily had a fine mill stream running through his rich meadows. They called upon him at the hotel where he put up, invited him to dine with some worthy bank directors, and gradually slided into his mind a strong notion to build a merchant mill upon his brooks, and enter upon the manufacturing of flour on a great scale. 'But I have no money to spare,' said the honest farmer. This was the very point they wished to bring him to; and now was opened to his eager comprehension, a way to get as much money as he wanted, so easy and so free from any danger of evil consequences, that the good farmer was surprised as well as delighted, at the prospect of having as much as he wanted, with never being obliged to pay anything but the interest. In short to make an end of a long story, he borrowed several thousand dollars, gave his note for it at sixty days, endorsed by his worthy friend the broker, and went home to build his mills, with the full conviction that banks were the greatest blessings that heaven ever showered down upon a country. The note was renewed several times without difficulty; the worthy farmer finished his mills, but owing to some oversight he never reverted to the fact, that there were already quite as many mills in the country as could find employment, and consequently he was without grist for his mill a good part of the time. To remedy this, he determined to purchase wheat to keep the mill a-going, and for this purpose he gave his note to the little bank, endorsed by his friend the broker, for a few thousand more to buy grain,—for it was nonsense to have a mill with nothing to do.—Still the good farmer was perfectly easy —his notes he was assured, might run on *till the day of judgment,* and his crops and the profits of his mill would enable him to pay all off in a few years. But the judgment of heaven was on him for his folly. His crops were smitten with the Hessian fly two or three years in succession, and not only his, but those of all the country round, so that his mill was entirely idle. He was consequently under the necessity of adding the interest to his notes every time he renewed them, and his good friend the broker, who having now a fair presumptive title to the poor man's estate was made a bank director, finding him getting to the proper pitch of difficulty, began to play off the various arts of the trade. He was consistently writing letters about the scarcity of money—the curtailing of discounts—the difficulty of obtaining a renewal of his notes, and playing on his fears by all that infamous cant with which these reptiles preface every new extortion. All this time the predestined victim was testifying his gratitude to the broker for his friendly exertions, in getting his notes renewed, by presents of flour, mutton, poultry and sometimes a fat beeve, on which the rascal regaled his brother rogues, the brokers and bank directors. At last, the broker had interest—that is to say, he consented to let his brother directors in for a share of the spoils, if they would refuse to discount the country gentleman's notes, to frighten him a little. The notes were thrown out and the worthy broker, to show his disinterested friendship, came forward, in the most liberal manner, and paid them himself, by advancing the money, for which he only charged him three per cent a month.

"The poor farmer was now out of the frying pan into the fire—his wants grew every day more pressing, and the more he wanted money, the more his friend the broker made him pay for it. By various arts, which these wretches know so well how to practise—by creating wants, and then taking advantage of them, by playing upon his fears, by cajolling, by threatening and by falsehood, he drew the unfortunate farmer every day deeper and deeper into his toils, until at last in the agony of his fears of immediate exposure to his friends and family, and to ward off for a little while the hour when he must blush to appear before them, he was induced to give a deed of trust of his whole estate for the mutual benefit of the broker and his worthy co-adjutors, the bank directors; who continued to furnish the farmer with money until his debt amounted to two thirds of his whole property. One day the bank *shaved* him, next the broker; and now in a few days they will divide the spoil of the whole estate, which is worth two hundred thousand dollars, but will probably be bought a great bargain by the broker and his sweet confederates. It is advertised for public sale, and a worthy, useful member of society together with his family, is thus ruined and turned adrift upon the world, for the benefit of a race of worthless drones—who destroy the wholesome prosperity of the farmer—who suck the heart's blood of the industrious—and who by the extensive seduction of these vile examples, have, in a great measure, destroyed the land marks of all honorable dealings between man and man, so that business is now little else than unprincipled cupidity; and trading and swindling are become synonimous."

The gentleman here ended his story, and I could not help reflecting on the importance of the lesson it conveyed. It was a practical exposition of some principles laid down by me in my essays on the paper system, and furnishes a striking example of the consequences of that system, to the other classes of the community. It is a true story—I know it to be a fact—and that I do not expose the vile actors in this scene of villainy and seduction, is because I regard the feelings of their victim rather than the resentment of his tempters. If there be any *thing* I despise, beyond the dirt on which I tread, it is these worthless beings, who at the very moment they are earning and enjoying the wages of the vilest roguery, have the insolence to associate and challenge an equality with the rest of their fellow creatures. They and their precious compeers, the numerous race of worthies, who descend to the lowest degradation of villainy, by counterfeiting money, which is itself a counterfeit, are equally the product of the paper system, and we may judge of the tree by its fruits.

I rejoice to see that you still continue to expose the monstrous abuses of this system, abuses that would not be tolerated but in a country ripe for the vilest species of slavery—submission to a beggarly, upstart, and unprincipled aristocracy. I rejoice, too, that you promise in due time to pay your respects to these thriving adjuncts of the beautiful system of paper, the lottery office gentry—who fill the newspapers with their disgusting and filthy garrulity—who pay the great prizes in gold of which they pick the pockets of the poor—and who invite honest labor, in delectable verses and seducing parodies, to come and gamble away its last shilling.—These are a precious brood, and highly deserving the attention of the curious in the reptile species. They furnish a most amusing study to the naturalist who wishes to investigate the sources of mischief possessed by the insect tribe—and to the philosopher who is at a loss for the connective link between man and beast. But after all, we ought not to throw all the blame on these worthy people. The different legislatures, who pass lottery laws with as little ceremony as they charter banks, are the real sources of the abuse. Where there is honey there will be flies—where there is a dead dog there will be maggots. I repeat again, we must thank the different legislative bodies, for furnishing nutriment to these mischievous and offensive creatures, by sanctioning lotteries with as little hesitation as they make laws against every other species of gambling! In truth, the state governments appear to monopolize all the profits of gambling, to the utter exclusion of every other species of blacklegs, except the lottery-office men.

You, sir, are the very man to rout this hitherto prosperous confederacy; at least to hold them up in their proper colours. They have laughed in their sleeves a long time at the world, and it is but justice the world should have its turn. Happily, you are not held in subjection to quack doctors who cure all diseases, and lottery-office men who make everybody rich—you publish none of those advertisements with which they fool mankind. Your paper, devoted as it has ever been to the support of national honor, and conducted as it is, in the spirit becoming an independent citizen of the United States, is beyond the petty malice of the race of rag barons of every class and degree, who dare to threaten ruin and persecution to those who are honest enough to expose their conduct or who possess the spirit to demand justice at their hands. What, sir!

is it come to this—shall a little upstart bank director—a moth, engendered and brought to maturity in a bundle of dirty rags, insolently threaten you and I with persecution, for saying of them what is true, and they dare not deny—that they will not and cannot, pay their debts in the manner other people pay them, and yet are running in debt deeper and deeper every day? Really, the times are come to a pretty pass if a man cannot call a rogue a rogue—a swindler a swindler—a rag a rag—without being persecuted by the whole tribe of rogues, swindlers and rag barons! Don't be alarmed, Mr. Niles, at the formidable confederacy of kites and crows you may chance to provoke. Remember that *virius mille scuta*—and truth is equal to a thousand weapons. You have already done great good— you have alarmed the dishonest banks for their very existence—and the honest ones, lest they should be involved in the general ruin that menaces the system. I am convinced you will do still more, although in sad and sober earnest, I am not so sanguine as to hope a thorough cure. It seems to me that the whole paper system is nothing more than a contrivance of knaves to cheat honest men, and that nothing but a complete union of the latter can make head against the combinations of the former. This is hardly to be expected, since experience everywhere demonstrates that rogues are much more gregarious and apt to stick together than honest men.

James Flint (1781–1855) was a Scotsman who traveled extensively through the Ohio River valley at the time of the Panic of 1819. As a foreigner his viewpoint, while not unprejudiced, had a critical detachment that most Americans would not have when viewing their own society. According to Flint, what impact did the increasing numbers of banks and paper money have on the American economy? Were there any advantages to this great increase in paper money? Any disadvantages? What was Flint's position on relief legislation—such as bankruptcy laws and property laws? "Flint's Letters from America" were first published in Edinburgh in 1822, but were edited and republished by Reuben Gold Thwaites in Volume IX of his *Early Western Travels, 1748–1846* (Cleveland, Ohio, 1904), pp. 132–34, 220, 225–28.

⊂⊒ Letters from America

JAMES FLINT

There is here much trouble with paper money. The notes current in one part, are either refused, or taken at a large discount, in another. Banks that were creditable a few days ago, have refused to redeem their paper in specie, or in notes of the United States' Bank. . . . The total number of these establishments in the United States, could not, perhaps, be accurately stated on any given day. The enumeration, like the census of population, might be affected by births and deaths. The creation of this vast host of fabricators, and venders of base money, must form a memorable epoch in the history of the country.—These craftsmen have greatly increased the money capital of the nation; and have, in a corresponding degree, enhanced the *nominal* value of property and labour. By lending, and otherwise emitting, their engravings, they have contrived to mortgage and buy much of the property of their neighbours, and to appropriate to themselves the labour of less moneyed citizens. Proceeding in this manner, they cannot retain specie enough to redeem their bills, admitting the gratuitous assumption that they were once possessed of it. They seem to have calculated that the whole of their paper would not return on them in one day. Small quantities, however, of it have, on various occasions, been sufficient to cause them to suspend specie payments. . . .

Of upwards of a hundred banks that lately figured in Indiana, Ohio, Kentucky, and Tennessee, the money of two is now only received in the land-office, in payment for public lands. Many have perished, and the remainder are struggling for existence. Still giving for their *rags* "bills as *good as their own;*" but, except two, none pay in specie, or bills of the United States Bank. Discount varies from thirty to one hundred per cent.

The recent history of banking in these western States, is probably unrivalled. Such a system of knavery could only be developed in a country where avarice and credulity are prominent features of character. About four years ago, the passion for acquiring unearned gains rose to a great height; banking institutions were created in abundance. The designing amongst lawyers, doctors, tavern-keepers, farmers, grocers, shoemakers, tailors, &c. entered into the project, and subscribed for stock. . . . A common provision in charters, stipulated, that the property of each partner was not liable, in security, to a greater amount than the sum he had subscribed. This exempted the banks from the natural inconveniences that might be occasioned by the insolvencies and elopements of members. Money was accumulated in great abundance, as they bought property; lent on security; and became rich. But their credit was of short duration. When it was found, that a few of them could not redeem their bills, the faith of the people was shaken. A run on the paper shops commenced; and a suspension of specie payments soon became general. . . .

The accounts given in my last letter of the depredations committed by bankers, will make you suppose that affairs are much deranged here. Bankruptcy is now a sin prohibited by law. In the Eastern States, and in Europe, our condition must be viewed as universal insolvency. Who, it may be asked, would give credit to a people whose laws tolerate the violation of contracts? Mutual credit and confidence are almost torn up by the roots. It is said that in China, knaves are openly commended in courts of law for the adroitness of their management. In the interior of the United States, law has removed the necessity of being either acute or honest.

The money in circulation is puzzling to traders, and more particularly to strangers; for besides the multiplicity of banks, and the diversity in supposed value, fluctuations are so frequent, and so great, that no man who holds it in his possession can be safe for a day. The merchant, when asked the price of an article, instead of making a direct answer, usually puts the question, "What sort of money have you got?" Supposing that a number of bills are shown, and one or more are accepted of, it is not till then, that the price of goods is declared; and an additional price is uniformly laid on, to compensate for the supposed defect in the quality of the money. Trade is stagnated—produce cheap—and merchants find it difficult to lay in assortments of foreign manufactures. . . .

Agriculture languishes—farmers cannot find profit in hiring labourers. The increase of produce in the United States is greater than any increase of consumption. . . . To increase the quantity of provisions, then, without enlarging the numbers of those who eat them, will be only diminishing the price farther. Land in these circumstances can be of no value to the capitalist who would employ his funds in farming. The spare capital of farmers is here chiefly laid out in the purchase of lands.

Labourers and mechanics are in want of employment. I think that I have seen upwards of 1500 men in quest of work within eleven months past, and many of these declared, that they had no money. Newspapers and private letters agree in stating, that wages are so low as eighteen and three-fourths cents (about ten-pence) per day, with board, at Philadelphia, and some other places. Great numbers of strangers lately camped in the open field near Baltimore, depending on the contributions of the charitable for subsistence. You have no doubt heard of emigrants returning to Europe without finding the prospect of a livelihood in America. Some who have come out to this part of the country do not succeed well. Labourers' wages are at present a dollar and an eighth part per day. Board costs them two three-fourths or three dollars per week, and washing three-fourths of a dollar for a dozen of pieces. On these terms, it is plain that they cannot live two days by the labour of one, with the other deductions which are to be taken from their wages. Clothing, for example, will cost about three times its price in Britain: and the poor labourer is almost certain of being paid in depreciated money; perhaps from thirty to fifty per cent. under par. I have seen several men turned out of boarding houses, where their money would not be taken. They had no other resource left but to lodge in the woods, without any covering except their clothes. They set fire to a decayed log, spread some boards alongside of it for a bed, laid a block of timber across for a pillow, and pursued their labour by day as usual. A still greater misfortune than being paid with bad money is to be guarded against, namely, that of not being paid at all. . . . Employers are also in the habit of deceiving their workmen, by telling them that it is not convenient to pay wages in money, and that they run accounts with the storekeeper, and that from them they may have all the necessaries they want very cheap. The workman who consents to this mode of payment, procures orders from the employer, on one or more of these citizens, and is charged a higher price for the goods than the employer actually pays for them. This is called *paying in trade.*

William Harris Crawford (1772–1834) was Secretary of the Treasury from 1816 to 1825. A candidate for President in 1824 until he suffered a stroke, Crawford, a Georgian, was the favorite of the Old Republican wing of the party which supported strict construction of the Constitution and state rights and which opposed the nationalist tendencies of the party such as federal funds for internal improvements, a protective tariff, and a national bank. What according to Crawford was the cause of the economic dislocation? What must be done to regain prosperity? What role should banks play in American society? This document, which is Crawford's report to Congress on the condition of the banks, may be found in the *Niles Weekly Register*, March 11, 1820.

⊂⊟ Report of the Secretary of the Treasury

W. H. CRAWFORD

In obedience to a resolution of the house of representatives, passed on the 1st of March, 1819, . . . the secretary of the treasury . . . [is transmitting] to congress, at an early period in the first session, a general statement of the condition of the bank of the United States, and its offices, similar to the return made by the bank; and a statement exhibiting, as nearly as may be practicable, the amount of capital invested in the different chartered banks in the several states and the district of Columbia. . . .

Such, it is believed, has been the process by which the capital of most of the banks has been formed, which have been incorporated since the commencement of the last war. Since that period, banks have been incorporated, not because there was capital seeking investment; not because the places where they were established had commerce and manufactures . . . but because men, without active capital, wanted the means of obtaining loans, which their standing in the community would not command from banks or individuals having real capital and established credit. Hence, the multiplicity of local banks, scattered over the face of the country, in particular parts of the union; which, by the depreciation of their paper, have levied a tax upon the communities, within the pale of their influence, exceeding the public contributions paid by them.

All intelligent writers upon currency agree that where it is decreasing in amount, poverty and misery must prevail. . . . The united voice of the nation attests its accuracy. As there is no recorded example in the history of nations of a reduction of the currency, so rapid and so extensive, and but few examples have occurred, of distress so general and so severe, as that which has been exhibited in the United States. To the evils of a decreasing currency are superadded those of a deficient currency. But, notwithstanding it is deficient, it is still depreciated. In several of the states the great mass of the circulation is not even ostensibly convertible into specie at the will of the holder. During the greater part of the time that has elapsed since the resumption of specie payments, the convertibility of bank notes into specie has been rather nominal than real in the largest portion of the union. On the part of the banks, mutual weakness had produced mutual forbearance. The extensive diffusion of bank stock among the great body of the citizens, in most of the states, had produced the same forbearance among individuals. To demand specie of the banks, when it was known that they were unable to pay, was to destroy their own interests, by destroying the credit of the banks, in which the productive portion of their property was invested. In favor of forbearance, was also added the influence of the great mass of bank debtors. Every dollar in specie drawn out of the banks, especially for exportation, induced the necessity of curtailments. To this portion of the community all other evils were light, when compared with the imperious demands of banks. Their exertions to prevent the drain of specie in the possession of those who controuled their destiny, equalled the magnitude of the evils which were to be avoided. In most parts of the union this forced state of things is passing away. The convertibility of bank notes into specie is becoming real wherever it is ostensible. If public opinion does not correct the evil in those states where this convertibility is not even ostensible, it will be the imperious duty of those who are invested with the power of correction to apply the appropriate remedy.

As the currency is, at least in some parts of the union, depreciated, it must, in those parts, suffer a further reduction before it becomes sound. The nation must continue to suffer until this is effected. After the currency shall be reduced to the amount which, when the present quantity of the precious metals is distributed among the various nations of the world, in proportion to their respective exchangeable values, shall be assigned to the United States; when time shall have regulated the price of labor, and of commodities, according to that amount; and when pre-existing engagements shall have been adjusted, the sufferings from a depreciated, decreasing, and deficient currency, will be terminated. Individual and public prosperity will gradually revive, and the productive energies of the nation resume their accustomed activity. But, new changes in the currency, and circumstances adverse to the perpetuity of the general prosperity, may reasonably be expected to occur. So far as the changes depend upon the currency, their recurrence, to an extent sufficient to disturb the prosperity of the nation, would be effectually prevented, if it could be rendered purely metallic. In that event, we should always retain that proportion of the precious metals which our exchangeable commodities bear to those of other nations. The currency would seldom be either redundant or deficient, to an extent that would seriously affect the interest of society. But when the currency is metallic, and paper convertible into specie, changes to such an extent, it is believed, will frequently occur.

There can be no doubt, that a metallic currency, connected with a paper circulation, convertible into specie, and not exceeding the demand for the facile transmission of money, is the most convenient that can be devised. When the paper circulation exceeds that demand, the metallic currency to the amount of the excess will be exported, and a liability to sudden fluctuations to the same extent will be produced.

If banks were established only in the principal commercial cities of each state; if they were restrained from the issue of notes of small denominations; if they should retain an absolute control over one half of their capital, and the whole of the credit which they employ, by discounting to that amount nothing but transaction paper payable at short dates; the credit and stability of the banks would, at least, be unquestionable. Their notes could always be redeemed in specie on demand. The remaining part of their capital might be advanced upon long credits to manufacturers, and even to agriculturalists, without the danger of being under the necessity of calling upon such debtors to contribute to their relief, if emergencies should occur. Such debtors are, in fact, unable to meet sudden exigencies, and ought never to accept of advances from banks, but upon long credits, for which timely provision may be made. The latter class, of all others, is the least qualified to meet the sudden demands which a pressure upon banks compels them to make upon their debtors. The returns of capital invested in agriculture are too slow and distant to justify engagements with banks, except upon long credits. If the payment of the principal should be demanded at other periods than those at which the husbandman receives the annual reward of his toil, the distress which would result from the exaction would greatly outweigh any benefit which was anticipated from the loan. That the establishment of banks, in agricultural districts, has greatly improved the general appearance of the country, is not denied. Comfortable mansions, and spacious barns, have been erected, lands have been cleared and reduced to cultivation, farms have been stocked and rendered more productive, by the aid of bank credits. But these improvements will eventually be found, in most cases, to effect the ruin of the proprietor. The farm with its improvements, will frequently prove unequal to the discharge of the debts incurred in its embellishment. Such, in fact, is the actual or apprehended state of things wherever banks have been established in the small inland towns and villages. Poverty and distress are impending over the heads of most of those who have attempted to improve their farms by the aid of bank credits. So general is this distress, that the principal attention of the state legislatures, where the evil exists, is at this moment, directed to the adoption of measures calculated to rescue their fellow citizens from the inevitable effects of their own indiscretion. If, in affording a shield to the debtor, against the legal demands of his creditor, the axe shall be applied to the root of the evil, by the annihilation of banks where they ought never to have existed, the interference, however doubtful in point of policy or principle, may, eventually, be productive of more good than evil.

The general system of credit, which has been introduced through the agency of banks, brought home to every man's door, has produced a fictitious state of things, extremely adverse to the sober, frugal, and industrious habits, which ought to be cherished in a republic. In the place of these virtues, extravagance, idleness, and the spirit of gambling adventure have been engendered and fostered by our institutions. So far as these evils have been produced by the establishment of banks where they are not required, by the omission . . . [of] wholesale restraints; and by the ignorance or misconduct of those who have been entrusted with their direction, they are believed to be beyond the control of the federal government. Since the resumption of specie payments, measures have been adopted in some of the states to enforce their continuance; in others, the evil has been left to the correction of public opinion. There is, however, some reason to apprehend, that the authority of law may be interposed in support of the circulation of notes, not convertible into specie.

But the federal government has, by its measures in some degree, contributed to the spirit of speculation, and of adventurous enterprise, which, at the moment so strongly characterise the citizens of the republic, the system of credit, which, in the infancy of our commerce, was indispensable to its prosperity, if not to its existence, has been extended at a period when the dictates of sound discretion seemed to require that it should be shortened. The credit given upon the sale of the national domain has diffused this spirit of speculation and of inordinate enterprise among the great mass of our citizens. The public lands are purchased, and splendid towns erected upon them, with bank credits. Every thing is artificial. The rich inhabitants of the commercial cities, and the tenant of the forest, differ only in the objects of their pursuit. Whether . . . splendid mansions, or public lands, be the object and desire, the means by which the gratification is to be secured, are bank credits.

The two following documents are from the *Argus of Western America* published in Frankfort, Kentucky, by editor Amos Kendall (1789–1869). Kendall later became a prominent member of an inner circle of advisors around President Andrew Jackson. Kentucky was hard-hit by the Panic of 1819; and to help alleviate the distress, the legislature in 1820 chartered the Bank of the Commonwealth of Kentucky. This bank, which was backed by no real capital, was authorized to print large sums of paper money and to lend it to needy Kentuckians. This paper money was to be received for all public debts as well as private ones. The law chartering the bank provided that if a creditor refused to accept the notes of the Bank of the Commonwealth, the debtor could defer payment of the debt for two years. The Kentucky Court of Appeals in 1823 ruled that this relief measure was unconstitutional. These two documents appeared in Kendall's paper immediately before the 1824 election in which the Relief party candidates won an overwhelming victory at the polls. Once in power, they abolished the "Old Court" which had struck down the Bank of the Commonwealth as unconstitutional and appointed a "New Court" friendly to relief measures. For several years afterward political battles in Kentucky were fought between the "New Court" party and the "Old Court" party. The speaker in the first document, Major William T. Barry, was a prominent Kentucky Democrat who was appointed by the Relief party to be the chief justice of the "New" Court of Appeals in 1825. President Andrew Jackson appointed him Postmaster General in 1829. What view do these partisan documents give of the contending political forces in Kentucky? What role is advocated for the state government in times of economic crisis? Why? Should any one branch of the government have precedence over the other? Why? These documents may be found in the *Argus* of March 3, 1824, and May 12, 1824.

⊂Ξ Major Barry's Address

Amos Kendall

Dinner to Maj. W. T. Barry

WILLIAM T. BARRY—The soldier, the statesman, the orator, the patriot; but above all THE FRIEND OF THE PEOPLE'S RIGHTS; long may he live to adorn society, and to serve the cause of his country and of human nature.

"Jefferson and Liberty"

On the above toast being drank, and after the repeated cheering had subsided, Maj. BARRY rose and addressed the company in the following impressive manner.

The attention shewn me to day, and the approbation expressed of my public conduct, affect me deeply. The applause of the people is what

I have sought for as the highest reward that I could obtain. My wishes have been gratified. The people of Kentucky have evinced their partiality for me whenever I have presented myself as a candidate for their suffrages, and now, in retiring it gives me pleasure to believe that I still have their confidence. . . . The utmost harmony prevailed with the democratic party with whom I acted on questions of State as well as National policy. This harmony was a little disturbed at home, in the contest for a new election that arose on the death of . . . [our late Governor.] I took an active part in that controversy, and was separated for a time from some of my democratic friends. When its agitations were subsiding, another of a more perplexing and difficult nature grew out of the pecuniary embarrassments of the country. I was one of those who thought Legislative interference necessary to mitigate the sufferings of society, and relieve the distressed. I stood foremost as advocating the measures that were adopted—I believed the crisis demanded them, and was satisfied that the Legislative had power to enact them. . . . I was embarking in the cause of humanity, and relied on the benevolent feelings of a generous community to excuse if they could not justify my course. From the first, my conduct on this subject has been open, uniform, and independent. . . . It is true I should have preferred a property Law. This was attempted and failed; I then advocated the Bank of the Commonwealth. I am satisfied it has been of great public utility, and that it has saved thousands from ruin. I regret to think that in some instances it has operated injuriously, but am happy in the belief that its general tendencies were beneficial, and that the balance of good is greatly in its favour. . . . These relief laws were adopted against violent opposition, and have been continued in the midst of bitter controversy. The authors and promoters have been abused and their motives impunged [sic]. . . . Pleading the cause of the weak and distressed, I did not wish to provoke unnecessarily the hostility of the rich and powerful. I will not now attempt to characterize the opposition,—the actors in this period of universal excitement are not qualified to judge each other;—the public mind is unhappily too much disturbed at this time for calm decision, it must be left to others when the excitement is over to judge our conduct, and to do justice to the motives of all parties. . . .

The contest about relief measures is nearly ended. If the opposition had been content to have addressed themselves to the intelligence of the people and waited for them to act through their representatives, all would soon have been quieted; the emergency having passed by, we could again have met in harmony and friendship. But they either did not confide in the people or were too impatient to wait on public opinion. They denied the power of the Legislature to pass the laws and called on the Judges to interpose between the people and their laws. After much time had elapsed, and thousands of transactions had taken place under the laws, the Appellate Court of the State at their Fall session, declared them unconstitutional. . . . I consider myself authorised at this time to say that the opinion is erroneous, as a large majority of the Legislature . . . has said so by the most solemn and responsible declaration. I am compelled to respect this declaration of the Legislature of my country, especially when it conforms to my own opinion. . . . I have mentioned this subject with a view to combat the dangerous doctrine advanced by a party in this state. It is useless to disguise; these are two parties in Kentucky.

One is in favour of judicial supremacy, and irresponsibility except in case of corruption: the other contending that the Judges are responsible for erroneous opinion, merely when these errors affect the vital interests of society; that this responsibility is by the theory of the constitution of the state to be enforced through the Legislature to which the power of removal by address is given, and that of course in the exercise of this high power the Legislature are of necessity made paramount to the Judges. The latter appeal to the theory and principles of a representative government as regulated by the actual provisions of our constitution for the truth of their doctrine. The power to declare a law unconstitutional is admitted in the Judges, in plain and palpable cases of violation. But a just respect for the Legislative department and the rights of the people, will not permit a judge who is influenced by a proper sense of duty, to interfere in doubtful cases, but rather leave the evil, if it be one, to be corrected by the good sense and intelligence of the people. If it becomes a practice for the Judge to interfere in doubtful cases, it will lead to the most deplorable consequence. Under the exercise of such a power our code of laws would become uncertain, and the statute book, instead of furnishing the rule of conduct, would prove a snare to the citizen. The people of Kentucky look to the acts of assembly for the law, read and understand it as printed by the authority of the Legislature—if it is a palpable violation of the terms of the constitution, the common mind sees it at once; the act is looked upon as a nullity and the evils of it avoided. But if the violation is to be sought for through a long train of Metaphysical reasoning that perplexes schoolmen and lawyers, such subtle principles elude the common mind, and the infraction of the constitution will not be seen until proclaimed by the learned judge: His judgment differing perhaps from that of nine tenths of society, only serves to perplex and confound. . . .

Why should judges be irresponsible? Are they infallible? No one believes this; and is it expected that a free people will tamely submit to the fatal consequences of error, where the corrective is in their own hands? Will they part with laws that are dear to them, surrender important rights and powers the exercise of which are essential to their happiness through mere tenderness to the judges? No, let the judge yield to the people. What man that has republican feelings would wish to hold an office, when he can no longer administer the law in a satisfactory manner to those that employ him and whose money he receives? Delicacy and a respect for the people should induce him voluntarily to retire and not to insist on ruling against their will. It should be recollected that this office was not made for the man who fills it, it is not his private property; it is the *people's* office, and when they are not satisfied for him to fill it, he should retire. . . .

I admit that there are many errors for which the Judge cannot be held responsible except to his own conscience and to God, in the application of an acknowledged rule, or in the interpretation of laws, when applied to the case of individuals. But when the law is admitted, the intention of the Legislature understood, and the Judge undertakes to annul the law, it is not an ordinary exercise of judicial power, but an assertion of the highest prerogative known to the constitution. He is no longer the mere Judge expounding and executing the law as prescribed to him; but he rises into the character of the statesman, mounts to the high source of power, explores it, invades the legislative province, sets limits to it and enlarges his own sphere of action. If in the exercise of great political power the judge errs, for such error he ought to be responsible: otherwise the judge may go on from one assumption of power to another, until the legislative power is destroyed and a judicial oligarchy established on its ruins. When the two departments differ as to the nature and extent of their constitutional powers, the appeal must be made to the people as the ultimate umpire. That appeal is now made to the people of Kentucky.—It is for them to say whether they will yield to Judicial supremacy, or retain to themselves the power of acting through their representatives in the emergencies that all states are destined to pass through, of famine and disease, of pestilence and war; and as occasion may require, stay the hand of the law until the destroying angel shall have passed by, or the war worn soldier returned from fighting the battles of his country. It is urged that the independence of the judiciary is attacked when judges are questioned for honest errors. There is no danger on this score when Judicial independence is properly understood. I hold it to consist in freedom from partiality and favour towards friends, exemption from the influence of particular classes of men and factions, from the influence of powerful and wealthy men, and above all exemption from the influence of those great monied corporations that threaten the liberties of the country; but not independence of the people. Independence of the corrupt and partial influences that I have named, is necessary to secure dependence on and responsibility to the people, and to make judges what all public functionaries ought to be, the faithful organs of the public will.

The Appeal of "Common Sense"

To the People of Kentucky, Exposing the "Exposers."

AMOS KENDALL

No. II.

Fellow-Citizens—We have had, and now have two parties in Kentucky and the United States, and it is high time for us to understand them. viz. A Court Party and a Country Party; (*alias*) a Tory Party and a Whig Party. The first of these parties always rally around offices for life, and commenced with Alexander Hamilton's project of a President and Senate for life. They are ever ready to support all measures calculated to throw power into the hands of *the few*, no matter how corrupt or destructive to the rights of the people. They love great men, and men who hold their power free from any disturbance from popular elections. The voice of the people gives them the cholic or hysterics. In a time of war, they are afraid to trust themselves in reach of gunpowder. They love their fire-sides, where they can grumble and growl at the *wicked* majority that called upon them to defend their constitution, the rights, honor and glory of their country. But when peace and sunshine returns, they come out, like the Locusts of Egypt, and their first motions are to eat up all the property of the brave soldier, who had but a short time before, defended them from the tomahawk and scalping knife. Their next step is to strut and swagger, look big and nod their towering heads, at all the poor plebeians who happen to come in their way, and tell them, that this republican government (which they had been fighting for) was not intended for such poor clodhoppers as they were; that the rich minority had exclusive rights, both to talk and manage affairs as to them seemed right. And to crown all, if the representatives of the people happen to think that *moral justice* ought, at all times, to constitute *legal justice*, then what an out-cry, and denunciation against the laws of their country! In answer to this party, let us for a moment ask ourselves, what is Justice? Does it consist in giving a man more than his due? No! Does it operate like the tyrant's bed in which a man was to be stretched or have his head or feet cut off in order to fit its dimensions? No! It cannot be, that it is justice, sacred justice, for the creditor to take his neighbor's plantation, worth a thousand dollars for one hundred, or his negro, his horse, or his other property at similar sacrifices. I never could see how a man, calling himself a Christian, could take one set of principles to church and another to his court house. To one place he goes with "*Father forgive my debts or trespasses as I forgive my debtors or those who trespass against me.*" To the other he goes with his bond in his hand, ready to take the life's blood of his debtor with the cry of "*justice and honesty*" in his mouth, and when his execution issues, *his conscience* permits him very *quietly* to take a plantation, a negro or a horse at *one tenth* of its value, because the *law allows* it. Yes, fellow-citizens, because the law of the country allows it! and our interest happens to be on that side. It is all right, it is all honest! The soldier who is fighting his country's battles may be ruined by that very country, for which he is hazarding his life; and this is the consequence, if this court party's principles succeed. Because, according to their doctrine, our laws, good or bad, ruinous or otherwise, must remain like the tyrant's bed, or like the laws of the Medes and Persians. You cannot be so deluded by a party mad to desperation because they cannot confront the people as they have done the courts, who are silently stealing away powers retained to the states and the people which are essential to their existence, their happiness and their safety. Then let me hear no more of their honesty, or their *cry of justice;* because *justice* is not their object, but the establishment of *principles* which *are to gag the people, bridle and saddle them, ready to be rode in any direction.* Common sense revolts at their syren songs, because every man of reflection must know, that when the Commonwealth's Bank was established, there was not as much silver in the country as would have more than paid the ordinary taxes, except in the hands of a few wealthy men; and while I admit that legislative measures of this nature should only pass in cases of the greatest emergency, yet there are times when it is necessary, and all governments have resorted to measures calculated to do *real justice* by delays or postponements as to the collection of specie. And a case of this kind did occur in Kentucky in the year 1819, when the United States Bank had swallowed up the specie of the country, and the Bank of Kentucky was driven to the wall, to the utter ruin and despair of many of her debtors.

JUSTICE

Hezekiah Niles (1777–1839) was one of the most famous editors in ante-bellum America. His widely circulated and influential *Niles Weekly Register* was published by him from 1811 to 1836. During this quarter of a century, Niles was an able advocate of economic nationalism, tirelessly promoting protective tariffs and internal improvement systems. Why, specifically, does Niles object to the relief laws? What should be done to meet widespread economic distress? This editorial may be found in the *Niles Weekly Register*, November 3, 1821.

⊂⊒ Relief Laws Condemned

HEZEKIAH NILES

RELIEF LAWS, &c. It is with much satisfaction that we notice the progress of good principles in the west, in regard to relief laws and local currencies, and refer our readers to the inaugural message of governor Carrol to the legislature of Tennessee, for some very sound common-sense remarks on those subjects. Had the legislators of Kentucky and Tennessee refused first to have sanctioned litters of banks, and afterwards rejected certain propositions that interfered between debtor and creditor and violated the obligation of contracts, the people of those states would have easily passed through the trials and difficulties which have been so generally encountered in Europe and America, in consequences of the great changes that have happened in the relation of things and condition of nations. But they attempted to legislate their people out of their difficulties, and the result has been, that every act for that purpose, producing momentary relief to some, has mightily added to the general stock of misery and distress—and caused the ruin of thousands through the sudden extension and contractions of the credit system—by outrageous depreciations of the local *currency*, which necessarily caused extraordinary appreciations of *money*.

Much has been said about "hard-hearted creditor"—it answers well to catch the vulgar, and may be very *profitably* employed by those who would live on the labor of their fellows: it is like the cry of "mad-dog" in the mouth of a malicious man:—but, as we have before observed, there is ten thousand times more injury sustained by dishonest debtors than from hard-hearted creditors. Now and then a wretch appears, and I think that I know two or three such, who would sell the widow's milk at auction, which nature had given her for the support of her orphan child, if it were possible to do it, rather than lose a part of their claims against her; but it is so generally the interest of creditors to deal tenderly with their *honest* debtors, that they rather sustain and encourage than oppress and dishearten them. The man that will not make an effort to pay his debts, or squander other people's money at the gaming table, racecourse, &c. more often receives mercy than justice,—for he is not entitled to commiseration; and it is for his own good, as well as that of the society in which he lives, that extensive suffering should teach him discretion, and compel him to live honestly or suffer him to exist ignominiously. If reformation is produced, there are few persons so destitute as to be without friends to help them onwards, unless their previous vices and crimes have exhausted the means of such friends, which is too often the case, especially in places where the payment of debts may be shoved off by long stays of execution or other regulations for "relief"; by which their friends, lending their names just as *matters of form,* are often-times involved in a common ruin.

I am not prepared to say, that no emergency can arise when it might not be sound policy to interpose between debtor and creditor, by legal provisions; but I never have heard of any thing of the kind being done, which did not add to the heap of suffering which it was presumed to be a panacea for. The dissolute and desperate as much *calculate* upon such procrastinated payments, as a prudent man does upon the money which he has on hand; and the result is, that they get not only deeper and deeper in debt, but involve others in their difficulties, who ought and would have assisted them to begin the world a-new, under different circumstances. As labor and abstinence are the only means by which certain cruel diseases of the human body can be relieved or cured, so there is no remedy for "hard times" but industry and economy. All else is quackery.

William M. Gouge (1796–1863) was an early critic of the banking system as it developed in the United States in the early nineteenth century, publishing in 1833 his most famous work, *A Short History of Paper Money and Banking in the United States.* As a "hard money" or anti-bank man, Gouge's economic and financial views were quite compatible with the Jacksonians, and he served as a clerk in the Treasury Department from 1834 to 1841. Gouge's writings, although written a decade or more after the Panic of 1819, represent a reaction common to many Americans. Not clearly understanding the complex economic forces which affect the business cycle, Gouge and his Jacksonian colleagues singled out the banks as being responsible both for the earlier economic collapse as well as for a continuing crisis in national morality. According to Gouge, what was the relationship between moral character and banking? How do or how can financial institutions have such an impact upon moral character? The following selection may be found in Gouge's *A Short History of Paper Money and Banking in the United States,* to which is prefixed "An Inquiry into the Principles of the System, with Considerations of its Effects on Morals and Happiness" (New York, 1835).

Banking and Moral Character

WILLIAM M. GOUGE

The practice of trade seems, in most countries, to fix the standard of commercial honesty. In the Hanse Towns and Holland, while they were rising to wealth, this standard was very high. Soldiers were not more careful to preserve their honor without stain, than merchants were to maintain their credit without blemish.

The practice of trade in the United States, has debased the standard of commercial honesty. Without clearly distinguishing the causes that have made commerce a game of hap-hazard, men have come to perceive clearly the nature of the effect. They see wealth passing continually out of the hands of those whose labor produced it, or whose economy saved it, into the hands of those who neither work nor save. They do not clearly perceive *how* the transfer takes place: but they are certain of the fact. In the general scramble they think themselves entitled to some portion of the spoil, and if they cannot obtain it by fair means, they take it by foul.

Hence we find men without scruple, incurring debts which they have no prospect of paying.

Hence we find them, when on the very verge of bankruptcy, embarrassing their friends by prevailing on them to endorse notes and sign custom-house bonds.

Instances not unfrequently occur of men who have failed once or twice, afterwards accumulating great wealth. How few of these honorably discharge their old debts by paying twenty shillings in the pound!

How many evade the just demands of their creditors, by privately transferring their property.

It is impossible, in the present condition of society, to pass laws which will punish dishonest insolvents, and not oppress the honest and unfortunate.

Neither can public opinion distinguish between them. The dishonest share the sympathy which should be given exclusively to their unfortunate neighbors: and the honest are forced to hear a part of the indignation which should fall entirely on the fraudulent.

The standard of commercial honesty can never be raised very high, while trade is conducted on present principles.

"It is hard," says Dr. [Benjamin] Franklin, "for an empty bag to stand up-right." The straits to which many men are reduced, cause them to be guilty of actions which they would regard with as much horror as their neighbors, if they were as prosperous as their neighbors.

We may be very severe in our censure of such men, but what else ought we to expect, when the laws and circumstances give to some men so great advantages in the great game in which the fortunes of the whole community are at issue—what else ought we to expect, but that those to whom the law gives no such advantage, should exert to the utmost faculties as remain to them in the struggle for riches, and not be very particular whether the meaning they use are such as the law sanctions or the law condemns.

Let those who are in possession of property which have been acquired according to the strict letter of the law, be thankful that they have not been led into such temptations as those on whom the positive institution of society have had an unfavorable influence.

But Banking has a more extensive effect on the moral character of the community, through that distribution of wealth which is the result of its various direct and remote operation. Moralists in all ages, have inveighed against luxury. To it they attribute the corruption of morals, and the downfall of nations. The word luxury is equivocal. What is regarded as a luxury in one stage of society, is in another, considered as a comfort, and in a still more advanced stage as a necessary. The desire of enjoyment is the great stimulus to social improvement. If men were content with bare necessaries, no people would, in the arts and sciences, and in whatever else renders life desirable, be in advance of the lowest caste of the Hindoos, or the unhappy peasantry of the most unhappy country of Europe.

But whatever moralists have said against luxury, is true when applied to that *artificial* inequality of fortune which is produced by *positive* institutions of an unjust character. Its necessary effect is to corrupt one part of the community, and debase the other.

The bare prospect of inheriting great wealth, damps the energies of a young man. It is well if this is the only evil it produces. "An idle man's brain," says John Bunyan, "is the devil's workshop." Few men can have much leisure, and not be injured by it. To get rid of the *ennui* of existence, young men of wealth resort to the gambling-table, the race-ground, and other haunts of dissipation. They cannot have these low means of gratification without debasing those less favored by fortune.

The children of the poor suffer as much in one way, as the children of the rich suffer in another. The whole energies of the father and mother are exhausted in providing bread for themselves and their family. They cannot attend properly to the formation of the moral character of their offspring—the most important branch of education. They can ill spare the means to pay for suitable intellectual instruction. Their necessities compel them to put their children to employments unsuited to their age and strength. The foundation is thus laid of disease which shorten and embitter life.

Instances occur of men, by the force of their innate powers, overcoming the advantages of excess or defect of wealth; but it is true, as a general maxim, that in early life, and in every period of life, too much or too little wealth, is injurious to the character of the individual, and when it extends through a community, it is injurious to the character of that community.

In the general intercourse of society, this artificial inequality of wealth produces baneful effects. In the United States, the pride of wealth has more force than in any other country, because there is here no other pride to divide the human heart. Some of our good republicans do, indeed, boast of a descent from the European nobility; but when they produce their coats of arms, and their genealogical trees, they are laughed at. The question propounded if their noble ancestors left them any *money*. Genious confers on its possessor a very doubtful advantage. Virtue, with us, as in the days of the Roman poet, is viler than seaweed, unless it has a splendid retinue. Talent is estimated only as a means of increasing riches. Wealth alone can give permanent distinction, for he who is at the top of the political ladder today, may be at the bottom tomorrow.

One mischief this state of things produces is, that men are brought to regard wealth as the *only* means of happiness. Hence they sacrifice honor, conscience, health, friends, every thing to obtain it.

The other effects of artificial inequality of wealth, have been treated of at large, by moralists, from Solomon and Socrates downwards. To their works and to the modern treatises on crime and pauperism, we refer the reader. The last mentioned treatises are, for the most part, only illustrations of the ultimate effects of positive institutions, which operate unequally on different members of the community.

Chapter

7: Young America, the Greek Revolt, and the Future of Mankind

⊂⊐ ROBERT D. ACCINELLI

On July 4, 1826, the fiftieth anniversary of the signing of the Declaration of Independence, Thomas Jefferson died. Less than two weeks earlier he reminded his countrymen that what happened in 1776 was but the beginning of a movement which would someday embrace the globe. The Fourth of July would sooner or later, he predicted, become for all the world "the signal of arousing men to burst the chains under which monkish ignorance and superstition had persuaded them to bind themselves, and to assume the blessings and security of self-government." Americans were familiar with the belief that providence had destined them to guide less fortunate people in other parts of the world down the path of revolution and republican government. In the years before the Civil War a series of revolutions—most notably in France in 1789, in Latin America beginning in 1809, in France and Central Europe in 1848, and in Greece in 1821—provided Americans with the opportunity to put this belief to the test. Each of these upheavals demanded of them that they decide what their own role should be. Would they endorse the revolution? What kind of support, if any, would they lend it? This chapter will examine their response to these questions during the Greek revolution.

In the spring of 1821, after four centuries of domination by the Ottoman Empire, the Greeks rebelled against their Turkish masters. The insurrection followed an erratic and bloody course until 1829, when the Greeks finally won their independence. In late 1823 the revolt captured the imagination of many Americans and "Greek fever" swept the country. The man most responsible for stimulating pro-Greek sentiment was Edward Everett, a Harvard professor and editor of the highly esteemed literary journal, *The North American Review*. In the issue for October, 1823, Everett printed an appeal to the American people from the Greek Senate of Calamata asking for assistance in the struggle against the

Turks. In invoking the name of liberty, the Greeks told the Americans, "we invoke yours at the same time, trusting that in imitating you, we shall imitate our ancestors, and be thought worthy of them if we succeed in resembling you." The appeal had already reached John Quincy Adams, Secretary of State in James Monroe's Cabinet, but had aroused no comment. Everett, however, stirred his readers with a dramatic plea of his own for assistance for the beleaguered rebels. Soon, in the words of Henry Clay, pro-Greek sentiment "blazed with the rapidity of electricity" from one end of the country to the other.

Popular feeling found expression in resolutions passed at mass meetings and by several state legislatures, in speeches in Congress, in pamphlets issued by committees organized to assist the Greeks, and in numerous sermons, editorials, and orations. Three illustrious survivors of America's own revolution—Jefferson, Madison, and John Adams—gave the rebels their blessing. Jefferson corresponded with the famous Greek scholar and patriot, Adamantios Korais, offering him advice on government matters based on the American experience. Madison suggested that Monroe invite the British government to join "in some declaratory act in behalf of the Greeks," while Adams admitted to Jefferson that his "old imagination" was "kindling into a kind of missionary enthusiasm for the cause of the Greeks. . . ." Private donors made available money, supplies, and some military equipment to the insurgents, and a handful of idealistic Americans even made the long trek to Greece to join in the fight. There were some individuals, however, in Washington and in the country at large (particularly in Boston) who remained immune to the "Greek fever."

The spread of the fever focused attention on the federal government's policy toward the revolutionaries. John Quincy Adams had outlined that policy in August, 1823, in response to a request from Andreas Luriottis, a representative of the revolutionary government, for recognition and extension of such aid as would enable the Greeks to call Americans "allies as well as friends." Adams turned down the request, though two other Cabinet members, Secretary of War John C. Calhoun and Secretary of the Treasury William H. Crawford, were inclined to be more generous with assistance. The issue reappeared at a Cabinet meeting in the late fall during a discussion of a draft of the President's annual message to Congress, in which Monroe acknowledged that he intended to extend recognition. But it was Adams who again had his way, for when the message reached Congress in December, it contained only an expression of hope that the Greeks would win their independence. In the meantime, Congress had begun to take an interest in the Administration's policy. On December 8 Daniel Webster of Massachusetts, then only a Congressman, introduced a resolution recommending an appropriation of funds to send an agent or commissioner to Greece whenever the President thought it expedient to make the appointment. The resolution received a full-dress debate in late January but never came to a vote. As it was, the government never assisted the Greeks and withheld recognition until 1831, by which time several European nations, including Czarist Russia, had already acknowledged their independence.

In reacting to events in Greece, Americans had to define their own and their country's relationship with European revolution. They did not, as is quite apparent, all hold the same opinions. Five interrelated considerations help to shed light on the process by which they arrived at their diverse conclusions. First, there was the spirit of nationalism present in the country. Second, there were those concrete ties which shaped American attitudes toward the Greeks and the Ottoman Empire. Third, there was the problem created by the opposition of the reactionary members of the Holy Alliance to nationalist revolutions. Fourth, there was the influence exerted by the isolationist tradition and by well-defined policies of neutrality and recognition. Fifth, there was the ambiguity inherent in the belief that America had an obligation to serve the cause of liberty in other lands.

The revolution occurred at a time when Americans were counting up the accomplishments of nearly a half century of independence and were overflowing with nationalistic pride and self-confidence. That spirit marked many a celebration in 1824, when the Marquis de La Fayette, who had served by Washington's side during the Revolution, returned from abroad after an absence of forty years. Wherever he went during his triumphant tour of the states, he was welcomed as a living symbol of the Revolution and of the stimulating effect it had had on the foes of tyranny in the Old World. The Americans who cheered him knew that he, like many other European liberals, was a warm admirer of the Greek cause.

Despite the distance separating the United States from the eastern Mediterranean, the conflict between the Greeks and Turks touched Americans directly in several ways. Boston merchants conducted a profitable trade (much of it in opium which was resold in China) with the Turkish port of Smyrna bordering on the Aegean. There were men in Boston and in Congress who feared that the "Greek fever" would harm this trade; similar concern about trade advantages was no doubt also present in the mind of Adams, who in late 1823 was in the process of arranging a commercial treaty with the Sultan of Turkey. Advocates of the Greek cause were less fearful of losing the trade with Smyrna ("A wretched invoice of figs and opium has been spread before us to repress our sensibilities and eradicate our humanity," declared Clay) and predicted an even more lucrative trade with an independent Greece. American Protestant missionaries were at work among the Greeks who, although already Christian, were affiliated with the Orthodox Church. Furthermore, many aspects of American life and culture bore the imprint of the heritage of ancient Greece. Americans did not forget that the Greek rebels were the descendants of the very men who had given the world the concepts of liberty and popular government. They were, in contrast, prone to identify the Ottoman Empire with an alien religion, autocracy, and barbarism, the last characteristic taking on an especially vivid reality because of stories in the press depicting atrocities committed against innocent Greeks by the ruthless Turks.

In addition, Americans associated the repressive policy of the Ottoman Empire with the Holy Alliance, a term which they loosely and inaccurately used to describe the European powers which banded together after the Napoleonic wars to maintain the balance of power and preserve conservative government. Strictly speaking, the Holy Alliance was a visionary and ineffective pact devised by the Czar of Russia in 1815 and eventually subscribed to by all the rulers of Europe, except the Pope, the Prince-Regent of Great Britain, and the Sultan of Turkey. The real source of power in Europe was the Quadruple Alliance formed in the same year by Austria, Prussia, Russia, and Great Britain, and expanded into the Quintuple Alliance in 1818 by the inclusion of France. Americans acquired the habit of mistakenly referring to this concert of powers as the Holy Alliance and, to avoid confusion, the term will be used here in the same imprecise sense. Between 1818 and 1822 the powers met in a series of congresses to discuss common issues. In 1820 Russia, Prussia, and Austria agreed to act jointly against revolutionary disturbances anywhere in Europe, a decision from which England dissented. In 1821 an Austrian army crushed an uprising in Italy and in the spring of 1823 the French government, which also looked askance at revolutionaries, restored the monarchy in Spain, thereby raising the possibility that the Alliance might try to reimpose Spain's rule over its former colonies in Latin America. By the latter part of 1823 the Holy Alliance had, in the eyes of many Americans, come to represent the greatest menace to liberty in both the Old and New World. In his message to Congress, Monroe confined himself to wishing the Greeks success but enunciated several ambitious principles regarding the New World which later came to be known as the Monroe Doctrine. In light of the policy followed toward Greece, it was significant that he stressed that Europe and the Americas belonged to two different political systems: as European powers would be expected to keep their hands off the New World, so the United States would not intervene in the Old.

In drawing the line between Europe and the Americas, Monroe expressed a fundamental assumption of the isolationist tradition. This tradition, already well entrenched by the 1820's, prohibited entanglement in European political affairs, particularly in the form of political or military commitments. The United States was to remain free to pursue its own ideals and interests with a minimum of outside interference. Despite its influence on the public and on government officials, isolationism had no standing in law. It was a habit of mind, not a legal statute or legislative enactment. In 1818 Congress had, however, taken a step to keep America aloof from foreign conflicts, including revolutions, by passing a neutrality act prohibiting certain kinds of assistance to combatants on either side of an international conflict. The legislation borrowed from earlier acts (the first enacted in 1794 after the outbreak of war between England and France) and became law at a time when some Americans were aiding insurgents in Latin America. The Neutrality Act of 1818 remained in force during the Greek revolution. One method of encouraging the Greeks which the Act did not prohibit was recognition of their government by the President. Yet here, too, official policy was, as the Greeks discovered, well defined and conservative.

In responding to the revolution, Americans had to grapple with the ambiguity underlying the popular conviction that they had a special mission to serve the cause of liberty. Even those sharing in this conviction might disagree with one another either about the form which their service should take or precisely where they should direct it. Some felt that people struggling for freedom should receive direct assistance, while others believed that America's proper role was to seek its own advancement and simply serve as a model for others to emulate through their own efforts. The country's duty toward Europe was a particularly troublesome problem. The Old World, with its monarchs and reactionaries, was obviously very much in need of political redemption, and the agitation of European liberals and nationalists made it seem possible, even inevitable, that the day of redemption was near at hand. There were Americans who felt it would be derelict to stand apart from this momentous struggle. Yet doubts persisted. Could the precedent set by the United States take root among people who did not enjoy its unique advantages? And did not the isolationist tradition counsel abstention from European entanglements and devotion to America's own interests? Was the nation prepared to risk war and jeopardize itself by becoming deeply involved in distant quarrels? These questions required an answer before passing judgment on the nation's obligation to revolutionaries across the Atlantic.

The Greek revolution put Americans to the test. They had to decide whether their own revolutionary past placed obligations on them and their nation and, if so, what they should do about the Greeks. The following selections were written in the six-month period from August, 1823, to January, 1824, and each illustrates the differing ways in which Americans attempted to resolve these fundamental issues.

Few Americans were better qualified to comment on Greek affairs than Edward Everett. After being appointed Eliot Professor of Greek Literature at Harvard in 1815, he studied and traveled in Europe for four years, deepening his knowledge of Greek language and literature and visiting Greece itself in 1819. He was personally acquainted with a number of Greek patriots and held the country and its heritage in high regard. Both his translation of the proclamation of the Greek Senate of Calamata and his own dramatic appeal for assistance, from which the following selection is taken, were printed in *The North American Review* for October, 1823 (Vol. XVII, pp. 415–24). According to Everett, what part is America to play in the spread of liberty? Does he make a distinction between its role in Europe and the New World? Does he ask for anything which violates the isolationist tradition?

⊂≣ The Independence of Greece

EDWARD EVERETT

Though we do not consider the foregoing address [the proclamation of the Greek Senate] to be in very good taste, nor in every part perfectly intelligible, it shows at least how soon and how spontaneously the eyes of Greece were turned to this country as the great exemplar of states in the agonies of contest for independence. Such an appeal from the anxious conclave of self-devoted patriots, in the inaccessible cliffs of the Morea, must bring home to the mind of the least reflecting American, the great and glorious part, which this country is to act, in the political regeneration of the world. It must convince us that what Burke[1] orignially said in eulogy of his own land, is going into its literal fulfilment here; and in a wider sense than he dared to speak it. Wheresoever the chosen race, the sons of liberty, shall worship freedom, they will turn their faces to us.— We have seen, in our own days, the oldest and most splendid monarchy in Europe, casting off its yoke, under the contagion of liberty caught from us; and why should the excesses of that awful crisis be ascribed to the new found remedy rather than to the inveterate disease? Through France, the influence of our example has been transmitted to the other European states, and in the most enslaved and corrupted of them, the leaven of freedom is at work. Meantime, at one and the same moment, we perceive in either hemisphere the glorious work of emancipation going on; and the name and the example of the United States alike invoked by both. From the earliest abodes of European civilization, the venerated plains

---

[1] Edmund Burke, the great English orator and conservative.

141

of Greece, and from the scarcely explored range of the Cordilleras, a voice of salutation and a cry for sympathy are resounding in our ears. While the great states of Europe, which for centuries have taken the lead in the affairs of the world, stand aghast at this spectacle, and know not if they shall dare to sanction what they cannot oppose, our envoys have already climbed the Andes and reached the Pacific, with the message of gratulation. We devoutly trust that another season will find them on their way to Greece. The recognition of South American Independence, in many respects of national policy a dubious measure, was adopted with the cheering unanimity of old revolutionary times; and the man who was not in his seat in Congress that day, felt that he had done himself and his constituents a wrong, in losing the opportunity to record his voice among those of his brethren. Not less popular, we venture to say, would be the recognition of the Independence of Greece. We feel none of the scruples, which perplex the cabinets of Europe. We see nothing but an enterprising, intelligent, christian population struggling against a ghastly despotism, that has so long oppressed and wasted the land; and if an animating word of ours could cheer them in the hard conflict, we should feel that not to speak it, were to partake the guilt of their oppressors.

Meantime there is something for the people of this country in their private capacity, to do for Greece. In Germany, and in France, large numbers of enthusiastic young men have devoted themselves personally to the cause, and flocked to Greece, as the same class of generous spirits did to this country, in the revolutionary war. Considerable sums of money have also been raised in those countries, and supplies of arms and ammunition sent to the Grecian armies. In England a benevolent association has been formed under the presidency of Lord Milton, a nobleman of one of the wealthiest and most powerful British families; and this association has entered into a correspondence with the Grecian authorities. Local political dissensions have unfortunately mingled themselves with the counsels adopted in England for the relief of the Grecians. Still, however, large subscriptions have been made and forwarded to that country. We are sorry for the fact, that America did not set this example also. The experience of our own revolutionary war is so recent, that we ought to have felt, how precious would be any aid from a distant land, however insignificant in amount. Who does not know that there were times in our own revolutionary war, when a few barrels of gunpowder, the large guns of a privateer, a cargo of flour, a supply of clothing, yea, a few hundred pairs of shoes, for feet that left in blood the tracks of their march, would have done essential service to the cause of suffering liberty. . . .

America has done something for Greece. Our missionary societies have their envoys in the Grecian church, with supplies of bibles and religious tracts for their benighted flocks. But in the present state of this unhappy people, this is not the only succor they require. They are laying the foundations of civil freedom, without which even the blessings of the Gospel will be extended to them in vain; and while they are cementing with their blood this costly edifice, they are in the condition of the returning Jews, of whom "every one with one of his hands wrought at the work, and with the other hand held a weapon." We would respectfully suggest to the enlarged and pious minds of those, who direct the great work of missionary charity, that at this moment, the cause of the Grecian church, can in no way be so effectually served, as by contributions directed to the field of the great struggle. The war is emphatically a war of the crescent against the cross. . . . At this crisis the messenger of the gospel fraternity should come in other guise than the distributor of the word; and could the broad and deep current of religious bounty be turned into a channel to reach the seat of the principal distress, it is not going too far to say, that it might be the means of giving another independent country to the church of Christ; and do more to effect the banishment of the crescent to the deserts of Tartary, than all that has yet been achieved by the counsels of christendom. . . .

In the few remarks, which we have taken the liberty to make on this occasion, we have not insisted on the topic of the glorious descent of the Greeks; of the duty of hastening to the succor of those whose fathers were the masters of the world, in the school of civilization. It is not because we are not sensible of the power of this appeal also; but because we think a much stronger appeal may be made. . . . It is not merely the countrymen of Aristides, the fellow-citizens of Phocian, the descendants of Aratus, that are calling upon us. These glorious names are a dead letter to two thirds of the community of christendom. But it is christians bowed beneath the yoke of barbarous infidels; it is fathers and mothers condemned to see their children torn from them and doomed to the most cruel slavery; it is men like ourselves bereft of all the bounties which providence has lavished on their land, obliged to steal through life, as through the passes of a mountain before the blood-hounds of the pursuer. . . .

In the great Lancastrian school of the nations, liberty is the lesson, which we are appointed to teach. Masters we claim not, we wish not, to be, but the Monitors we are of this noble doctrine.[2] It is taught in our settlement; taught in our revolution; taught in our government; and the nations of the world are resolved to learn. It may be written in sand and effaced, but it will be written again and again, till hands now fettered in slavery shall boldly and fairly trace it, and lips, that now stammer

---

[2] Joseph Lancaster (1778–1838), an Englishman, devised an educational system in which advanced pupils called monitors taughts the students below them.

at the noble word, shall sound it out in the ears of their despots, with an emphasis to waken the dead. Some will comprehend it and practice it at the first; others must wrestle long with the old slavish doctrines; and others may abuse it to excess, and cause it to be blasphemed awhile in the world. But it will still be taught and still be repeated, and must be learned by all; by old and degenerate communities to revive their youth; by springing colonies to hasten their progress. With the example before them of a free representative government—of a people governed by themselves,—it is no more possible that the nations will long bear any other, than that they should voluntarily dispense with the art of printing or the mariner's compass. It is therefore plainly no age for the Turks to be stirring. It is as much as men can do, to put up with christian, with civilized, yea, with legitimate masters. . . . The idea that the most honorable, the most responsible, the most powerful office in the state, can, like a vile heirloom, follow the chance of descent, is quite enough to task the forbearance of this bold and busy time. What then shall become of viziers and sultans, when ministers are bewildered in their cabinets, and kings are shaken on their thrones? . . .

Secretary of State John Quincy Adams was the architect of American policy toward the revolution. A brilliant diplomat, he was dedicated to keeping the country out of European entanglements, extending its rule across the North American continent, and enlarging its influence in Latin America. Hard-boiled and intensely nationalistic, he opposed any policy based on sentiment rather than self-interest, even when dealing with revolutionary struggles. America is "the well-wisher to the freedom and independence of all," he said in 1821. "She is the champion and vindicator only of her own." He put this dictum into practice in August, 1823, when the Cabinet discussed a proposal from a representative of the Greek revolutionary government forwarded to Washington by the American Minister in London, Richard Rush. The first selection printed below, an account by Adams of what happened in the Cabinet, is taken from his private diary (Charles Francis Adams, ed., *Memoirs of John Quincy Adams*, Philadelphia, 1875, Vol. VI, pp. 172–73). The second, a response to the Greek proposal sent by him to Rush, is from the *American State Papers, Foreign Relations*, Class I, Vol. V, p. 257. Together, the selections reveal the distance separating the most extreme interpretation of America's obligations to the insurgents from the policy actually followed by the government. Was the suggestion made by Calhoun and Crawford compatible with isolationism? On what grounds does Adams reject their suggestion and the Greek proposal? What policy does he adopt toward the revolution?

⊂≡ Peace and Neutrality

JOHN QUINCY ADAMS

[August] 15th. Cabinet meeting at the President's at one. . . . The subject first mentioned by the President for consideration was a letter to me from Andreas Luriottis at London, styling himself Envoy of the Provisional Government of the Greeks, a copy of which was sent to me some months since by R. Rush. This letter, recommending the cause of the Greeks, solicited of the United States recognition, alliance, and assistance. It was proper to give a distinct answer to this letter, and I had asked the President's directions what the answer should be.

The President now proposed the question. Mr. Gallatin [1] had proposed in one of his last dispatches, as if he was serious, that we should assist the Greeks with our naval force in the Mediterranean—one frigate, one corvette, and one schooner. Mr. Crawford and Mr. Calhoun inclined to

[1] Albert Gallatin, then serving as Minister to France, had recommended giving the Greeks a loan and naval assistance. An American naval squadron had been stationed in the Mediterranean ever since the War with Tripoli (1801–1805).

countenance this project. Crawford asked, hesitatingly, whether we were at peace with Turkey, and seemed only to wait for opposition to maintain that we were not. Calhoun descanted upon his great enthusiasm for the cause of the Greeks; he was for taking no heed of Turkey whatever. In this, as in many other cases, these gentlemen have two sources of eloquence at these Cabinet meetings—one with reference to sentiment, and the other to action. Their enthusiasm for the Greeks is all sentiment, and the standard of this is the prevailing popular feeling. As for action, they are seldom agreed; and after two hours of discussion this day the subject was dismissed, leaving it precisely where it was— nothing determined, and nothing practicable proposed by either of them. Seeing their drift, I did not think it necessary to discuss their doubts whether we were at peace with Turkey, their contempt for the Sublime Port, or their enthusiasm for the cause of the Greeks.[2] I have not much esteem for the enthusiasm which evaporates in words; and I told the President I thought not quite so lightly of a war with Turkey. I said I would prepare an answer to Mr. Luriottis and an instruction to Mr. Rush for his consideration. . . .

⊂⊟   A Response to the Greek Proposal

JOHN QUINCY ADAMS

Department of State, Washington, August 18, 1823

Sir:

I have the honor of inclosing herewith an answer to the letter from Mr. Luriottis, the agent of the Greeks, addressed to me, and a copy of which was transmitted with your despatch, No. 295.

If upon the receipt of this letter Mr. Luriottis should still be in London, it will be desirable that you should deliver it to him in person, accompanied with such remarks and explanations as may satisfy him and those whom he represents, that, in declining the proposal of giving active aid to the cause of Grecian emancipation, the Executive Govern-

---

[2] "Sublime Porte" or "Porte" were often used to refer to the government of the Ottoman Empire.

ment of the United States has been governed, not by its inclinations or a sentiment of indifference to the cause, but by its constitutional duties, clear and unequivocal.

The United States could give assistance to the Greeks only by the application of some portion of their public force or their public revenue in their favor, and it would constitute them in a state of war with the Ottoman Porte, and perhaps with all the Barbary powers. To make this disposal either of force or treasure, you are aware, is by our Constitution, not within the competency of the Executive. It could be determined only by an act of Congress, which would assuredly not be adopted, should it even be recommended by the Executive.

The policy of the United States with reference to foreign nations has always been founded upon the moral principle of natural law— *peace* with all mankind. From whatever cause war between other nations, whether foreign or domestic, has arisen, the unvarying law of the United States has been *peace* with both belligerents. From the first war of the French Revolution to the recent invasion of Spain, there has been a succession of wars, national and civil, in almost every one of which *one* of the parties was contending for liberty or independence. To the first revolutionary war a strong impulse of feeling urged the people of the United States to take side with the party which, at its commencement, was *contending*, apparently at least, for both. Had the policy of the United States not been essentially pacific, a stronger case to claim their interference could scarcely have been presented. They nevertheless declared themselves neutral, and the principle then deliberately settled has been invariably adhered to ever since.

With regard to the recognition of sovereign States, and the establishment with them of a diplomatic intercourse, the experience of the last thirty years has served also to ascertain the limits proper for the application of principles in which every nation must exercise some latitude of discretion. Precluded by their neutral position from interfering in the question of right, the United States have recognized the *fact* of foreign sovereignty only when it was undisputed, or disputed without any rational prospect of success. In this manner the successive changes of government in many of the European States, and the revolutionary Governments of South America, have been acknowledged. The condition of the Greeks is not yet such as will admit of the recognition upon these principles.

Yet as we cherish the most friendly feelings towards them, and are sincerely disposed to render them any service which may be compatible with our neutrality, it will give us pleasure to learn from time to time the actual state of their cause, political and military. Should Mr. Luriottis be enabled and disposed to furnish this information, it may always be communicated through you, and will be received with satisfaction here.

The public accounts from that quarter have been of late very scanty, and we shall be glad to obtain any authentic particulars which may come to your knowledge, from this or through any other channel. . . .

On January 19, 1824, Daniel Webster rose in the House of Representatives, where he had served for eleven years, to defend the resolution he introduced in early December recommending an appropriation for an agent to be sent to Greece at Monroe's discretion. Though cautiously worded, the resolution was clearly intended as an official gesture of support for the insurgents and perhaps as the first step toward recognition. Webster's brilliant oration created a sensation everywhere and touched off a debate in the House on the entire Greek issue. In the excerpts printed here, Webster places the revolution and America's mission within a global context. (The complete speech may be read in *The Writings and Speeches of Daniel Webster*, Boston, 1903, Vol. V, pp. 61–93.) Why does he think America has a duty to oppose the principles of the Holy Alliance? What does the Greek revolution have to do with this obligation? Does the policy he advocates differ significantly from Adams's?

America's Global Mission

DANIEL WEBSTER

As it is never difficult to recite commonplace remarks and trite aphorisms, so it may be easy, I am aware, on this occasion, to remind me of the wisdom which dictates to men a care of their own affairs, and admonishes them, instead of searching for adventures abroad, to leave other men's concerns in their own hands. It may be easy to call this resolution *Quixotic*, the emanation of a crusading or propagandist spirit. All this, and more, may be readily said; but all this, and more, will not be allowed to fix a character upon this proceeding, until that is proved which it takes for granted. Let it first be shown, that in this question there is nothing which can affect the interest, the character, or the duty of his country. Let it be proved, that we are not called upon, by either of these considerations, to express an opinion on the subject to which the resolution relates. Let this be proved, and then it will indeed be made out, that neither ought this resolution to pass, nor ought the subject of it to have been mentioned in the communication of the President to us.[1] But, in my opinion, this cannot be shown. In my judgment, the subject is interesting to the people and the government of this country, and we are called upon, by considerations of great weight and moment, to express our opinions upon it. These considerations, I think, spring from a sense of our own duty, our character, and our own interest. I wish to treat the subject on such grounds, exclusively, as are truly American; but then, in considering it as an American question, I cannot forget the age in which we live, the prevailing spirit of the age, the interesting questions which agitate it, and our own peculiar relation in regard to these interesting questions. . . .

I might well, Mr. Chairman, avoid the responsibility of this measure, if it had, in my judgment, any tendency to change the policy of the country. With the general course of that policy I am quite satisfied. The nation is prosperous, peaceful, and happy; and I should very reluctantly put its peace, prosperity, or happiness at risk. It appears to me, however, that this resolution is strictly conformable to our general policy, and not only consistent with our interests, but even demanded by a large and liberal view of those interests. . . .

In the next place, I take it for granted that the policy of this country, springing from the nature of our government and the spirit of all our institutions, is, so far as it respects the interesting questions which agitate the present age, on the side of liberal and enlightened sentiments. The age is extraordinary; the spirit that actuates it is peculiar and marked; and our own relation to the times we live in, and to the questions which interest them, is equally marked and peculiar. We are placed, by our good fortune and the wisdom and valor of our ancestors, in a condition in which we *can* act no obscure part. Be it for honor, or be it for dishonor, whatever we do is sure to attract the observation of the world. . . .

It cannot be denied that the great political question of this age is that between absolute and regulated goverments. The substance of the controversy is whether society shall have any part in its own government. Whether the form of government shall be that of limited monarchy, with more or less mixture of hereditary power, or wholly elective or representative, may perhaps be considered as subordinate. The main controversy is between that absolute rule, which, while it promises to govern well, means, nevertheless, to govern without control, and that constitutional system which restrains sovereign discretion, and asserts that society may claim as matter of right some effective power in the establishment of the laws which are to regulate it. The spirit of the times sets with a most powerful current in favor of these last-mentioned opinions. . . .

What part it becomes this country to take on a question of this sort,

[1] Monroe's Message to Congress, December 2, 1823.

so far as it is called upon to take any part, cannot be doubtful. Our side of this question is settled for us, even without our own volition. Our history, our situation, our character, necessarily decide our position and our course, before we have even time to ask whether we have an option. Our place is on the side of free institutions. From the earliest settlement of these States, their inhabitants were accustomed, in a greater or less degree, to the enjoyment of the powers of self-government; and for the last half-century they have sustained systems of government entirely representative, yielding to themselves the greatest possible prosperity, and not leaving them without distinction and respect among the nations of the earth. This system we are not likely to abandon; and while we shall no farther recommend its adoption to other nations, in whole or in part, than it may recommend itself by its visible influence on our own growth and prosperity, we are, nevertheless, interested to resist the establishment of doctrines which deny the legality of its foundations. . . .

I will now, Mr. Chairman, advert to those pretensions put forth by the allied sovereigns of Continental Europe, which seem to me calculated, if unresisted, to bring into disrepute the principles of our government, and, indeed, to be wholly incompatible with any degree of national independence. . . .

Every body knows that, since the final restoration of the Bourbons to the throne of France, the Continental powers have entered into sundry alliances, which have been made public, and have held several meetings or congresses, at which the principles of their political conduct have been declared. These things must necessarily have an effect upon the international law of the states of the world. If that effect be good, and according to the principles of that law, they deserve to be applauded. If, on the contrary, their effect and tendency be most dangerous, their principles wholly inadmissable, their pretensions such as would abolish every degree of national independence, then they are to be resisted. . . .

The first of these principles is, that all popular or constitutional rights are held no otherwise than as grants from the crown. Society, upon this principle, has no rights of its own; it takes good government, when it gets it, as a boon and concession, but can demand nothing. It is to live by that favor which emanates from royal authority, and if it have the misfortune to lose that favor, there is nothing to protect it against any degree of injustice and oppression. It can rightfully make no endeavor for a change, by itself; its whole privilege is to receive the favors that may be dispensed by the sovereign power, and all its duty is described in the single word *submission*. . . .

But the second, and, if possible, the still more objectionable principle . . . is the right of forcible interference in the affairs of other states. A right to control nations in their desire to change their own governments, wherever it may be conjectured, or pretended, that such change might furnish an example to the subjects of other states, is plainly and distinctly asserted. . . .

No matter what be the character of the government resisted; no matter what weight the foot of the oppressor bears on the neck of the oppressed; if he struggle, or if he complain, he sets a dangerous example of resistance,—and from that moment he becomes an object of hostility to the most powerful potentates of the earth. I want words to express my abhorrence of this abominable principle. I trust every enlightened man throughout the world will oppose it, and that, especially, those who, like ourselves, are fortunately out of the reach of the bayonets that enforce it, will proclaim their detestation of it, in a tone both loud and decisive. The avowed object of such declarations is to preserve the peace of the world. But by what means is it proposed to preserve this peace? Simply, by bringing the power of all governments to bear against all subjects. Here is to be established a sort of double, or treble, or quadruple, or, for aught I know, quintuple allegiance. An offence against one king is to be an offence against all kings, and the power of all is to be put forth for the punishment of the offender. . . . What is to be the limit to such a principle, or to the practice growing out of it? What, in any case, but sovereign pleasure, is to decide whether the example be good or bad? And what, under the operation of such a rule, may be thought of our example? Why are we not as fair objects for the operation of the new principle, as any of those who may attempt a reform of government on the other side of the Atlantic? . . .

It may now be required of me to show that interest *we* have in resisting this new system. What is it to *us*, it may be asked, upon what principles, or what pretences, the European governments assert a right of interfering in the affairs of their neighbors? The thunder, it may be said, rolls at a distance. The wide Atlantic is between us and danger; and, however others may suffer, *we* shall remain safe.

I think it is a sufficient answer to this to say, that we are one of the nations of the earth; that we have an interest, therefore, in the preservation of that system of national law and national intercourse which has heretofore subsisted, so beneficially for all. Our system of government, it should also be remembered, is, throughout, founded on principles utterly hostile to the new code; and if we remain undisturbed by its operation, we shall owe our security either to our situation or our spirit. The enterprising character of the age, our own active, commercial spirit, the great increase which has taken place in the intercourse among civilized and commercial states, have necessarily connected us with other nations, and given us a high concern in the preservation of those salutary principles upon which that intercourse is founded. We have as clear an interest in international law, as individuals have in the laws of society.

But apart from the soundness of the policy, on the ground of direct interest, we have, Sir, a duty connected with this subject, which I trust we are willing to perform. What do *we* not owe to the cause of civil and religious liberty? to the principle of lawful resistance? to the principle that society has a right to partake in its own government? As the leading republic of the world, living and breathing in these principles, and advanced, by their operation, with unequalled rapidity in our career, shall we give *our* consent to bring them into disrepute and disgrace? It is neither ostentation nor boasting to say, that there lies before this country, in immediate prospect, a great extent and height of power. We are borne along towards this, without effort, and not always even with a full knowledge of the rapidity of our own motion. Circumstances which never combined before have cooperated in our favor, and a mighty current is setting us forward which we could not resist even if we would, and which, while we would stop to make an observation, and take the sun, has set us, at the end of the operation, far in advance of the place where we commenced it. Does it not become us, then, is it not a duty imposed on us, to give our weight to the side of liberty and justice, to let mankind know that we are not tired of our own institutions, and to protest against the asserted power of altering at pleasure the law of the civilized world? . . .

It may, in the next place, be asked, perhaps, Supposing all this to be true, what can *we* do? Are we to go to war? Are we to interfere in the Greek cause, or any other European cause? Are we to endanger our pacific relations? No, certainly not. What, then, the question recurs, remains for us? If we will not endanger our own peace, if we will neither furnish armies nor navies to the cause which we think the just one, what is there within our power?

Sir, this reasoning mistakes the age. The time has been, indeed, when fleets, and armies, and subsidies, were the principal reliances even in the best cause. But, happily for mankind, a great change has taken place in this respect. Moral causes come into consideration, in proportion as the progress of knowledge is advanced; and the public opinion of the civilized world is rapidly gaining an ascendency over mere brutal force. It is already able to oppose the most formidable obstruction to the progress of injustice and oppression; and as it grows more intelligent and more intense, it will be more and more formidable. It may be silenced by military power, but it cannot be conquered. . . .

We see here [in Greece], Mr. Chairman, the direct and actual application of that system which I have attempted to describe. . . . We learn, authentically and indisputably, that the Allied Powers, holding that all changes in legislation and administration ought to proceed from kings alone, were wholly inexorable to the sufferings of the Greeks, and entirely hostile to their success. Now it is upon this practical result of the principle of the Continental powers that I wish this House to intimate its opinion. The great question is a question of principle. Greece is only the signal instance of the application of that principle. If the principle be right, if we esteem it conformable to the law of nations, if we have nothing to say against it, or if we deem ourselves unfit to express an opinion on the subject, then, of course, no resolution ought to pass. If, on the other hand, we see in the declarations of the Allied Powers principles not only utterly hostile to our own free institutions, but hostile also to the independence of all nations, and altogether opposed to the improvement of the condition of human nature; if, in the instance before us, we see a most striking exposition and application of those principles, and if we deem our opinions to be entitled to any weight in the estimation of mankind,—then I think it is our duty to adopt some such measure as the proposed resolution. . . .

Silas Wood (1769–1847) was a Congressman from New York who had taught at Princeton and practiced law before being elected to the House in 1818. Although unable to match Webster's oratorical skills, he did raise a number of the most important objections directed against the resolution during the debates. His speech was transcribed by a special reporter and printed in the *Annals of Congress* (18th Cong., 1st Sess.), 1132–39. How does Wood believe America can best serve the cause of liberty? What consequences does he foresee if the resolution is adopted? How does his image of the Greeks differ from Everett's? How is the policy he endorses related to what Adams said in his response to the appeal from the Greek envoy?

⊂⊋ A Model for Mankind

Silas Wood

He [Wood] observed, that the resolution, as explained by its advocates, implies that the United States are the guardians of liberty, and are bound to propagate it among all nations. Sir, said Mr. W., this is the doctrine of the Pope, of Mahomet, and Bonaparte, and leads to universal war— to universal power. Before we admit this doctrine, it would be well to examine what was our duty as a nation. The duties of every nation are limited to the prosperity and security of its own citizens; it owes nothing to other nations but the duties of humanity. This is more particularly the case with a government like ours, which is only intrusted with certain specific powers. . . .

Because the world is full of oppression, is this Government the Hercules that is to free it from the monsters of tyranny and slavery? And are we bound to emulate the chivalrous achievements of the renowned Knight of La Mancha, by engaging in conflict with every windmill that we may, in the delirium of our frenzy, imagine to be a tyrant?

It will be asked, is our Government to be of no use to mankind? I answer yes; but not by its fleets and armies—not by embarking in a military crusade to establish the empire of our principles—not by establishing a corps of diplomatic apostles of liberty, but by the moral influence of its example.

It presents to the world a model by which the rights of men may be secured, and the benefit of good government may be obtained, with the least sacrifice of individual independence. It excites inquiry—it invites examination; the knowledge of it will be conveyed, by our flag, to every region of the earth. Foreigners will visit our shores; they will examine its structure; they will witness its practical operation; they will discover its excellence; and it will thus diffuse a spirit of reformation throughout the world.

Much has been said, during this debate, about the spirit of the age. The present age is distinguished from the last by liberality of sentiment in religion and politics. The American Revolution, Bible societies, and Christian missions, aided by the extension of commerce, have produced this change. It does not need the aid of physical means—such aid would obstruct its influence. This moral influence is all powerful, but does not irritate—does not excite alarm—does not provoke opposition. But, let it be connected with physical means, and it instantly will meet with resistance. Let it, then, operate as it has done, and we may expect it will continue to produce more and more important results, till the governments of the world are reformed. . . .

Sir, it is very doubtful whether the Greeks possess the elementary principles that are necessary to form a free State. If a people possess the elements of freedom, they cannot be long held in slavery; and if they are destitute of these, no efforts they may make will terminate in the establishment of free institutions.

The love of liberty is so ingrained into the heart of every American, that we are apt to overlook the difficulties in the way of free government, and to conclude that every effort in favor of liberty will be successful.

It is a deception to compare the situation of other countries with ours, at the commencement of our Revolution.

We inherited the principles of liberty from our ancestors; we were educated in the free principles of the common law. We enjoyed the protection of person and property, the right of suffrage, and trial by jury; in which it would require a century for any people who have been born under the civil law to be instructed, and much longer to acquire by their own exertions.

Sir, are gentlemen aware of the value of the inheritance which they have derived from their ancestors? The privilege we enjoy is the result of a struggle of virtuous and enlightened men for more than six hundred years, with ignorance, superstition, and tyranny. They were extorted piecemeal, with incredible labor and perseverance. It was more than two hundred years from the Great Charter to the Bill of Rights.[1] From the time of the Great Charter to the American Revolution, distinguished individuals continued the conflict, breaking one fetter after another, until their persevering efforts terminated in a complete emancipation of this country from the shackles of superstition and tyranny, and in the establishment of civil and religious liberty, by political institutions conformable to the principles of natural liberty, and calculated to secure it. . . .

Do the Greeks possess the elementary principles of freedom? This is very doubtful. They are represented by the travellers who have visited them, in general, as grossly ignorant of political principles—as by no means distinguished for a scrupulous sense of moral obligation, and as unequal with regard to property. There are some intelligent men among them, who have been educated in Italy, Germany, or France, but the great mass of the people have very little knowledge of the free States that once existed in that country; it is but recently that their ambition has extended further than to re-establish the Greek Empire without any design to form a free State. The Ottoman Empire has been decaying ever since the discovery of a passage to India by the Cape of Good Hope. The provinces are becoming independent, and new sects are dissolving the only bond that held them together. The Greeks also constitute the largest part of the population of Europe. They will probably succeed in rendering themselves independent of the Porte, and will, most probably, transfer their allegiance to a Russian Prince and erect a new Grecian monarchy. They may lighten their chains, but will not at present establish a free State.

The adoption of the resolution, under these circumstances, would be premature, and might involve us in the absurdity of recognizing as a fact what does not exist. But the strongest objection I have to the adoption of the resolution is, that it may involve us in a war with the nations of Europe. . . .

War with all Europe would be extremely pernicious to us; not that

---

[1] Wood had his dates confused. The Great Charter or Magna Charta was signed in 1215 and the Bill of Rights, which limited royal authority and protected the rights of citizens, enacted by Parliament in 1689.

I have any apprehensions of our being subdued; but, by its wasting energies, it would be less injurious to them than to us. We are not able to contend with them on equal terms; our incapacity arises from the felicity of our condition.

They have an accumulation of capital, the product of ages of industry —they have a surplus population which is a burden to them, and from which war would relieve them. They can embark in war without interrupting the common pursuits of life, or materially affecting their revenue. On the contrary, we need our whole capital for public improvements, and to lay the foundations of the institutions which are necessary for the development of domestic industry. We have no mendicant population to form an army. Our soldiers must be taken from the plough, and the common pursuits of life.

War with us deranges industry, interferes with our private pursuits— affects every cottage—arrests the progress of our improvement—annihilates our ordinary revenue, and augments the necessity, while it diminishes our ability, of contributing to the public energies. . . .

What is the true policy of this country in relation to foreign nations?

The common Father of our Country, among the treasures of wisdom he has bequeathed to us in his Farewell Address, conjures us, in extending our commercial connexions with foreign nations, to have as little political connexion as possible, and the Sage of Monticello, in his inaugural speech, which is the text book of his political opinions, councils us to cultivate peace, commerce, and honest friendship, with all nations, but to form entangling alliances with none.

The same course of policy is dictated by our physical and moral condition. Providence has prepared the people of this country for high destinies. When a new empire of civil and religious liberty was to be established, he selected a site three thousand miles from the corruptions of Europe, which would have checked the growth of the institutions that were to secure them. When we were ripe for independence, it was achieved, and now, to favor the prosperity of this great moral empire, which he has evidently destined to be the scene of higher degrees of moral excellence, and of a greater perfection of the human character, and of civil society, than has ever before been witnessed, he has connected our felicity with an incapacity for wars of ambition, or conquest, which would impair it. Is not this a mark of divinity? and is not the monition as authoritative as a voice from Heaven? . . .

Chapter
8: Women in the Age of the Common Man

⊂⊃ EDWARD PESSEN

The forgotten person of the so-called era of the common man was the American woman. Lacking in power and public influence, she has been largely ignored by historians. It is not necessary to be a woman's liberationist to feel that this neglect is unwarranted, due more to faulty assumptions on the part of scholars than to the lack of importance of the subject. That the political or social role of women may have been limited during the pre-Civil War decades does not mean that the topic is an insignificant one. If power were the decisive criterion, there would be little point to discussing the millions of slaves, than whom no group was more politically impotent—or for paying much attention to the common man himself, since recent evidence discloses that his actual influence on his time has been much exaggerated. Another explanation for the slight attention paid heretofore to the status and condition of women in the ante-bellum era is the lack of abundant evidence or documentary material on the subject.

We have recently learned a great deal, however, about the ideal of womanhood that prevailed during the period. A cult of "true womanhood" flourished in women's magazines, gift annuals, and religious literature. It stressed four great virtues: piety, purity, submissiveness, and domesticity. Like her counterpart in early Victorian England, the American girl's purpose in life was to marry. Foreign visitors found that a single girl of twenty was considered old, while at twenty-five she was regarded as an old maid. All of her training and experience prior to marriage were designed to prepare her for that ecstatic state. Education, for example, was to be pursued neither out of a mistaken zeal for abstract learning nor from a utilitarian desire to master a skill. The purpose of education, like the purpose of other activities engaged in by young women, was to increase their marriageability. George Templeton Strong, well-to-do son of an old New York City family, confided to his diary that he would abandon bachelorhood only for a young woman of sound education, by which he meant a smattering of "literary taste." Other necessary traits, according to Strong, were "piety"; a "talent for obedience and submission"; "agreeableness"; "personal attractions—A No. 1"; "music"; and "from $50,000 to $100,000."

After marriage, the ideal state of wifely behavior was equally obvious. Whatever their social or economic class might be, women were directed toward essentially similar goals. The one exception was the Negro woman. To judge from the comments of many Southerners, black and white, the female slave's purpose was to work hard and above all to breed. Piety and domesticity were irrelevant in her case. Not purity but its opposite was expected. Submissiveness in her was to be directed not toward her husband—if she were permitted one—but toward her master.

Although reflective Americans, such as James Fenimore Cooper and John Quincy Adams, had interesting comments to make on the situation of American women, most of the discussion was confined to foreign visitors. These travelers evidently regarded America's treatment of females as one of the most fascinating features of the civilization of the "young republic." Perhaps it was a sign that even the visitors, respectful though they were, were not altogether free of condescension toward women that they directed so much of their attention to the American woman's physical attractiveness. Bitter critics agreed with yankophiles that no women surpassed and very few could match the beauty of American women. Young Alexis de Tocqueville and his companion, Gustave de Beaumont, were filled with admiration. The prettiest women in the world, exclaimed Captain Frederick Marryat. While the girls of New York City and Philadelphia were praised, Baltimore and New Orleans attracted the most attention. Europeans raved over the beauty of these women. Special notice was paid the devastating beauty of the mulatto, quadroon, and octaroon females of the Louisiana city. Mrs. Frances Trollope "never saw anywhere so many beautiful women at one glance" as she saw at Baltimore. A number of contemporaries, however, felt that this beauty faded in a short time. Mrs. Trollope and Charles Dickens thought that defects in their upbringing and intellect detracted from the beauty of American women as from their appeal to discerning persons: they were thus handsome but limited, pretty but insipid.

European visitors found the American woman's situation emancipated in comparison to the restricted life led by females on the Continent. According to Tocqueville, American girls were bold, independent, and forthright, precisely as women were supposed to be in the logical model of a Democratic society he appeared to carry in his mind. The visiting actress, Fanny Kemble, who was not at all interested in theories, found American women to be very much as Tocqueville described them, although Miss Kemble cautioned that no simple generalizations could account for so large and diverse a female population. Henry Tudor thought them uppity and was struck by the fact that a small number of young women in Auburn prison caused more trouble than all the men combined. The English phrenologist, George Combe, felt the American female head and found that it showed unusual "moral and intellectual development."

Visitors were struck by the physical freedom in everyday matters enjoyed by women here. The relative absence of chaperones was a source of much comment. Yet according to Arthur Calhoun, the author of the last comprehensive history of the American family (written fifty years ago), "such 'equality' as was enjoyed by [the American] woman in the nineteenth century was a stingy concession, even though it may have looked large to European visitors."

Legally the American woman's situation was one of inequality and strict dependence. Commencing with New York in 1778 and concluding with New Jersey in 1844, one state after another deprived her of the suffrage rights that she had possessed during the first years of the Revolution. Paradoxically, then, from the point of view of women's political rights the significance of the "era of the common man" is that it witnessed the completion of the retrograde and undemocratic tendency that had begun a half century earlier. In the words of the English visitor, Harriet Martineau, one of this country's chief features was the "political non-existence of women."

Many relics of "medievalism" encumbered woman's status down to the Civil War. Marriage was "permeated with injustice": in a legal sense the wife to all practical purposes belonged to her husband. He had a right to her person and he possessed the sole right to redress legal wrongs committed against her person. During marriage he asserted absolute power over any property she may have brought to the marriage. He could use "gentle restraint upon her liberty to prevent improper conduct"; in fact he could beat her within an inch of her life without being liable for prosecution. He could reclaim her if she went away. The woman who won a divorce because of her husband's infidelity, forfeited claims to children, home, and property earned during the marriage. Legally the unmarried woman was a perpetual minor. As for her married sister, the era's legal formula held that "the wife is dead in law."

On the other hand, some gains were registered during the era. The relative shortage of women and the new economic opportunities that stemmed from the youthful nation's growth may have accounted for the advances made in some states. The most important of these permitted women to retain possession after marriage of property that had belonged to them before. The developing factory system in New England beckoned young women out of the home. The closely supervised boarding houses in Lowell, Waltham, and Chicopee provided reassurance to anxious parents, while the new textile machinery offered income, albeit little, to the young women themselves. A controversy has raged from that time to our own day over the quality of life in these Massachusetts mill towns. Yet even sharp critics of the new system conceded that work outside the home, no matter how unattractive and poorly paid for, had a liberating effect on women.

Opinions also differed sharply over the quality of marriages and of the relationship between the sexes in this country. Some observers thought American marriages as much a matter of convenience as they were elsewhere, while others found them uniquely romantic and thus a sign of the greater respect accorded the female personality in America. Most people conceded that in this country wives were everywhere treated with every outward sign of respect and deference. To such women as Frances Wright, Margaret Fuller, Abby Kelley, the Grimké sisters, and others of that striking band of feminist leaders who emerged during the era, public gallantry or deference was precisely the rub.

Surface pleasantries, gallant tenderness, exaggerated politeness, were only one side of the coin. The other side inevitably was the subordination, even subjugation, of the sex so flattered. It was not admirers of the great feminist leader, Mary Wollstonecraft alone who held to this view of things, by any means. Both Miss Martineau and Mrs. Trollope were critical of a regime which compelled women to separate from men at social gatherings. In Mrs. Trollope's striking phrase, American women were "guarded by a sevenfold shield of habitual insignificance." The English ladies believed that American marriages doomed women to insipid and meaningless lives, devoted to gossip, clothing, and often to no greater ambition than merely getting through the day. One reason women were believed to throw themselves into religion with the abandon they did was that their usual routines were otherwise totally devoid of significance.

Discerning male observers also found fault. Even Tocqueville, who so admired both American women and the treatment they were accorded, conceded that marriage confined them to a narrow circle, requiring "much abnegation on the part of a woman and a constant sacrifice of her pleasures to her duties, which is seldom demanded of her in Europe." Another of his criticisms was made from the standpoint, not of a male who believed women should have greater opportunity to flourish as full persons, but rather from that of the male who wanted his women more "delightful" for his own pleasure. Thus, he wrote, American marriages tended "to make cold and virtuous women instead of affectionate wives and agreeable companions to men." Captain Basil Hall found that for all the kindness shown women here, there was no mutual understanding between the partners. Francis Grund, typically most approving of American democracy, was sharply critical of its marriage institution. If marriages here appeared to work fairly well, it was because so little was expected of them. Significant relationships between husbands and wives were out of the question in view of the inequality of the latter. Nor was there real communication between the partners. If American women were reputed to be good mothers, it was due to the fact that the inattention of their husbands permitted women to devote all their energies to their children.

Southern women were regarded as a group apart. White women, particularly the wives of well-to-do planters and of the many who aped their ways even though they lacked their means, were exalted, their virtue, charms, and femininity praised to the heavens. According to Calhoun, however, this was "the gallantry of the harem. Nowhere in the world were women shown more surface respect than in the South, yet degradation of the sex was obvious." If they were prized for their "delicacy"—the euphemism used for their tendency to be spared the earthy pleasure of fornication—it was, according to some observers, due in part to the fear of contaminating them with the veneral disease believed to be prevalent in the section. President Madison's sister had said of Southern white women, "we are only mistresses of seraglios." Southern white males, married and unmarried, had easy access to the quarters of female slaves and were believed to have taken full advantage of it. As for the Negro woman, her marriage to a slave was treated with contempt. In the judgment of some contemporaries, the South was spared the "free-love" associations that sprang up elsewhere not because it was imbued with a keener sense of morality, but because of the easy availability of slave women to white men. Calhoun's conclusion was that "American slavery almost universally debauched slave women."

Feminists did grant that divorce was relatively easy in America. To the champion of women's rights, liberal divorce laws promoted those rights in the same sense that the frontier's safety-valve allegedly improved the lot of the eastern worker. In the one case as in the other, the opportunity for freedom or escape, whether acted on or not, had a salutary effect on would-be oppressors. Growing economic opportunities, even in the form of unattractive and low-paying factory jobs, were prized by some women's spokesmen as the means by which the sex could attain economic and ultimately other forms of independence.

Tocqueville completed his chapter on "the equality of the sexes," with the remarkable statement that "the singular prosperity and growing strength of [the American] . . . people ought mainly to be attributed . . . to the superiority of the women." Harriet Martineau, on the other hand, believed that if the test of a civilization were its treatment of women, the United States would come off badly. In her view, American practice fell not only "below their own democratic principles, but the practice of some parts of the old world." Woman's intellect was confined here, she was subjected to a double standard that crushed true morality. She was made subservient and ignorant, as unfit for life as for a truly admirable marriage. "Indulgence [was] . . . given her as a substitute for justice." To Tocqueville, the admittedly limited life that was the lot of most women was a minor vagary of a marvelously exciting civilization. It was hardly a serious flaw to a young man who shared the common notion that woman was essentially an adornment. His criticism was directed only at a system of education that unfortunately made this delicious creature less attractive than she could be. Like Tocqueville, Miss Martineau also marveled at this civilization. Unlike him, however, she regarded women as more than ornaments or mere appendages to men. Contemporaries who shared her view of woman's worth invariably found fault with American society, believing that it was seriously flawed by its maltreatment of roughly half its members.

Some of the most discerning comments about American society in the 1830's and 1840's were made by European observers. One of the most able and respected of these visitors was the English woman, Harriet Martineau. Certainly she was one of the friendliest, for she cheerfully applauded American traits and institutions that were roundly condemned by most of her fellow travelers. Yet Miss Martineau was sharply critical of the status of American women. As the following passages make clear, she believed that in the United States women were treated with a contempt that was all the more unattractive for being hypocritical or masked. In Miss Martineau's judgment, Americans had somehow convinced themselves that they treated woman as an equal, when in reality they regarded her as an appendage to man—albeit a charming and occasionally pampered one. The following excerpts are from *Society in America* (2 vols., New York, 1837), II, pp. 226–30, 245, 255–57.

⊂⊋ The American Woman Is Indulged

Harriet Martineau

If a test of civilisation be sought, none can be so sure as the condition of that half of society over which the other half has power,—from the exercise of the right of the strongest. Tried by this test, the American civilisation appears to be of a lower order than might have been expected from some other symptoms of its social state. The Americans have, in the treatment of women, fallen below, not only their own democratic principles, but the practice of some parts of the Old World.

The unconsciousness of both parties as to the injuries suffered by women at the hands of those who hold the power is a sufficient proof of the low degree of civilisation in this important particular at which they rest. While woman's intellect is confined, her morals crushed, her health ruined, her weaknesses encouraged, and her strength punished, she is told that her lot is cast in the paradise of women; and there is no country in the world where there is so much boasting of the "chivalrous" treatment she enjoys. That is to say,—she has the best place in stage-coaches: when there are not chairs enough for everybody, the gentlemen stand: she hears oratorical flourishes on public occasions about wives and home, and apostrophes to woman: her husband's hair stands on end at the idea of her working, and he toils to indulge her with money: she has liberty to get her brain turned by religious excitements, that her attention may be diverted from morals, politics, and philosophy; and, especially, her morals are guarded by the strictest observance of propriety in her presence. In short, indulgence is given her as a substitute for justice. Her case differs from that of the slave, as to the principle, just so far as this; that the indulgence is large and universal, instead of petty and capricious. In both cases, justice is denied on no better plea than the right of the strongest. In both cases, the acquiescence of the many, and the burning discontent of the few, of the oppressed, testify, the one to the actual degradation of the class, and the other to its fitness for the enjoyment of human rights.

The intellect of woman is confined. I met with immediate proof of this. Within ten days of my landing, I encountered three outrageous pedants, among the ladies; and in my progress through the country I met with a greater variety and extent of female pedantry than the experience of a lifetime in Europe would afford. I could fill the remainder of my volume with sketches: but I forbear, through respect even for this very pedantry. Where intellect has a fair chance, there is no pedantry, among men or women. It is the result of an intellect which cannot be wholly passive, but must demonstrate some force, and does so through the medium of narrow morals. Pedantry indicates the first struggle of intellect with its restraints; and it is therefore a hopeful symptom.

The intellect of woman is confined by an unjustifiable restriction of both methods of education,—by express teaching, and by the discipline of circumstance. The former, though prior in the chronology of each individual, is a direct consequence of the latter, as regards the whole of the sex. As women have none of the objects in life for which an enlarged education is considered requisite, the education is not given. Female education in America is much what it is in England. There is a profession of some things being taught which are supposed necessary because everybody learns them. They serve to fill up time, to occupy attention harmlessly, to improve conversation, and to make women something like companions to their husbands, and able to teach their children somewhat. But what is given is, for the most part, passively received; and what is obtained is, chiefly, by means of the memory. There is rarely or never a careful ordering of influences for the promotion of clear intellectual activity. Such activity, when it exceeds that which is necessary to make the work of the teacher easy, is feared and repressed. This is natural enough, as long as women are excluded from the objects for which men are trained. While there are natural rights which women may not use, just claims which are not to be listened to, large objects which may not be approached, even in imagination, intellectual activity is dangerous: or, as the phrase is, unfit. Accordingly, marriage is the only object left open to woman. Philosophy she may pursue only fancifully, and under pain of ridicule: science only as a pastime, and under a similar penalty. Art is declared to be left open: but the necessary learning, and, yet more, the indispensable experience of reality, are denied to her. Literature is also said to be permitted: but under what penalties and restrictions? . . . Nothing is thus left for women but marriage.—Yes; Religion, is the reply.—Religion is a temper, not a pursuit. It is the moral atmosphere in which human beings are to live and move. Men do not live to breathe: they breathe to live. A German lady of extraordinary powers and endowments, remarked to me with amazement on all the knowledge of the American women being based on theology. She observed that in her own country theology had its turn with other sciences, as a pursuit: but nowhere, but with the American women, had she known it make the foundation of all other knowledge. Even while thus complaining, this lady stated the case too favourably. American women have not the requisites for the study of theology. The difference between theology and religion, the science and the temper, is yet scarcely known among them. It is religion which they pursue as an occupation; and hence its small results upon the conduct, as well as upon the intellect. We are driven back upon marriage as the only appointed object in life: and upon the conviction that the sum and substance of female education in America, as in England, is training women to consider marriage as the sole object in life, and to pretend that they do not think so.

The morals of women are crushed. If there be any human power and business and privilege which is absolutely universal, it is the discovery and adoption of the principle and laws of duty. As every individual, whether man or woman, has a reason and a conscience, this is a work which each is thereby authorised to do for him or herself. But it is not only virtually prohibited to beings who, like the American women, have scarcely any objects in life proposed to them; but the whole apparatus of opinion is brought to bear offensively upon individuals among women who exercise freedom of mind in deciding upon what duty is, and the methods by which it is to be pursued. There is nothing extraordinary to the disinterested observer in women being so grieved at the case of slaves,—slave wives and mothers, as well as spirit-broken men,—as to wish to do what they could for their relief: there is nothing but what is natural in their being ashamed of the cowardice of such white slaves of the north as are deterred by intimidation from using their rights of speech and of the press, in behalf of the suffering race, and in their resolving not to do likewise: there is nothing but what is justifiable in their using their moral freedom, each for herself, in neglect of the threats of punishment: yet there were no bounds to the efforts made to crush the actions of women who thus used their human powers in the abolition question, and the convictions of those who looked on, and who might possibly be warmed into free action by the beauty of what they saw. . . .

The greater number of American women have home and its affairs, wherewith to occupy themselves. Wifely and motherly occupation may be called the sole business of woman there. If she has not that, she has nothing. The only alternative, as I have said, is making an occupation of either religion or dissipation; neither of which is fit to be so used: the one being a state of mind; the other altogether a negation when not taken in alternation with business.

It must happen that where all women have only one serious object, many of them will be unfit for that object. In the United States, as elsewhere, there are women no more fit to be wives and mothers than to be statesmen and generals; no more fit for any responsibility whatever, than for the maximum of responsibility. There is no need to describe such: they may be seen everywhere. I allude to them only for the purpose of mentioning that many of this class shirk some of their labours and cares, by taking refuge in boarding-houses. It is a circumstance very unfavourable to the character of some American women, that boarding-house life has been rendered compulsory by the scarcity of labour,—the difficulty of obtaining domestic service. The more I saw of boarding-house life, the worse I thought of it; though I saw none but the best. Indeed, the degrees of merit in such establishments weigh little in the consideration of the evil of their existence at all. . . .

As for the occupations with which American ladies fill up their leisure; what has been already said will show that there is no great weight or diversity of occupation. Many are largely engaged in charities, doing good or harm according to the enlightenment of mind which is carried to the work. In New England, a vast deal of time is spent in attending preachings, and other religious meetings: and in paying visits, for religious purposes, to the poor and sorrowful. The same results follow from this practice that may be witnessed wherever it is much pursued. In as far as sympathy is kept up, and acquaintanceship between different classes in society is occasioned, the practice is good. In as far as it unsettles the minds of the visitors, encourages a false craving for religious excitement, tempts to spiritual interference on the one hand, and cant on the other, and humours or oppresses those who need such offices least, while it alienates those who want them most, the practice is bad. I am disposed to think that much good is done, and much harm: and that, whenever women have a greater charge of indispensable business on their hands, so as to do good and reciprocate religious sympathy by laying hold of opportunities, instead of by making occupation, more than the present good will be done, without any of the harm.

All American ladies are more or less literary: and some are so to excellent purpose: to the saving of their minds from vacuity. Readers are plentiful: thinkers are rare. Minds are of a very passive character: and it follows that languages are much cultivated. If ever a woman was pointed out to me as distinguished for information, I might be sure beforehand that she was a linguist. I met with a great number of ladies who read

Latin; some Greek; some Hebrew; some German. With the exception
of the last, the learning did not seem to be of much use to them, except
as a harmless exercise. I met with more intellectual activity, more general
power, among many ladies who gave little time to books, than among
those who are distinguished as being literary. I did not meet with a
good artist among all the ladies in the States. I never had the pleasure
of seeing a good drawing, except in one instance; or, except in two, of
hearing good music. The entire failure of all attempts to draw is still a
mystery to me. The attempts are incessant; but the results are below
criticism. Natural philosophy is not pursued to any extent by women.
There is some pretension to mental and moral philosophy; but the less
that is said on that head the better.

This is a sad account of things. It may tempt some to ask 'what then
are the American women?' They are better educated by Providence than
by men. The lot of humanity is theirs: they have labour, probation, joy,
and sorrow. They are good wives; and, under the teaching of nature,
good mothers. They have, within the range of their activity, good sense,
good temper, and good manners. Their beauty is very remarkable; and,
I think, their wit no less. Their charity is overflowing, if it were but
more enlightened: and it may be supposed that they could not exist
without religion. It appears to superabound; but it is not usually of a
healthy character. It may seem harsh to say this: but is it not the fact
that religion emanates from the nature, from the moral state of the
individual? Is it not therefore true that unless the nature be completely
exercised, the moral state harmonised, the religion cannot be healthy?

One consequence, mournful and injurious, of the 'chivalrous' taste
and temper of a country with regard to its women is that it is difficult,
where it is not impossible, for women to earn their bread. Where it is a
boast that women do not labour, the encouragement and rewards of
labour are not provided. It is so in America. In some parts, there are
now so many women dependent on their own exertions for a maintenance,
that the evil will give way before the force of circumstances. In the
meantime, the lot of poor women is sad. Before the opening of the
factories, there were but three resources; teaching, needle-work, and
keeping boarding-houses or hotels. Now, there are the mills; and women
are employed in printing-offices; as compositors, as well as folders and
stitchers.

I dare not trust myself to do more than touch on this topic. There
would be little use in dwelling upon it; for the mischief lies in the system
by which women are depressed, so as to have the greater number of
objects of pursuit placed beyond their reach, more than in any minor
arrangements which might be rectified by an exposure of particular evils.

Mrs. Frances Trollope, mother of the Victorian novelist Anthony Trollope, wrote a detailed account of American manners and values. Many Americans were stung by her criticisms, but few denied that she was an honest and accurate reporter. No one has given a fuller report of how women of the middle and upper classes actually spent their days. The problem, according to Mrs. Trollope, was not one of physical or material deprivation, but rather of spiritual or emotional emptiness. The woman she describes is engaged in insipid activities designed above all to killing time; and, if she is married, to permit her husband to do his business without her presence or interference. The following passage is from Mrs. Trollope's *Domestic Manners of the Americans* (London, 1832), pp. 280–85.

The Insignificance of Women's Lives

FRANCES TROLLOPE

Let me be permitted to describe the day of a Philadelphian lady of the first class, and the inference I would draw from it will be better understood.

It may be said that the most important feature in a woman's history is her maternity. It is so; but the object of the present observation is the social, and not the domestic influence of woman.

This lady shall be the wife of a senator and a lawyer in the highest repute and practice. She has a very handsome house, with white marble steps and door-posts, and a delicate silver knocker and door-handle; she has very handsome drawing-rooms, very handsomely furnished, (there is a sideboard in one of them, but it is very handsome, and has very handsome decanters and cut glass water-jugs upon it); she has a very handsome carriage, and a very handsome free black coachman; she is always very handsomely dressed; and, moreover, she is very handsome herself.

She rises, and her first hour is spent in the scrupulously nice arrangement of her dress; she descends to her parlour neat, stiff, and silent; her breakfast is brought in by her free black footman; she eats her fried ham and her salt fish, and drinks her coffee in silence, while her husband reads one newspaper, and puts another under his elbow; and then, perhaps, she washes the cups and saucers. Her carriage is ordered at eleven; till that hour she is employed in the pastry-room, her snow-white apron protecting her mouse-coloured silk. Twenty minutes before her carriage should appear, she retires to her chamber, as she calls it, shakes, and folds up her still snow-white apron, smooths her rich dress, and with nice care, sets on her elegant bonnet, and all the handsome *et cætera;* then walks down stairs, just at the moment that her free black coachman announces to her free black footman that the carriage waits. She steps into it, and gives the word, "Drive to the Dorcas society." Her footman stays at home to clean the knives, but her coachman can trust his horses while he opens the carriage door, and his lady not being accustomed to a hand or an arm, gets out very safely without, though one of her own is occupied by a work-basket, and the other by a large roll of all those indescribable matters which ladies take as offerings to Dorcas societies. She enters the parlour appropriated for the meeting, and finds seven other ladies, very like herself, and takes her place among them; she presents her contribution, which is accepted with a gentle circular smile, and her parings of broad cloth, her ends of ribbon, her gilt paper, and her minikin pins, are added to the parings of broad cloth, the ends of ribbon, the gilt paper, and the minikin pins with which the table is already covered; she also produces from her basket three ready-made pincushions, four ink-wipers, seven paper-matches, and a paste-board watch-case; these are welcomed with acclamations, and the youngest lady present deposits them carefully on shelves, amid a prodigious quantity of similar articles. She then produces her thimble, and asks for work; it is presented to her, and the eight ladies all stitch together for some hours. Their talk is of priests and of missions; of the profits of their last sale, of their hopes from the next; of the doubt whether young Mr. This, or young Mr. That should receive the fruits of it to fit him out for Liberia; of the very ugly bonnet seen at church on Sabbath morning, of the very handsome preacher who performed on Sabbath afternoon, and of the very large collection made on Sabbath evening. This lasts till three, when the carriage again appears, and the lady and her basket return home; she mounts to her chamber, carefully sets aside her bonnet and its appurtenances, puts on her scolloped black silk apron, walks into the kitchen to see that all is right, then into the parlour, where, having cast a careful glance over the table prepared for dinner, she sits down, work in hand, to await her spouse. He comes, shakes hands with her, spits, and dines. The conversation is not much, and ten minutes suffices for the dinner; fruit and toddy, the newspaper and the work-bag succeed. In the evening the gentleman, being a savant, goes to the Wister society, and afterwards plays a snug rubber at a neighbor's. The lady receives at tea a young missionary and three members of the Dorcas society.

And so ends her day.

For some reason or other, which English people are not very likely to understand, a great number of young married persons board by the year, instead of "going to house-keeping," as they call having an establishment of their own. Of course this statement does not include persons of large fortune, but it does include very many whose rank in society would make such a mode of life quite impossible with us. I can hardly imagine a contrivance more effectual for ensuring the insignificance of a woman, than marrying her at seventeen, and placing her in a boarding-house. Nor can I easily imagine a life of more uniform dulness for the lady herself; but this certainly is a matter of taste. I have heard many ladies declare that it is "just quite the perfection of comfort to have nothing to fix for oneself." Yet despite these assurances I always experienced a feeling which hovered between pity and contempt, when I contemplated their mode of existence.

How would a newly-married Englishwoman endure it, her head and her heart full of the one dear scheme—

Well ordered home, *his* dear delight to make?

She must rise exactly in time to reach the boarding table at the hour appointed for breakfast, or she will get a stiff bow from the lady president, cold coffee, and no egg. I have been sometimes greatly amused upon these occasions by watching a little scene in which the bye-play had much more meaning than the words uttered. The fasting, but tardy lady, looks round the table, and having ascertained that there was no egg left, says distinctly, "I will take an egg if you please." But as this is addressed to no one in particular, no one in particular answers it, unless it happen that her husband is at table before her, and then he says, "There are no eggs, my dear." Whereupon the lady president evidently cannot hear, and the greedy culprit who has swallowed two eggs (for there are always as many eggs as noses) looks pretty considerably afraid of being found out. The breakfast proceeds in sombre silence, save that sometimes a parrot, and sometimes a canary bird, ventures to utter a timid note. When it is finished, the gentlemen hurry to their occupations, and the quiet ladies mount the stairs, some to the first, some to the second, and some to the third stories, in an inverse proportion to the number of dollars paid, and ensconce themselves in their respective chambers. As to what they do there it is not very easy to say; but I believe they clear-starch a little, and iron a little, and sit in a rocking-chair, and sew a great deal. I always observed that the ladies who boarded wore more elaborately worked collars and petticoats than any one else. The plough is hardly a more blessed instrument in America than the needle. How could they live without it? But time and the needle wear through the longest morning, and happily the American morning is not very long, even though they breakfast at eight.

It is generally about two o'clock that the boarding gentlemen meet the boarding ladies at dinner. Little is spoken, except a whisper between the married pairs. Sometimes a sulky bottle of wine flanks the plate of one or two individuals, but it adds nothing to the mirth of the meeting, and seldom more than one glass to the good cheer of the owners. It is not then, and it is not there, that the gentlemen of the Union drink. Soon, very soon, the silent meal is done, and then, if you mount the stairs after them, you will find from the doors of the more affectionate and indulgent wives, a smell of cigars steam forth, which plainly indicates the felicity of the couple within. If the gentleman be a very polite husband, he will, as soon as he has done smoking and drinking his toddy, offer his arm to his wife, as far as the corner of the street, where his store, or his office is situated, and there he will leave her to turn which way she likes. As this is the hour for being full dressed, of course she turns the way she can be most seen. Perhaps she pays a few visits; perhaps she goes to chapel; or, perhaps, she enters some store where her husband deals, and ventures to order a few notions; and then she goes home again—no, not home—I will not give that name to a boarding-house, but she re-enters the cold heartless atmosphere in which she dwells, where hospitality can never enter, and where interest takes the management instead of affection. At tea they all meet again, and a little trickery is perceptible to a nice observer in the manner of partaking the pound-cake, &c. After this, those who are happy enough to have engagements, hasten to keep them; those who have not, either mount again to the solitude of their chamber, or, what appeared to me much worse, remain in the common sitting-room, in a society cemented by no tie, endeared by no connection, which choice did not bring together, and which the slightest motive would break asunder. I remarked that the gentlemen were generally obliged to go out every evening on business, and, I confess, the arrangement did not surprise me.

It is not thus that the women can obtain that influence in society which is allowed to them in Europe, and to which, both sages and men of the world have agreed in ascribing such salutary effects. It is in vain that "collegiate institutes" are formed for young ladies, or that "academic degrees" are conferred upon them. It is after marriage, and when these young attempts upon all the sciences are forgotten, that the lamentable insignificance of the American women appears, and till this be remedied, I venture to prophesy that the tone of their drawing-rooms will not improve.

Not many American males have expressed a sensitive awareness of the plight or complex status of women in America. H. L. Mencken, better known for his magnificently savage satirical attacks on the stupidities of the 1920's, is one of the few who has. Francis Grund is another. Grund came to this country from Germany as a young man and fell so in love with the burgeoning democracy of the Jacksonian era that he decided to make America his permanent home. Grund had a reporter's eye and a marvelous ear for American speech. He was also equipped with a refined understanding that permitted him to discern the tension generated by a treatment which publicly adored but privately ignored women, as the following passage indicates, from his *Aristocracy in America* (2 vols., London, 1839), I, pp. 84–90.

⊂⊋ American Ladies Are Worshipped; But . . .

FRANCIS GRUND

When we entered the dining-room, soup and fish were already removed, and active operation commenced on chickens, ducks, turkeys, beef, veal, mutton, and pork,—the seven standing dishes in the United States. We were fortunate enough to obtain seats not far from the landlady, right in the middle of a garden of blooming beauties. The ladies were all *en grande toilette*, though among the gentlemen not one appeared to be dressed for dinner. The conversation was very loud; but, notwithstanding, completely drowned in the clatter of knives and forks. I perceived that the women talked, not only much more, but also much louder than the men; American gentlemen of the higher classes being indeed the most bashful creatures, in the presence of ladies of fashion, I ever saw. They approach women with the most indubitable consciousness of their own inferiority, and, either from modesty or prudence, seldom open their lips except to affirm what has been said by the ladies. One is always reminded of poor Candide's honest prayer, "*Hélas! madame; je répondrai comme vous voudrez.*" I have seen one of the most distinguished old gentlemen in the United States,—one who held the highest rank in the gift of the American people, and whose learning and knowledge on most subjects rendered him a most pleasing and entertaining companion of men,—betray as little self-possession in the presence of women as if he had been making his *début* in society, and this too in the house of one of his most intimate friends.

This excessive awkwardness in the men, to which even the most distinguished of their race make no exception, must be owing to something radically wrong in the composition of American society, which places men as well as women in a false position. The conviction of this fact must force itself on the mind of every impartial observer who has had an opportunity of making himself familiar with the customs and manners of the higher classes. There appears to be a singular mixture of respect and want of sincerity on the part of the men with regard to the women, produced, I believe, by the unnatural position which the latter hold wherever they are brought into contact with the former.

In the first place, American ladies occupy, from mere courtesy, a rank in society which is not only opposed to that which they hold in private life and in their own families, but which is actually incompatible with the exercise of discretion on the part of the gentlemen. "The ladies must be waited upon;" "the ladies must be helped;" "the ladies must be put into the carriage;" "the ladies must be taken out of the carriage;" "the ladies must have their shoe-strings tied;" "the ladies must have their India-rubber shoes put on;" "the ladies must be wrapped up in shawls;" "the ladies must be led up stairs and down stairs;" "the ladies must have their candles lit for them when they go to bed." On every occasion they are treated as poor helpless creatures who rather excite the pity than the admiration of men; and as the services they require are numerous, just in proportion to the scarcity of hired servants, the gentlemen are obliged to officiate in their stead.

These continual exigencies cannot but render the society of women often irksome to men who are daily engaged from ten to twelve hours in active business, before they dress to do the agreeable at a party; and hence the retiring of the ladies is but too frequently hailed as the signal for throwing off restraint, or, as I once heard it called, "for letting off the steam," and being again natural and easy. If in any of these matters the men were allowed to use their own discretion in bestowing attention on those only whom they like, all would be well enough. The ladies would receive a great deal of voluntary tribute; and the gentlemen, delighted with the privilege of a choice, would be more prodigal of their *petits soins* to those who would have a smile in return for their devotion. But, instead of this, a fashionable American is harassed by an uninterrupted series of exactions, made for no other purpose than for gratifying "the ladies;" while the rules of society are such, that he can scarcely ever find a chance of making himself agreeable to a particular individual. Hence an American *salon* exhibits nothing but generalities of men and women, in which no other merit is recognised but that which belongs to the sex. In this manner American ladies are worshipped; but the adoration consists in a species of polytheism, in which no particular goddess has a temple or an altar dedicated to herself.

Whenever an American gentleman meets a lady, he looks upon her as the representative of her sex; and it is to her sex, not to her peculiar amiable qualities, that she is indebted for his attentions. But look upon the same lady when she returns home from a party, or after the company has been dismissed at her own house! She is indeed honoured and respected, a happy mother, a silent contented wife, and complete mistress at home; but how seldom is she the intimate friend of her husband, the repository of his secrets, his true and faithful counsellor,—in one word, the better half of his existence! And yet what woman would not rather be *that*, than an idol, placed on an artificial elevation in society, in order to be deprived of her true influence on the deliberations and actions of men. I have undoubtedly seen American ladies who were all a woman could wish to be to their husbands; but I scarcely remember one, especially in fashionable life, who was not quoted to me as an exception to the rule.

If the plight of upper-class white women was a subtle affair, marked by psychological rather than by material deprivation, the case was altogether different for black slave women. The difficulties they suffered were tangible, often brutal. The observations by Fanny Kemble offer testimony that is perhaps more fascinating for what it reveals of the mind of the observer than what she observed. Miss Kemble was a well-known English actress, who had married a Southern planter. The interest of her hearsay accounts of the sufferings and humiliations experienced by female slaves is increased by the fact that they involve her husband's own "property" and by the evidence that Miss Kemble was by no means totally free of feelings of paternalism and condescension. Above all, however, she felt a bitterness and frustration over the inhumanities of slavery that seemed to be more typical of visitors than of natives. The following passages, in the form of letters, are from Frances Anne Kemble, *Journal of a Residence on a Georgia Plantation in 1838–1839* (New York, 1863), pp. 174–75, 189–92, 198–200.

❧ How Miserable the Condition of These Poor Creatures

FANNY KEMBLE

Dear E——,—I can not give way to the bitter impatience I feel at my present position, and come back to the North without leaving my babies; and though I suppose their stay will not in any case be much prolonged in these regions of swamp and slavery, I must, for their sakes, remain

where they are, and learn this dreary lesson of human suffering to the
end. The record, it seems to me, must be utterly wearisome to you, as
the instances themselves, I suppose, in a given time (thanks to that
dreadful reconciler to all that is evil—habit), would become to me.

This morning I had a visit from two of the women, Charlotte and
Judy, who came to me for help and advice for a complaint, which it
really seems to me every other woman on the estate is cursed with, and
which is a direct result of the conditions of their existence; the practice
of sending women to labor in the fields in the third week after their
confinement is a specific for causing this infirmity, and I know no specific
for curing it under these circumstances. As soon as these poor things had
departed with such comfort as I could give them, and the bandages they
especially begged for, three other sable graces introduced themselves,
Eddie, Louisa, and Diana; the former told me she had had a family of
seven children, but had lost them all through "ill luck," as she de-
nominated the ignorance and ill treatment which were answerable for
the loss of these, as of so many other poor little creatures their fellows.
Having dismissed her and Diana with the sugar and rice they came to
beg, I detained Louisa, whom I had never seen but in the presence of her
old grandmother, whose version of the poor child's escape to, and hiding
in the woods, I had a desire to compare with the heroine's own story.
She told it very simply, and it was most pathetic. She had not finished
her task one day, when she said she felt ill, and unable to do so, and had
been severely flogged by Driver Bran, in whose "gang" she then was.
The next day, in spite of this encouragement to labor, she had again
been unable to complete her appointed work; and Bran having told her
that he'd tie her up and flog her if she did not get it done, she had left
the field and run into the swamp. "Tie you up, Louisa!" said I; "what is
that?" She then described to me that they were fastened up by their wrists
to a beam or a branch of a tree, their feet barely touching the ground,
so as to allow them no purchase for resistance or evasion of the lash,
their clothes turned over their heads, and their backs scored with a
leather thong, either by the driver himself, or, if he pleases to inflict their
punishment by deputy, any of the men he may choose to summon to
the office; it might be father, brother, husband, or lover, if the overseer
so ordered it. I turned sick, and my blood curdled listening to these
details from the slender young slip of a lassie, with her poor piteous face
and murmuring, pleading voice. "Oh," said I, "Louisa; but the rattlesnakes—the dreadful rattlesnakes in the swamps; were you not afraid
of those horrible creatures?" "Oh, missis," said the poor child, "me no
tink of dem; me forget all 'bout dem for de fretting." "Why did you come
home at last?" "Oh, missis, me starve with hunger, me most dead with
hunger before me come back." "And were you flogged, Louisa?" said I,
with a shudder at what the answer might be. "No, missis, me go to

hospital; me almost dead and sick so long, 'spec Driver Bran him forgot 'bout de flogging." I am getting perfectly savage over all these doings, E——, and really think I should consider my own throat and those of my children well cut if some night the people were to take it into their heads to clear off scores in that fashion. . . .

Old Molly, of whom I have often before spoken to you, who lived here in the days of the prosperity and grandeur of "Hampton," still clings to the relics of her old master's former magnificence, and with a pride worthy of old Caleb of Ravenswood showed me through the dismantled decaying rooms and over the remains of the dairy, displaying a capacious fish-box or well, where, in the good old days, the master's supply was kept in fresh salt water till required for table. Her prideful lamentations over the departure of all this quondam glory were ludicrous and pathetic; but, while listening with some amusement to the jumble of grotesque descriptions, through which her impression of the immeasurable grandeur and nobility of the house she served was the predominant feature, I could not help contrasting the present state of the estate with that which she described, and wondering why it should have become, as it undoubtedly must have done, so infinitely less productive a property than in the old major's time.

Before closing this letter, I have a mind to transcribe to you the entries for to-day recorded in a sort of daybook, where I put down very succinctly the number of people who visit me, their petitions and ailments, and also such special particulars concerning them as seem to me worth recording. You will see how miserable the physical condition of many of these poor creatures is; and their physical condition, it is insisted by those who uphold this evil system, is the only part of it which is prosperous, happy, and compares well with that of Northern laborers. Judge from the details I now send you; and never forget, while reading them, that the people on this plantation are well off, and consider themselves well off, in comparison with the slaves on some of the neighboring estates.

Fanny has had six children; all dead but one. She came to beg to have her work in the field lightened.

Nanny has had three children; two of them are dead. She came to implore that the rule of sending them into the field three weeks after their confinement might be altered.

Leah, Cæsar's wife, has had six children; three are dead.

Sophy, Lewis's wife, came to beg for some old linen. She is suffering fearfully; has had ten children; five of them are dead. The principal favor she asked was a piece of meat, which I gave her.

Sally, Scipio's wife, has had two miscarriages and three children born, one of whom is dead. She came complaining of incessant pain and weakness in her back. This woman was a mulatto daughter of a slave called

Sophy, by a white man of the name of Walker, who visited the plantation.

Charlotte, Renty's wife, had had two miscarriages, and was with child · again. She was almost crippled with rheumatism, and showed me a pair of poor swollen knees that made my heart ache. I have promised her a pair of flannel trowsers, which I must forthwith set about making.

Sarah, Stephen's wife—this woman's case and history were alike deplorable. She had had four miscarriages, had brought seven children into the world, five of whom were dead, and was again with child. She complained of dreadful pains in the back, and an internal tumor which swells with the exertion of working in the fields; probably, I think, she is ruptured. She told me she had once been mad and had ran into the woods, where she contrived to elude discovery for some time, but was at last tracked and brought back, when she was tied up by the arms, and heavy logs fastened to her feet, and was severely flogged. After this she contrived to escape again, and lived for some time skulking in the woods, and she supposes mad, for when she was taken again she was entirely naked. She subsequently recovered from this derangement, and seems now just like all the other poor creatures who come to me for help and pity. I suppose her constant childbearing and hard labor in the fields at the same time may have produced the temporary insanity.

Sukey, Bush's wife, only came to pay her respects. She had had four miscarriages; had brought eleven children into the world, five of whom are dead.

Molly, Quambo's wife, also came to see me. Hers was the best account I have yet received; she had had nine children, and six of them were still alive.

This is only the entry for to-day, in my diary, of the people's complaints and visits. Can you conceive a more wretched picture than that which it exhibits of the conditions under which these women live? Their cases are in no respect singular, and though they come with pitiful entreaties that I will help them with some alleviation of their pressing physical distresses, it seems to me marvelous with what desperate patience (I write it advisedly, patience of utter despair) they endure their sorrow-laden existence. Even the poor wretch who told that miserable story of insanity, and lonely hiding in the swamps, and scourging when she was found, and of her renewed madness and flight, did so in a sort of low, plaintive, monotonous murmur of misery, as if such sufferings were all "in the day's work."

I ask these questions about their children because I think the number they bear as compared with the number they rear a fair gauge of the effect of the system on their own health and that of their offspring. There was hardly one of these women, as you will see by the details I have noted of their ailments, who might not have been a candidate for a bed in a hospital, and they had come to me after working all day in the fields. . . .

I have been interrupted by several visits, my dear E——, among other, one from a poor creature called Judy, whose sad story and condition affected me most painfully. She had been married, she said, some years ago to one of the men called Temba, who, however, now has another wife, having left her because she went mad. While out of her mind she escaped into the jungle, and contrived to secrete herself there for some time, but was finally tracked and caught, and brought back and punished by being made to sit, day after day, for hours in the stocks—a severe punishment for a man, but for a woman perfectly barbarous. She complained of chronic rheumatism, and other terrible ailments, and said she suffered such intolerable pain while laboring in the fields, that she had come to entreat me to have her work lightened. She could hardly crawl, and cried bitterly all the time she spoke to me.

She told me a miserable story of her former experience on the plantation under Mr. K——'s overseership. It seems that Jem Valiant (an extremely difficult subject, a mulatto lad, whose valor is sufficiently accounted for now by the influence of the mutinous white blood) was her first-born, the son of Mr. K——, who forced her, flogged her severely for having resisted him, and then sent her off, as a farther punishment, to Five Pound—a horrible swamp in a remote corner of the estate, to which the slaves are sometimes banished for such offenses as are not sufficiently atoned for by the lash. The dismal loneliness of the place to these poor people, who are as dependent as children upon companionship and sympathy, makes this solitary exile a much-dreaded infliction; and this poor creature said that, bad as the flogging was, she would sooner have taken that again than the dreadful lonely days and nights she spent on the penal swamp of Five Pound.

I make no comment on these terrible stories, my dear friend, and tell them to you as nearly as possible in the perfectly plain, unvarnished manner in which they are told to me. I do not wish to add to, or perhaps I ought to say take away from, the effect of such narrations by amplifying the simple horror and misery of their bare details.

My dearest E——,—I have had an uninterrupted stream of women and children flowing in the whole morning to say "Ha de, missis?" Among others, a poor woman called Mile, who could hardly stand for pain and swelling in her limbs; she had had fifteen children and two miscarriages; nine of her children had died; for the last three years she had become almost a cripple with chronic rheumatism, yet she is driven every day to work in the field. She held my hands, and stroked them in the most appealing way while she exclaimed, "Oh my missis! my missis! me neber sleep till day for de pain," and with the day her labor must again be resumed. I gave her flannel and sal volatile to rub her poor swelled limbs with; rest I could not give her—rest from her labor and her pain—this mother of fifteen children.

Another of my visitors had a still more dismal story to tell; her name was Die; she had had sixteen children, fourteen of whom were dead; she had had four miscarriages: one had been caused with falling down with a very heavy burden on her head, and one from having her arms strained up to be lashed. I asked her what she meant by having her arms tied up. She said their hands were first tied together, sometimes by the wrists, and sometimes, which was worse, by the thumbs, and they were then drawn up to a tree or post, so as almost to swing them off the ground, and then their clothes rolled round their waist, and a man with a cowhide stands and stripes them. I give you the woman's words. She did not speak of this as of any thing strange, unusual, or especially horrid and abominable; and when I said, "Did they do that to you when you were with child?" she simply replied, "Yes, missis." And to all this I listen—I, an English woman, the wife of the man who owns these wretches, and I can not say, "That thing shall not be done again; that cruel shame and villainy shall never be known here again." I gave the woman meat and flannel, which were what she came to ask for, and remained choking with indignation and grief long after they had all left me to my most bitter thoughts.

Chapter

9: The Evolution of a New England Town

⊆ **CARROLL PURSELL**

"The prosperous situation of all the lesser divisions of a state," wrote an early historian of Newburyport, Massachusetts, "is essential to the true greatness of the state itself; and therefore, in examining the character of towns, we become insensibly led upwards to that of nations. And the several doings, which tend to promote the well-being of petty communities, are the same in nature, although not in extent, with those, which give wealth to the most opulent empires." Newburyport itself was a case in point. On the one hand the great questions of national policy which shaped the United States as a whole were reflected in the town's activities and prosperity which, in turn, contributed to the forming of national policies and to well-being. The whole was certainly greater than the sum of of its parts, but the two were just as certainly wedded in intimate interaction.

When the Founding Fathers established what they liked to call the new American empire, they realized that, like the British empire after which it was modeled, its economy must be in some measure balanced. Agriculture, commerce, and manufactures were the three pillars upon which any empire must rest—a fact which was obvious from experience and reinforced by the economic theories of Mercantilism. During the colonial period, the first two of these had flourished, but the third had languished under the twin handicaps of economic immaturity and governmental disfavor. Like all underdeveloped nations, America suffered from a shortage of capital, labor, and technical know-how. What she did possess of these was most often invested in subsistence farming, the culture of staple crops for export, and in trade itself.

All of this changed in the late eighteenth century. Two great revolutions—one political and the other economic and technical—made it possible for the new United States to actually create that empire of which its leaders dreamed. The War for Independence cut us off from the protection but also the confinements of the British imperial system. The Industrial Revolution, which was going on at the same time, brought forward the techniques which would enable Americans to establish a flourishing manufacture of their own. Politics gained for us new territory and the freedom to exploit it. Technology enabled us to tame that land and tie it together.

Cities and towns played a key role in this transformation. Although as late as 1800 only about one out of fifteen of the nation's 5¼ million souls lived in towns; these few had always played a disproportionately large part in the making of America. Furthermore, as the nineteenth century progressed, the nation's urban centers grew in number, size, and influence. From the establishment of the American colonies, towns had served as centers of trade and communication. Now, however, cities began to be centers of manufacture as well. The coming of the steam engine, as improved by James Watt in the 1760's and 1770's, made it possible for factories to be located in towns, far from water power of streams which had given the earliest impetus to the Industrial Revolution.

Added to this new role as manufacturing center, and closely tied to it, was the coming of increasing numbers of immigrants to the nation's urban centers. The most conspicuous of these, during the ante-bellum period, were the Irish, but they came as well from other parts of western Europe. Altogether they numbered some 5 million persons, and between 1860 and 1890 they were joined by another 10 million. Although a few of these new settlers went immediately to the agricultural lands of the frontier, the vast majority stayed on in cities to fill the slums and man the growing factories.

All of these massive alterations in the country's condition were reflected in Newburyport, Massachusetts. Located near the mouth of the Merrimack River, in the northeastern corner of the state 40 miles north of Boston, the town had a population of nearly 6,000 in 1800. During the colonial years it had been a trading center and, by the 1760's, a merchant aristocracy of some two hundred men dominated the town, basing their wealth on a lucrative trade within the British empire. Most of these supported independence, but were ruined by the depression which followed the war. A second group of merchants rose to exploit the neutral trade which flourished during the Napoleonic wars, but the Jeffersonian Embargo and subsequent War of 1812 ruined this group also.

By 1815 the town was once again beset by depression. For the next quarter of a century, until the 1840's, the town continued to deteriorate. The population fell and property valuation declined. The sea, once a source of wealth in the form of trade routes, fisheries, and shipbuilding facilities, no longer provided a prosperous existence for the population. Many other towns, especially in New England, had embarked on new careers as manufacturing centers, but this option appeared closed to Newburyport. In 1826 Caleb Cushing wrote, discouragingly, that the Industrial Revolution offered no hope for the town: "as Newburyport possesses no site with water power, it does not afford facilities for the establishment of those manufactories which require the application of a great moving force to complicated machinery."

Then, in the 1840's, the tyranny of geography was broken. The city's population and wealth both doubled in a decade and nearly six hundred new houses were erected. The cause of this new prosperity was the establishment of five large cotton factories, all powered by steam. The first two of these were set to work in the late 1830's. Within twelve years some 1,500 people were employed in cotton factories in the city.

The coming of the Industrial Revolution to Newburyport was not, for everyone, an unmixed blessing. Like other towns, it experienced a significant influx of population, both rural native Americans and recent arrivals from foreign lands, both groups hoping to improve their lot in the city. Under the impact of industrialization and urbanization, the old social structure of Newburyport disintegrated. The traditional institutions of the church, the family, and the merchant aristocracy proved no longer able to exert social control. By 1853 something like one out of ten families (about half of these foreign-born, and most of them Irish) were on public assistance.

The cotton mills which had moved Newburyport into the nineteenth century had lost their central importance in the economy by 1880, but by then the manufacture of shoes had taken hold in the city. Both were mechanized and factory-organized enterprises, however, and the impact of the change on social structure was apparently minimal. After mid-century, the city continued on a plateau of unspectacular existence which allowed for some social mobility but no dramatic change in the fortunes of the city as a whole. Well into the twentieth century it remained a small and fairly typical New England city—holding its own but little more, as industry moved west and south.

In all of these evolutions of fortune, technology played a role perhaps as large as that of public policy. The need for adequate transportation and power runs through all the changes in the local economy. The evolution of ever larger ocean-going ships until the river could no longer accommodate them; the failure to build a canal when other cities were building theirs; the pulling power of Boston as it built its own transportation network for the express purpose of confiscating for itself the trade of satellite communities; the lack of water power from natural streams and the failure to build hydraulic works (as at nearby Lowell) to provide artificial sources of water power; and finally the use of steam engines, themselves dependent upon the cheap transport of coal for fuel.

Nor were the effects economic only. In pre-industrial Newburyport about half the adult males were artisans, a quarter were merchants, and the rest common laborers (sailors, teamsters, and so forth). With the coming of factories, the category of machine operative was established— not quite an artisan, but not a laborer either. The new situation not only increased the numbers of the city's lower class—it made them at the same time more visible and less easily controlled.

The documents which follow address themselves to many of these problems. At every stage of the city's life, serious commentators and ambitious boosters sought to assess the promise of the city by looking at its history and showing wherein past failure could be turned into future success. There was a large area of agreement on what had gone wrong in the past—the river bar, the fire, the Embargo—and tacit agreement on what the future should hold—industrialization. Caleb Cushing's shrewd analysis of what had been, Charles James's bold assertion of what might be, John Parson's hearty but essentially rhetorical invitation to progress, and the calm appraisal of the social scientist W. Lloyd Warner—all attest to the importance of the mid-century watershed when industry replaced commerce as the city's basic economic activity.

Population of Newburyport, Mass. 1790–1960 (U.S. Census Data)

1790	4,837
1800	5,946
1810	7,634
1820	6,852 (down 10.2 percent, largest for any decade)
1830	6,375
1840	7,161
1850	9,572
1860	13,401 (increase of 40 percent, largest for any decade)
1870	12,595
1880	13,538
1890	13,947
1900	14,478
1910	14,949
1920	15,618
1930	15,084
1940	13,916
1950	14,111
1960	14,004

Caleb Cushing (1800–1879) was a young lawyer recently settled in Newburyport when he wrote his book, *The History and Present State of the Town of Newburyport* (Newburyport, 1826). He had before him a long career in public life, first as representative to the state legislature, then to Congress, and finally in a succession of diplomatic and executive positions in Washington. In 1826, however, he was concerned with the depressed state of his adopted home, caught in the economic slough between bustling commercial port and humming industrial center. Why did the city decline? To what extent did he attribute the city's problems to poor politics and how much to changed technology? The merchant class of the city had been on the edge of secession by 1815, so little sympathy did it have with President Madison's policies. Eleven years after the end of the war—during the Era of Good Feelings—how were those policies viewed? The expectation of economic (and every other kind of) growth has become ingrained in the American mind. What did Cushing think was the possibility and acceptability of a state of stability rather than growth?

☞ What Went Wrong?

CALEB CUSHING

The rise of Newburyport to wealth and consequence was extremely rapid. This elevation was not capable of being ascribed entirely, or for the greater part, to intrinsic, local, or peculiar sources of property. . . . We had not the extraordinary advantage, which New Orleans and New York possess, of being the natural depot of an immense interior country of unexampled fertility and richness. There were no inexhaustible coal mines wrought in the town or its vicinity, as at Birmingham or Manchester, to facilitate the establishment of manufactories. Nor had we, within our narrow six hundred acres of territory, the waterfalls of the Pawtucket or the Powow, to be subjected, by human art, to the noblest objects of human convenience, industry, and happiness. Our peculiar local advantages extended but little beyond the single business of shipbuilding.

From what, then, sprung the prosperous energies and the speedy increase of the town, in its best days?—They arose, it is believed, *mainly*, from the address, enterprise, and good fortune of its citizens, in seizing upon the propitious opportunities afforded by the situation of the United States. Newburyport rose with the commercial rise of the county, and with that alone kept even pace. True it is, that the town stood somewhat in advance, in the celerity of its progress, of the nation at large; and this advancement, it is repeated, we must attribute to the character of its inhabitants,—which their staple manufacture contributed to develope. Their success was in maritime commerce, and in the arts subsidiary to, and dependant upon, maritime commerce.—And their skill in ship-building, created by their local advantage for that manufacture, empowered them the more easily to gain the start of other places in marine trade. For this business had enabled them to accumulate some capital. It made it easy, also, with a very small expense of outfit, to obtain a bottom for the transportation of goods. And by placing the means of foreign commerce constantly before the eyes of the people, in the shape of their staple product, it naturally tempted them the more to adventure in maritime speculations.

Thus matters stood, so long as the wonderful commercial prosperity of this country lasted. During this period, when the neutral position of America was so extraordinary, so unparalleled in the history of commerce, our citizens pushed their advantage to the utmost. The profits of commerce were immense. We had the carrying trade of the whole universe, almost, in our hands. Our proximity to the European colonies in America co-operated, with other things, to fill the horn of our abundance to overflowing. The industrious mechanic of the Merrimac found a demand for his manufacture:—the enterprising merchant could obtain his vessel on easy terms, and in a very short period she would earn her whole original cost. All the departments of industry connected with the ocean were thus stimulated to the highest degree, and universal prosperity and the easy acquisition of a competence, were the natural result.

France and England soon became jealous of this our rapid approach to the very empire of the seas and the monopoly of marine commerce. Previous to this, however, our trade to the French islands had begun to decline. The business was overdone by competition.—Their markets became drugged with our produce, as, indeed, they have continued to be ever since. They began to be more directly supplied with foreign manufactures, thereby diminishing the profits of our commerce with Europe. And no slight injury was sustained by our commerce, in consequence of the disorders in the West Indies occasioned by the French revolution.

But the deadly blow to our commercial prosperity was more directly struck by the insolence and cupidity of the great belligerents of Europe. Without entering into the broad question whether the system of restrictions on our commerce adopted by the government was or was not vindicated by the issue, thus much may be confidently affirmed: our government was forced into it by the injustice of foreign powers. It was a choice of evils. England,—France,—Holland,—Naples,—Denmark, —were committing the most flagitious depredations upon the property of

our citizens. They were heaping insult upon insult, and injury upon
injury.—They were sweeping our ships from the ocean with fearful
rapacity, and profligate disregard of every law, divine or human. This
it was, which drove our government into that series of restrictive measures, finally terminated in war. During that calamitous period, our seamen were thrown out of employment; our traders lost their customers;
the farmers, who had looked to us for foreign commodities, and of whom
we had purchased lumber, and provisions, left our market,—and our
merchants were compelled to sit down idly and see their ships rotting
in the docks. True it is that, had the uncalculating enterprise of our
capitalists been left to itself, their ships and property would have been
captured or confiscated abroad; and the millions of our foreign claims
would have been swelled incalculably; but, in either alternative, the
loss must have been, as it was, deplorable.

In the midst of all these misfortunes came the fire of 1811, which
destroyed a great amount of our property, and diverted too much of
what remained from more profitable channels into the form of buildings.
But a conflagration, destructive as it may be of property, is not of a
nature to produce any permanent injury to the prosperity of a town. The
skill, the talents, the industry, which regard the piles, devoured by the
flames, are capable of soon repairing the damage by a little added exertion. Of course, the fire could have had but partial influence, in producing the decline of Newburyport. The genuine difficulty to be solved, the
question really needing an answer, is, why Newburyport did not resume
its prosperity, and continue to rise, when all the temporary causes of
misfortune alluded to had ceased to operate. We shall not find the
explanation of this point in the fire of 1811, nor in the embargo, nor in
the war. It is to be sought further. New York and Boston have grown as
rapidly since the pressure of those restrictions on commerce was taken
off, as they did before. But various circumstances contributed to retard
the increase of Newburyport, as is usual in similar cases.

Some of these were local. Thus the bar is undoubtedly some impedi-
ment to our prosperity,—because it confines our navigation to vessels
of the smaller class; and, contrary to what was customary twenty years
ago, the present exigencies of foreign trade require the use of large
vessels. The falls and rapids in the Merrimac are also a local difficulty.
They deprive us of the benefit of supplying with heavy goods the inhabitants of the interior along the river, above the actual head of navigation.
The business of these persons is diverted, by means of the Middlesex
canal, from Newburyport, its natural resort, to Boston. This advantage
might be remedied, in a great degree, by the completion of the long
talked of canal around the remaining obstructions in the bed of the
Merrimac.

Every small sea-port competes, to great disadvantage, with any large one near to it. The greatest market will inevitably tend to swallow up others in its vicinity. This law of trade has undoubtedly operated to the serious injury of Newburyport. Like other sea-ports of the second class in Massachusetts bay, it has withered under the influence of Boston. There are but few exceptions to this remark, and those exceptions confirm the rule. Thus New-Bedford and Nantucket are sustained by their possession of the whale-fishery; Salem, also, had its advantage in the East India trade, so long as that continued peculiarly lucrative. But the bad effects of the vicinity of Boston are constantly and seriously experienced here, in leading the importer to make sales of large cargoes, or heavy goods, almost universally in Boston; and the retailer to resort there for his supplies.

Within the last fifteen years, many other towns along the sea-coast of New England have entered into competition with this, in what formerly constituted a very important part of its business, namely, the exportation of lumber and fish, and the carriage of the products of the West Indies to a market. The competition has, of course, in all cases diminished the profits. And Portland and other places in Maine can export lumber at less charge than ourselves, and therefore to greater advantage.

All these different causes have their influence. But the most efficient and comprehensive reason of the decline of the town is, in truth, the immense alteration of the general condition of business during the last fifteen years. The whole of Europe, with the exception of its extreme eastern regions, is in a state of peace. We are no longer the carriers for its many nations. The sphere of our commercial enterprize is wonderfully narrowed. Our capital is now driven into new channels, and the entire circle of the relations of business and trade has undergone a radical revolution. Foreign commerce now requires a larger capital than formerly, and the profits on it are less. We are beginning to perceive and appreciate the importance of encouraging and protecting domestic industry, for the most substantial reasons; and if we did not, the impossibility of employing all the resources of the country in commerce would force open our eyes to see the necessity of investing a portion of it in manufactures. Here, then, we lose our population, whilst other towns gain it. Boston, for instance, by reason of the immense accumulations of wealth in the hands of its inhabitants, becomes, by the laws of political economy, a permanent market as well for domestic manufactures and products, as for imported articles. Amesbury, Lowell, Dover, are the site of vast manufactories, and thither our mechanics and traders emigrate, following the concentration of capital, wherever it takes place. But we, on the other hand, have neither natural sites for manufactories, nor that immense accumulation of riches, which should secure to us, at present, the means of successful competition with any of those places, to which the recent revolutions in the conduct of business have imparted such great accession of wealth or population.

If these remarks are entitled to any weight, they may serve to reconcile us to the diminution of population and of taxable property, which a comparison of the state of the town in 1810 and 1820 exhibits, by showing that it was inevitable. No efforts of our own could have prevented it. Some injudicious kinds of trade were, it is true, entered upon by the citizens on the restoration of peace, whose unprofitableness ere long was discovered and caused them to be abandoned. And had the canal been constructed when it was originally projected, it would have undoubtedly enlarged our trade, and might also have been used advantageously for the location of manufactories. But these things were not the great causes of the check in our prosperity. For after all, the present condition of the town is by no means a state of decline. It has not now the riches, the population, or the business, which it once possessed. But it is no worse off than many other sea-ports on the New-England coast of the same general description. And its actual state is not so much a state of decline, as of slow and gradual, but sure, consolidation and advancement. We Americans, and especially we New-Englanders, are an enterprising, restless, impatient race. We are not content with living, or living well with long continued industry, as in the old countries. We are ambitious to make large fortunes, and to make them quickly, and as it were *extempore*. Our national and individual energies have been evoked by a sort of unnatural and hot-bed process of developement. And while the inhabitants of Newburyport have, in a most remarkable manner, at a former period, been thus hurried on to prosperity, they can the less easily accommodate themselves to a stationary condition, or one of mere simple well-being.

But the author feels admonished that these remarks have been pursued at sufficient length. It is more grateful to inquire how the town might be enabled to regain its ancient standing. But there is no royal road, no convenient short cut, to national wealth or public prosperity. It is pleasing to reflect . . . that while some occupations are in a less thriving state than formerly, yet others are much improved. The fisheries and the coast-wise trade of the town, departments of industry every way preferable, in respect to questions of political economy, over foreign commerce, have steadily gained upon the latter, in profitableness and in amount of tonnage. To be speedily restored to its old prosperity, some great revolution must take place, either in external affairs, or in the internal resources of the town. Such a revolution in foreign affairs is a most improbable event. But the creation of sites for manufactories in the place, or the establishment here of any species of manufacture which do not require the application of water-power, would produce a revolution in the internal resources of Newburyport. Whether such a thing is practicable or not is too wide an inquiry to be pertinent or otherwise proper in this connexion. But the facility and usefulness of extending the manufacture of vessels are too prominent and obvious to pass unnoticed, in any consideration of the means of stimulating our domestic industry by adequate rewards. . . .

The true policy of communities, whether large or small, like the best interest of individuals, is to cultivate industry, economy, regularity, temperance, and the higher principles of virtue, and to obey the dictates of pure religion. Without this policy, all advantages of locality, or circumstances, or fortune, and all the accumulated blessings of the richest soil, the healthiest climate, and the most transcendant bounties of nature, are utterly unavailing to confer prosperity upon a nation, a state, or a town. And with this policy, everything else is easy of accomplishment. The most sterile soil may be converted into a garden, and the wilderness caused 'to bloom as a rose.' Commerce, the arts, literature, may be made to pour forth their golden streams of plenty, and comfort, and refinement, to enrich the land. For there is a secret of public welfare, which political economy does not teach. It lies at the foundation of every prosperous community, and it is capable of retrieving the most adverse fortunes. Though it be not learned in the schools, the fate of empires and the destinies of mankind impress it visibly upon the face of the universe.— It is, unwavering obedience to the lessons of morality and piety. Be this the noble aim, then, of all our actions.

Cushing had hesitated to predict that Newburyport could ever become a center of manufactures, because it lacked natural water power. But within little more than a decade the widespread adoption of steam engines for use in manufactures had made it possible for many cities to develop into industrial centers. By 1838 the Secretary of the Treasury was able to count 1,860 steam engines so used, a figure certainly less than the actual number in use. Philadelphia, Pittsburgh, New York, Boston, and a host of lesser cities each had scores of engines applied to industry. In 1840 James Montgomery had published a pamphlet attempting to show that steam could seldom compete with water in the cotton manufacture. To counter this argument, Charles T. James, a Newburyport engineer who had built steam mills there as well as in other parts of the nation, wrote a pamphlet (under the pen name of "Justitia"), *Strictures on Montgomery on the Cotton Manufactures of Great Britain and the United States* (Newburyport, 1841), in which he not only defended cotton factories in general, but steam mills in particular. Using figures based on Newburyport's Bartlett Mills, he held out the hope that both the mills and the city would survive and prosper. What are the social implications (and the economic advantages) of locating a cotton mill in a city rather than at a water power site in the country? If James was correct, could the city hope to overcome the handicaps described by Cushing?

⊂⊅ The Coming of Industrialization

CHARLES T. JAMES

From the first attempts to manufacture goods in the United States, by means of steam power, most people have been, or appeared to be, quite skeptical as to the practicability of the profitable application of that power for such a purpose. It has been the general, and almost universal impression, that steam could not, by any possibility, be employed at a cost so low as water. With people in general, on this, as on all other practical subjects, argument is of no avail, even if sustained by known facts, and proved true by the incontrovertible laws of nature. Practical illustration is demanded in each individual case. Persons when comparing steam and water power, seem to forget that the latter costs any thing, either originally or in its application; and would appear to think it as free for manufacturing as for domestic purposes, and as cheaply applied.

People either forget, do not know, or do not take the trouble to consider, that steam-mills may be erected and put in operation, at one half the expense, generally, which is required for water-mills, exclusive of machinery, and that thus a large amount of interest on the original investment of capital is annually saved. Nor yet do they appear to take into the account the well-known fact, that steam-mills erected and operated contiguous to navigable waters, save all the heavy expense of inland transportation. . . .

One more item of the advantage of location to the steam mill. Proprietors of water mills, generally, in the interior, are under the necessity of purchasing land, and erecting dwellings, for the accommodation of their operatives. This requires a very considerable amount of capital, which is thus diverted from other objects. In seaports, this necessity does not exist. Dwellings are generally found in abundance, already erected; and any deficiency is readily supplied by the owners of real estate themselves. Added to this, there is another consideration. There is, in general, to be found in maritime places, an abundance of help, of nearly all descriptions wanted in the mill. A vast proportion of these persons either cannot or will not leave their homes, to labor in distant establishments, without the inducement of high wages; and many not even for that inducement. But they readily and gladly go into mills in their immediate vicinity, will work for less wages than would command their services abroad, and in fact can well afford to do so, as they can live as well with their own families and friends, at much less expense. This is a very important consideration; and the difference it makes in favor of the steam mill, is, in many cases, sufficient to pay the daily expenditure of the power to drive it. And finally, to all this is to be added the vast difference in the original cost of the water mill and the steam mill, making a corresponding saving to the latter, in the annual interest on the original outlay.

I have now given the reader some of the data which are to serve as the basis of my estimates and comparisons. In them it is believed a case will be made out, sufficiently plain and clear for every one to understand, and sustained by proofs sufficiently strong to satisfy even the most incredulous; and those proofs drawn from actual results, capable of ocular practical demonstration.

The writer has not asserted, nor is he about to assert, or to attempt to show, that steam-power has ever, in all cases, been applied to the manufacture of cotton goods, with a profitable result, in this country. In some cases, he is aware it has not; and the same may truly be said of water-power. But in neither case has the power been in the fault. Other circumstances have operated unfavorably. In the application of steam-power, a great deal depends on the judicious construction of engines and other machinery, and a proper adaptation of the means to ends; and very much, indeed, to strict attention and judicious management. When all these particulars are attended to, and the principles they suggest fully carried out, steam power can be as profitably employed, to say the least, in our maritime towns, as water power can be in any part of New-England.

The coming of the Industrial Revolution to Newburyport—in the form of the Essex and Bartlett cotton mills—opened a new era of prosperiy for the city. Steam factories were joined by steam railroads, and both were surrounded by the social and political currents of Jacksonian America. The picture of mid-century Newburyport presented by E. Vale Smith, *History of Newburyport: From the Earliest Settlement of the Country to the Present Time* . . . (Newburyport, 1854), is almost a classic portrait of nineteenth century, small-town America. Smith makes it perfectly clear that such political events as the distribution of surplus funds from the Federal Treasury in January, 1837, and social movements like the extension of educational opportunities to girls (a kind of investment in human capital) contributed to the town's new prosperity. What social consequences does Smith attribute to the new economic activity of the town? As you follow the author on a tour of this town, can you distinguish any geographical sorting out of different social or economic strata or activities? In other words, if you were a stranger taking this walking tour in 1854, what could you tell of the social and economic divisions and activities of the town?

⊂┇   A City Revivified

E. VALE SMITH

The revival of enterprise in Newburyport, its increase in population, and the gradual breaking up of the stereotyped complaints, that "Newburyport plans were especially distasteful to Providence," are mainly attributable to the introduction of the cotton manufacture, though the first established mill (the "Essex," in 1834,) failed to bring heavy dividends to the first stockholders. But since the erection of the Bartlett Mills, in 1838, followed in quick succession by the James, Globe, and Ocean, a new impetus was given to the whole business of the town, which gradually began to change its outward appearance, with the influx of a large floating population. State street, the principal rendezvous of the dry goods merchants, doffed its old exterior of small windows, carefully curtained, lest the sun or customers should see the goods intended for sale, and in their place appeared large plate glass, granite fronts, and a liberal display of colors, in cheerful contrast to the old secretive style of doing business.

The addition of several hundred to the population in so short a time, tended to modify the exclusiveness of old established castes in society, which forty years of comparative inertia had produced, and strangers received a readier admission to guarded circles, as they became more numerous. Business was also revivified. The fifteen hundred added to the manufacturing population are all consumers, and brought in their train an increase of retail traders; while other concurring events favored that elasticity of the public mind which opens the way to public improvements and municipal prosperity. Among these was the distribution of the surplus revenue, the opening of the Eastern Railroad to Newburyport, the change in regard to public sentiment on female education, the temperance reformation, the maturity of the Putnam School fund, the opening of the Magnetic Telegraph line, the Newburyport Railroad, &c. . . .

Newburyport, as now defined, lies on the southern bank of the Merrimac river. The closely built portion of it extends some three miles in length, and less than a quarter of a mile in width; this narrow parallelogram gradually ascending from the river to High street, or "the Ridge." The streets are regularly laid out, running from the ridge to the river, and crossed by transverse ways at nearly right angles, with some few exceptions. The place is noted for its cleanliness, the general appearance of thrift and comfort among its inhabitants, and the number and beauty of the trees which adorn the streets.

Back of "the Ridge" lies an agricultural district, which may be reached from any part of the town in fifteen minutes; while the river, lying at its feet, gives to it that vitality and spirit which characterize a seaport town. Towards the north, a part of the town, called Belleville, concentrates the ship-building interest. Here are four ship-yards, three large and one smaller; the products of which may now be found in every quarter of the globe. In the central portion of the town are gathered the merchants and retail traders, the City Hall, Banks, Market House, &c., and through it runs the railroad, penetrating the ridge by a tunnel, and being carried by a bridge, elevated some twenty-five feet, across Merrimac street, and leading thence directly across the river, over which, many times a day, rushes the screaming locomotive. Towards the southerly part of the town, we find the fishermen, many of whom in winter work at shoemaking. And here too is one of the primitive ship-yards, long dedicated to the exclusive production of schooners. This section of of the town owns to the common appellation of "Joppa;" and leading directly from this, in a south-easterly direction, is the Plum Island turnpike, which by a bridge connects the island to the main land, at a distance of nearly two miles from the southern extremity of Water street. Hence, the inhabitants of Newburyport have within the compass of a moderate walk, the choice of turning to the green fields, with the West Newbury hills forming a background to the picture; to the inland river scenery, over which presides the "bald summit of old Powow;" or to the dashing waves of the free Atlantic, which spend their unobstructed strength on the yielding shores of Plum Island; while interspersed everywhere over the town, rise the church spire and the schoolhouse, and those emblems of industry, the cotton factories, which pour out into the streets some six times a day, their fifteen hundred well-paid and well-cared-for operatives. A few rods distant from the southern extremity of the thickly settled part of the town, is "Pettingell's," formerly "Pierce's" farm, upon which stands an ancient stone house, built about 1660 or 1670 used in the early days of Newbury to store the town's powder; a portion of which on one occasion exploded and blew out a side of the house, lodging a woman, a negro slave of Mr. Pierce's, bed and all, in the branches of a large apple tree. From the Pierce family who occupied this estate, is descended Franklin Pierce, President of the United States; Benjamin Pierce, of Hillsborough, being descended from Benjamin Pierce of Newbury, who is buried in Byfield Parish, Newbury, and, if we may believe his epitaph, like his descendant, a "pillar i' th' State he was."

Following up the street, along the water-side, the southern half of which is called Water street, and the northern Merrimac street; commencing at the southern extremity, the following varieties of business may be observed, with many others which we have not space to enumerate. At the starting-point is located the gas factory, which, with its iron arms, diffuses its light through all parts of the town; from which, following up Water street, through "Joppa," we find the shore lined with small boats and nets, which latter may often be seen drying in the sun; while on vacant lots to the left in the latter part of summer, it is not uncommon to see the fish-flakes reared, and the cod, which the fishermen have brought home ready salted, spread out to dry, preparatory to packing. Attached to many of the houses in this vicinity are small workshops, which in winter are occupied by groups of four, six, or eight shoemakers, busily plying awl and thread, while they watch for the opening spring, which will lead many of them to the "banks" and the "Labrador," in pursuit of the mackerel and cod. In this vicinity, and both above and below it, for some distance, the shore consists of flats, which are only deeply covered with water at full tide. From this position, perhaps one or more pilot boats may be seen putting out after some ship or barque, whose white sails may be discerned on looking down the harbor, between Salisbury point and Plum Island, standing up to the bar, where, if she is a stranger, she must wait for a guide.

Above Bromfield street, anciently the southern limits of Newburyport, the wharves jut out in quick succession, one after another, into the stream, and fishing schooners, coasters, West India traders, eastern vessels, with wood from the Provinces, fill up the docks. To the left stands the James cotton mill; and at little less than a mile from our starting-place, we come to Lunt's mast-yard, where the long pine timbers are shaped into spars and masts for the schooners we have passed, and the ships which we shall come to, and for others which may never see the Merrimac. Not far from here are the boat-builders, Orne & Rolfe, and Pickett, the latter of whom, in 1846, built a splendid thirty-oared barge for the Government, to be used in the war with Mexico.

Nearly opposite to them is Huse's cigar factory; and in this vicinity are found the importers of West India goods, coal, lumber, and grain; and a little farther on, we approach the Custom House, a substantial granite building, which contains not one square foot of wood-work from the cellar to the cupola; and just beyond, is the primitive ferry-way established by Andros, where now, as then, the Merrimac may be crossed in the style of our ancestors a century and a half ago, the traveller being rowed across at a nominal price, and at a pace which gives ample opportunity to examine all the beauties of the harbor, the river, and the Salisbury shore with which it connects.

Above this a few rods, we leave Water street, which terminates in Market square—an open space into which leads the central business street, (State street,) and at a few rods from the foot of which, stands the Market House. From the north side of Market square, the water street is continued under the name of Merrimac street. Walking on in this direction, we have, on Brown's wharf, the iron foundry, and then pass the machine-shop of Mr. Lesley, the marble-yard of Mr. Ira Davis; and a little beyond the railroad bridge, the distillery of Mr. Caldwell. The first ship-yard we approach, is that of Messrs. Manson & Fernald; then comes a tannery, which business has been carried on on the same spot nearly ever since the "water-side" was settled. Soon appear the black-smith shops, the adjuncts to the larger ship-yards. Here we shall probably see several clippers on the stocks in various degrees of progress, and perhaps a steamboat building. Passing the several ship-yards, the road leads directly to the "Chain bridge," (the Essex Merrimac,) which crosses the river at little more than four miles above the gas factory.

Parallel with the water-side street, and at little less than a quarter of a mile from it, runs High street, where the "retired merchants most do congregate;" and at a central point on its line, on the westerly side, is situated the "Bartlett Mall," an enclosed piece of ground on the centre of which stands the County Court House, and at either end, a brick school-house. Back of the Mall lies a beautiful pond, surrounded with terrace walks, elevated from twenty to forty feet above its level. The general appearance of this vicinity is extremely pleasing and picturesque, the effect being heightened by an ancient burying hill lying just beyond its westerly limits. Between High and Water streets, the upper ship-yard and the gas factory, is contained the mass of the population of the city.

"The avenue known as High street, in this city, is remarkable for its location, extent, and beauty. Many portions of it not only afford an extensive view of the scenery for ten miles in the surrounding country, the full extent of the handsomest portion of the city, and the numerous private residences, gardens, lawns, and landscapes, but it commands a most beautiful marine panoramic view of our coast from the Isles of Shoals to Cape Ann, including Plum Island and the harbor. The location of this street is the admiration of strangers from all parts of the country. The many tasty dwellings located along its entire length, extending a distance of over six miles, from Parker river to Chain bridge, its wind-ing way through Belleville and Newbury, together with the beautiful foliage intermingled with the waving elms, the sturdy oak, and the majestic forest trees of a century's growth, arching their spreading branches in luxuriant grandeur, united with songs of the forest birds, and enlivened by fragrant aromatic breezes constantly sweeping their course from hundreds of highly cultivated exotic plants and gardens on either side, cooled by refreshing air from the ocean, contribute to make this avenue of our city a delightful promenade and fashionable retreat during the summer season. The number of shade trees on High street, embracing that portion within the limits of Newburyport, (from the 'Three Roads' on the north, to Marlborough street on the south,) is *eleven hundred and forty-seven.*"

After the coming of industrialization in the 1830's and 1840's, there was little change in the economic structure of Newburyport, in part because there was little significant change in the basic technological nature of local activities. Cotton manufacture was gradually replaced by shoemaking as the city's leading economic activity, but both were machine-dominated, factory activities. Economic growth, of course, continued to be the ideal here as elsewhere, and in the absence of dramatic changes small accretions of industry were sought and en-couraged. In this age of civic boosterism after the Civil War, many schemes were promoted by chambers of commerce and boards of trade in order to attract business. One was the publication of the type of promotional literature represented by John D. Parsons, *Newbury-port: Its Industries, Business Interests and Attractions* (Newburyport, 1887). What were the attractions which the city was supposed to have for industry? How did these differ from what was available a half century earlier? Is it either possible or useful to separate these ad-vantages into technological versus political?

Boosterism in a Period of Stability

JOHN D. PARSONS

Newburyport extends a cordial invitation to the wide-awake, active, energetic business man, wherever he may be, to come and locate within her borders, invest his capital here, and identify himself with the interests of the city. That the people are thoroughly in earnest in this matter is

evinced by the public meetings which have been held, the interest manifested, and the character and business standing of the men who are
identified with the movement. At a meeting held May 13 the following
circular was issued:

To Manufacturers and Capitalists:

At a meeting of the citizens of Newburyport held May 13, 1887, an executive committee, consisting of the Mayor, and Aldermen Richardson and Houston,
and Councilmen Besse, Gurney and McGlew, on the part of the city council,
and Messrs. E. P. Dodge, Edward P. Shaw, A. F. Ross, Frank W. Hale, W. A.
Stiles, Charles H. Goodwin and Albert Currier in behalf of the citizens at large,
was appointed to mature plans and take such steps as may be necessary to develop and extend the business and industrial enterprises of the city.

In the performance of this duty we desire to call your attention to the following facts: Land and rents are comparatively cheap here; labor can be had
in abundance; the cost of living is exceedingly moderate when compared with
that in any city of the same size in New England; the facilities for the transportation of merchandise by land or by water are unequalled; four national
banks with a combined capital of over $800,000 (including surplus) are pre-
pared to furnish reasonable accommodation to all worthy and laudable manufacturing enterprises.

The city has already three cotton mills, two silverware manufactories, one
wool and fur hat shop, eight shoe factories, one street railway car manufactory,
one brass and one iron foundry, two comb factories, besides other smaller industries, in successful operation.

The committee having the matter in charge desire to increase the number
of useful and profitable enterprises now established here, and therefore invite
manufacturers seeking a favorable location to make personal application to, or
communicate with, the undersigned.

                                                          Frank W. Hale, Secretary.

John J. Currier, Chairman.

At the same meeting a resolution was adopted as follows:

That although the laws of the State are such that exemption from taxation
is illegal, it is the judgment of this meeting that the assessors should adopt a
liberal policy in regard to the matter of taxing new industries.

The above is indicative of the feeling of the people on the subject,
and the new-comer may be assured of a cordial welcome.

Newburyport offers superior advantages both as a home, and as a
place for carrying on business. Its connections with the rest of the world,
by land and water, are unrivalled. The Boston & Maine Railroad, Eastern
division, passes through the city, and a branch line connects us with the
other cities and towns of Essex county that the Eastern does not touch.
A freight line, the City railroad, connects the wharves with the two
branches of the Boston & Maine, so that the union of water and land
commerce is perfect, and transfers are avoided. The special advantages

of a seaport town are so apparent as to need no enumeration. The one fact that the cost of coal is from fifty to eighty cents per ton less than it can be put down for in cities a few miles inland is of itself an unanswerable argument. The cheapness of freights by water, as compared with railroads, is a matter of common knowledge. The value of real estate in Newburyport is very low. Desirable locations for erecting buildings can be obtained at sums far less than the average in other New England cities, and the supply is large. The city is provided with all modern improvements. It has complete systems of gas and water works. The Newburyport Electric Light and Power Company light the principal streets with electricity, and are prepared to furnish buildings and factories with both light and power. A street railway connects the city with Amesbury and Salisbury, on the one side and Plum Island on the other. The fire department is a model of excellence, and the electric fire alarm system is used. . . .

It will be seen, therefore, that the manufacturing industry is no new thing in Newburyport, only its progress and growth were retarded by causes easy of explanation. For a hundred or more years it was secondary, while commerce was first. The latter had played such a part in the history of the old town, that when it began to decline and the signs of its dissolution approached, so far as Newburyport was concerned, the good people who had always looked upon commerce as the vital part of business life imagined that business of all sorts was "going to the dogs." Those who had money held on to it and were slow to embark in new enterprises. It was a transition period in two ways—transition from the commercial to the mechanical, from the days of hand work to those of machinery. The first was the greater to the people of Newburyport and they were long in getting accustomed to the change. Other cities did not have this to contend with, and there was no apparent halt in the transition from hand to machine. The change was almost imperceptible. Newburyport had the two to contend with, but finally conquered. Conservatism was forced to give way step by step to the spirit of the times, and with the infusion of a little new blood the victory was gained. Newburyport took its place among the manufacturing cities of New England, and it proposes to go ahead, hold all it has got and get all it can hold. Whether or not it has made any strides since entering on its new epoch, the following pages of this little book will show.

The manufacture of cotton goods in Newburyport dates from 1834, when the Essex steam mill was incorporated, with a capital of $100,000, divided into 200 shares. A wooden structure for manufacturing purposes was erected on the wharf property where the bakery of John Pearson & Son now stands. The company, particularly during the first years was not successful, and on the destruction of the building by fire, March 8, 1856, the corporation ceased to exist. Meanwhile, in 1837, the Wessacumcon Company was incorporated, with a capital stock of $350,000, divided into 350 shares. The principal projectors were Messrs. Ebenezer Moseley, Richard S. Spofford, John Chickering, Samuel T. DeFord, Philip Johnson, William Ashby, and T. M. Clark. Work was commenced in 1838, and two years later a second mill was erected and the name changed to Bartlet Steam Mills. In 1845 the shares of stock were made 700, reducing the par value from $1000 to $500. The mills employed 275 hands, operated 448 looms and 22,000 spindles, and made about 4,000,000 yards of cloth annually. March 18, 1882, the mills were totally destroyed by fire. A year or two previously the number of shares had been reduced three-fifths, and an assessment made. The latter years of the company were anything but prosperous ones to the shareholders, and it was voted by a large majority not to rebuild, the stockholders preferring to invest their insurance money in other channels.

Although within a half dozen years one corporation operating two mills has been wiped out of existence, yet those that remain have made such additions and improvements and have enlarged their capacity to such an extent that today the cotton industry is just about equal to what it was before the disastrous fire. For instance over a thousand hands are employed today against 1125 in 1881; 85,216 spindles and 1771 looms were operated then, 82,872 spindles and 1789 looms now.

All of the commentators on Newburyport thus far, from Cushing through Parsons, were speaking for and to the business and professional classes of the city. Furthermore, they were concerned more with growth than with welfare—that is, with the size of the economic pie rather than with the sharing of it. In the days before the steam mills came, about half the men in Newburyport were artisans, a quarter were merchants, and the remainder were laborers, sailors, etc. With the factories came the Irish and other immigrant groups, as well as formerly rural Americans looking for work in the cities. There was an unofficial assumption that among these workers those who were moral and hard-working would share in the prosperity which everyone wanted for their city. The obligation to better oneself was felt by all the classes—but was it equally possible for all classes? When Newburyport hummed again with economic activity, did all the people share it? Stephan Thernstrom made a careful investigation of the problem and discovered some of the dimensions of the life lived by nineteenth-century workmen in America. Many were drifters, failing to gain establishment in one city and then moving to another. For those who stayed, the native-born fared better than did the immigrant, and most found it easier to accumulate some property in the form of a family home than to move from one job category to a better one. Do you consider Thernstrom's questions to be an advance over the concerns of the previous writers? Did the kind of city described by Smith and hoped for by Parsons have any reality for the workers described by Thernstrom? Do you have any reason to believe that growth automatically benefits all the classes of a city? (Selection abridged by permission of the publishers from pp. 198–206 of Stephan Thernstrom, *Poverty and Progress: Social Mobility in a Nineteenth-Century City,* Harvard University Press, Copyright, 1964, by the President and Fellows of Harvard College.)

⊂≣ Who Knew Poverty, and Who Progress?

STEPHAN THERNSTROM

It is reasonable to anticipate that the level of opportunities in other American communities undergoing urbanization and industrialization in these years resembled the Newburyport pattern to at least some degree. . . . It is very clear, for example, that the marked volatility of the Newburyport population was not at all unusual, and it is likely that the selective character of the working class migration cycle revealed by the Newburyport evidence was common to other American cities of the age. The rate of population turnover in Rochester, New York, for 1849–1859 was even higher than in Newburyport, we know, and other studies indicate the extreme instability of the manual labor force in such communities as Biddeford, Maine, and Lowell, Holyoke, and Chicopee, Massachusetts. In Massachusetts, then the leading industrial state in the country, the State Census of 1885 showed that little more than a third of the state's population had been born in their city of current residence; even when native-born Americans alone were taken into account, the figure was less than 50 percent. Thus one striking characteristic of working class life in Newburyport—the fact that so many workmen were transients, drifting from city to city according to the dictates of the labor market—was a local reflection of a national phenomenon of major importance.

Nor does it seem likely that the remarkable property mobility achieved by the settled segment of the Newburyport laboring class was peculiar to this small community. It is difficult to believe that, on the whole, conditions in Newburyport were uniquely conducive to working class prosperity. Quite the contrary. After the boom of the 1840's the local economy was notably sluggish by comparison with cities like Portsmouth, New Bedford, Lynn, and New Haven. From the point of view of economic growth Newburyport represents anything but a favorable case, and any variations from the Newburyport pattern of working class property mobility turned up by future investigators may well lead to a more optimistic view of the lot of the workman in nineteenth century America. True, many scholars have ventured rather pessimistic judgments about working class savings and home ownership in particular cities, but since none of these writers have actually traced individuals, it would be well to be skeptical of their conclusions. The opinion that working class savings in Chicopee were small enough to melt away during periods of recession, for example, has been advanced on the basis of accurate knowledge of wage levels and dubious guesses as to "minimum" family budgets. The Newburyport evidence casts considerable doubt on such estimates of minimum consumption standards, and fragments of data from Lawrence and Holyoke in this period reinforce these doubts.

It is likely, too, that the patterns of occupational mobility for unskilled laborers and their sons in other nineteenth century industrial cities did not often differ radically from those described here. For the immigrant sector of the working class, at least, relevant evidence exists in the form of a Bureau of the Census monograph analyzing the occupational distribution of the nation's immigrant groups from 1850 to 1950. The fact that the unit of analysis was not individuals but groups whose composition was changing—the "born in Ireland" group of 1850 includes only a fraction of the "born in Ireland" group of 1880—precludes a detailed comparison with the Newburyport findings, but these national data tell a broadly similar story. In Newburyport and in the United States generally the Irish immigrants entered the labor market at the bottom and climbed slowly;

if a substantial minority of them advanced within the working class occupational world, only a select elite rose into nonmanual positions. The sons of these men found greater opportunities in business and white collar callings, but they too remained disproportionately concentrated in manual occupations; characteristically, though, the son of an Irish immigrant became a semiskilled factory operative rather than an unskilled day laborer, and signficant numbers of them entered the skilled trades.

The Newburyport evidence suggests that much the same pattern held for unskilled migrants from rural America, with the difference that the native-born laborer, somewhat less successful than the immigrant at accumulating property, tended to rise a little more rapidly in the occupational sphere. Whether or not these ethnic differences in types of social mobility were the rule in other American cities is a question which merits investigation. A recent analysis of data from the Census of 1930 has shown that in Detroit, Los Angeles, Chicago, and Philadelphia foreign-born residents were more likely to own their own homes than the sons of immigrants, who in turn had higher home ownership rates than the sons of native-born parents. This fits with the Newburyport findings, and suggests the interesting possibility that in these major twentieth century cities too some immigrant groups may have invested in real estate at the cost of other forms of social mobility.

It may seem outrageous to suggest that a study of the experiences of manual laborers in Newburyport can reveal anything of interest about the working class of Boston or New York. In their comprehensive survey, *Social Mobility in Industrial Society,* Lipset and Bendix confidently assert that "in a small city like Newburyport . . . which has not increased in population for a century, the chances for a lower-class individual to rise must necessarily be less than in a large city in which new positions of higher status are constantly being created." This judgment, however, rests on questionable premises. It is not at all clear that the process of urban growth in the nineteenth century produced a disproportionately greater expansion of high status positions in large cities than in smaller ones. Nor can one assume a simple relationship between the stability or instability of a city's total population and the fluidity of its occupational structure. Even in a community with a declining population, exceptionally high emigration of high status individuals could create a vacuum drawing large numbers of lower class persons up the occupational scale.

Some empirical evidence which suggests the inadequacy of the Lipset and Bendix formulation is supplied in [the] Table, which compares the Newburyport findings concerning the career patterns of ordinary laborers with the results of mobility inquiries dealing with Norristown, Pennsylvania, between 1910 and 1950, and with six major American cities in the 1940–1950 decade. The Norristown population in 1910 was more than twice that of Newburyport, and it continued to grow rapidly

Table. Occupational status attained by unskilled laborers over ten-year periods, selected cities, 1850–1950.

	Un-skilled	Semi-skilled	Skilled	Non-manual	Number in sample
Newburyport					
1850–1860	64%	16%	15%	5%	55
1860–1870	74	12	8	5	74
1870–1880	79	6	10	5	102
Norristown					
1910–1920	70	14	6	10	825
1920–1930	70	12	10	8	925
1930–1940	52	30	10	8	1180
1940–1950	51	26	12	12	1065
Chicago, Los Angeles, New Haven, Philadelphia, St. Paul, San Francisco					
1940–1950	65	26		9	—

for another quarter of a century. The chances for a man from the unskilled labor class to ascend the occupational scale should therefore have been greater in Norristown than in supposedly static Newburyport, and they should have been greater still in Chicago, Los Angeles, and the other burgeoning metropolises studied in the 1940–1950 period. This expectation is not borne out by the evidence. The mobility patterns of common laborers in these cities of radically different size and growth patterns display an impressive resemblance. Movement into a nonmanual occupation was somewhat rarer in Newburyport than in the other communities, it is true, but this probably indicates a trend toward greater opportunities in twentieth century American cities regardless of size and rate of growth. If size and rate of growth were as important as Lipset and Bendix claim, the six large cities should have shown higher rates of mobility than Norristown, while in fact their rates were slightly lower. A further difficulty with the Lipset-Bendix theory is that as the Norristown population leveled off (1930–1950), mobility from the bottom of the occupational ladder did not decline correspondingly; instead there was a marked increase in movement into semiskilled positions, and a slight increase in movement into skilled and nonmanual callings. . . .

The evidence is admittedly fragmentary, and it is obvious that information about mobility patterns in certain large cities in recent decades provides but a slender basis for speculation about the large cities of the nineteenth century. Nevertheless, these suggestive similarities in the rates of occupational advance of unskilled laborers and their sons in a variety of American cities are sufficient to call into question the assumption that differences in community size and rate of population growth result in very drastic intercity differences in the structure of opportunities. They suggest instead that the patterns of working class mobility found in Newburyport in the latter half of the nineteenth century were the result of forces which were operating in much the same way in cities throughout the entire society.

It is worth observing that, even if it could be shown that with respect to working class mobility opportunities the differences between the great metropolitan centers and Newburyport were differences of kind rather than simply of scale, Newburyport was perhaps more representative of the nineteenth century American city than New York. In 1850 only a seventh of the American urban population lived in cities as large as 250,000 and two thirds lived in cities of less than 50,000. Several giant cities grew up in the next five decades, but their growth was not at the expense of the small and medium-sized communities of the land. The importance of the glamorous big city in the social history of nineteenth century America should not be exaggerated; New York, Chicago, Philadelphia, Boston, and the others were part of the urban landscape, but only one part.

If the mobility prospects of working class families in the great metropolitan centers of the nineteenth century did diverge much from the Newburyport norm, it is likely that they differed not in being more favorable, as Lipset and Bendix hold, but in being less favorable. The moderate occupational advances and the impressive property accumulations of Newburyport's laborers were in part a result of the fact that pressures to migrate from the community operated selectively on men at this social level; the working class family which failed to advance itself significantly simply did not stay in Newburyport very long. Little is known about the stability of the working class populations of the large cities of this period, but it seems unlikely that after arriving in Boston or New York a completely destitute laboring family would ever return to a small community like Newburyport. For this reason, a city like Boston soon developed an "unskilled, resourceless, perennially unemployed Irish proletariat." Unlike the smaller community, the metropolis provided a haven for the demoralized and destitute, and they probably clustered there in disproportionately large numbers. In the big city slums, therefore, it is quite possible that a somewhat smaller proportion of laboring families became savings bank depositors and home owners. Nevertheless, it is doubtful that the difference was as dramatic as might be thought. The workmen of the large cities too climbed the occupational ladder in time, and left the slums for better neighborhoods; an exhaustive analysis of building permits issued in three of Boston's "streetcar suburbs" in the last quarter of the nineteenth century supplies some valuable hints on the gradual operation of this process in one major city. Nineteenth century

Boston indeed had its proletariat, but on the whole the composition of this group was constantly changing.

The greatest variations from the social patterns described in this book are likely to be found not in the great cities but in the small towns. Even in 1900 the United States still contained quiet villages and market towns in which the factory and the immigrant were unknown. The myth of Yankee City should be a vivid reminder of the dangers of inferring an absence of economic and social change from a superficial index like population stability; nevertheless it is true that there were American towns in this period which remained relatively static and traditional. Precisely what this means as to social mobility opportunities is unknown, since such a community has yet to be studied thoroughly. Many of these may have lacked a substantial working class and have been virtually unstratified; in preindustrial Newburyport and some other old New England towns, however, class lines appear to have been sharp and movement out of the lower class difficult. Further research will be necessary before we can speak about the openness of the class structure in communities of this type.

To emphasize that this study of one small New England city provides some insights into the position of the working class in other American communities of the period is not to claim that Newburyport was representative of the United States in any statistical sense. The point is rather that this was a community undergoing a process of transformation that eventually affected all American cities and towns to one or another degree, and that it is likely that there were important uniformities in the social consequences of urbanization and industralization in each of these communities.

During the 1930's a team of social scientists, led by W. Lloyd Warner, picked Newburyport for an intensive study of social structure in a typical American town. Calling it Yankee City, the resulting study ran to many volumes. It was weakened by an anti-historical bias which distorted changes in the past, but it presented an accurate picture of what the town was like at the time the study was made during the Depression. The following description was taken from the first volume of the series, W. Lloyd Warner and Paul S. Lunt, *The Social Life of a Modern Community* (New Haven, copyright © 1941 by Yale University Press). Giving themselves only a few pages for describing the town, in what terms do the authors choose to do it most effectively? Does anything about the town appear to be inconsistent with the picture painted a half century previously by Parsons? Is there a meaningful distinction between "stability" and "stagnation" in the condition of cities? How might we explain why so little had changed in so many years?

⊂⊇   A Picture of Yankee City

W. LLOYD WARNER and PAUL S. LUNT

Yankee City is situated on a harbor at the mouth of a large river in New England. The pilot of an airplane looking down some 10,000 feet might see the harbor as the dark hand of a giant with its five fingers reaching for the sea, and the river flowing through the brown land toward the white sandy shores as an arm extended straight back from the hand and then bending sharply some few miles from the sea. The streets of the town run along the banks of the river for a few miles up from the harbor until they almost reach the bend in the river.

In shape the town is a long thin rectangle which bends at each end. Near the center of the rectangle at the bank of the river is a square around which the business district is located. The residential area covers the two ends of the rectangle as they extend up and down the river. From the two ends of the town square a highway runs out along the water front for the full length of the town. This river street is paralleled, on the other long side of the rectangle, by another broad street which runs along a ridge of high ground from one end of the city to the other. In the center of the city the residential area projects beyond the outline of the rectangle for a few blocks, and a number of dwellings are found outside the rectangle at either end, but, generally speaking, the population is concentrated within the few blocks of streets between the river and the broad street which parallels it on the ridge. The town sits on high ground with a river on one side and flatlands on the other.

The two long avenues are connected by a large number of side streets which cross several short streets as they climb from the river to the summit of the hill. A highway, one of the more important motor roads connecting southern with northern New England, crosses the center of Yankee City and leaves it over a large bridge. A railway line parallels this highway and has a station in the town.

Along the river are a large number of wharves and shipyards which were once employed in the sea trade but which were abandoned when the town turned to manufacturing. Most of the factory sites are in and near the business district, but a few are situated in each arm of the rectangle. The residences tend to be larger and better kept on the Hill Street than on the River Street side of the town. There are six cemeteries in the community and one fairly large park and a few small ones.

Several smaller towns are situated in the surrounding countryside. Yankee City maintains its own economic life and is not a satellite community to a large city. It does, however, look to Boston as its metropolis, and movement to and from Boston by automobile and train is frequent. Some of its citizens look ultimately to New York, but none of them would admit it; a very few of them look to Europe for their social centers, and all of these admit it.

Yankee City has some 17,000 people. There are a few more women in its population than there are men. Slightly over 50 per cent of the population were born in or near Yankee City; 23.50 per cent were foreign-born; and the remainder were born elsewhere in the United States. The first impression one gains of the town is that it has a living tradition inherited from generations of Yankee forebears. Yankee City is "old Yankee" and proud of it.

About one fourth of the employable population are in the shoe industry. The other principal but smaller economic activities are silverware manufacturing, the building trades, transport, and electric shops. The clamming industry, the only remaining economic activity of the town which depends on the sea, employs about 1 per cent of those who work for a living.

The semiskilled workers constitute the largest group (46.19 per cent) in our occupational sample. The workers in the factories compose the great bulk of this group. Only 5.28 per cent are classifiable as unskilled. The professional, proprietary, and managerial group comprise a seventh of those economically occupied; wholesale and retail store managers and similar proprietors, 7.92 per cent; clerks and kindred workers, 14.90 per cent; and skilled workers, 11.37 per cent. When the unemployment study was made in 1933, 50.73 per cent of those who were employable had jobs at which they were working, 30.61 per cent were employed part-time, and 18.66 per cent were without work. A little over 13 per cent of the total population were recipients of relief.

According to ethnic affiliations, the Yankees comprised 53.80 per cent (9,030) of the 16,785 individuals represented in our study, and the nine other ethnic groups, 45.55 per cent (7,646). There were 3,943 Irish, 1,466 French Canadians, 397 Jews, 284 Italians, 677 Poles, 412 Greeks, 246 Armenians, and 141 Russians. The Negroes, with 80 individuals, constituted the smallest group in the population. The Irish are the oldest ethnic group in Yankee City, other than the Yankees, and the Jews next in order of age. The Russians, Poles, Greeks, and Armenians are comparatively recent migrants.

Yankee City is one of the oldest Yankee cities in the United States. It was founded early in 1600 and by shipbuilding, fishing, and sea trade grew into one of the most prominent of the colonial New England communities. It quickly became a city of several thousand inhabitants. After certain fluctuations in size it attained approximately its present population and has succeeded in maintaining but not in adding to it. At one time the town was of sufficient commercial importance to compete on equal terms with Boston in its trade activities. The histories of the state in which it is located tell of its importance politically and socially and of the role it played in the life of New England at a period of its greatest prosperity. While still an important shoe and silverware manufacturing center, Yankee City is no longer of the same comparative importance; with the general growth of population and industry throughout the United States, like many other New England communities it has not grown but maintained a stable population in a stable society.

The city's earlier farming and shipping industries have largely gone. They helped employ the early Irish immigrants, but with the appearance of the factory the Irish and new immigrant groups were recruited for less skilled jobs in the shoe, textile, and other industries. The older ethnic groups have moved into varying occupations, and some of them have succeeded in climbing to the top of the occupational ladder.

Economically and socially Yankee City is organized very much like other American industrial towns. Its business district is supported by the residential area which surrounds it, and the residential area is supported, at the base at least, by workers who are largely maintained by the wages and salaries of the factories. The town has a city government with a mayor and council; city officials, boards, and committees direct such activities as the school, police, and fire departments. The mayor, council, and school board are elected by the voters.

There are a number of grade schools, parochial and public, and one public high school. There are a large number of Protestant churches, the principal ones belonging to the Congregational, Presbyterian, Unitarian, Baptist, Methodist, and Episcopalian denominations. The two Catholic churches are staffed primarily by Irish and French-Canadian priests and nuns; the congregation of the largest Catholic church is Irish, and of the other, French-Canadian. The Jews have one synagogue in the community and the Russians and Greeks have remodeled a Protestant church into a Greek Orthodox house of worship. There are thousands of members of lodges, secret societies, and fraternities, and of organizations such as the Rotary, Kiwanis, and Chamber of Commerce.

Yankee City is an American town. Its people live a life whose values are in general as understandable to Middle Westerners as they are to men from the Pacific and Atlantic coasts. Specific differences are present; certain kinds of behavior are more definite and more highly developed than elsewhere in the United States, and other ways of life are not quite so heavily accented in Yankee City as in the South or in the West. But while it is important, for a full understanding of the community, to know these differences, it would be erroneous to emphasize them and to forget the fundamental similarity to other American towns.

Chapter
10: Slavery and Politics in 1860

⊂⊃ RALPH E. MANN, II

Negro slavery was the most divisive issue faced by citizens of the United States in the nineteenth century. Could a man morally hold another in bond because of his race? The spectrum of attitudes on the slavery question was enormous. Some thought the institution damned America to destruction; others saw it as the cornerstone of the highest civilization the world had known. Almost always accompanying this issue was its complement, the place of the black in American life. Almost all whites believed in the necessity of subordinating the black; the controversy over his role therefore had narrower limits than the argument over slavery. Should he have political rights, particularly suffrage, natural rights, usually defined as personal liberty, or limited legal rights within slavery? The inability of the nation to find a solution to the problem of slavery led to a civil war, with the loss of over 600,000 lives. The inability to agree on the Negro's place in society was the chief complicating factor preventing those who opposed slavery from taking a unified stand. The status of the Negro was also an important emotional factor in internal Northern politics, even when slavery was not at issue.

The last full-scale debate on these questions before the Civil War took place during the first session of the Thirty-sixth Congress, which met in the winter and spring of 1860. On February 29, 1860, William Seward of New York, in the course of an extended oration, drew a comparison between the free North and slave South. His statement and its rebuttals, from both North and South, offer a convenient focal point for the consideration of differing opinions on slavery and the potential status of the Negro.

The Thirty-sixth Congress first came to order on December 5, 1859, three days after John Brown had been hung for leading a raid on the federal arsenal at Harpers Ferry, Virginia. Sectional tensions were at a new height, for Brown's purpose had been to secure weapons to arm a slave insurrection which he hoped would ultimately destroy slavery in the South. Brown, a Northerner, was loosing the South's greatest nightmare, the slave revolt. The rapid canonization of Brown by an important element of the North's intellectual leadership made the South even more bitter and fearful.

The abolitionists had begun decades before as moral crusaders, hoping to convince slaveholders to free their slaves by appeals to their consciences and denunciations of their sins. The South had resisted these efforts by burning anti-slavery literature and sometimes threatening abolitionists with physical violence. The national political parties, fearing sectional disruptions that would result in electoral defeats, attempted to ignore slavery. Some abolitionists refused to attempt to work through a government tainted by slavery, and withdrew in disgust to construct, in theory, social and racial utopias. A few believed with Brown that slavery, being based on force, could only be ended through violence. The majority continued to try political means, either by forming anti-slavery parties or by influencing existing parties to take an anti-slavery stand. In 1860, the Republican party was the vehicle of those who wanted to destroy slavery by sanctions of the federal government.

The Southern senators, who saw Brown's raid as the logical culmination of the anti-slavery agitation in the North, demanded and obtained a Congressional investigation into its genesis and its Northern support. They obviously hoped to implicate the Republican party, which they identified with extreme abolitionism, in a plot to attack the South, thus discrediting the party nationally. The year 1860 was a presidential election year, and a victory for the Republicans, whose support was almost entirely Northern, would constitute the gravest direct threat yet to the slave South.

The Republicans were pledged to follow the Constitutional definition of states' rights and not to interfere with slavery where it already existed. But they were also committed to preventing the further expansion of slavery. Free soil and free labor were central to their ideology; the Republicans' stated goal was to further the interests of the common man by allowing him to work without the competition of slaveholders. The Republican constituency was the North's independent farmers and entrepreneurs; America's western territories were the obvious place for the continuing development of their kind of society. Therefore, the territories must be kept free of slavery. Complicating Republican free soil views were two other stances taken by party members. One group insisted that free soil meant the exclusion of all Negroes, slave or free, from the territories. They feared miscegenation and the loss of racial identity, and believed that Negroes fleeing slavery would become an economic burden on white settlers in free areas. Another group wanted to use the exclusion of slavery as an indirect means of attacking slavery in the South. "To restrict slavery within its present limits," said Horace Greeley, "is to secure its speedy and ultimate extinction."

The South, dominated politically by the Democratic party, and itself dominant within that party nationally, had obvious political reasons for opposing the Republicans. More important was a belief that Southerners shared with the radical wing of the Republicans, that slavery must expand in order to survive. Slave agriculture was wasteful and inefficient, and slaves were not considered capable of undertaking careful, scientific farming. Cotton and tobacco, the most important agricultural staples, both depleted the soil. The combination of crude farming and soil depletion meant that old lands rapidly lost their agricultural value. This loss generated a continual demand for virgin soil. In addition, the accepted mode of success in the South was to acquire land and slaves, and join the planter society. As new men and new generations rose, more land was needed if they were to follow the model set by those who already owned plantations. Finally, the prospect of a constricted slave society raised the specter of slave revolt and racial inundation caused by a concentration of more and more slaves in an economy that would be becoming less and less productive.

Such considerations, more than the hysteria over John Brown, led Southern senators to introduce resolutions which, if passed, would effectively neutralize the Republican platform. These resolutions would guarantee federal protection of existing slavery within the territories, would prevent the citizens of a territory from refusing entry to slaves, and would deny the right of citizens of any state to interfere with slavery anywhere else. The second provision had a wider target than the Republican party; it was intended also to damage an element within the Democratic party.

The central political ideal of many Northern Democrats was popular sovereignty, which gave the residents of a territory the opportunity to vote whether or not slavery would be admitted. Some men saw popular sovereignty as a fair means of settling sectional rivalries over territories; however, among its supporters, as among the believers in free soil, were those who believed the principle could be used to exclude the Negro. Popular sovereignty would force slaveholders into competition with free labor if they wished to win land for expansion, and potentially would expose the slaves to abolitionist sentiments. The South knew that slavery could flourish only where it enjoyed complete legal protection, and popular sovereignty would therefore operate to exclude slavery from the western territories. At one time popular sovereignty had been part of the Democratic party platform, but through Southern influence on the last two Democratic Presidents, Franklin Pierce and James Buchanan, and because the growth of the Republicans had cut into party strength in the North, Southern Democrats had been able to turn the party to the idea of nationwide protection of slave property. The resolutions were intended to make sure the Southern element continued to lead both the Democratic party and the national government.

Other conflicts between rival sections and rival ideologies marked the Thirty-sixth Congress. The South frustrated Northern interests by preventing an increase in tariff levels, and by withholding federal funds to be used for the improvement of navigation in the Great Lakes. A Homestead Act, dear to free-labor Republicans, which would help open western lands for settlement by individual farmers, was also thwarted by Southern efforts, as was an attempt to obtain funds for a railroad connecting the west coast with the midwest. Northerners, especially Republicans, thought these measures were vital to the nation's future prosperity; Southerners feared they would damage the South economically and dangerously increase the powers of the federal government.

These were the controversies that had created the atmosphere of tension in Congress when Seward triggered a political examination of slavery. Probably none of the men who rose successively to attack or defend slavery hoped to make converts to his position; the Senate was a theater where he performed for his constituents, declaiming on the most dangerous questions ever faced by the nation. All the actors were defining their political positions, taking stances they hoped the voters would endorse. The human importance of the question of slavery was often obscured. Each of the first three who spoke, William Seward of the Republicans, Stephen Douglas of the Northern Democrats, and Jefferson Davis of the Southern Democrats, was recognized as the leader and spokesman of his faction. Seward and Douglas were both convinced that they would be the presidential nominees of their respective parties in the upcoming election; Davis, too, probably entertained presidential hopes. Seward and Davis probably were mostly interested in solidifying support in their sections; Douglas was advancing a formula he hoped could be acceptable to both sections. Lyman Trumbull and Charles Sumner attempted to meet the arguments of Davis and Douglas, and also represented different sub-groups within the Republican party. According to these political leaders, what ought to be the condition of the Negro in America?

The speeches consider three answers to that question: slavery, freedom under various disabilities, and full equality. Only the most radical thinkers of the day would have argued that the words of the Declaration of Independence, "that all men are created equal," meant exactly what they said. This position was considered too advanced to be politically safe. The advocates of racial equality of course saw slavery as the worst of abominations, a practice that kept America in a state of barbarism. America could never fulfill its destiny until its black population was given full social and political rights. Since their position was

radical to the point of excluding them from national politics, they felt no
necessity to moderate their condemnations of slavery, or to try to placate
either the South or the nation's voters. Their role was simply to denounce sin.

The majority of Northerners had first come to condemn slavery because it deprived the Negro of his natural right to liberty; the abolitionists
had then convinced them that it was a cruel and inhumane institution.
They further believed, however, that the Negro's inherent inferiority
denied him the rights of citizenship, particularly the vote. There was
some tendency for men of this viewpoint to emphasize the democratic
right of all white men to participate in government; their leaders believed
themselves the representatives of the common man, the "real" American.
The importance they attached to government by and for white men
could lead some, even of those who agreed that slavery was in the
abstract wrong, to indifference to it in practice.

Over against both these positions stood the argument that slavery
was a positive good. The South extolled the aristocratic society it had
founded on the institution of slavery, and presented Biblical and "scientific" evidence in its own support. The South's most important argument,
however, held that the black's abilities limited him to the role of slave,
and that he was happiest in bondage. Slavery was, therefore, a boon
to both races. A romantic description of Southern social relations, contrasting the condition of the slave favorably with that of the free Negro
in the North or in Africa, was often used to illustrate this point. Racial
equality was unthinkable to men who held these views, and even a little
freedom a great wrong to the black.

These speeches are of course the products of white politicians discussing the future of black people. The Negro himself had no part in the
political debates that concerned him; in 1860, public opinion would
permit no black officeholders, and there were only five states which
permitted Negroes even to vote. Frederick Douglass' newspaper, in
which he editorially condemned Seward for concessions to the South in
his speech and enthusiastically approved Sumner's sentiments, represented the extreme limit of black political influence, and Douglass reached
only a small audience. While Seward and Stephen Douglas jockeyed for
the presidency, the most Frederick Douglass could do was participate in
a losing campaign for Negro suffrage in New York state.

Even though the ultimate purpose of political parties was and is to
win elections and control government in order to implement their policies,
neither the Republicans nor the Southern Democrats were willing to
give up enough of their diametrically opposed principles to allow the
machinery of the federal government to continue to operate. Their
beliefs, especially concerning slavery, were not to be compromised. The
Southern Democrats failed to carry their anti-Republican resolutions, and

they fielded a rival Democratic candidate, John Breckinridge, rather than allow a popular sovereignty man, Stephen Douglas, to represent the party. Following the Republican victory of 1860, the second session of the Thirty-sixth Congress saw Southern senators give farewell speeches and return to their home states to play their parts in the Confederacy. Slavery had divided the Union.

The five documents that follow, all of them taken from the Senate debate, supply different perspectives on slavery, race, and national politics in 1860. The first four were given in sequence, all on February 29, 1860. Each speaker is responding directly to the statements made that day; only the first, Seward's, is a carefully prepared speech. The last selection, Charles Sumner's, was delivered several months later, on June 4, and included both a direct answer to Southern views expressed in the other selections, and a formal statement as to the nature of slavery. Several of the most important themes of the sectional debate are included in these selections. The range of convictions here expressed demonstrates the painful division between sections and races and the impossibility of reaching an acceptable compromise on slavery, and indicates how this debate could lead to war. John J. Crittenden of Kentucky, after the last attempt at compromise failed, despairingly cried out, ". . . the country trusted to our hands is going to ruin. . . . We see the danger, we acknowledge our duty; and yet with all this before us, we are acknowledging before the world that we can do nothing. . . ."

William H. Seward (1801–1872) was the best-known Republican politician. He had long been dominant in New York state politics as a Whig and had been one of the most important early converts to the Republican party. First elected to the Senate in 1848, he had taken advanced stands against slavery and against compromise with the South. He had argued that there was a "higher law" than the Constitution that prohibited slavery, and that the South's favorite institution was bringing "an irrepressible conflict" between the sections. Fearing that his identification as a radical would deny him his party's presidential nomination, Seward made his speech as conciliatory as he could without denying his principles. Its purpose was to make him acceptable as a candidate to the more conservative Republicans. How does Seward obscure his basically radical opposition to slavery? How does he try to bring the average man to his support? The speech is excerpted from the *Congressional Globe* (36th Cong., 1st Sess., February 29, 1860), pp. 910, 912.

⊆ On Slavery

WILLIAM H. SEWARD

It will be an everflowing source of shame, as well as of sorrow, if we, thirty millions—Europeans by extraction, Americans by birth or discipline, and Christians in faith, and meaning to be such in practice—cannot so combine prudence with humanity, in our conduct concerning the one disturbing subject of slavery, as not only to preserve our unequaled institutions of freedom, but also to enjoy their benefits wtih contentment and harmony.

Wherever a guiltless slave exists, be he Caucasian, American, Malayan, or African, he is the subject of two distinct and opposite ideas—one that he is wrongly, the other that he is rightly a slave. The balance of numbers on either side, however great, never completely extinguishes this difference of opinion, for there are always some defenders of slavery outside, even if there are none inside of a free state, while also there are always outside, if there are not inside, of every slave state, many who assert with Milton, that "no man who knows aught can be so stupid to deny that all men naturally were born free, being the image and resemblance of God himself, and were by privilege above all the creatures, born to command and not to obey." It often, perhaps generally happens, however, that in considering the subject of slavery, society seems to overlook the natural right, or personal interest of the slave himself, and to act exclusively for the welfare of the citizen. But this fact does not materially affect ultimate results, for the elementary question of the rightfulness or wrongfulness of slavery inheres in every form that discussion concerning it assumes. What is just to one class of men can never be injurious to any other; and what is unjust to any condition of persons in a State, is necessarily injurious in some degree to the whole community. An economical question early arises out of the subject of slavery—labor either of freemen or of slaves is the cardinal necessity of society. Some States choose the one kind, some the other. Hence two municipal systems widely different arise. The slave State strikes down and affects to extinguish the personality of the laborer, not only as a member of the political body, but also as a parent, husband, child, neighbor, or friend. He thus becomes, in a political view, merely property without moral capacity, and without domestic, moral, and social relations, duties, rights, and remedies—a chattel, an object of bargain, sale, gift, inheritance, or theft. His earnings are compensated and his wrongs atoned, not to himself, but to his owner. The State protects not the slave as a man, but the capital of another man, which he represents. On the other hand, the State which rejects slavery encourages and animates and invigorates the laborer by maintaining and developing his natural personality in all the rights and faculties of manhood, and generally with the privileges of citizenship. In the one case capital invested in slaves becomes a great political force, while in the other labor thus elevated and enfranchised, becomes the dominating political power. It thus happens that we may, for convenience sake, and not inaccurately, call slave States capital States, and free States labor States.

So soon as a State feels the impulses of commerce or enterprise or ambition, its citizens begin to study the effects of these systems of capital and labor respectively on its intelligence, its virtue, its tranquillity, its integrity or unity, its defense, its prosperity, its liberty, its happness, its aggrandizement, and its fame. In other words, the great question arises, whether slavery is a moral, social, and political good, or a moral, social, and political evil? This is the slavery question at home. But there is a mutual bond of amity and brotherhood between man and man throughout the world. Nations examine freely the political systems of each other, and of all preceding times, and accordingly as they approve or disapprove of the two systems of capital and labor respectively, they sanction and prosecute, or condemn and prohibit commerce in men. Thus, in one way or in another, the slavery question which so many among us, who are more willing to rule than patient in studying the conditions of society, think is a merely accidental or unnecessary question that might and ought to be settled and dismissed at once, is, on the contrary, a world-wide and enduring subject of political consideration and civil administration. Men, states, and nations entertain it, not voluntarily, but because the progress of society continually brings it into their way. They

divide upon it, not perversely, but because owing to differences of constitution, condition, or circumstances, they cannot agree.

The fathers of the Republic encountered it. They even adjusted it
so that it might have given us much less than our present disquiet, had
not circumstances afterwards occurred which they, wise as they were,
had not clearly foreseen. Although they had inherited, yet they generally
condemned the practice of slavery and hoped for its discontinuance.
They expressed this when they asserted in the Declaration of Independence, as a fundamental principle of American society, that all men
are created equal, and have inalienable rights to life, liberty, and the
pursuit of happiness. Each State, however, reserved to itself exclusive
political power over the subject of slavery within its own borders. . . .

Mr. President, did ever the annals of any Government show a more
rapid or more complete departure from the wisdom and virtue of its
founders? Did ever the Government of a great empire, founded on the
rights of human labor, slide away so fast and so far, and moor itself
so tenaciously on the basis of capital, and that capital invested in laboring
men? Did ever a free representative Legislature, invested with powers
so great, and with the guardianship of rights so important, of trusts so
sacred, of interests so precious, and of hopes at once so noble and so
comprehensive, surrender and renounce them all so unnecessarily, so
unwisely, so fatally, and so ingloriously? If it be true, as every instinct
of our nature, and every precept of political experience teaches us, that

> Ill fares the land, to hastening ills a prey,
> Where wealth accumulates, and men decay,

then where in Ireland, in Italy, in Poland, or in Hungary, has any ruler
prepared for a generous and confiding people disappointments, disasters,
and calamities equal to those which the Government of the United States
holds now suspended over so large a portion of the continent of North
America?

Citizens of the United States, in the spirit of this policy, subverted the
free Republic of Nicaragua,[1] and opened it to slavery and the African
slave trade, and held it in that condition waiting annexation to the United
States, until its sovereignty was restored by a combination of sister
Republics exposed to the same danger, and apprehensive of similar subversion. Other citizens reopened the foreign slave trade in violation of
our laws and treaties; and, after a suspension of that shameful traffic for
fifty years, savage Africans have been once more landed on our shores
and distributed, unreclaimed and with impunity, among our plantations.

[1] William Walker, a Southern-born adventurer, had seized control of the Nica-
raguan government. He had embraced slavery in the hopes of winning support from
Southerners in the United States government for his policy.

For this policy, so far as the Government has sanctioned it, the Democratic party avows itself responsible. Everywhere complaint against it is denounced, and its opponents proscribed. When Kansas was writhing under the wounds of incipient, servile war, because of her resistance, the Democratic press deridingly said, "let her bleed." Official integrity has been cause for rebuke and punishment, when it resisted frauds designed to promote the extension of slavery. Throughout the whole Republic there is not one known dissenter from that policy remaining in place, if within reach of the executive arm. Nor over the face of the whole world is there to be found one representative of our country who is not an apologist of the extension of slavery. . . .

We have loved not freedom so much less, but the Union of our country so much more. We have been made to believe, from time to time, that, in a crisis, both of these precious institutions could not be saved together, and therefore we have, from time to time, surrendered safeguards of freedom to propitiate the loyalty of capital and stay its hands from doing violence to the Union. The true state of the case, however, ought not to be a mystery to ourselves. Prescience, indeed, is not given to statesmen; but we are without excuse when we fail to apprehend the logic of current events. Let parties, or the Government, choose or do what they may, the people of the United States do not prefer the wealth of the few to the liberty of the many, capital to labor, African slaves to white freemen, in the national Territories and in future States. That question has never been distinctly recognized or acted on by them. The Republican party embodies the popular protest and reaction against a policy which has been fastened upon the nation by surprise, and which its reason and conscience, concurring with the reason and conscience of mankind, condemn. . . .

Stephen A. Douglas (1813–1861) was the accepted leader of the popular sovereignty wing of the Democratic party. Rising to prominence in Illinois politics as a vigorous expansionist, he had accomplished his greatest congressional service as chairman of the Senate territorial committee. He was an advocate of sectional compromise, and had managed the passage of the Compromise of 1850, which had temporarily lessened sectional tensions by the means of popular sovereignty. He had been a candidate for the Democratic presidential nomination in 1852 and 1856 and almost certainly would have been the nominee in 1860, except that his stand for popular sovereignty was unacceptable to the Southern Democrats. He had already lost support in the North over his Kansas-Nebraska bill, which had introduced popular sovereignty into an area previously closed to slavery. He had said that he did not care if slavery was voted up or down, and his speech was intended to make Seward, his chief rival, seem too radical for the common voter. What is his view of the Negro's place in politics and society? How does he attempt to use the race issue against Seward? The speech is taken from the *Congressional Globe* (36th Cong., 1st Sess., February 29, 1860), pp. 914–15.

Speech Before the Thirty-sixth Congress

STEPHEN A. DOUGLAS

But, sir, the whole argument of that Senator [Seward] goes far beyond the question of slavery, even in the Territories. His entire argument rests on the assumption that the negro and the white man were equal by Divine law, and hence that all laws and constitutions and governments in violation of the principle of negro equality are in violation of the law of God. That is the basis upon which his speech rests. He quotes the Declaration of Independence to show that the fathers of the Revolution understood that the negro was placed on an equality with the white man, by quoting the clause, "we hold these truths to be self-evident, that all men are created equal, and are endowed by their Creator with certain inalienable rights, among which are life, liberty, and the pursuit of happiness." Sir, the doctrine of that Senator and of his party is—and I have had to meet it for four years—that the Declaration of Independence intended to recognize the negro and the white man as equals under the Divine law, and hence that all the provisions of the Constitution of the United States which recognize slavery are in violation of the Divine law. In other words, it is an argument against the Constitution of the United States upon the ground that it is contrary to the law of God. The Senator from New York has long held that doctrine. The

Senator from New York has often proclaimed to the world, that the Constitution of the United States was in violation of the Divine law, and that Senator will not contradict the statement. I have an extract from one of his speeches now before me, in which that proposition is distinctly put forth. In a speech made in the State of Ohio, in 1848, he said:

Slavery is the sin of not some of the States only, but of them all; of not one nationality, but of all nations. It perverted and corrupted the moral sense of mankind deeply and universally, and this perversion became a universal habit. Habits of thought become fixed principles. No American State has yet delivered itself entirely from these habits. We, in New York, are guilty of slavery still by withholding the right of suffrage from the race we have emancipated. You, in Ohio, are guilty in the same way by a system of black laws still more aristocratic and odious. It is written in the Constitution of the United States that five slaves shall count equal to three freemen as a basis of representation; and it is written, also, in violation of Divine law, that we shall surrender the fugitive slave who takes refuge at our fireside from his relentless pursuer.

There you find his doctrine clearly laid down, that the Constitution of the United States is in violation of the Divine law, and, therefore, is not to be obeyed. You find the declaration that the clause relating to fugitive slaves, being in violation of the Divine law, is not binding on mankind. This has been the doctrine of the Senator from New York for years. I have not heard it in the Senate to-day for the first time. I have met in my own State, for the last ten years, this same doctrine, that the Declaration of Independence recognized the negro and the white man as equal; that the negro and white man are equals by Divine law, and that every provision of our Constitution and laws which establishes inequality between the negro and the white man, is void, because contrary to the law of God.

The Senator from New York says, in the very speech from which I have quoted, that New York is yet a slave State. Why? Not that she has a slave within her limits, but because the constitution of New York does not allow a negro to vote on an equality with a white man. For that reason he says New York is still a slave State; for that reason every other State that discriminates between the negro and the white man is a slave State, leaving but a very few States in the Union that are free from his objection. Yet, notwithstanding the Senator is committed to these doctrines, notwithstanding the leading men of his party are committed to them, he argues that they have been accused of being in favor of negro equality, and says the tendency of their doctrine is the equality of the white man. He introduces the objection, and fails to answer it. He states the proposition and dodges it, to leave the inference that he does not indorse it. Sir, I desire to see these gentlemen carry out their principles to their logical conclusion. If they will persist in the declaration that the negro is made the equal of the white man, and that any inequality is in violation of the Divine law, then let them carry it out in their legislation by conferring on the negroes all the rights of citizenship the same as on white men. For one, I never held to any such doctrine. I hold that the Declaration of Independence was only referring to the white man—to the governing race of this country, who were in conflict with Great Britain, and had no reference to the negro race at all, when it declared that all men were created equal. Sir, if the signers of that Declaration had understood the instrument then as the Senator from New York now construes it, were they not bound on that day, at that very hour, to emancipate all their slaves? If Mr. Jefferson had meant that his negro slaves were created by the Almighty his equals, was he not bound to emancipate the slaves on the very day that he signed his name to the Declaration of Independence? Yet no one of the signers of that Declaration emancipated his slaves. No one of the States on whose behalf the Declaration was signed, emancipated its slaves until after the Revolution was over. Every one of the original colonies, every one of the thirteen original States, sanctioned and legalized slavery until after the Revolution was closed. These facts show conclusively that the Declaration of Independence was never intended to bear the construction placed upon it by the Senator from New York, and by that enormous tribe of lecturers that go through the country delivering lectures in country schoolhouses and basements of churches to Abolitionists, in order to teach the children that the Almighty has put his seal of condemnation upon any inequality between the white man and the negro.

Mr. President, I am free to say here—what I have said over and over again at home—that, in my opinion, this Government was made by white men, on the white basis, for the benefit of white men and their posterity forever, and should be administered by white men, and by none other whatsoever. . . .

Mr. President, I am in favor of throwing the Territories open to all the white men, and all the negroes, too, that choose to go, and then allow the white men to institute the government and govern the Territory. I would not let one of the negroes, free or slave, either vote or hold office anywhere, where I had the right, under the Constitution, to prevent it. I am in favor of each State and each Territory of this Union taking care of its own negroes, free or slave. If they want slavery, let them have it; if they desire to prohibit slavery, let them do it; it is their business, not mine. We in Illinois tried slavery while we were a Territory, and found it was not profitable; and hence we turned philanthropists and abolished it, just as our British friends across the ocean did. They established slavery in all their colonies, and when they found they could not make any more money out of it, abolished it. I hold that the question of slavery is one of political economy, governed by the laws of climate, soil, productions, and self-interest, and not by mere statutory provision.

I repudiate the doctrine, that because free institutions may be best in one climate, they are, necessarily, the best everywhere; or that because slavery may be indispensable in one locality, therefore it is desirable everywhere. I hold that a wise statesman will always adapt his legislation to the wants, interests, condition, and necessities of the people to be governed by it. One people will bear different institutions from another. One climate demands different institutions from another. I repeat, then, what I have often had occasion to say, that I do not think uniformity is either possible or desirable. I can see no two States precisely alike in their domestic institutions in this Union. Our system rests on the supposition that each State has something in her condition or climate, or her circumstances, requiring laws and institutions different from every other State of the Union. . . .

Jefferson Davis (1808–1889) of Mississippi was probably the leading exponent of the Southern cause in the Senate. He had been a planter and a soldier, and had served with distinction in the Mexican War. He had become important in Democratic national politics and had been very influential in the formation of the policies of both Pierce and Buchanan. He had been a successful Secretary of War under Franklin Pierce. In 1860 he had outlined the South's demands, emphasizing the necessity of guaranteed safety for slave property in the territories if the South was to remain in the Union. In these last stages of the sectional crisis, Davis was considered a Southern moderate because he resisted calls for immediate secession. In this speech he answers Seward with a defense of Southern civilization and the effects of the institution of slavery. In what ways does he claim slavery to be beneficial? How does he defend the South against charges of cruelty to the slaves? This speech is condensed from the *Congressional Globe* (36th Cong., 1st Sess., February 29, 1860), pp. 917–18.

⊂⊒   A Defense of Southern Civilization

JEFFERSON DAVIS

There is nothing, Mr. President, which has led men to greater confusion of ideas than this term of "free States" and "slave States;" and I trusted that the Senator [Seward], with his discriminating and logical mind, was going to give us something tangible, instead of dealing in a phrase never applicable. He applied another; but what was his phrase? "Capital States" and "labor States." And where is the State in which nobody labors? The fallacy upon which the Senator hung adjective after adjective was, that all the labor of the southern States was performed by negroes. Did he not know that the negroes formed but a small part of the people of the southern States? Did he suppose nobody labored but a negro, there? If so, he was less informed than I had previously believed him to be. Negro slavery exists in the South, and by the existence of negro slavery, the white man is raised to the dignity of a freeman and an equal. Nowhere else will you find every white man superior to menial service. Nowhere else will you find every white man recognized so far as an equal as never to be excluded from any man's house or any man's table. Your own menial who blacks your boots, drives your carriage, who wears your livery, and is your own in every sense of the word, is not your equal; and such is society wherever negro slavery is not the substratum on which the white race is elevated to its true dignity. We, however, have no theory to press upon you; we leave you to such institutions as you may prefer; but when you assail ours, we come to the vindication of our institutions by showing you that all your phrases are false; that we are the freemen. With us, and with us alone, as I believe, the white man attains to his true dignity in the Government. So much for the great fallacy on which the Senator's argument hangs, that the labor of the South is all negro labor, and that the white man must there be degraded if he labors; or that we have no laboring white men. I do not know which is his opinion; one of the two. The Senator has himself resided in a southern State, and therefore I say I believed him to be better informed before he spoke. I must suppose him to be as ignorant as his speech would indicate. No man, however, who has seen any portion of southern society, can entertain any such opinion as that which he presents; and it is in order that the statement he has made may not go out to deceive those less informed than himself, that I offer at this time the correction. . . .

But the Senator in his zeal depicts the negro slave of the South as a human being reduced to the condition of a mere chattel. Is it possible that the Senator did not know that the negro slave in every southern State was still a person, protected by all the laws which punish crime in other persons? Could the Senator have failed to know that no master could take the life of or maim his slave without being held responsible under the criminal laws of any southern State, and held to a responsibility as rigid as though that negro had been a white man? How, then, is it asserted that these are not persons in the eye of the law, not protected by the law as persons . . . ?

Several southern Senators around have spoken to me to the effect that in each of their States the protection is secured, and a suit may be instituted at common law for assault and battery, to protect a negro as well as a white man. The condition of slavery with us is, in a word, Mr. President, nothing but the form of civil government instituted for a class of people not fit to govern themselves. It is exactly what in every State exists in some form or other. It is just that kind of control which is extended in every northern State over its convicts, its lunatics, its minors, its apprentices. It is but a form of civil government for those who by their nature are not fit to govern themselves. We recognize the fact of the inferiority stamped upon that race of men by the Creator, and from the cradle to the grave, our Government, as a civil institution, marks that inferiority. In their subject and dependent state, they are not the objects of cruelty as they would be if left to the commission of crime, for which they should be incarcerated in penitentiaries and work-houses, and put under hired overseers, having no interest in them and no relation to them, no affiliation, growing out of the associations of childhood and the tender care of age. Is there nothing of the balm needed in the Senator's own State, that he must needs go abroad to seek objects for his charity and philanthropy? What will he say of those masses in New York now memorializing for something very like an agrarian law? What will he say to the throngs of beggars who crowd the streets of this great commercial emporium? What will he say to the multitudes collected in the penitentiaries and prisons of his own State? I seek not, sir, to inquire into the policy and propriety of the institutions of other States; I assume not to judge of their fitness; it belongs to the community to judge, and I know not under what difficulties they may have been driven to what I cannot approve; but never, sir, in all my life, have I seen anything that so appealed to every feeling of humanity and manliness, as the suffering of the poor children imprisoned in your juvenile penitentiaries—imprisoned before they were old enough to know the nature of crime—there held to such punishment as we never inflict save upon those of mature years. I arraign you not for this; I know not what your crowded population and increasing wants may demand; I know not how far it may be the necessary result of crime which follows in the footsteps of misery; I know not how far the parents have become degraded, and how far the children have become outcast, and how far it may have devolved on the State to take charge of them; but, I thank my God, that in the state of society where I reside, we have no scenes so revolting as these.

Why then not address yourselves to the evils which you have at home? Why not confine your inquiries to the remedial measures which will relieve the suffering of and stop the progress of crime among your own people? Very intent in looking into the distance for the mote in your brother's eye, is it to be wondered that we turn back and point to the beam in your own?

Lyman Trumbull (1813–1896) had made a name in Illinois politics as a Democrat, serving as Illinois Supreme Court Justice and as Congressman, but had broken with the party over Douglas' Kansas-Nebraska bill. He had been elected to the Senate as an anti-slavery Democrat when Abraham Lincoln, the Whig candidate, threw his support to Trumbull to prevent the election of a pro-slavery Democrat. Trumbull and Lincoln both soon joined the new Republican party. In the Senate, Trumbull was a fierce opponent of Douglas and a leading speaker for the anti-slavery forces. It was his purpose here to refute Douglas' charges against the Republican party, and to define his interpretation of the Negro's rights. What limitations does he put on these rights? How does he agree and disagree with Douglas on the Negro's place? This speech is condensed from the *Congressional Globe* (36th Cong., 1st Sess., February 29, 1860), pp. 918, 921.

⊂⊇ The Negro's Place

LYMAN TRUMBULL

Now, sir, I know that my colleague [Douglas] has battled against negro equality in Illinois, and he may have battled, for aught I know, against the idea that the Constitution conflicted with the Divine law, and was therefore void; but if he has so battled, he has battled Don Quixot-like, against windmills rather than realities. He is very much in the habit of setting up a principle and then knocking it down, talking about negro equality as if somebody was for it, and then assailing it. Now, sir, I am glad to have my colleague face to face, where I can put it to him and tell him he never heard such a declaration of principles from the Republican party of Illinois, nor the Republican party of the Union. I tell him now in his face, and to his teeth, that when he charges upon the Republican party of Illinois, or of the country, that it has advocated negro equality, he charges that which is wholly untrue, wholly without foundation, so far as the Republican party is concerned.

But, sir, he says that we believe in the Declaration of Independence. I do. I do believe in the Declaration of Independence; and has my colleague yet to learn the distinction between a natural right and a right in organized society; the distinction between the gift of God and the gift of man? I do believe in the Declaration of Independence, and so does the Republican party believe in it, that all men were endowed by their Creator with certain inalienable rights. I do believe that all men were born with the same natural rights; and that is what the Declaration of Independence declares; that is what, if he has listened to the Republicans in Illinois, he has heard many a time enunciated as the doctrine of the Republican party, that all men were created equal, not made equal by human society, by human laws. We know that the very idea of government creates an inequality among men. To have government, you must have rules and regulations; you must have magistrates, those who command, and those who obey; and, of course, there is an inequality. But, sir, does that militate against the God-given right that all were created equal? How were they created, if not equal? Was there any human government from God? Destroy all human government; wipe out all organized society; take man as he came from the hands of his Maker, and tell me, if you please, what superior authority one has over another? If one has superior authority over another, how did he get it before government was organized?

The object of inserting the words in the Declaration of Independence has been proclaimed a thousand times. It was this: our ancestors were a people fleeing from the tyranny and the despotisms of the Old World; escaping from countries where the idea prevailed that one man had a Divine right to rule over another; and they meant, when they were proceeding to form a government, as the first thing they did, to write it down in that immortal Declaration, that their posterity in all time might see it; that they might look to it as the polar star by which they should ever be guided in their future legislation, and should never forget it— the great natural right of all men to life, liberty, and happiness. Now, keeping that in view, with your eye fixed upon that star of the equal rights of all, go on and frame your government, infringing as little as possible upon that great natural right. That you must infringe somewhat we know; but we repudiate and trample under foot, for ourselves and forever, the idea that one man is born with a right over another. That is what the Declaration of Independence meant, and no such thing as that in organized society we must have perfect equality—an impossibility; and the Republican party in Illinois has contended for no such thing, as its principles, proclaimed in its platform, will show. . . .

He has asked here to-day, whether we claim that negroes are created by the Almighty with the same natural rights as the white man? I answer him, that I do claim it. Well, then, said he, does not the Declaration of Independence declare that they are endowed with certain inalienable rights, among which are life, liberty, and the pursuit of happiness; and if you deny any of these rights, do you not violate the law of God? That is the way my colleague put the question. Now let me answer him. I will apply his own mode of reasoning to white men, and see if his construction does not violate the laws of God equally with mine.

He claims the Declaration of Independence applies to white men. If it applies to white men, then white men are endowed by their Creator with certain inalienable rights, among which are life, liberty, and the pursuit of happiness. What right has he to take the life or liberty of a white man? Is he opposed to the criminal code of the State of Illinois, which subjects the horse thief to imprisonment in the penitentiary, and takes away his inalienable right to liberty? He says this inalienable right is secured to him, being a white man, by the great Creator; and yet he is for taking it away, I presume. If the Declaration of Independence applies to white men, I ask him, by virtue of what authority it is that he violates the law of God, and sends the horse thief to the penitentiary, or the murderer to the gallows? Ah! sir, he does it because the exigencies of society require it. We deny to the negro equal political and civil rights because the exigencies of society require it. And if he can press the argument upon me, that I have no right to deny an inalienable right to a negro, then I say he has no right to deny an inalienable right to a white man, and he must abolish the criminal code, and let murderers and robbers, thieves and perjurers, go unwhipped of justice through the land. This shows the utter fallacy of his attempt to make Republicans the advocates of negro equality, because they say all men are created equal, and endowed with certain inalienable rights.

Charles Sumner (1811–1874) was the radical Republicans' most outspoken leader. A thorough abolitionist, he had involved himself in several other reform crusades. He had helped form the Republican party in Massachusetts and had been one of the first radical antislavery men elected to the Senate. Sumner was notorious for violent verbal attacks on the South and Southerners, as well as on slavery. After one such oration, in 1856, he had been publicly caned by a Representative from South Carolina. Broken in health, Sumner undertook lengthy trips to Europe and had consulted many doctors before he felt able to return to the Senate. Slightly over four years had passed when, on June 4, 1860, Sumner again addressed the Senate on the question of slavery. He had lost none of his old ardor or vindictiveness. Although the Republicans had recently nominated Lincoln for President and were running him on a moderate platform, Sumner refused to compromise his radical position. How does he counter Davis' description of the South? What does he say about racial equality? This speech is excerpted from "The Barbarism of Slavery" in *Charles Sumner's Complete Works* (Boston, 1900), pp. 127–32, 162–63, 220–21.

⊂⊋ The Barbarism of Slavery

CHARLES SUMNER

Barbarous in origin, barbarous in law, barbarous in all its pretensions, barbarous in the instruments it employs, barbarous in consequences, barbarous in spirit, barbarous wherever it shows itself, Slavery must breed Barbarians, while it develops everywhere, alike in the individual and the society to which he belongs, the essential elements of Barbarism. In this character it is conspicuous before the world. . . .

I know well the difficulty of this discussion, involved in the humiliating truth with which I begin. Senators, on former occasions, revealing their sensitiveness, have even protested against comparison between what were called "two civilizations,"—meaning the two social systems produced respectively by Freedom and Slavery. The sensibility and the protest are not unnatural, though mistaken. "Two civilizations!" Sir, in this nineteenth century of Christian light there can be but one Civilization, and this is where Freedom prevails. Between Slavery and Civilization there is essential incompatibility. If you are for the one, you cannot be for the other; and just in proportion to the embrace of Slavery is the divorce from Civilization. As cold is but the absence of heat, and darkness but the absence of light, so is Slavery but the absence of justice and humanity, without which Civilization is impossible. That slave-masters should be disturbed, when this is exposed, might be expected. But the assumptions so boastfully made, while they may not prevent the sensibility, yet surely exclude all ground of protest, when these assumptions are exposed.

I begin with the Law of Slavery and its Origin; and here this Barbarism sketches itself in its own chosen definition. It is simply this: Man, created in the image of God, is divested of the human character, and declared to be a "chattel,"—that is, a beast, a thing, or article of property. That this statement may not seem made without precise authority, I quote the statutes of . . . South Carolina, whose voice for Slavery has always unerring distinctiveness. According to the definition supplied by this State, slaves

shall be deemed, held, taken, reputed, and adjudged in law to be chattels personal in the hands of their owners and possessors, and their executors, administrators, and assigns, to all intents, constructions, and purposes whatsoever.

. . . Sir, look at its plain import, and see the relation which it establishes. The slave is held simply for the use of his master, to whose behests his life, liberty, and happiness are devoted, and by whom he may be bartered, leased, mortgaged, bequeathed, invoiced, shipped as cargo, stored as goods, sold on execution, knocked off at public auction, and even staked at the gaming-table on the hazard of a card or a die,—all according to law. Nor is there anything, within the limit of life, inflicted on a beast, which may not be inflicted on the slave. He may be marked like a hog, branded like a mule, yoked like an ox, hobbled like a horse, driven like an ass, sheared like a sheep, maimed like a cur, and constantly beaten like a brute,—all according to law. And should life itself be taken, what is the remedy? The Law of Slavery, imitating that rule of evidence which in barbarous days and barbarous countries prevented the Christian from testifying against the Mahometan, openly pronounces the incompetency of the whole African race, whether bond or free, to testify against a white man in any case, and thus, after surrendering the slave to all possible outrage, crowns its tyranny by excluding the very testimony through which the bloody cruelty of the Slave-Master might be exposed. . . .

Foremost, of course, in these elements, is the impossible pretension, where Barbarism is lost in impiety, by which man claims property in man. Against such blasphemy the argument is brief. According to the Law of Nature, written by the same hand that placed the planets in their orbits, and, like them, constituting part of the eternal system of the Universe, every human being has complete title to himself direct from the Almighty. Naked he is born; but his birthright is inseparable from the human form. A man may be poor in this world's goods; but he owns himself. No war or robbery, ancient or recent,—no capture—no middle passage,—no change of clime,—no purchase-money,—no transmission from hand to hand, no matter how many times, and no matter at what price, can defeat this indefeasible, God-given franchise. And a divine mandate, strong as that which guards Life, guards Liberty also. Even at the very morning of Creation, when God said, "Let there be Light," —earlier than the malediction against murder,—he set the everlasting difference between man and chattel, giving to man "dominion over the fish of the sea, and over the fowl of the air, and over every living thing that moveth upon the earth." . . . Slavery tyrannically assumes power which Heaven denied,—while, under its barbarous necromancy, borrowed from the Source of Evil, a man is changed into a chattel, a person is withered into a thing, a soul is shrunk into merchandise. Say, Sir, in lofty madness, that you own the sun, the stars, the moon; but do not say that you own a man, endowed with soul to live immortal, when sun and moon and stars have passed away. . . .

It is in the Character of Slavery itself that we are to find the Character of Slave-Masters. I need not go back to the golden mouth of Chrysostom to learn that "Slavery is the fruit of covetousness, of extravagance, of insatiable greediness"; for we have already seen that this five-fold enormity is inspired by the single idea of compelling men to work without wages. This spirit must naturally appear in the Slave-Master. But the eloquent Saint did not disclose the whole truth. Slavery is founded on violence, as we have already too clearly seen; of course it can be sustained only by kindred violence, sometimes against the defenceless slave, sometimes against the freeman whose indignation is aroused at the outrage. It is founded on brutal and vulgar pretensions, as is unhappily too apparent; of course it can be sustained only by kindred brutality and vulgarity. The denial of all rights in the slave can be sustained only by disregard of other rights, common to the whole community, whether of the person, the press, or speech. Where this exists there can be but one supreme law, to which all other laws, statute or social, are subordinate,—and this is the pretended law of Slavery. All these things must be manifest in Slave-Masters; and yet, unconscious of their true condition, they make boasts which reveal still further the unhappy influence. Barbarous standards of conduct are unblushingly avowed. The swagger of a bully is called chivalry; a swiftness to quarrel is called courage; the bludgeon is adopted as substitute for argument; and assassination is lifted to be one of the Fine Arts. Long ago it was fixed certain that the day which makes man a slave "takes half his worth away,"—words from the ancient harp of Homer, sounding through long generations. Nothing here is said of the human being at the other end of the chain. To aver that on this same day all his worth is taken away might seem inconsistent with exceptions which we gladly recognize;

but, alas! it is too clear, both from reason and from facts, that, bad as Slavery is for the Slave, it is worse for the Master. . . .

The law of life is labor. Slavery is a perpetual effort to evade this law by compelling the labor of others; and such an attempt at evasion is naturally supported by the pretension, that, because the African is inferior, therefore he may be enslaved. But this pretension, while surrendering to Slavery a whole race, leaves it uncertain whether the same principle may not be applied to other races, as to the polished Japanese who are now the guests of the nation, and even to persons of obvious inferiority among the white race. Indeed, the latter pretension is openly set up in other quarters. The "Richmond Enquirer," a leading journal of Slave-Masters, declares, "The principle of Slavery is in itself right, and does not depend on difference of complexion." And a leading writer among Slave-Masters, George Fitzhugh, of Virginia, in his "Sociology for the South," declares, "Slavery, black or white, is right and necessary. Nature has made the weak in mind or body for slaves." In the same vein, a Democratic paper of South Carolina has said, "Slavery is the natural and normal condition of the laboring man, black or white."

These more extravagant pretensions reveal still further the feebleness of the pretension put forth by the Senator [Davis], while instances, accumulating constantly, attest the difficulty of discriminating between the two races. Mr. Paxton, of Virginia, tells us that "the best blood in Virginia flows in the veins of the slaves"; and more than one fugitive has been advertised latterly as possessing "a round face," "blue eyes," "flaxen hair," and as "escaping under the pretence of being a white man."

This is not the time to enter upon the great question of race, in the various lights of religion, history, and science. Sure I am that they who understand it best will be least disposed to the pretension which, on an assumed ground of inferiority, would condemn one race to be the property of another. If the African race be inferior, as is alleged, then unquestionably a Christian Civilization must lift it from degradation, not by the lash and the chain, not by this barbarous pretension of ownership, but by a generous charity, which shall be measured precisely by the extent of inferiority.

Chapter
11: Reconstruction: The Fourteenth Amendment

⊑ **WILLIAM HANCHETT**

The problems involved in making peace at the end of a long and bloody war are seldom simple. They were especially complicated in the United States after the Civil War because, as Lincoln observed in an important speech on Reconstruction, April 11, 1865, there was no political authority in the South with whom the victorious government could deal. "We simply must begin with, and mould from, disorganized and discordant elements," he said. To make the task even more difficult, "we, the loyal people, differ among ourselves as to the mode, manner, and means of reconstruction." Indeed, the differences between loyal men over Reconstruction policy became so great and bitter that Democrats and Republicans fought each other in the postwar years with a fervor almost as passionate as that displayed by Rebels and Yankees during the war.

Supporters of the policies of President Andrew Johnson insisted that he was only carrying out the generous peace program originated by Lincoln. In a Proclamation of Amnesty and Reconstruction issued December 8, 1863, Lincoln had announced that he would give full pardon to all supporters of the rebellion (with certain exceptions) who would take oaths to be loyal to the United States and the Constitution in the future. As soon as 10 percent of the voters in any rebel state had taken the oath, they could proceed to reorganize their government, and upon amending the state constitution to provide for the permanent freedom of the former slave population, this government would "be recognized as the true government of the State. . . ."

Before his death Lincoln began the reconstruction of four states on these easy terms. When Johnson became President, he continued with the same policy. He, too, issued a generous proclamation of amnesty, pardoning most participants in the rebellion upon the swearing of an oath of future loyalty, and stating that the rest could apply directly to him for pardons, which he promised would be "liberally extended." He appointed provisional governors in the seven states where they had not already been appointed by Lincoln, and, like Lincoln, instructed them to supervise the establishment of loyal governments.

By December, 1865, when Congress convened for the first time since the end of the war, the President maintained that reconstruction was almost over. In the months since Appomattox, he told Congress, "I have acted, and have gradually and quietly, and by almost imperceptible steps, sought to restore the rightful energy of the General Government and of the States." State constitutions had been amended, governors, state legislators, and United States Senators and Representatives had been elected, federal courts, customs houses, and post offices were once again functioning, and, best of all, the return of the authority of the United States was known "only as a beneficence" in the South. The Thirteenth Amendment, which would become part of the Constitution two weeks later, "reunites us beyond all power of disruption," the President continued; "it heals the wound that is still imperfectly closed; it removes slavery, the element which has so long perplexed and divided the country; it makes of us once more a united people, renewed and strengthened, bound more than ever to mutual affection and support." All Congress had to do was to allow the Senators and Representatives from the Southern states to take the seats to which they had been elected, and the reconstruction of the Union was complete.

But American Congresses are seldom so obliging as to accept a presidential program without studying it. The day after listening to Johnson's message, Congress took steps to establish a joint committee, consisting of six Senators and nine Representatives, "to inquire into the condition of the States which formed the so-called Confederate States," and to determine if they were entitled to Congressional representation. The Joint Committee on Reconstruction divided into sub-committees to investigate the various states, collected large quantities of documents illustrative of public opinion in the South, and summoned witnesses for questioning. By March, 1866, its preliminary investigations were complete, and on April 30 it reported to the floor of Congress the text of another amendment to the Constitution of the United States. On June 13, after extended debate and revision, this amendment, which became the Fourteenth, was passed by more than the necessary two-thirds vote in both houses, and sent to the states for ratification.

In passing the Fourteenth Amendment, Congress rejected the President's program for Reconstruction and submitted its own.

There were two principal reasons for its action, the first of short-run significance, the other of long-run significance: first, Johnson's lenient policy permitted the same men who had led the rebellion against the United States to remain in political power; and second, that policy allowed the white people of the South to keep the black people in such an inferior legal position as to make a mockery of the Emancipation

Proclamation and the Thirteenth Amendment. To Congress, the first reason represented an unconscionable threat to national security, and the second a violation of a moral responsibility to see that the freedmen actually received their freedom.

While conceding that Lincoln had indeed initiated the so-called Ten Per Cent Plan which Johnson completed, most Republicans believed that by the time of his death he had seen the need to modify it. Early in 1865, Congress had refused to seat the Senators and Representatives sent to Washington by the Lincoln-sponsored government of Louisiana for the same reasons it refused to seat the delegations from the Johnson-sponsored governments a year later. Johnson tried to force Congress to accept his governments; the flexible and pragmatic Lincoln would never have done so. Indeed, he admitted that he had perhaps been too hasty in his quest for a quick and easy return of normal relations, and in his Reconstruction speech hinted that he might become more demanding. "In the present situation . . .," he declared, "it may be my duty to make some new announcement to the people of the South." Had he lived to make it, so these Republicans believed, no one would make the mistake of referring to the "Lincoln-Johnson Plan" for Reconstruction.

In fact, Lincoln did not have a "plan" for Reconstruction, and said so himself. Circumstances were so different from state to state and could change so suddenly within a state, he said on April 11, "that no exclusive, and inflexible plan can safely be prescribed as to details and collaterals." Such an exclusive and inflexible plan would surely become a new entanglement.

It was Andrew Johnson who had a plan and who adhered rigidly to it despite the strength of the opposition he knew existed in Congress. His inflexibility, in turn, prompted Congress to propose its own plan, to which it also adhered rigidly. The "entanglement" of these two irreconcilable plans is the central theme of the political history of Reconstruction.

Of course simple political partisanship was an important factor in the conflict. Congress was overwhelmingly Republican, and it was easy for Republicans to convince themselves that the Union was safe only in their hands. The nation's enemies, men who had come very close to destroying it, were, after all, Democrats. The President himself was a Democrat and a Southerner, who had been nominated for Vice-President on the Lincoln ticket in 1864 to attract the votes of other loyal Democrats. But now he was betraying the party which had elevated him, and making common cause with rebels and traitors, whose influence in the government would be stronger than ever if he had his way. Before the war, the Southern states had counted only three-fifths of their slave populations in determining representation in the House of Representatives; with slavery abolished, they could now count their entire black populations. Yet none of them permitted blacks to vote. The President was, in effect, seeking to reward disloyalty and treason, and abandoning the loyal black people of the South to their disloyal former masters.

It was just as easy for Johnson and the Democrats to convince themselves that they were the custodians of the principles of justice and democracy, and that the Republicans were the enemies of the Union. The Republican party was a purely Northern party. It had represented only a minority of the people of the United States when it came to power in 1861, and it could remain in power only by keeping Southern Democrats out of Congress. The claim of Republicans that in denying representation to the Southern states they were only protecting the nation against disloyalty was spurious, for no Democrat, least of all the President, was asking that disloyal men be seated in Congress. The fact was that the Republicans were denying the South any representation at all, even when the individuals concerned had sworn their loyalty or received presidential pardons. For the most contemptible political motives, they were prolonging disunion and division, repudiating the fundamental democratic principle that citizens are entitled to be represented by leaders of their choice, and violating the Constitution. Their demand that blacks be given equal civil rights and allowed to vote was pure political opportunism, for they showed little interest in such subjects in their own states.

Because the controversy between the Republican Congress and the Democratic President was so intense, and because the race question continued to divide the nation more than one hundred years later, it is perhaps not surprising that many historians of Reconstruction have been themselves partisans in the dispute, have denounced the opposition with almost as much intolerance as the original participants. Thus Congressional Republicans have been called "malicious" and "vindictive," and accused of wishing to humiliate the penitent Southerners and the well-intentioned President who was only trying to follow in Lincoln's footsteps. On the other hand, Johnson and his supporters in both North and South have been condemned as traitors and bigots who thwarted the will of the loyal people of the United States, and who finally succeeded through force and violence in substituting legalized white supremacy for the civil equality envisioned by the Fourteenth Amendment.

The documents in this chapter illustrate the thinking and the conditions in both the defeated South and the victorious North which caused Congress to make its momentous decision to reject President Johnson's Reconstruction plan and to force its own upon the South. They also provide clues to explain the ultimate nonenforcement of the Fourteenth Amendment, and perhaps they will suggest that Reconstruction failed, not because it was too radical or not radical enough, but because the fundamental problem was insoluble, except for a future generation.

President Johnson's first annual message to Congress early in December, 1865, asserted in general terms that the authority of the United States government was once again accepted and operative in the Southern states, and urged that they be restored to their full rights and privileges under the Constitution by the admission to Congress of their Senators and Representatives. Since the Constitution makes each House the judge of its own membership, the decision was Congress's alone to make. The following excerpts from the lengthy and seldom reprinted introduction to the *Report of the Joint Committee on Reconstruction* (39th Cong., 1st Sess., Washington, D.C., 1866), pp. x–xiii, xvi–xvii) summarize the Committee's findings and conclusions, and give the reasoning behind some of the provisions of the Fourteenth Amendment. Was Congress justified in refusing admission? Was its decision consistent with the North's wartime claim that the Southern states had never seceded because there was no such thing as secession? Were those who demanded immediate admission being realistic?

⊂ᴱ Introduction to the Report of the Joint Committee on Reconstruction (1866)

A claim for the immediate admission of senators and representatives from the so-called Confederate States has been urged, which seems to your committee not to be founded either in reason or in law, and which cannot be passed without comment. Stated in a few words, it amounts to this: That inasmuch as the lately insurgent States had no legal right to separate themselves from the Union, they still retain their positions as States, and consequently the people thereof have a right to immediate representation in Congress without the imposition of any conditions whatever; and further, that until such admission Congress has no right to tax them for the support of the government. It has even been contended that until such admission all legislation affecting their interests is, if not unconstitutional, at least unjustifiable and oppressive.

It is believed by your committee that all these propositions are not only wholly untenable, but, if admitted, would tend to the destruction of the government.

It must not be forgotten that the people of these States, without justification or excuse, rose in insurrection against the United States. They deliberately abolished their State governments so far as the same connected them politically with the Union as members thereof under the Constitution. They deliberately renounced their allegiance to the federal government, and proceeded to establish an independent government for themselves. In the prosecution of this enterprise they seized the national forts, arsenals, dock-yards, and other public property within their borders, drove out from among them those who remained true to the Union, and heaped every imaginable insult and injury upon the United States and its citizens. Finally, they opened hostilities, and levied war against the government. They continued this war for four years with the most determined and malignant spirit, killing in battle, and otherwise, large numbers of loyal people, destroying the property of loyal citizens on the sea and on the land, and entailing on the government an enormous debt, incurred to sustain its rightful authority. Whether legally and constitutionally or not, they did, in fact, withdraw from the Union and made themselves subjects of another government of their own creation. And they only yielded when, after a long, bloody, and wasting war, they were compelled by utter exhaustion to lay down their arms; and this they did, not unwillingly, but declaring that they yielded because they could no longer resist, affording no evidence whatever, of repentance for their crime, and expressing no regret, except that they had no longer the power to continue the desperate struggle.

It cannot, we think, be denied by any one, having a tolerable acquaintance with public law, that the war thus waged was a civil war of the greatest magnitude. The people waging it were necessarily subject to all the rules which, by the law of nations, control a contest of that character, and to all the legitimate consequences following it. One of those consequences was that, within the limits prescribed by humanity, the conquered rebels were at the mercy of the conquerors. That a government thus outraged had a most perfect right to exact indemnity for the injuries done, and security against the recurrence of such outrages in the future, would seem too clear for dispute. What the nature of that security should be, what proof should be required of a return to allegiance, what time should elapse before a people thus demoralized should be restored in full to the enjoyment of political rights and privileges, are questions for the law-making power to decide, and that decision must depend on grave considerations of the public safety and the general welfare.

It is moreover contended, and with apparent gravity, that, from the peculiar nature and character of our government, no such right on the part of the conqueror can exist; that from the moment when rebellion lays down its arms and actual hostilities cease, all political rights of rebellious communities are at once restored; that, because the people of a State of the Union were once an organized community within the Union, they necessarily so remain, and their right to be represented in Congress at any and all times, and to participate in the government of the country under all circumstances, admits of neither question nor dispute. If this is indeed true, then is the government of the United States powerless for its own protection, and flagrant rebellion, carried to the extreme of civil war, is a pastime which any State may play at, not only certain that it can lose nothing in any event, but may even be the gainer by defeat. If rebellion succeeds, it accomplishes its purpose and destroys the government. If it fails, the war has been barren of results, and the battle may be still fought out in the legislative halls of the country. Treason, defeated in the field, has only to take possession of Congress and the cabinet. . . .

It is most desirable that the Union of all the States should become perfect at the earliest moment consistent with the peace and welfare of the nation; that all these States should become fully represented in the national councils, and take their share in the legislation of the country. The possession and exercise of more than its just share of power by any section is injurious, as well to that section as to all others. Its tendency is distracting and demoralizing, and such a state of affairs is only to be tolerated on the ground of a necessary regard to the public safety. As soon as that safety is secured it should terminate.

Your committee came to the consideration of the subject referred to them with the most anxious desire to ascertain what was the condition of the people of the States recently in insurrection, and what, if anything, was necessary to be done before restoring them to the full enjoyment of all their original privileges. It was undeniable that the war into which they had plunged the country had materially changed their relations to the people of the loyal States. Slavery had been abolished by constitutional amendment. A large proportion of the population had become, instead of mere chattels, free men and citizens. Through all the past struggle these had remained true and loyal, and had, in large numbers, fought on the side of the Union. It was impossible to abandon them, without securing them their rights as free men and citizens. The whole civilized world would have cried out against such base ingratitude, and the bare idea is offensive to all right-thinking men. Hence it became important to inquire what could be done to secure their rights, civil and political. It was evident to your committee that adequate security could only be found in appropriate constitutional provisions. By an original provision of the Constitution, representation is based on the whole number of free persons in each State, and three-fifths of all other persons. When all become free, representation for all necessarily follows. As a consequence the inevitable effect of the rebellion would be to increase the political power of the insurrectionary States, whenever they should be allowed to resume their positions as States of the Union. As representation is by the Constitution based upon population, your committee did not think it advisable to recommend a change of that basis. The increase of representation necessarily resulting from the abolition of slavery was considered the most important element in the questions arising out of the changed condition of affairs, and the necessity for some fundamental action in this regard seemed imperative. It appeared to your committee that the rights of these persons by whom the basis of representation had been thus increased should be recognized by the general government. While slaves they were not considered as having any rights, civil or political. It did not seem just or proper that all the political advantages derived from their becoming free should be confined to their former masters, who had fought against the Union, and withheld from themselves, who had always been loyal. Slavery, by building up a ruling and dominant class, had produced a spirit of oligarchy adverse to republican institutions, which finally inaugurated civil war. The tendency of continuing the domination of such a class, by leaving it in the exclusive possession of political power, would be to encourage the same spirit, and lead to a similar result. Doubts were entertained whether Congress had power, even under the amended Constitution, to prescribe the qualifications of voters in a State, or could act directly on the subject. It was doubtful, in the opinion of your committee, whether the States would consent to surrender a power they had always exercised, and to which they were attached. As the best if not the only method of surmounting the difficulty, and as eminently just and proper in itself, your committee came to the conclusion that political power should be possessed in all the States exactly in proportion as the right of suffrage should be granted without distinction of color or race. This it was thought would leave the whole question with the people of each State, holding out to all the advantage of increased political power as an inducement to allow all to participate in its exercise. Such a provision would be in its nature gentle and persuasive, and would lead, it was hoped, at no distant day, to an equal participation of all, without distinction, in all the rights and privileges of citizenship, thus affording a full and adequate protection to all classes of citizens, since all would have, through the ballot-box, the power of self-protection. . . .

Examining the evidence taken by your committee still further, in connexion with facts too notorious to be disputed, it appears that the southern press, with few exceptions, and those mostly of newspapers recently established by northern men, abounds with weekly and daily abuse of the institutions and people of the loyal States; defends the men who led, and the principles which incited, the rebellion; denounces and reviles southern men who adhered to the Union; and strives, constantly and unscrupulously, by every means in its power, to keep alive the fire of hate and discord between the sections; calling upon the President to violate his oath of office, overturn the government by force of arms, and drive the representatives of the people from their seats in Congress. The national banner is openly insulted, and the national airs scoffed at, not only by an ignorant populace, but at public meetings, and once, among other notable instances, at a dinner given in honor of a notorious rebel who had violated his oath and abandoned his flag. The same individual is elected to an important office in the leading city of his State, although an unpardoned rebel, and so offensive that the President refuses to allow him to enter upon his official duties. In another State the leading general of the rebel armies is openly nominated for governor by the speaker of the house of delegates, and the nomination is hailed by the people with shouts of satisfaction, and openly indorsed by the press.

Looking still further at the evidence taken by your committee, it is found to be clearly shown by witnesses of the highest character and having the best means of observation, that the Freedmen's Bureau, instituted for the relief and protection of freedmen and refugees, is almost universally opposed by the mass of the population, and exists in an efficient condition only under military protection, while the Union men of the south are earnest in its defence, declaring with one voice that without its protection the colored people would not be permitted to labor at fair prices, and could hardly live in safety. They also testify that without the protection of United States troops, Union men, whether of northern or southern origin, would be obliged to abandon their homes. The feeling in many portions of the country towards emancipated slaves, especially among the uneducated and ignorant, is one of vindictive and malicious hatred. This deep-seated prejudice against color is assiduously cultivated by the public journals, and leads to acts of cruelty, oppression, and murder, which the local authorities are at no pains to prevent or punish. There is no general disposition to place the colored race, constituting at least two-fifths of the population, upon terms of even civil equality. While many instances may be found where large planters and men of the better class accept the situation, and honestly strive to bring about a better order of things, by employing the freedmen at fair wages and treating them kindly, the general feeling and disposition among all classes are yet totally averse to the toleration of any class of people friendly to the Union, be they white or black; and this aversion is not unfrequently manifested in an insulting and offensive manner.

When the Joint Committee on Reconstruction reported out its text of the Fourteenth Amendment at the end of April, 1866, it also submitted a bill providing that when any of the ex-confederate states ratified the amendment, its Senators and Representatives would be admitted to Congress. Tennessee, where there had been substantial Unionist sentiment all during the war, did ratify it. Its Congressional delegation was thereupon promptly seated, and the state was exempted from the Reconstruction Acts later passed by Congress. In very nearly a formal sense, therefore, the Fourteenth Amendment was a "treaty of peace" with the Southern states. Was it a reasonable one? How much more or less should have been demanded of the South? What could Congress do if the remaining Southern states simply refused to ratify the amendment, thus effectively preventing it from becoming part of the Constitution?

⊂≣ Congress's "Treaty of Peace," the Fourteenth Amendment

Section 1: All persons born or naturalized in the United States, and subject to the jurisdiction thereof, are citizens of the United States and of the State wherein they reside. No State shall make or enforce any law which shall abridge the privileges or immunities of citizens of the United States; nor shall any State deprive any person of life, liberty, or property, without due process of law; nor deny to any person within its jurisdiction the equal protection of the laws.

Section 2: Representatives shall be apportioned among the several States according to their respective numbers, counting the whole number of persons in each State, excluding Indians not taxed. But when the right to vote at any election for the choice of electors for President and Vice President of the United States, Representatives in Congress, the Executive and Judicial officers of a State, or the members of the Legislature thereof, is denied to any of the male inhabitants of such State, being twenty-one years of age, and citizens of the United States, or in any way abridged, except for participation in rebellion, or other crime, the basis of representation shall be reduced in the proportion which the number of such male citizens shall bear to the whole number of male citizens twenty-one years of age in such State.

Section 3: No person shall be a Senator or Representative in Congress, or elector of President and Vice President, or hold any office, civil or military, under the United States, or under any State, who, having previously taken an oath, as a member of Congress, or as an officer of the United States, or as a member of any State legislature, or as an executive or judicial officer of any State, to support the Constitution of the United

States, shall have engaged in insurrection or rebellion against the same, or given aid or comfort to the enemies thereof. But Congress may by a vote of two-thirds of each House, remove such disability.

Section 4:   The validity of the public debt of the United States, authorized by law, including debts incurred for payment of pensions and bounties for services in suppressing insurrection or rebellion, shall not be questioned. But neither the United States nor any State shall assume or pay any debt or obligation incurred in aid of insurrection or rebellion against the United States, or any claim for the loss or emancipation of any slave; but all such debts, obligations and claims shall be held illegal and void.

Section 5:   The Congress shall have power to enforce, by appropriate legislation, the provisions of this article.

It was ironic that in 1866 the only former Confederate state to ratify the Fourteenth Amendment—or, to put it another way, to accept the Congressional "treaty of peace"—was Tennessee, Andrew Johnson's home state. The President himself was vigorously opposed to Congress's Reconstruction policy, as the two documents excerpted here demonstrate. In the first, his Second Annual Message, he holds Congress responsible for the unnecessary perpetuation of disunion by its refusal to seat the Senators and Representatives from the ten Southern states still not represented in Congress. In the second, his veto of the Civil Rights Act of 1866, he implies a repugnance at the idea of black equality which was shared by many whites, and warns against the expanding power of the federal government. The Civil Rights Act, which incorporated in ordinary legislation the same principle of equal rights found in the Fourteenth Amendment, was passed over Johnson's veto in April. Both documents are readily available in *Messages and Papers of the Presidents*, VI, pp. 446–47, 448–49, and 405, 406–08, 412–13. Should Congress have screened the elected Senators and Representatives individually, as the President wanted? Why do you suppose it did not? Was Johnson's fear that civil rights legislation would lead to a centralization of power in Washington only a rationalization?

On Congressional Policy

ANDREW JOHNSON

December 3, 1866

SECOND ANNUAL MESSAGE TO CONGRESS

I deem it a subject of profound regret that Congress has thus far failed to admit to seats loyal Senators and Representatives from the other States whose inhabitants, with those of Tennessee, had engaged in the rebellion. Ten States—more than one-fourth of the whole number—remain without representation; the seats of fifty members in the House of Representatives and of twenty members in the Senate are yet vacant, not by their own consent, not by a failure of election, but by the refusal of Congress to accept their credentials. Their admission, it is believed, would have accomplished much toward the renewal and strengthening of our relations as one people and removed serious cause for discontent on the part of the inhabitants of those States. It would have accorded with the great principle enunciated in the Declaration of American Independence that no people ought to bear the burden of taxation and yet be denied the right of representation. It would have been in consonance with the express provisions of the Constitution that "each State shall have at least one Representative" and "that no State, without its consent, shall be deprived of its equal suffrage in the Senate." These provisions were intended to secure to every State and to the people of every State the right of representation in each House of Congress; and so important was it deemed by the framers of the Constitution that the equality of the States in the Senate should be preserved that not even by an amendment of the Constitution can any State, without is consent, be denied a voice in that branch of the National Legislature.

It is true it has been assumed that the existence of the States was terminated by the rebellious acts of their inhabitants, and that, the insurrection having been suppressed, they were thenceforward to be considered merely as conquered territories. The legislative, executive, and judicial departments of the Government have, however, with great distinctness and uniform consistency, refused to sanction an assumption so incompatible with the nature of our republican system and with the professed objects of the war. . . .

In the admission of Senators and Representatives from any and all of the States there can be no just ground of apprehension that persons who are disloyal will be clothed with the powers of legislation, for this could not happen when the Constitution and the laws are enforced by a vigilant and faithful Congress. Each House is made the "judge of the elections, returns, and qualifications of its own members," and may, "with the concurrence of two-thirds, expel a member." When a Senator or Representative presents his certificate of election, he may at once be admitted or rejected; or, should there be any question as to his eligibility, his credentials may be referred for investigation to the appropriate committee. If admitted to a seat, it must be upon evidence satisfactory to the House of which he thus becomes a member that he possesses the requisite constitutional and legal qualifications. If refused admission as a member for want of due allegiance to the Government and returned to his constituents, they are admonished that none but persons loyal to the United States will be allowed a voice in the legislative councils of the nation, and the political power and moral influence of Congress are thus effectively exerted in the interests of loyalty to the Government and fidelity to the Union. Upon this question, so vitally affecting the restoration of the Union and the permanency of our present form of government, my convictions, heretofore expressed, have undergone no change, but, on the contrary, their correctness has been confirmed by reflection and time. If the admission of loyal members to seats in the respective Houses of Congress was wise and expedient a year ago, it is no less wise and expedient now. If this anomalous condition is right now —if in the exact condition of these States at the present time it is lawful to exclude them from representation—I do not see that the question will be changed by the efflux of time. Ten years hence, if these States remain as they are, the right of representation will be no stronger, the right of exclusion will be no weaker.

The Constitution of the United States makes it the duty of the President to recommend to the consideration of Congress "such measures as he shall judge necessary and expedient." I know of no measure more imperatively demanded by every consideration of national interest, sound policy, and equal justice than the admission of loyal members from the now unrepresented States. This would consummate the work of restoration and exert a most salutary influence in the reestablishment of peace, harmony, and fraternal feeling. It would tend greatly to renew the confidence of the American people in the vigor and stability of their institutions. It would bind us more closely together as a nation and enable us to show to the world the inherent and recuperative power of a government founded upon the will of the people and established upon the principles of liberty, justice, and intelligence. . . .

In our efforts to preserve "the unity of government which constitutes as one people" by restoring the States to the condition which they held prior to the rebellion, we should be cautious, lest, having rescued our nation from perils of threatened disintegration, we resort to consolidation, and in the end absolute despotism, as a remedy for the recurrence of similar troubles. The war having terminated, and with it all occasion for the exercise of powers of doubtful constitutionality, we should hasten to bring legislation within the boundaries prescribed by the Constitution and to return to the ancient landmarks established by our fathers for the guidance of succeeding generations.

Veto of Civil Rights Act

March 7, 1866

I regret that the bill, which has passed both Houses of Congress, entitled "An act to protect all persons in the United States in their civil rights and furnish the means of their vindication," contains provisions which I can not approve consistently with my sense of duty to the whole people and my obligations to the Constitution of the United States. I am therefore constrained to return it to the Senate, the House in which it originated, with my objections to its becoming a law.

By the first section of the bill all persons born in the United States and not subject to any foreign power, excluding Indians not taxed, are declared to be citizens of the United States. . . . Four millions of them have just emerged from slavery into freedom. Can it be reasonably supposed that they possess the requisite qualifications to entitle them to all the privileges and immunities of citizens of the United States? Have the people of the several States expressed such a conviction? . . . Besides, the policy of the Government from its origin to the present time seems to have been that persons who are strangers to and unfamiliar with our institutions and our laws should pass through a certain probation, at the end of which, before attaining the coveted prize, they must give evidence of their fitness to receive and to exercise the rights of citizens as contemplated by the Constitution of the United States. The bill in effect proposes a discrimination against large numbers of intelligent, worthy, and patriotic foreigners, and in favor of the negro, to whom, after long years of bondage, the avenues to freedom and intelligence have just now been suddenly opened. He must of necessity, from his previous unfortunate condition of servitude, be less informed as to the nature and character of our institutions than he who, coming from abroad, has, to some extent at least, familiarized himself with the principles of Government to which he voluntarily intrusts "life, liberty, and the pursuit of happiness." Yet it is now proposed, by a single legislative enactment, to confer the rights of citizens upon all persons of African descent born within the extended limits of the United States, while persons of foreign birth who make our land their home must undergo a probation of five years, and can only then become citizens upon proof that they are "of good moral character, attached to the principles of the Constitution of the United States, and well disposed to the good order and happiness of the same."

The first section of the bill also contains an enumeration of the rights to be enjoyed by these classes so made citizens "in every State and Territory in the United States." These rights are "to make and enforce contracts; to sue, be parties, and give evidence; to inherit, purchase, lease, sell, hold, and convey real and personal property," and to have "full and equal benefit of all laws and proceedings for the security of person and property as is enjoyed by white citizens." So, too, they are made subject to the same punishment, pains, and penalties in common with white citizens, and to none other. Thus a perfect equality of the white and colored races is attempted to be fixed by Federal law in every State of the Union over the vast field of State jurisdiction covered by these enumerated rights. In no one of these can any State ever exercise any power of discrimination between the different races. In the exercise of State policy over matters exclusively affecting the people of each State it has frequently been thought expedient to discriminate between the two races. By statutes of some of the States, Northern as well as Southern, it is enacted, for instance, that no white person shall intermarry with a negro or mulatto. Chancellor Kent says, speaking of the blacks, that—

Marriages between them and the whites are forbidden in some of the States where slavery does not exist, and they are prohibited in all the slave-holding States; and when not absolutely contrary to law, they are revolting, and regarded as an offense against public decorum.

I do not say that this bill repeals State laws on the subject of marriage between the two races, for as the whites are forbidden to intermarry with the blacks, the blacks can only make such contracts as the whites themselves are allowed to make, and therefore can not under this bill enter into the marriage contract with the whites. I cite this discrimination, however, as an instance of the State policy as to discrimination, and to inquire whether if Congress can abrogate all State laws of discrimination between the two races in the matter of real estate, of suits, and of contracts generally Congress may not also repeal the State laws as to the contract of marriage between the two races. Hitherto every subject embraced in the enumeration of rights contained in this bill has been considered as exclusively belonging to the States. They all relate to the internal police and economy of the respective States. They are matters which in each State concern the domestic condition of its people, varying in each according to its own peculiar circumstances and the safety and well-being of its own citizens. I do not mean to say that upon all these subjects there are not Federal restraints—as, for instance, in the State power of legislation over contracts there is a Federal limitation that no State shall pass a law impairing the obligations of contracts; and, as to crimes, that no State shall pass an ex post facto law; and, as to money, that no State shall make anything but gold and silver a legal tender; but where can we find a Federal prohibition against the power of any State to discriminate, as do most of them, between aliens and citizens, between artificial persons, called corporations, and natural persons, in the right to hold real estate? If it be granted that Congress can repeal all State laws discriminating between whites and blacks in the subjects covered by this bill, why, it may be asked, may not Congress repeal in the same way all State laws discriminating between the two races on the subjects of suffrage and office? If Congress can declare by law who shall hold lands, who shall testify, who shall have capacity to make a contract in a State, then Congress can by law also declare who, without regard to color or race, shall have the right to sit as a juror or as a judge, to hold any office, and finally, to vote "in every State and Territory of the United States." As respects the Territories, they come within the power of Congress, for as to them the lawmaking power is the Federal power; but as to the States no similar provision exists vesting in Congress the power "to make rules and regulations" for them. . . .

I do not propose to consider the policy of this bill. To me the details of the bill seem fraught with evil. The white race and the black race of the South have hitherto lived together under the relation of master and slave—capital owning labor. Now, suddenly, that relation is changed, and as to ownership capital and labor are divorced. They stand now each master of itself. In this new relation, one being necessary to the other, there will be a new adjustment, which both are deeply interested in making harmonious. Each has equal power in settling the terms, and if left to the laws that regulate capital and labor it is confidently believed that they will satisfactorily work out the problem. Capital, it is true, has more intelligence, but labor is never so ignorant as not to understand its own interests, not to know its own value, and not to see that capital must pay that value.

This bill frustrates this adjustment. It intervenes between capital and labor and attempts to settle questions of political economy through the agency of numerous officials whose interest it will be to foment discord between the two races, for as the breach widens their employment will continue, and when it is closed their occupation will terminate.

In all our history, in all our experience as a people living under Federal and State law, no such system as that contemplated by the details of this bill has ever before been proposed or adopted. They establish for the security of the colored race safeguards which go infinitely beyond any that the General Government has ever provided for the white race. In fact, the distinction of race and color is by the bill made to operate in favor of the colored and against the white race. They interfere with the municipal legislation of the States, with the relations existing exclusively between a State and its citizens, or between inhabitants of the same State—an absorption and assumption of power by the General Government which, if acquiesced in, must sap and destroy our federative system of limited powers and break down the barriers which preserve the rights of the States. It is another step, or rather stride, toward centralization and the concentration of all legislative powers in the National Government. The tendency of the bill must be to resuscitate the spirit of rebellion and to arrest the progress of those influences which are more closely drawing around the States the bonds of union and peace.

In passing the Fourteenth Amendment, Congress assumed authority over civil rights, a subject which had previously been left mostly to the states. Inevitably, some critics charged that it had gone too far, others that it had not gone far enough. Among the latter was Frederick Douglass. Born a slave on a Virginia plantation around 1817, Douglass escaped to Massachusetts in 1838, and became the best-known and most influential of the black abolitionists. In his autobiography, *Narrative of the Life of Frederick Douglass* (1845), and in innumerable lectures and articles, he educated the northern public on the institution of slavery, and impressed it with his own character and devotion to the principles of freedom and justice. The following article, published in *The Atlantic Monthly*, XVIII (December, 1866), pp. 762–65, explains why he believed the Fourteenth Amendment was inadequate. Was he reasonable in insisting that men who had so recently been slaves be made full-fledged voters?

☞ A Black Man Protests

FREDERICK DOUGLASS

The arm of the Federal government is long, but it is far too short to protect the rights of individuals in the interior of distant States. They must have the power to protect themselves, or they will go unprotected, [in] spite of all the laws the Federal government can put upon the national Statute-book.

Slavery, like all other great systems of wrong, founded in the depths of human selfishness, and existing for ages, has not neglected its own conservation. It has steadily exerted an influence upon all around it favorable to its own continuance. And to-day it is so strong that it could exist, not only without law, but even against law. Custom, manners, morals, religion, are all on its side everywhere in the South; and when you add the ignorance and servility of the ex-slave to the intelligence and accustomed authority of the master, you have the conditions, not out of which slavery will again grow, but under which it is impossible for the Federal government to wholly destroy it, unless the Federal government be armed with despotic power, to blot out State authority, and to station a Federal officer at every cross-road. This, of course, cannot be done, and ought not even if it could. The true way and the easiest way is to make our government entirely consistent with itself, and give to every loyal citizen the elective franchise,—a right and power which will be ever present, and will form a wall of fire for his protection.

One of the invaluable compensations of the late Rebellion is the highly instructive disclosure it made of the true source of danger to republican government. Whatever may be tolerated in monarchial and despotic governments, no republic is safe that tolerates a privileged class, or denies to any of its citizens equal rights and equal means to maintain them. What was theory before the war has been made fact by the war.

There is cause to be thankful even for rebellion. It is an impressive teacher, though a stern and terrible one. In both characters it has come to us, and it was perhaps needed in both. It is an instructor never a day before its time, for it comes only when all other means of progress and enlightenment have failed. Whether the oppressed and despairing bond-man, no longer able to repress his deep yearnings for manhood, or the tyrant, in his pride and impatience, takes initiative, and strikes the blow for a firmer hold and a longer lease of oppression, the result is the same,—society is instructed, or may be.

Such are the limitations of the common mind, and so thoroughly engrossing are the cares of common life, that only the few among men can discern through the glitter and dazzle of present prosperity the dark outlines of approaching disasters, even though they may have come up to our very gates, and are already within striking distance. The yawning seam and corroded bolt conceal their defects from the mariner until the storm calls all hands to the pumps. Prophets indeed, were abundant before the war; but who cares for prophets while their predictions remain unfulfilled, and the calamities of which they tell are masked behind a blinding blaze of national prosperity?

It is asked, said Henry Clay, on a memorable occasion, Will slavery never come to an end? That question, said he, was asked fifty years ago, and it has been answered by fifty years of unprecedented prosperity. Spite of the eloquence of the earnest Abolitionists,—poured out against slavery during thirty years,—even they must confess, that, in all the probabilities of the case, that system of barbarism would have continued its horrors far beyond the limits of the nineteenth century but for the Rebellion, and perhaps only have disappeared at last in a fiery conflict, even more fierce and bloody than that which has now been suppressed.

Without attempting to settle here the metaphysical and somewhat theological question (about which so much has already been said and written), whether once in the Union means always in the Union,—agreeably to the formula, once in grace always in grace,—it is obvious to common sense that the rebellious States stand to-day, in point of law, precisely where they stood when, exhausted, beaten, conquered, they fell powerless at the feet of Federal authority. Their State governments were overthrown, and the lives and property of the leaders of the Rebellion were forfeited. In reconstructing the institutions of these shattered and overthrown States, Congress should begin with a clean slate, and make clean work of it. Let there be no hesitation. It would be a cowardly deference to a . . . treacherous President, if any account were made of the illegitimate, one-sided, sham governments hurried into existence for a malign purpose in the absence of Congress. These pretended governments, which were never submitted to the people, and from participation in which four millions of the loyal people were excluded by Presidential order, should now be treated according to their true character, as shams and impositions and supplanted by true and legitimate governments, in the formation of which loyal men, black and white, shall participate.

It is not, however, within the scope of this paper to point out the precise steps to be taken, and the means to be employed. The people are less concerned about these than the grand end to be attained. They demand such a reconstruction as shall put an end to the present anarchial state of things in the late rebellious States,—where frightful murders and wholesale massacres are perpetrated in the very presence of Federal soldiers. This horrible business they require shall cease. They want a reconstruction such as will protect loyal men, black and white, in their persons and property; such a one as will cause Northern industry, Northern capital, and Northern civilization to flow into the South, and make a man from New England as much at home in Carolina as elsewhere in the Republic. No Chinese wall can now be tolerated. The South must be opened to the light of law and liberty, and this session of Congress is relied upon to accomplish this important work.

The plain, common-sense way of doing this work, as intimated at the beginning, is simply to establish in the South one law, one government, one administration of justice, one condition to the exercise of the elective franchise, for men of all races and colors alike. This great measure is sought as earnestly by loyal white men as by loyal blacks, and is needed alike by both. Let sound political prescience but take the place of an unreasoning prejudice, and this will be done.

Men denounce the Negro for his prominence in this discussion; but it is no fault of his that in peace as in war, that in conquering Rebel armies as in reconstructing the rebellious States, the right of the Negro is the true solution of our national troubles. The stern logic of events, which goes directly to the point, disdaining all concern for the color or features of men, has determined the interests of the country as identical with and inseparable from those of the Negro.

The policy that emancipated and armed the Negro—now seen to have been wise and proper by the dullest—was not certainly more sternly demanded than is now the policy of enfranchisement. If with the Negro was success in war, and without him failure, so in peace it will be found that the nation must fall or flourish with the Negro.

Many witnesses appeared before the Joint Committee on Reconstruction—whites, blacks, Northerners, Southerners, Republicans, Democrats, soldiers, civilians, celebrities, nonentities. The end product of their testimony as analyzed by the Committee was, of course, the Fourteenth Amendment, and for that reason the Committee's extensive and detailed transcriptions deserve more close study than they have received. Much of the individual testimony, furthermore, is uniquely valuable for the insights it gives into the attitudes and opinions of people of the time, and the question-and-answer format never lets the reader forget that he is dealing with real people, and real attitudes and opinions. The following views and assumptions of an educated white Virginian, B. R. Grattan, are taken from the Committee's massive *Report*, Part II, pp. 161–63. How much reliance could be placed upon Grattan's assurance that the "results of the war" were accepted in good faith by Southern whites? Was his attitude toward blacks malicious in character? Was it subject to change by reasoning?

A Southern White Man Protests

Testimony of B. B. Grattan
Before the Joint Committee

B. R. GRATTAN

February 10, 1866

Question: Where do you reside?
Answer: Richmond, Virginia.
Question: Are you a native of Virginia?
Answer: Yes, sir: I was raised in the valley of Virginia.
Question: Do you hold any public position?
Answer: I am a member of the present house of delegates of Virginia.
Question: Is that the only public position you have held?
Answer: I held the office of reporter to the court of appeals since January, 1844.
Question: I speak of two classes of people in Virginia for the sake of convenience, not with a view of offending anybody. I speak of secessionists and Union men. By secessionists I mean those who have directly or indirectly favored the rebellion; and by Union men I mean those who opposed the rebellion; and by the rebellion I mean the war which has taken place between the two sections of the country. What is the

general feeling among the secessionists of Virginia towards the government of the United States, so far as your observation extends?

Answer: So far as I know, the sentiment is universal that the war has decided the question of secession entirely, that it is no longer an open question, and that we are all prepared to abide by the Union and live under it.

Question: You mean to be understood as saying that they suppose that the sword has settled the abstract right of secession?

Answer: Yes; we consider that we put it to the arbitrament of the sword, and have lost.

Question: What proportion of the legislature of Virginia are original secessionists, have in view the definitions I gave?

Answer: I would suppose that there are few members of the legislature who are less able to judge of that matter than myself, for my acquaintance as a member is very limited; but I should suppose, from the general sentiments of the people of Virginia, that while probably a very large proportion of those who are now members of the legislature were not in favor of secession or a dissolution of the Union originally, yet nearly all of them went with their State when it went out. They went heartily with it.

Question: How have the results of the war affected the feelings of Virginians generally? What is the sentiment left in their hearts in regard to satisfaction or dissatisfaction with the government of the United States—love or hatred, respect or contempt?

Answer: I cannot undertake to say generally; my intercourse is very limited. I would rather suppose, however, that while the feeling against the government was originally very strong, that feeling has been very much modified; it is nothing like as strong as it was, and is gradually declining.

Question: You think that the feeling is gradually changing from dislike to respect?

Answer: Yes, I think so.

Question: Have you any reason to suppose that there are persons in Virginia who still entertain projects of a dissolution of the Union?

Answer: None whatever. I do not believe that there is an intelligent man in the State who does.

Question: In case of a war between our country and any foreign power, such as England or France, one that should put the government to the exercise of all its powers in order to secure its safety, and in case it should become apparent that there was a chance for secessionism to become a success hereafter, would you anticipate that any considerable portion of the people of Virginia would join the enemy?

Answer: No, sir.

Question: Would there be many who would be likely to do so?

Answer: No, sir; I do not think there would be. You might find some boys who would do so. I think that the people have made up their minds to become a part of this Union and to perform every duty connected with that relation. I speak with confidence on that subject, for while I was not an original secessionist, I am certain that nobody ever suffered more at its failure than I did, and I know what my own sentiments are, and judge other people by myself.

Question: What has been, in your judgment, the effect, in the main, of President Johnson's liberality in bestowing pardons and amnesties on rebels?

Answer: I think it has been very favorable; I think President Johnson has commended himself very heartily. There is a very strong feeling of gratitude towards President Johnson.

Question: Has that liberality in your judgment, increased or diminished the respect of these same persons towards the government of the United States?

Answer: It has increased it.

Question: Is that increase of respect towards the government, or is it especially towards President Johnson?

Answer: It is to Mr. Johnson, as the representative of the government.

Question: Are you aware of the nature of the constitutional amendment now pending in the Senate of the United States in reference to the basis of representation?

Answer: Yes, sir.

Question: You know its effect?

Answer: Yes.

Question: It places the basis of representation upon numbers, including all classes and all races, but at the same time declares that in case any State shall exclude from the right of suffrage any portion of its population on account of race or color, the whole of the people of that race or color shall be excluded from the count, thus leaving the entire option with the States whether they shall exclude or include persons of color in the right of suffrage. I want to ascertain your opinion on that subject, whether you think the people of Virginia are likely ever to consent to let negroes vote?

Answer: I should say not, sir, under no circumstances.

Question: Do you think that the interests of the States would finally so operate as to induce them to take off the unkind proscription of the black race?

Answer: I do not think so. I would like to explain that. I, perhaps, ought not to undertake to express an opinion for the people of Virginia. My intercourse for years has been very limited. I have been confined very closely to my own duties as a lawyer, and I have mingled very little with the people. Perhaps I speak rather from my own sentiment and opinion. My own opinion about that is, that the very worst thing that can occur to the negro, (and I believe that will be the sense of the people) the very worst consequence to the negro, will be the attempt to give him political power; and I believe that really the desire to preserve the negro himself, to take care of him, and to prevent the consequences which will arise to him from such an effort would, of itself, preclude his admission to political rights.

Question: What, in your judgment, would be the consequences of such an infranchisement: would it produce scenes of violence between the two races?

Answer: I believe it would. I have very great apprehension that an attempt of that sort would lead to their extermination, not immediately, but to their gradual extinction. It would set up really an antagonistic interest, which would probably be used as a power, because I have no doubt that the negro vote would be under the influence of white people. You are to recollect that this is not simply a prejudice between the white and black races. It has grown to be a part of our nature to look upon them as an inferior; just as much a part of our nature as it is a part of the nature of other races to have enmity to each other; for instance, between the Saxon Irish and the Celtic Irish, or between the English and the French. You must change that nature, and it takes a long time to do it. I believe that if you place the negro on a footing of perfect equality with the white, it would actually increase the power of the white race, which would control the negro vote; yet it seems to me that nothing can reconcile the white people to that short of equal political power, and I fear, therefore, very much the consequences of any attempt of that sort upon the black race in Virginia.

Question: Would not that prejudice become modified a great deal in case the blacks should be educated and rendered more intelligent than they are now?

Answer: You would have to change their skin before you can do it. I beg leave to say this, so far from there being any unkind feeling to the negro, I believe that there is, on the part of the white race, towards the negro, no feeling but that of kindness, sympathy, and pity, and that there is every disposition to ameliorate their condition and improve it as much as possible; but it is that difference which has existed so long in their obvious distinction of color and condition—

Question: But suppose the condition of the negro should change?

Answer: The condition is annexed to the color. We are accustomed to see the color in the condition.

Question: But the condition may be changed by education and enlightenment?

Answer: You are to recollect, as to that, that they are a people who now have no property, who are not accustomed, from their former condition, to any sort of providence for themselves; that they are not accustomed to take care of themselves; that they are a people who have always depended upon others; and, therefore, unless there is some power or person who is to give them wealth and to educate them, you can never expect that they will be in a condition to rise. They cannot educate themselves: they are not disposed to educate themselves. They live in the very lowest condition of life. They are not disposed to work if they can help it, as nobody else is, I suppose; so that I see no help or expectation that by their own exertions they are going to acquire that amount of property which will enable them to educate themselves. If they rise, it will be by the effort of the white race, among whom they live, to raise them.

Question: Is there a general repugnance on the part of whites to the acquisition and enjoyment of property by the blacks?

Answer: I do not know. I do not think there is. Far from it. We would be very glad to see them all doing well and improving their conditon.

Question: Do you find a similar repugnance to the acquisition of knowledge by blacks?

Answer: No, sir; far from it; on the contrary, we are trying, so far as we can, to educate them; but we are too poor ourselves to do much in educating other people, and they are certainly too poor to educate themselves.

Question: You would, then, anticipate a struggle of races in case the right of suffrage was given to the blacks?

Answer: Yes, sir; I think so.

Question: You would not anticipate it in case the blacks should vote in the interests of the white race?

Answer: As I said before, I believe that if the blacks are left to themselves, if all foreign influence were taken away, the whites would control their vote. It is not in that the difficulty lies, but it is in the repugnance which the white race would feel to that sort of political equality. It is the same sort of repugnance which a man feels to a snake. He does not feel any animosity to the snake, but there is a natural shrinking from it; that is my feeling. While I think I have as much sympathy for the black race, and feel as much interest in them as anybody else, while I can treat them kindly and familiarly, still the idea of equality is one which has the same sort of shrinking for me, and is as much a part of my nature, as was the antagonism between Saxon and Celt in Ireland.

Question: You are aware that that state of feeling does not exist in Ireland, England, or Scotland towards the blacks?

Answer: No; because they never had them; because they never saw them in their constant condition. So that difference of alienation between Saxon and Celt does not exist here, but it exists in Ireland. It is where that has been the feeling operating for so long that it has become a part of our nature. It is not a simple prejudice, but it becomes part of the nature of the man. . . .

Question: You have not much reason to expect that the legislature of Virginia will adopt this constitutional amendment in case it shall pass both houses of Congress?

Answer: I cannot speak for others, but for myself I say certainly not. No political power would ever induce me to vote for it. That form is much more objectionable than even a proposition to make them voters. It is giving you all the advantages of numbers, while you are taking that from us which, according to the original constitution, we had— three-fifths of the slave population—and no political power will force me to consent to that.

Chapter

12: Violence and Social Change: The Homestead Strike

⊂Ð EDWARD A. PURCELL, JR.

In the summer of 1965, President Lyndon Johnson, who several months before had ordered the full-scale bombing of North Viet Nam, told blacks rioting in the Los Angeles suburb of Watts that nothing of value could be won through violence. Rather than indicating the necessary incorrectness of either of those courses, that glaring contradiction simply emphasized the extremely confused manner in which most Americans have considered the problem of violence. Though its role has been continually de-emphasized and ignored, violence is an important and integral part of American history.[1]

To some extent the failure of Americans to recognize the role of violence has been due to a kind of ideological blindness. The moralistic tradition of American politics condemned the use of violence as evil, while the same tradition also proclaimed the righteousness of violent means in the service of justice. The democratic ideal rejected the coercion and oppression of one man by another, but the same principle also justified majorities in suppressing small and unpopular minorities. The ideal of equality stood for a fraternal relationship among all men, but it led in practice to an intense effort to prevent various individuals from trying to be "different." The goal of freedom called for broad areas of unrestrained human activity, but historically that freedom helped create immense wealth and power in the hands of a few and economic sub-

---

[1] For discussions of violence in America, see Hugh Davis Graham and Ted Robert Gurr, eds., *Violence in America: Historical and Comparative Perspectives*, A Report to the National Commission on the Causes and Prevention of Violence (New York, 1969); James F. Kirkham, Sheldon G. Levy, and William J. Crotty, *Assassination and Political Violence*, A Report to the National Commission on the Causes and Prevention of Violence (New York, 1970); Thomas Rose, ed., *Violence in America: A Historical and Contemporary Reader* (New York, 1970); Richard Hofstadter and Michael Wallace, eds., *American Violence: A Documentary History* (New York, 1971). For a more theoretical discussion, see Hannah Arendt, *On Violence* (New York, 1969).

servience on the part of many. Thus while the nation's most revered ideals declared violence both useless and wrong, those ideals at the same time helped create the very conditions and attitudes that led to violence.

While ideological commitments thus help obscure the true role of violence in American history, the idea of "violence" itself contributes to the confusion. In spite of a general consensus about certain acts such as murder and rape, people mean very different things when they use the term. Any definition, such as "the violation of a human being" or "the destruction or injury to life or property," remains problematical. When is a person "violated"? How broadly is the term "injury" to be interpreted? What, in short, does "violence" actually mean?

That confusion is increased by the fact that the term "violence" is generally employed, not in a descriptive, but rather in a moral sense. In common usage, violence connotes "bad" or "unjust" actions. In a good cause the most destructive actions are normally referred to as "manliness" or "protective reaction" rather than simply "violence." Where and how is such a line to be drawn?

However one answers that moral question, a discussion of the actual use of violence in social and political affairs necessitates several distinctions. Both theoretically and historically, differences in who is employing violence and what means they use are crucial. Violence can be perpetrated by random individuals, spontaneous mobs, organized groups, or socially powerful institutions. Their methods can range from overt physical assault to the subtlest psychological coercion. The full meaning and practical implications of violence in social and political affairs vary greatly, depending on the nature of both the agent and the method.

The pragmatic utility of violence is another problem. Though morally repudiated, violent means have sometimes proven effective in achieving desired ends. Historically the probable success of violence has depended on several factors: social approval, relative power, legality, and specificity of purpose. Violence that enjoyed widespread social approval could be successful, as were the efforts of the Ku Klux Klan in the late nineteenth century. When one side was immensely more powerful than the other, it could often make violence effective, as did companies which hired thugs to beat up or kill union organizers who entered the towns they controlled. The cover of legality frequently permitted successful violence, such as the brutal removal and destruction of Indian tribes during the nineteenth century. Finally, the more specific and direct the purpose of a violent act, the greater were its chances of success. Many frontier towns found it quite easy to lynch accused horse-thieves, but impossible to create through violence a crimeless society.

Among the numerous violent episodes in American history, the Homestead strike of 1892 stands out as one of the most spectacular and revealing. Varieties of violence abounded, from attempted assassination to a ten-hour pitched battle, and they made the name Homestead infamous. "Europe has rung with Homestead, Homestead, until we are all sick of the name," Andrew Carnegie, who owned the Homestead plant, cabled his partners from Rome.[2] Though Carnegie eventually won the fight and thereby helped drive unionism out of the steel industry for forty-five years, the memory of Homestead did not die. In 1936, beginning the final successful campaign to unionize the industry throughout the United States, the Steel Workers Organizing Committee held a special memorial meeting at Homestead and marched to the cemetery that held the graves of four of the strikers killed in the conflict. The name today conjures up bitter memories to both workers and owners.

Located in a small town of 12,000 from which it derived its name, the Homestead plant was the largest and most efficient open-hearth steel mill in America. A major cog in the complex of mills that covered the area east of Pittsburgh, Homestead stretched for a mile along the increasingly dirty Monongahela River, whose banks were lined with cinders, refuse, and scrap metals. "No respectable microbe would live in it," commented one resident.[3] At the edge of the mill a small hill sloped up southward on which the town had been built. With neither paved streets nor a sewage system, it was jumbled, crowded, and dirty.

In spite of the generally poor living conditions, some of the workers enjoyed a reasonably good position, due to the efficiency of the mill, the high demand for its steel, and the power of the Amalgamated Association of Iron and Steel Workers. Organized in 1876, the Amalgamated Association was the strongest union in America, enjoying national, industry-wide power. Organized in strict craft lodges and composed of only the most skilled workers, the union represented about 325 of Homestead's 3,800 workers. A few of the most skilled Amalgamated men made very high wages, while the rest received pay they generally regarded as good. The wages of the other 3,400 workers ranged from adequate to abysmal. Twenty-eight hundred of them made less than $2.50 a day, and over 1,600 of those averaged less than $1.40 per day.[4] Most of the men worked twelve hours a day, often seven days a week. The labor was backbreaking and dangerous, especially during the last few hours of a shift, when reflexes were slowed and muscles exhausted.

On July 1, 1889, the Amalgamated had negotiated a new three-year contract at Homestead that consolidated its favorable position. In addi-

---

[2] John K. Winkler, *Incredible Carnegie: The Life of Andrew Carnegie* (New York, 1931), p. 219.

[3] Leon Wolff, *Lockout: The Story of the Homestead Strike of 1892: A Study of Violence, Unionism, and the Carnegie Steel Empire* (New York, 1965), p. 29.

[4] Joseph Frazier Wall, *Andrew Carnegie* (New York, 1970), p. 554. For another general study of Homestead, see Henry David, "Upheaval at Homestead," in Daniel Aaron, ed., *America in Crisis: Fourteen Crucial Episodes in American History* (New York, 1952), pp. 132–70.

tion to high tonnage rates, the union won acceptance of certain work rules in the mill and a rather effective grievance procedure that gave the men some control over their job situation. That demonstration of success, together with the general leadership the union provided, won the widespread support of the rest of Homestead's unorganized workers.

When the contract came up for renewal in 1892, however, conditions had changed. The new chairman of the company, Henry Clay Frick, was the most determined anti-union man in the whole industry. On more than one occasion, he had used state militia and private guards to ruthlessly break strikes. More importantly, Carnegie, who owned 55 percent of the company's stock, had changed his earlier pro-union stance, and in early 1892 gave Frick free rein to negotiate with and hopefully destroy the Amalgamated. Both men felt that the union exerted too much influence over labor policy and prevented them from realizing sufficiently increased profits from the introduction of technological improvements.

In addition to the new attitude of the company, changed economic conditions increased the Amalgamated's vulnerability. Whereas in 1889 the company had been flooded with orders, in 1892 the market was overcrowded and continued high production was unnecessary. Additionally, recent technological improvements had seriously diminished the importance of the Amalgamated's highly skilled craftsmen. Since inexperienced workers could be more quickly trained to handle the new and more efficient machinery, skilled workers were no longer irreplaceable. Finally, because of the continued growth of urban populations, there was a ready surplus of individuals who badly needed jobs.[5] The time was perfect, Frick and Carnegie believed, for a final showdown.

Rejecting the union's proposal that the 1889 agreement be extended, Frick countered with a contract that offered a lower union minimum wage scale, 15 percent cuts in tonnage rates, and a new expiration date of December 31, 1894. The changes would have meant a wage cut of between 15 and 25 percent for the Amalgamated men. Also, the new termination date would have given the company an additional lever over the workers. If a strike were ever necessary, July, not January, was the time to have it. Gradually during the spring, when Frick refused to consider compromise offers and then constructed around the mill a three-mile wooden fence with regularly spaced, three-inch holes that suggested gun portals, the Amalgamated came to believe that Frick and Carnegie were indeed out to destroy them.

When his June 24 deadline passed with no surrender, Frick announced that the company would cease dealing with the Amalgamated and in the future bargain only with individual workmen. On June 28 he began shutting down the departments employing union men, and on

[5] *Ibid.*, pp. 539–41.

July 1, the non-union men walked out in support of the Amalgamated. If the skilled workers were defeated, they reasoned, harsh cuts would face them in their turn. The huge mills then lay dark and quiet, while Frick completed plans to bring in 300 Pinkerton guards to secure the property and prepare for its reopening as a non-union plant.

Since the late 1870's the Pinkerton Detective Agency had become a major weapon against labor, participating on the side of owners who could afford their services in over seventy major labor disputes. In spite of a few state laws restricting their actions, the Pinkertons flourished and in practice enjoyed the complete cover of both law and money. "It would be next to impossible to convict a Pinkerton of any crime," declared one labor leader, "for he operates against the poor." [6] Their most recent appearance had been during the New York Central strike of 1890, in which they had killed five persons.[7] The irony was, of course, that by and large it was only the poor and desperate who took employment as actual Pinkerton guards in the first place; and hence it was the very poor, rather than the wealthy, who bore the actual burden and danger of breaking the strikes of other poor men. By the nineties the Pinkertons were among the most hated symbols of industrial oppression for workers across the country.

Up to July 1, events followed a pattern that was similar to any number of past strikes and lockouts. What made Homestead unusual was that the strike Advisory Committee proceeded to organize the workers into three semi-military divisions, each responsible for guarding the mill and town in consecutive eight-hour shifts, and sent men out along the roads and rivers to watch for the expected Pinkertons and replacement workers. With the full cooperation of the citizenry and the town government, the Advisory Committee took charge of the whole area, including the mill. The sheriff of Allegheny County, though allowed to inspect the mill, was unable to raise a force of deputies from the population, and retired helplessly to Pittsburgh. The workers made it clear that there would be no destruction of company property, but also that no strikebreakers would be allowed into Homestead.

During the still dark morning of July 6, the Pinkertons moved up the Monongahela on two armor-plated barges. Though the plan was to sneak into the mill before dawn, the workers' lookout system reported their approach long before they arrived. Sirens and factory whistles sounded throughout the town and thousands of residents grabbed weapons and rushed toward the riverbank and the mill docks. When the guards tried to land, some of the residents opened fire, driving them back inside the barges. For the next ten hours sporadic firing continued until at four in

---

[6] United States House of Representatives, 52nd Congress, 2nd sess. (1892–1893), *House Reports*, volume 3, number 2447, p. 222.

[7] Wolff, *Lockout*, pp. 69–70.

the afternoon the Pinkertons surrendered. Though guaranteed safe conduct by the strike leaders, the Pinkertons were beaten, kicked, and
clubbed by an enraged mob, composed mainly of women and children,
before they at last reached safety. Three Pinkertons and ten strikers died,
and hundreds of others were wounded.

Five days later the Governor of Pennsylvania sent in 8,000 militiamen
who took over the town. Shortly thereafter the furnaces were relit and the
company began bringing in and training new workers. When sympathy
strikes erupted at many of the other Carnegie mills, they were quickly
stopped or broken. Though the Homestead strike continued and the
company was hampered, production began to rise by early autumn.

On July 23, Alexander Berkman, a young Russian immigrant who
hoped to dramatize the plight of the workers, attempted to assassinate
Frick in his office. Though he shot him twice and stabbed him three
times, Berkman failed to kill the company chairman. Rather than rallying
the workers, he succeeded mainly in turning Frick from a villain to a
hero in the eyes of many people. While there was no connection whatever between Berkman and the Homestead workers, many tried to blame
them for the attempt. "The leaders who organized the attack upon the
Pinkertons three weeks ago, and who have never expressed any regret for
the act," declared *The Nation*, "are morally responsible for Berkman's
performance." [8] Once admit violence of any kind, the argument ran, and
all other kinds logically followed.

On November 20 the Amalgamated officially ended the five-month
strike. While many at the time, including the strike leaders, claimed
that the attack on Frick had ruined the workers' chances, it is clear in
retrospect that they had lost when the company began replacing its
workers under protection of the state militia. In spite of the long shut-
down at Homestead, the company's profits fell only $300,000 under those
of 1891, and still equaled a more than satisfactory 16 percent on its total
capitalization.[9] By the end of the year Homestead was once more in full
operation. The new non-union scale cut tonnage rates approximately
55 percent; the union work rules and grievance procedures were dis-
carded; and the minimum wage-scale was soon abolished.[10] Though
supported by contributions from groups throughout the United States
and Europe, the workers could not hold out indefinitely. Carnegie and
Frick could.

[8] *The Nation*, 55 (July 28, 1892), p. 60.
[9] George Harvey, *Henry Clay Frick: The Man* (New York, 1928), p. 178.
[10] Wall, *Andrew Carnegie*, p. 579.

Born into an established and socially prominent New England family, the brother of one Supreme Court Justice and the son-in-law of another, George Ticknor Curtis graduated from Harvard in 1832 and soon took up the study of law himself. Enjoying a long and prominent career, he made innumerable appearances before the United States Supreme Court and wrote extensively on both history and law. When in 1889 he published the first volume of his *Constitutional History of the United States from the Declaration of Independence to the Close of the Civil War,* he was widely recognized as one of the most learned constitutional authorities in the country. The following selection appeared in *The North American Review* just two months after the July battle at Homestead. What are the strengths and weaknesses of his highly legalistic approach? What does Curtis mean by the terms "liberty" and "right"? What assumptions does he make about the nature of American society and the nature of violence?

⊂⊋ Labor and the Law

GEORGE TICKNOR CURTIS

In the Homestead case, the existing agreement between the Carnegie Steel Company and their workmen about wages, had run out. Mr. Frick, the managing agent of the company, had an interview with the men, and offered a new scale of wages. This the men refused to accept. Mr. Frick then closed the mills. After this the workmen seized the mills, excluded the owners from their property by an overwhelming force, and prevented the employment of non-union men. Obviously, it was indispensable that something should be done to restore law and order, and to reinstate the owners of the mills in their property. The local officer of the law, whose duty it was to do this, was the sheriff of Allegheny County. His means consisted only of special deputy sheriffs appointed from the citizens at large, and sworn in as a temporary and extemporized force. In a population consisting largely of the striking workmen and their sympathizers, a force adequate to do what had to be done could not be obtained.

Thereupon the Carnegie Steel Company applied to the Pinkerton Agency for a body of watchmen to protect their property. The agency refused to supply the men unless they should be sworn in as deputy sheriffs before going to Homestead. . . .

The men were sent down the Allegheny River on barges. It is immaterial whether there is or is not a law of Pennsylvania which prohibits the sending of a body of armed men into the State for any purpose. I understand that there is no such law in Pennsylvania, although there is such a law in some of the New England States. But the Pinkerton men were within the limits of the state before they were armed or needed to be. The boxes containing arms and ammunition were shipped from Chicago, *and were to be delivered at the Homestead yards.* These boxes, on board the barges, were not opened and the contents distributed until after the strikers had begun firing from the shore on the watchmen and it had become an evident matter of self-defence. Klein, one of the Pinkerton watchmen, had been killed by the strikers, and about five other men shot and wounded before the Pinkerton men began their fire in self-defence. Then it was impossible to shoot those firing from the shore at the barges, because the strikers had made a breastwork for themselves by placing women and children in front and firing from behind them.

The Pinkerton men were obliged to capitulate before they were allowed to land, and even then they were not permitted to go to the mills which they had been employed to protect. They were conducted by an overwhelming force of the strikers to Labor Hall, the place of meeting of the strikers. There they were made to promise to quit Homestead and never again to serve the mill owners. On their way from the hall they were insulted and brutally assailed by a mob, among whom the women were the most violent. They were withdrawn from the State by the agency, and thus the whole object for which they had been employed was prevented.

Under these circumstances, the sheriff of Allegheny County applied to the Governor of the State for a military force. The Governor declined to order out any of the troops of the State, until the sheriff had exhausted his means of restoring law and order by the appointment of special deputies. The sheriff made an ineffectual effort to do this, but the citizens responded in such few numbers that it would have been idle to rely on the civil arm alone. When the Governor was officially informed of this, he ordered out the entire division of the State militia, about 6,000 men, under General Snowden, a capable, prudent and experienced officer. The troops were marched to Homestead, and encamped on a hill that overlooks the town. It is only necessary to say, concerning this part of the history, that at the time at which I am writing there is every prospect that the strike will be completely put down, and thus the State of Pennsylvania will have rendered a great service to the whole country, employers and employed, capitalists and laborers.

On the indubitable facts of the Homestead case, which I have taken great pains to gather from authentic sources, I have no hesitation in expressing my opinion, as follows:

First, That the owners of the mills had a perfect legal right to employ any necessary number of men to defend their property.

Secondly, That all the acts of the Pinkerton men at Homestead were lawful; and that, as watchmen, they had a right to bear arms on the premises of the Carnegie company in order to protect life and property, whether they were or were not deputized by the sheriff of Allegheny County; and that the agency had the right to ship arms for such purposes from Chicago to the Carnegie yards at Homestead; and that, in view of the attack on the barges, the watchmen had the right to bear arms and defend themselves; and that all their acts in firing in self-defence from the barges after the attack on them were legally justifiable under the laws of the United States and the State of Pennsylvania.

Thirdly, That the killing of Klein by one or more of the riotous strikers was a murder.

Fourthly, That all who stood by, sympathizing with and encouraging the strikers, or not exerting themselves to prevent the strikers who were armed from firing on the barges, were accessories to the murder. . . .

The first duty of the legislative power is to emancipate the individual workman from the tyranny of his class. Unless this be done, capitalists can afford no aid to the solution of any labor problem whatever. Of what avail is it that a mill owner or a railroad company is willing to make fair terms with workmen if the state of things is such that they cannot employ whom they please, on such terms as will be agreed to by the men who want employment? It is only by making the individual laborer a perfectly free man that society can do its duty to him and to those who wish to buy his labor for a price that he is willing to take, and which it is for the interest of those who are dependent upon him to have him take.

In opposition to this view, it will be said that the individual workman is a free agent now, and that if he choose to join a trades-union and bind himself not to work for wages less than what the union permits him to take, it is his own affair; he is acting in his own right. There is a wide distinction between the physical power to do a thing and the moral and legal right to do it. Men have the physical power to commit suicide, but society does not allow that they have a moral or a legal right to do it. On the same principle, the individual workman should not be allowed to commit moral suicide by surrendering his liberty to the control of his fellow workmen. His labor is his capital, all that he has in the world, all that he and his family have to depend upon for subsistence from day to day. It is to him and them what money invested in real estate, machinery, etc., is to the capitalist. Deprive the capitalist of the power to determine what remuneration he shall derive from the employment of his invested money, and you do the same wrong as when you deprive the laborer of the free power to determine what remuneration he will be content to take for the employment of his capital, which consists of his muscular power and his acquired skill.

These doctrines may not be popular. They may not meet at once with universal acceptance. But until they are accepted and carried out in legislation, there can be no successful reconcilement between the interests of capital and the interests of labor; no adjustment of the rights of society and the rights of employers and employed.

In order that I may not be misunderstood, I will now draw the line between what it may and what it may not be permitted to workmen to do. Associations of workmen, formed for the purpose of discussing the subject of wages with their employers, of obtaining and diffusing information about the price of labor in different places, and of mutual assistance in time of sickness, are beneficial and should be encouraged. But the trades-unions do not confine themselves to these objects. They transcend the line which divides what they may from what they may not rightfully do. In this respect they do a double wrong:

First, They bind their members to strike when ordered to do so by the governing authority of the union. Now the right to renounce an employment is an individual and not a corporate right. The corporate body of a trades-union should not be permitted to bind their members to quit work, as a body, when ordered to do so by the governing authority of the association.

Secondly, The trades-unions, as most of them are now organized, prevent non-union men from getting employment, by every species of intimidation, even by personal violence, and sometimes by murder.

This coercion of non-union men, however attempted and in whatever it ends, should be made a crime, and be punished with severity. It is contrary to the fundamental principles of our institutions. The Declaration of Independence says "we hold these truths to be self-evident, that all men are created equal; that they are endowed by their Creator with certain inalienable rights; that among these are life, liberty and the pursuit of happiness. That, to secure these rights, governments are instituted among men, deriving their just powers from the consent of the governed."

Be it observed that these are individual rights; that they are inalienable by the individual himself. We should not permit a man to sell himself into slavery or to sell his own life. He cannot alienate his right to life or his right to liberty. No more should he be permitted to alienate his right to the pursuit of happiness, by giving up his power to consult his own individual welfare, in obtaining the means of happiness; and by putting it in the power of those who are engaged in the same employment to take the bread out of his mouth. We have emancipated the colored race from slavery; certain portions of our own race need emancipation from a slavery that is just as bad.

One of twelve children of Irish immigrant parents, Terence V. Powderly went to work as a railroad switchman at the age of thirteen and joined his first labor union in 1871 when he was twenty-two. Likable, energetic, and effective as an orator, he rose through the ranks of the Knights of Labor to become Grand Master Workman in 1879, a position he held until 1893. Powderly rejected craft unionism in the belief that skilled workers should join with and help the unskilled, and he opposed the strike in favor of impartial arbitration in industrial disputes. Though he consistently urged a nonviolent policy for American workers, emphasizing the educational role unions should play, he was outraged at the actions of the Carnegie Steel Company, especially at the use of the Pinkertons. His essay appeared along with Curtis' in *The North American Review*. In what ways does he differ from Curtis in tone and method of argument? What assumptions does he make about the nature of American society and the role of violence? Does Powderly justify labor in the use of violence?

⊂⊋ Human Realities at Homestead

TERENCE V. POWDERLY

The principle involved in the Homestead trouble is the same as that by which the founders of this republic were governed in rebelling against the British government. To have accepted decisions, decrees, and laws without question, and without a voice in their making, would have stamped the colonists as slaves. To accept, without inquiring the why or wherefore, such terms and wages as the Carnegie Steel Company saw fit to offer would stamp the brand of inferiority upon the workmen of Homestead. Independence is worth as much to the workingman as it can be to the employer. The right to sell his labor in the highest market is as dear to the workman as the right of the manufacturer to sell the product of that labor can possibly be to the latter. It is folly to assert that the workman has no right to a voice in determining what the minimum rate of compensation shall be. If the manufacturer is permitted to invade the market place and undersell competitors a reduction in the wages of his employees must inevitably follow. It was to protect the manufacturer as well as the workman that the Amalgamated Association insisted on a minimum rate of pay. The fixing of that rate imposed no hardship on the manufacturer; it gave no competitor the advantage over him, for the majority of mills were operated under the Amalgamated scale, and this of itself fixed a rate below which manufacturers would not sell. The minimum rate was therefore as advantageous to the manufacturer as to the workman in the steel trade. The question at issue between the

Carnegie Steel Company and the steel workers does not so much concern the price as the right to a voice in fixing that price.

Individual employers no longer exist; the day no longer dawns on the employer taking his place in the shop among the men. When that condition of workshop life existed employer and employee experienced a feeling of lasting friendship for each other; the interests of each were faithfully guarded by the other. Now the employer of men may be three thousand miles away from the workshop; he may be a part of a syndicate or corporation which deals with the employees through a special agent or superintendent, whose desire to secure the confidence and good will of the corporation may cause him to create friction in order to demonstrate that he is vigilant in looking after the interests of those to whom he looks for favors. The corporation, composed of many men, is an association of capital which delegates its authority to an agent whose duty it is to deal with the workmen and make terms with them. The Amalgamated Association, and all other bodies of organized workmen, stand in the same relation to the men as the corporation does to the capitalists whose money is invested. One invests money, that is, his capital; the other invests his labor, which to him is not only his capital but his all. That the workman should have the same right to be heard through his legitimately appointed agent, the officer of the labor organization, that the corporation has to be heard through the superintendent or agent, is but equity. This is the bone of contention at Homestead, and in fact everywhere else where a labor organization attempts to guard the rights of its members.

Every law, every right, every concession which the workingmen now enjoy has come to them through the labor organization. Philanthropists have spoken honeyed words for the laboring man, but he has always been forced to knock, and knock hard, with his organization in order to take what equity would have accorded him without a struggle if greed had not entered its protest. Equality of rights is what the workmen are contesting for, and because of its immense wealth the Carnegie Steel Company denies that right. It is argued that this trouble is between the employer and the employed and that no other has the right to interfere. That is a doubtful position to take. In a store, in a small shop, or where but a few persons are interested, a strike or lockout may be said to affect only those directly engaged in it, but in the present instance the case presents a different aspect to the thoughtful person. If the great steel plant were not just where it is the town of Homestead would not be the flourishing place that it is. The establishment of that plant attracted workmen to the spot; they built homes, raised their families, and invested every dollar of their earnings there. Business men, professional men, and clergymen followed them, and a community of well-behaved, respectable citizens surrounds the steel works. The workmen by their labor made the steel works prosperous and great; on the other hand they made Homestead what it is. The men depend for their support on steady work, and the community back of them depends on their steady employment. Three parties are interested in this struggle, the Carnegie Steel Company, the employees of that concern, and the community. By community I mean the whole people. Other towns have grown up as Homestead grew, by the labor of workmen, and each one is to a certain extent interested in the welfare of the other. The articles manufactured in one place are sold in another, and a mutuality of interests exists to-day which did not, and could not, exist years ago when men required but few things to serve the every-day needs of life. The manager of the Carnegie Steel Company is asserting that he has the right to turn the makers of a prosperous town out of employment and out of the town,—for that naturally follows,—stands upon treacherous ground, for the makers of towns have equally as good a right to be heard as have the investors of money. If we go to a higher law than that of the land, the moral law, there will be no disputing the assertion that flesh and blood should receive more consideration than dollars and cents. . . .

At the hands of the law-making power of State and nation the Knights of Labor demand "the enactment of laws providing for arbitration between employers and employed, and to enforce the decision of the arbitrators." It should be a law in every State that in disputed cases the employer should be obliged to select two arbitrators and the employees two, these four to select the fifth; this arbitration commission to have access to all books, papers, and facts bearing on the question at issue from both sides. It goes without saying that the commission should be made up of reasonable, well-disposed men, and that publicity would not be given to such information as they might become possessed of. . . .

In no case should the introduction of an armed force, such as the Pinkerton detective agency arms and equips, be tolerated. The system which makes one man a millionaire makes tramps and paupers of thousands. The thousands go down to the brothels and slums, where they sprout the germs of anarchy and stand ready for any deed of desperation. The millionaire becomes more arrogant and unreasonable as his millions accumulate. Victimizing and blacklisting are the concomitants of the rule of industrial establishments by our millionaire "lords of industry," and these measures furnish recruits for the army of greed when organized labor enters its protest against such acts of injustice as has made tramps of other men under like circumstances. The employer who is satisfied with a reasonable profit will not fear to intrust his case to such a board of arbitrators as I have described. The employer who refuses arbitration fears for the justice of his cause. He who would acquire legitimately need not fear investigation; he who would steal must do it in the dark in order to be successful.

Those who harshly criticize the workmen of Homestead should put themselves in the place of these workmen for a few brief moments of thought. Picture the skill required to turn out faultless work, the loss of eyesight which follows a few years of toil before the seething furnace, the devotion to duty which must be shown in order to succeed. Then step outside of the mill and witness the erection of a high fence and its armament. Consider what it means and that it is being erected before a threat has been made or a disagreement considered among the possibilities. Think of the stigma which the erection of that fence casts on the man who works, the builder of the town; and then reflect that it is being built to serve as a prison-pen for those who must work so cheap that they will not be able to erect homes or maintain families in respectability. Ponder over the fact that when cheap men take the places of well-paid men, they do not buy carpets, organs, pianos, decent, respectable furniture or raiment, and that the makers of these articles elsewhere will be thrown out of employment, and that other manufacturers will be driven to bankruptcy because of a falling off in the demand for their product. Then read what Mr. Carnegie said six short years ago in speaking of the question of employing non-union, cheap men:

To expect that one dependent upon his daily wage for the necessaries of life will stand by peaceably and see a new man employed in his stead is to expect much. This poor man may have a wife and children dependent upon his labor. . . .

[The] employer of labor will find it much more to his interest, whenever possible, to allow his works to remain idle and await the result of a dispute than to employ the class of men that can be induced to take the place of other men who have stopped work. Neither the best men as men, nor the best men as workers, are thus to be obtained. There is an unwritten law among the best workmen: "Thou shalt not take thy neighbor's job." No wise employer will lightly lose his old employees. Length of service counts for much in many ways. Calling upon strange men should be the last resort.

The introduction of an armed body of men at the outset was an indication that some man would be expected to "take his neighbor's job," and at once. The arbitrament of the sword was the first thought with the Carnegie Steel Company. The laws of Pennsylvania were disregarded in arming citizens of other States and assigning them to duty at Homestead. In that awful spectacle to which the eyes of humanity turned on the 6th of July could be seen the final abolition of brute force in the settlement of strikes and lockouts. What the law will not do for men they must do for themselves, and by the light of the blazing guns at Homestead it was written that arbitration must take the place of "Pinkertonism."

Abandoning his middle-class Jewish home at the age of sixteen, Alexander Berkman emigrated from Russia to the United States in 1888. He quickly associated himself with the small anarchist groups, composed mainly of immigrant Russians and Germans, which congregated in New York. Known for his extreme views, Berkman judged the Homestead strike as an important step toward the radicalization of American labor and an appropriate setting for an *attentat,* an act of political assassination known as "the propaganda of the deed." Though legally liable for only seven years in prison for attempted murder, Berkman was sentenced to a term of twenty-one years by a court that unfairly manipulated charges in order to punish him more severely. He served fourteen of those years before a parole in 1906. The following selections are taken from his *Prison Memoirs of an Anarchist,* published in 1912. The first describes his attitude immediately before the assault of Frick. The second, from a letter written to his lover and fellow anarchist Emma Goldman, contains his reflections on the assassination of President William McKinley in 1901 by the anarchist Leon Czolgosz. In the first selection, notice Berkman's use of a medical metaphor to justify assassination. Such a metaphor, in one form or another, often undergirds defenses of violence (a search-and-destroy mission "sanitizes" an "infested' area; advocates of air power call for "surgical" bombing; repressive governments urge "amputation" of "diseased" parts of the "body politic"). How valid is such a metaphor, and why does it so consistently appear? The argument of the second selection is highly condensed. In what specific ways has Berkman changed? What does he mean by "the real despotism of republican institutions"? When can violence be effective, and when self-defeating?

Violence and Social Progress

ALEXANDER BERKMAN

I

My purpose is quite clear to me. A tremendous struggle is taking place at Homestead: the People are manifesting the right spirit in resisting tyranny and invasion. My heart exults. This is, at last, what I have always hoped for from the American workingman: once aroused, he will brook no interference; he will fight all obstacles, and conquer even more than his original demands. It is the spirit of the heroic past reincarnated in the steel-workers of Homestead, Pennsylvania. What supreme joy to aid in this work! That is my natural mission. I feel the strength of a great undertaking. No shadow of doubt crosses my mind. The People

—the toilers of the world, the producers—comprise, to me, the universe. They alone count. The rest are parasites, who have no right to exist. But to the People belongs the earth—by right, if not in fact. To make it so in fact, all means are justifiable; nay, advisable, even to the point of taking life. The question of moral right in such matters often agitated the revolutionary circles I used to frequent. I had always taken the extreme view. The more radical the treatment, I held, the quicker the cure. Society is a patient; sick constitutionally and functionally. Surgical treatment is often imperative. The removal of a tyrant is not merely justifiable; it is the highest duty of every true revolutionist. Human life is, indeed, sacred and inviolate. But the killing of a tyrant, of an enemy of the People, is in no way to be considered as the taking of a life. A revolutionist would rather perish a thousand times than be guilty of what is ordinarily called murder. In truth, murder and *Attentat* are to me opposite terms. To remove a tyrant is an act of liberation, the giving of life and opportunity to an oppressed people. True, the Cause often calls upon the revolutionist to commit an unpleasant act; but it is the test of a true revolutionist—nay, more, his pride—to sacrifice all merely human feeling at the call of the People's Cause. If the latter demand his life, so much the better.

Could anything be nobler than to die for a grand, a sublime Cause? Why, the very life of a true revolutionist has no other purpose, no significance whatever, save to sacrifice it on the altar of the beloved People. And what could be higher in life than to be a true revolutionist? It is to be a *man*, a complete MAN. A being who has neither personal interests nor desires above the necessities of the Cause; one who has emancipated himself from being merely human, and has risen above that, even to the height of conviction which excludes all doubt, all regret; in short, one who in the very inmost of his soul feels himself revolutionist first, human afterwards.

II

I followed the newspapers with great anxiety. The whole country seemed to be swept with the fury of revenge. To a considerable extent the press fanned the fires of persecution. Here in the prison very little sincere grief was manifested. Out of hearing of the guards, the men passed very uncomplimentary remarks about the dead president. The average prisoner corresponds to the average citizen—their patriotism is very passive, except when stimulated by personal interest, or artificially excited. But if the press mirrored the sentiment of the people, the Nation must have suddenly relapsed into cannibalism. There were moments when I was in mortal dread for your very life, and for the safety of the other arrested comrades. In previous letters you hinted that it was official rivalry and jealousy, and your absence from New York, to which you owe your release. You may be right; yet I believe that your attitude of proud self-respect and your admirable self-control contributed much to the result. You were splendid, dear; and I was especially moved by your remark that you would faithfully nurse the wounded man, if he required your services, but that the poor boy, condemned and deserted by all, needed and deserved your sympathy and aid more than the president. More strikingly than your letters, that remark discovered to me the great change wrought in us by the ripening years. Yes, in us, in both, for my heart echoed your beautiful sentiment. How impossible such a thought would have been to us in the days of a decade ago! We should have considered it treason to the spirit of revolution; it would have outraged all our traditions even to admit the humanity of an official representative of capitalism. Is it not very significant that we two—you living in the very heart of Anarchist thought and activity, and I in the atmosphere of absolute suppression and solitude—should have arrived at the same evolutionary point after a decade of divergent paths? . . .

And you, my dear friend, with the deeper insight of time, you have yet happily kept your heart young. I have rejoiced at it in your letters of recent years, and it is especially evident from the sentiments you have expressed regarding the happening at Buffalo. I share your view entirely; for that very reason, it is the more distressing to disagree with you in one very important particular: the value of Leon's act. I know the terrible ordeal you have passed through, the fiendish persecution to which you have been subjected. Worse than all must have been to you the general lack of understanding for such phenomena; and, sadder yet, the despicable attitude of some would-be radicals in denouncing the man and his act. But I am confident you will not mistake my expressed disagreement for condemnation.

We need not discuss the phase of the *Attentat* which manifested the rebellion of a tortured soul, the individual protest against social wrong. Such phenomena are the natural result of evil conditions, as inevitable as the flooding of the river banks by the swelling mountain torrents. But I cannot agree with you regarding the social value of Leon's act.

I have read of the beautiful personality of the youth, of his inability to adapt himself to brutal conditions, and the rebellion of his soul. It throws a significant light upon the causes of the *Attentat*. Indeed, it is at once the greatest tragedy of martyrdom, and the most terrible indictment of society, that it forces the noblest men and women to shed human blood, though their souls shrink from it. But the more imperative it is that drastic methods of this character be resorted to only as a last extremity. To prove of value, they must be motived [sic] by social rather than individual necessity, and be directed against a real and immediate enemy of the people. The significance of such a deed is understood by the

popular mind—and in that alone is the propagandistic, educational importance of an *Attentat*, except if it is exclusively an act of terrorism.

Now, I do not believe that this deed was terroristic; and I doubt
whether it was educational, because the social necessity for its performance was not manifest. That you may not misunderstand, I repeat: as an
expression of personal revolt it was inevitable, and in itself an indictment of existing conditions. But the background of social necessity was
lacking, and therefore the value of the act was to a great extent nullified.

In Russia, where political oppression is popularly felt, such a deed
would be of great value. But the scheme of political subjection is more
subtle in America. And though McKinley was the chief representative of
our modern slavery, he could not be considered in the light of a direct
and immediate enemy of the people; while in an absolutism, the autocrat
is visible and tangible. The real despotism of republican institutions is
far deeper, more insidious, because it rests on the popular delusion of
self-government and independence. That is the subtle source of democratic tyranny, and, as such, it cannot be reached with a bullet.

In modern capitalism, exploitation rather than oppression is the real
enemy of the people. Oppression is but its handmaid. Hence the battle
is to be waged in the economic rather than the political field. It is therefore that I regard my own act as far more significant and educational
than Leon's. It was directed against a tangible, real oppressor, visualized
as such by the people.

As long as misery and tyranny fill the world, social contrasts and consequent hatreds will persist, and the noblest of the race—or Czolgoszes
—burst forth in "rockets of iron." But does this lightning really illumine
the social horizon, or merely confuse minds with the succeeding darkness?
The struggle of labor against capital is a class war, essentially and chiefly
economic. In that arena the battles must be fought.

Born into a devoutly religious family of New Englanders in 1854, Richard T. Ely rejected the strict Presbyterian Calvinism of his father and embraced instead a more optimistic and humanitarian version of Christianity. Winning a fellowship that allowed him to travel to Germany, the intellectual training ground for many Americans in the latter half of the nineteenth century, Ely studied economics, history, and philosophy at the Universities of Halle and Heidelberg. When he returned to the United States, he soon established himself as an important innovator and organizer in the field of economics and began to develop his own brand of Christian social ethics. A strong advocate of social reform, he wholly rejected anarchism and warned against its dangerous influence. He published the following essay in *Harper's Weekly* for December 23, 1893, clearly thinking of such events as Homestead and the assault on Frick. What are the logical and historical connections between "authority" of various kinds, including "God," and the use of violence? Why does Ely find it necessary to attack the anarchists so sharply while presenting his own ideas of reform so mildly? What are the advantages and disadvantages of the two possible methods for dealing with movements such as anarchism, repression, and reform?

⊂⊋   Christian Ethics and Social Problems

RICHARD T. ELY

There are various groups among the anarchists, but they are agreed in one fundamental and most dangerous doctrine, namely, that man has no moral right to exercise authority over his fellows. To the exercise of authority of some men over other men they trace the social and individual evils of our time. It is authority, they claim, which protects privilege, exploits labor, maintains wage slavery, and stands athwart the pathway which leads to the promised land of plenty and peace secured by co-operation. Men are held by anarchy to be naturally good, and to be restrained from brotherly co-operation by the authority of a few oppressors maintained through church and state. The evil of evils, then, is authority. Even this may not suggest at once its full meaning to the reader. Let him remember, however, what consequences naturally flow from the principle that authority has no ethical or religious basis. Does not government then become simply a combination of individuals exercising force merely for personal advantage? If government has the character of any private combination of strong men to pursue their own advantage to the detriment of others by downright physical force, does not resistance to it become a duty? We are now brought face to face with one of the most serious problems of modern times, namely, the true seat of authority in government and its ethical justification. The anarchist can look upon resistance to government at a particular time at the best as only a question of expediency. You may take the position that it is better to submit to a certain injustice from a pugilist rather than to resist him with your insufficient physical strength. You wish that you had the power and the skill to knock him down; you know that should you punish him as the brutal fellow deserves your conduct would be only praiseworthy. There are anarchists who say that resistance to government at present is folly, because it has no outlook for success; but there are no anarchists, so far as the writer knows, who look upon resistance as morally wrong. It is this refusal to recognize anything but ordinary brute force in government which renders anarchy the most extreme social theory in the world's history, and the most dangerous theory which civilization has ever had to encounter. . . .

As the anarchists are rebels against human authority, they are, with perhaps scarcely an exception, rebels against divine authority. The flag which they wave is the flag of atheism and materialism. Voltaire said that if God did not exist it would be necessary to invent Him, because he felt the need of the idea of God as a social force. The anarchist says, however, in the words of Bakounin, "If God existed it would be necessary to abolish Him." The meaning of this is that the source of all authority is God, and it is possible to get authority out of the world only by driving out of the minds of men the idea of God. . . .

The first impulse is to determine to attack these wild beasts of society, to exterminate them as enemies of their kind. Yet the first impulse here is not wholly reliable. Looking at the matter thoughtfully, we find it is necessary to make distinctions. The "propaganda of the deed" must, in fact, be suppressed. Violence must be punished with severity; public peace must be preserved at all costs. The power of society must be brought to bear upon rebellion and put it down; and society, we may all rest assured, is equal to this task. But this is not sufficient. The philosophy underlying anarchy cannot be rooted out by physical force. Wise thinkers have long recognized that the only cure for a bad philosophy is a good philosophy. We must replace the philosophy of freedom and happiness through rebellion with the philosophy of real freedom and real happiness through obedience. We must learn to recognize the state as something sacred, or else we must be prepared to deal with anarchy as a perpetually menacing force. We must establish upon a firm foundation the right of man to exercise authority over his fellows, showing in what this right originates, what maintains it, and what holds it within desirable limits. Indeed, if government is mere brute force, why should it not be resisted by brute force? Is the policeman's club the beginning and the end of authority? If this is so, what ethical reason can be deduced to show that a stronger man than he should not wrest his club from him? . . .

But this question of anarchy is also a question of economics. It is important to add to our ethical and religious teaching a sound political economy, and this political economy will show the impossibility of the attainment of the end proposed by the anarchists by the means which they propose, altogether apart from the ethical nature of these means. The economic impossibility of anarchism is a topic which is worthy of serious treatment.

There are dangers against which we must guard in the present emergency. One of these is that the strength of the anarchists will be over-estimated. They are but a handful of people, and perhaps in a dozen years have not been weaker than they are now. . . .

Another danger is that society will fail to discriminate between the various social movements, and thus, on the one hand, lose much useful support, and, on the other, by acts of persecution, will tend to drive some to the anarchistic philosophy and practices. The chief discrimination which should be made at the present time is that between socialism and anarchy, which have so recently been confounded. The two are far enough apart, and where the one thrives the other languishes. The most effective force, for example, in keeping anarchy out of Germany has been social democracy. And if this social democracy were stronger in Spain, there would be less anarchy there. . . .

There is, no doubt, very much to be condemned in social democracy, but this is something different enough from anarchy. It is one of the most useful antagonists of anarchy, because it opposes the social demand of anarchy from a stand-point which the masses can understand. It is something which is to be attacked and overcome by very different methods.

Born in rural Wisconsin in 1860, Hamlin Garland early learned to hate the dull drudgery of farm life. His father, Richard Garland, had typified the restless westward movement of Americans in the nineteenth century, having moved first from Maine to Wisconsin, then with his new family to the rich farm lands of Iowa, and finally to the Dakota territory. Richard Garland was never able to win the economic prosperity that the West had promised, and young Hamlin rebelled bitterly against what he considered a pointless and profitless existence. At twenty-one he left home and headed back east. Embarking on a strenuous program of self-education, he moved to Boston in 1884, where he eventually attracted the attention of several prominent literary figures, including William Dean Howells. In 1891, Garland published his *Main-Travelled Roads*, a poignant account of harsh midwestern farm life that would later become a recognized classic of American realism. He continued to write both novels and journalistic pieces, expressing his deep concern over problems of poverty and the need for economic reform. In early 1894 he visited the Homestead mills, which were once again running smoothly, and published his impressions in *McClure's Magazine* in June. To what extent does Garland think the Homestead workers are free men? Does the concept of violence need to be broadened beyond such acts as bombing and shooting in order to be a valid and just social concept? What does the essay suggest about the relationship between violence and the degree of meaningful control that individuals have over the conditions that affect their lives?

⏚ Homestead Two Years After

HAMLIN GARLAND

The streets of the town were horrible; the buildings were poor; the sidewalks were sunken, swaying, and full of holes, and the crossings were sharp-edged stones set like rocks in a river bed. Everywhere the yellow mud of the street lay kneaded into a sticky mass, through which groups of pale, lean men slouched in faded garments, grimy with the soot and grease of the mills.

The town was as squalid and unlovely as could well be imagined, and the people were mainly of the discouraged and sullen type to be found everywhere where labor passes into the brutalizing stage of severity. It had the disorganized and incoherent effect of a town which has feeble public spirit. Big industries at differing eras have produced squads of squalid tenement-houses far from the central portion of the town, each plant bringing its gangs of foreign laborers in raw masses to camp down like an army around its shops.

Such towns are sown thickly over the hill-lands of Pennsylvania, but this was my first descent into one of them. They are American only in the sense in which they represent the American idea of business.

The Carnegie mills stood down near the river at some distance from the ferry landing, and thither I took my way through the sticky yellow mud and the gray falling rain. I had secured for my guide a young man whose life had been passed in Homestead and who was quite familiar with the mills and workmen. I do not think he over-stated the hardships of the workmen, whose duties he thoroughly understood. He spoke frankly and without undue prejudice of the management and the work.

We entered the yard through the fence which was aggrandized into a stockade during the riots of a year ago. . . .

The great building which we entered first was a beam mill, "one of the finest in the world," my guide said. It was an immense shed, open at the sides and filled with a mixed and intricate mass of huge machinery. On every side tumultuous action seemed to make every inch of ground dangerous. Savage little engines went rattling about among the piles of great beams. Dimly on my left were huge engines, moving with thunderous pounding. . . .

Everywhere in this pandemoniac shed was the thunder of reversing engines, the crash of falling iron, the rumbling growl of rollers, the howl of horrible saws, the deafening hiss of escaping steam, the wild vague shouts of workmen. . . .

"That looks like hard work," I said to one of them to whom my companion introduced me. He was breathing hard from his work.

"Hard! I guess it's hard. I lost forty pounds the first three months I came into this business. It sweats the life out of a man. I often drink two buckets of water during twelve hours; the sweat drips through my sleeves, and runs down my legs and fills my shoes."

"But that isn't the worst of it," said my guide; "it's a dog's life. Now, those men work twelve hours, and sleep and eat out of ten more. You can see a man don't have much time for anything else. You can't see your friends, or do anything but work. That's why I got out of it. I used to come home so exhausted, staggering like a man with a 'jag.' It ain't any place for a sick man—is it, Joe?"

Joe was a tall young fellow, evidently an assistant at the furnace. He smiled. "It's all the work I want, and I'm no chicken—feel that arm."

I felt his arm. It was like a billet of steel. His abdomen was like a sheet of boiler iron. The hair was singed from his hands and arms by the heat of the furnace.

"The tools I handle weigh one hundred and fifty pounds, and four o'clock in August they weigh about a ton."

"When do you eat?"

"I have a bucket of 'grub'; I eat when I can. We have no let-up for eating. This job I'm on now isn't so bad as it might be, for we're running easy; but when we're running full, it's all I can stand.". . .

Everywhere in this enormous building were pits like the mouth of hell, and fierce ovens giving off a glare of heat, and burning wood and iron, giving off horrible stenches of gases. Thunder upon thunder, clang upon clang, glare upon glare! Torches flamed far up in the dark spaces above. Engines moved to and fro, and steam hissed and threatened.

Everywhere were grimy men with sallow and lean faces. The work was of the inhuman sort that hardens and coarsens.

"How long do you work?" I asked of a young man who stood at the furnace near me.

"Twelve hours," he replied. "The night set go on at six at night and come off at six in the morning. I go on at six and off at six."

"For how much pay?"

"Two dollars and a quarter."

"How much do those men get shoveling there in the rain?"

"One dollar and forty cents." (A cut has since taken place.)

"What proportion of the men get that pay?"

"Two-thirds of the whole plant, nearly two thousand. There are thirty-five hundred men in the mills. They get all prices, of course, from a dollar and forty cents up to the tonnage men, who get five and ten dollars per day when the mills run smooth."

"I suppose not many men make ten dollars per day."

"Well, hardly." He smiled. "Of course the 'rollers' and the 'heaters' get the most, but there are only two 'rollers' to each mill, and three 'heaters,' and they are responsible for their product. The most of the men get under two dollars per day."

"And it is twelve hours' work without stop?"

"You bet! And then again you see we only get this pay part of the time. The mills are liable to be shut down part of the year. They shut down part of the night sometimes, and of course we're docked. Then, again, the tendency of the proprietors is to cut down the tonnage men; that is, the 'rollers' and 'heaters' are now paid by the ton, but they'll some day be paid by the day, like the rest of us.". . .

We passed on into the older mills, where cruder methods are still in use. Man seems closer to the hot iron here. Everywhere dim figures with grappling hooks worked silently and desperately, guiding, measuring, controlling, moving masses of white-hot metal. High up the superintending foremen, by whistle or shout, arrested the movement of the machinery and the gnome-like figures beneath.

Here were made the steel rails for street railways. . . . Each crude mass of metal was heated in oven-like furnaces tended by dim figures of bare-armed men, thence drawn by cranes and swung upon a roadway and thrust into the rollers. Then it ran back and forth, back and forth, lengthening into a swift and terrible serpent of red. One that I saw had split at the end, and its resemblance to a serpent was startling as it shot toward us in sinuous thrust. Upon such toil rests the splendor of American civilization. . . .

"Yes, the men call this the death-trap," repeated my guide, as we stood in the edge of the building; "they wipe a man out here every little while."

"In what way does death come?" I asked.

"Oh, all kinds of ways. Sometimes a chain breaks, and a ladle tips over, and the iron explodes—like that." He pointed at the newly emptied retort, out of which the drippings fell into the water which lay beneath like pools of green gold. As it fell, each drop exploded in a dull report.

"Sometimes the slag falls on the workmen from that roadway up there. Of course, if everything is working all smooth and a man watches out, why, all right! But you take it after they've been on duty twelve hours without sleep, and running like hell, everybody tired and loggy, and it's a different story."

My guide went on:

"You take it back in the beam mill—you saw how the men have to scatter when the carriers or the cranes move—well, sometimes they don't get out of the way; the men who should give warning don't do it quick enough."

"What do those men get who are shoveling slag up there?"

"Fourteen cents an hour. If they worked eight hours, like a carpenter, they'd get one dollar and twelve cents."

"So a man works in peril of his life for fourteen cents an hour," I remarked.

"That's what he does. It ain't the only business he does it in, though."

"No," put in a young villager, who was looking on like ourselves. "A man'll do most anything to live."

"Just as everywhere, the man who does the hardest work gets the poorest pay," I said, remembering Shelley's discovery. . . .

My guide looked serious. "You don't notice any old men here." He swept his hand about the building. "It shortens life, just like mining; there is no question about that. That, of course, doesn't enter into the usual statement. But the long hours, the strain, and the sudden changes of temperature use a man up. He quits before he gets fifty. I can see lots of fellows here who are failing. They'll lay down in a few years.". . .

"I'm glad I don't have to work here for a living," said the young man of the village, who stood near me looking on.

"Oh, this is nothing," said my guide. "You should see it when they're running full in summer. Then it gets *hot* here. Then you should see 'em when they reline the furnaces and converting vessels. Imagine getting into that Bessemer pot in July, hot enough to pop corn; when you had to work like the devil and then jump out to breathe."

"I wouldn't do it," said the young villager; "I'd break into jail first." He had an outside job. He could afford to talk that way.

"Oh, no, you wouldn't; you'd do it. We all submit to such things, out of habit, I guess. There are lots of other jobs as bad. A man could stand work like this six hours a day. That's all a man ought to do at such work. They could do it, too; they wouldn't make so much, but the hands would live longer."

"They probably don't care whether the hands live or die," I said, "provided they do every ounce they can while they do live."

"I guess that's right," said the other young fellow with a wink. "Mill-owners don't run their mills for the benefit of the men."

"How do you stand on the late strike?" I asked another man.

"It's all foolishness; you can't do anything that way. The tonnage men brought it on; they could afford to strike, but we couldn't. The men working for less than two dollars can't afford to strike."

" 'While capital wastes, labor starves,' " I ventured to quote.

"That's the idea; we can't hurt Carnegie by six months' starving. It's *our* ribs that'll show through our shirts."

"Then the strikes do not originate among the men of lowest pay?"

"No; a man working for fourteen cents an hour hasn't got any surplus for a strike." He seemed to voice the general opinion.

A roar as of a hundred lions, a thunder as of cannons, flames that made the electric light look like a twinkling blue star, jarring clang of falling iron, burst of spluttering flakes of fire, scream of terrible saws, shifting of mighty trucks with hiss of steam! This was the scene upon which I looked back; this tumult I was leaving. I saw men prodding in the deep soaking pits where the ingots glowed in white-hot chambers. I saw other men in the hot yellow glare from the furnaces. I saw men measuring the serpentine rosy beams. I saw them send the saw flying into them. I saw boys perched high in cages, their shrill voices sounding wild and animal-like in the midst of the uproar: a place into which men went like men going into war for the sake of wives and children, urged on by necessity, blinded and dulled by custom and habit; an inhuman place to spend four-fifths of one's waking hours. I crawled dismally back to my boarding-place, in the deep darkness, the chill, and the falling rain. The farther I got from those thundering beams and screaming saws, the deeper I drew my breath. Oh, the peace and sweetness of the dim hills across the river!

I ate breakfast the next morning with two of the men I had seen the evening before. There was little of grace or leisurely courtesy in their actions. Their hearts were good, but their manners were those of ceaseless toilers. They resembled a Western threshing crew in all but their pallor.

"The worst part of the whole business is this," said one of them, as I was about saying good-by. "It brutalizes a man. You can't help it. You start in to be a man, but you become more and more a machine, and pleasures are few and far between. It's like any severe labor. It drags you down mentally and morally, just as it does physically. I wouldn't mind it so much if it weren't for the long hours. Many a trade would be all right if the hours could be shortened. Twelve hours is too long."

Again I boarded the little ferry and crossed the Monongahela on my way to the East. Out of those grim chimneys the belching smoke rose, defiling the cool, sweet air. Through this greenish-purple cloud the sun, red and large, glowed like an ingot of steel rising from a pit, filling the smoke with flushes of beautiful orange and rose amid the blue. The river was azure and burning gold, and the sun threw the most glorious shadows behind the smoke. Beyond lay the serene hills, a deeper purple.

Under the glory of gold and purple I heard the grinding howl of the iron-saws, and the throbbing, ferocious roar of the furnaces. The ferry-boat left a wake of blue that shone like the neck of a dove; and over the hills swept a fresh, moist wind. In the midst of God's bright morning, beside the beautiful river, the town and its industries lay like a cancer on the breast of a human body.

Chapter
13: Social Welfare in the Industrial Era

☞ ROY LUBOVE

The depression of the 1890's posed a unique challenge to American welfare institutions. They confronted an unprecedented relief problem on the one hand and a growing contempt for charitable relief on the other. An aggressive, strike-conscious trade-union movement represented one expression of the revolt against charity and the paternalism it embodied. The industrial armies of 1894 and their assertion of a "right to work" doctrine also challenged traditional assumptions about dependency and welfare policy. The right to work concept, in essence, clashed with the conventional view of charity as a mainly voluntary responsibility through which benefits were dispensed to the "worthy." The right to work, which implied an expanded governmental welfare role, can be interpreted as an early expression of the social security principle of the right to economic assistance or public services.

Far from endorsing any claims to a publicly guaranteed right to work, private relief agencies during the depression emphasized the need to limit public provision for the poor. This view was consistent with the philanthropic division of labor which evolved in the nineteenth century. Ideally, public agencies would assume a routine caretaker responsibility for the non-able-bodied poor (aged, handicapped); and they would serve as an instrument of discipline for the able-bodied who were unwilling to support themselves. Private or voluntary organizations were delegated the more "constructive" character-building task. They would influence the attitudes and behavior of the poor, above all enhancing their capacity for self-support. The voluntary sector was also assigned an important economic relief function. Presumably, the commitment of private charitable agencies to elevating the character of the poor insured that relief would not degenerate into a mechanical dole.

The nineteenth-century philanthropic division of labor was rooted in a fear of undermining work incentive. It was widely assumed that voluntary welfare organizations were less likely to encourage pauperism than public agencies. Private agencies not only combined relief with religious and moral training; equally important, they were comparatively immune to the political pressures which might force public officials to increase relief expenditures. The generosity of these officials would, in turn, increase the number of paupers and the demands upon the public treasury would become limitless.

Widespread unemployment during the depression of the 1890's intensified concern over the dangers of public relief. And at the height of the depression, unemployment totaled 20 percent of the labor force. Depression-enforced idleness, combined with readily obtainable alms, represented a disastrous combination; hitherto respectable workers might make the "fatal discovery . . . that living and labor are not interchangeable terms." The charitably disposed had to "bear in mind the importance of not letting men discover that they can have all they need . . . without work." [1] An overly generous relief policy which created paupers ran contrary to the laws of nature and thus threatened the survival of society: "Nature enacts that if a man be profligate he must suffer therefor disease and death; but we pick up this wretched rake from the midst of his diseases and nurse him back to health at the expense of the upright and sober and then we send him out to repeat his folly." [2]

The tramp and vagrant, the pauper generally, dramatized the key challenge confronting welfare institutions in the American work culture. How could society provide economic relief without increasing dependency? How much economic security, and what kind, could be offered without undermining work incentvie or labor force participation? The depression crisis, in relation to these issues, was significant in two respects. First, it stimulated interest in work relief as a means of reconciling the conflict between relief and incentive objectives. Second, it led to the assertion of the right to work doctrine which anticipated social security ideals of the twentieth century.

Welfare leaders could not endorse any doctrine, including the right to work, which sanctioned an arbitrary redistribution of wealth. They were, to the contrary, anxious to insure that the depression emergency did not lead to heresies which increased the claims of the poor and unemployed upon society. Thus Josephine Shaw Lowell, founder of the New York Charity Organization Society, vehemently criticized relief programs during the winter of 1893–94 which "seemed ingeniously devised to offer a temptation to dependence for all sorts and conditions of men." Among the worst offenders were the newspaper relief funds which "sent

[1] J. J. M'Cook, "The Tramp Problem: What It Is and What to do About It," National Conference of Charities and Correction, *Proceedings* (1895), pp. 295, 297.
[2] Samuel Lane Loomis, "The Tramp Problem," *The Chautauquan* (June, 1894), p. 312.

wagons blazoned with their names and errands into the crowded tenement streets, and called aloud the names of those for whom they had a charity package." These practices, Miss Lowell objected, "fostered the socialistic teaching that such gifts were not a favor received, but only a small part of what was due from the rich to the poor." The depression experience reinforced the conviction of charity societies that relief had to be limited and carefully controlled. The most "painful revelation" during the first winter of depression was the "willingness of those who have not hitherto been paupers to avail themselves of the public provision for the poor." The "melancholy" truth was that a liberal "distribution of alms tends to weaken the self-respect and independence of many who have hitherto taken care of themselves." [3]

Interest in work relief was stimulated by the belief that it would minimize the conflict between assistance and incentive. However, work relief could not compete with private employment if it was to be "beneficial" and not "injurious." It had to be "continuous, hard, and underpaid." Otherwise, it might still encourage individuals to depend on charitable resources rather than seek employment in the private market. Important in the formulation of a work relief program was the need to distinguish between the temporarily unemployed and the chronic mendicant. Workhouses had to be established for the latter, the "incorrigible idlers and tramps," who required a semi-correctional regime. A model existed in the European labor colonies where an attempt was made to teach the worker a skill so that he could regularly support himself.

Both public and private agencies undertook work relief schemes during the depression of the 1890's. They often involved heavy outdoor labor for men, and sewing or laundry work for women. But work relief differed from the assertion of the right to work. The former remained a charitable endeavor, always paternalistic and often punitive as well. The right to work implied the liberation of the worker both from charitable caprice and a market economy which deprived him of employment through no fault of his own.

The industrial army movement in the spring and summer of 1894 was described as an "American adoption of a familiar Russian mode of airing grievances and of protesting against abuses." [4] The indigenous ideological roots included Populism, the Greenback and Anti-Monopoly crusades and, to some extent, nativism. These various traditions of social protest were exemplified in the preamble to the constitution of General

[3] Mrs. C. R. Lowell, "The Unemployed in New York City, 1893–94," *Journal of Social Science* (November, 1894), pp. 19, 20; Charles D. Kellogg, "The Situation in New York City During the Winter of 1893–94," National Conference of Charities and Correction, *Proceedings* (1894), p. 29; Washington Gladden, "Relief Work,—Its Principles and Methods," *Review of Reviews* (January, 1894), p. 38.

[4] W. T. Stead, " 'Coxeyism': A Character Sketch," *Review of Reviews* (July, 1894), p. 48.

Lewis C. Fry's Los Angeles Army: "The evils of murderous competition; the supplanting of manual labor by machinery; the excessive Mongolian and Pauper immigration; the curse of alien landlordism; the exploitation by rent, profit and interest, of the products of the toiler, has centralized the wealth of the nation into the hands of the few, and placed the masses in a state of hopeless destitution."[5] Fry's contingent demanded government employment for all unemployed citizens, a ten-year moratorium on immigration, and the prohibition of real estate ownership by aliens. The right to work program devised by Charles T. Kelly's San Francisco army stressed employment on arid land reclamation projects in the west.

The west produced the largest and most turbulent of the industrial armies, but the best-known was Jacob S. Coxey's "Commonweal of Christ." Originating in Massillon, Ohio, the Coxey group clearly illustrated the link between the right to work idea and Greenback ideology. The Commonwealers' march on Washington was designed to promote the passage of two bills. A Good Roads Bill would have required the Secretary of the Treasury to print $500 million in notes for use in the construction of roads. A Non-Interest-Bearing Bond Bill would have authorized communities to deposit non-interest-bearing bonds with the Secretary of the Treasury. The bonds could total up to one-half the assessed value of property in the community. The Secretary would then print notes equal to the face value of the bonds, and the money would be used to employ any man seeking work.

Contemporaries differed in their evaluation of the industrial armies. They were condemned as the harbinger of anarchy, "simply organized bands of wandering mendicants, with little regard for law or the rights of property." Other critics, with an eye on the opposite end of the ideological continuum, saw an "essentially socialistic" threat; "if government is bound to furnish every man with work fitted to his capacity, and pay him enough to support life in comfort then the ideal of individual responsibility, one of God's grandest gifts to men, is utterly overthrown." The industrial armies also triggered apocalyptic visions. The nation was resting on the crater of a "volcano." If it continued to ignore the "cry of the poor and downtrodden," then class war was inevitable.[6] The worker would no longer accept charity in place of justice.

A more realistic evaluation of the right to work episode was suggested by the economist John R. Commons. It implied the development of a new system of industrial relations in which the worker acquired a right "not to the entire product, but to a definite standing supported by law within

[5] Donald L. McMurray, *Coxey's Army: A Study of the Industrial Army Movement of 1894* (Boston, 1929), p. 304.

[6] Shirley Plumer Austin, "The Downfall of Coxeyism," *The Chautauquan* (July, 1894), p. 452; A. Cleveland Hall, "An Observer in Coxey's Camp," *Independent* (May 17, 1894), p. 616; Henry Frank, "The Crusade of the Unemployed," *Arena* (July, 1894), pp. 239, 242.

industry along with the capitalist proprietors." [7] In other words, if a society required labor force participation as a condition of survival, then it was obliged to guarantee that work would be available. Succeeded by an organized movement for comprehensive social insurance in the early twentieth century, the right to work idea marked a phase in the broader quest for social security in America.

[7] John R. Commons, "The Right to Work," *Arena* (February, 1899), p. 138.

In the selection, "Plea for Organized Charity" (editors' title), a social worker describes the response of a leading industrial community to large-scale unemployment during the winter of 1893–94. The Pittsburgh experience was typical in at least two important respects. First, a large number of emergency relief funds sprung into existence, supplementing the efforts of the regular public and private agencies. Experienced charity workers complained that these frequently did more harm than good. The depression reinforced the conviction that a community's charitable work had to be coordinated and managed by experts. Second, Pittsburgh's response to the depression was typical in the emphasis on work relief. This device presumably would safeguard the self-respect of the unemployed, and at the same time prevent an increase in the pauper population. From a reading of this selection, could one conclude that work relief was a charitable expedient which prevented unemployment? Did it achieve a more efficient balance between supply and demand in the labor market? As a charitable resource, was its value limited because it could not be allowed to compete with private employment in terms of product or pay? The following article, by R. D. McGonnigle, originally entitled "The Winter in Pittsburg," is taken from the *Proceedings* of the National Conference of Charities and Correction, 1894, pp. 36–42.

Plea for Organized Charity

R. D. McGonnigle

The recent industrial depression has not been without its silvery lining. This was the spontaneous impulse of enthusiasm that rose out from the hearts of the more fortunate, and illustrated itself in a feeling of true brotherliness. It was a beautiful exemplification of a distinctive characteristic of the American nation, fellow-feeling, which prompted immediate and thorough action, and brought about relief in a condition of affairs such as the world has fortunately not often witnessed.

We know how in all the larger cities self-constituted committees, with and without the aid of municipal governmental assistance, sprang into rapid existence; and, while they may not have been equally effective in alleviating the demands made by every individual, their intentions were good. And that a great deal was accomplished, and that in some instances wonders were achieved, is not to be doubted.

In Pittsburg the necessity for relief was especially augmented on account of the large number of its idle industrial establishments, which threw out of work thousands of men.

All during the summer of 1893 increasing want was noticeable. Many of the iron mills, the steel works, and the glass works shut down. While the weather was warm, there was not much cause for alarm, and those who had no work were able to exist on their savings; but, as soon as the trees had shed their leaves, poverty made itself perceptibly felt. The local department of charity and charitable institutions were overrun with demands from the hungry and needy, and could not cope with them successfully. The clamor for bread and clothing grew very rapidly, until on the 12th of December Mayor McKenna, of Pittsburg, called a public meeting. The call struck a sympathetic chord; and the meeting was a representative gathering of the best and wealthiest men of the city, who voiced a unanimous willingness to do all in their power to quell the ravages of destitution.

At this meeting several committees were appointed: on finance, on employment, and to lay out plans as to the best means of aiding those in want. Voluntary subscriptions of money were asked, and it was decided to furnish employment. The city had recently acquired parks of some three hundred acres, and it was deemed advisable to employ the workmen on these.

To this end the committees entered into co-operation with the Department of Public Works. It was agreed that the city was to furnish foremen and engineers, while the committee selected the time-keepers. The uniform price of $1 per day per man, irrespective of duties, was decided upon.

In the mean time subscriptions had been coming in, amounting to nearly $50,000. The city ordered the police department to take a census of the unemployed, the report showing that there were 5,300 heads of families out of work. This ended the preliminary work, and the committee established an office in the city hall. It was a regular business establishment, with clerks, book-keepers, and heads of departments, all employed at $1 a day, the members of the committee of course receiving no compensation. Public announcement was made, and everybody out of employment and wanting to earn $1 a day was invited to come to the city hall.

Names and addresses were taken on a blank form, giving age, married or single, nationality, residence, occupation, time out of work, number of family at work, number of family dependent.

These applications were divided by district among the police, who were asked to investigate the statements of the applicants. The police returned such cards to the committee next day; and, according to the result of the investigation, the applicant was or was not accepted there and then.

If accepted, he received an order blank for work, which he took to the park, and was put to work at ten cents an hour. The orders were not transferable.

A record of every man put to work was kept at the office of the committee by a simple system of cards, while the workman himself received at the park a brass check, which he retained while at work.

The committe endeavored to give work first to men who had families depending upon them, and in all cases American citizenship was made a proviso.

The Citizens' Relief Committee set the first men at work on Jan. 1, 1894, and continued until April 5, 1894. During that time 22,528 different applications for work were received.

Mr. Andrew Carnegie offered to duplicate all subscriptions received for a period of two months, commencing with Dec. 28, 1893. The amount thus paid by him was $125,922.19. The next largest subscription came from the Westinghouse interests, amounting to $10,000.

The total amount paid out by the committee up to April 5, 1894, was $256,416.02. Out of this sum $3,290.02 was paid for clerk hire and printing expenses, leaving $253,124 paid out for labor performed.

During the entire period 13,224 individuals received work. The smallest number on any one day was 2,000 men at work, and the largest 4,571, an average per day of 2,907.

Of the 13,244 men employed there were married 11,202; their dependants, 42,712; single, 1,841; their dependants, 4,257; not classed, 181; total employed, 13,224; total dependants, 46,969. Hence a total of 60,193 were benefited by this work.

The employees represented 80 different occupations, and were divided in the following four classes:—

Professionals	6
Commercial	30
Skilled laborers	1,810
Laborers	11,378
Total	13,224

Of the entire number 39.55 per cent. were classed as American born; English speaking, 71.217 per cent.; foreign speaking, 28.782 per cent.

It was fortunate that the committee was able to provide this work, not only because it furnished those in want with the means of earning a little money, but because it was also a saving to the city, as much work was accomplished which the city would have had done some time probably at a higher price than it cost just then. The men in the parks were employed in laying out roads, building an artificial lake, and grading.

Schenley and Highland Parks are some distance from the business portion of the city; but the Baltimore & Ohio Railroad Company furnished free transportation in the morning and evening to one, and the Allegheny Valley Railroad Company to the other.

Also, owing to the distance of the parks from the workmen's homes, food was distributed to the men; and in some cases shoes and clothing were given.

This system of helping the poor prevented much hunger, starvation, and even crime. It gave the man in want an opportunity of maintaining his independence, because he gave his work for the money he obtained; it kept thousands who saw starvation staring them in the face out of the workhouse; it obviated the necessity of begging; it helped hundreds to retain their own personal pride and self-respect; and it put up a barrier against the temptation of theft, robbery, murder, and suicide.

In no case was politics allowed to interfere either for or against any applicant; and the greatest tribute that can possibly be paid to the committee lies in the fact that, out of the 13,224 men, no one had any complaint to make against the committee.

Apart from this Citizens' Relief Committee there were started in Pittsburg a number of other organizations,—missions, leagues, clubs, unions, etc.,—one of which established a soup-house that did more harm than good. In these there was no organized method for distribution of charity; and want was not decreased, but apparently grew day by day. Some of these mushroom organizations sought honor for their work through the newspapers, with the result that Pittsburg became the Mecca for all the tramps and vagabonds in Western Pennsylvania, Eastern Ohio, and West Virginia. The Department of Public Safety in Pittsburg had to inaugurate a special department of food supply, to feed all the loungers at the crowded police stations.

The kind-heartedness of the people was also much abused. A little coterie, headed by one of the most notorious beggars in Allegheny County, established a place ostensibly for the benefit of the poor and suffering. They gathered clothes, money, food, and everything they could get in the name of charity, and then disposed of it to make money for themselves.

Still, much good was accomplished, and for that we ought to be thankful; but to the thinking mind this period of depression in Pittsburg afforded a great lesson, and showed the importance and necessity of organizing all the charities of the city.

The City Department of Charities and the regularly organized Society for the Improvement of the Poor worked in harmony as far as possible; but there was no regular interchange between the various relief agencies, such as would prevent duplication and imposition.

The two agencies above named met all the demands made upon them promptly, and their work was as well done as it could be under the circumstances; but, of the relief societies that sprang up in the emergency, many did more harm than good, and, not being accountable to any authority, so far as I am informed, no report has been made of their receipts or disbursements.

Pittsburg needs a complete organization, all its charities working through one channel in a systematic, business-like way, taking up work on hand, and carrying it forward every day in the year.

As an example of what can be done in this way, I take pleasure in reporting the work of the Christian Aid Association of the East End. This is largely a residence section, and has a population of about fifty thousand. When it became apparent that there was unusual destitution in the city, and that help was needed, representatives of all the churches in the territory met, and an organization effected for work from December to March 1. An office was opened, and a census of the unemployed was taken by enumerators employed for the purpose, all other information was put into intelligent shape, visitors were employed, and the territory was laid out in districts, in each of which a volunteer committee of ladies was appointed. District conferences, and also general conferences of all district committees and visitors, were held from time to time. Relief was only given out after the most searching investigation of the circumstances of each applicant. The Department of Charities and all other agencies for granting relief were notified by the Association that it would care for all persons in need of relief in its territory, and thus duplication was avoided. Physicians volunteered to attend to cases of sickness sent them by the Association, and druggists and dispensaries agreed to fill prescriptions free of charge. All the churches agreed to provide for any members sent them by the Association, so there was no repeating in this direction. A storehouse was rented, groceries and provisions were purchased at whole-sale rates, and the goods were issued on orders from the general office.

Cash subscriptions received $11,512.31

EXPENDITURES

Supplies	$ 4,448.24
Labor	5,089.61
Sundry expenses	1,636.81
	$11,174.66
Balance	$ 337.65

The balance of $337.65 was turned over to the Society for the Improvement of the Poor.

Visits made by physicians	574
Office patients attended	208
Prescriptions furnished, amounting to	$107.95
Number of cases investigated	2,192
Number of cases relieved	1,424
Number of cases supplied with clothing	618
Number of cases supplied with coal	534

Even in providing work, the East End Committee was successful. You will remember that the Citizens' Relief and Employment Committee provided only for American citizens. Now, there were a number of

Italians and others not naturalized, yet in great want, and as much in need of bread and butter as anybody.

The West Pennsylvania Hospital grounds of Pittsburg needed grading badly; and it was here these men were set at work by the East End Society at fifty cents per day. For this purpose $5,089.61 was spent, representing 10,178 days' work.

The work of the Association is a practical illustration of organized charity in contrast with the work done or attempted by the many unorganized charities in other portions of the city, which speak volumes for the newer method of work. The management of the Association was in the hands of business men, who took up the work without sentiment; and, although they had had no experience previously in this line, they carried it forward in accordance with their ideas of common sense and business training, and they may well feel proud of their work. Their report, now being made up, shows in detail their entire operations; and, while they have laid down their work, they have their organization records, blanks, etc., and are prepared to take it up again if it should be required at any time. As already stated, what Pittsburg needs is organization of all her charities on these lines.

Washington Gladden (1836–1918), a Congregational minister, was noted for his efforts to apply religious principles to the solution of social problems. In the following selection he clarifies the broader implications and objectives of work relief. Apart from its value as a charitable expedient during the depression emergency, Gladden sees work relief as a tool to eradicate pauperism and mendicancy entirely. A comprehensive system of work relief would enable the community to abolish outdoor relief, provide work for the involuntarily unemployed, and consign the incorrigible mendicant to reformatory institutions.

Gladden's program is progressive in its effort to differentiate between categories of dependency, and treat the involuntarily unemployed more favorably. To what extent does Gladden share the nineteenth-century tendency to view unemployment in a moralistic and paternalistic framework? How much emphasis does he place upon questions of character as opposed to labor market organization in explaining unemployment? On the whole, does Gladden treat the total problem of unemployment in terms of charity and relief strategy? Or does he see the issue as one involving community economic policy? The article, under its original title "Relief Work—Its Principles and Methods," appeared in the *Review of Reviews* (January, 1894), pp. 38–40.

Work Relief and Social Reform

Washington Gladden

Want and destitution are always at our doors, but they are upon us just now in stronger force than we have been wont to encounter. It is doubtful whether in any year of this century so large a proportion of the population of the United States has been unemployed and destitute. In most of our cities and towns numbers of workingmen can be found who have had little or no remunerative labor for weeks or months, whose savings are exhausted, whose credit is badly strained, and who are facing hunger and cold. "But these men have had good wages for a long time," it will be said; "why have they not a surplus in the savings-bank?" Some workingmen have a surplus, and they are fortunate; but the lack of a hoard is not a sure sign of unthrift. Many of these hardworking people have been trying to pay for homes, and all their savings, month by month, have gone into these investments; the interest and the taxes and the street assessments and the payments due upon their property are now a heavy additional burden; the fear of losing what they have saved is one cause of their present distress.

Among the destitute will be found a good many others, who, if not quite so thrifty as those of whom I have spoken, are yet industrious and self-reliant, and not at all in the habit of asking for alms. In every large town a considerable number of these industrious mechanics and laborers are now in very needy circumstances. A great many people are asking for help to-day who never before in their lives were compelled to seek assistance. The charitable societies of our cities find themselves confronted with an army of applicants; the overseers of the poor are overwhelmed by the burden thrown upon them; special relief committees have been formed in many places to meet the emergency.

It must not be supposed, however, that these applicants for aid all belong to the class which I have described. If this were so, the problem before the relief agencies would be a simple one. The great majority of these applicants are well known to the overseers of the poor and to the charitable visitors. They are chronic paupers; the names of many of them will be found on the books of the city authorities as recipients of relief last winter and for many previous winters. And even if their names have never appeared on these lists before, they may still belong to this class; for the population of all our cities is being largely recruited by the shiftless poor from the country. In all our cities a great deal of reckless charity is dispensed; and the opportunity of the mendicant is constantly enlarging. Thrifty country folk who have poor relations on their hands sometimes find it easier to maintain them in the city. I know a woman with a small family whose relatives in the country pay her rent, which is only three or four dollars a month; the city furnishes her coal; one of the benevolent societies supplies her with groceries; from one of the restaurants she gets broken victuals enough to feed herself and her children, and her clothing has been mainly provided by one of the churches. There appears to be no urgent reason why she should look for work, and she is not, apparently, anxious about the morrow. I dare say that her acquaintances in the country have heard how comfortably she is getting on, and that we shall see some of them moving in to try the same experiment. The number of those in our cities who expect to get a portion, at least, of their living in this way is steadily and rapidly increasing. And this class of persons is sure to come directly to the front in the present distribution of relief. The woman of many resources, of whom I have just spoken, found her way to the special relief committee of our city as soon as its doors were open. No matter what other income they may have, whether from earnings or from gratuities, people of this class will never fail to embrace any opportunity that is offered them of getting something for nothing. Like Dr. Eggleston's Hoosier economist, their motto is, "Git a plenty while you're a gittin'." If they have employment by means of which they could earn a livelihood, the appearance of a relief fund is very likely to undermine their health.

The melancholy fact is that a free distribution of alms tends to weaken the self-respect and independence of many who have hitherto taken care of themselves, but who are living near the borders of mendicancy. The fact that food and fuel can be had for the asking is a temptation which some of the weaker ones will not resist. Many whose earnings have been somewhat reduced, but who might with frugality live upon them, are now coming forward with the rest to get their share of the relief funds. The most painful revelation to me of this winter's experience has been the willingness of those who have not hitherto been paupers to avail themselves of the public provision for the poor.

Such are the conditions which the relief committees must face. To some of them the problem must, I am sure, have already become disheartening. The difficulty of sorting out the chronic mendicants from the industrious and self-reliant working people is very great. Yet it is evident that the treatment accorded to the one class ought to differ radically from that bestowed upon the other. Measures which would be safe and wise in the one case would be mischievous in the other. We may admit that the mendicants, as well as the industrious poor, are entitled to our compassion; but there are different ways of expressing compassion.

The great need of all these people is remunerative employment. This is what the industrious ones want. Charity they do not want; it will be a bitter humiliation to them if they are compelled to take it; all they ask is the chance to earn their livelihood. The chronics also tell the same story, but a little investigation shows that their appetite for work does not amount to a craving; they always ask for it, but you soon discover that they could manage to get along without it if you should not happen to have any to offer them. We read of a Chicago professor, accompanied by a staff of student investigators, who passed through the serried ranks of the tramp brigade, reposing in the corridors of the city hall, questioning them as to their wants. They were unanimous, we are told, in expressing a desire for work. None of them preferred to beg. Really the question was superfluous. Nobody ever heard these people express any other sentiment.

The great army of applicants at the doors of the relief committee will all be asking for work, some because they hope to get it, and some with the strong hope that they will not get it. Both classes ought to have it—those who do not want it as well as those who do. We ought not to make the independent workingman take charity when he does not want it; we ought not to let the chronic mendicant have it because he does want it. Work is food for the one and medicine for the other; but the shirk needs the medicine not less than the honest man needs the food.

The problem, then, is to find work for the unemployed. And it is highly desirable that as much as possible of this work be furnished by individuals or firms or companies, acting independently and of their own motion. A large share of the unemployed in every city might be taken care of in this way if good people would only set their wits at work to find and furnish them employment. These idle people are not going to starve. There is food and fuel and shelter enough for them all, and they will not be allowed to perish for the lack of it. The only question is whether they shall receive this relief as earnings or as gratuity. It will cost the community no more to pay it to them as wages than to bestow it upon them as alms. But the economical and moral advantage to the recipients themselves and to the community of putting it in the form of wages is simply immeasurable. It is, therefore, the duty of every citizen to exhaust his ingenuity in inventing ways of furnishing work to persons whom he knows to be in need of it. These lines will fall under the eyes of many men and women of good will who know that they will be required to give during this winter some portion of their income for the relief of want. If all these would invent some way of spending this money for work, and would find some unemployed persons, male or female, who are suffering for the need of work, and would permit them to earn this money, a large share of the existing want would be immediately relieved. The problem of making work and of bringing the task and the toiler together is one that requires some thought and ingenuity, some trouble and pains, no doubt; but many of my readers can solve it, if they will give it half as much study as they will expend upon the costume for the next high tea, or the plans for the holiday vacation. Some job may be found in the garret or in the cellar; some work of repairing; some rearrangement of the store or the office; some ditching or plumbing or cleaning or painting; some new piece of furniture that an idle cabinetmaker can construct for you; some renovation of the wardrobe with next spring's wants in prospect; it may be any one of a thousand things that wit can devise. I know a builder, with this end in view, who has begun the erection of a few houses. I know a gas company, which, for the same purpose, has put one or two hundred men at work laying mains in a part of the city not yet occupied. I have heard of many individuals who, on a smaller scale, have found and furnished work to the unemployed. Any one who will spend his money in this way will do about twice as much good with it as if he sent his check for the same amount to the charitable society or the relief committee.

The best work that the relief committee can do is that of an employment bureau in keeping classified lists of the unemployed, and thus co-operate with those who are willing to furnish work. Whenever it is possible this committee should organize some sort of industry—a wood yard, or stone pile, or laundry, or sewing room, by means of which all able-bodied applicants for aid should be enabled and required to pay by their labor for all that they receive. All honest and self-respecting applicants would vastly prefer to earn their bread, even by the most menial service, and those who are not willing to earn it in this way should be permitted to go hungry.

Whatever relief is furnished by the municipality should also take the form of wages for work. Fear of socialistic tendencies has restrained municipal authorities from making work for the unemployed, but it is difficult to see that paying people for work out of the public treasury is any more socialistic than supporting them gratuitously from the same source.

Serious practical difficulties will be found in the application of the work-test. Those benevolent individuals who undertake to assist their neighbors in this manner will sometimes be greatly disappointed and incensed by the response which is made to their overtures. Some of those to whom work is offered will be indifferent and unreasonable. Work which is provided in this way, at an unseasonable time and in anticipation of future needs, cannot, of course, be paid for at the highest rate of wages; the stipend must needs be small. A good many of those who are asking for charity promptly refuse work when it is offered them at low wages. Several men who had been subsisting for some time upon the charity of their neighbors have, to my knowledge, refused employment at a dollar and a dollar and a half a day. Such beggars should be permitted to choose starvation.

The rules of the trades-unions forbidding members to work for less than a certain wage must be relaxed in these times. The discipline of the trades-union is necessary; but there is reason in all things, and it is not rational to insist that men shall not work for less than a stipulated rate of wages, when there is no economic demand at all for their labor. If the trades-unions are able to support their members in idleness they have a right to do so; but they are hardly justified in saying to their neighbors, "You must either pay us two dollars and a half a day for our work or else support us by your charity."

It will not be possible to furnish work, this winter, to all who will need relief. That is the thing to aim at, and the nearer we can come to it the better. But the need is so unusual and so urgent, and the machinery of relief is in most places so new and inadequate, that we shall sometimes be compelled to give aid to those, whether willing or unwilling to work, for whom we cannot find employment.

The establishment of soup houses and charitable bakeries for the gratuitous distribution of food is the first impulse of many kind-hearted people; but experience proves that the injury outweighs the benefit. It may, however, be safe and wise to establish soup kitchens and cheap restaurants, where nutritious food can be sold at cost. The relief committees might establish such kitchens, in connection with their industries, and pay for their work in orders for food.

The relief committees will, of course, undertake some sort of investiga-

tion into the circumstances and needs of applicants. Those who are new
to this business will imagine, at first, that they are getting, in a single
hurried interview, the truth concerning the applicant; there will be
evidence enough of poverty; and the explanation of it will be plausible;
but after a few months' experience it will be clear that considerable
acquaintance is necessary in order to deal wisely with most of these
families. One of the facts most commonly concealed is the existence of
relatives who are able to afford the necessary relief and who ought to
be shamed into doing so. In many ways the relief committees will find the
problem of helping these poor people becoming more and more difficult
the longer they study it. Probably it will soon become clear to them that
no temporary organization can dispose of the business which they have in
their hands; and that there ought to be in every considerable town a
thorough systematization of the business of charity. In some of our cities
the business has been pretty well systemized, and these cities are much
better prepared to meet this emergency than those in which no such
organization exists. Yet even here the work of charity organization has
been sorely crippled by the sentimental skepticism of multitudes. It
has never been possible to convince a great many well-meaning people
of the mischief wrought by indiscriminate and misdirected almsgiving.
The attempt to combine the charitable workers in such a manner as
to prevent the growth of pauperism is always resisted and ridiculed
by a class of effusive philanthropists, who have very little practical
knowledge of existing conditions. In cities where the charities are well
organized, and where every case of want could be promptly attended
to if the applicant were sent to the central office, the majority of the
citizens still persist in giving to tramps and beggars at their doors. It
is to be hoped that this winter's experiences may throw some light
upon this matter, and that the people of this country may come to
some realization of the magnitude of the task which confronts them in
dealing with the evil of increasing pauperism. It is to be hoped that
in communities where the charities are already organized a more cordial
co-operation of societies and churches and all philanthropic agencies
may be secured; and that in communities where no such organization has
been attempted the need of it will be clearly seen. For in dealing with
this emergency a great many people are likely to discover that we are
confronted with something worse than an emergency; that the acute
disorder is terribly complicated with a chronic complaint; and that a
thorough course of constitutional treatment is clearly indicated.

There is no room here to discuss the nature of the remedies. I think
that they are likely to include:

1. The abolition of gratuitous, official, outdoor relief.
2. The care of the helpless and friendless poor, who are dependent
upon the state, in infirmaries, hospitals, almshouses and orphanages.

3. The establishment of work-houses, to which all able-bodied and chronic mendicants should be committed, with in[de]terminate sentences. These incorrigible idlers and tramps need a thorough course of reformatory treatment. A work-house to which they can only be sent for brief terms of a few weeks or months is a doubtful good; they should be kept in confinement until their bodies, which are generally saturated with alcohol, are renovated and brought under normal conditions; until they have received some necessary industrial training, and until there is some fair assurance that they will become, if discharged, producers instead of parasites.

4. The provision of some kind of relief institution in every community, in which persons in temporary straits may obtain employment, and support themselves by their labor. It is vastly preferable, I think, that such relief institutions should be organized and managed by private charity; but, as I have already said, it is far better that the municipality should furnish work to able-bodied applicants for aid than that it should support them gratuitously for any length of time. The invariable rule of such relief institutions, whether under public or private management, should be to furnish work that is not particularly desirable, at low wages. The compensation offered should be distinctly less than is given for the same kind of labor in the market.

The thing to be aimed at is this: To enable every able-bodied person to obtain the bare necessaries of life by his labor; and to prevent able-bodied persons from obtaining a living without labor. Our charities will not be properly organized until both these ends are practically secured.

When all this is done there will still be ample scope for Christian benevolence in ministering to the sick, the infirm and the helpless poor, who ought not to be permitted to become a charge upon the state, but should be cared for in their own homes.

Washington Gladden was troubled by the conflict between relief and work incentive. He feared that readily obtainable relief funds would discourage labor force participation. Unless relief was carefully controlled in amount and character, workers would be tempted to join the ranks of the professional mendicants discussed in the following selection. The author, Samuel Lane Loomis, was a Congregational minister and author of *Modern Cities and Their Religious Problems* (1887).

The tramp was the nemesis of the nineteenth-century charity official. The aversion, as Loomis's article makes clear, was rooted in a sharp cultural conflict. What values and attitudes attributed to "the tramp" caused him to be thought "a subversive influence"? Was society justified in adopting repressive measures in self-defense, including involuntary confinement? In what ways might the general public's view of tramps have affected notions about welfare and charity? The following excerpt is taken from Loomis's article, "The Tramp Problem," published in *The Chautauquan* (June, 1894), pp. 308–09.

⊂⊒ The Tramp Problem

SAMUEL LANE LOOMIS

The tramp is a historic figure. His name is indeed new, the word tramp with its present signification has been in general use only a few years, but the man himself with all his essential traits,—the self-same idle, impudent, unclean, lawless, aimless wanderer, under the various titles of sturdy beggar, bandit, vagrant, and vagabond, has constantly held his place in European society ever since the Middle Ages. In periods of distress he has been wont to appear in numbers so great and threatening that the severest measures have been adopted for his repression. It will be remembered, for example, that in the early days of Elizabeth the magistrates of Somersetshire captured one hundred such offenders at a time and forthwith proceeded to hang fifty, complaining bitterly because they were forced to await the assizes "before they could enjoy the spectacle of the fifty others hanging beside them."

From the midst of the dark pestilential and hunger bitten days of the fourteenth century William Langland in the "Vision of Piers the Plowman" has given us a picture of the tramp of the times which, with slight modification, would well fit his modern counterpart.

"Filling their bags and stomachs by lies, sitting at night over at hot fire while they untie their legs, which have been bound up in the daytime, and lying at ease roasting themselves over the coals and turning their

back to the heat,—drinking gallantly and deep, after which they draw
to bed and arise when they are in the humor. Then they roam abroad
and keep a sharp outlook where they may soonest get a breakfast or a
rasher of bacon or money or victuals or sometimes both,—a loaf or a
half loaf or a thick piece of cheese which they carry to their own cabin,
and contrive to live in idleness and ease by the labors of other men." [1]

The tramps of this country constitute a class by themselves with well
recognized traits, habits, and pursuits. They have not yet attained so
high a degree of organization as their cousins, the beggars of Paris, who
hold regular weekly meetings, have their routes mapped out for them
by a standing committee, and even publish, twice a week an organ of
their own, *Le Journal des Mendicants;* but the American tramps are thorough-going professionals with fixed customs, regulations, routes, and
rendezvouses. They even have their own vernacular, a rude and mutilated
English. In tramp language a member of the profession is not known as
a tramp but a "hobo," or a "bum"; police are "screws"; the poorhouse,
"pogus"; the prison, "the pen"; liquor drinking is "rushing the growler,"
etc.

The number of these vagabonds in the whole country is reckoned
to be from forty to sixty thousand, of whom the great majority are natives.
The Irish are the most numerous among the foreigners; next to them are
the Germans; of French, Italians, and other Europeans there are very
few.

They are nearly all men between the ages of twenty and forty. A few
boys are found among them, and occasionally a woman of the lowest
type. They are not illiterate. Those who know them intimately affirm that
they nearly all can read and write. As a class they are drunken and
vicious. Many of them are criminals and a great majority have been
inmates of prisons and reformatory institutions.

The leading characteristic of the tramp is homelessness. He will style
himself "Chicago Slim" or "Baltimore Bill" but he belongs nowhere in
particular, has no folks and no possessions except the rags he wears and
the whisky bottle that gurgles in his pocket. Even a family name he
eschews and goes by some rough nickname. A fugitive and a vagabond
he wanders aimlessly through the land. He sleeps in sheds and outhouses,
in barns and deserted dwellings, beneath haystacks and in camps in the
woods or beside the track, warmed by heaps of blazing railway ties.
When cold rough weather approaches he comes to town. You will find
him in the casual wards at the police stations, in the almshouses, in the
county jails, and especially in the low dives and lodging houses. He
counts it good luck to be stricken with sickness in early winter and it is
said to be common among them to court disease of the vilest sort at this

---

[1] Quoted by J. R. Turner. "A History of Vagrants," etc. London, 1887.

time of year, because it assures one of comfortable quarters in the paupers' hospital for a month or two.

Of a piece with the tramp's wandering disposition is his fondness for railway travel. Although he never pays his fare, your thoroughgoing tramp has ridden thousands of miles by rail and knows all the trunk lines of the country and most of the minor routes. His usual mode of conveyance is the freight train, where he rides comfortably in an empty box car, or a trifle less comfortably on the bumpers between two cars. The brakemen are rarely unfriendly. When the tramps are in large enough gangs they often intimidate the train's crew and ride as they please. Another way to travel is on the trucks beneath the passenger coaches. This mode of locomotion is swift, but it is arduous and is apt to be a trifle too dusty even for a tramp. As a rule, not being pressed for time, he prefers the freight.

The tramp is exceedingly fond of the railway and rarely leaves it. Its water tanks are his register on which, upon arriving at a town, he hastens to enroll his name, searching among those that have been inscribed before his own for the names of cronies and companions.

The other great characteristic of the tramp is his aversion to work. He is able-bodied and idle. He is idle on principle. He will not work unless he is compelled to do so by prison discipline. He is always searching for employment, but can never find it. There are certain half-breeds who will engage in special kinds of labor, such as harvesting and hop-picking in the season, but it is characteristic of the full-blooded tramp that he hates nothing, not even cleanliness itself, so much as honest toil, and he will go any length to avoid it.

Here is the distinction between the tramp and other vagrants—among whom there are multitudes of honest laborers wandering about in search of work, eager for employment and worthy of sympathy and assistance.

Producing nothing himself this parasite preys on other men. He gets his living in three ways: by stealing, by availing himself of public provisions for the needy, and by begging. Upon occasion he plays the part of highwayman or burglarizes lonely dwellings, but this is rare. His thieving is oftener that of a *dilettante*, confined to such small matters as a shirt from the line, a brace of chickens from the roost, or a hatful of potatoes from the field. His main reliance is on public charity and begging, and he well knows how to make the most of these two resources.

America's general response to the industrial army movement in the spring of 1894 undoubtedly suffered from intense middle-class hostility to the tramp. It seems that trampdom, flushed with depression-spawned recruits, had become unusually well organized and assertive. However, the following account of the industrial army crusade by the English journalist, W. T. Stead (1849–1912), does not support an interpretation of the armies as a collection of outcasts.

Although Stead recognized that the right to work crusade generated some bizarre characters and strange events, he was more concerned with its underlying significance. Basically, he interpreted the movement as a disciplined quest for social justice, one which received considerable support from the working-class population. What values and objectives did Stead find in the "petition in boots"? Does Stead's portrayal of "Coxeyism" suggest that a vast ideological gulf separated workers from charity leaders? Or does his account suggest a "mere gap"? " 'Coxeyism': A Character Sketch" was published in the *Review of Reviews* (July, 1894), pp. 48–49, 55–56.

"Coxeyism": A Character Sketch

W. T. STEAD

There is nothing new in Coxeyism. It is as old as the hills. The only novelty is to find in this respect, as in many others, Russian methods reproduced in the American Republic. Try as one may, one never escapes free from Muscovy in the Western World. Coxeyism in its methods of organizing petitions in boots is an American adoption of a familiar Russian mode of airing grievances and of protesting against abuses. Professor Hourwitch, an able Russian statesman, of the University of Chicago, to whose painstaking researches we are indebted for much authentic information as to the constitution of the Coxeyite armies, has pointed out that in this respect, as in many others, the Americans are but English-speaking Muscovites. He says:

In Russia it frequently happens that the peasants of some remote village or group of villages, finding no relief for their grievances with the home authorities, send their delegates to bring "petitions in boots" to the seat of the central government. The weary "walkers," as they are called in Russia, march thousands of miles, very often begging "for Christ's sake." That men should come to the adoption of such methods of petitioning in America is a phenomenon so extraordinary that it deserves study from another than a policeman's standpoint.

The petition in boots has at least succeeded in achieving a phenomenal success. This, no doubt, it owed chiefly to the immense publicity which it

secured through the newspapers; but the art of converting the Press
into a sounding board is one of the most indispensable for all those who
would air their grievances, and Coxey by instinct seems to have divined
how to do it.

Every one in America knew of the existence of the unemployed. Every
newspaper reader had grown weary of the discussion as to what should
be done with tramps and out-of-works. It seemed almost impossible to
contrive any device by which this grim and worn-out topic could be served
up in good salable newspaper articles. But Coxey did the trick. Coxey
compelled all the newspapers of the Continent to devote from a column
to six columns a day to reporting Coxeyism, that is to say, with echoing
the inarticulate clamor for work for the workless. That was a great
achievement. To have accomplished it shows that Coxey is not without
genius. No millionaire in all America could, without ruining himself, have
secured as much space for advertising his wares as Coxey commanded
without the outlay of a red cent, by the ingenious device of his petition
in boots.

The origin of Coxeyism, the source and secret spring of all its power,
is to be found in the existence of an immense number of unemployed men
in the United States.

Yet America is very wealthy. It is the land of millionaires. But as in
England in 1842, "in the midst of plethoric plenty the people perish; with
gold walls and full barns no man feels himself safe or satisfied. Have we
actually got enchanted, then—accursed by some god?" To that question
Coxey and his penniless pilgrims of industry have compelled all men to
make some answer.

Coxey, who has given his name to the movement, is little more than a
figure-head. The real man on the horse is not Coxey, but Browne; and
even Browne is without influence or authority outside the Ohio contingent of the Coxeyite forces. The movement is not that of any one
man. Coxeyism is as little the handiwork of Coxey as the French Revolution was the work of Mirabeau or of Robespierre. Coxeyism is a kind
of sporadic growth—the adoption of petitions in boots by widely scattered
groups of miserable men, all of whom have but one idea and one prayer.
"Work, give us work," is their cry; and as it is to the government they
address their prayer, they set their faces towards Washington. Every
newspaper in the country blames the party to which it does not belong
for the bad times. Party politicians in the States habitually speak as if
prosperity were in the gift of the administration. The Federal government with its tariffs and its subsidies is constantly called upon to play
the part of an earthly providence to the classes. Coxeyism only asks
that the same *Deus ex machinâ* which has for a whole generation been
invoked to fatten millionaires should exert a little of its omnipotence to
secure work for the unemployed. As the throng of Parisians led by

Demoiselle Theroique poured tumultuous upon Versailles to demand bread, so Coxeyism with its multitudinous ragged regiments bent its steps towards Washington. Versailles is within easy marching distance from the Hotel de Ville of Paris. In America space is a great obstacle, how great no one adequately realizes until he has been there. Hence the great difficulty of Coxey. But from an advertising point of view the parade was all the longer and the more drawn out. . . .

The march to Washington from Massillon was child's play compared with the enterprise undertaken by the Commonwealers who started for Washington from the Pacific Slope. The distance, some 3,000 miles, was a longer walk than the Crusaders of the Middle Ages who started for the Holy Land, and the armies no sooner began to march than they discovered it was indispensable they should go by rail. As they had no money to pay for their freight, this necessity led them naturally to seize railway trains. Sometimes they succeeded in inducing the railway companies to carry them. More frequently they seized goods trains and compelled the conductor to bring them along. But for this expedient they never could have crossed the great desert. There were two armed bodies: General Frye's, who started from Los Angeles, and General Kelly's, which came from Sacramento. Of these Kelly's was much the larger and more formidable. It was twice threatened with Gatling guns. At Sacramento and at Utah it traveled alternately on foot, by rail, and in flat-bottomed boats, which it built on the Des Moines River. It was sometimes menaced by the authorities, and then *fêted* by the people. The Pacific armies said little about good roads. Their cry was State aid for the irrigation of the desert. They do not seem to have been acting in concert with Coxey, and General Kelly expressed himself freely in criticism of Coxey's tactics. The most notable feature about their movements was the sympathy which they commanded along the line of their march. Not even the seizing of trains to the general dislocation of railway transit could alienate the support of the masses.

Journalists laugh at Coxeyism. The laboring people sympathize, and in the end it is the latter who will prevail. We are not unfamiliar with similar petitions in boots in London. Lazarus showed his sores in Trafalgar Square, and the unemployed tramped their shoes off their feet in 1886–87 demonstrating their desire for work. London newspapers, with one or two exceptions, scoffed and flouted the agitators. The metropolitan police broke up the processions and cleared the Square amid the cheers of Dives and his myrmidons. John Burns and Cunningham Graham were flung into prison, and for a time there was peace, the peace and the silence of the grave. But in two short years London elected its first County Council, and John Burns fresh from prison became the most influential member of the new governing body. The men at Trafalgar Square became the rulers of Spring Gardens, and the greatest movement of our time in the direction of municipal socialism is being conducted at this moment in the name of the London Council by the representatives of the army of discontent which bivouacked at the base of Nelson's Column only seven years ago.

There is something so abhorrent to human reason in the waste of the labor of a million willing workers in a continent which has not yet made decent roads through its most populous districts, that every one must sympathize with the attempt by pacific, although irregular, methods to force the subject upon the attention of the government. Coxey may be mad, and Kelly may be visionary, but America needs good roads and the arid lands of the West await irrigation. General Frye's demands are more extensive. He wants government employment, the prohibition of all immigration for ten years, and the prevention of all aliens holding land in the United States. If a hostile power were to invade the United States, the necessity of repelling the enemy would compel the government to find means wherewith to utilize this waste mass of human force in making fortifications, roads, and other indispensable necessaries of successful war. But as there is no enemy in the field save Hunger and Cold, the government is paralyzed. It has neither funds nor initiative now. So it has come to pass that these workless workers are endeavoring, more or less aimlessly, to force on a crisis that may be as effective although not so bloody a stimulant to action as actual war. They realize, do these unemployed industrials, that governments when threatened with destruction by war can find at least rations for all the troops they can raise. What then if they are equally threatened by armies of industrials marching resolutely onward to the capital? Of the capacity of the industrial armies to place whole districts in a state of siege, there is already evidence enough and to spare. The seizure of railway trains, the suspension of traffic along whole lines of rail, the calling out of the militia, the parading of Gatling guns, the pursuit and capture of trains by United States cavalry, all this may be regarded as but playful, somewhat tragically playful reminders that even in a free Republic the condition of governments going on is that men must somehow or other be fed. What will be the end of it all who can say? No prophecy can be made with any degree of certainty, excepting this, that the end is not yet. A revival of trade may postpone further developments at present, but unless all the lessons drawn from past history are mistaken, Coxeyism will in future assume much more menacing dimensions, unless forestalling the evil betimes the Americans decide upon adopting a policy which will give the workless something better to do than the organizing of petitions in boots.

Chapter
14: Cincinnati's Boss Cox

⊂⊇ ZANE L. MILLER

Perhaps the most pervasive and certainly the most controversial political phenomenon on the early twentieth-century urban scene was the big city boss. None was more powerful or nationally prominent than George B. Cox of Cincinnati. He headed the local Republican organization for nearly thirty years and compiled an impressive winning record. Between 1885 and 1911 the Queen City GOP lost but two city elections and its grip on the county was almost as tight. Like other bosses before and since, Cox became a household word in the United States. One nationally read journalist declared that "Cox's System" was "one great graft,"—"the most perfect thing of the kind in this country." And another called him "The Biggest Boss of Them All," asserting that he had an organization "more compact and closely knit than any of the political machines which have dominated New York, Philadelphia, Chicago, St. Louis, or San Francisco."

Despite these tributes, Cox was not unique. Reuf in San Francisco, Croker and Murphy in New York, Crump in Memphis, the Pendergasts in Kansas City, and a dozen others, all exerted extraordinary influence. Like Cox, moreover, all were persistently opposed and denounced by a steadfast though diverse group of anti-machine spokesmen. And both the bosses and their opponents were products of general processes which profoundly transformed American cities in the late nineteenth century and unleashed forces which led a generation of city dwellers to examine the practice and future prospects of democratic politics in urban America.

Industrialization, immigration, and the flight of whites and blacks from the countryside to the city all played a part in reshaping the form and patterns of metropolitan life. Innovations in intra-city transportation technology were equally important. The introduction of the horse-drawn railway, the cable car and finally the electric trolley generated a remarkable expansion in the physical proportions of cities and set the stage for the emergence of a new kind of urban politics.

Mid-nineteenth-century Cincinnati, like other major American towns, was a walking city. Despite a burgeoning population, the lack of rapid mass transit facilities dictated that men and women go about their daily tasks on foot, and thus restricted the geographic flexibility of the city. The upper strata of society tended to huddle near the central business district while the poor, the greenest immigrants, and the blacks were pushed out to the periphery. By the turn of the century, however, all this had changed. Liberated by the new modes of transportation, both people and businesses began a relentless push outward. Commercial, financial, and factory districts shifted, old neighborhoods changed, and new communities sprang up on the urban fringe only to be engulfed by the expanding metropolis. The modern city had arrived, with the poor and the newcomers packed in the central slums, the blue and the white collars crowded nervously in a ring about that core, and the prosperous and successful sprawled around the cool green suburban rim.

For the first time a generation of urban Americans had to face the consequences of a significant freedom of intra-mural mobility and to adjust and accommodate to widespread uprootedness and constant flux. Life for slum dwellers was particularly grim. Poor, unskilled, ill-educated, and strangers to city life, they desperately needed jobs, decent housing, medical care, and a sense of belonging, status, and self-pride. Eagerly they sought out reliable and sympathetic guides who could show them the way out of the congestion, noise, vice, crime, violence, disease, and disorder haunting the checkerboard of ethnic ghettos which made up the slums. While some rose up the social and economic scale and moved out, many barely managed to hold their own. Others failed and slipped into permanent dependency or joined the flourishing escapist cultures of crime, alcohol, or drugs.

Inhabitants of the adjacent residential band, dubbed the "Zone of Emergence" by social workers, fared somewhat better. Here the physical environment, though by no means posh, was relatively safe, clean, and healthy, and the incidence of social and economic distress declined. Yet most teetered on the razor's edge of insecurity. Many of the lower-middle and middle-class inhabitants of these neighborhoods were recent graduates of the slums who lived in perpetual dread of reabsorption into the expanding central ghettos. Their wages and salaries were meager, their job security marginal. Burdened with the dual domestic responsibility of assuring success to their children and caring for their elders they, too, lived in anxiety.

The professional and business men inhabiting the outlying fashionable districts, by contrast, maintained a significant degree of control over their lives. Though harried by the searing competition of the city's private enterprise economy, they possessed the resources to improve their neighborhoods and adjust their social activities to suit their tastes and desires. Separated physically from the inner city, they were tempted to ignore its social and political problems. But they could not escape the disorder endemic in the metropolis. Annexation kept most of them within the urban political arena and they were bound to the fate of the city by a network of economic, occupational, educational, religious, and sentimental ties. Their daily trips to the central business and entertainment districts alone made it difficult for them to remain indifferent to the lack of stability, order, and prosperity which characterized the new conditions of life.

City hall seemed overwhelmed by the chaos. The clash of cultures between ghettos and along the cutting edge of the swelling central slums set off riots, brawls, and acrimonious controversies among religious, ethnic, and neighborhood factions. Strikes erupted into violence and elections were regularly accompanied by brutal conflict. As the physical area of the city expanded, officials were besieged by demands for the extension, improvement, and inauguration of public services of all kinds and for lower taxes. Existing municipal institutions and agencies, established to meet the needs of the walking city, became overburdened, outmoded, and dilapidated.

The response to the crisis was a general cry for positive governmental action to mitigate the chaos. As often as not the clamor produced a boss. His special genius was his ability to mobilize and organize the potential political power of those caught in the slums. There the machine supplied jobs, rent money, and coal in bad times, legal aid and advice, and a sense of status in return for votes. Armed with the solid support of one-third of the city, the boss then fished among the varied interests within the Zone and suburban fringe and attracted enough allies to finance his organization and carry citywide elections. By the repeated improvisation of these diverse coalitions the machine contrived to hold power long enough to get things done.

Cox mastered this strategy. A product of a marginal neighborhood on the edge of the Democratic slum wards, he rose to power in the 1880's by cooperating with the Republican reformers whose power base lay in the suburban fringe. The city's affairs were in such a state of disarray that even minimal reforms seemed striking, and Cox went just fast enough and far enough to convince the reformers that here, at last, was someone who could get something done. Party regulars were even more impressed by the growing Republican vote. By eliminating election violence, reducing the incidence of petty graft, suppressing blatant violations of gambling and vice laws, and by streamlining the structure of municipal government while improving the more obvious public services and curbing the competitive excesses in the street railroad, gas and electric fields, Cox managed to unite the peripheral districts in a push for moderate reform.

Yet the boss's relentless search for an unbeatable alliance led him into deep trouble. While continuing his strategy of meeting at least some of the demands for reform, he managed, after 1900, to bring the inner city wards into the GOP camp. The cost was high. With the composition of the coalition altered, the attack on the social, physical, and economic problems of the new city sputtered as laws were bent, ignored, or unevenly enforced to fit the special interests of particular neighborhoods. Cox found it increasingly difficult to maintain the credibility of his reform image. To the growing force of dissenters the pace of change seemed agonizingly slow and Republican performance unforgivably ragged. In this context the "new" reformers' critique of the origins and essence of bossism generated a broad discussion of the nature, possibilities, and prospects of democracy in modern urban America.

The most articulate of the political analysts were the anti-boss spokesmen. They had much in common. Almost invariably they spoke from the perspective of the residents of the periphery, that section of the city dominated by the ideals of the relatively wealthy, well-educated, Protestant middle classes. Accustomed to controlling their own lives, they were sure of their ability to shape the future of the city. Most, at bottom, had confidence in "the people," yet they differed over whether the masses could lead or ought to be led. They also disagreed over how politicians should go about courting voter support. Both they and machine supporters, moreover, also divided on the root cause of bossism. Did it flourish because men placed their self-interest above civic welfare? If so, was this tendency a natural product of imperfect human nature, of temporary and remedial ignorance, or moral indifference? Or did it grow out of the contemporary emphasis on individual enterprise and upward social mobility?

The anti-boss forces also sought out solutions. Could the political system be made more democratic without also democratizing social and economic institutions, or would it suffice merely to alter the city charter and institute election and civil service reforms? Assuming ignorance, apathy, or greed were at fault, could they be overcome by the moral regeneration of individuals, by education, or through astute psychological manipulation of the electorate by an elite leadership? Was the situation hopeless short of revolution or a miracle, or were the forces already at work within the city destined to produce a more democratic politics by evolution?

Candid defenders of the machine, though fewer and generally less articulate, nonetheless addressed themselves to the same kinds of issues. They, too, analyzed the relationship between the social-economic system and politics. They, too, took a stand on the reliability of the people, the role of the political leader, the place of special interests in a democratic system, and the political mechanisms appropriate in the new city. Both sides, in short, asked who governs, why, how, and to what ends? In the final analysis their preoccupation was with the nature and potential of democracy in modern urban America.

The following documents were all produced by close students of urban politics who had a special knowledge of conditions in Boss Cox's Cincinnati. All but one represent the anti-machine forces and, though similar in some respects, each of these has its own peculiar emphasis. Together they reflect the general divisions among the most influential anti-machine spokesmen at the turn of the century. The single pro-machine statement was written by Cox near the end of his long career in public life. Though defensive in tone and rambling in organization, it well represents the arguments marshaled in behalf of the boss and the assumptions which supported those arguments.

Frederic C. Howe was an earnest student of economics, city growth, and urban politics in both the United States and Europe. He was also an active participant in local political campaigns and in municipal government. Perhaps his most significant experience in this respect was his tenure as an advisor to the administration of Tom Johnson, a reform mayor of Cleveland, Ohio, during the early years of the 1900's. The following selection comes from the introduction to a book Howe wrote in 1905 called *The City: The Hope of Democracy* (New York, 1905), pp. 1–8. As the title suggests, Howe was optimistic about the future of urban politics in America. Yet he belonged to a group of politicians and students who prided themselves on their realism, and as if to confirm this assessment, he described his book as "an attempt at the Economic Interpretation of the City." Does that description summarize Howe's introductory remarks? Is his optimism based on an analysis of the economic facts of life, or does his faith rest on some other unstated yet implied belief? If the introduction is an "economic interpretation," does it suggest that a wholesale restructuring of the economic base of urban life was necessary to rid the cities of bossism? And how "realistic," given the nature of the turn of the century city, was his position?

⊂⊋   A "Realistic" View

FREDERIC C. HOWE

Distrust of democracy has inspired much of the literature on the city. Distrust of democracy has dictated most of our city laws. Many persons are convinced that mass government will not work in municipal affairs. Reform organizations have voted democracy a failure. Beginning with a conclusion, they have aimed to temper the failures of an experiment that has never yet been fully tried. They have petitioned State Legislatures to relieve the overburdened city of the duty of self-government. To these men of little faith, we have too much democracy, too wide a suffrage, too many people in our confidence. From their point of view corruption is fivefold. Its origins may be traced to the spoils system, the party machine, the saloon, the foreign voter, and faulty charter provisions. According to them democracy has broken down of its own weight. They conceive our mistake to be an attempt to extend government to the many, and believe that it should be left to the few.

To such persons, the cure seems as simple as the disease. They would limit the suffrage. They would divorce national issues from city politics. They would pass civil service reform laws. They would elect better men to office. They would treat the city as a business concern, and put its affairs in the hands of commissions or experts. A business man's government is their highest ideal.

We are beginning to see that such analyses as well as such reforms are inadequate. The evil is not only personal—it is industrial and economic. The mass of the people are not corrupt. We have not too much democracy. In all probability we have too little. The spoils system is pernicious, but it is not maintained by democracy so much as by business interests which use it for private ends. As a matter of fact we nowhere have a democratic government. What we really have is government by special privileges and big business men. These privileges are owned by leading members of the community. And they give us such government as best serves their business. Any government which is good for the people is bad for privilege, for privilege cannot be secured from honest officials, while disinterested men are kept out of politics not so much by the people as by the system of government which has grown up about these business interests.

Nor is the foreign voter greatly at fault, for Philadelphia is more corrupt than New York, although Philadelphia is a city of American-born citizens. Moreover, Chicago, Boston, and New York have known corruption under the merit system just as do Cincinnati, Pittsburg, and St. Louis under the spoils system. The election returns in almost any city show that as discriminating voting is done in the mill districts as in the well-to-do, brownstone wards. Apparently the poor are not wholly to blame. Nor is the foreign voter. And while the spoils system is an evil, it does not explain the big corruption. The machine finds the model charter as easy to control as the earlier forms which it has superseded. While reform halts in Philadelphia, Pittsburg, and New York, where model charters, designed by the best talent of the community, have been adopted, it proceeds to success in Cleveland, Chicago, Detroit, and elsewhere where discredited forms of government survive. Something more than the legal framework is at fault.

Any one familiar with political conditions in any one of our large cities knows that the largest campaign contributions invariably come from the street railways, the gas and electric-lighting companies. These contributions are sometimes made to the Republican, sometimes to the Democratic party. Officials of these companies control the party committees. They name candidates for mayor, for tax officials, and for the council. In the aldermanic districts the agents of the corporations supply the candidates with funds. In many of the wards they nominate the candidates upon both tickets. In addition to this they control the county auditor, who fixes the appraisal of their property for taxation.

On the organization of the council, the managers of franchise corporations choose the members, select the candidates for president and clerk, and through them make up the committees. These officials form the lobby in the council chamber.

Wherever one may go the same phenomena appears. Always the boss is the recognized agent of the public service corporations. Everywhere campaign contributions come from the same source; everywhere hostility or apathy on the part of big business, everywhere the cry of socialism, of anarchy, whenever reform touches vested interests, everywhere a class-conscious distrust of democracy and an organized alliance between what President Roosevelt has termed "the criminal rich and the criminal poor." And when Mr. Steffens lent his open-minded skill to the task of reporting St. Louis, Pittsburg, Philadelphia, and Chicago, as well as the states of Missouri, Illinois, New Jersey, and Wisconsin, the truth became even more apparent, and the root of the disease that is responsible for the "shame of the city" more clearly appeared.

In city and in state it is the greed for franchise grants and special privileges that explains the worst of the conditions. This is the universal cause of municipal shame. By privilege, democracy has been drugged. And this explanation is susceptible of deductive as well as inductive proof. The franchises are the most valuable gift in the possession of the city. Those to whom our cities have given millions, those who have been enriched by the city's liberality, those who have grown in wealth by the mere growth of population, have not been content with the city's generosity; but, like the serpent in the fable, have turned and stung the breast of those who have befriended them.

The fact that Cincinnati is governed by an ex-saloon keeper, that St. Louis has been ruled by a blacksmith, and that in every large city this type of boss appears, is not conclusive that we are governed by saloon keepers, blacksmiths, or prize-fighters. Neither Cox, Butler, nor Croker govern their respective cities. They are but representatives of privileged interests. They sit on the throne of power. But the real authority is behind them, invisible and secure, in the office of the big business men. Not the wholesale nor retail dealer, not even the jobber nor the manufacturer; nor these any more than the spoilsman, the petty grafter, or the saloon keeper. The latter are but camp followers, who join in the looting and form but the fringe of the system. . . .

Despite current pessimism, the outlook for the American city is reassuring. The city contains the independent vote. Here are the militant forces of our politics. As time goes on this independence will be extended to the state and the nation as well, with a consequent toning up of the larger issues in American life. To the city, we are to look for a rebirth of democracy, a democracy that will possess the instincts of the past along with a belief in the power of co-operative effort to relieve the costs which city life entails. We already see this manifest in many forms, in our schools, libraries, parks, playgrounds, kindergartens, bath houses, where conservatism has not been so strengthened by vested interests as to be able to resist democracy's coming.

And if democracy has not justified its highest ideals, it has at least given assurances of great vitality in many cities. The city is the hope of the future. Here life is full and eager. Here the industrial issues, that are fast becoming dominant in political life, will first be worked out. In the city, democracy is organizing. It is becoming conscious of its powers. And as time goes on, these powers will be exercised to an increasing extent for the amelioration of those conditions that modern industrial life has created. And to those who are fearful of this tendency towards increased activities and larger municipal powers, the words of Macaulay, in his essay on Milton, are suggestive:

There is only one cure for the evils which newly acquired freedom produces; and that cure is freedom. When a prisoner first leaves his cell he cannot bear the light of day; he is unable to discriminate colors, or recognize faces. But the remedy is, not to remand him into his dungeon, but to accustom him to the rays of the sun. The blaze of truth and liberty may at first dazzle and bewilder nations which have become half blind in the house of bondage. But let them gaze on, and they will soon be able to bear it. In a few years men learn to reason. The extreme violence of opinion subsides. Hostile theories correct each other. The scattered elements of truth cease to contend, and begin to coalesce. And at length a system of justice and order is educed out of the chaos.

Many politicians of our time are in the habit of laying it down as a self-evident proposition, that no people ought to be free till they are fit to use their freedom. The maxim is worthy of the fool in the old story, who resolved not to go into the water till he had learnt to swim. If men are to wait for liberty till they become wise and good in slavery, they may indeed wait forever.

Lincoln Steffens was one of the most brilliant of a band of muckraking journalists who startled the reading public at the turn of the century with well-researched and sensational exposés of the ills of American society. Writing for a national urban audience, he specialized, at this stage of his career, in the dissection of bossism in cities across the country. In 1905 he visited Cincinnati to investigate Cox's system and published his findings a year later in a book entitled *The Struggle for Self-Government: Being an Attempt to Trace American Political Corruption to Its Sources in Six States of the United States with a Dedication to the Czar* [of Russia] (New York, 1906). Steffens and Howe came out of similar backgrounds and both were particularly sensitive to the connections between economics and politics. Does the following selection from Steffens' book (pp. 198–203, 206) suggest that they had arrived at similar or different conclusions about the source of boss rule? And do their analyses imply radically different solutions to the problem? Finally, how important is it that Steffens, as a muckraker, hoped his writing would act as a direct stimulus to reform?

⊂⊒ The Struggle for Self-Government

LINCOLN STEFFENS

Let's run down there again to see what Cox has done since 1898 to make Cincinnati the model Ohio city. He has "Russianized" it. His voting subjects are all down on a card catalogue, they and their children and all their business, and he lets them know it. The Democratic Party is gone. Cox has all the patronage, city, county, State and federal, so the Democratic grafters are in Cox's Republican Club. That club contains so many former Democrats that "Lewie" Bernard, John R. McClean's political agent, says, happily, that he is waiting for a majority, to turn it into a Democratic club. And "Lewie" Bernard's machine remnant is in touch with Cox when "John," as Cox calls McClean, doesn't want anything, either office or revenge. Conventions are held, and Cox plans them in detail. If he has been hearing mutterings among his people about the boss, he is very ostentatious in dictation; otherwise he sits in his favorite beer hall and sends in slips containing the motions and nominations each is to make. But there must be no nominating speeches. "Takes time; all foolishness; obey orders and get done." He picks ward leaders, and they deliver the votes. The citizens have no choice of parties, but they must get out and vote. Cox is good to some of them. If they knuckle under, he puts respectable men up for the school board. He has little use for schools; not much graft in them; except to cut down their appropriations in favor of fatter departments, and as a place to try respectable men. If these take orders on the school board, Cox tries them higher up, and he has a-plenty. The press is not free. *The Post* and the *Citizens' Bulletin,* the last a weekly organ of the smallest but one of the most enduring groups of reformers in America—these are the only papers that speak out honestly for the public interest. Official advertising, offices for the editors, public-service stock and political prospects for the owners, hold down the rest. It is terrible. The city is all one great graft; Cox's System is the most perfect thing of the kind in this country, and he is proud of it.

"What you think of it?" he asked, when I had finished and was taking leave.

"Pretty good," I said.

"Pretty—!" He was too disgusted to finish. "Best you ever saw," he retorted, firmly.

"Well, I can't tell," I said. "My criterion for a graft organization is, How few divide the graft. How many divide it here?"

"Ain't no graft," he grumbled.

"Then it's a mighty poor thing."

He pondered a moment. Then, "How many do you say divides up here?"

"Three at least," I said. "You and Garry Herman and Rud Hynicka."

"Ugh!" he grunted, scornfully, and, wagging one finger slowly before my face, he said: "There's only one divides up here."

Of course, that isn't true. He must mean only political graft, the campaign fund, police blackmail, contracts, etc., etc. . . .

But there is lots of graft besides political graft in Cincinnati, bankers's and business men's graft. Cox is reaching for that, too. Some Cleveland and Cincinnati financiers organized a trust company in Cincinnati, and they took Cox in for his pull and the public moneys he could have deposited there. A quarrel arose, and Cox, taking one side, told the others to buy or sell. They sold, of course, and Cox, becoming president, wrote a letter to officeholders, inviting them to use his bank; the letter to the school teachers was published. Certain financiers of Cleveland and Cincinnati got up a scheme to take over the Miami and Erie Canal. They gave Cox stock for Cox's pull on the Legislature, and his letter to the legislators was published. The bill was beaten; business men all along the canal were grafting the water for power, and they fought for *their* graft. The company had floated its stock and bonds, and the failure of the Legislature threw the "canals Scandal" into a receivership. Some of the financiers are in trouble, but Cox is safe, and the scheme was to go through next year. Cox was in on the scheme to sell or "lease" the Cincinnati Southern, the only steam railroad under municipal ownership. Leading citizens of Cincinnati concocted this grab, but the Germans beat it; and, though it went through later, the city got much better terms.

So, when Cox says only one divides the graft in Cincinnati he probably means that one man can dispose as he will of all of it, police, political, and financial, as the examples cited indicate, but he has let all sorts of men in on it. And he does. And that is his best hold on the graft. They talk in Cincinnati, as they do in Philadelphia, of apathy. Apathy! Apathy is corruption. Cincinnati and Philadelphia are not asleep; they are awake, alive. The life is like that in a dead horse, but it is busy and it is contented. If the commanding men, of all the natural groupings of society, were not interested in graft, no city would put up with what satisfies Cincinnati. For Cincinnati is not unhappy. Men like Elliot H. Pendleton, Rufus B. Smith, and a dozen others, are eating their hearts out with impotent rage, but as for the rest—

The rest are in it for profit or fear. The bums get free soup; the petty criminals "get off" in court; the plain people or their relatives get jobs or a picnic or a friendly greeting; the Germans get their beer whenever they want it; the neighborhood and ward leaders get offices and graft; "good" Democrats get their share of both; shopkeepers sell to the city or to politicians or they break petty ordinances; the lawyers get cases, and they tell me that the reputation of the bench is such that clients seek lawyers for their standing, not at the bar, but with the ring; the banks get public deposits and license to do business; the public utility companies get franchises and "no regulation"; financiers get canals etc., they "get blackmailed," too, but they can do "business" by "dividing up"; property owners get low assessments, or high; anybody can get anything in reason, by standing in. And anybody who doesn't "stand in," or "stand by," gets "nothing but trouble." And there is the point that pricks deepest in Cincinnati. Cox can punish; he does punish, not with physical cruelty, as a Czar may, but by petty annoyances and "trouble," and political and business ostracism. The reign of Cox is a reign of fear. The experience that made my visits there a personal humiliation was the spectacle I saw of men who were being punished; who wanted to cry out; who sent for me to tell me facts that they knew and suffered and hated; and these men, after leading me into their back offices and closing the door, dared not speak. It was rumored that I was shadowed, and that made them afraid. Afraid of what? They were afraid of their government, of their Czar, of George Cox, who is not afraid of them, or of you, or of me. Cox is a man, we are American citizens, and Cincinnati has proved to Cox that Americans can be reduced to craven cowards. . . .

The signs of promise? . . . The people are beginning to see things. Even in Cincinnati (Cox scoffed when I told him so) there is some discontent, and the nucleus of veteran reformers are finding recruits willing to line up against Cox, "just Cox," for a fight, not to throw out the slot machines, not to ameliorate particular evils, but to restore representative government and be free, wholly free. . . .

The material reprinted here is taken from a speech, "The Moral Aspect of the Political Situation in Cincinnati," delivered by the Rev. John Howard Melish during the 1903 mayoralty campaign. Melish was not only an opponent of bossism, but an exponent of the controversial notion that the churches ought to take an active and direct role in politics. The talk, available in pamphlet form at the Cincinnati Historical Society, was given before a federation of Protestant ministers, most of whom served congregations in the two outer residential districts of the city. At the conclusion of the address the clergymen endorsed the reform candidate for mayor. He was overwhelmingly defeated. Although hardly a successful campaign appeal, the document is representative of one kind of turn-of-the-century campaign rhetoric. Compared to the two previous selections, how "radical" and "realistic" is Melish's statement? In what ways does it differ from both? What, if any, assumptions do all three men hold in common? Why was Melish so strikingly unsuccessful as a politician in the new city?

⊂⊒ The Moral Aspect

Rev. John Howard Melish

Our political situation to-day has a distinctly moral side, and it is this side which, it seems to me, we should, as ministers, bring to the knowledge of our city. I want to make clear four parts of this moral problem: gambling, the social evil, the decline in civic patriotism and the lowering of moral standards. I take it that what you gentlemen want of me is what I actually know. A gentleman who has been in politics many years said to me the other day that I have not mentioned one-half of what may be said about the evil way the machine has ruled our city. I hope he is wrong for the sake of our city, but what I have said and say to-day I know from personal experience or careful investigation, and stand ready to prove. . . .

Inquiries among members of our men's club showed me that gambling houses were flourishing all over the city. On the same block with Christ Church a game of hazard ran in Heil's saloon Saturday night and Sunday. I have stood on the corner of Broadway and Fifth at one o'clock on Sunday morning and heard the calls of the game keeper and the sound of money. A policeman came by but paid no attention to that saloon. O'Brien's saloon, on Sixth street, was the most brazen place I visited. It was about 1.30 when I came by there. Light streamed through the stained glass window across the sidewalk, showing a patrolman standing there talking to some cabmen. The noise from within was heard across the street. Some employe spoke to me there, and seeing I was somewhat green, explained stud poker, and told me of games which had lasted from Saturday night to Tuesday morning. . . . I visited several other notorious places myself, and then had some trustworthy men make a careful investigation of the situation in the city. As was afterwards made public we were ready to prove that 38 places ran gambling games, and knew of about 75 places which permitted games of chance, such as poker, craps and hazard. Of that published list only one man denied our charge and threatened suit, but when he beheld the array of evidence we had against him he subsided.

I have mentioned the facts, and have shown that the police were doing nothing to close those gambling houses. Let me now speak of their protection by government.

In no case was a lieutenant of police implicated in receiving blackmail. The patrolmen received cigars, and we were told in two places that the policemen "were fixed," and would notify the gamblers in case of a contemplated raid. One of the Police Commissioners told me that he and the Chief of Police once made an investigation of gambling houses. But they found that their coming had been tipped off, for when they entered men were sitting around doing nothing, and without any thing to bring them together unless it was some game which had been hurriedly hidden. . . .

What was it that gave gambling houses protection, if the police department did not receive blackmail? . . .

We were told in a number of places that they made liberal contributions to the Republican campaign fund, and it was understood that the party would look after their interests. . . .

The men, so licensed as it were, pay for their privilege either by controlling votes for the party or by contributing to the campaign fund. . . .

When a gambler wins his ward the machine adopts him, and lets him do as he pleases within certain limits, and the control of the police force is within those limits. . . .

To my mind the issue is perfectly clear, and it is up to the public. I take it that one of the first duties of good government is to limit the number of those who seek vicious pleasures, and to make the road to vice hard and dangerous. Judged by that first principle of good government the present administration has been weighed and found wanting. Though not criminals themselves, they have allowed the police force to be terrorized by the politicians, and as Judge Smith has put it, "made to connive at this vice." "Criminally Weak," that is the writing on the wall over the tables where the present administration is feasting. . . .

I want to speak frankly about a subject which we . . . have long shunned. . . .

On both sides of Longworth and George streets, for squares, nearly every house is used openly for immoral purposes, with the madams' names upon the doors. Scattered through the city are other houses of prostitution. In addition to the houses of ill-fame are the houses of assignation. I have had two good men make an investigation of the number of these houses. They can prove that 58 houses are given up to that evil; they know of 60 more; and the cabmen, who know this evil best of any one, by reason of their business, have told them that there are simply hundreds. . . . In the opinion of our Health Officer, Cincinnati is one of the worst cities morally in the United States, and I have heard that statement verified by newspaper men, traveling men and physicians, whose experience includes many of the large cities of our country. My calling as a minister has brought me face to face with the social evil again and again, and for years I have been trying to diagnose the situation in our city. Cincinnati, one of the worst cities morally in the United States! That is a matter which should concern us ministers. . . .

The cause of the social evil, of course, lies way back in human nature. Its extent and prevalence can be traced to the crowding of the population, to bad amusements, the conditions of labor, especially female labor, inadequate moral education, and communicable disease. But in these respects Cincinnati is like all great modern cities. If this were all our city should be no worse than others; it should be better, because our population has such large German and Jewish elements, both descendants of moral races. I believe there is a reason for this serious moral situation. . . .

There is a law on the statute books which makes it a crime for any person to rent or maintain a house for immoral purposes. . . .

At present the law is a dead letter. It is worse than dead, for it is a fruitful source of blackmail. *With that law on the statute books it is to the interest of a corrupt machine not only to allow as many houses to run as wish, but actually induce others to open up.* It makes it possible for a corrupt machine to levy tribute, called campaign contributions, upon every immoral house, and if it refuses to pay, the machine can use the police power to put it out of business instantaneously. Every additional house means additional income to the machine. When houses renting ordinarily for $50 a month are rented for immoral purposes at $175 and $200 a month it is easy to see what a lucrative income may accrue. Our laws also make it possible for the clerk of the Police Court to arrest individual prostitutes whenever he pleases and then let them out on a bond signed by a professional bondsman with whom he has formed a partnership. This source alone would bring in about $17,000 a year. . . .

The second cause of the extent and prevalence of the social evil is the failure of government to enforce the law of nuisances.

Associated with these immoral houses are various enticements, such as dancing, music, drinking, card playing. I have known many young men to go to those places, especially on winter nights, merely for those social pleasures. Once there, the step beyond was easily taken. . . . Those enticements come, or ought to come, under the law of nuisances. If such things were forbidden, and wise, practical regulations enforced, vice to-day in this city would not be so attractive, or so extensive, and many a men and woman would have had a better chance to be morally clean. . . .

The present administration has practically licensed prostitution. It has put the approval of government upon the traffic in woman's shame. Not content with levying blackmail and flaunting vicious pleasures in the faces of our young men and young women, it has issued certificates to the women to prove to the men that they need have no fear of communicable disease. Cincinnati is the only city in the United States which has licensed this vice. And it did this when the present administration went into power. If for no other reason than this, I say, this administration is unworthy of our continued support. Prostitution is inevitable and we must reluctantly admit it. But, I do not believe that Anglo-Saxon men will ever put the stamp of government upon a trade in their women's honor. . . .

Another moral problem is forced upon us in the spirit of unbelief, which is taking possession of countless numbers of our people. The present political domination of our city has had a stifling influence upon the patriotism of our people. . . .

Civic patriotism is dying, crushed by the apparent irresistible strength of the machine. Many men whisper their sentiments under the pledge of confidence as though they were citizens of Russia, not free men of America. The sentiment of the citizen toward the city is one of shame, deepening occasionally into indignation. This, gentlemen, is a moral problem far more serious than gambling or prostitution. These vices touch only a portion of our people, and that the weak; this evil touches the majority, and those who are strong. To me the saddest experience I have had is seeing splendid young men, men of ability and leadership, men who have believed in the principles of American government, lose their faith in government of the people, by the people and for the people, devote their abilities to a system of boss rule, which in their souls they hate, give their good names to the machine, and, as they express it, "climb into the band wagon." I suppose Moses must have found this spirit among his people when in Egypt. A people under a master's yoke or a boss' lash loses its grit, its hope and its patriotism. Every year which delays the exodus will make the work of our Moses harder when he comes. . . .

It is the conviction of workers in our poorer districts . . . that one of the greatest evils which we have to fight is the constant lowering of moral standards due to political organization. I know a councilman in our city who is enthusiastically voted for by the men of his ward, praised by the women as the friend of the poor, and worshipped by the boys as a hero. He has won this support by distributing the public patronage among the voters, having today some 400 people in various positions in city departments and public service corporations. He has been the good Samaritan in his ward for years, heading subscription lists to bury the dead, distributing coal and groceries in hard times, and rescuing his constituents when they chance to fall into the clutches of the law for selling inferior milk, breaking city ordinances and highway robbery. In this way he has built up a ward machine within the city machine, which on his own statement is copied after Tammany, with improvements of his own.

I do not wish to be unjust to that gentleman. I admire many of his qualities, and believe that he can teach reformers a much needed and valuable lesson. But my appreciation of his good side does not blind me to the fact that his influence on the rising generation is pernicious. He is teaching the boys that law is the handmaid of political pull, which destroys their reverence for law. He is dulling their sense of justice. . . .

Before the American boy Benjamin Franklin was once held up as worthy of imitation; and the lesson was that the road to honor lay through plain living and high thinking. At a later time Abraham Lincoln taught our boys to rise above political expediency and stand on the principles of justice and eternal right. To-day our boys are drawing their lessons from this councilman. And the lesson which I find our boys have learned is that the way to office, and to the glory of philanthropy as well lies through bribery, the tampering with justice and political corruption. This lowering of moral standards, due to political organization, is one of the most important moral problems confronting this country to-day. . . .

In conclusion, gentlemen, I would have you fix the responsibility for many of these evils where, it seems to me, it belongs in no small degree, namely upon the political machine calling itself Republican, though the disgrace of the "grand old party" and its undoing in this State. Back of that whole gambling situation we found the hand of the machine. When publicity was given to the matter it was the machine's tip that went down the line, telling gambling houses to close down for the present. And they obeyed their master. Four weeks later they were wide open again. More publicity and the nearness of the election required something radical to be done. Then the Mayor acted. That time the police went down the line and the gambling houses closed. What was shown in that whole agitation was the hand of the machine, and this is what the citizens should remember now. No one asks, or has asked, that gambling be suppressed. What we demand is that our government shall not be used by gambling politicians to protect their trade in vice.

Back of this social evil also is seen the hand of the machine. We do not ask that this evil be suppressed. That were folly. We simply demand that our government shall not be used to license a traffic in woman's shame, and turn the terrible money into the pockets of politicians.

Back of the decline of civic patriotism stands that machine, brazen in its intrenched security, making, so far as this city is concerned, free America a despotic Russia, the refutation and denial of "government of the people, by the people, and for the people."

Back again of the lowering of moral standards stands that same machine which knows no party, has no enthusiasm, and refuses to use no method, however harmful to the true welfare of the community, so long as it maintains its power. . . .

If boss rule and machine domination were inevitable and necessary there would be no moral aspect to our political situation to-day, and I would have nothing to say. But democracy is no failure and will yet be vindicated before the world. What she needs in our cities is worthy leaders; a boss is a leader gone wrong. What she further needs is a worthy organization; a machine is an organization gone wrong. Let us keep faith in our great republic, stand shoulder to shoulder with all men who are working for her vindication, and above all, pray—

"God give us men. A time like this demands strong minds, great hearts, true faith and ready hands; men whom the lust of office does not kill; men whom the spoils of office can not buy; men who possess opinions and will; men who have honor; men who will not lie; men who can stand before a demagogue and scorn his treacherous flatteries without winking; tall men, sun-crowned, who live above the fog in public duty and in private thinking."

In 1911 a strong anti-boss coalition emerged in Cincinnati and a Democratic reform administration, led by Henry T. Hunt, took office. Both his administration and his long campaign for mayor reflected his analysis of bossism and his conclusions about the political strategy most likely to succeed in an urban democracy. Though Hunt's winning margin came from the peripheral wards, he hoped to make his coalition citywide and adjusted his actions accordingly. Nonetheless, in 1913 he lost his bid for reelection by a narrow margin due to defections in Zone wards. Shortly thereafter, A. Julius Freiberg, an ally of Hunt in Cincinnati politics, wrote an article describing the campaign tactics and policies of the Hunt movement and dissecting the causes for its defeat. The piece, reprinted here in slightly abbreviated form, appeared in the *National Municipal Review*, III (July, 1914), pp. 517–24, a journal established by the National Municipal League to improve city government in the United States. To what extent did Hunt follow the advice of Howe, Steffens, and Melish? Does Freiberg's tone and emphasis suggest that there was a fourth school of municipal reformers? Would you characterize Freiberg as a cynic, optimist, or realist?

Mayor Hunt's Administration in Cincinnati

A. JULIUS FREIBERG

Up to above eight years ago, Cincinnati, to borrow the phrase of one of our most accomplished muck-rakers, was sleeping contented in the arms of as powerful a clan of unpatriotic politicians as ever held a city in its grasp. . . .

Henry T. Hunt was then just out of college, one of a group of young men alive to the situation and eager to begin the fight. . . . They managed in an off year to nominate Hunt and elect him to the legislature. . . . A legislative committee was sent down [to Cincinnati] to take testimony. Hunt did brilliant work in assisting the committee. The testimony forced from many unwilling witnesses opened the eyes of the people. There was good fighting for the young men. Hunt was at once an idol and there was no trouble at all in electing him as prosecuting attorney of the county.

Here is one of the elements in the psychology of electorates. . . . The people love the dramatic; not merely the poor, but the rich and the middle class as well. They will not elect Nathan, but give them a David who has just slain his Goliath and they will raise him to a kingdom and keep him there—for awhile. The reformer and his fellow students may sit about the table and evolve high principles for action, but the people, even those of his own stratum, will not be fed those principles unless there is a dramatic setting, and the favorite dramatic setting is the killing of a dragon. This is not intended to be a reflection on the voting public; it is an inexorable fact that no true student of American government can afford to ignore. . . .

Mr. Hunt proceeded vigorously with his new duties as prosecuting attorney. He began at once to lay plans for bringing to book the boss himself—a thing that had never been dared before. . . . Mr. Hunt surrounded himself with the best talent he could get for his assistants. Two of the most learned and best equipped lawyers in the city, at much sacrifice to themselves, joined with him. The boss was indicted, and people were correspondingly elated. But the boss was not convicted. The judges on technical grounds released him. Hunt quarreled with the judges; he taunted them and whether rightly or wrongly, he defied them. So he had his victory after all; for the people who had enjoyed the spectacle of the fight were with him. . . .

The mayoralty campaign was soon on. . . . Much against his will, because his term as prosecutor had not yet ended, Hunt consented to stand for mayor. He could afford to be independent, however, and he insisted that the ticket nominated with him should comprise the best men available. His advice was heeded, the ticket was elected, and the result was that Cincinnati never had a better opportunity for good government. . . .

The people were delighted with their choice. . . . Business men and conservatives of the old school who were always good citizens but afraid of the so-called vagaries of the reformer came over in large numbers. . . . Nor was there anything sanctimonious in the flavor of the new administration. It was soon understood that there was to be no intolerance or unnecessary restraint of decent liberties. The administration had the council with it, too—on the whole, a reformer's paradise.

If there were nothing further to record until the defeat of the administration at the last election, the gain notwithstanding this defeat, would have been and is still inestimable. The old order is gone forever. While the people are fickle and sometimes disposed to regard the mote instead of the sunbeam, they will never tolerate a complete retrogression. The pendulum of the popular mind will swing, but never so far back as the first beat, because the popular mind has been educated—at least it has had its primary lesson. This is point number two in the psychology of the voting mass.

The first note struck by the Hunt administration was the adherence to the campaign declaration that there was to be no wholesale turning out of the old place-holders. . . . Through the influence of the mayor, a civil service commission was appointed, consisting of three dyed-in-the-wool civil service reformers, good men and true, who immediately set about the institution of a thorough-going system of examinations.

Then came the constructive work, into which Mayor Hunt put himself with all his heart and soul. Among the first jobs he tackled was the removal of the delinquent and dependent children of the house of refuge, an old ramshackle building, to buildings in the country. He then delved deep into the tenement question—housing reform. He had appointed as building inspector, a ruggedly honest man, who though perhaps lacking in tact was uncompromising in his opposition to law violators. The building inspector, being no respecter of persons, would now and then step on the toes of a vigorous Hunt supporter; and before the end of the term, legions of such toes were stepped on.

Practical reformers have learned that to succeed with reform one must be a conservative reformer. Point three in the psychology of the voter is that his toes must not be stepped on.

From housing reform, Hunt branched away into railroad extension. He soon saw that unless the small-home territory is enlarged and suburban territory made available, the tenement problem will remain practically unsolvable. Thereby hung, however, a long tale. The Cincinnati Traction Company, or rather its lessor, obtained some years ago, through an act of the legislature, a fifty-year franchise for the exclusive use of the streets. . . . There is a provision, however, in the franchise contract under which the traction company must submit to revision of fares in 1916. Mayor Hunt very wisely and with great discernment approached the traction people with an anticipatory compromise proposition, embracing, (1) the features of a valuation of the company's plant to be agreed upon an equitable basis; (2) the exchange of the company's fifty-year franchise for a so-called "indeterminate permit"; (3) the building by the city of a rapid transit right of way over an abandoned canal bed in conjunction with an underground city loop, the traction company to operate the rapid transit system, the company also to provide for suburban extensions when demanded by the city; the whole object being to bring suburban cars into the city proper with great speed, thus opening up an enormous undeveloped suburban territory. . . .

While the laying down of these comprehensive plans was agreed on every hand to be a vital necessity for the city's future growth, naturally the more the thing was talked about, the greater was the opportunity for criticism. In the first place, the traction interests and other allied interests . . . were averse to being hectored into any kind of a traction settlement at this time. The plan would, of course, involve a valuation of the plant, and there was much wailing and gnashing of teeth at the bare thought of the possibility of reduction in the stock value of the Cincinnati Street Railroad Company. This stock is very widely held among all classes of our citizens. In the next place, the employment of experts from outside the city, though they were the only men who could be secured for the purpose, was used by the old organization. . . . Point four in the psy-

chology of the average voter is that notwithstanding his general desire
to have an efficient administration, his misplaced patriotism resents the
employment of experts from outside the city. . . .

Notwithstanding all the criticism, Mayor Hunt went on with his work
and was in a fair way to succeed, when another disturbing event took
place. The radical element in the city, headed by Herbert Bigelow,
began to make clamor against the large capitalization Mayor Hunt was
about to agree upon with the traction company for the purpose of basing
fares and other calculations. . . . The radical element had supported
Mayor Hunt in his campaign for election, and the demoralized leaders of
the old organization began to rub their hands with glee.

Meantime, [a] cloud erstwhile no bigger than a man's hand, began to
grow. I refer to the disgruntled Democrats who had waited and waited
for their jobs, always hoping that the mayor had not really meant what
he had said. It soon became apparent that notwithstanding all the good
work that Mayor Hunt and his associates had done, the dogs of war were
loosing themselves and the serenity attending the opening of the administration was wellnigh dispelled. . . .

Then came another blow, Strikes sprang up in the textile and shoe
trades. The mayor was be-labored by the manufacturers for police assistance. The mayor at first conceived that the manufacturers wanted him
to help suppress a legitimate strike. So, while he did his duty, he did
not accede to all of their demands. This took from him the support of
many good citizens who had been loudest in their approval of him when
he ran at the polls. When later, after certain acts of violence startled
the community, the mayor strengthened the police protection, he incurred
to some extent, the ill-will of the unions.

Finally, there came a strike of the employees of the traction company.
All the lines were tied up. Popular opinion was with the strikers. Nevertheless the mayor gave what police protection he could to the company.
Strike-breakers were imported; the police became worn out with their
long vigil, and it was no longer possible to run cars. The mayor asked the
governor for the militia. Whereupon the latter refused to send it. The
radical element of course resented the call for the militia. The city solicitor
thereupon brought an action in the common pleas court, asking for a
receiver for the company on the ground that it was not performing its
public duty. This action brought the company to terms, arbitration was
agreed upon, and the strike was settled. But it was at a tremendous cost
to the mayor and his friends, for not merely the traction company but
all of the capitalistic class, many of them the mayor's strongest friends,
bitterly resented the action of the solicitor. . . . The strike was over, but
it left the political future of the mayor in the balance. The radical element was stirred up against him, the capitalistic element likewise. He

was charged with playing to the galleries, with vacillating, with breathing hot and cold. It was a most difficult situation. . . .

As a result of all of these happenings, it was felt, along towards the summer, that the mayor's chances for re-election were not at all rosy. Between this time and the election, however, the atmosphere being once more peaceful, a slight reaction did set in in favor of the mayor. It was whispered about that the old organization had helped foment the troubles. Loyalty to the administration for its good work re-asserted itself. The campaign was well planned and vigorously conducted. Both evening papers were plainly on the side of the mayor, and even the strong morning newspaper.

It looked like a close election, and, indeed, on the eve of the contest the Republican organization had practically conceded its defeat. So that when the votes were counted and it was found that by a small majority Mayor Hunt had lost, every one was surprised. . . .

It was a great pity. The fruition of a great many constructive policies seemed close at hand. . . . It seems a shame to say that one must "play politics" and take account of the feministic tendency of the elector. And perhaps it is not quite true; but in the present state of public education (one cannot always find dragons to kill), it is plain that unless all the conditions are just right, it is difficult for a thorough-going reform administration to survive for long. . . .

The present administration has promised constructive reform. The time is too short to judge whether the promise will be fulfilled. It is enough to say that the good done by the former administration is by no means forgotten. A standard has been set, and if it is not quite lived up to, at least there will be no going backward.

Cox, of course, looked at his role as an urban politician from an altogether different perspective from that of his critics. He did not, however, take up the question in detail until near the end of his career. In 1911, while under indictment for perjury in a graft case involving the ultimate disposition of interest paid on county funds,* Cox described what bossism meant to him and tried to explain his view of the origins and nature of the phenomenon. In the process he took into account, either directly or by implication, most of the criticisms of himself and his machine raised by his antagonists. Cox's apologia, printed here with only minor deletions, appeared first in the New York *World*, May 14, 1911, and was carried locally the next day by the *Cincinnati Enquirer*. In his few previous public remarks, Cox consistently claimed that his organization and the candidates it supported gave the city, considering the extraordinary circumstances produced by the urban explosion, good government. How do you reconcile his account of his leadership with those of his critics? Was he more or less "democratic" than they? How optimistic was he about the ability of men to control their future through political action? Was he sensitive to what Freiberg called "the psychology of the voter"? Why does he prefer the term "leader" to describe his role in politics?

The "Boss" Himself

George B. Cox

This is the age of the boss. And it is not surprising when one understands what a boss really is.

A boss, in the accepted usage of the word, is the dictator of a political party. As a matter of fact, a boss is more often simply the leader of a political party. The term is partly relative. And nine times out of ten it is applied by those who wish to vilify a successful political leader. This is true in my case. I have been so uniformly successful since I rose to the leadership of the Republican Party in Cincinnati and Hamilton County in 1884 that my enemies and vilifiers for 27 years have been calling me a boss. They are at perfect liberty to do so. However, I maintain that I am nothing more or less than the leader of the Republican Party in Cincinnati and Hamilton County. But since the public seems to prefer the incorrect term of boss to the correct term of political leader, I will use that term throughout this article. . . .

In the first place, I want to say that a boss is evolved—not self-made. He is a product of evolution—a natural product of American political

---

* Cox was acquitted. Subsequent research has thus far failed to turn up substantial evidence of his guilt or innocence on this and other charges.

life. Every community has developed bosses. The successful ones, naturally, have obtained more or less fame or notoriety. There have always been political leaders from the earliest days of civilization. The men best fitted for leadership became the leaders. In the old days strength and physical prowess were the chief attributes of the successful leader or boss; to-day the ability to control men is the most essential quality.

I had no ambition to become a boss—I am using the incorrect term instead of the correct term, political leader—when I entered politics as a young man. But because of my peculiar fitness I evolved into a boss.

Right here I want to say that the success I have met with I owe to the loyalty of my friends. I have never made a dollar out of politics. For 27 years my enemies have been investigating me, but even the bitterest of men will have to admit that they have never been able to prove the slightest dishonesty. . . .

How did I make my millions? Principally in real estate and investments. I am interested in 31 different business enterprises, representing almost as many different kinds of business. For instance, I own half the Shubert Theatrical Company. Business with me comes first. But I have no personal or private interests when it comes to a question of doing that which is to be for the benefit of the party.

While I have taken an active interest in politics since I was 18 years of age, I have never neglected my business. I have always had my business on my mind. That is one of the reasons why I have been successful. In political matters I have never allowed personal feelings to sway me. I use my own judgement as to the class of candidates most acceptable to the people. Whenever I have defaulted in that I have been unsuccessful. Naturally I have met with some reverses, but since 1884, when I became leader of the Republican Party, Cincinnati has had only two Democratic Mayors. Their administrations were so unsatisfactory that the Republicans were returned at the next elections by large majorities. . . .

Cincinnati is the best governed city in the United States. There is less graft, less dishonesty among its office-holders than in any of the larger cities in the country. Why? Because I have prevented graft. Because I have seen to it that the city had the right kind of men to serve it. Back in the early eighties I brought about honest elections, and since that time I have seen to it that the city officials gave honest administrations.

The fact that all the investigations by self-styled reformers for the past 27 years have not even resulted in the finding of seven illegal votes out of a total population of 400,000 is pretty good proof of my statements. It is in this very work of seeing that the city has honest and efficient servants, and that there is not the slightest graft, that a boss is most successful. The people do the voting. I simply see that the right candidates are selected. The fact that they are elected settles all argument on that score. Furthermore, it costs a candidate nothing to run and be elected. I have eliminated the use of big sums for election purposes.

What do I consider my greatest achievement? I take great pride in my achievement of taking the schools, the Fire and Police Departments out of politics. This was my first work after I became boss of Cincinnati. . . . Since I brought it about, practically every city has tried to accomplish the same thing. Many have been successful, but it is still a deplorable fact that the Police Departments in many cities are dominated by politics.

It was through my efforts that Cincinnati obtained its water-works, but my chief work as boss has been in preventing graft and seeing that the city has had the right men to serve it. A boss is not necessarily a public enemy.

At the present time I am striving to get the city home rule. The question of home rule is the greatest problem before the cities of this country to-day. No further progress can be made in municipal affairs until the cities become free. I am striving to have Cincinnati make its own laws instead of being ruled by legislators from rural districts. The cities of this country should make their own laws and I believe the time is close at hand when they will do so. . . .

I was born in Cincinnati on April 29, 1853, in a quarter that was peopled largely by the poor. My father was an Englishman, who came to this country in 1847. He was a very pious man, but he died when I was only 8 years of age, without leaving a dollar. I had to leave school and help support my mother. The only work I was fitted for was selling newspapers, so I began at once to peddle them on the city's streets. I was successful from the start, and I was soon able to give my mother several dollars every week for our support. I suppose there was little difference between my early life and that of a newsboy in New York today. It was a hard battle, but I was a husky lad and I stood it well. I was as fond of a scrap as any one, and I dare say that I fought a good many times, and if my memory serves me right I was the victor on most occasions.

In addition to selling papers I blacked boots. I ran errands and made small sums by doing such odd jobs as a small boy has the opportunity to do. From the very first I knew what poverty meant, and for that very reason I began to save small amounts every week. The first $1,000 I ever possessed I saved in small amounts. It took years to do it and it was the hardest money I ever earned, but it taught me the value of saving, for with it I got my start in life.

When I grew too big to sell papers I became a butcher's boy at the munificent salary of $5 a week. To earn a larger salary I next became a wagon driver, and after I had saved a nest egg I became a tobacco salesman. . . .

I was 18 years of age at that time and I made my first entry into politics. I allied myself with the Republican Party (for one reason because my father had been a Republican) and served as a challenger at the polls on election day. I was a big, husky young fellow and was especially useful when it became necessary to throw illegal voters out of line.

I drifted into the liquor business, becoming a bartender. I was at that trade for several years, eventually becoming proprietor of a saloon at Central Avenue and Longworth Street. Of course, as soon as I was of age, I voted and I became active in ward politics. At 24 I was elected to the City Council. In those days the Democrats had everything their own way. We had no election laws to speak of, and citizens not only voted as many times as they wanted to, but the officials who counted the votes counted in or counted out the candidates, just as they pleased. I decided that if the Republicans were ever to have a fair deal in Cincinnati it would be necessary to pass strict election laws, and accordingly I set about to have such laws passed. It took many years, but eventually I was successful in having such laws passed by the Legislature, and I was equally successful in having them enforced. Needless to say, conditions were greatly improved. . . .

As I said before, Cincinnati is the best governed city in the United States. It is not "wide open" in the popular usage of that term, but a liberal policy is observed. It is possible to get a drink on Sunday. More than one third of our population is composed of Germans, and they demand that privilege. The gambling houses were driven out many years ago, and the social evil is regulated as far as it is possible to regulate it. Cincinnati has all the problems of the large cities of America, and, of course, there is a certain amount of vice and crime. But I do not hesitate to say that we have come nearer to solving these vexatious problems than has any other municipality of our size.

While I have always taken an interest in state politics I have never been very active in them. I find it takes enough of my time to look after Hamilton County, and there are 87 other counties in Ohio. To be the boss of Cincinnati is a big enough job. I have had no ambition to extend my scope. The only other public office I ever held was that of State Oil Inspector, to which I was appointed by Governor Foraker in 1888. . . .

I arise every morning at 6:30 and am through breakfast by 7:30. I take a 25 or 30 mile ride in my automobile before going to my office at the Cincinnati Trust Company. I always arrive there at 9 o'clock and, except for an hour or so at noontime, I am there until 5 o'clock in the afternoon. I am accessible to every one except bores and pests. I take dinner at one of the hotels or clubs with my business or political associates and arrive home about 8 o'clock in the evening. I get my pleasure in my home life, for, while I have no children, I have a loving and devoted wife. Although I have large theatrical interests I rarely go to the theater. When I do go I attend matinees so as not to waste an evening.

Next to my home life I get the greatest pleasure out of politics. After all, politics is a game. I like it because I am successful. One usually likes to play the game in which one is successful. It's human nature.

Naturally, my success as a boss has brought all manner of attacks upon me. I have been assailed from every quarter, and on every pretext. I am attacked for two reasons: First, because most people suppose a boss is dishonest; and, secondly, because I've been so successful. Success is one thing disappointed office-seekers can never forgive in a boss. I believe the bitterest attacks that have been made on me have emanated from the disappointed office-seekers—men within the ranks of the Republican party who have been turned down by me because of their unfitness.

If people wish to believe every political boss dishonest, that is their privilege. I challenge anyone to prove that I have been dishonest or that I have ever made a dollar out of politics. My indictment at the present time is simply a political move on the part of my enemies. I will clear myself of the charge at the proper time. I am hardened to attacks by the press. I am living my life as I believe I should live it. My enemies cannot affect me. . . .

I would strenuously advise young men not to enter politics. If I had a son I would forcibly prevent him from taking any kind of an active part in it. In the first place there is no money in it for the honest man, and in the second place there is only abuse, whether you are successful or unsuccessful. In fact, the more successful you are the most abuse will be heaped on you. Politics as a profession doesn't pay. . . .

What would happen if I should resign or die? Of course I don't know. I am not gifted with second-sight. But I am inclined to believe that another leader would soon develop to take my place. And I venture to predict that if he met with success for any length of time he would be called the new boss of Cincinnati.

This is the age of the boss. No one must lose sight of this fact for a second.

Chapter

15: The Preparedness Controversy, 1914–1917

⊂⊅ KEITH L. NELSON

During the years before America's entry into World War I, as citizens agonized and disputed over their government's policies toward the European belligerents, a significant and related struggle was taking place among them in regard to the nation's basic military posture. The issue was whether or not to increase the size of the armed forces, and the battle was a bitter one, involving as it did the profoundest beliefs Americans possessed about themselves and their role in history. Only after a serious polarization of opinion had occurred between the proponents and opponents of "preparedness" was a way found past the extremists to what seemed for a time to be a reasonably realistic compromise.

Unfortunately, American belligerency after 1917 did not necessarily confirm the wisdom of the chosen course, and has left, for historians judging it, as many questions as contemporaries faced. Indeed, today, just as before, an individual's conclusions in the matter depend upon his interpretation of the World War itself, and upon what he conceives to be the dynamics (including the effects) of such cataclysms. If he contends, for instance, that it was historically possible for the United States to refrain from participating in the conflict, his explanation as to how this might have been achieved relates directly to his opinions about preparedness. Similarly, if he believes that America was bound to be drawn in and that it was only possible to alter the manner in which we fought, this view, too, affects his judgments regarding the adequacy of our preparation.

Thus, certain very difficult queries must be confronted at the outset of our study. Assuming that Americans had a choice, was it really to our advantage to participate in the First World War? Or would we have been better off in letting it run its course, or in inducing the belligerents to negotiate among themselves? Conversely, assuming that sooner or later war was inevitable (or perhaps that it was advantageous to fight), what would have been the optimal time to enter upon the conflict? In any case, how much "preparedness" would have been required to enable us to carry out our plans? And how much could have been mounted without triggering unacceptable side effects or running inadmissible risks, either at home or overseas? (Obviously, if the cost of "preparedness" had been too high, either in domestic or in foreign terms, it would have been desirable for policymakers to compromise with the "ideal" wartime solution.)

Parenthetically, it might be remarked that such questions as these are not unlike those which we face today in judging the appropriateness of current defense policies. Before we can decide, for example, whether or not the capacity for "flexible military response" (which President John F. Kennedy designed as a means of contending with so-called "brush-fire" wars) is truly adequate to our needs, we must first ask ourselves whether or not it is to our advantage to be able to participate in wars like that in Vietnam. We must also inquire about the costs involved in maintaining this capability, both on the domestic front (e.g., postponed school construction) and on the foreign (e.g., hostility toward our country).

The selections which follow this introduction, and which recapture a portion of the preparedness debate, cannot suffice to answer questions of this nature, which in fact demand the widest possible historical perspective. Nevertheless, by enabling us to understand what the various leaders and groups believed and what they did, these statements can throw light upon what was possible and desirable in the context of 1914–1917. And when, with the assistance of this information, one has made up his mind (at least tentatively) about some of the larger issues involved, he will be in a better position to estimate which of the specific policies or programs would have been effective in accomplishing the tasks which were constructive.

Looking back now, even briefly, it is hard to escape the impression that the entire debate over preparedness was conditioned by a deep American complacency regarding our own security. In truth, it would seem that almost all sides of the controversy made at least two remarkable assumptions: that the western hemisphere was and could remain essentially independent of the eastern, and that the Allies were going to win the war, anyway. What this meant was that the discussion could be carried on in pretty much the same form that it had taken since the 1890's and the very advent of the European arms race. If the argument was now more heated, it remained, as before, relatively general and concerned with hypothetical dangers. For conservatives, who had been preaching for over two decades the duty ethic, the idealism of manhood, and the necessity of national power, the war was simply a particularly excellent proof of the threatening nature of the world outside, and therefore of the need to arm. For reformers and radicals, who had devoted so much effort to the burgeoning peace movement of the last few years, the conflagration across the waters was only an especially impressive argument against abandoning that traditional anti-militarism which was to them the best guarantee against war.

At first, the "pacifists" (as anyone who compaigned against armament was likely to be called) seemed to have much the better of the confrontation. They derived considerable advantage, for example, from their opponents' tendency to picture the danger to the United States in terms of a massive and absurd invasion from overseas. They also received a boost from President Woodrow Wilson, who spoke out as early as the autumn of 1914 against those who would have "aroused" the nation and have disturbed the atmosphere of calm which he considered essential to his attempts at mediation. The result was that not even such new preparedness organizations as the National Security League were able to make much headway, and soon found themselves confronting competitive groups like the American Union Against Militarism and the Women's Peace Party.

A series of events of 1915 brought the preparedness movement to life, perhaps not so much because they altered American assumptions about the war as because they provoked a feeling of impotence and rage throughout the nation. The first and most important of these developments was the sinking of the *Lusitania* in May, but the exposure of German attempts at espionage in American factories (which were producing arms for sale to the Allies) was also significant, as was the growing fear that, in any crisis, the German-American minority would not be loyal to its adopted land. In the wake of all this, large numbers of opinion leaders, particularly among such groups as the clergy, began to take up the cry for armament.

Moreover, Wilson himself was now reworking his position on the military question. In July, a few weeks after his "pacifist" Secretary of State William Jennings Bryan had resigned in dismay at the President's "harsh" (second) *Lusitania* note, Wilson instructed his Secretaries of War and Navy to begin to draw up plans for what they considered an "adequate preparation for national defense." On October 20, he approved a proposal for a five-year naval building program involving the, at that time, immense sum of $502 million. (The total federal budget for 1916 was only $713 million.) On November 4, he announced in a formal address his intention to expand the regular army and to create a sizable new reserve, the "continental army," under federal control.

Naturally, neither extreme of opinion in the country was placated by the President's actions. Theodore Roosevelt called the program a "sham," and other advocates of military strength demanded an even larger army, and compulsory training as well. Yet it was on the Left that the most violent reaction took place, for as historian Arthur Link has pointed out,

Wilson seemed by implication to be questioning two of the most basic beliefs of many of his progressive followers: that America's unique historical mission was to purify herself of such Old World corruptions as large military establishments; and that any modern war was necessarily evil because industrialists seeking markets were among its chief promoters and beneficiaries. The result was a critical split in reformist ranks, with Bryan, Representative Claude Kitchin of North Carolina (the majority leader in the House), Senator Robert LaFollette of Wisconsin, and other Democratic and Republican progressives of the South and West, pulling out to oppose the President. Farmer and labor organizations went on record as objecting almost unanimously to military and naval increases. The liberal majority of the House Military Affairs Committee and its chairman, James Hay of Virginia, were particularly critical of the "continental army" scheme, which Secretary of War Lindley Garrison had championed as a necessary alternative to the National Guard (state militia).

The President attempted in January and February to take his arguments to the people in a tour through the Middle West, but although he met with considerable public enthusiasm wherever he spoke, he found on his return to Washington that there was no escaping the need for compromise. To get any bill at all out of Hay's committee, Wilson was forced to abandon the "continental army" and accept "federalization" of the National Guard, thus making a concession which cost him his Secretary of War, who felt compelled at this point to resign in protest. As it turned out, however, the incident may have been the key to the entire preparedness dispute, because Wilson's new flexibility, together with Garrison's departure and the appointment of Newton Baker (a man of known "pacifist" leanings) as his successor, seemed to reestablish a degree of faith in the President among many of his former supporters. In March the House was able to ratify its committee's recommendations, which increased the size of the army from 100,000 to 140,000 and brought the National Guard under War Department control.

Opposition to preparedness continued, of course, led by a determined band of liberal progressives and socialists, but by the spring of 1916 resistance to the President's program appeared to be disintegrating. Too many of his earlier critics were coming over to his side to leave anything like a united front against him, even among radical groups. By late April the preparedness movement had taken on somewhat the aspect of a patriotic revival, and the Mexican and Sussex crises of the spring enabled the Senate to pass a bill which embodied virtually the original Garrison plan, increasing the regulars to 250,000 and establishing a volunteer reserve of 261,000. Under presidential pressure a compromise between the House and Senate verisons was achieved in May, more than doubling the authorized peacetime army (from 5,029 officers and 100,000 men to 11,327 officers and 208,338 men) and making further provision for expansion to 254,000 men in case of emergency. The National Guard was integrated into the federal establishment and was to be increased to 17,000 officers and 440,000 men within five years. Later laws established a government armor plate factory and provided for a Council of National Defense, designed to facilitate and coordinate any wartime mobilization.

On the naval side, a similar story was unfolding. In May the House of Representatives had turned down the President's five-year building program even while it conceded more tonnage for one year than Wilson had requested. Yet the more conservative Senate, inspired by the battle of Jutland (May 31), astonished the nation by providing for completion of the full administration proposal in three years, not five. At this juncture, the President threw his full weight behind the Senate bill, and this was finally accepted by the House in August. A few days later Congress also passed a much-revised shipping bill, the first version of which it had rejected in 1914, and which now appropriated $50 million for the construction or purchase of merchant ships usable as naval auxiliaries.

Anti-preparedness leaders were bitterly disappointed by what had happened. Though some claimed that they had compelled the President to accept "reasonable preparedness," most found relatively little satisfaction in the minor successes which they had achieved. Their only real solace, and it was not much, lay in the fact that they now forced Congress to pay for the new armaments by enacting a progressive revenue bill, doubling the income tax, increasing the surtax on incomes over $20,000, and levying new corporate taxes including a 12½ percent tax on the gross receipts of munitions industries.

While this was going on, the country was being treated to a presidential campaign in which both major parties espoused preparedness and often sponsored preparedness parades as a means of politicking. The fact that the Democrats ran with Wilson on the slogan "he kept us out of war" did not prevent them from posing as the champions of a powerful America. As a party, only the Socialists continued to attack the expansion of the army and the navy.

Yet throughout 1916 the speeches of preparedness advocates were distinguished by their vagueness and their lack of any new reasoning. Almost no one suggested, for instance, that America's security depended upon the preservation of a European balance of power. Almost no one talked of the possibility of an expeditionary force to Europe. And that such thoughts were as foreign to the administration as to everyone else is apparent from the astonishing fact that when war was finally declared in April, 1917, fully eleven months after the National Defense Act had been passed, the United States Army still numbered only 5,791 officers and 121,797 enlisted men, and the National Guard only 181,000 officers and men. It would not be until February, 1918, that the nation could provide more than one division of infantry to the fighting front in France.

All of which raises several interesting questions:

What, really, had Wilson been doing in striving for "preparedness"? What had his opponents been attempting to accomplish?

How wise, or realistic, were the several contending schools of thought in their attitudes toward the war and national security?

Is it true, perhaps, as one commentator maintains, that the whole preparedness debate actually amounted to a miseducation of the American public, presenting security as some abstract condition to be achieved quite apart from the process of relating day-to-day policies to changing world conditions? Or does this do injustice both to Wilson and his critics?

The European war was just ten weeks old when Representative Augustus P. Gardner (1865–1918), Republican from Massachusetts and Henry Cabot Lodge's son-in-law, fired the opening gun of the preparedness controversy in a sensational speech on behalf of a resolution calling for an investigation of the military establishment. Later in December he was joined by Lodge himself in reintroducing this resolution, a move which so distressed President Wilson that he called Gardner to the White House and attempted in vain to dissuade him from the project. Though Gardner's initiatives stimulated considerable activity among advocates of military expansion, his vigorous partisanship and frankly pro-Allied bias were such as to weaken the appeal of his argument to the public at large. The full text of his address can be found in the *Congressional Record* (63rd Cong., 2nd Sess., October 16, 1914), pp. 16745–47. What, in your opinion, did Gardner seem to be implying about the motivations of men and nations? Why did he make so little reference to the European war?

⊂⊒ The Argument for Preparedness

AUGUSTUS P. GARDNER

For a dozen years I have sat here like a coward, and I have listened to men say that in time of war we could depend for our defense upon our National Guard and our Naval Militia, and I have known all of the time that it was not so. I am a former militiaman myself. I am a veteran of the Spanish War, and I tell you that any such doctrine is the supremest folly. Under that delusion in 10 short years we have allowed our Navy to slough away from a strong second to England, until now it is a very bad third and is fast sinking to fourth or fifth place. The theory in this country that we can create an army and a navy right off the reel is totally and entirely wrong. After war breaks out you can not improvise a dreadnought, you can not improvise a torpedo, you can not improvise a 42-centimeter howitzer, you can not improvise a traveling concrete plant, you can not improvise plants for inflating Zeppelin balloons, you can not improvise sailors. . . .

"Oh, yes," somebody says to me, "that is the same old story that we have been hearing so long—that the United States is not prepared for war." My friends, it is the same old story, and it is a true old story. We were not prepared for the war when the Spanish War broke out in 1898 and we were not prepared for war when the Spanish War ended. . . .

Let us see if the situation is much better to-day. The naval board is continually dinning into our ears a story of the unpreparedness of the

United States for war. Every time he issues a report, Gen. Wood [1] tells us the same thing about the Army. He appeals to us to arise from our lethargy and take an interest in these questions which are vital to the Nation. Yet we go on slumbering and gibbering and scattering money for all sorts of projects wherever the votes grow thickest, and I am just as bad as anyone else in that respect. . . .

We Congressmen have been salving our consciences by trying to believe that no one would dare attack the United States. Are you so confident of that assumption now, gentlemen? Do you believe that if, after this war, Germany found the Monroe doctrine standing in her way—Germany or any other powerful nation—do you feel so sure that she would pay any attention to that doctrine of ours if the redundancy of her population forced her to look about for colonial outlets?

The United States by the Monroe doctrine has said to the world, "You must not colonize in Mexico and you must not colonize in South America—rich, fertile South America. We do not intend to colonize there ourselves, but you shall not colonize there, either. You shall not be allowed to overflow America with colonies recruited from your teeming population." Do you believe that we can maintain any such doctrine unless we are prepared to fight for it? Then, again, we have looked square in the eye of the most military nation which Asia has ever known, and we have said, "We will have none of you within our borders." Do you suppose a proud people like the Japanese will continue to listen with equanimity to a doctrine like that, unless behind that doctrine lies a force which can put it into effect? Perhaps men may say that the Monroe doctrine and the Asiatic exclusion doctrine are prompted by national selfishness. So be it. I concur in both doctrines. I am ready to battle for them and I am ready to pay the bill for enforcing them. . . .

How many men do you think we need in order to man the modest Navy which we have? We need from 75,000 to 100,000 men. And how many do you think that we have? We have just about 50,000 men and some 9,000 Naval Militia. Before we can mobilize our entire fleet, if it is all worth mobilizing, which it is not, we must enlist approximately 41,000 raw recruits, many of whom never saw the sea in their whole lives. . . .

The plans of modern warfare on the sea require fast scouts to keep in touch with the enemy and find out where he is. These scouts must have a minimum speed of 30 knots an hour. How many such scouts do you suppose we have? Mr. Speaker, we have only three of these scouts with which to obtain our information. Germany has 14 fast scouts, and Great Britain has 31. How about the great fighting weapon, the ship which must lie across the ocean paths and intercept the enemy? How

[1] Leonard Wood, Commander of the "Rough Riders" in the Spanish-American War and close friend of Theodore Roosevelt, was Chief of Staff of the Army, 1910–1914.

about the dreadnought and the dreadnought cruiser, the great, strong fighting men-of-war? Let us see how we stand in that respect. Great Britain has 42 dreadnoughts and dreadnought cruisers built and building. Germany has 26. We have only 12, and 3 just authorized. "Oh," you say, "the day of the dreadnoughts has gone by; it is submarines which we want." I do not agree with you that the dreadnought's day has passed, but most certainly I believe that we need a powerful fleet of submarines. Let us see how we stand in that respect. Great Britain has 64 submarines, and we are fourth on the list. So it goes—we are short of nearly every kind of vessel and nearly every kind of armament. The longer it takes to build things, by some strange chance it seems as if the shorter we were of them.

Now, if we have not a fleet, ship for ship, which matches the fleet which comes against us, we probably can not stop that opposing fleet. If we can not stop his fleet, the enemy can land his troops anywhere on the coast of the United States that he sees fit. We have no Army wherewith to oppose him.

Do you know what we have got in the way of an Army? Do you know what we have got with which to oppose 4,000,000 trained men, which happens to be the war strength of the German Army? Do you realize that we have only about 85,000 regulars and about 120,000 militia? Are those militia trained? Why, Mr. Speaker, 60 per cent of the men in the militia who are armed with a rifle do not know how to use it properly. Sixty per cent last year were unable to qualify even as third-class marksmen. . . .

Of course, it is evident that our main defense must be the Navy. This country will not tolerate these huge European land armaments. But at all events, we can vastly increase the Regular Army without putting an undue burden on the taxpayers. Furthermore, we can equip it with plenty of the latest artillery; we can equip it with plenty of the latest machines for fighting in the air; we can double the number of our officers; we can treble the number of our noncommissioned officers. . . .

I know there has been an improvement in artillery, but what I am contending for is a radical change, not a palliative. The whole matter lies deeper than Congress. The trouble is that we have never dared to tell the people that they are living in a fool's paradise, for fear that we should antagonize somebody and perhaps incur the charge that we are revealing our weakness to foreign nations, as if there were any secret about our weakness which we could conceal if we tried. The truth is that each one of us is afraid that some National Guard man in his district will say, "Why, that man GARDNER says I am no good. I will teach him." That is why the people of the United States have not yet awakened to the understanding that 42-centimeter guns and superdreadnoughts present stronger arguments than past victories and present treaties.

President Woodrow Wilson (1856–1924) had no intention in 1914 of allowing "nervous and excited" people to upset the balance of the country and deprive it of its acceptability as a mediator in the eyes of the belligerents. In his Annual Message to Congress of December 8, he went out of his way to minimize the actual danger to America, remind the nation of its traditions of antimilitarism, and call it forth to its highest ideals of international service. The reception of the message was generally enthusiastic. The following is excerpted from *The New York Times*, December 9, 1914, p. 6. Where, in your view, was the root of the President's disagreement with individuals like Representative Gardner? How dissimilar (and how similar) were their fears and their intentions?

⊂⊃ A Declaration of Friendship

WOODROW WILSON

[The subject of national defense] cannot be discussed without first answering some very searching questions. It is said in some quarters that we are not prepared for war. What is meant by being prepared? Is it meant that we are not ready upon brief notice to put a nation in the field, a nation of men trained to arms? Of course we are not ready to do that; and we shall never be in time of peace so long as we retain our present political principles and institutions. And what is it that is suggested we should be prepared to do? To defend ourselves against attack? We have always found means to do that, and shall find them whenever it is necessary without calling our people away from their necessary tasks to render compulsory military service in times of peace. . . .

We are at peace with all the world. No one who speaks counsel based on fact or drawn from a just and candid interpretation of realities can say that there is reason to fear that from any quarter our independence or the integrity of our territory is threatened. Dread of the power of any other nation we are incapable of. We are not jealous of rivalry in the fields of commerce or of any other peaceful achievement. We mean to live our own lives as we will; but we mean also to let live. We are, indeed, a true friend to all the nations of the world, because we threaten none, covet the possessions of none, desire the overthrow of none. Our friendship can be accepted and is accepted without reservation, because it is offered in a spirit and for a purpose which no one need ever question or suspect. Therein lies our greatness. We are the champions of peace and of concord. And we should be very jealous of this distinction which we have sought to earn. Just now we should be particularly jealous of it, because it is our dearest present hope that this character and reputation may presently, in God's providence, bring us an opportunity such as has seldom been vouchsafed any nation, the opportunity to counsel and obtain peace in the world and reconciliation and a healing settlement of many a matter that has cooled and interrupted the friendship of nations. This is the time above all others when we should wish and resolve to keep our strength by self-possession, our influence by preserving our ardent principles of action.

From the first we have had a clear and settled policy with regard to military establishments. We never have had, and while we retain our present principles and ideals, we never shall have, a large standing army. If asked, Are you ready to defend yourselves? we reply, Most assuredly, to the utmost; and yet we shall not turn America into a military camp. We will not ask our young men to spend the best years of their lives making soldiers of themselves. There is another sort of energy in us. It will know how to declare itself and make itself effective should occasion arise. And especially when half the world is on fire we shall be careful to make our moral insurance against the spread of the conflagration very definite and certain and adequate indeed. . . .

In the months after the *Lusitania* crisis President Wilson changed his mind about preparedness, apparently coming to believe that if Americans were going to "keep a free hand to do the high things that we intend to do," it would be necessary to look to a strengthening of the national defense. After a number of preliminary announcements regarding his new views, Wilson publicly summarized his reassessment of the situation in an address to the Manhattan Club of New York City on November 4, 1915. The complete text is in the *The New York Times*, November 5, 1915, pp. 1, 4. Note the President's concern to present a plan in conformity with the ancient "traditions" of the nation. Why do you think this was so important to him? What was the point in developing a force of "citizen soldiers" apart from the National Guard?

⊂⊋ A Decision for Compromise

WOODROW WILSON

Within a year we have witnessed what we did not believe possible, a great European conflict involving many of the greatest nations of the world. The influences of a great war are everywhere in the air. All Europe is embattled. Force everywhere speaks out with a loud and imperious voice in a titanic struggle of governments, and from one end of our own dear country to the other men are asking one another what our own force is, how far we are prepared to maintain ourselves against any interference with our national action or development.

In no man's mind, I am sure, is there even raised the question of the willful use of force on our part against any nation or any people. No matter what military or naval force the United States might develop, statesmen throughout the whole world might rest assured that we were gathering that force, not for attack in any quarter, not for aggression of any kind, not for the satisfaction of any political or international ambition, but merely to make sure of our own security.

We have it in mind to be prepared, but not for war, but only for defense, and with the thought constantly in our minds that the principles we hold most dear can be achieved by the slow processes of history only in the kindly and wholesome atmosphere of peace, and not by the use of hostile force. The mission of America in the world is essentially a mission of peace and good-will among men. She has become the home and asylum of men of all creeds and races. Within her hospitable borders they have found homes and congenial associations and freedom and a wide and cordial welcome, and they have become part of the bone and sinew and spirit of America itself. America has been made up out of the nations of the world and is the friend of the nations of the world. But we feel justified in preparing ourselves to vindicate our right to independent and unmolested action by making the force that is in us ready for assertion.

And we know that we can do this in a way that will be itself an illustration of the American spirit. In accordance with our American traditions we want and shall work for only an army adequate to the constant and legitimate uses of times of international peace. But we do want to feel that there is a great body of citizens who have received at least the most rudimentary and necessary forms of military training; that they will be ready to form themselves into a fighting force at the call of the nation; and that the nation has the munitions and supplies with which to equip them without delay should it be necessary to call them into action. We wish to supply them with the training they need, and we think we can do so without calling them at any time too long away from their civilian pursuits.

It is with this idea, with this conception, in mind that the plans have been made which it will be my privilege to lay before the Congress at its next session. That plan calls for only such an increase in the regular army of the United States as experience has proved to be required for the performance of the necessary duties of the army in the Philippines, in Hawaii, in Porto Rico, upon the borders of the United States, at the coast fortifications, and at the military posts of the interior.

For the rest it calls for the training within the next three years of a force of 400,000 citizen soldiers to be raised in annual contingents of 133,000, who would be asked to enlist for three years with the colors and three years on furlough, but who during their three years of enlistment with the colors would not be organized as a standing force but would be expected merely to undergo intensive training for a very brief period of each year. Their training would take place in immediate association with the organized units of the regular army. It would have no touch of the amateur about it, neither would it exact of the volunteers more than they could give in any one year from their civilian pursuits.

And none of this would be done in such a way as in the slightest degree to supersede or subordinate our present serviceable and efficient National Guard. On the contrary, the National Guard itself would be used as part of the instrumentality by which training would be given the citizens who enlisted under the new conditions, and I should hope and expect that the legislation by which all this would be accomplished would put the National Guard itself upon a better and more permanent footing than it has ever been before, giving it not only the recognition which it deserves, but a more definite support from the National Government and a more definite connection with the military organization of the nation.

What we all wish to accomplish is that the forces of the nation should indeed be part of the nation and not a separate professional force, and the chief cost of the system would not be in the enlistment or in the training of the men, but in the providing of ample equipment in case it should be necessary to call all forces into the field.

Moreover, it has been American policy time out of mind to look to the navy as the first and chief line of defense. The navy of the United States is already a very great and efficient force. Not rapidly, but slowly, with careful attention, our naval force has developed until the navy of the United States stands recognized as one of the most efficient and notable of the modern time.

All that is needed in order to bring it to a point of extraordinary force and efficiency as compared with the other navies of the world is that we should hasten our pace in the policy we have long been pursuing, and that chief of all we should have a definite policy of development, not made from year to year, but looking well into the future and planning for a definite consummation. . . .

No thoughtful man feels any panic haste in this matter. The country is not threatened from any quarter. She stands in friendly relations with all the world. Her resources are known and her self-respect and her capacity to care for her own citizens and her own rights. There is no fear amongst us. Under the new-world conditions we have become thoughtful of the things which all reasonable men consider necessary for security and self-defense on the part of every nation confronted with the great enterprise of human liberty and independence. That is all.

William Jennings Bryan (1860–1925), spokesman of agrarian radicalism, three-time presidential nominee, and Wilson's former Secretary of State, was shocked at the President's reversal of position on preparedness. During the summer and fall, Bryan had been touring the West and South calling for peace at almost any price and defending the soundness of the militia idea. Now, from his home in Washington, he issued a stinging attack on Wilson's New York speech and an ardent appeal to the nation to fight against the administration's program. See *The New York Times*, November 6, 1915, pp. 1, 3, for the full statement. What was probably the most effective argument which Bryan used against the President? What is the most persuasive to you today? What do you make of his assertion that "There has not been a time in fifty years when there was less reason" to arm?

The Plea of Idealism

WILLIAM JENNINGS BRYAN

The President says that we should be prepared "not for aggression but for defense." That is the ground upon which all preparation for war is made. What nation has ever prepared for war on the theory that it was preparing for aggression? It is only fair to assume that the European rulers who are involved in the present war thought that they were contributing toward the maintenance of peace when they were making elaborate preparations for defense. It is a false philosophy, and, being false, it inevitably leads into difficulties.

The spirit that makes the individual carry a revolver—and whoever carries a revolver except for defense?—leads him not only to use it on slight provocation, but to use language which provokes trouble. "Speak softly but carry a big stick" is one of the delusive maxims employed by those who put their faith in force. There are two answers to it—first, the man who speaks softly has not the disposition to carry a club, and if a man with a soft voice is persuaded to carry a club his voice changes as soon as he begins to rely upon the club.

If there is any truth in our religion, a nation must win respect as an individual does, not by carrying arms, but by an upright, honorable course that invites confidence and insures good-will. This nation has won its position in the world without resorting to the habit of toting a pistol or carrying a club. Why reverse our policy at this time? The President himself admits that there is no reason for a change. He says:

The country is not threatened from any quarter. She stands in friendly relations with all the world. Her resources and her self-respect and capacity to care for her own citizens and rights are well known.

And to make the statement more emphatic he adds: "There is no fear among us."

If we're not threatened by any nation, if our relations with all nations are friendly, if everybody knows if we're able to defend ourselves if necessary, and if there is no fear among us, why is this time chosen to revolutionize our national theories and to exchange our policy for the policy of Europe? Why abandon the hope that we have so long entertained of setting an example to Europe? Why encourage the nations of Europe in their fatal folly by imitating them? Why impose upon the Western Hemisphere a policy so disastrous?

May we not expect all Latin America to be stimulated to preparation if we enter upon a new era of preparation? And will not such a policy make conflicts between these republics more probable? We shall do infinite harm to the neighboring nations as well as to ourselves if we are drawn into this policy which provokes a war by a preparation which is impossible without a large increase in taxation and the arousing of a military system which sets up false standards of honor.

We are now spending more than $250,000,000 a year on preparedness —ten times as much as we are spending on agriculture—and I feel sure that the taxpayers are not in favor of increasing this sum at this time when a change is not only unnecessary, but a menace to our national ideals.

There has not been a time in fifty years when there was less reason to add to the expense of the army and navy, for we are not only without an enemy, but our preparedness is increasing relatively as other nations exhaust themselves. And there never was a time, and there never has been a time, in our whole history when our duty to the world more imperatively demanded self-restraint and the counsels of peace.

In 1916, Arthur Capper (1865–1951) was a progressive Republican governor of Kansas and at the beginning of a distinguished political career which would include thirty years of service in the United States Senate. Like many other Westerners at the time, he had become convinced that President Wilson and the nation were being stampeded into "preparedness" by their old enemies: the bankers, capitalists, and jingoes. In statements like the following, which bear a startling resemblance to present-day charges regarding the so-called "military-industrial complex," Capper urged his fellow citizens to reject the counsel of "excitable persons" and "interests having ulterior motives" and to retain their allegiance to "right rather than might." This selection is excerpted from an article entitled 'The West and Preparedness," *Independent*, LXXXV (January 10, 1916), pp. 49–50. Why do you believe Capper was so sure that his diagnosis of the problem was the correct one? What kinds of evidence did he offer to support it? Do you see any connection between his opinions on preparedness and his attitudes regarding an "international league"?

Accusations of Conspiracy

ARTHUR CAPPER

Here is a list of organizations that have formally gone on record against so-called "preparedness" in Kansas:

The Kansas State Teachers' Association, in a convention of 6,000; the Kansas State Grange, with 24,000 members; the Kansas State Farmers' Union, with 21,000 members; the Kansas State Federation of Labor, with 30,000 members; the Kansas State Mutual Insurance Association, with 60,000 members; the Kansas Association of Machinists, with 7,200 members; more than 100 churches, 150 fraternal organizations and 40 women's clubs.

Up to this time not one organization of any description has declared for the "preparedness" program in the State of Kansas.

Our people are convinced this clamor for increased armament comes from two easily traced sources.

On the one hand, we have emotional, excitable persons who become alarmists, who see a spook in every shadow and a murderer in every stranger. They are easily played upon by the demagog. A sensational article in a magazine; a subsidized picture at a movie show; a melodramatic grouping of waxworks in a window display—for which some financially interested person pays—is sufficient to upset them. They are given to violent action and re-action. They are temperamentally hysterical, unsafe, a constant menace to their community and the nation. Their alarm is genuine; their fears frightful to them; but it is the duty of sane and better balanced citizens to quiet their fears, allay their alarms and help them regain poise.

On the other hand, we have quite apparently a well-organized propaganda systematically and cruelly promoting this war hysteria in the United States. Manufacturers who see fat contracts looming ahead of them are deliberately playing upon the imaginations of the excitable and the fears of the timid, in order to stampede the nation into a campaign of extravagant expenditures, regardless of all other consequences.

Back of the manufacturers are the professional fighting men of the nation whose trade is war—men whose training and environment have made them military above everything else and warped them to the narrow point of view of the military specialist. They are schooled to glory in war. Their life-long ambition is to practice actual warfare in a great campaign conducted on a modern scale. They believe might makes right. In bloodshed they see the regeneration of the race, the development of the stern and manly virtues and a panacea for all life.

The manufacturers, with their heads turned by the prospect of easy profits and the men of war aroused by the prospect of a real fight, or by greater professional opportunities, fully realize that they must strike now if they are to gain their ends. They must take advantage of the scare. Hence the adroitly worked-up panic and the insistent demand that war preparations begin *now*—without waiting the outcome of the European war or to see what lessons may be learned from that conflict.

We can see, therefore, only unending misfortune in this preparedness step. Let the United States arm itself to the teeth and straightaway the rapidly growing republics of South America, with their enormous natural resources and teeming populations, will take up arms in self-protection. . . . Then a coalition against the feared and misunderstood United States by these South American Latins will bring about the inevitable conflagration we now see as a result of this policy in Europe, but long before this we shall lose their trade. They will fear to build up a dreaded rival by buying goods of him.

But more than the commercial loss, a greater calamity even than the loss of human lives which attend warfare, is the deterioration of national character which follows the policy of militarism. We now are a peaceful people, loving the ways of peace. Given over to the rule of jingoes we shall become a swaggering, aggressive, bullying nation that puts its trust in might rather than right. The reign of peace on earth may, as the alarmists tell us, be a long way off, but surely it cannot be hastened by transforming this great nation into a military camp.

I have great faith in the efficacy of economic pressure as a defensive measure. I do not think that the idea embodied in the proposal of a "League to Enforce Peace" is at all visionary. An international court is as possible among civilized nations as are courts for the adjustment of disputes between individuals. The combined forces of the powers, economic and military, against any one of their number who fails to take its case before an international court, could hardly fail to keep the peace. A cycle of preparedness in Europe and of the very sort now demanded with such clamor for the United States, has resulted in the greatest cataclysm of history. Are we prepared to pay that price?

I think not. I do not believe that the sober-minded people of this country will be frightened by any bogeyman into so wicked a program. Unless we go mad in the heat of a political campaign, the wave of hysteria will recede and the United States will again put her trust in open dealing in diplomacy; in common honesty between nations; in right rather than in might.

No critic of Woodrow Wilson was more vigorous or severe than former President Theodore Roosevelt (1858–1919). A believer in bold national assertion on behalf of self-interest and of "righteousness," he grew steadily more wrathful during these years at what he considered the administration's cowardly behavior and irresponsible idealism in the face of repeated German violations of international law. Of all the President's policies, nothing exasperated T.R. more than Wilson's caution about "preparedness," and, as he inaugurated his unsuccessful campaign for the Republican presidential nominations in 1916, he gave vent to his feelings regarding this in a speech before the Illinois Bar Association in Chicago. *The New York Times*, April 30, 1916, sec. I, pp. 1, 3, carries the complete address.

To what constituencies would you estimate that Roosevelt was appealing here? How would his statements have affected the Congress, then engaged in enacting "preparedness" legislation? How did his view of an "international league" compare with that of Capper?

The Demand for Realism

THEODORE ROOSEVELT

Every nation in the world now realizes our weakness, and no nation in the world believes in either our disinterestedness or our manliness. The effort to placate outside nations by being neutral between right and wrong, and to gain good-will along professional pacifist lines by remaining helpless for self-defense, has resulted, after two fatuous years, in so shaping affairs that the nations either already feel, or are rapidly growing to feel for us, not only dislike but contempt. . . .

Our prime duty, infinitely our most important duty, is the duty of preparedness. Unless we prepare in advance we cannot when the crisis comes be true to ourselves. If we cannot be true to ourselves, it is absolutely certain that we shall be false to every one else. If we are not able to safeguard our own national honor and interest, we shall make ourselves an object of scorn and derision if we try to stand up for the rights of others. We have been sinking into the position of the China of the Occident; and we will do well to remember that China—pacifist China— has not only been helpless to keep its own territory from spoliation and its own people from subjugation but has also been helpless to exert even the most minute degree of influence on behalf of right dealing among other nations.

There are persons in this country who openly advocate our taking the position that China holds, the position from which the best and wisest Chinamen are now painfully trying to raise their land. Nothing that I can say will influence the men and women who take this view. The holding of such a view is entirely incompatible with the right to exercise the privileges of self-government in a democracy, for self-government cannot permanently exist among people incapable of self-defense.

But I believe that the great majority of my fellow-countrymen, when they finally take the trouble to think on the problem at all, will refuse to consent to or acquiesce in the Chinafication of this country. I believe that they will refuse to follow those who would make right helpless before might, who would put a pigtail on Uncle Sam, and turn the Goddess of Liberty into a pacifist female huckster, clutching a bag of dollars which she has not the courage to guard against aggression. . . .

I speak of the United States as a whole. Surely it ought to be unnecessary to say that it spells as absolute ruin to permit divisions among our people along the lines of creed or of national origin as it does to permit division by geographical section. We must not stand merely for America first. We must stand for America first and last; and for no other nation second—except as we stand for fair play for all nations. There can be no divided loyalty in this country. The man who tries to be loyal to this country and also to some other country is certain in the end to put his loyalty to the other country ahead of his loyalty to this.

The politico-racial hyphen is the breeder of moral treason. We are a new nation, by blood akin to but different from all the nations of Europe.

Preparedness must be both of the soul and of the body. It must be not only military but industrial and social. There can be no efficient preparedness against war unless there is in time of peace economic and spiritual preparedness in the things of peace. Well-meaning men continually forget this interdependence. Well-meaning men continually speak as if efficient military preparedness could be achieved out of industrial and social chaos, whereas such military preparedness would represent merely a muscular arm on a withered body.

To mobilize our resources, and introduce efficiency everywhere in business would merely make us a more attractive and a more helpless prey unless we in similar fashion develop our power and purpose for self-defense. I stand heartily for protection. By that I mean not only protection to American industries and to the material interests of American workingmen, farmers, and business men. I also mean, and with even greater emphasis, protection for the whole American nation, protection for American honor, protection for America's self-respect, protection for America's position among the nations, protection for her when she strives, as she ought to strive, to bring peace to the rest of the world. And there can be no such protection without thoroughgoing preparation—military, social, and industrial.

We need, beyond anything else, a first-class navy. We cannot possibly get it unless the naval program is handled with steady wisdom from the standpoint of a nation that accepts the upbuilding and upkeep of such a navy as cardinal points of continuous policy. There should be no party division along these lines. A party which, whatever its views are on other subjects, stops the upbuilding of the navy or lets it be impaired in efficiency should be accepted as false to the vital interests of the American people. The navy should be trained in deep water, in salt water, and it should be trained always with one end in view, to increase its fighting efficiency. It is not an educational institution. It is Uncle Sam's right arm of defense; and that arm is meant to hold the sword, and not the pen. The minute the effort is made to turn a battleship into an ambulatory schoolhouse, we spoil the battleship without getting the schoolhouse. . . .

The navy stands foremost. But to rely only on the navy would be as foolish as in a battle to rely only upon infantry or only upon artillery or only upon trench digging. Back of the navy must stand the regular army; and back of the regular army must stand the trained strength of the nation.

The regular army is indispensable. Here again, gentlemen, let me ask you to do your part in seeing that our people understand the utter folly of embarking on a policy unless we have the means to enforce that policy. A treaty has recently been proposed by the Governmental authorities in Washington under which we would guarantee the territorial integrity of all the South American republics, with, as a quid pro quo, the assurance of these republics (Honduras, Nicaragua, and Ecuador for instance) that they will guarantee our territorial integrity. Translate this into terms of fact. If the treaty does not mean what it purports to mean it is insincere, and worse. If it does mean what it purports to mean, then we are to guarantee that we will go to war to defend, say, Terra del Fuego on behalf of somebody else.

Yet the upholders of this proposal in the same breath announce that we are not to go to war for our own rights or our own citizens. It is possible to defend either proposition with sincerity (although not with wisdom,) but it is not possible to defend both propositions with either sincerity or wisdom. Well-meaning people propose that we shall enter into an international league to enforce peace, by making treaties under which we would pledge ourselves, if for instance Belgium were invaded, to back Belgium in war by the two or three million men without whom our unsupported backing would amount to little.

Before going into any more grandiose promises, let us keep the moderate promises we made in The Hague Conventions; and before we promise action on behalf of others which might necessitate an army of two or three million men being sent abroad to fight in a quarrel in which interest was purely altruistic, let us ponder the fact that in order to send an army after a Mexican bandit, although this army was operating in company with the forces of the de facto Government of Mexico, we had to strip our country of regular soldiers until we did not have enough left to patrol the border.

The Mexican affair, by the way, offers the best possible example of the need that this country should deal with things and not merely with words. For some years Mexico has stood to us much as the Balkan peninsula with its weak and turbulent States once stood to Europe. Success or failure in our Mexican policy is no mere local matter; if in this place our foreign policy fails, it means general failure. The problem is not primarily a military one, although now unfortunately our failure to grapple with it intelligently and in terms of fact may well mean that there may have to be a military prelude to the real settlement. The settlement itself will come only when we make up our minds to render constructive and disinterested service on a common sense basis, as we so successfully did in Cuba.

The preparedness of a big, highly efficient navy and a small, highly efficient regular army will meet our immediate needs, and can be immediately undertaken. But ultimately, and to meet our permanent needs, I believe with all my heart in universal training and universal service on some modification of the Swiss and Australian systems adapted to the needs of our American life. Such training would not merely—indeed, perhaps not primarily—be of benefit from the military standpoint, although the good from this standpoint would be inestimable; it would not take our young men away from their life work; it would, on the contrary, help fit them for their life work, make them more valuable socially and industrially, train them to order, discipline, the power to enjoy and make use of self-respecting liberty, the power to co-operate with their fellows.

It would be an antiseptic to militarism; for Switzerland and Australia are the least militaristic and most democratic of Commonwealths. It would be done in the schools, and then by four to six months' work in the field when they leave the schools. It would mean only extending the system already admirably applied in Wyoming. With such a system we should be guaranteed forever against the kind of conflict which is known as a rich man's war and a poor man's fight. We should never have a war unless the people who were to fight it deliberately determined upon it. It would be a war waged by the people for the people.

Newton D. Baker (1871–1937), the "pacifist" mayor of Cleveland whom Wilson appointed Secretary of War in March, 1916, was quick to take his pen in hand to defend the administration's record. Ultimately one of America's most dynamic wartime leaders, in the summer of 1916 Baker was fully satisfied that the nation was on its way to "preparedness," and he attempted to justify his opinion in articles such as that which follows (*The Outlook*, July 5, 1916, pp. 550–52). Significantly enough, the "measure" which he mentions regarding a "council of executive information" (later called the Council of National Defense) had been proposed and drafted by Baker himself, and was enacted by Congress with scarcely a ripple of public notice. Is it clear why Baker was convinced that the additions to the army and navy had been "necessary"? Do you think that his concept of mobilization was a realistic one, considering the situation? Did it differ so much from Roosevelt's?

⊂≣ A Defense of the President's Course

Newton D. Baker

At first this question revolved around mere military preparation in the narrowest sense—the number, weight, and armament of our ships; the length of the guns of our coast defenses; the amount of ammunition of various kinds in store; the number of trained men to officer impromptu armies. But as the war developed in Europe we learned that these things are but a part of preparation, and a relatively useless part, unless they are based upon other things very much more difficult to secure—things which must be secured long in advance of a crisis or else be then obtainable only with peril and fearful unnecessary loss. We have witnessed the nations of Europe preparing as they fought, and have come to realize that perhaps the most important kind of preparedness is a kind which is equally available and useful in times of peace, and which, if secured, will not only render our military preparation more effective, but will steady and strengthen and inspire the Nation when engaged in peaceful pursuits.

The war in Europe is teaching us many lessons. For one thing, we have learned that the whole art of war has changed in character. The forces concerned are more extensive, the instruments used more deadly, their preparation involves more time. The spectacle in Europe to-day is that of millions of men fighting underground—a war in which machinery is king. The ingenuity and the inventiveness of these people have been long busy with its preparation. And one lesson for us is that any degree of preparation requires more forethought than was formerly necessary. If America should ever be called upon to defend the rights of her citizens in any such contest as is now being waged, it would mean either our destruction or the summoning of every vital energy of our people to our defense.

I have no hysterical notion that war is like the plague, and that we are going to catch it from mere proximity; nor have I the slightest fear that the great people of this Nation are going to lose their heads and embark upon a career of combat and conquest out of a mere desire to be heroic or to attain glory. As a matter of fact, the glory of war has largely disappeared, and the magnitude of the sacrifices entailed makes of it a stern business to be entered upon only as an alternative to impossible conditions of peace. This Administration has taken note, however, of the fact that this is an age in which the principles of mechanics, the output of the workshops, and the preparation made by industry and commerce are a part—a necessary part—of the preparation for National security.

The Congress has now passed an army reorganization bill, creating no great standing army, enforcing by no compulsion a universal sacrifice from the manhood of the Nation of years out of careers devoted to industry and commerce, but providing a first-line of defense. The bill will give us a National force large enough to maintain order in those outlying places where we have assumed responsibilities and to protect our own borders against any aggression. It provides an experiment in Federalizing the militia of the States, making it a safer reliance for the National defense and recognizing the sacrifice and patriotism of those who prepare to serve their country by enlistment in these State forces. Some increases in the navy are also authorized. And by a measure now under consideration, suggested by the President, a council of executive information is proposed which will bring the Government into such intimate relations of knowledge and sympathy with labor and business and industry as to make possible, should it ever be necessary, an instant mobilization of the great resources of this Nation for the common defense.

I am persuaded that the additions to the army and navy were necessary, and that common prudence requires and justifies the expenditures and reorganizations here proposed.

Threefold mobilization is necessary in any country for war, and of these three elements two are as valuable and as vital in times of peace as in times of conflict.

In the first place, there must be, of course, arms and soldiers, ships and sailors, and these must be modern and adequate. A fourth and fifth arm—aircraft and submarine—have been added. No nation can with justice summon embattled farmers with the rude firearms which were adequate a few decades ago. Regimentation, discipline, and knowledge are more important than they used to be, and the masses and the maneuvers are on a more intricate and difficult scale. . . .

The second mobilization necessary is that of our industries and commerce. The war in Europe had been under way more than a year before some of the countries were able to equip the men who volunteered for their armies. With all the zeal which their governments could display, the mobilization of their industries yet lagged, not from unwillingness, but from lack of forethought. Perhaps no other lesson of the great war is so impressive as its universality. In the warring countries this war and its demands sit at the table of every family, from that of the king to that of the peasant. Each is contributing his share, each is suffering his loss. The farmer is no longer growing grain merely to sell, but for the national welfare. The railways are no longer carrying passengers or freight merely for hire, but for the national defense. The soldier is no longer a tradesman in war, but is a part of the large regiment which includes his entire country, and in which each man is assigned a necessary part. So in America, if the test ever comes, the army in the field will be merely the advance guard resting on a mobilized, patriotic, industrial co-ordination. Back of it will be every factory and every workshop, every bank, and every farm, and this industrial co-ordination is as valuable to us in peace as it is in war. We now have the impulse and the opportunity to give to our daily life a National purpose. Every occupation in America now takes on a patriotic aspect. It is not merely a means of gaining a livelihood, but a contribution to the common interest. It is therefore of the utmost importance that we should know what our reliance is; that careful, continuous, scientific studies should be made of our industrial and commercial capacity and adaptation; that we should card-index our industrial strength so that we can know it and summon it into instant co-operation when needed. And very much more than that, we must gain this knowledge and arrange for this co-operation in such a fashion as to take away from it all profit in war. If the hour of trial should ever come, there must be no war stocks, no war brides, no war fortunes made out of the National danger. . . .

The third mobilization that is necessary is spiritual. In order to make sacrifices for America we must be sure that our stake in the country justifies it. Our institutions must be so just, our arrangements so fair, that every man in this Nation will realize how completely his opportunity and that of those who come after him rest upon the continuing prosperity of the Nation as a whole.

The military mobilization will take place easily and need not be upon a magnificent scale in advance. The industrial and spiritual mobilization ought to be constant and as wide as the country. . . .

One of the very few men in the United States who faced up unafraid to the meaning of the new armaments was Herbert Croly (1869–1930). Editor of *The New Republic,* Croly also authored that influential work, *The New Nationalism,* upon which Theodore Roosevelt leaned so heavily. A long-time proponent of socially constructive centralization, Croly was willing to recognize that the preparedness program constituted a violation of America's historic traditions, but he felt that it was a necessary part of the nation's "growing up" and of returning to the mainstream of world history. He saw that the new weapons brought with them the power of "aggressive" as well as defensive action, but he remained hopeful that America would be inspired to employ them in a positive and useful way. This excerpt is taken from an essay which Croly wrote for *The Annals* of the American Academy of Political and Social Science, 66 (July, 1916), pp. 157–72. Would you conclude that Croly's accusations against President Wilson were generally accurate and fair? Do you agree with him that the country was in need of "serious moral adventure"? Was this an indirect plea for American participation in the World War?

⊂⊐ Hope of "Serious Moral Adventure"

HERBERT CROLY

Last summer when President Wilson decided to include in the legislative program of the administration provision for a large army he ordered his Secretary of War to make the plans for an increase confoming to the existing American military tradition. What the President had in mind is clear. He had decided that more soldiers must be enlisted and trained presumably because they might be needed for certain practical purposes. But after having reached this decision he was chiefly preoccupied, not with the number and kind of soldiers demanded by these practical needs, but with the effect of any increase at all upon the opinions and traditions of his fellow-countrymen. He knew his proposals would meet with lively opposition based chiefly on the presumptive un-Americanism of large armies, and he preferred to bestow on the plans of the administration not so much the positive merit of careful adaptation to the practical need as the negative merit of conformity to a prevailing tradition. In order to make them politically acceptable the administration plans should look unoffensive and not too unfamiliar. The American army had always been the creature of domestic political policy and so it must remain.

In adopting this course President Wilson was behaving like a shrewd and cautious political leader. It was the course calculated to effect a certain result with the smallest friction. He has been rewarded by the practical collapse of the opposition to his program. It has been an adroit achievement and an important success. But the fullest possible recognition of the achievement should not blind us to the disadvantages of the method. The success was purchased by a lack of thoroughness in framing the details of the plans and by a lack of frankness in explaining their meaning and consequences. The technical obstacles to adequate preparation and its political penalties and dangers have been underestimated and evaded rather than courageously confronted and definitely overcome. As a result the American people are acting in a grave national crisis without any sufficient understanding of the bearing of the new policy on their past and its probable effects on their future.

The American tradition of military organization and policy which President Wilson wished to preserve was not on its merits worth so much anxious solicitude. It called for a small standing professional army which was really no more than a national police force. Its members, organization and equipment were not adjusted to a foreign policy or an international condition. Invasion was not considered a danger against which any elaborate precautions needed to be taken. In the event of war the navy would act as a screen, behind which could be trained around a nucleus furnished by the state militia a volunteer citizens' army. The aspect of this system which Mr. Wilson probably considered most precious was its underlying and almost complete civilianism. It included a professional army, to be sure, but only in insignificant numbers. The United States depended ultimately for its soldiers upon its citizens and it had consequently no reason to fear the corruption of its democratic institutions and ideals by a military caste or spirit. All this is true, but it is also true that the system was a tissue of inadequacies and contradictions. It evaded every difficulty and ignored every serious responsibility involved by military preparedness.

A democracy should depend ultimately for its soldiers on its citizens; but our traditional system only pretended to create an armed citizenry. Its trained soldiers were prevented from being citizens; its citizens were never sufficiently trained to be good soldiers. The American people had no reason to fear their army, but neither had the possible enemies of the American people. It was not intended to be dangerous to anybody but a few foreign or domestic marauders. Congress always refused to incorporate in it a coherent formative idea. It was partly professional and partly amateur, partly under national and partly under state jurisdiction, partly based upon the idea of service and partly upon an appeal to mercenary motives. But above all it was wholly and intentionally innocuous. It was essentially an attempt to assure civilian control over the military machine less by making the civil authority strong, clearsighted, able and worthy, than by making the army feeble and incompetent.

If, as President Wilson decided last summer, the American democracy was finally faced by the necessity of seriously preparing during peace for the possibility of war, this national tradition in military organization needed to be radically modified rather than loyally cherished and preserved. The traditional military system can be fairly characterized as organized unpreparedness. Americans had believed themselves immune from the grim necessity of anticipating and providing either against social evils at home or the defense of national policies abroad. America was the promised land precisely because it was delivered from such moral and physical stresses and from the structural reenforcement, necessary to withstand them. Some years ago one-half of these expectations began to be abandoned. It became only too apparent that American domestic economy is not a stream which purified itself in the running. It had developed the same social disorders as the older European societies and similar precautions must be taken against them. The decision to increase the army and navy means the abandonment also of the other half. The organized unpreparedness of our military system had been based upon a conception of international relationships and of ensuing American dangers, opportunities and responsibilities which had ceased to be true. The indispensable condition of any effective military preparation was a declaration of war against an essential aspect of the very tradition which the President was seeking so sedulously to preserve.

In so far as the American tradition in military organization consisted in the strict and absolute subordination of the military and naval machines to ultimate civilian control and their employment for valid political purposes, every good American will attach the utmost importance to its preservation. But in so far as the civilian control was obtained by paralyzing the army rather than by organizing the nation, strengthening its government and clarifying its policy, the existing tradition manifestly constitutes an insuperable obstacle to effective military preparation. The larger army and navy must be intended and made ready for actual definite service. In so far as it is ready for specific service the army must be a dangerous weapon. It must be dangerous to the possible enemies of the United States; and it must be dangerous to our traditional internal equilibrium. Unless the American people are willing and ready to create a powerful weapon, which if misused would prove to be harmful to them no less than to their possible enemies, the money and energy spent on military preparations will continue to be a colossal waste. As a matter of fact the American people proved more willing to create a powerful weapon than its chosen leaders imagined. The original program of the administration was indeed framed to look innocuous rather than dangerous. It was based chiefly upon the principle of amplifying our deficiencies. But the original program has been radically modified, and every modification has tended to make it less innocuous and more dangerous. A reluctant Democratic administration and Congress, which had every disposition to keep down the scope and cost of military "preparedness," have been forced by the logic of their own decision to build very much more than they intended. The final legislation is likely to provide for a really formidable fighting force—one which will be measurably adjusted in size, training and equipment to the probable needs of national policy. . . .

The new American army will be unsafe for two reasons. An army of this kind is really adapted chiefly to service abroad and consequently to something more than a defensive foreign policy. It is also the kind of an army which will have a profound reaction on American domestic life, because as a consequence of its increased size and authority it will be constantly making imperative demands upon the civil authorities which they will be reluctant to grant and which will raise the issue between civil and military control over American policy. These are precisely the questions which the President wished to avoid, as they have been avoided in the past, but from now on they will wax increasingly troublesome. The new army could not be made serviceable, without becoming unsafe, because in the opinion of too many American citizens, a safe army meant an imperilled country. In truth there was no way in which the domestic life and institutions of the nation could be guaranteed against far-reaching modifications as a consequence of substituting organized preparedness for organized unpreparedness. An efficient new military and naval establishment is bound in the end to do something important to the American people, and the certainty of a drastic result should be recognized in advance. Confident prophecies are being made as to what this drastic result will be. Many good Americans predict that our democracy will be ruined by their new and dangerous servant. Others predict with equal confidence that a more powerful army and widespread military training is necessary not merely to save the nation from its possible foreign enemies but to preserve it from its domestic infirmities. Neither of these predictions need be taken too seriously. They are the expression of fears and hopes rather than a disinterested estimate of the action of social forces. Although drastic result will certainly follow, what that result will be is by no means so certain. It will depend less upon the size and organization of the army and the navy than upon the way in which the nation decides to use them.

At present the American people have not made up their mind how they will use their new army and navy, and anti-militarists are insisting that the creation of the larger army and navy should be postponed until they do. I cannot agree with them. We shall have to take the risk of preparing first and of deciding later just what we are preparing for. To have refused to prepare would under the circumstances have been an indication of inertia and weakness. To have begun to prepare is on the whole a symptom of self-confidence. It indicated that the country is not afraid to plunge forward even though somewhat blindly and to risk the assumption of a perilous and costly responsibility which before it is redeemed may diminish many prescriptive rights, damage many vested interests and perhaps change the whole outlook of the American democracy.

The American nation needs the tonic of a serious moral adventure. It has been too safe, too comfortable, too complacent and too relaxed. Its besettting weakness is the prevalence of individual and collective irresponsibility, based on the expectation of accomplishing without effort. Living as it did in a favored land which was not exposed to attack from without and which offered to good Americans surpassing opportunities to satisfy their own special and individual purposes, our democracy has not been required to pull itself together. It has depended for its cohesion upon loyalty to an achieved and essentially complete constitutional system, and upon a suppositious harmony between individual or local, and public or national interests. Unlike European countries, it could afford to leave the satisfaction of many public objects to the results of an accidental concert among individuals, groups of individuals, or local political units. It has been reluctant to create powerful political or economic organs for the accomplishment of its national purposes, and when instruments of this kind came into existence as the result of automatic economic and political forces, the instinct of the democracy was to dissolve, rather than to discipline and use its own unmanageable servants. It has not liked the responsibility of turning such potentially dangerous agents as a centralized administration, an authoritative legislature, an efficient army or any concentrated embodiment of industrial power to beneficial public use. . . .

Chapter

16: Government and the Economy in the 1920's: The Struggle Over Muscle Shoals

⊂⊋ MICHAEL E. PARRISH

The Tennessee River, from its beginning four miles above Knoxville to where it joins the Ohio River at Paducah, Kentucky, flows for 650 miles, south through the Cumberland Plateau, west across northern Alabama and northeast Mississippi, and finally, north across western Tennessee and Kentucky. Near the towns of Sheffield and Florence in northern Alabama the river makes a great bend north into Tennessee. Here, the water once fell 130 feet in 30 miles, producing the tortuous rapids and navigational hazards known as Muscle Shoals. This portion of the Tennessee River, with its whirlpools and jagged rocks, became the focus of one of the most prolonged, bitter, and complex political contests in American history.

At the heart of the struggle over Muscle Shoals, which spanned seventeen years from 1916 to 1933, were two inseparable questions: (1) Who would control and develop the potential water resources of this strategic area of the Tennessee River? (2) How would the resources be utilized and for whose benefit? The resolution of these questions involved rival philosophies of government, economic groups, political parties, geographic regions, and engineering-scientific preferences. Should control and development of the water resources at Muscle Shoals be vested in private corporations, the Federal government, or a mixture of private and public authorities? Should hydroelectric power, flood control, navigation, or nitrate-fertilizer production be the principal objective of development?

In 1933, during the early days of the New Deal, these issues were settled by the creation of the Tennessee Valley Authority. The TVA law, written by Senator George Norris of Nebraska and supported enthusiastically by Franklin Roosevelt, required multiple-purpose development of the entire Tennessee River under a corporation owned by and operated by the Federal government. Muscle Shoals then became a central link in the hydroelectric, flood-control, reclamation, navigation, and fertilizer production activities of the Tennessee Valley Authority. But 1933 was a quiet ending to the furious controversy of the previous decade when the many alternative proposals for Muscle Shoals were first set forth to be praised by, denounced by, and pigeonholed by Congressional committees and rejected by two Presidents. The real climax came in 1931 when Herbert Hoover vetoed for the second time Senator Norris's legislation calling for government operation of Muscle Shoals.

The Norris-Hoover confrontation over Muscle Shoals was a legacy of World War I. Prior to 1916 the United States depended upon Chilean nitrates for the manufacture of munitions. Fearing interruption of these supplies in the event of war, Congress passed the National Defense Act which authorized the President to select one or more sites where cheap water power could be developed for the purpose of extracting nitrogen from the air through the cyanamid process. The nitrates produced were to be used for munitions in time of war and in the manufacture of commercial fertilizer and other products in time of peace. This final provision was popular with Southern and Western agricultural representatives in the Congress.

President Wilson chose the Muscle Shoals site. The work schedule called for the construction of three dams (two for navigation and one for power), two nitrate plants, two electrical steam plants, a power house, and an industrial village; the purchase of a large tract of land, and a lime quarry. By 1918 the government had expended $105 million on Muscle Shoals. Two nitrate plants and the steam plants were then complete. Work had only begun on the power and navigation dams, and with the signing of the armistice, the most urgent need for nitrates passed. The question of the disposition of Muscle Shoals was thrown back to the Congress.

Progressives in the Wilson Administration and in Congress hoped to extend government operation of Muscle Shoals after the armistice. They rallied behind the Wadsworth-Kahn bill of 1919, drafted by Secretary of War Newton D. Baker, which placed the Muscle Shoals properties under the control of a government-owned corporation. The corporation would produce nitrogen products, initially for defense purposes, but also for sale to farmers and fertilizer manufacturers. Wilson Dam, the only hydroelectric facility then under construction at Muscle Shoals, would be complete; surplus power, not utilized by the corporation for nitrogen production, would be sold at the switchboard to private utility companies and municipalities. With strong backing from Southerners and Westerners, interested in cheap electricity for industrial development and in fertilizer for farmers, the Wadsworth-Kahn bill passed the Senate. It was defeated, however, in the House Military Committee, largely by Republican votes. The House also rejected temporarily further appropriations for Wilson Dam. Republican victories in the Presidential and Congressional elections of 1920 dealt another severe blow to the proponents of government operation.[1]

Presidents Harding, Coolidge, and Hoover, as well as a sizable number of Republicans in the Congress, worked assiduously over the next eleven years to defeat all variations of the Wadsworth-Kahn bill which threatened governmental control of Muscle Shoals. They preferred to lease the nitrate and power properties to private business. The Republican position, following defeat of the Wadsworth-Kahn measure, also attracted temporary support from many Southern Democrats who were not committed in principle to government operation of Muscle Shoals but who were attracted by the possibility of cheap electricity and fertilizer through either public or private development. This left a small, but tenacious band of Progressive Congressmen, led by Senator Norris, who were dedicated to the broad objectives of the Wadsworth-Kahn bill.

Even with their absolute political advantage, the Republicans and their erstwhile Southern supporters were not able to dispose of Muscle Shoals to private bidders who, while fighting each other, helped to produce a legislative stalemate. Henry Ford's offers in 1921 and 1922 to develop the nitrate and power properties on the basis of a perpetual lease and an annual rental fee of $1.4 million fired the imagination of farmers generally and Southerners particularly to whom he promised low-cost fertilizer, abundant power, and a new city at Muscle Shoals to rival the industrial might of Detroit. But Ford's audacious scheme, which involved a hidden government subsidy of $50 million, called down the wrath of the Alabama Power Company and its financial allies who wanted Muscle Shoals for themselves, alarmed the chemical and aluminum companies who feared the possibility of Ford's diversification into their product areas, provoked the National Fertilizer Association, and even antagonized many Southern businessmen who believed Ford would monopolize the entire output of Muscle Shoals power and thus retard the economic growth of nearby regions. Legislation approving the Ford offer passed the House in 1924, but died in the Senate. A similar fate befell all other private leasing measures designed to turn Muscle Shoals over to the Alabama Power Company, American Cyanamid, or Union Carbide.

Senator Norris exploited the rivalry of private groups brilliantly. As chairman of the Senate Agriculture Committee which had jurisdiction over all Muscle Shoals proposals, he encouraged the various interests to checkmate each other, allowed the private leasing measures to stagnate in his committee, and organized successful filibusters against those which reached the Senate floor. In addition to these daring parliamentary

[1] Under incessant pressure from Southern Democrats, Congress finally appropriated additional funds for Wilson Dam in 1922. The dam and power house were completed by 1925 under the supervision of the Army Corps of Engineers.

maneuvers, he kept the issue of government operation alive by sponsoring his own Muscle Shoals legislation and recapturing the support of Southern Democrats who were exhausted by the failure of private development schemes.

Under Norris's leadership, the nitrate and fertilizer aspects of Muscle Shoals were subordinated to the other multiple-purpose projects of hydro-electric power, flood control, and navigation. Norris hoped that the generation and distribution of power by the Federal government would reduce prices to the consumer. At the very least, he believed, the rates offered by a public authority at Muscle Shoals could function as a "yard-stick" to test the fairness of rates charged by private utilities. Norris's proposals, solidly backed by Southern and Western votes, passed the Congress in 1928 and again in 1931, but were vetoed by Coolidge and Hoover. Both measures provided for operation of the existing Muscle Shoals power facilities by a government corporation; construction of an additional dam at Cove Creek for power and flood control; and the building of transmission lines to enable the corporation to market its electricity. Municipalities and other public agencies were given priority over private utilities in the purchase of the power. In order to satisfy the agricultural bloc in the Congress, the Norris bills permitted a private agency to lease the nitrate plants at Muscle Shoals and guaranteed the leasee sufficient electricity at a reasonable rate to manufacture fertilizer. If the President could not lease the nitrate facilities within one year, however, the government corporation would enter the fertilizer business directly by operating the plants for both research and commercial production.

The following documents address themselves to the Norris plan of 1931 and President Hoover's veto. They discuss many of the technical issues raised by the possibility of operation of Muscle Shoals as well as the political and philosophical positions of the protagonists on the larger question of the proper role of the government in the American economy.

In his message to Congress on March 3, 1931, President Hoover outlined his reasons for not signing Norris's Muscle Shoals bill, which had been approved by the Senate, 55–28, and the House, 216–153. The President's objections to the Norris plan were two: (1) it was unsound economically and (2) it would violate what he believed to be basic American political principles. Can you distinguish the two arguments? Which one did Hoover emphasize more? What did Hoover hold to be the proper relationship between government and the people? The message has been edited here, but may be read in full in *The State Papers and Other Public Writings of Herbert Hoover*, pages 521–29 (William Starr Myers, ed., Vol. I, Doubleday, Doran, 1934).

⊂ The Hoover Veto

HERBERT HOOVER

This bill proposes the transformation of the war plant at Muscle Shoals, together with important expansions, into a permanently operated Government institution for the production and distribution of power and the manufacture of fertilizers.

Disregarding for the moment the question of whether the Federal Government should or can manage a power and fertilizer manufacturing business, we should examine this proposal from the point of view of the probabilities of success as a business. . . .

The following properties and proposed extensions are embraced in the proposed project:

(a) Wilson Dam and its hydroelectric equipment valued at $37,000,000 being the original cost of $47,000,000 less $10,000,000 applicable to navigation.

(b) The steam power plant at Muscle Shoals valued at $5,000,000 being a reduction for depreciation of $7,000,000 from the original cost of $12,000,000.

(c) Proposed further additions to the electrical plant at Muscle Shoals costing $9,000,000.

(d) Proposed construction of Cove Creek Dam with hydroelectric plant with transmission line to Wilson Dam $41,000,000 of which $5,000,000 may be attributed to flood control and improvement of navigation or, say, $37,000,000.

(e) Proposed construction of transmission lines for wholesale distribution of power within the transmission area—$40,000,000.

(f) Nitrate plants, quarries, etc., at Muscle Shoals which originally cost $68,555,000 but upon which no valuation is placed at present.

The total valuation of the old property to be taken over for the power portion of the project is . . . $42,000,000 after the . . . deductions from original cost. The new expenditures from the Treasury applicable to the power business are estimated at $90,000,000, less $5,000,000 which might be attributable to flood control, or a total of $127,000,000 of capital in the electrical project. This sum would be further increased by accumulated interest charge during construction. . . . Several millions further would be required for modernizing the nitrate plants. The total requirement of new money from the Federal Treasury for the project is probably $100,000,000. . . .

Assuming the additional power given by the construction of the Cove Creek Dam and the use of steam power for five months in the dry season each year, and taking the average [power] load factor from experience in that region, about 1,300,000,000 kilowatt-hours of continuous power could be produced annually. . . . A portion of this must be held in reserve to protect consumers, leaving a net of about 1,000,000,000 kilowatt-hours annually of salable power. This amount would be somewhat increased if a large proportion of 24-hour load were applied to fertilizer manufacture.

The secondary power for a period of less than seven months in the year is not regarded as of any present commercial value.

The following is the estimated annual overhead and operating cost of the electrical end of the project including the steam plant necessary to convert 7-month secondary power into primary power as stated above:

Interest at 4 per cent per annum on capital of $127,000,000	$5,080,000
Amortization	1,890,000
Operating and maintenance cost of hydroelectric plant	775,000
Operating and maintenance cost of steam plant	850,000
Operation and maintenance cost of transmission lines	550,000
Total	$9,145,000

The estimated cost of production and distribution is, therefore, about 9.1 mills per kilowatt-hour. If only part of the transmission lines were constructed it would decrease capital and operating charges but would not comply with the requirement of equitable distribution through the transmission area.

The purpose of the bill is to provide production and wholesale distribution of surplus power and to give preference to states, municipalities, and cooperative organizations. It further provides that the policy of the Government must be to distribute the surplus power equitably amongst states, counties, and municipalities within transmission distance of Muscle Shoals and provides for the construction of transmission lines to effect this purpose. Such a transmission system for wholesale purposes only is estimated to cost $40,000,000. . . .

The average gross income of the [private] power companies in that territory, including retail as well as wholesale power, is about 12 mills per kilowatt-hour. This includes retail residential power averaging something over 50 mills per kilowatt-hour. Miscellaneous industrial power realizes about 10 mills per kilowatt-hour. The power sold wholesale to other companies and those engaged in municipal distribution average about 7.2 mills per kilowatt-hour.

It is impossible to compute Muscle Shoals income under this project upon a basis which includes retail power sales, as this is a project for wholesale distribution only. . . .

Assuming that the whole 1,000,000,000 kilowatt-hours should be sold to municipalities or other power distributors, it would on the basis of the realization of the private companies of 7.2 mills yield a gross annual income to this project of about $7,200,000, or a loss upon this basis of nearly $2,000,000 annually. This territory is now supplied with power and to obtain such an income it would be necessary to take the customers of the present power companies. To secure these customers it would be necessary to undercut the rates now made by them. It is difficult to estimate the extent to which it would be necessary to go in such rate cutting in order to secure the business. In any event it would of course diminish estimated income and increase the losses. . . . Any estimate of the income of the project as set up by this legislation will show a loss.

This bill provides that the President for a period of 12 months may negotiate a lease of the nitrate plants for fertilizer manufacture . . . but in failure to make such a lease the bill makes it mandatory upon the Government to manufacture nitrogen fertilizers at Muscle Shoals by the employment of existing facilities or by modernizing existing plants. . . . The leasing provision is . . . of no utility; it may at once be dimissed. In consequence the project we have to consider under this bill is the manufacture of fertilizers by the Federal Government.

The Department of Agriculture reports that these plants are now more or less obsolete and that with power at even 2 mills per kilowatt-hour, with proper charges included, could not produce the products for which they are constructed as cheaply as these products are now being sold in the wholesale markets. Therefore, it would be necessary to modernize the equipment at an unknown cost in millions. . . .

I am firmly opposed to the Government entering into any business the major purpose of which is competition with our citizens. . . . There are many localities where the Federal Government is justified in the construction of great dams and reservoirs, where navigation, flood control, reclamation or stream regulation are of dominant importance, and where they are beyond the capacity or purpose of private or local government capital to construct. In these cases power is often a by-product and should be disposed of by contract or lease. But for the Federal Government deliberately to go out to build up and expand such an occasion to the major purpose of a power and manufacturing business is to break down the initiative and enterprise of the American people; it is destruction of equality of opportunity amongst our people; it is the negation of the ideals upon which our civilization has been based.

This bill would launch the Federal Government upon a policy of ownership and operation of power utilities upon a basis of competition instead of by the proper Government function of regulation for the protection of all the people. I hesitate to contemplate the future of our institutions, of our government, and of our country if the preoccupation of its officials is to be no longer the promotion of justice and equal opportunity but is to be devoted to barter in the markets. That is not liberalism, it is degeneration. . . .

The establishment of a Federal-operated power business and fertilizer factory in the Tennessee Valley means Federal control from Washington with all the vicissitudes of national politics and the tyrannies of remote bureaucracy imposed upon the people of that valley without voice by them in their own resources, the overriding of state and local government, the undermining of state and local responsibility. . . .

The real development of the resources and the industries of the Tennessee Valley can only be accomplished by the people in that valley themselves. Muscle Shoals can only be administered by the people upon the ground, responsible to their own communities, directing them solely for the benefit of their communities and not for the purpose of pursuit of social theories or national politics. Any other course deprives them of liberty. . . .

John Bauer, director of the American Public Utilities Bureau, an organization which had been critical of the financial and rate-making practices of private electric companies during the 1920's, was highly regarded by political liberals as an expert on the economics of public utilities, including construction costs, rates of service, and the benefits of multiple-purpose development. In this article, which appeared in the *National Municipal Review*, XX (April, 1931), pages 231–34, he sought to answer many of the objections raised by Hoover's veto of the Norris bill. What is his position on the issue of private versus public development at Muscle Shoals? What portions of the Hoover message does Bauer single out for criticism and what areas does he tend to ignore? Why?

⊂⊱   An Expert's Response

JOHN BAUER

The President's veto was based upon *general* political and *specific* economic objections—that the project violated proper governmental policy, and was unsound as a financial undertaking.

The first objection follows the deeply-riveted views of the President, that government should keep out of business; that public ownership and operation destroys private initiative and results in destructive competition with private individuals. . . .

The President, of course, would not perceive what is obvious commonplace to students of history, political science and economics—that government always has been in business, always has competed with business, and has always interfered with and also stimulated private initiative. Its embarking upon a particular economic activity, does not prove that it would or should undertake another specific enterprise. Each project stands on its own merits. Nor could the President sense the fact that any line of demarcation between governmental and economic functions is largely artificial. The President's veto can be understood only if one comprehends his indoctrination with respect to business and public operation.

The President's specific economic objection can be summarized: That the cost of furnishing power would come to about 9 mills per kilowatt hour sold, while the revenue received would amount to about 7 mills; that this net loss of about 2 mills per kilowatt hour would render the project unsound as a financial undertaking.

The question is whether the costs and revenues have been properly computed to gauge the profitableness of the power enterprise. This correct test of the costs appears in what would be saved by the government if the power project is not carried out. Only those costs should be counted which would be incurred directly or additionally because of the power undertaking. Costs that have been incurred, or will be incurred by the government, even if the power project is not carried out, should obviously not be included. . . . Let us apply this test to the following costs charged by the President to power:

	Annual Costs
Interest at 4% on capital of $127,000,000	$5,080,000
Amortization	1,890,000
Operating and maintenance of hydro-electric plant	775,000
Operating and maintenance of steam plant	850,000
Operating and maintenance of transmission lines	550,000
Total annual cost	$9,145,000
Estimated annual kilowatt hours sold	1,000,000,000
Average cost per kilowatt hour	9 mills

These costs are grossly excessive, if tested from the standpoint of what would be saved if the project were abandoned, or what additional costs would be directly due to power development and operation. Let us consider briefly each cost element.

The largest single item is interest on investment. The aggregate investment allocated to power amounts to $127,000,000, but the special or additional capital outlay required for power would be a minor fraction of that huge sum. The President's figures consist of the following items:

Existing Properties:

Wilson Dam and hydro-electric properties, total cost $47,000,000; allocated to power	$37,000,000
Steam power at Muscle Shoals, original cost $12,000,000; present value allocated to power	5,000,000
Total existing properties	$42,000,000

New Construction:

Cove Creek Dam, with hydro-electric plant and transmission lines to Wilson Dam, total cost $41,000,000, of which $5,000,000 is allocated to navigation and flood control, and the remainder allocated to power	$36,000,000

Additions to electrical plant at Muscle Shoals	9,000,000
Transmission lines	40,000,000
Total new construction	$85,000,000
Total capital cost assigned to power	$127,000,000

Take the first two items together, the existing Wilson Dam, with the hydro-electric properties and the steam power plant. They make up a total of $42,000,000, charged by President Hoover to power; but all these costs have already been incurred by the government, and they cannot be avoided, if it does not go on with the power plan. They should, obviously, be excluded from the calculation, to test the financial soundness of the power operation.

With regard to the new construction, the cost of all the facilities that would be directly required by power, should, of course, be charged to power. But the situation is altogether different with regard to Cove Creek Dam, which, according to the President himself, should be built by the government in the interest of flood control. But of the aggregate cost of $41,000,000, the President assigns only $5,000,000 to flood control and improvement of navigation, as against $36,000,000 for power. Since the dam would be required for the other purposes, the allocation to power is manifestly excessive. . . . The allocation to power should probably not exceed $25,000,000.

The final item in Mr. Hoover's capital figures is $40,000,000 for the construction of transmission lines. This figure is wholly arbitrary. It appears to represent an aggregate construction of 3,500 miles of transmission lines, and contemplate extensive duplication of existing facilities; but no such result is implied by the bill. . . .

Suppose we allow, generally, $6,000,000 for transmission lines, $25,-000,000 for Cove Creek dam and its connections with Muscle Shoals, and $9,000,000 for steam plant additions—then we have a total of $40,000,000 direct additional costs due to power development, instead of President Hoover's $127,000,000.[1] At 4 per cent, the annual interest would be $1,600,000, instead of $5,080,000 charged to power by the President.

Amortization is placed at $1,890,000 per year, and is figured at about 1.5 per cent per annum upon the $127,000,000. The charge should be based upon only $40,000,000, and should be computed at 1 per cent. The rate of 1.5 per cent exceeds the reasonable requirement, and the usual allowance is 1 per cent upon capital cost. . . . The proper charge would be $400,000 instead of $1,890,000.

[1] While Hoover's $40,000,000 figure for transmission lines was, as Bauer noted, wholly arbitrary, so, too, was the $6,000,000 estimate made by the utility expert. The Norris bill did not include a precise funding level for transmission lines. It merely stated that the government was to distribute surplus power "equitably among States within transmission distance." [Ed.]

The operating and maintenance cost of the hydro-electric plant is placed at $775,000. If this is to include depreciation, the figure does not appear greatly excessive, and the same may be said of the $850,000 charged to operation and maintenance of the steam plant. But the $550,000 for operation and maintenance of transmission lines has no justification; at most, the figure should not exceed $100,000 a year for the limited transmission lines that would probably be included in the system.

On the basis of our analysis, the aggregate direct costs due to power development would not exceed $3,725,000 per year, as follows:

	Annual Cost
Interest, 4% on capital of $40,000,000	$1,600,000
Amortization, 1% capital	400,000
Operating expenses and maintenance	1,725,000
Total additional cost due to power	$3,725,000

These figures, of course, are rough approximations, but they probably exceed substantially the additional cost imposed on the government by power development. This assumes that the Cove Creek Dam is needed for flood control and improvement of navigation, and the President in his veto message subscribes to that view.

If we take the total annual cost of $3,750,000 and divide by the President's estimate of 1,000,000,000 kilowatt hours of annual sales, we have a cost of only 3.75 mills per kilowatt hour, instead of 9 mills. This would make power an economical undertaking even if the rest of Mr. Hoover's assumptions and computations were to be accepted at par. . . .

The actual project . . . must be considered, first from the standpoint that, to a large extent, costs have already been incurred and are, therefore, unavoidable, whatever may be done as to power; and, second, that the new construction involves joint undertakings needed for flood control and aid to navigation, as well as for power. The costs, therefore, must be considered for all the purposes, and cannot be validly assigned exclusively to power.

If Muscle Shoals, including the proposed construction, is considered from the standpoint of reality, there seems little doubt but what the project as a whole is justified, and that power can be economically developed. Whether the operation should be by government or by private agency, is another question. . . . For our part, however, we see no reason why there should not be government operation, in which we see distinct advantages, while, under the special circumstances, we cannot discover any particular advantage in private operation.

Public operation of this one project cannot possibly endanger the foundations of our economic system.

George Norris, who had served Nebraska in the United States Senate since 1912, replied to the President's veto in a long, passionate speech which appeared in the *Congressional Record* (71st Cong., 3rd Sess., 1931), pp. 7084–89. How does Norris's analysis of his own legislation for Muscle Shoals differ from Hoover's? What, according to Norris, should be the most important consideration of the government in dealing with the issue? To whom does he attribute the defeat of his proposal?

⊂Ξ   Senator Norris's Rebuttal

GEORGE NORRIS

According to the first part of the President's message the Government has nothing to do with [Muscle Shoals] and ought to get rid of it. Then he turns around and says the solution of the problem is to turn it over to Alabama and Tennessee, and he tells us what they can do. . . . In the first part of his message he said the nitrate plants are of no account whatever and of no value. . . . It is a useless, worthless property that the Federal Government can not operate and get anything out of, but he proposes to turn it over to Alabama and Tennessee and tells them that they have a great thing in it, that they can help agriculture, that they can make some money out of it and use it to help agriculture. I wonder if the President of the United States can be so cruel to some of the States in our Union as to give them what he has just said is a gold brick? He said it is worthless for the Federal Government, but it is valuable for a State government to operate it. . . . Either the Federal Government is incompetent—and he is at the head of it—or he is blackmailing the States, one or the other. . . .

It is not going to cost 9 mills to make electricity at Muscle Shoals, especially when the plant shall be completed. I think it will be made for less ultimately than 1 mill per kilowatt-hour. The President's own engineers . . . have shown and have testified before the committees of Congress that at Muscle Shoals power would cost 1.36 mills. If the entire plant were completed, if Cove Creek Dam were in operation, and the flow of the Tennessee River were adjusted, as that dam would adjust it—and perhaps later additional flood-control dams will be constructed—there could be produced at Muscle Shoals some of the cheapest water power in the world.

The power is there; all that has to be done is to regulate the flow of the Tennessee River. The President bases his calculation again upon some erroneous figures. He estimates $41,000,000, as I recall, as the cost of Cove Creek Dam, and allows only $5,000,000 of that to be charged up to flood control, when everybody who knows anything about the subject knows that Cove Creek Dam is a flood-control proposition; that power is only incident. We were anxious to provide for its construction in the bill because it would be an economic sin to let any private party build Cove Creek Dam.

If private parties built it, they, of course, would want to make all the money they could out of it for power; they would let the reservoir fill up and would never let the water out, because, as water was allowed to flow out of the reservoir, the power generated would decrease, until, when all the water was out, there would be no power; but when the Government owns it, it is a flood-control proposition. It could let out that water or a great share of it, perhaps all of it in some years. After the experience of a few years it would be possible to determine just how much ought to be let out. When the water was let out the power generated there would decrease very materially. A private party would not let it out. So the chief value of Cove Creek and Cove Creek Reservoir is flood control; its next value is for navigation purposes, and power comes third. . . .

So when the President only charges off about one-eighth, according to his figures, or a little less than one-eighth of the cost, he is not fair. He ought to charge off at least three-fourths of it for flood control and navigation.

The Tennessee River is one of the largest streams in the country, but sometimes in the neighborhood of Chattanooga and between Cove Creek and Muscle Shoals the water gets down so low that there is no navigation in the river. When it gets down that low navigation ceases, and power at Muscle Shoals decreases. However, by the use of Cove Creek Dam the power at Muscle Shoals would be increased, and the navigability of the stream would be increased for 300 miles. . . .

Cove Creek is valuable as one of the ways of controlling the flood waters of the Mississippi River. . . . The basin in the vicinity of Cove Creek is the largest basin on the east side of the Mississippi River. It will hold 3,500,000 acre-feet of water. That is a large volume of water. The impounding of that water alone would have a very material effect upon the flood waters of the Mississippi River. So the President is not fair when he says we will charge up all of this flood control and this navigation proposition to power.

Of course, it is an engineering proposition, and if the great engineer had referred it to an engineer instead of to somebody else, he would have obtained better information. He himself ought to know better. If he remembers what he read when he went to school, and studied engineering, he ought to know that the prime reason for the construction of Cove Creek Dam is flood control and navigation. I never would advocate the Government building a dam at Cove Creek for power purposes. Power is the third consideration. . . . So the President, when he arrives at the figure of 9 mills a kilowatt-hour, is figuring on an exorbitant price for Cove Creek Dam, and is figuring on an unfair distribution of that cost. Nobody else would figure it in any such way. . . .

It does not cost, and it will not cost, 9 mills to make electricity at Muscle Shoals. It does not cost that much at other places where they have the same advantages, where they have the same natural resources that exist there. . . . When Cove Creek Dam is finished, and the machinery is put in the dam that is there now, waiting for the machinery, we will have perhaps 500,000 horsepower owned by the Government for sale to municipalities and counties and individuals. . . .

It is not a question of putting the Government into the power business. It is there now. We own it. It is not like going into it as a power proposition. . . . It is a question of whether the Government should keep its own property. . . .

I am sorry to say that our President—perfectly conscientious in his belief, I think—is with the Power Trust.

This is a great victory for the Power Trust. If we had had our way and this bill had gone into effect, Muscle Shoals would not only have been beneficial to all of the South, new factories would not only have sprung up, but, in addition to that, it would have been a yardstick for the whole Nation. . . .

It would have developed the natural resources which God gave to our people. God did not intend that they should be given away to the Power Trust or to any other monopoly. It would have turned the falling water into electricity, which would have gone into the homes, thousands of homes, all through the South . . . besides, as I have said, setting the example all over the United States. But the President has killed the bill. He has vetoed it, and to-night the Power Trust are in high jubilee. . . .

There is not a place in the political firmament where the Power Trust has not its servants, its faithful servants, stationed to-night, right now, living off the fat of the land, taking their toll from the poor people of the land, taxing every home, taxing every factory, taxing every citizen, and doing it out of property which belongs to the people, the streams which flow down hill, which God intended should be a blessing to people rather than to the power interests.

That is what this meant, that is what was in this measure, and that is what the President of the United States has taken away from the American people by his wicked, his cruel, his unjust, his unfair, his unmerciful veto.

Representative Allen Treadway, a Massachusetts Republican, had served in the House of Representatives since 1913. As a dedicated partisan of Presidents Coolidge and Hoover, he voted against the Norris measure twice—in 1928 and 1931. In this speech from the *Congressional Record* (71st Cong., 3rd Sess., 1931), pp. 5556–58, Treadway reaffirmed his opposition to Norris and endorsed Hoover's veto message. What is Treadway's principal objection to the Norris plan? Do his arguments cast any new light or provide additional evidence in support of the President's position?

⊂⊒ Hoover Defended

ALLEN TREADWAY

If . . . this bill eventually becomes law, I do not think the United States can ever again object to other countries becoming socialistic. To my mind this is the nearest approach to a socialistic doctrine that has ever been advanced in Congress.

We have expended already at Muscle Shoals $125,000,000, and we are now asked to expend at least $50,000,000 more on the Cove Creek Dam proposition; and, in addition to that, to build transmission lines and to set up a governmental corporation, the directors of which are to be appointed by the President of the United States for the purpose of carrying on that business. It is true that the suggestion of a lease is made, and the advocates of the legislation say that the lease will be taken up. . . .

To my mind that is a smoke screen and nothing else; an effort to fool the people into thinking there is likelihood of a lease being made, when back of it all there is really a plan to set the Government up in business. I for one am opposed to that proposition. . . .

This resolution . . . purports to be for the primary purpose of manufacturing nitrates and other products for use as fertilizer bases, fertilizers, and national defense. The resolution, however, provides for placing the Government in the business of distributing electrical energy from Wilson Dam, the steam plant as now constituted, and such other modifications and additions as may be necessary, and provides for the construction of Cove Creek Dam and the distribution of the power therefrom.

Both the hydroelectric and steam power companies of southeastern United States during the period from 1923 to 1928 were selling well under 25 per cent of their productive capacity of electrical energy, and the net increase of sales between 1923 and 1928 was less than 1 per cent per year, which clearly indicates that the existing power companies in this locality will not be able to sell their efficient productive capacity in the next 30 years at the present rate of growth.

From an economic standpoint, it is obvious that the power market, the condition of annual floods, and the price of fertilizer, do not warrant the construction of Cove Creek Dam or the extension of the Muscle Shoals project to meet any public need within the next 30 years.

The cost of Wilson Dam, the steam plant, and the anticipated cost of the projected Cove Creek Dam, are such as will not result in cheap fertilizers if the project contemplated by the Norris resolution is carried out.

Wilson Dam, the steam plant at nitrate plant No. 2, and the Cove Creek Dam, combined, would produce approximately 225,000 kilowatts of prime power, and would represent an investment of over $100,000,000. Applying ordinary business principles to an investment of this character, the cost of operation, depreciation, and maintenance costs, together with a reasonable amortization factor, the result would be an annual deficit of at least $5,000,000 per year, and could not possibly obtain the object of supplying fertilizer at a rate cheaper than the present market, unless Congress by appropriation provides a subsidy to reduce such costs. . . .

It is clear that the effect of the [Norris bill] . . . would be to launch the Government in the power business in direct competition with privately and State owned power developments in the Tennessee River Valley. There are projected developments of the Tennessee River and its tributaries costing hundreds of millions of dollars for the production of hydroelectric power to the amount of approximately 3,000,000 kilowatts, and if the Federal Government enters into competition therewith, it may well with its unlimited financial resources drive these weaker groups entirely out of business by the mere force of economic pressure. That the Government has a clear right to operate Wilson Dam for its own purpose and to place on the market for sale the surplus power therefrom, as it is now doing, is to be conceded. To lease its nitrate plants to private industry for the manufacture of fertilizer bases, and so forth, is also, if practicable, a laudable purpose. But the program of power development and operation by the Government set forth in the proposed resolution furnishes an entirely different picture, one in fact that I can find no excuse for in the category of the legitimate functions of the Federal Government. It should be clear to any reasonable mind that such a proposition is not a proper Government function. . . .

Hugo Black, first elected to the Senate in 1926, became a leader of the Southern Democrats who supported the Norris plan in 1928 and 1931. Black, an Alabaman, tended to emphasize those aspects of the Norris plan which were of immediate, practical interest to tobacco and cotton farmers in the South. What was the basis of Black's agreement with Norris? Did he share any of Hoover's objections to the Norris proposal? Black's remarks are taken from the *Congressional Record* (71st Cong., 3rd Sess., 1931), pp. 7071–77.

⊂⊋   For the South and the Farmer

Hugo Black

I . . . call attention to the fact that in the year 1929 there were used in this country a total of 513,300 tons of nitrogen. There were imported into the country a total of 239,500 tons. Without that 239,500 tons of nitrogen, even in a time of peace when we were not called upon for explosives in order to protect our country, it was necessary to import 239,500 tons of nitrogen. . . .

This is the only civilized country in the world, except Russia, that is not independent of other countries for its nitrogen, and it is because of the same interests that have worked year in and year out against a bill which would provide for the operation of the nitrate plants at Muscle Shoals. . . .

We imported last year 180,000 tons, or practically 40 per cent of the total amount that was used; and if this country should become involved in war to-day it would send its $40,000,000 battleships down to protect the coast of Chile.

But what difference does that make? The operation of the nitrate plants [at Muscle Shoals] will interfere with the Guggenheims. The Guggenheims have a half control of the nitrate beds in Chile. The southern farmer pays 25 per cent of the entire taxes of the Chilean Government. The farmers of the States of Alabama, Louisiana, Georgia, Mississippi, North Carolina, and South Carolina, pay practically 25 per cent of every dollar of revenue that goes into the Chilean Government's treasury. Why is that? It is because we are afraid, as alleged, that if we provide for a lease to be made at Muscle Shoals it will interfere with private initiative and destroy individualism in America. . . .

This issue is as plain as it can be. It is an issue between those who seek, as best they can, to represent the best interests of the plain people of this Nation, as against those who depend upon the untold wealth, the incalculable millions of the beneficiaries of special privilege and predatory greed to stifle the voice of the people and defeat legislation intended for their benefit. . . .

Those who oppose this measure belong on the side of special privilege and greed. They belong on the side of those who have gained immense wealth by extracting it from the pocketbooks of the poor people whom they have had under their heel through the years of their oppression. . . .

This Muscle Shoals measure is dying at this session of Congress because the power companies and the fertilizer companies and those who control the wealth of this Nation want it to die. It is dying because it is known that if it should be signed and become a law the farmers of this Nation would have for one time the privilege and opportunity of buying fertilizer at a reasonable rate. It is dying because of the fear of those who sit in the high places and who extract their millions from the pockets of the people of this country who pay an extortionate price for the electric current which turns the washing machine, which illuminates the humble home, which revolves the wheels of industry, and which operates the great business of this Nation. . . .

The statement is also made . . . by the Department of Agriculture that fertilizer could not be manufactured at Muscle Shoals as cheaply as it is sold to-day on the wholesale market. Chilean nitrate is bringing $39 per ton at the port, or it was a few days ago. Thirty-nine dollars per ton at the port is 13 cents a pound wholesale. In a test run at Muscle Shoals immediately after the project was completed, valuing the power at 4 mills when it only cost 1.36 mills to produce it, nitrogen was manufactured at a cost of 8.75 cents per pound. Ten years ago, without the new and modern improvements, with a test run at 4 mills per kilowatt for the power, nitrogen was produced at 8.75 cents per pound, and Chilean nitrate is selling to-day wholesale at the port for 13 cents per pound. . . .

It is but another of the glaring inaccuracies and misconceptions that appear . . . from the first to the last page of this veto message. Having no case to build upon facts, it became necessary to send to the departments to obtain information which could be exploded in the records of these departments. . . .

I do not stand here as an exponent of Government operation in business; I favor the operation of private business by private initiative whenever it can be accomplished. I would not break down a single one of the traditional principles underlying American achievement; but, Mr. President, the time is coming in this Nation when something must be done in order to curb the growing power of those who themselves seek to destroy the private initiative and competitive business system upon which this Nation has been built. They want no competitive business system; they desire a government of monopoly for monopoly and by monopoly. . . .

Mr. President, who is benefiting? The Alabama Power Company and the fertilizer companies. The Alabama Power Co. continues to buy at 2 mills this power [from Wilson Dam] that the President says costs 9 mills to produce. Have you stopped to think that if those figures are correct, the Alabama Power Co. has received a bonus running up into the millions and millions and millions of dollars during the past few years that they have bought this power at Muscle Shoals? [1]

I maintain that if it costs the United States Government 9 mills to produce that power, and they continue to sell it for 2 mills, Al Capone and his bunch of racketeers and buccaneers never picked a pocket or robbed a man any more successfully than the people of the United States are being robbed to-day to benefit the Alabama Power Co. . . .

We gave the President a year in which to find a leasee [for the nitrate plants]. It was not supposed that one would be found in four days. I have not the slightest shadow of doubt but that if this bill were signed a lease would and could be obtained, and that the plants would be operated to their full and complete capacity. . . .

The fact remains that Muscle Shoals is still unsettled; that it could have been settled by President Hoover; that he has declined to do it. The farmers of this Nation are suffering from it. The people who are entitled to buy power at a reasonable rate are suffering from it. The power companies and their stockholders are growing richer from it. The fertilizer companies and their stockholders are growing richer from it. . . .

[1] When Wilson Dam was completed in 1925, the War Department entered into a contract with the Alabama Power Company under which the private utility purchased test power at the dam for 2 mills per kilowatt hour. The contract was renewed after the test period. At the same time, the Secretary of War, with the approval of Presidents Coolidge and Hoover, refused to sell Wilson Dam power to the town of Muscle Shoals or other nearby municipalities.

At the age of seventy, Simeon D. Fess of Ohio was one of the Senate's oldest members in 1931. First elected in 1922, he had taught American history at Ohio Northern University and was chairman of the Republican party's National Committee from 1930 to 1932. His objections to the Norris bill are set forth in this excerpt from the *Congressional Digest,* Vol. 9, No. 5 (May, 1930) "Federal Operation of Muscle Shoals, Pro & Con," pages 143–46. Compare and contrast Fess's conceptions of opportunity and liberty with those offered by Hoover, Norris, and Black.

⊂⊐   A Threat to Opportunity and Liberty

Simeon D. Fess

Our problem today is, What are we going to do with the Muscle Shoals property? We have it on our hands. The Government owns it. Shall we junk it? I would not think so. . . .

The other plan that might be open to consideration would be for the Government to sell the property outright and pass title to it, if it could find a purchaser. . . . Then there is another opposition to the sale of the property, and that is because of the tremendous possibilities which are involved in the future development of hydro-electric power. It would appear that it would be wiser for us not to dispose of the property in fee simple unless we could do it for a very reasonable consideration. I think we might as well pass that over. . . .

The two alternatives left would be for the Government, owning it, to lease it under proper terms and acceptable considerations, or to operate it as a Government project. . . . Every time the matter has come up for final decision I have opposed Government operation of the property. I have been convinced that it would be much better for us to secure a lease under satisfactory conditions, so that not only would we be safeguarding the rights of the public but also we would have a recapture clause, so that the property would ultimately be back in the hands of the Government, either to re-lease it, or for whatever operation we might at that time decide upon. . . .

I think everybody must admit that if the Government is launched into any commercial transaction in which there are any great number of units it is unfair for the Government to compete with those private industries. The danger is that the Government's competition will put out of business the independent units, and it seems to me that it is not a fair proposition. . . .

There is a great drift today toward concentration throughout the world. I do not think it would be wise for us to attempt to interfere with that general drift. It is in the interest both of lower cost to the public and more efficient production. But it will never do to allow the concentration to go uncontrolled. The Government must keep its regulatory power over all units of production which might become monopolistic. . . . But when we are considering an industry [i.e., fertilizer production] in which many citizens are engaged, if the Government goes into competition with those citizens, the Government does not count the elements of cost those citizens must count, and if the Government does not proceed in a way that will lead to a profit, but runs the business at a loss, and then out of the Treasury makes up the loss, it is unfair to the individual producer who is in competition with the Government.

What strikes me as strange, having some fair familiarity with the position of the fathers throughout the South on questions of this kind, is the changed attitude of the people of the South. Jefferson said that that is the best government which governs least. Jefferson never wanted to put the Government into competition with individuals. Jefferson did not want to meet the Government in every person he met on the street. He did not want to multiply Government agents; and that was a sound rule, and it permeated the whole country.

The one reason why I am opposed to the Government going into business like this is that it has such a deadening effect. The routine, the deadly uniformity, the deadening effect upon individuals employed is obvious to everybody. There is no liberty. Bureaucracy spreads its net and kills the spirit. What I want to see is the liberalism in the life of the Nation that we see in the freedom of the press, the freedom of speech, the freedom of assembly, the open door of opportunity, the freedom of leadership where leadership does not come through seniority in service but comes through the rugged struggle of merit in the work. I want to see those avenues kept open, and they cannot be kept open under Government operation.

Chapter

17: The Strategy of Mass Protest: The Sitdown Strikes of 1936–1937

⊂⊐ **JAMES T. PATTERSON**

To many Americans the Christmas season of 1936 called for peace and good will. Not so for workers in Detroit, Flint, and scores of industrial towns. At that time 150,000 employees of General Motors defied both management and officials of their unions by refusing to work. They were not ordinary strikers, because they insisted on staying in their factories, remaining stubbornly by their machines for more than a month.

By early February the strikers had won most of their demands, forcing management to recognize the United Auto Workers (U.A.W.) as the collective bargaining agent for its members. It was the first time that G.M. had signed a national agreement with a union. Success then bred imitation, and similar "sitdown" strikes erupted or threatened to erupt in other mass production industries. Soon U.S. Steel, long the citadel of the open shop, capitulated without a struggle, granting the steelworkers of the Committee for Industrial Organization (C.I.O.) a contract. When the Chrysler Corporation resisted, 65,000 workers sat down; in a short time Chrysler also relented. Encouraged, thousands of workers across the country in hotels, restaurants, department stores, cigar factories, and other manufacturing companies followed suit. Organized labor had never seemed so militant or management so vacillating and ineffectual.

Conservatives reacted furiously. "Down that road lurks dictatorship," one senator declaimed. Another branded John L. Lewis, the fiery, bushy-browed leader of the C.I.O., a "traitor to American ideals and a menace to the peace and prosperity of the Nation." Terrified management officials predicted class war, and congressmen angrily introduced resolutions calling for investigations of the radicals who were shattering industrial harmony.

These responses, while exaggerated, were understandable, for the sit-downs presented management with very difficult choices. Some employers talked of calling in police to evict the strikers. But at Flint in the "battle of the bulls," strikers repulsed police by hurling hinges and pop bottles and by dousing them with fire hoses. It seemed possible, indeed likely, that strikers would resist with even stronger measures if necessary, and that violence would ensue. What then? One result would be bashed heads and a wave of popular sympathy for the workers. Worse, the confrontations would inevitably occur on company property. Damage to expensive machinery, especially in the depression-ridden 1930's, was hardly an alluring prospect. Cooler heads usually called for court injunctions demanding the eviction of the workers. But most strikers ignored the courts, and industrialists usually shied from challenging them. Governor Frank Murphy of Michigan, a liberal Democrat, refused to call out the militia to enforce a court order against the strikers and in so doing deprived angry businessmen of the state support they had so often enjoyed in the past. Harassed employers, like university administrators responding to student protesters three decades later, seemed to have little alternative to recognizing the workers, and by the end of 1937 most of the major industries—autos, glass, steel, rubber—were partially unionized.

A few stubborn, strong-willed business leaders continued to defy labor; Henry Ford, employing hard-fisted security forces, was one. The leaders of smaller steel companies (so-called "Little Steel"), utilizing police to cut down pickets in Chicago, were others. But these were the exceptions willing to respond to peaceful sitdowns with violent countermeasures. The sitdown tactic, it seemed, had achieved suddenly what decades of union activity had failed to produce: free collective bargaining in the new mass production industries. Since that time most unions have been more able to negotiate with management, and they have posed a political pressure group which few astute politicians in industrial areas have dared to ignore. Of the many remarkable developments during the depression decade, none has proved more profound than the growth of organized labor in the mass production industries, and while the sitdowns themselves by no means produced this growth, they were an essential ingredient.

The initial successes of the sitdowns stimulated much speculation. For years labor leaders had tried lobbying, picketing, striking, and every other conceivable means of protest against the often unyielding attitudes of many American employers, but had achieved very little. In 1936, for instance, some 20 million of 27 million American laborers did not even belong to a union. Moreover, sporadic sitdowns in the past had failed to evoke the remarkable chain reaction which developed in 1937. Yet suddenly, it seemed, small groups of workers, ignoring cautious union leaders, were taking matters into their own hands, defying courts, risking pitched battles, and cowing the great corporations hitherto deemed unassailable.

The obvious question was why. Why did the sitdowns so excite workers and so terrify employers? These questions are not only challenging in themselves, but they inevitably invite comparisons with the equally dramatic (if often short-lived) results achieved by small bands of civil rights activists who "sat in" at lunch counters in the early 1960's and by little groups of disenchanted college students who sat down in the sacrosanct offices of university administrators in the late 1960's and early 1970's. How much credit for such success is due the tactic itself? Do these tactics, in winning small skirmishes against unprepared opponents, create the enthusiasm which unleashes mass movements? Are they manifestations of deep social tensions which must culminate in some sort of confrontation? Or is there operating an interactive process by which a combination of real grievances, grass roots indignation, and skillful strategy combine to lead personal protests into avenues of mass social change?

The sitdown strikes, and later the sit-ins, raise still broader questions. One is the role of the mass media. In 1885 striking railroad workers seized company property, and management met their demands. Working conditions in that unhappy era were frightful, and the Knights of Labor was at its peak, yet no chain reaction occurred. Perhaps, some have argued, the incalculable influence of radio and of mass circulation newspapers and magazines (in the fashion of television in the 1970's) explains the apparent ease with which local disputes quickly become confrontations of national significance.

The sitdown strikes also forced people to examine the role of leadership. Many officials of the well-established American Federation of Labor opposed the sitdowns, partly because workers in the rival C.I.O. were conducting them, but also because they foresaw a backlash which would wipe out the remarkable progress in unionization of the early 1930's. Even John L. Lewis was cautious, defending but hardly encouraging the sitdowns. Perhaps, people have argued, a movement of mass protest cannot be planned by leaders—there can be no grand strategy, certainly no "conspiracy." On the contrary, observers say, successful mass movements must be spontaneous, and the militants must never feel that they are being directed or manipulated. Whatever the truth, many of the sitdowns in 1937 occurred without the foreknowledge or approval of union officials. The result was that some of these leaders, like the so-called "Uncle Toms" of the NAACP in the late 1960's, were ignored by the rank and file.

The leaders of embattled management also came under fire in 1937. Many Americans, cherishing law and order, regarded them with the same mixture of disbelief and contempt which they have flung at "soft" college administrators in more recent times. And thoughtful commentators began to ask whether the submissive attitude of employers might be a sign of guilt, or even of a dangerously unjust, sick society. From such a perspective, tactics seemed relatively unimportant: what mattered was the existence of smoldering resentments merely awaiting a spark to set them ablaze. Because this thesis presupposes an unhealthy society, many Americans have been uncomfortable with it, preferring to believe that determined responses from wise leaders could have prevented serious trouble. To many observers in the tense 1960's, however, more pessimistic interpretations have seemed plausible, and recent views of the sitdowns in 1937 often reflect this point of view.

While all these theories are provocative, it is a mistake to jump to conclusions about the sitdowns without understanding the milieu in which they took place. American labor unions had always confronted hostile public opinion, and resentment against organizing campaigns in 1919 had sapped the strength of many unions in the 1920's. Hard times after 1929 struck another blow, for workers could not pay union dues, let alone risk their jobs by protesting against managers who were looking for ways to cut labor costs. American unions, never strong in comparison to those in most industrialized nations, fell to low ebb in 1932.

By 1936 the picture had brightened tremendously. The New Deal of Franklin D. Roosevelt, forced by circumstances to worry about mass unemployment, pushed through the National Industrial Recovery Act (N.I.R.A.) in 1933. This historic law included a provision (Section 7-a) which gave an unambiguous federal guarantee to free collective bargaining. Encouraged, leaders like Lewis went about saying "the President wants you to join a union." Militant workers began asking why the A. F. of L. continued to support skilled craft unions without doing much to organize the much larger number of non-union workers in the emerging mass production industries. These militants wished to set up unions by industry (glassworkers, steelworkers, autoworkers, etc.) rather than by crafts within these industries, for they believed that industry-wide unions alone could bargain on an equal basis with large employers. When A. F. of L. leaders refused to heed their warnings, Lewis and others broke away in 1935 to form the C.I.O. Organizing campaigns among unskilled workers then accelerated at a feverish pace. Although the conservative Supreme Court had declared the N.I.R.A. unconstitutional in May, 1935, the Wagner Act, passed shortly thereafter, established a National Labor Relations Board whose appointees proved partial to the C.I.O.

The ensuing changes were amazing. C.I.O. unions more than doubled their strength in 1936 and already claimed 2,000,000 workers at the time of the sitdowns, compared to 2,750,000 in the much older A. F. of L. organization. Membership in those C.I.O. unions involved in sitdowns increased strikingly—the steelworkers union from 8,000 to nearly 200,000 members in a year, and autoworkers from 20,000 to 75,000. The expansion of these unions was so rapid and their expectations so great that many employers were simply unprepared to grant their sudden demands for recognition and improved working conditions. From this perspective, some sort of confrontation seems highly likely in retrospect.

Meanwhile, other developments suggested tactical approaches. Workers abroad, also trapped by depression, had staged successful sitdown strikes in Yugoslavia, Hungary, and Poland in 1934. In 1936 a million workers in France sat down, causing immediate passage of laws favoring unions and improving working conditions. Rubber workers in Akron in 1934 had also applied the tactic successfully, and strikers at the Bendix Company in South Bend in early 1936 were perhaps the first in America to remain overnight in the plants. While few workers at General Motors consciously imitated these tactics, the precedent was there—and it had often been successful.

Finally, while far from prosperous by the standards of the more affluent 1920's, the year 1936 witnessed improved economic conditions. Union leaders have often regarded the onset of recovery from hard times as auspicious for better contracts: workers had suffered badly during the depression, they argued, and management would surely be able to pay more in good times than in bad. It is hard to prove that such considerations motivated the sitdown strikers, but the fact remains that the economic situation encouraged some workers to think that they deserved (and that management could afford) better terms.

After early 1937, sitdowns occurred less often, partly because many employers, afraid of such tactics in their plants, capitulated before strikes had to be called. Perhaps more important, conditions changed considerably during 1937. The New Deal, hitherto so popular and powerful, seemed to lose favor, as Roosevelt became embroiled in a series of debilitating battles with Congress. The C.I.O., closely associated in the public mind with the New Deal, suffered accordingly. And in late 1937 a sharp recession set in, changing completely the temporary optimism which had developed earlier in the year. Where militant tactics promised to be productive in January, 1937, they seemed extreme a year later.

By 1939, sitdowns had become an almost forgotten tactic. For one thing, the Supreme Court ruled them illegal and said the N.L.R.B. might not reinstate workers discharged for taking part in such strikes. Moreover, better times returned, this time for an extended period. As pay checks became fatter, the militance of workers declined. Though a few unions continued to agitate for better terms throughout the 1940's, as many more were captured by moderate leaders more interested in union treasuries than in mass protest. By the 1950's, the once militant C.I.O. had become hardly distinguishable from the A. F. of L., and was regarded by new generations of activists as part of the "establishment."

The sitdowns of the middle and late 1930's were of epochal significance, helping to produce perhaps the most lasting social consequences of a dramatic decade, for they helped transform organized labor from a relatively feeble voice into a powerful, if often divided, national institution. The following selections suggest some of the excitement which surrounded this important movement. They also reveal the confusion which beset spokesmen as they came face to face with what many regarded as a prelude to revolution.

Louis Adamic was a widely read writer sympathetic to ordinary workers and to the causes of organized labor. He was also one of the very few to perceive the potential of the sitdown tactic before it achieved such publicity in the General Motors strike of December, 1936. Writing in the liberal journal, *The Nation*, two weeks before the disturbances in Michigan ("Sitdown," Dec. 5, 1936, pp. 652–54), Adamic offered a colorful description of the sitdown strikes in Akron, which is reprinted here. Although other writers later argued that the Akron workers were more aware of European precedents for sitdowns than Adamic was willing to say, his account suggests some of the spirit of the strikers. How does the sitdown strike differ from more traditional strikes? How important is the morale of the workers? To what extent is successful protest necessarily spontaneous?

A Social Affair

LOUIS ADAMIC

. . . The rank-and-file movement really got under way in a curious and peculiarly American way. The story goes that one Sunday afternoon a couple of baseball teams composed of workers employed in two big rubber factories suddenly refused to play a scheduled game because they found out that the umpire—to whom some of them objected, incidentally, also as a person and an umpire—was not a union man. The players just *sat down* literally, some on the grass, others on the benches beneath the grandstand, while the crowd, consisting mainly of working-men—partly "for the hell of it" and partly in seriousness—yelled for an umpire who was a union member, cheered the NIRA, and generally raised a merry din, till the non-union umpire withdrew and a union man called the game. It is said that the expression "sitdown" was first used in the discussions that followed that game.

Not long afterward a petty dispute over a point in working conditions developed between the workers and the superintendent of a department in one of the great rubber factories. The superintendent would not yield and, annoyed, made an indiscreet remark which angered the workers in question; about a dozen in all. They had been on the verge of dropping their demand or complaint, whatever it was; now, remembering the sit-down at the ball game, one of them blurted out, "Aw, to hell with 'im, let's sit down!" And they sat down.

In a few minutes several other departments of the extremely complex and delicately organized production process in the factory, which employed 7,000 men, were in a mess. What had happened? The question was asked all over the plant. The answer quickly spread through the place: There was a sitdown in such-and-such a department! A sitdown? Yeah, a sitdown; don't you know what a sitdown is, you dope? Like what happened at the ball game the other Sunday!

Hundreds of workers who did not know what the sitdown was about but who belonged more or less to the rank-and-file element experienced a thrill. A sitdown in the plant! In no time the most important departments of the factory were at a standstill. Thousands of workers sat down. Some because they wanted to, more because everything stopped anyhow.

And sitting by their machines, caldrons, boilers, and work benches, they talked. Some realized for the first time how important they were in the process of rubber production. Twelve men had practically stopped the works! Almost any dozen or score of them could do it! In some departments six could do it! The active rank-and-filers, scattered through the various sections of the plant, took the initiative in saying, "We've got to stick with 'em!" And they stuck with them, union and non-union men alike. Most of them were non-union. Some probably were vaguely afraid not to stick. Some were bewildered. Others amused. There was much laughter through the works. Oh boy, oh boy! Just like at the ball game, no kiddin'. There the crowd had stuck with the players and they got an umpire who was a member of a labor union. Here everybody stuck with the twelve guys who first sat down, and the factory management was beside itself. Superintendents, foremen, and straw bosses were dashing about. They looked funny, these corporals, sergeants, and shavetails of industry. Telephones were ringing all over the plant. This sudden suspension of production was costing the company many dollars every minute. . . . In less than an hour the dispute which had led to the sitdown was settled—full victory for the men!

Walking out of the factory gates that evening, the men laughed. They told the night shift about it. The thing got into the Akron newspapers. There was no little talk about the affair, most of it perhaps, to the effect that the sitdown was a good joke on the factory management. The rank-and-file leaders, some of whom were more or less leftist, others mainly inspired by the New Deal and its Section 7-a, did their best to keep the talk going. They reiterated that, as had been demonstrated by the sitdown on the baseball diamond and the sitdown in the factory, workers could get somewhere only collectively, by sticking and working together. The thing to do was to join the unions. Many did join and new federal unions were organized.

Some of the leftist rank-and-filers realized that the sitdown might have revolutionary implications or possibilities—workers stopping production, sitting down, and taking possession of plants! So many of them, free-lance agitators without authority from any union, what the bosses called "trouble-makers," began to encourage sitdowns. Working in various departments in the several Akron rubber plants, they subtly organized sitdowns when disputes arose. As a result of late there have been scores of sitdowns, some lasting only an hour or even less, others several hours or most of the day, running into the next shift; and a few stretching over two, three, four, or more days, thus becoming "stay-ins."

Some sitdowns tied up production only in parts of a given factory, other paralyzed the whole plant. When the sitdowns became longer, the men sitting in their working places took to whiling away the time by playing cards or checkers, telling yarns, singing, or reading. Some of them simply stretched on the benches or on the floor and went to sleep. When a sitdown ran into the next shift, the incoming workers relieved the old shift and did the same thing—sat, talked, sang, played cards or checkers, and slept on the floor—till the dispute that had produced the sitdown was settled; or else they gave their dinner pails to the sitters-down and went home—which made the sitdown a stay-in.

Of course, like the original sitdown, several sitdowns—perhaps a majority of them—in the Akron rubber plants have occurred without encouragement from any rank-and-file organizer. They have been sudden, spontaneous affairs springing out of immediate conditions in a department.

Nearly all the sitdowns have been effective, winning the demands of the men who started them. So far as I know, only one or two have fizzled out. The men in other departments almost invariably back the initiators of the sitdowns. Why? Let me give a list of the virtues and advantages of the sitdown as a method of labor aggression from the point of view not so much of the rank-and-file organizer or radical agitator as of the average workingman in a mass-production industry like rubber.

1. The sitdown is the reverse of sabotage, to which many workers are opposed. It destroys nothing. Before shutting down a department in a rubber plant, for instance, the men bring the compounded rubber from the mills, or they finish building or curving the tires then being built or curved, so that nothing is needlessly ruined. Taking the same precautions during the sitdown as they do during production, the men do not smoke in departments where benzine is used. There is no drinking. This discipline —of which more in a moment—is instinctive.

2. To say, as did a New York *Times* reporter, writing from Akron last winter, that the sitdown "resembles the old Oriental practice of passive resistance" is a bit farfetched, but it probably is a sort of development of the old I.W.W.[1] "folded-arm" strike and of "striking on the job"; only it is better, manlier than the latter, which required men to pretend they were working, and to accomplish as little as possible without being discharged, which was more fatiguing than to work according to one's

[1] Industrial Workers of the World, a militant labor organization especially prominent prior to 1917. [Ed.]

capacity, as well as contrary to the natural inclinations of the best class of workers.

3. The sitdown is the reverse of the ordinary strike. When a sitdown is called, a man does not walk out; he stays in, implying that he is willing to work if——

4. Workers' wives generally object to regular strikes, which often are long, sometimes violent and dangerous, and as likely as not end in sell-outs and defeat. Sitdowns are quick, short, and free of violence. There are no strikebreakers in the majority of instances; the factory management does not dare to get tough and try to drive the sitting men out and replace them with other workers, for such violence would turn the public against the employers and the police, and might result in damage to costly machinery. In a sitdown there are no picket-lines outside the factories, where police and company gunmen have great advantage when a fight starts. The sitdown action occurs wholly inside the plant, where the workers, who know every detail of the interior, have obvious advantages. The sitters-down organize their own "police squads," arming them—in rubber—with crowbars normally used to pry open molds in which tires are curved. These worker cops patrol the belt, watch for possible scabs, and stand guard near the doors. In a few instances where city police and gunmen have entered a factory, they were bewildered, frightened, and driven out by the "sitting" workers with no difficulty whatever.

5. Most workers distrust—if not consciously, then unconsciously—union officials and strike leaders and committees, even when they themselves have elected them. The beauty of the sitdown or the stay-in is that there are no leaders or officials to distrust. There can be no sell-out. Such standard procedure as strike sanction is hopelessly obsolete when workers drop their tools, stop their machines, and sit down beside them. The initiative, conduct, and control of the sitdown come directly from the men involved.

6. The fact that the sitdown gives the worker in mass-production industries a vital sense of importance cannot be overemphasized. Two sitdowns which completely tied up plants employing close to 10,000 men were started by half a dozen men each. Imagine the feeling of power those men experienced! And the thousands of workers who sat down in their support shared that feeling in varying degrees, depending on their individual power of imagination. One husky gum-miner said to me, "Now we don't feel like taking the sass of any snot-nose college-boy foreman." Another man said, "Now we know our labor is more important than the money of the stockholders, than the gambling in Wall Street, than the doings of the managers and foremen." The sitdown technique is still in the process of development, but already one man's grievance, if the majority of his fellow-workers in his department agree that it is a just grievance, can tie up the whole plant. He becomes a strike leader; the

other members of the working force in his department become members of the strike committee. *They* assume full responsibility in the matter: form their own patrols, keep the machines from being pointlessly destroyed, and meet with the management and dictate their terms. *They* turn their individual self-control and restraint into group self-discipline— which probably is the best aspect of the sitdown. *They* settle the dispute, not some outsider.

7. Work in most of the departments of a rubber factory or any other kind of mass-production factory is drudgery of the worst sort—mechanical and uncreative, insistent and requiring no imagination; and any interruption is welcomed by workers, even if only subconsciously. The conscious part of their mind may worry about the loss of pay; their subconscious, however, doesn't care a whit about that. The sitdown is dramatic, thrilling.

8. All these factors were important in the early sitdowns. They still are important. In addition now there is in Akron the three-year-old tradition that when a sitdown begins anywhere along the line of production everybody else is to sit down, too. And while we are explaining the men's solidarity in sitdowns, we mustn't forget also that the average worker in a mass-production plant is full of grievances and complaints, some of them hardly realized, and he knows or feels instinctively that when he and his fellow-workers get ready to act, they will need the support of all the labor in the place, and they will get it only if they back the men who have initiated the current sitdown.

9. The sitdown is a purely democratic action, as democracy is understood in America within the capitalist system.

10. The sitdown is a social affair. Sitting workers talk. They get acquainted. And they like that. In a regular strike it is impossible to bring together under one roof more than one or two thousand people, and these only for a meeting, where they do not talk with one another but listen to speakers. A rubber sitdown holds under the same roof up to ten or twelve thousand idle men, free to talk among themselves, man to man. "Why, my God, man," one Goodyear gum-miner told me, "during the sitdowns last spring I found out that the guy who works next to me is the same as I am, even if I was born in West Virginia and he is from Poland. His problems are the same. Why shouldn't we stick?"

Few syndicated columnists have been more conscious of the rights of property than George E. Sokolsky. When he realized what was happening in labor-management relations in early 1937, he published an article in *The Atlantic Monthly* ("The Law and Labor," April, 1937, Vol. 159, pp. 429–39). His comments suggest the sense of frustration—and at times of outrage—felt by many employers at the time. How does his basic attitude toward the sitdowns differ from that of Adamic? What does he have to say about the minority rights of those workers—perhaps, he thinks, a majority—who did not want to sit down but did not want to leave their fellow workers exposed? Finally, Sokolsky's definition of the "law," and of what is "lawless," raises the question of how one interprets legal precedents in a time of rapid social change.

⊂⊟ The Law and Labor

GEORGE E. SOKOLSKY

. . . The principle of the sit-down is not new. It is a development of sabotage which used to be advocated by the syndicalists, anarchists, I.W.W., and which has been practised in many countries. Chinese workers have for ages struck by folding their arms on the job; Chinese merchants effect great political changes by putting up the shutters of their shops. The recent election of Premier Blum of France was accompanied by a series of sit-down strikes in French factories.

The novelty of the current form of sabotage is that a small group of workers actually seizes the property of the employer. In the Goodyear, Goodrich, Bendix plants, and in many other enterprises, this form of sabotage has been practised.

The seizure of the property of the employer does not require the participation of a large number of workers. Consider the recent sit-down of seventeen men in the mixing room of the Goodrich plant in Akron. These seventeen men threw 10,000 out of work. Their action was not approved by their fellow workers. It was not approved by the labor union. It was not even approved by all the workers in the mixing room. Yet seventeen men were able to close down a plant for several days.

Mass-production industries cannot defend themselves easily against this device except through the enforcement of the law protecting property rights. As it is impossible for a mass-production industry to operate a part of a line unless there is a continuous flow of raw or semi-fabricated goods, the employer is at the mercy of a sit-down group; and when that is a fractional minority the worker is also at its mercy. If the law does

not function, there is no way of ending a sit-down except by compromise
or the forcible expulsion of the sit-downers on some legal basis.

Under the law, the normal remedy in such a procedure is for the
owner of the property to appear in a court of law to seek relief in accordance with the law. These measures General Motors proceeded to use on
two occasions. The first injunction apparently fouled because it was
found that the judge who issued it was a General Motors stockholder.
But on the second occasion a restraining order was issued by the court in
language and under circumstances which permit of no misunderstanding.
Judge Paul V. Gadola in this injunction said in opening:—

This proceeding involves a simple legal question that would be of relatively
little importance except to the litigants involved, other than that it is of great
public interest because of the relationship existing between the parties litigant
at the present time and as they affect the general public and welfare of all of
our people. The question involved is solely as to the right of the defendants to
occupy the premises involved in this litigation described in the amended bill
of complaint of the plaintiff.

And the Judge closed with the following order:—

It therefore follows that the relief asked for by plaintiffs in this action must
be granted. The injunction shall be issued out of this court commanding the
defendants that have appeared, and all defendants, and all persons operating
through, under or by virtue of any contact with these defendants, to evacuate
the premises in question, and further that they shall be restrained from picketing
the plants of the plaintiff.

This order further provides that the Sheriff of this county shall read the
order of this court in the premises described to the parties therein, and that
shall be sufficient notice of the order of the court to all parties involved. And
further providing that the evacuation shall be done within twenty-four hours
from this time.

The decision was later read to the strikers by the Sheriff. This order
was disobeyed. It has, in effect, been suspended. According to the best
information available, it was suspended by order of the Governor of the
State of Michigan. A further court order involving the arrest of certain
persons has also been suspended. The suspension of a court order by the
executive is an unusual procedure, setting a precedent which may be
applied to matters unrelated to labor problems. The Governor's excuse is
significant. He sought to avoid bloodshed. He believed that the operation
of the law would lead to a riot and a massacre.

Accepting the Governor's attitude as representing a decent regard
for human life, we still face the question of due process of the law, the
rights to possession of private property, the enforcement of law and
order, the control of mob violence by the exercise of police power.
These the Governor's policy and practice utterly disregard.

For instance, Governor Hoffman of New Jersey has already declared that he would forbid sit-downs in his state, even if force had to be used. In effect, his statement is an order to the C.I.O. to stay out of New Jersey. Although this may give comfort to employers, it is part of the same process that was evident in Michigan—namely, that of an executive official acting outside of the due process of the law. . . .

It is obvious that here is an utterly lawless situation. The law of the land, the Wagner Act, is suspended. An injunction is suspended. A court writ is suspended. Property is held by trespassers with the connivance of government. An admittedly minority labor group can throw 125,000 men out of work, while refusing to permit the workers themselves to decide who is to represent them. Unions within the American Federation of Labor are refused the right to representation. A public body of workers in Flint is denied a voice.

No law of the land, no law of the State of Michigan, is permitted to function. Hundreds of millions of dollars' worth of property, wages, and income are imperiled. The remedy of the law is avoided, and the reason, the judgment, of one individual is substituted.

This even raises the question as to whether there is any law in labor disputes. It has been suggested that a Labor Court be created to provide a lawful but compulsory medium for the settlement of labor disputes. Such a court would have to be empowered to compel attendance and to compel the enforcement of its decisions. Organized labor dislikes this form of compulsion, and the employers would fear it because of its possible political complexion.

The weakness of the National Labor Relations Board lies in its partisan character and in its unwillingness to render a decision in cases involving conflicts in jurisdiction between A. F. of L. and C.I.O. unions. Were it not for this weakness, this Board might have developed juridical characteristics which would have supported the conception of a Labor Court.

Furthermore, the agitation over the revision of the United States Supreme Court, whatever its outcome, and the flouting of the courts in the General Motors Strike, leave the authority of the courts in a questionable position. A new court, such as the Labor Court, would have to create its own prestige at a moment when the country is divided in its opinion concerning the Courts and the Law.

A labor law is needed, one that fits American conditions, that does not force the worker to sacrifice the weapon of the strike, but at the same time protects the employer from being compelled to accept one, and only one, labor union as representing all of his workers, with or without the consent of the workers.

The British Trade Disputes and Trade Unions Act of 1927, adapted to American conditions, affords the basis for such a law.

Before discussing this measure it needs to be pointed out that numerous laws exist which limit the functions of the employer and which place upon him onerous responsibilities. Child-labor laws, workmen's compensation acts, safety acts, building regulations, the SEC,[1] the income-tax law and the documents that must be filled out by individuals and corporations in connection therewith, the Wagner Act, the Walsh-Healy Act [2]—a host of laws and regulations have been passed by both Federal and state governments to fix employer responsibility. Not a single law exists to fix labor-union responsibility.

This inequality of legislation makes for disorders in industrial relations. The trade unions have no legal responsibilities as organizations. They are above the law. I recall that a New York judge recently said that they are outside the law. It is inherently wrong in a democracy that any group of citizens should be above the law or outside the law or without any law. Democracy must stand on the foundation of equality before the law, as difficult as that always is to achieve. . . .

In a word, the Act calls for what in the United States would be the incorporation of labor unions; for the publication of financial accounts broken down as corporation returns must be broken down for income-tax and SEC purposes; for a definition and limitation of picketing, so that the rights of the individual in private property would be amply protected and the rights of the public fully protected. Under this act the sit-down would be altogether unlawful. Under this act the half-million-dollar campaign contribution of the United Mine Workers to Mr. Roosevelt's reëlection would be difficult.

The British found a basis for national harmonious coöperation in the solution of national problems. At a time when, in a score of European and Asiatic countries, the people were forced to go through fundamental economic and political revolutions in the course of which they were deprived of their liberties, British Democracy stood firm. Yet in 1926, before this act was passed, Great Britain was actually at the beginning of a revolution. The rôle of the Labor Disputes Act in England has never been underestimated in that country. If it is not adequately understood in America—that is our misfortune. . . .

There can be only one remedy for this, and in my opinion that remedy must be in Federal law, even if an amendment to the Constitution is necessary to effect it. That remedy is:—

1. Let every labor organization be required, like a corporation, to receive a state charter setting forth its rights, obligations, and responsibilities.

2. Let every labor organization be required to file annually with a public authority a statement of accounts, so broken down that the mem-

[1] Securities and Exchange Commission. [Ed.]
[2] Passed in 1936, the Walsh-Healey Act regulated labor conditions in businesses contracting with the government. Healey is misspelled by *Atlantic*. [Ed.]

bers of the union as well as the public may know how these funds are spent.

3. No labor union should be permitted to expend funds for political purposes without the personally confirmed consent of the membership, and all such expenditures should be made public.

4. The checkoff should be forbidden by law, and both employers and labor leaders should be made liable for its practice.

5. The workers' representatives should be elected annually, with the right of recall, at a secret, democratic election held for each plant, on the basis of proportional representation. Strict regulations concerning these elections should be incorporated in the labor law. The rights of majorities, minorities, and individual workers should be made clear and should be fully protected.

> The president of the American Federation of Labor in 1937 was William Green, then serving his thirteenth year in that capacity. A firm believer in craft unions, he was less prepared to encourage industry-wide unions of unskilled workers. Chastened by frustrating experiences in the 1920's, Green was acutely conscious of the anti-labor nature of much of American public opinion, and fearful of the reaction which would ensue from the use of such radical measures as sitdowns. In this spirit he issued a press release on March 29, 1937 (reprinted in the *Congressional Digest*, Vol. 16, No. 5 [May, 1937], "Congress and the Sit-Down Strikes, Pro & Con," p. 150), stating the official position of the A. F. of L. It poses directly the question of what the tactics of labor ought to be. To what extent should militants trust in official spokesmen? Does spontaneous mass protest inevitably lead to excesses? If so, are the short-run gains worth the long-run backlash? Green also comments on the role of government; is labor better off without any federal activity at all?

⊂⊟   What About the Backlash?

WILLIAM GREEN

The sit-down strike has never been approved or supported by the American Federation of Labor. Because there is involved in its application grave implications detrimental to labor's interests, it must be disavowed by the thinking men and women of labor.

First, public opinion will not support sit-down strikes. That means labor loses public support when any part of it engages in sit-down strikes. Without such support organized labor cannot win strikes or establish and maintain itself as a vital force in the economic and industrial life of the nation. Labor cannot afford to lose the support of public opinion.

Second, temporary advantages gained through sit-down strikes will inevitably lead to permanent injury. The public generally will not long tolerate the illegal seizure of property. If persisted in it will through State and Federal law-making bodies force the enactment of legislation providing for compulsory arbitration, the incorporation of unions and other repressive forms of legislation which will deprive organized labor of freedom of association and liberty of action within the limitations of both moral and statutory law. Such action would be a severe blow to labor. Labor should refrain from engaging in sit-down strikes and maintain its freedom of action and association rather than experiment with it and as a result be subjected to oppressive legal regulation and compulsory arbitration. Labor therefore runs the risk of losing more than can be gained by engaging in sit-down strikes. It must be free to strike against injustice and oppression and for higher wages and better living standards. It must be permitted to picket when strikes occur. It may be greatly restricted and perhaps denied the exercise of these elemental rights if it persists in engaging in sit-down strikes.

I therefore publicly warn labor against this illegal procedure. Both personally and officially I disavow the sit-down strike as a part of the economic and organization policy of the American Federation of Labor.

For John L. Lewis, the 1930's were rejuvenating. Long the leader of the United Mine Workers, he had been forced by economic conditions and hostile public opinion to preside over the sharp decline of a once-proud industrial union. But the New Deal encouraged him, and he quickly became the leader of the militant faction within the A. F. of L. Breaking away in 1935, he formed the C.I.O. and presided over it during its most militant phase between 1935 and 1940. A master of rhetoric, Lewis proved an exciting, if unpredictable leader. At the peak of the troubles at General Motors, he offered his view of the causes of labor-management tension (Radio address, reprinted in the *Congressional Digest*, Vol. 16, No. 5 [May, 1937], "Congress and the Sit-Down Strikes, Pro & Con," pp. 157–58). What seems to be Lewis's attitude toward the sitdown tactic? How does he try to place management on the defensive? Compare his expectations of labor as a pressure group with those of Green, his rival in the labor movement.

John L. Lewis Speaks

JOHN L. LEWIS

The Committee for Industrial Organization is carrying its plans forward. Extensive unions have been promoted and expanded in the steel, automotive, glass, shipbuilding, electrical manufacturing, oil and by-product coke industries. Tremendous enrollment of the workers is under way. Unabashed by employer opposition, they are joining the unions of their industries, literally by the thousands.

The year 1936 witnessed the beginning of this great movement in the mass production industries. The year 1937 will witness an unparalleled growth in the numerical strength of labor in the heretofore unorganized industries, and the definite achievement of modern collective bargaining on a wide front, where it heretofore has not existed. Not only the workers, but our nation and its entire population, will be the beneficiaries of this great movement. Labor demands collective bargaining and greater participation by the individual worker, whether by hand or brain, in the bountiful resources of the nation, and in the fruits of the genius of its inventors and technicians.

Employers talk about possible labor trouble interfering with continued expansion and progress of industry. They ignore the fact that unless people have money with which to buy, the wheels of industry slow down, and profits and likewise capital disappear. It would be more fitting and accurate to talk about "employer trouble"—that is something from which wage earners are suffering. I refer you to the refusal of some of the largest and most powerful corporations in this country to follow modern labor practice, or to obey the law of the land. They deny the entirely reasonable and just demands of their employees for legitimate collective bargaining, decent incomes, shorter hours, and for protection against a destructive speed-up system.

It is the refusal of employers to grant such reasonable conditions, and to deal with their employees through collective bargaining, that leads to widespread labor unrest. The strikes which have broken out in the last few weeks, especially in the automotive industry, are due to such "employer trouble." Modern collective bargaining, involving negotiations between organized workers and organized employers on an industry basis, would regularize and stabilize industry relations, and reduce the economic losses occasioned by management stupidity. The sit-down strike is the fruit of mismanagement and bad policy towards labor. Employers who tyrannize over the employees, with the aid of labor spies, company guards, and the threat of discharge, need not be surprised if their production lines are suddenly halted.

Huge corporations, such as United States Steel and General Motors, have a moral and public responsibility. They have neither the moral nor the legal right to rule as autocrats over the hundreds of thousands of employees. They have no right to transgress the law which gives to the worker the right of self-organization and collective bargaining. They have no right in a political democracy to withhold the rights of a free people.

The workers in the steel industry are organizing; the workers in the automotive industry are organizing; the workers in other industries are organizing; any sane concept of industrial relations would indicate that the labor problems of these industries should be settled across the council table.

The unlicensed and unrestrained arming of corporations against the workers has no place in any political or industrial democracy. Recent revelations before the LaFollette Subcommittee of the Senate have revealed in part the plans of industry to club, gas and cripple workers with the lethal weapons of warfare. Huge stocks of such weapons have been purchased at enormous expense, and over five hundred thousand dollars worth of tear and mustard gas has been delivered to industrial plants, and the expenditure necessary for the purchase of these war supplies is charged to the cost of production.

This real alternative to industrial democracy has been slightly exposed by the LaFollette Committee. This alternative is what industrialists want left undisturbed under this sudden "era of good feeling." They do not want the Senate and workers to discover how the anti-labor policies of great industrialists have filled the land with a fat business of spying and armed strike-breaking and civic corruption. They have stored mills and plants with the paraphernalia of war and its mercenaries; they suborn police and the judiciary, and they want the Senate and workers to blind their eyes to their warfare and their plan in the name of "good feeling."

May I respectfully suggest to the LaFollette Committee, which has hauled before it a few of industry's criminal agents, that it summon industry's brass hats, however eminent, to answer why they hire and feed this anti-labor army, and why they maintain warehouses overflowing with industrial war munitions and paraphernalia. May I humbly warn the Senate that labor wants this investigation pressed home, and wants industry disarmed, lest labor men on their march to industrial democracy should have to take by storm the barbed-wire barricades and machine gun emplacements, builded and maintained by the rapacious moguls of corporate industry. The agents of the Federal Government should enter these plants and gut them of their deadly weapons, so that Americans in the industrial communities may walk erect and enjoy, with the pride of free men, their inherent and rightful privileges.

Labor now demands the right to organize, and the right to bargain. Labor demands a new deal in America's great industries. Labor holds in contempt those who for mercenary reasons would restrict human privileges. Labor demands legislative enactments, making realistic the principles of industrial democracy. It demands that Congress exercise its constitutional powers and brush aside the negative autocracy of the Federal judiciary, exemplified by a Supreme Court which exalts property above human values. Either by constitutional amendment or statutory enactment, the right of Congress to legislate for the welfare of the people and the perpetuity of the Republic must be assured. The court has over-stepped the bounds of its own authority and has gratuitously offended over two-thirds of the nation's citizens. Labor will support the elected representatives of the Republic in any attempt to restore to the Federal Congress the legislative powers of which it has gradually been stripped by the judicial encroachment and arbitrary decrees of the Supreme Court.

Labor desires a peaceful solution of the problems of its relationships in the mass production industries. The organizations associated with the Committee for Industrial Organization are not promoting industrial strife —they are hoping for industrial peace on a basis that recognizes the rights of the workers, as well as the employers. Peace, however, cannot be achieved by employers' denial of the right to organize; by denial of conferences for bargaining purposes; by the purchase and use of arms, ammunition and tear gas; by a continued policy of arrogance and re-pression.

The time has passed in America when the workers can be either clubbed, gassed, or shot down with impunity. I solemnly warn the leaders of industry that labor will not tolerate such policies or tactics. Labor will also expect the protection of the agencies of the Federal Government in the pursuit of its lawful objectives.

The stage is set. Industry can go forward with profit to its investors, and with security to our citizenship; or it can elect to destroy itself by blindly following its unreasoning prejudices, and refusing to conform to the modern concept of proper industrial relationships.

The leaders of industry will decide, and upon them rests the responsibility of deciding wisely.

Few important magazines at the time of the sitdowns could resist the opportunity to denounce or extol the sitdown strikers. *The Nation* was no exception. In one issue the editors reflected on the legal aspects of the problem ("Making Sitdowns Legal," Vol. 144, March, 1937, p. 340). Its point of view is particularly interesting, for the 1930's witnessed a historic confrontation between the conservative Supreme Court, adhering to what it regarded as constitutional precedents, and an activist New Deal, reflecting a more flexible view of what was "legal" and "illegal." Where does *The Nation* stand on this controversy? Which position seems more sound in general, and in this instance? What, in short, is "the law" in times of acute social tension?

⊂⊐ Editorial: Making Sitdowns Legal

THE NATION

Never in our memory has anything happened in America that so completely illumines the uses of law in our society as the controversy over the sitdown strike. The speed with which the sitdown has spread in the highly industrial states shows of course that it is deeply related to a felt need among our workers. . . . And the response of the law itself to this need is a stiff-necked assertion of illegality.

Let us not be misunderstood. Given the law as it stands, interpreted narrowly, there can be little doubt that the sitdown is illegal. There have been those who have urged the opposite, and we have ourselves pointed to the property rights that a worker has in his job. But it is terribly important to make a distinction here. Are we talking about the law that *exists* or the law that *is emerging?* If we take Justice Holmes's excellent behavioristic definition of law—"law is what the courts are likely to decide"—and if we couple that with what we know about most American judges today, the answer is clear. We could, of course, write an editorial on what the judges *should* decide. Or we could ruminate on what *we* should decide if we were judges. But the hard reality is that we are not.

Unless we make this distinction, we obscure the uses of law in social struggles and the manner in which law grows. Law at any given period is a crystallization of past growths and past struggles. It is a response to the felt impulsions of the past. In America today our law reflects the desperate need for protecting property in a rapidly growing, mushrooming frontier society that turned in an amazingly brief span of time into the most highly developed capitalist state in the world. It reflects also the fears that our industralists felt when faced by the growth of trade unionism and democratic feeling. This need and these fears have been written —have written themselves—into the law. The use of the injunction in the past, even more than today, as a strike-breaking weapon is a prime example of how law can be used to favor one side in the capital-labor relationship. Today such a use of the injunction is illegal in sixteen states and in the federal courts. And not only the injunction. The strike itself was once illegal. It is now, in theory at least, legal. The labor boycott was illegal. It is now, under certain circumstances, legal. Picketing was once illegal. It is now legal. Mass picketing was once illegal. It is now generally legal. What we call "the law" has on these subjects changed as social realities have somehow got themselves into peoples' heads and become recognized as realities.

The "law" on the sitdown will also change—is, in fact, changing under our very hands. Judges are human, and even judges are not entirely impervious to realities outside the courtroom. . . . For they will come to understand that there is more in the heaven and earth of the sitdown than is dreamt of in the doctrine of simple trespass. You do not dispose of the controversy between the Chrysler corporation and its workers by recourse to an eighteenth-century idea of private property. Such a controversy is infinitely involved. On its settlement depend not only the livelihoods of thousands, even of millions, but the social health of the state. Whoever you are—judge, corporation head, newspaper publisher—you must recognize that the stake these workers have in their livelihoods and the stake the nation has in healthy and decent industrial conditions are far greater than your narrow and static legalism. You cannot chase these men out as you would chase out a trespasser from your back yard.

Even on the score of strict legality, the total case is far from clear. Every day, throughout the nation, the corporate employers are breaking laws in their struggle against collective bargaining. Every day the Labor Relations Board is defied, labor spies are used, men are discharged for union activities. Every day police brutality is used to smash strikes and break up picket lines. Two wrongs, of course, do not make a right. But we cite these facts because we are convinced that the objection of the corporations to the sitdown is not that it is illegal but that it levels out the immense advantage they have thus far had in the bargaining struggle. That is what they cannot endure—not the trespass, but the fact that they are now compelled to put their houses in order and accept the workers' demands for collective bargaining.

In legal terms the sitdown must therefore be seen as part of the no man's land where the law is, except in the narrowest and most mechanical sense, still undetermined. In such an area the considerations that should be decisive are those leading to a decent living standard for all.

Where *The Nation* considered legal aspects of the sitdowns, its chief rival among liberal journals, *The New Republic,* concerned itself with the related question of what was fair ("Is the Sitdown Unfair?" Vol. 90, Feb. 17, 1937, pp. 32–33). Accordingly, it focused on the technological and economic changes of the decade which had led up to the crisis, and it asked, in effect, how organized labor could have unionized the mass production industries by any means other than sitdowns. A key question raised by the article is the extent to which ends, however desirable, are justified by the means. A second issue is whether existing law ought to count much (or at all) if changing economic reality makes it seem obsolete.

Editorial: Is the Sitdown Unfair?

THE NEW REPUBLIC

Many persons who are as a rule friendly to the cause of organized labor are gravely troubled about the sit-down strike. Their feeling, as reflected in numerous letters received by *The New Republic,* is that it is clearly illegal and that it constitutes a sort of blackmail by which a small minority of the employees of an industrial corporation seek to dictate both to management and to their fellow workers, who may be entirely out of sympathy with the aims of those who are "sitting down." This attitude is probably well expressed by one correspondent of ours who remarked in effect: I am a farmer and I own an apple orchard. If I hired a man to pick apples and he sat down under the tree, I would be well within my rights, morally and legally, to throw him out.

The point missed by this correspondent, and by many other persons, is that simple analogies about an apple picker sitting under a tree have no meaning in relation to an affair like the General Motors strike. This corporation has some 235,000 employees, scattered through the United States. It is . . . owned . . . by some 329,000 stockholders, who are also scattered through the United States. Probably 99 percent of them have no first-hand knowledge of the labor policies of their company, and even if they had, and if they objected to the actions that are being taken, they have no real means of indicating their disapproval or altering the policy. . . . Ownership and control are now distinct from one another; all that the average stockholder demands is that dividends should be regular and large. When you hire one man to pick apples in your orchard, you know how he and his family are getting along and you would probably be distressed if they were in a state of semi-starvation. But there is no contact at all between any of the 329,000 owners and any of the 235,000 workers except through the tiny group of [managers] who probably own little if any stock and over whom the only real social control is the approval of their fellow big-business men in Wall Street or near to it.

Let it be remembered that this group as a whole has always been and is now 100-percent anti-union. . . . What they really want is no collective bargaining at all. If they can't have that, then they want fake company unions, or numerous employee groups that will be weak and ineffective just because none of them speaks for the whole mass of the workers. It is the standard history of strikes that the management always complains that the strike leaders are arrogant or radical or ambitious and that it weeps crocodile tears over the non-union workers who are deprived of the right to earn a living. Change the union leadership, change the personnel of the groups on strike, and the complaints from the bosses still go on.

The sit-down strike is not illegal. It is so new that no existing law has any relevance in regard to it. Statutes against trespass are clearly intended to prohibit the entry of thieves and other criminals who break in for the purpose of damaging property. But the sit-down strikers enter upon the property with the knowledge and consent of management. They have no desire to steal or damage any property, and whenever damage has occurred it has been incidental to brutal tactics of the police. The sit-down strikers are just as anxious to get back to work as anyone else is to have them to do so. All they ask is decent treatment enforced through collective bargaining.

Vast quantities of nonsense have been printed lately about the immorality of a strike conducted by less than a majority of the employees. If the UAW, according to this argument, had 117,501 members, the strike would be perfectly proper. If it has only 117,499, then we must have nothing to do with it. To argue this way is to misunderstand the whole history of the labor movement. Unions do not win strikes by having an overwhelming majority of the workers in their ranks before trouble arises. They get such majorities by winning strikes. The fact remains that all previous attempts to unionize the automobile industry have failed; that the effort to operate with groups of small unions was tried in 1934 and proved a disastrous failure. If the automobile industry really wanted collective bargaining on the only basis on which it has any reality, it would accept the UAW and work with it. A ten-word announcement by [management] that this was being done would bring 95 percent of the GM employees into the union in forty-eight hours. A majority of any group of employees will almost always favor a union strong enough to enforce their right to be heard. But instead, the General Motors Corporation has fought this union and any other effective one. It has spent vast sums on a spy system. It has violated the terms of the Wagner Labor Relations Act in the hope that the law would be declared unconstitutional. It has exerted every sort of bribery and coercion to keep men out of the union.

The sit-down strike is here to stay, and industry would be well advised to come to terms with it. Even if the present strikers are forced out by the bayonet, on the day that operations are resumed, the possibility of another sit-down will appear. Dismiss every union man, and it will still exist; the conditions which force one group of employees to organize and fight in self-protection will eventually cause any other group to do the same thing. Modern industry, through technological advance, has itself created conditions under which its workers can no longer be treated as abject serfs. If the managers were really intelligent—which they are not —and if they were not controlled by patterns of thinking carried over from a dead past—which they are—they would make the decision their fellow industrialists in Great Britain made a quarter of a century ago. They would accept collective bargaining, would help the process instead of hindering it, and would agree to American standards of life for American workers.

Chapter

18: The Truman Doctrine and America's Mission in World Affairs

⊂Ξ RICHARD P. TRAINA

On March 12, 1947, President Truman addressed a joint session of Congress. Speaking in a manner both grave and blunt, he pronounced in a single sentence those words which immediately became known as the Truman Doctrine: "I believe that it must be the policy of the United States to support free peoples who are resisting attempted subjugation by armed minorities or by outside pressures." The President then requested $400 million in military and economic assistance for the Greek and Turkish governments.

About three weeks earlier, on February 21, British officials had quietly informed the Department of State of an imminent crisis in the eastern Mediterranean. In Greece, civil war had been raging for many months between royalist government forces and communist elements. The British, having long provided assistance to the Greek government, were now facing bankruptcy at home and would have to withdraw from Greece by April. The British foreign office simultaneously informed American officials that Turkey—while relatively stable internally—was encountering continued difficulties with its Russian neighbor. The contention was that the Turks required outside assistance if they were to resist that pressure. Would the United States assume the burden of supporting the Greek and Turkish governments upon the departure of the British? This was the immediate question to which the President responded on March 12.

Among the claims made for the historical importance of the Truman Doctrine, one stands out: it has been commonly judged a turning point in the history of American foreign policy. The reason for this view is not simply that the President called for assistance to two Mediterranean nations in a time of international peace, but that he couched this call in a broad-gauged pronouncement capable of being used to explain, justify, or rationalize global intervention against the spread of communism. The general terms of the doctrine resulted in confusion as to what precisely the President intended beyond aid to Greece and Turkey. But probably every public figure who became involved in the controversy assumed that it was a rejection of isolationism, an acknowledgment of the existence of a kind of "cold war" with the Soviet Union, and the first step of a probable series to counter communist expansion. It is widely believed that the continual enlargement of American foreign commitments since the spring of 1947 was ideologically rooted in the Truman Doctrine.

There have been dissenters from the "turning point" opinion. Two objections are common. First, it was argued that Truman was in effect continuing a long tradition of policy-making guided by realistic self-interest (with the claim, for example, that the Truman Doctrine was simply an extension of the Monroe Doctrine in a shrunken world). Second, it was proposed that Truman was merely giving an updated expression to an enduring missionary zeal of the American people to make their impact upon the world. It is the last issue—that of the American mission —which is the focus of this chapter, and it leads to many other questions.

No presidential address as critical as this could avoid widespread debate, and around one common assumption all the disputes took place —America has a mission. But what mission? How should it be accomplished? What values and traditions are at stake? It is with such questions that Americans elevated the issue of the Truman Doctrine into a vital public controversy. From this debate, one may begin to judge what many Americans in 1947 thought their role in the world should be, whether their ideas were realistic or unrealistic, and also whether their views represented continuity with or departure from previous American experience.

Three interrelated considerations provide some background for analyzing the debate over the doctrine. First, there was the poor state of Soviet-American relations by the winter of 1947. Second, there were the general circumstances in Greece and Turkey. And third, there were the conflicting guidelines which Americans proposed concerning the proper role for the United States in international affairs.

Relations between the United States and Soviet Russia were in a decline well before the end of the world war, and with its conclusion the pace accelerated. Simply the number of major setbacks to Soviet-American cooperation was disquieting. American insistence on "satisfactory" arrangements in postwar eastern Europe appeared to Russian leaders an unwarranted interference in a Russian security zone. The decision of the United States government to manage the occupation of Japan without Soviet involvement seemed calculated to irritate Stalin. And the agreement for a large loan ($3.75 billion) which the Americans concluded with Britain in December, 1945, emphasized for the Russians the already obvious American preference for its British ally. In stark contrast to that British loan, a $6 billion loan proposed for Russia never materialized. As important as these events was the favorable reception Americans gave to Winston Churchill's "iron curtain" speech in March, 1946. It was in this address, delivered at Fulton, Missouri, with President Truman in the audience, that the prime minister made his dramatic appeal for Western unity.

From the American point of view the list of disappointments was growing distressingly long. The Russians by denying the West a voice in realigning eastern Europe showed their unwillingness to abide by pledges made at Yalta. Their persistent refusal, on a variety of issues, to cooperate with the West on the administration of Germany resulted in even greater distrust. A belief that the Russians were assisting the Chinese Communists, in violation of both the Yalta agreements and the Sino-Soviet Treaty of 1945, helped extend the area of poor relations to the Far East. The Russians' persistent use of the Security Council veto to frustrate United Nations operations, and their constant refusal to discuss even the most liberal international atomic control schemes, convinced American officials that the Soviet Union desired to pursue an independent and antagonistic course.

There was, therefore, a substantial background of discord between the Russians and the Americans by the time of the Greek and Turkish issues of March, 1947. To that point, the Soviet Union's disagreements in the Balkans, Dardanelles, and Asia Minor were primarily with Great Britain. In fact, the two powers had historically pursued conflicting policies in those areas. With the pronouncement of the Truman Doctrine, the United States began to assume from Great Britain the burden of these disputes.

The most recent British concern in the eastern Mediterranean began before the world war ended. As Russian troops overran the Balkans, Churchill became fearful that Greece would go the way of Romania, Bulgaria, and Yugoslavia and fall into the Russian orbit. The prime minister rushed British troops to Greece and even made a personal visit to Athens in December, 1944, for the precise purpose of combating Russian influence. When peace came to the peninsula the following spring, the British were there. A subsequent plebiscite conducted with Allied supervision approved a right-wing, anti-Soviet government under the Greek king. Inefficient, corrupt, and weak, this government met with communist-led guerrilla resistance. Assisted by Moscow's new allies and satellites, these bands made constant use of the borders of Albania, Yugoslavia, and Bulgaria. British garrisons managed to hold the guerrillas in check until in 1947 Great Britain could no longer afford the expense.

Russian interest in Greece was an extension of its interest in the Dardanelles (and the Aegean Sea) as an opening to the Mediterranean. A Greek government friendly to the Soviet Union would be beneficial to Russian aspirations in that quarter. Stalin was encouraged for a time by the assistance communist governments were giving the Greek rebels, but he did not himself provide direct aid. Turkey, because it borders Russia and flanks the Dardanelles, was also important to the Soviet Union. And Stalin did renew historic Russian pressures upon its Turkish neighbor.

In the summer of 1945, the Russians put three demands before the Turks: (1) the cession of the regions of Kars and Ardahan, which had been Russian between 1878 and 1918; (2) Soviet military bases inside the Bosporus and the Dardanelles; and (3) a new convention on the Dardanelles which would substitute for the existing international control of the strait an exclusive joint control by Turkey and the Soviet Union. This last item was the paramount one, and the Turks would not accede to it for fear of becoming a virtual Russian satellite. Faced with these demands, the Turks maintained military readiness at considerable expense and requested financial assistance from Great Britain. Like the royalist Greek government, the Turkish regime was not the kind to excite the enthusiasm of Western liberals. But unlike Greece, Turkey was not rent with internal disruption, and it had already entered a period of modernization which, however agonizing, was to make it a hope for political and economic transformation in the Middle East.

Such were the general political and diplomatic conditions in Greece and Turkey when the British made known their need to withdraw. What remains to be considered is the general theoretical context of the public controversy over the Truman Doctrine. What principles had Americans been advocating as the proper ones upon which to base a foreign policy?

Three suggested guidelines for American foreign policy were vigorously debated in the immediate postwar period. Each of these antedated World War II, and each subsequently became part of the disputes over the Truman Doctrine. Although the lines separating them were often blurred, they may be stated simply: isolationism, collective security, and balance of power.

Isolationist sentiment, always strong except in the heat of war, reappeared in some quarters after the defeat of the Axis powers. The main, minimal tenet of isolationism was opposition to political and military commitments beyond the western hemisphere. (There is justification for the contention that this view was not so much isolationism as it was a kind of "continentalism" spanning North and South America.) Isolationism meant opposition to collective security arrangements, such as Woodrow Wilson had hoped the League of Nations would provide, as well as to foreign alliances such as at least a few Americans in the 1930's would like to have seen with Great Britain and France against Hitler's Germany.

Advocates of collective security, many of them having known the frustrations and failures of the 'twenties and 'thirties, received new hope and strength during World War II with the creation of the United

Nations Organization. Many Americans were thus once more encouraged
by the possibility of nations collectively organizing and utilizing power
in such ways as to enforce peace among themselves. It was not a mani-
festation of a desire for world government. It came primarily from a
hope for a world organization to keep peace.

All through the interwar years the champions of collective security
had confronted, as their main ideological and political opposition, the
isolationists. In the 'forties the situation changed. The most powerful
opposition now came from increasingly influential opinion leaders who
counciled the need for power politics. It had been nearly thirty years
since "balance of power diplomacy" had been widely and persuasively
advocated in the United States. During the two decades following the
peace at Versailles, one could hardly have found an audience to listen
to the idea of making alliances in either Europe or Asia, or of building
up and using American power in attempts to correct imbalances in those
spheres. The tremendous military capability developed by the United
States after 1940, the rise of a powerful and antagonistic Soviet Russia
in both Europe and Asia, and the distressing weakness of America's other
wartime allies were the primary conditions which by 1946 made balance
of power ideas attractive to many Americans who previously considered
them unthinkable.

The political/ideological environment into which President Truman
cast his "doctrine" very largely determined the tone and direction the
debate was to assume. The arguments were loud and angry, but political
strength lay with those who felt it necessary to stand four-square against
Communist Russia. Congress eventually voted the economic and military
aid to Greece and Turky which the President requested. But it did so
only after eight weeks of acrimonious controversy. During this time the
administration received invaluable assistance from Senator Arthur Vandenberg, Republican Chairman of the Foreign Relations Committee and
a converted isolationist. It was Vandenberg who contrived a successful
amendment aimed at satisfying a number of objections. It stipulated that
the program would end whenever the recipients desired, the United
Nations took action making such American involvement unnecessary, or
the President found its purpose fulfilled (or incapable of being fulfilled).
With those modifications, both the Senate and the House approved the
legislation by large majorities—67 to 23 and 287 to 107. This vote was not,
legally speaking, on the merits of the Truman Doctrine itself. But the
memorable language of the Doctrine became psychologically, ideologically, and even morally inseparable from the decision to assist the Greek
and Turkish governments.

All five of the following documents raise the issue of what America's
role should be in world affairs, and all five were written in March, 1947.
Each author was concerned with the specific challenges presented by

conditions in the eastern Mediterranean and with the manner in which the United States ought to respond. Finally, each author laid down certain principles or guidelines by which he believed America's foreign policy as a whole should be determined—and these were of necessity closely tied to his vision of what America's mission should be in world affairs.

Taken altogether, these selections reveal the nature of the debate that occurred over the Truman Doctrine. A variety of political, historical, and moral judgments find expression in these selections; and they show the extent to which many Americans believed that fundamental values were at stake in whatever decision was made and implemented.

When President Truman addressed Congress on March 12, 1947, he raised almost all the issues around which the controversy would gather. The basic difficulty for anyone interpreting his words is to discern how much weight he was giving to the freedom versus tyranny issue on the one hand and to the Middle Eastern and European balance of power questions on the other. To what extent was the President talking about "an American mission" writ large? What kind of mission did he believe this should be? And in what specific terms did he describe the tasks he thought should be performed in Greece and Turkey? Each of the four documents following this one is, in its own way, a comment on the President's position; and an understanding of what Harry Truman said is basic to an understanding of the entire debate. The speech, which is here only slightly edited, may be found in its complete form in *A Decade of American Foreign Policy, 1941–1949*, pages 1253–57 (81st Cong., 1st Sess., Sen. Doc. 123, Senate Foreign Relations Committee).

⊂⊃ The Truman Doctrine

HARRY S TRUMAN

The gravity of the situation which confronts the world today necessitates my appearance before a joint session of the Congress.

The foreign policy and the national security of this country are involved.

One aspect of the present situation, which I wish to present to you at this time for your consideration and decision, concerns Greece and Turkey.

The United States has received from the Greek Government an urgent appeal for financial and economic assistance. Preliminary reports from the American Economic Mission now in Greece and reports from the American Ambassador in Greece corroborate the statement of the Greek Government that assistance is imperative if Greece is to survive as a free nation.

I do not believe that the American people and the Congress wish to turn a deaf ear to the appeal of the Greek Government.

Greece is not a rich country. Lack of sufficient natural resources has always forced the Greek people to work hard to make both ends meet. Since 1940 this industrious and peace-loving country has suffered invasion, four years of cruel enemy occupation, and bitter internal strife. . . .

As a result of these tragic conditions, a militant minority, exploiting human want and misery, was able to create political chaos which, until now, has made economic recovery impossible.

420

Greece is today without funds to finance the importation of those goods which are essential to bare subsistence. Under these circumstances the people of Greece cannot make progress in solving their problems of reconstruction. Greece is in desperate need of financial and economic assistance to enable it to resume purchases of food, clothing, fuel, and seeds. These are indispensable for the subsistence of its people and are obtainable only from abroad. Greece must have help to import the goods necessary to restore internal order and security so essential for economic and political recovery.

The Greek Government has also asked for the assistance of experienced American administrators, economists, and technicians to insure that the financial and other aid given to Greece shall be used effectively in creating a stable and self-sustaining economy and in improving its public administration.

The very existence of the Greek state is today threatened by the terrorist activities of several thousand armed men, led by Communists, who defy the Government's authority at a number of points, particularly along the northern boundaries. A commission appointed by the United Nations Security Council is at present investigating disturbed conditions in northern Greece and alleged border violations along the frontier between Greece on the one hand and Albania, Bulgaria, and Yugoslavia on the other.

Meanwhile, the Greek Government is unable to cope with the situation. The Greek Army is small and poorly equipped. It needs supplies and equipment if it is to restore authority to the Government throughout Greek territory.

Greece must have assistance if it is to become a self-supporting and self-respecting democracy.

The United States must supply that assistance. We have already extended to Greece certain types of relief and economic aid, but these are inadequate.

There is no other country to which democratic Greece can turn.

No other nation is willing and able to provide the necessary support for a democratic Greek Government.

The British Government, which has been helping Greece, can give no further financial or economic aid after March 31. Great Britain finds itself under the necessity of reducing or liquidating its commitments in several parts of the world, including Greece.

We have considered how the United Nations might assist in this crisis. But the situation is an urgent one requiring immediate action, and the United Nations and its related organizations are not in a position to extend help of the kind that is required. . . .

No government is perfect. One of the chief virtues of a democracy, however, is that its defects are always visible and under democratic processes can be pointed out and corrected. The Government of Greece is not perfect. . . .

The Greek Government has been operating in an atmosphere of chaos and extremism. It has made mistakes. The extension of aid by this country does not mean that the United States condones everything that the Greek Government has done or will do. We have condemned in the past, and we condemn now, extremist measures of the right or of the left. We have in the past advised tolerance, and we advise tolerance now.

Greece's neighbor, Turkey, also deserves our attention.

The future of Turkey as an independent and economically sound state is clearly no less important to the freedom-loving peoples of the world than the future of Greece. The circumstances in which Turkey finds itself today are considerably different from those of Greece. Turkey has been spared the disasters that have beset Greece. And during the war the United States and Great Britain furnished Turkey with material aid.

Nevertheless, Turkey now needs our support.

Since the war Turkey has sought additional financial assistance from Great Britain and the United States for the purpose of effecting that modernization necessary for the maintenance of its national integrity. That integrity is essential to the preservation of order in the Middle East.

The British Government has informed us that, owing to its own difficulties, it can no longer extend financial or economic aid to Turkey.

As in the case of Greece, if Turkey is to have the assistance it needs, the United States must supply it. We are the only country able to provide that help.

I am fully aware of the broad implications involved if the United States extends assistance to Greece and Turkey, and I shall discuss these implications with you at this time.

One of the primary objectives of the foreign policy of the United States is the creation of conditions in which we and other nations will be able to work out a way of life free from coercion. This was a fundamental issue in the war with Germany and Japan. Our victory was won over countries which sought to impose their will, and their way of life, upon other nations.

To insure the peaceful development of nations, free from coercion, the United States has taken a leading part in establishing the United Nations. The United Nations is designed to make possible lasting freedom and independence for all its members. We shall not realize our objectives, however, unless we are willing to help free peoples to maintain their free institutions and their national integrity against aggressive movements that seek to impose upon them totalitarian regimes. This is no more than a frank recognition that totalitarian regimes imposed upon free peoples, by direct or indirect aggression, undermine the foundations of international peace and hence the security of the United States.

The peoples of a number of countries of the world have recently had totalitarian regimes forced upon them against their will. The Government of the United States has made frequent protests against coercion and intimidation, in violation of the Yalta Agreement, in Poland, Rumania, and Bulgaria. I must also state that in a number of other countries there have been similar developments.

At the present moment in world history nearly every nation must choose between alternative ways of life. The choice is too often not a free one.

One way of life is based upon the will of the majority, and is distinguished by free institutions, representative government, free elections, guaranties of individual liberty, freedom of speech and religion, and freedom from political oppression.

The second way of life is based upon the will of a minority forcibly imposed upon the majority. It relies upon terror and oppression, a controlled press and radio, fixed elections, and the suppression of personal freedoms.

I believe that it must be the policy of the United States to support free peoples who are resisting attempted subjugation by armed minorities or by outside pressures.

I believe that we must assist free peoples to work out their own destiny in their own way.

I believe that our help should be primarily through economic and financial aid which is essential to economic stability and orderly political processes.

The world is not static, and the *status quo* is not sacred. But we cannot allow changes in the *status quo* in violation of the Charter of the United Nations by such methods as coercion, or by such subterfuge as political infiltration. In helping free and independent nations to maintain their freedom, the United States will be giving effect to the principles of the Charter of the United Nations.

It is necessary only to glance at a map to realize that the survival and integrity of the Greek nation are of grave importance in a much wider situation. If Greece should fall under the control of an armed minority, the effect upon its neighbor, Turkey, would be immediate and serious. Confusion and disorder might well spread throughout the entire Middle East.

Moreover, the disappearance of Greece as an independent state would have a profound effect upon those countries in Europe whose peoples are struggling against great difficulties to maintain their freedoms and their independence while they repair the damages of war.

It would be an unspeakable tragedy if these countries, which have struggled so long against overwhelming odds, should lose that victory for which they sacrificed so much. Collapse of free institutions and loss of independence would be disastrous not only for them but for the world. Discouragement and possibly failure would quickly be the lot of neighboring peoples striving to maintain their freedom and independence.

Should we fail to aid Greece and Turkey in this fateful hour, the effect will be far-reaching to the West as well as to the East.

We must take immediate and resolute action.

I therefore ask the Congress to provide authority for assistance to Greece and Turkey in the amount of $400,000,000 for the period ending June 30, 1948. In requesting these funds, I have taken into consideration the maximum amount of relief assistance which would be furnished to Greece out of the $350,000,000 which I recently requested that the Congress authorize for the prevention of starvation and suffering in countries devastated by the war.

In addition to funds, I ask the Congress to authorize the detail of American civilian and military personnel to Greece and Turkey, at the request of those countries, to assist in the task of reconstruction, and for the purpose of supervising the use of such financial and material assistance as may be furnished. I recommend that authority also be provided for the instruction and training of selected Greek and Turkish personnel.

Finally, I ask that the Congress provide authority which will permit the speediest and most effective use, in terms of needed commodities, supplies, and equipment, of such funds as may be authorized. . . .

The seeds of totalitarian regimes are nurtured by misery and want. They spread and grow in the evil soil of poverty and strife. They reach their full growth when the hope of a people for a better life has died.

We must keep that hope alive.

The free peoples of the world look to us for support in maintaining their freedoms.

If we falter in our leadership, we may endanger the peace of the world—and we shall surely endanger the welfare of our own Nation.

Great responsibilities have been placed upon us by the swift movement of events.

I am confident that the Congress will face these responsibilities squarely.

Henry Agard Wallace (1888–1965) had a long public career, most notably as Secretary of Agriculture during the New Deal and as Franklin Roosevelt's third-term Vice-President. In 1948 he ran for the presidency under the Progressive party banner. He had served briefly under Truman as Secretary of Commerce, but angry, open disputes with both Truman and Secretary of State James Byrnes forced his resignation in 1946. Wallace subsequently wrote a weekly column for *The New Republic* in which he continued to express opposition to the administration's foreign policies, and the selection below is taken from his column of March 24, 1947, "The Fight for Peace Begins." (Reprinted by Permission of *The New Republic* © 1947, Harrison-Blaine of New Jersey, Inc.) What were Wallace's attitudes toward the United Nations, the governments of Greece and Turkey, and the behavior of the Soviet Union? How did these views relate to his ideas about American foreign policy and the nation's proper role in world affairs?

⊂ϴ Opposition on the Left

Henry A. Wallace

March 12, 1947, marked a turning point in American history. On that day President Truman confronted the world with a crisis, not of the Greek economy, but of the American spirit. . . . Only the American people, fully aroused and promptly acting, can prevent disaster.

In the name of democracy and humanitarianism, President Truman proposes a military lend-lease program. He proposes a loan of $400 million to Greece and Turkey as a down payment on an unlimited expenditure aimed at opposing Communist expansion. He proposes in effect that America police Russia's every border. There is no regime too reactionary for us; provided it stands in Russia's path.

In three weeks' time Congress is asked to make one of the most radical changes ever proposed in American foreign policy. Congress is asked to make this change with insufficient evidence, with few facts, with no knowledge of where this program will end. President Truman justifies this extraordinary procedure in the name of a crisis. It is as if tomorrow the heavy-booted soldiers of the Soviet Union will be heard tramping through the streets of Athens. What is this crisis that necessitates the President going to Capitol Hill as if the Soviet army were on the march or as if another Pearl Harbor were upon us?

There is a world crisis. It is not a war crisis; the Soviet Union has made no warlike moves. The real world crisis is the crisis of millions of people left homeless, hungry, disease-ridden, orphaned and ravaged by years of fighting. Of course this crisis demands action. The peoples of Italy, Poland, Yugoslavia, France, Greece, Hungary, China and other lands urgently need American food and supplies. The peoples of Russia suffered greater losses and contributed more to the defeat of Germany than those of any other nation. They need American supplies for reconstruction. . . .

The program proposed by President Truman bears almost no relation to the real crisis of today and no relation to the real needs of the peoples of the world. It is a program for the purchase of mercenaries and the widening of the conflict against the Soviet Union.

One-half of the loan of $250 million to Greece is to be used, according to government sources, to provide guns, signal equipment, army trucks and the services of American Army officers—all for the present Greek army. Very little of the remainder will serve the immediate needs of the Greek people. . . .

The $150 million loan to Turkey bears no relation to democracy or the economic needs of the Turkish people. There is no Communist problem in Turkey and Turkey is not in need of relief. The Turkish government is not democratic and we have no intention of promoting democracy in Turkey. . . .

Like all Americans I want to see freedom enjoyed by all peoples everywhere. This program is a program for the destruction, not the extension, of freedom. Once American loans are given to the undemocratic governments of Greece and Turkey, every reactionary government and every strutting dictator will be able to hoist the anti-Communist skull and bones, and demand that the American people rush to his aid. Today we are asked to support Greece and Turkey. Tomorrow Peron and Chiang Kai-shek may take their turn at the head of the line. American dollars will be the first demand, then American Army officers and technicians, then American GI's.

I say that this policy is utterly futile. No people can be bought. America cannot afford to spend billions and billions of dollars for unproductive purposes. The world is hungry and insecure, and the peoples of all lands demand change. American loans for military purposes won't stop them. Once America stands for opposition to change, she will become the most hated nation in the world. . . .

Coming two days after the opening of the Moscow Conference, President Truman's speech has undermined General Marshall's assignment of cooperating with Great Britain, France and Russia in writing the peace.[1] The United Nations, our great hope for peace, rests on the continued cooperation of these nations and will be gravely weakened if America

---

[1] The Council of Foreign Ministers was then meeting at Moscow. These sessions, with Secretary Marshall in attendance, failed to produce the agreements for which many hoped concerning the future of Germany. [Ed.]

follows the course that Truman recommends. A United Nations commission is now in Greece investigating the threat to Greek security. If Greece is in danger, let the United Nations tell us the facts and recommend action.

When President Truman proclaims the worldwide conflict between East and West, he is telling the Soviet leaders that we are preparing for eventual war. They will reply by measures to strengthen their position in the event of war. Then the task of keeping the world at peace will pass beyond the power of the common people everywhere who want peace. As our obligations around the world increase, Americans must give up hope of reduced national debt, of any relief from the burden of taxation. Pressure will increase for restoring conscription, for universal military training. Civil liberties will be restricted; standards of living will be forced downward; families will be divided against each other; none of the values we hold worth fighting for will be secure. . . .

As one American citizen I say: *No loan to undemocratic and well fed Turkey; no loan to Greece until a representative Greek government is formed and can assure America that our funds will be used for the welfare of the Greek people.*

No one wants war. If war comes one day, it will be because we have failed to think on the scale required for peace. Roosevelt thought on that scale. He foresaw generations of peace and plenty. Two years later President Truman asks us to look forward to generations of want and war. President Truman has summoned in a century of fear. I say this can be the century of the fulfillment of the American dream.

This is the time for an all-out worldwide reconstruction program for peace. This is America's opportunity. The peoples of all lands say to America: Send us plows for our fields instead of tanks and guns to be used against us. The United Nations is waiting, ready to do the job. We should start with an economic plan for the Near East financed by the International Bank and backed by the United Nations. The dollars that are spent will be spent for the production of goods and will come back to us in a thousand different ways. Our program will be based on service instead of the outworn ideas of imperialism and power politics. It is a fundamental law of life that a strong idea is merely strengthened by persecution. The way to handle communism is by what William James called "the replacing power of the higher affection." In other words, we must give the common man all over the world something better than communism. I believe we have something better than communism here in America. But President Truman has not spoken for the American ideal. It is now the turn of the American people to speak. Peace-minded people must act. Every church should organize. Every woman's club should pass resolutions. Every citizen should write to Congress. There is opportunity for great good as well as great evil in this hour.

John F. Kennedy (1917–1963) was in 1947 a first-term Congressman, destined to serve six years in the House and eight years in the Senate before reaching the presidency in 1961. Late in March, 1947, Congressman Kennedy spoke at the University of North Carolina on the subject of President Truman's recent proposal. (The address was subsequently entered into the *Congressional Record*, 80th Cong., 1st Sess., Vol. 93, Pt. 10, *Appendix*, pages 1422–23.) The organization of this speech almost makes it appear an intentional attempt to rebut Henry Wallace's position point by point. The kind of argument advanced by Kennedy reflected the "tough idealism" then entering American political life. The President benefited from such support in 1947, but by 1949 the young Congressman from Massachusetts was a critic of Truman's foreign policy. Kennedy would then charge the administration with not living up to the world-wide demands it had itself recognized by the Truman Doctrine. Did Kennedy add any perspectives or dimensions to the arguments advanced by Truman concerning American assistance to the governments of Greece and Turkey? In what ways did Kennedy and Wallace disagree on these issues: the ambitions of the Soviet Union, the appropriate role for the United Nations, and the character of the Greek and Turkish governments? Finally, how did their ideas differ on the larger question of "America's mission"?

⊂⊒ Tough Idealism

John F. Kennedy

Tonight I wish to discuss briefly the President's proposal for aid to Greece and Turkey, which illustrates clearly the direction and meaning of American foreign policy in the year 1947. . . .

This preoccupation of the United States with those countries that form the bridgehead between the peoples and civilizations of the East and the once powerful, now destitute and suffering people of Europe, is no new one for the United States. It was not President Truman who said, "a strong hope has long been entertained, founded on the heroic struggle of the Greeks, that they would succeed in their contest and resume their equal station among the nations of the earth. It is believed that the whole civilized world would take a deep interest in their welfare." It was not President Truman but that able, cautious man, who first enunciated the doctrine that placed American strength behind the guarantee of freedom for the Western Hemisphere, James Monroe.

I support the President's proposal for assistance to the Governments of Greece and Turkey. I feel it to be essential to the security of our country. I propose here to give the reasons for my belief.

428

Long a cornerstone of our foreign policy has been the belief that American security would be dangerously threatened if the continent of Europe or that of Asia were dominated by any one power. We fought in 1917 when it appeared that Germany would break the thinning lines of the French and the British and win through to domination of the European Continent. We fought again in 1941 to oppose the domination of Asia by the Empire of Japan. We fought in Europe to prevent the fall of Britain and of Russia and the consequent subjugation of Europe and Africa and the Middle East.

The atomic bomb and guided missile has not yet weakened that cornerstone. We would still fight, I believe, to prevent Europe and Asia from becoming dominated by one great military power and we will oppose bitterly, I believe, the suffering people of Europe and Asia succumbing to the false, soporific ideology of Red totalitarianism.

Our proposed assistance to Greece and Turkey, therefore, is not turning the page to a new chapter in American foreign policy. Our foreign policy is the same as it has always been from the day that the discerning Monroe first enunciated the principles of the Monroe Doctrine. It merely means that time and space have brought a new interpretation to that historical document.

We have only to look at the map to see what might happen if Greece and Turkey fell into the Communist orbit. The road to the Middle East would be flung open. The traditional goal of the Russian foreign policy, an opening to the Mediterranean, with all of its strategic implications, would be gained. If we give way and Greece and Turkey succumb it would have tremendous strategic and ideological repercussions throughout the world. It would be a sign to all of those hard-pressed governments now resisting those disciples of the party line, who feed on the misery and despair of the postwar world. Our neutrality would strengthen greatly the prestige of Soviet Russia. The barriers would be down and the Red tide would flow across the face of Europe and through Asia with new power and vigor.

I should like to deal with some of the objections which have been made with regard to the proposals for assistance. One of the most frequent objections, and one which is to be carefully considered, is that the proposed loans are unfriendly acts and enhance the prospects of war. . . .

I do not believe that Russia wants war now. Nevertheless, as General Eisenhower said the other day, "All wars are stupid and they can occur stupidly." There is real danger that Russia may stumble into a war which she may not want because of a series of bad guesses and bad information. The Russian information and intelligence services are, I believe, among the poorest in the world despite all the glamorous nonsense which seems to be written about them. . . .

This, to my mind, enhances the short-term danger of a conflict with the Soviet Union. Let us suppose that puppet governments are installed in Greece and Turkey which then establish still closer relations with Poland, Rumania, Yugoslavia, Albania, and the Soviet Union. The centuries-old Russian dream of domination of the straits and access to the vast areas to the south and east would be realized, and realized with practically no sacrifice. We may then well imagine that she might decide to round out her Mediterranean bastion by annexing a few crumbs of territory here and there, say in northern Iran or the eastern provinces of Turkey. She would expect to get such trifles at little cost only to be bitterly shocked and surprised to discover that she had touched off a world war.

If you consider this fantastic, look for a moment at Hitler's Reich. After the diplomatic failures at Munich and the subsequent swallowing up of Czechoslovakia, Hitler's information services told him that the British and French and Americans would do nothing about Poland. They were wrong about Britain and France, and the result we know.

To me all this adds up to the fact that the use of American dollars and credits in Greece and Turkey now will make it possible for us to avoid sending men later, and will avert a repetition of the process I have just described.

The second objection to the President's proposals, and one which is most often heard, I believe, is that we are willfully bypassing the United Nations. It is extraordinary what strange bedfellows this crisis has made and what sudden friendships have come to the aid of the United Nations! Imagine Henry Wallace and Senator Wherry [1] on the same side!

Many people do, however, sincerely feel that the United Nations has been slighted. I think the feeling arises from some confusion as to what the United Nations can do. It is not equipped to deal with every problem in international affairs nor is there anything in the concept of the United Nations which precludes one nation from asking another for assistance as Greece has asked the United States. . . .

The United Nations has had neither the funds nor the organization to do a job of this character. We cannot afford to wait until it has, or even to go through a long pro forma effort which we know will be futile in the end.

Moreover, we must remember that the whole concept of the United Nations is that of the evolution of law backed up by force utilized under the guidance and restraint of the Security Council. So far, no progress has been made in establishing the military contingents which are to back up Security Council decisions. Why? Because the Soviet Union has dragged its feet constantly in the discussions of the military staff com-

---

[1] A conservative and an isolationist, Senator Kenneth S. Wherry (Republican, Nebraska) vehemently opposed Truman's proposal. [Ed.]

mittee which was to draw plans for the enforcement measures. Besides all this, there is yet no settlement of the territorial problems arising from the last war, no peace settlement in fact, and no generally accepted plan for the control of atomic weapons, nor for the regulation of armaments.

Nevertheless, the United Nations is the great hope for the future. I do hope personally that the administration will inform and keep the United Nations abreast of all moves that it will take in this Greek and Turkish matter. We already have the administration's assurance that it is studying measures whereby the United Nations can help. . . . It would, however, mean an early collapse of the United Nations organization if we were to place on its infant shoulders a burden which it cannot yet bear and with which it was, in fact, never intended it should deal.

Another objection to the President's plan is based on the allegedly undemocratic and reactionary Greek Government, which our loan would support in power. The facts are these: In accordance with the Yalta agreement, a civil mission composed of the representatives of the United States, England, and France (Russia refused to join) was sent to Greece to determine the fairness of the recent election. In the conclusion of the report this mission unanimously stated "that notwithstanding the present intensity of political emotions in Greece, conditions were such as to warrant the holding of elections, that the election proceedings were on the whole free and fair, and that the general outcome represented the true verdict of the Greek people." Not only were the elections closely observed by the mission, but polls were taken which substantiated the results: 1,117,000 votes were recorded out of a possible 1,850,000. The Communist-dominated EAM [2] as a matter of policy abstained from voting, and it is estimated by the mission that they reduced the number of those voting by about 15 percent. Thus the election was free and fair. The Greek Government now contains elements of all parties with the exception of Communists.

The United States Government is not, as the President stated, endorsing or in any way condoning any of the past actions of the present Greek Government. But it recognizes full well that the alternative to the present government is not liberal democracy, but communism. An orderly liberal government will come into being when an orderly middle class exists in Greece.

The President has called for a loan to Greece and Turkey of $400,-000,000. One hundred and fifty million dollars will go for relief of the civilian population of Greece, whose suffering during the war was well known. . . .

An additional $150,000,000 will be devoted to making available to the Greek armed forces the clothing, arms, food, and equipment to deal

[2] The EAM was the National Liberation Front in Greece. [Ed.]

effectively with the guerrillas and to place some stability in the military position of Greece as a whole. . . .

The remaining $100,000,000 goes to the Turkish Government. The general economic conditions in Turkey are more favorable than those in Greece, and thus nearly the entire $100,000,000 will be devoted to equipment for the Turkish armed forces and for projects such as the rehabilitation of the Turkish railroad system which will contribute most directly to the maintenance of security in Turkey. Turkey occupies a strategic position of great importance, and lives under a heavy shadow thrown by its great neighbor to the north and to the east.

The proposed assistance to Greece and Turkey is an integral part of American foreign policy of 1947. It is part of the policy developed by Secretary Byrnes to prevent the spread of communism by supporting those governments that are standing up against Russian expansion. To some of those countries we have given outright loans, such as our recent loan to Great Britain; to others, relief shipments which have helped prevent sheer misery and starvation from driving the sufferers into the hands of the Communists. In Italy, Japan, and Germany, we have kept occupation troops. In Korea and China we retained elements of the American Army and Marines, and we have taken a firm stand on Trieste, the Dardanelles, and the freedom of the Danube. All of these independent events add up to the central theme of our American foreign policy—the prevention of Russian domination of Europe and Asia. This is the foreign policy that I support most vigorously. Upon it depends our security, and I believe the best hope of peace. . . .

Our aim is not to dominate by dollar imperialism the Governments of Greece and Turkey, but rather it is to assist them to live in freedom.

From Greece has come much of the culture and civilization upon which the institutional and political life of this nation has been based. We seek to give to the Greeks an opportunity to rebuild their country; and to the Turks an opportunity to maintain their security. . . .

The decision is up to us. The path is clearly marked. It must be clearly followed. It is the only path by which we will reach security and peace.

The following selection is taken from a lengthy editorial published by The Value Line Investment Survey, a New York corporation which has for many years provided a number of services for investors. Among these services has been its *Fortnightly Commentary*, the purpose of which is to provide "editorial appraisal of general political and economic trends that bear on investments." The selection here is from an editorial dated March 17, and entitled "Intervention in Greece." The editorial was actually written on the eve of Truman's address. It was subsequently printed as a three-column advertisement in *The New York Times* (March 23, 1947, financial section, page 3) and then appeared in the *Congressional Record* (80th Cong., 1st Sess., Vol. 93, Pt. 10, *Appendix*, pages 1270–71). It should be added that, in that substantial portion of the editorial which has not been reprinted here, the editors opposed political and military commitments in Europe and Asia expressly because these would require high taxes which would, over the long haul, lead the nation to socialism. The argument advanced in the paragraphs below is more ideological and more radical than conventional isolationist opinion—but it does reflect a number of sentiments common in isolationist circles. According to the editors, what was the extent of the sphere of legitimate foreign involvement for the United States? What reasons were given for this limitation? Did any of these reasons coincide with ones provided by Henry Wallace, who also wanted to limit (in another way) American involvement in other nations' affairs?

Editorial: Wall Street Isolationism

FORTNIGHTLY COMMENTARY

No one could be naive enough to imagine that the United States of America could gain permanent possession of a flank on the Dardanelles, Russia's only outlet to the Mediterranean, for $250,000,000.[1] The cost will come much higher than that, not only in terms of the commitment in Greece but also in the collateral undertakings in the Near East, in Europe, and in Asia—wherever in fact the Russian expansion will have to be bottled up if the new foreign policy is to carry through.

The investor can find no prospect of tax reduction in such a foreign policy. The question he must answer is whether he has a better chance to resist communism by strengthening capitalism or by aiming a gun at the Russians. . . .

The Russian people have a sincere admiration for America and American achievement, as attested by the dispatches of many responsible men

[1] The editors did not yet know of the administration's intention to request funds for Turkey as well. [Ed.]

who have visited Russia. Why, then, is it necessary to prove to them at the point of a gun that our way of life is superior to their own? Especially so when pointing the gun requires that we weaken our own way of life?

It is necessary to be practical. There must be some lines within which the contest for men's loyalties can be fought out by force of example. We are not yet such a perfect race that we can eliminate power politics altogether. But in the practical application of power politics, the first rule is not to bite off more than can be chewed. The natural—the practical sphere—in which to prove the superiority of capitalism and individualism is North and South America and the islands of the Caribbean and Pacific. These happen also to be the territories that the United States has traditionally defended. The area is large enough to be economically self-sustaining. Yet one imagines that if any responsible government authority advocated intervention in South American political and economic affairs, he would be denounced as an imperialist by the very same people who shout isolationist at anyone who is reluctant to see America control the Government of Greece.

There is not such a vast gulf between the Russians and ourselves that we could not live together in peace in our own parts of the world. It is implicit in the Russian program to relax the present regimentation of the individual's life. When that happens the difference between us will be no greater than that between us and the socialist state of Great Britain.

The contest of capitalism versus communism will then get down to a question of which works better. That could be settled without warfare. It would seem to be the part of wisdom for America to strengthen capitalism by removing as many as possible of the controls that make it unworkable, such as tariffs, cartels, subsidized prices, labor monopolies, and income taxes that prevent constructive enterprise. Nobody is going to stop the expansion of communism by sticking a $250,000,000 thorn into the side of Russia. Communism will be stopped by something that works better. Russian Communists are men. They have the same love of God and their fellowmen that other people have. They can learn, but they will not be taught at the point of a foreign gun. Nor will they learn to admire the capitalist economy unless we capitalists see to it that it works. We have more to do in North and South America than on the flanks of the Dardanelles.

The danger to Americans is not the activity of Communist agents but the deterioration of capitalism itself. Sensing our own weakness we look for a foreign devil to blame it on. But this is self-deception. Communism would have no chance at all in a world, or even in a part of a world, in which capitalism was working. Rome did not fail because of the power of the barbarians but because of the weakness of the Romans. In weakening capitalism in order to contain Russia by naked military force, we do not defend ourselves intelligently.

Alfred M. Landon (1887–   ) is a former governor of Kansas and was the Republican presidential nominee in 1936. He remained an active participant in public affairs for a good many years, counseling political candidates, officeholders, and the general public, on a variety of issues. He had been acutely concerned over the course of American foreign policy under Franklin Roosevelt, and in a number of public statements Landon made clear his desire that Harry Truman pursue a tougher policy toward the Soviet Union. In the political environment of those years, Landon was a moderate and, more importantly, a plains state moderate with a reputation for straight talking. In the opinion of the editors of the Scripps-Howard newspapers, Landon reflected "the thinking and sturdy confidence of the solid Americanism at the nation's grass roots." The passages below, selected from his Wichita speech of March 19, 1947, reflect his midwestern, no-nonsense style. The most convenient source for the full text of this speech is the *Congressional Record* (80th Cong., 1st Sess., Vol. 93, Pt. 10, *Appendix*, pages 1109–11). Did Landon have any misgivings about Truman's speech? What convinced him of the necessity of a global effort to contain communist expansion? What judgments did he make about views like those held by Henry Wallace on the one hand and the *Fortnightly Commentary* editors on the other? Finally, how did his vision of America's mission in the world relate to the others you have read?

⊂≡ No-Nonsense Power Politics

ALFRED M. LANDON

The biggest lesson the American people have to learn in foreign affairs is the ultimate end of their commitments. It is time we recognize where internationalism of the "hallelujah" brand brings us.

We have created our present situation by acting weak and foolish instead of wise and strong in our foreign affairs. Our foreign policy in recent years has been a thing bent quickly to solve each momentary crisis or a political campaign at home. We need some plain, simple guideposts. . . .

We have been on the wrong track. We have been running away from reality by crying, "Let the United Nations do it." Not only is the United Nations only in its infancy, but our policy has been infantile. We lent Tito $650,000,000 to make the Balkans safe for communism; now we are loaning Turkey and Greece $400,000,000 to save the Balkans from communism. We sold our own ally, Poland, the first to fight Germany, into the hands of Stalin. Now we are desperately trying to stop what we helped start—the spread of Communism in Europe. Only gross inept handling of foreign affairs could have brought us into our present position, and that is exactly what we have had to date. It is the sad result of a decade of patty-cake foreign policy and now we have reached the point where the chips are down. It is now beyond partisanship; it is a matter of patriotism.

President Truman not only brought the issue out into the open. He recommended more—much more—than a mere financial or humanitarian policy. He did not make a bellicose speech. At the same time he was extending to Russia our hand through Secretary of State Marshall at Moscow—if she chooses to accept it. But he did throw down the gauntlet to the imperialist and aggressive policies of Russia.

The President announced that not only were we anti-Comintern—but that we proposed to do something about it. Here is what we are doing.

In effect, we are forming a western bloc with Britain, et al., in the Mediterranean to stop Soviet expansion.

Of course, it naturally follows that we will be forced to a similar course of forming an eastern bloc with China, Australia, etc., in the Orient.

Despite political or wishful protestation—it is the old balance-of-power game. And we might as well face an additional fact—it bypasses the United Nations. It is Marshallian militaristic realism versus one-worldian star gazing. In short, we are in European power politics up to our necks, and in it to stay—right out in the open.

I believe it is imperative that the American people should know what they are doing. Mr. Truman and Mr. Marshall should place their cards face up on the table at all times.

As I see it—we may be at this moment deciding for war with Russia —just as much as we decided for war with Germany, when lend-lease was passed.

People ought to understand that this decision is being made and, if they want, express themselves on the subject.

But listen, if we had asserted ourselves when Hitler went into Czechoslovakia or Japan into Manchuria, there would have been no Dunkerque or Pearl Harbor. . . .

Russia is already vigorously carrying on acts of aggression in Cuba, Mexico, Canada—in fact, all the countries of the Western Hemisphere, including the United States.

Furthermore, everywhere communism only rules as a minority dominating the majority by force. The conflict is not economic. It is more the age-old attempt of Asia to conquer Europe—of paganism against Christianity. . . .

The military dictatorship of Russia is not content to demonstrate in one country the workings of communism by the trial and error method. But has reverted to original Marxism and is undertaking to impose it on the whole world by force. . . .

President Truman's request for authority to block Russian aggression also means the end of the old give a yard and gain an inch—of our tragic comedy billed as the firm but friendly policy with Russia. . . .

The more we protest that the new Turko-Grecian policy is not pressure on Russia—the more we destroy its benefits to us and the world.

Only by frankly and boldly proving that we are through with concessions and that our purpose is to put a stop to Russian imperialism and expansion—can the loans accomplish the ends desired by the liberty loving democracies of the world. . . .

Now is the time to exert our strength—our determination to have peace—or fight if need be. There is no other nation, or combination of nations that can lick us, and the other democracies. This is not war talk; this is just common sense. I am simply trying to say that in strength and a sure knowledge of that strength is the only road to peace.

If Greece falls into the Soviet group so will Turkey, Iran, Egypt, Italy, and most of Europe. Unless we help China she, too, will eventually become a Russian satellite. But we have pulled out of China because of conditions that are duplicated in Greece. We should return.

Therefore the controlling factor of the Turko-Grecian loan is not only its over-all purpose—but how our other policies are to match this step. That is the crux of the whole matter.

We must make our moves in a way that will leave other democracies in no doubt as to our long-range policies. . . .

In all this we must not cease to recapture a sense of the principles for which America stands almost alone in the world today.

Under the new deal and the war to beat the Nazis we went half down the road to socialism. There is great danger that we could go even more totalitarian in our struggle with Russian aggression.

Unless we are on our guard we may not have anything left of our Republic to show for it after it is all over. . . .

In my judgment only by giving the President everything that he asks—and only by the President on his part developing a definite, strong, consistent, and intelligent foreign policy in place of a vacillating to the point of nonexisting foreign policy can we hope to achieve a secure and free life.

Chapter
19: The Southern Black Confronts the Northern City

⊂⊃ **JOSEPH T. TAYLOR**

In 1968, the Kerner Report [1] pointedly asserted that race relations had seriously worsened in the United States. In asserting that black people and white people have seriously and dangerously polarized along color lines, the report dramatized a startling outcome to the great increase in internal migration during the past half century.

In 1790, when the first census of the United States was taken, there were approximately four million people in the new nation. Of these, nearly eight hundred thousand, about 20 percent, were Negroes. During the next century, the abolition of legal slavery along with a marked increase in European immigration produced a steady proportionate decrease in the Negro population in the United States. There has been no marked change in the ratio of the Negro population to the total population since 1900. In 1900, nearly nine million Negroes constituted 12 percent of the total United States population. In 1966, the 21.5 million Negroes represented 11 percent of the total population of the United States, reflecting a net change of only 1 percent in nearly seventy years.

Negroes have never participated as equals in American life. At first they were indentured servants, then slaves. Even when the United States became a nation, its black population did not share in the guarantees provided the rest of the population by the Constitution. During the past half century, there have been slow but significant changes in the legal position of Negroes in the United States. These changes have been accompanied by improvements in their socio-economic position. Even so, these modifications have not been sufficient to insure an equal competitive opportunity for individual Negroes. Consequently, they have had reason to make continuous reassessment of their life chances wherever

[1] *Report of the National Advisory Commission on Civil Disorders* (New York, Bantam Books, Inc., 1968).

they happen to be located. This reassessment has resulted in significant changes in the distribution of the Negro population in the United States.

The proportion of the Negro population living in the South changed very little until the twentieth century. In 1790, 90 percent of all the black population in the United States lived in the South. In 1910, the figure was 91 percent of the 9.8 million blacks. World War I provided the impetus for the first sustained wave of internal migration by Negroes from the South to the North. The most intense movement was along routes leading to Chicago, Detroit, Philadelphia, and New York.

The war involved some nations from which large numbers of recent immigrants had come. Questions were raised by native-born Americans about the loyalty of newly arrived immigrants—most notably German-Americans—in a war involving their homelands. There were peculiarly vexing problems involving the loyalty of persons from the countries against which America and her allies fought. When the war ended, there were serious economic and social problems involved in making the transition from a wartime to a peacetime economy. One approach to these problems was the passage of more restrictive immigration laws. Fewer foreign persons were permitted to enter the country.

Several factors combined to make migration to northern cities attractive to Negroes of the South. Their living conditions were poor; wages were low. Recurring crop failures made their meager wages and sharecroppers' income more uncertain and less adequate. The southern agricultural system, under the influence of which most blacks lived, afforded little justice or equitable treatment for them. Negro newspapers, particularly the *Chicago Defender*, became highly vocal organs of protest. They pointed out the disadvantages and hopelessness of continuing to remain in the South. At the same time, they emphasized the advantages to be gained from moving North. This was done in dramatic and most attractive ways. In the decade 1910–1920 more than 500,000 blacks from the South moved to northern cities.

The movement of Negroes—mostly to the northern cities—has been steady for much of the past sixty years. In 1910, 91 percent of all Negroes in the United States were located in the South. By 1964, only about 54 percent of all Negroes in the United States lived in the South. During the same period, the number of Negroes living in the North had risen to 38 percent of the total Negro population in the United States. There has also been a dramatic increase in the concentration of Negroes in the western part of the United States—chiefly during the past thirty years. In 1940, only 1 percent of the Negro population was found in the West. By 1968, approximately 8 percent of the total Negro population lived in the West—on the Pacific Coast.

The rate of migration slowed considerably during the depression of the early 1920's. For a brief period there was even some reverse migration, as some blacks returned to their points of origin in the South. The rate of northward migration also slowed considerably during the depression of the 1930's; and it increased dramatically during the period immediately following World War II. Migration to the North and West continues.

Not only has there been increased migration to the cities of the North and West, but the direction of this migration within the target cities has been distinctive. Negroes, because of restrictive housing patterns, have been forced to concentrate in the least desirable sections of these cities. The areas are usually older and suffer greatly from obsolescence and neglect. Here most of the dwellings are outmoded and deteriorating. Here health and safety standards are least enforced. Here population density is highest; unemployment is consistently higher and family income is lowest.

To a degree, these undesirable features have characterized urban life for a series of migrants who preceded Negroes in the ghettos of northern cities. These earlier migrants found the ghetto more than a place where mass discrimination was practiced. It was also a place where people with common problems, aspirations, and life styles assisted one another, making group survival and growth against great odds possible. Such migrants, notably the Germans, Irish, Italians, Poles, and Jews, were all subjected to great inconvenience; and all suffered discrimination during the period that they spent in the ghettos of American cities.

The group solidarity and cohesion which these migrants sought and achieved helped to provide both motivation and opportunity for the individual growth and development of their members. Increasingly, members of these minority groups found ways of competing more effectively in American society. In growing numbers, these persons lost their identity as members of restricted minorities. For them, a measure of assimilation became both possible and desirable. For the black minority, the option of assimilation was not readily available. No other minority had such high visibility.

Blacks were restricted to the ghetto because they were identifiable. Life in the ghetto rather than a fortifying experience preparing blacks for full participation in the institutional life of American society has instead been a distinct liability. That is, the subcultures developed in the restrictive environment of the ghetto, while highly efficient for survival there, contained values and traditions that were undesirable when measured by the standards of the dominant society.

The concentration of Negroes in the least desirable parts of northern cities was not accidental. In numerous instances, the settlement options for these new migrants have been planned with some detail. Until relatively recently, this type of discriminatory planning could be achieved with official sanction. Segregated living has been preserved through practices and policies that have been highly effective. Discriminatory selling practices are illustrative of the devices used to restrict movement from the ghetto.

There is no easy scheme through which heavy concentrations of Negroes can be absorbed in the larger community. The barriers to freedom of movement by individual Negroes are based on racial identity. This identity cannot be changed as could the cultural patterns which differentiated the earlier migrant groups who preceded Negroes to the ghettos of our large cities. The argument was advanced that these earlier migrants were discriminated against because they behaved differently. Therefore, they could, if they desired, change their behavior and presumably eliminate the basis of discrimination. If the discrimination is based on innate characteristics, such as color, rather than acquired or learned characteristics, changing group behavior to eliminate the cause of discrimination is not a very effective option.

The concentration of countless black citizens in sprawling, rapidly changing cities constitutes a real crisis which threatens the economic and social health of entire cities. Problems of housing, health, education, unemployment, recreation, police protection—all are aggravated where large incoming populations must be absorbed and accommodated. In too many of these areas, little tangible progress is being made. This leads to increased frustration, disillusionment and impatience on the part of persons who migrated because of real or implicit promises that life for them would be better in the areas to which they migrated.

No serious comparison can be made between the progress made by Negro migrants and that made by the migrant groups which preceded them can be cited with optimism or satisfaction. Comparisons between the rate of progress of the average Negro with his non-Negro counterpart in terms of either personal or family achievement are discouraging.

In every significant category, black citizens in the urban setting are competing poorly with their white counterparts for the goods of life. A comparison of per capita income figures during the last decade is disturbing. While per capita income figures for Negroes have increased substantially, during this decade, the gap between incomes for Negro and white workers has widened. Moreover, Negro workers tend to be concentrated in jobs where skills are least required. Such jobs are most susceptible to automation and easy elimination. The Negro worker is thus more vulnerable to unemployment and all the consequences that attend it.

The work that one does and the benefits that he receives for this work have a telling effect on where he is able to live. The net result of the economic opportunities available to blacks when combined with other discriminatory practices insures that most blacks will be found in the least desirable residential areas of the cities in which they live. It is easy to predict that neighborhoods in such areas will assume that run-down appearance—one that endangers both the physical health and the social outlook of the residents of the area.

A residential area that is characterized by widespread physical deterioration and social disorganization can hardly be expected to develop and maintain highly attractive and efficient school facilities. This is doubtless due, in part, to the pervasiveness of neglect and apathy which one may expect to find in such a setting. It is also an indication of the powerlessness—economic, social, and political—of the residents of the area. Such an area scarcely receives the effective planning needed to provide opportunities for equal access to an education for all children of the city. Children attending schools in the ghetto generally do not perform on the same level as children who live in the midst of greater affluence. The attitudes, values, skills, and aspirations of these children are significantly affected by the different exposure that they have to the material goods of the urban environment in which they live.

In American society, if a group competes poorly in the three closely related areas of education, employment, and housing, it is caught in a vicious cycle. This is the plight of Negroes in some of our large urban areas. To break this cycle will require widespread institutional change. This change to be effective must be of such urgency and magnitude that it inevitably will create tension and unrest. Any plan designed to bring about meaningful social change must be so comprehensive that it infuses all of our major institutions with the impetus to entertain drastic but orderly change. Otherwise it will only increase unrest, tension, mistrust, and disillusionment among all segments of the population.

Our cities present an embarrassing contrast. We have a high level of national prosperity, but at the same time an uncomfortably large number of families live in abject poverty. There is a demonstrable inequity in the distribution of economic goods in the urban community. Policy changes are indicated at a time when there is increasing political participation by new and sometimes unsophisticated constituencies. The social problems of the inner city are becoming more numerous and critical at the very time that they must be borne by those persons least able to bear them. Financially able whites as they migrate to the suburbs are being replaced by blacks who are even less well equipped with the skills and resources to meet the complex challenges found in the inner city of the modern metropolis.

At this critical time in the development of urban America, migration to the city by black citizens to escape discrimination has produced disappointing results. It has given rise to an even more complex problem: how can we minimize the task of absorbing the nation's largest minority more completely into the life of the American city? To date we have had little success in achieving this goal. Makers of public policy have a real challenge to create means of dealing with the crisis facing black migrants to the city. For them the city has too often become a source of continued discrimination and disillusionment rather than an escape from the demeaning effects of unequal treatment based on race. Indeed, over the past half century, the experience of southern black migrants to the northern city must be viewed as movement from one frustration to another. This experience, in myriad forms, finds expression in the increasing racial tension, unrest, and polarization which characterize the social environment in which the American city dweller lives today.

The selections which are presented below relate to some specific problems that have persisted in the rural to urban migration. The first item consists of letters from would-be migrants to northern black benefactors. These letters stress the concerns, aspirations, and expectations of persons who yet remain in a hostile southern environment.

An excerpt from an article written during the height of the World War I migrations is included next. It deals with the tensions and conflict that resulted as a large and unwanted minority group sought to settle in a midwestern satellite city.

A portion of the introduction to a recent book is included next. It presents clearly the persisting image that the northern city is the promised land for the black from the rural South.

The next reading deals with conditions confronting migrants to northern cities fifty years after the first great wave of northern migration. It provides an opportunity to compare the factors leading to migration with the treatment accorded the migrants when they reached their target cities after a half century of social change in America. The next item outlines some of the high social costs which must be faced by most black migrants to the American city. Finally, details are presented which describe the process of transplanting a black migrant family from the deep South to a large midwestern metropolis. These selections taken together provide a background against which one can begin to view the efforts of black Americans to improve their status by migrating from the rural South to the urban North and West.

The following letters, written anonymously by black migrants to the editors of black newspapers, point up graphically both the pressures and restraints of their southern environment. They also suggest what the writers expect to find by migrating North. What kind of communications chain existed between the black man in the North and the black man in the South? What are the chief concerns of these letter writers as they contemplate migrating North? How do you account for the priorities expressed in these letters?

These letters were selected from a collection presented by Emmett J. Scott, long-time secretary to Booker T. Washington. Published shortly after World War I, "Letters of Negro Migrants of 1916–1918," are from *The Journal of Negro History*, Vol. IV (1919), pp. 291–94, 297–98, 308, 333–34. Copyright © by The Association for the Study of Negro Life and History, Inc.

⊂⊒ We Want to Come North
Letters of Black Migrants

HOUSTON, TEXAS, April 30, 1917

Dear Sir: wanted to leave the South and Go and Place where a man will be any thing Except a Ker I thought would write you for Advise as where would be a Good Place for a Comporedly young man That want to Better his Standing who has a very Promising young Family.

I am 30 years old and have Good Experience in Freight Handler and Can fill Position from Truck to Agt.

would like Chicago or Philadelphia But I dont Care where so long as I Go where a man is a man.

NEW ORLEANS, LA., April 23, 1917

Dear Sir: Reading a article in the 21st issue of the Chicago Defender about the trouble you had to obtain men for work out of Chicago and also seeing a advertisement for men in Detroit saying to apply to you I beg to state to you that if your could secure me a position in or around Chicago or any northern section with fairly good wages & good living conditions for myself and family I will gladly take same and if ther could be any ways of sending me transportation I will gladly let you or the firm you get me position with deduct transportation fee out of my salary. as I said before I will gladly take position in northern city or county where a mans a man here are a few positions which I am capable of holding down. Laborer, expirance porter, butler or driver of Ford car. Thaking you in advance for your kindness, beg to remain.

CEDAR GROVE, LA., April 23, 1917

Dear Sir: to day I was advise by the defendent offices in your city to communicate with you in regards to the labor for the colored of the south as I was lead to beleave that you was in position of firms of your city & your near by surrounding towns of Chicago. Please state me how is the times in & around Chicago place to locate having a family dependent on me for support. I am informed by the Chicago Defender a very valuable paper which has for its purpose the Uplifting of my race, and of which I am a constant reader and real lover, that you were in position to show some light to one in my condition.

Seeking a Northern Home. If this is true Kindly inform me by next mail the next best thing to do Being a poor man with a family to care for, I am not coming to live on flowry Beds of ease for I am a man who works and wish to make the best I can out of life I do not wish to come there hoodwinked now knowing where to go or what to do so I Solicite your help in this matter and thanking you in advance for what advice you may be pleased to Give I am yours for success.

P.S. I am presently imployed in the I C RR. Mail Department at Union Station this city.

SAVANNAH, GA., April 24, 1917.

Sir: I saw an advertisement in the Chicago Ledger where you would send tickets to any one desireing to come up there. I am a married man with a wife only, and I am 38 years of age, and both of us have so far splendid health, and would like very much to come out there provided we could get good employment regarding the advertisement.

FULLERTON, LA., April 28, 1917

Dear sir: I was reading about you was neading labor ninety miles of Chicago what is the name of the place and what R R extends ther i wants to come north and i wants a stedy employment ther what doe you pay per day i dont no anything about molding works but have been working around machinery for 10 years. Let me no what doe you pay for such work and can you give me a job of that kind or a job at common labor and let me no your prices and how many hours for a day.

MARCEL, MISS., October 4, 1917

Dear Sir: Although I am a stranger to you but I am a man of the so called colored race and can give you the very best or reference as to my character and ability by prominent citizens of my community by both white and colored people that knows me although am native of Ohio whiles

I am a northern desent were reared in this state of Mississippi. Now I am a reader of your paper the Chicago Defender. After reading your writing every wek I am compell & persuade to say that I know you are a real man of my color you have I know heard of the south land & I need not tell you any thing about it. I am going to ask you a favor and at the same time beg you for your kind and best advice. I wants to come to Chicago to live. I am a man of a family wife and 1 child I can do just any kind of work in the line of common labor & I have for the present sufficient means to support us till I can obtain a position. Now should I come to your town, would you please to assist me in getting a position I am willing to pay whatever you charge I dont want you to loan me not 1 cent but *help* me to find an occupation there in your town now I has a present position that will keep me employed till the first of Dec. 1917. now please give me your best advice on this subject. I enclose stamp for reply.

The black migrant going North not only was not always welcomed, he was, on more than one occasion, met with open hostility. The following commentary suggests how whites reacted to the arrival of blacks in East St. Louis, Illinois. Why did whites resent the black migrant's presence in the city? What do you think of the reactions of southern spokesmen to the riot in East St. Louis? In retrospect, does it seem that they were sincere in their inducements to have black migrants return to the South? This commentary is extracted from "The Illinois Race War and Its Brutal Aftermath," *Current Opinion*, August, 1917, pp. 75–77. Copyright, Time, Inc.

⊂⊱ The Illinois Race War and Its Brutal Aftermath

CURRENT OPINION

East St. Louis (1917).

It is not without a certain irony that, at the very moment when this country is entering the war to "make the world safe for democracy," a race riot of unexampled brutality should take place in East St. Louis, Illinois. On the two days preceding July 4, the Negroes of that city were anything but "safe." There had been trouble last May, but it was insignificant as compared with the July riots. Forty or fifty of the Colored people were killed; nearly a hundred were taken to hospitals; more than three hundred houses in the Negro quarter were burned to the ground. Thousands of militiamen were summoned to the scene and at last succeeded in quieting the tumult.

How East St. Louis Was Turned into a Shambles

No two writers agree entirely in their accounts of the beginning of the massacre. Henry M. Hyde, a correspondent of the *Chicago Tribune*, says that on the evening of Sunday, July 1, a Ford automobile, occupied by four men, was driven rapidly through the Negro districts of the city. The four men yelled, cursed and fired revolvers right and left. Some of the shots are said to have entered adjacent buildings, one of them a church, whose bell was rung later. At the ringing of the bell—evidently a preconcerted signal—two hundred armed Negroes assembled and, marching two abreast, started downtown. They were met by a police automobile, also a Ford car and also containing four men, who proved to be police officers in plain clothes. The officers started to explain, but the Negroes refused to listen, and when the car turned fired a volley at the fleeing officers. One of them was instantly killed, another died later. Then hell broke loose. For the greater part of thirty-six hours, Negroes were hunted through the streets like wild animals. A black skin became a death warrant. Man after man, with hands upraised, pleading for his life, was surrounded by groups of men who had never seen him before and who knew nothing about him except that he was Black, and stoned to death. A Negro girl, seeking safety from a band of White men, was attacked by White women, and despite her pleas for mercy had her face smashed by a club wielded by one of the White women. An aged Negro, tottering from a weakness, was seized and hanged to a pole. Three million dollars' worth of property was destroyed. State guardsmen were called out but did nothing. The police seemed helpless or acquiescent. A number of arrests were made, but hardly any one was held. "I have heard of St. Bartholomew's Night," writes Carlos F. Hurd, in the *St. Louis Post-Dispatch*, "I have heard stories of the latter-day crimes of the Turks in Armenia, and I have learned to loath the German army for its barbarity in Belgium. But I do not believe that Moslem fanaticism or Prussian frightfulness could perpetrate murders of more deliberate brutality than those which I saw committed, in daylight, by citizens of the State of Abraham Lincoln."

Invasion of Negro Labor as a Cause of the Rioting

The cause of the riot in East St. Louis is found by most commentators in the sudden influx of Negroes from the South and in the economic rivalries engendered. Race hatred has doubtless played its part, but the "scab" Negro, coming north to take the place of a White laborer on strike, is held to have been the chief factor in recent disturbances. The low immigration from Europe since the beginning of the war has helped to create an abnormal situation. East St. Louis is a great railroad and manufacturing center, with coal mines near at hand. Employers have been glad to avail themselves of Negro labor. Ray Stannard Baker writes in *The World's Work* of this shifting of Negro labor:

The earlier manifestations of the movement were more or less sporadic, due largely to the activities of northern labor agents, especially those representing railroad companies. Trains were backed into several southern cities and hundreds of Negroes were gathered up in a day, loaded into the cars, and whirled away to the North. I was told of instances in which Negro teamsters left their horses standing in the streets, or deserted their jobs and went to the trains without notifying their employers or even going home. But this spring the movement has become more or less organized, and, while not so spectacular, is probably more widespread.

Mr. Baker tells us further that great manufacturing and railroad corporations in the North have regular agents to direct the importations of Negro laborers, and that members of the Negro colonies already established in Pennsylvania, New York and southern New England, are drawing strongly from their compatriots in the South. In certain parts of Georgia and Alabama, especially where the larger tenant farming is still practiced, whole neighborhoods have been depleted of Black men of the best working ages, and often entire families have moved. Between 75,000 and 100,000 have settled in Pennsylvania alone, a large number being employed by the Pennsylvania and Erie Railroads, and still larger numbers by the steel mills, the munition plants and other manufacturing establishments. Mr. Baker calculates that, in all, 400,000 Negroes have gone north during the last eighteen months.

Plans for Preventing Race Riots in the Future

Federal, state and municipal investigations have all been undertaken to determine where the responsibility for the recent outbreak in East St. Louis belongs. Senator Sherman, in urging the necessity of congressional action, has declared his conviction that "there is as much influence in securing acquittal of guilty men in Illinois as there ever was in Georgia." The Senator stated on the floor of the Senate that the part played by liquor in the course of the trouble had made him from henceforth a "bone-dry Prohibitionist." *The New York Sun* indicts the East St. Louis city administration, and recalls the fact that its own officials have openly admitted that the law is not enforced. Other papers urge the necessity of establishing in Illinois a state constabulary of the kind now existing in Pennsylvania. But these and similar suggestions deal with symptoms rather than causes. Many of the southern papers take the view that the only real solution of present difficulties is for the Negroes to return to the South. There is a widespread disposition in the South to offer Negroes inducements to return. *The Nashville Tennessean* acknowledges a moral obligation to "protect and care for a race which we alone seem to understand"; and the *Jacksonville Times-Union* remarks:

The Negroes of the South may see in this East St. Louis affair just what will happen all over the North when there is no longer enough work for all and White men want their jobs. Where are they safest—in a section where a certain offense insures their summary death and good behavior assures them safety, or in a section that in time of passion gives them no assurance of safety at all, and where their color will mark them for assault?

The *Galveston Daily News* is convinced that the true and fundamental solution of this grave problem lies as a matter of duty and policy with the South. It says:

The South is the Negro's natural habitat, and the South has an economic need of him. The interests of the South and of the Negro are complementary in the truest sense. A policy of justice is likewise the policy of expedience. The Negro labor, which the South indispensably needs for its own economic well-being, can be retained if the South will, in its treatment of the Negro, conform its practices to the chivalrous precepts with which it decorates itself. When the Negro goes north, he is moved more by the repulsion of the conditions that beset him in the South than by the attraction of those that invite him to the North. His natural preference is to live in the South, but that preference is not so strong that it cannot be nullified by the injustices which are done him too frequently in the South. The Negroes of the South are not seeking social equality. They do, however, crave a larger opportunity for educational, economic, and social progress than they enjoy, and it is the denial of this which makes so many of them yield to the lure of the North. The South has only to reform its own habits of conduct toward the Negro to keep him contented, and, by doing that, preclude a repetition of the exhibition of savagery which the country has been called on to witness at East St. Louis.

In the foreword to his autobiography, Claude Brown makes a current assessment of the black migrant's status in New York (Harlem) a generation after his exodus from the South. As Brown sees it, what were the conditions the black migrant sought to escape? What conditions did he find in the North? Why is the persisting disillusionment of the migrant of significance in understanding the problems of urban America?

This foreword is reprinted by permission of the publisher from Claude Brown's *Manchild in the Promised Land* (New York: Macmillan, 1965).

⊂⋑ Are Times Any Better?

CLAUDE BROWN

I want to talk about the first Northern urban generation of Negroes. I want to talk about the experiences of a misplaced generation, of a misplaced people in an extremely complex, confused society. This is a story of their searching, their dreams, their sorrows, their small and futile rebellions, and their endless battle to establish their own place in America's greatest metropolis—and in America itself.

The characters are sons and daughters of former Southern sharecroppers. These were the poorest people of the South, who poured into New York City during the decade following the Great Depression. These migrants were told that unlimited opportunities for prosperity existed in New York and that there was no "color problems" there. They were told that Negroes lived in houses with bathrooms, electricity, running water, and indoor toilets. To them, this was the "promised land" that Mammy had been singing about in the cotton fields for many years.

Going to New York was good-bye to the cotton fields, good-bye to "Massa Charlie," good-bye to the chain gang, and, most of all, good-bye to those sunup-to-sundown working hours. One no longer had to wait to get to heaven to lay his burden down; burdens could be laid down in New York.

So, they came, from all parts of the South, like all the black chillun o' God following the sound of Gabriel's horn on that long-overdue Judgment Day. The Georgians came as soon as they were able to pick train fare off the peach trees. They came from South Carolina where the cotton stalks were bare. The North Carolinians came with tobacco tar beneath their fingernails.

They felt as the Pilgrims must have felt when they were coming to

450

America. But these descendants of Ham must have been twice as happy as the Pilgrims, because they had been catching twice the hell. Even while planning the trip, they sang spirituals as "Jesus Take My Hand" and "I'm On My Way" and chanted, "Hallelujah, I'm on my way to the promised land!"

It seems that Cousin Willie, in his lying haste, had neglected to tell the folks down home about one of the most important aspects of the promised land: it was a slum ghetto. There was a tremendous difference in the way life was lived up North. There were too many people full of hate and bitterness crowded into a dirty, stinky, uncared-for closet-size section of a great city.

Before the soreness of the cotton fields had left Mama's back, her knees were getting sore from scrubbing "Goldberg's floor." Nevertheless, she was better off; she had gone from the fire into the frying pan.

The children of these disillusioned colored pioneers inherited the total lot of their parents—the disappointments, the anger. To add to their misery, they had little hope of deliverance. For where does one run to when he's already in the promised land?

The material following is taken from an article by Dr. Robert Coles, an outstanding research psychiatrist. During the past decade, Dr. Coles has been an active participant-observer in interracial activity in the United States. This experience includes in-depth studies with black children in the deep South as well as the northern city.

This article provides an opportunity to compare the reception given the Negro migrant today with the reception he received half a century ago. What evidence is there of a generation gap between the attitudes of young black migrants and the attitudes of their parents? How helpful are these materials in understanding current race tensions in our cities? The complete article is available: Robert Coles, "The Southern Negro Moves North," *The New York Times Magazine*, September 17, 1967, Sec. 6, p. 25. "© 1967 by The New York Times Company. Reprinted by permission."

⊂⊋   Going North Today

ROBERT COLES

Since this century began, and particularly in the last three decades, millions of Negroes have abandoned the rural South to go North. Voteless, only recently declared "free," incredibly poor and heavily illiterate, they were nevertheless hopeful enough to risk a long trip into strange and not always friendly territory.

Had Northern cities received hundreds of thousands of immigrants from Europe in the past few decades no doubt all sorts of emergency provisions would have been made to help settle the newcomers, make them welcome, provide food, clothing and shelter for them, and enable them to find work. Southern Negroes obtained no such courtesy, and what recognition they did get was calculated to remind them that white Americans may fight among themselves but in the clutch know how to stand together as a race. Called "in-migrants" rather than immigrants, the newcomers were quickly made to know their "place."

Still, for a few years it had all seemed clear-cut: America was divided into the oppressive South and the promising North, a "land of freedom," or a place "up there where it's better," as I've heard rural Negroes from the Mississippi Delta put it. When the civil-rights struggle of the early nineteen-sixties came along, that seemed to offer even more hope. Whites flocked South to help change things faster, and in 1964 I heard this from a Negro in Alabama:

"I wish I had left here a long time ago. When my brother went up to Chicago I told him he was a fool for going there, because it's the

452

same all over, a little better here or there, but not really, only the frills. Now, I figure I was wrong. These whites keep coming down here, and I guess they must like us; and if they do, then it must better up there, where they live all the time."

He never did leave Alabama; and now he has little reason to envy his brother up North, though he lets you know how mean and hard life is for him. Recently he told me: "We went up there, a lot of us colored people like my brother and his family, and it was the way I first said it was, it was a hoax if you ask me. It's as if you've been cheated—you know, led down the wrong road.

"Now my brother says I'm the one who is lucky. I live poorer down here, but up there they don't live at all. They have more money than we can get down here, but they're packed tight into the buildings and they can't do anything, not even dream of going North, the way I do when it gets rough. It's bad, real bad; and they hate it."

Apparently they do—hate and resent the Northern sanctuary that has turned out to be little more than a new and different kind of hell. In June of this year, as riots broke out yet again in one Northern city after another, an interesting and carefully done report from Brandeis University's new Center for the Study of Violence offered evidence that "a high proportion of Southern-born Negroes living in the ghetto increases the possibility that a city will have a riot"—particularly when they feel themselves aggrieved, insulted, put upon and in general reminded of the "old days." My own work with individual families in a Boston ghetto confirms that finding almost daily—to the point that at times I have wondered not why we have riots regularly each summer but how so much anger and frustration manages to stay under reasonable control most of the time, week after week.

One family I have come to know rather well after three years of visiting can be called the Carrolls. They now live in the very center of a Boston slum, in a building that has been condemned again and again for its rats, its faulty plumbing and heating systems, its poorly lighted halls, its garbage-strewn yard that takes up the slack when two—exactly two!—cans become filled with the refuse of ten families. The Carrolls have lived in that building for five years now, ever since they came North from Marengo County, Alabama.

Why did they leave? What has happened to them since they came to Boston? Why did two young men in the family take part in a serious riot that took place in Boston early this summer? I ask these questions not to "answer" them with all sorts of sociological and psychiatric "explanations" and "conclusions," eagerly awaited by a public that wants things simplified and generalized. The obvious "answers" are that the Carrolls left to improve their lot; they eventually became disenchanted in Boston because they remained poor, still put down and looked down upon by the white man; and they rioted because they are sick and tired of losing, of wanting, of traveling, of searching, or being pushed aside and scorned.

All that is true, yet the whole truth is more complicated and I fear both more ambiguous and more horrible. . . . [Note Mrs. Carroll's concern for her children:]

"The kids would never go back even if I wanted to, which I don't really, I guess. The little ones are already used to it here, and the big ones, they'd be killed down there for the way they talk. The way things are going, they may even get killed up here, I'll tell you. At night, when I have a little time to clean things up I hear them talk to one another in bed, and believe me it's terrible what they pick up on the street. Up here the colored man lets it all out of his system, that's what I believe. They been beating on him and they'd come and tell me all the stories, and then they stopped. That's when I knew they were *really* changed—it was all second nature, and they were all just part of the scenery down there, I guess. So when the riot came, they joined like everyone else."

Her sons don't quite put it as she does. The oldest youth speaks bluntly and sarcastically. He asks me as many questions as he answers; "Why do *you* think we riot? Don't you know? You must by now, or you're pretty slow. We've had enough. They push you so far, then you can't let it go further. That's it. In Alabama they keep us down with guns. Here they say we're 'free.' But if we try to act free, then they pull their guns, anyway."

I knew him well enough to risk asking him what he meant by "acting free." Well, he meant acting like "whitey." "Look. You're upset by something, so you go raise your voice and get it stopped. We're told we can't. That's what they taught us in Marengo County; be quiet, obey the 'bossman,' and wait until heaven for your kicks. Here they teach you in school about that 'equality' stuff, and Washington and Lincoln and how they freed us, and everyone is the same—American. Then you look around and you see what a lot of lousy lies they peddle to you.

"In the South you couldn't look around much, or they'd take care of you for life—I mean they'd kill you. Well, up here they say they're not going to kill us. Maybe they should. If they killed us, everyone of us, they wouldn't have their trouble any more. But if they don't kill us, we're human, we're men, and we'll catch them in their lies, and it's only natural we'll try to get ours. That's what you're supposed to do in America, isn't it—get yours?"

That is that. I hear it again and again from him when I stupidly try to ask—once again—what angers him, and how he became involved in the rampant violence that destroyed so much of his own neighborhood: "First of all, it's not *our* place. We came here, and they soak us for rent. Whitey owns the place. It's *his* place. And besides, we're trying to get ours, like you have yours. We hear a fight, and man, we rush to the scene. We figure, this is our chance to do something. Sometimes I see the cops go by, and I wish I was them, I wouldn't mind the uniform and the car with the siren and all that. But I know the cops are here to keep their eyes on us, and they won't do a thing for us but shoot us."

Like his younger brother, he can identify for a moment with the police, the armed white man, the only white man he really knows today. I've even heard him echo his parents' sentiments—"maybe it's better down South." But he knows it "really" isn't better in Alabama, and he knows he can never be a white policeman or, in view of his "educational background," a Negro one.

When I ask him what he'd like to be and do, I hear this: "Maybe a pilot, or a president of something, or an official of some kind. But no kidding, something even half good, even half good; something that I could hold in my hands and know it'll stay there, like anyone else's job."

A seasoned black observer of the urban scene, Sterling Tucker, an executive of the National Urban League, describes in eloquent detail some of the problems confronting residents of the black ghetto today. How do some of the practices described give credence to the claim that ghetto residents are exploited? How does the operation of pawnshops, as described, affect respect for the law? How do you assess the role generally ascribed to the police by residents of the Black ghetto? How are these attitudes related to the generalized unrest in the ghetto? The excerpts presented here are taken from Sterling Tucker, *Beyond the Burning: Life and Death of the Ghetto* (New York: Association Press, 1968), pp. 28–33, by permission of the publisher.

⊂⊇ Social Costs of Ghetto Living

STERLING TUCKER

A TAX ON BEING BLACK

The shabby ghetto homes and the schools that teach despair have their parallels in other areas of ghetto life. Indeed, ghetto dwellers see only decay unless they venture forth outside the walls. *Decaying* or *inadequate* describes accurately everything from the barroom to the schoolroom, the alley to the park. *Decadent* describes accurately the absence of all that is cultural, the presence—the overabundance—of things that corrupt, the bar, the junkie, the pimp, the runner, the pawn shop, the fortune teller.

The ghetto store is one monument to graying mediocrity, uncaring neglect. Aisles are narrow, lighting is low-keyed, walls remain unpainted, attractive displays seem a contradiction in terms. Floors that aren't yellow from years of encrusted wax are gray from ground-in dirt. Merchandise is rarely encased; it is more often strewn about on worn tables, no pattern to the disorder. To establish a pattern would take time, and time costs money.

The ghetto store owner knows he need use little, if any, of his profit for improvements. He knows the ghetto is captive market and learned early that business will prosper without the frills. So, the ghetto store is one more reminder to the ghetto dweller that he isn't worth much anyway, not even the cost of a few amenities. His kind are not entitled to a few of the niceties of life, not even from the man whose profit they insure. . . .

People who live in the ghetto are also forced to pay more for less. . . .

THE GHETTO TODAY

A supermarket chain in the riot area of Watts was found to charge an average of 3 per cent more than a Beverly Hills store in the same chain. A recent study by the Federal Trade Commission charged that a special brand of inflation plagues the Washington, D.C., ghetto resident. A portable television set selling in any department store for $129.95 would cost $249.95 in the "low-income market" store. In Hough, prices go up on the tenth day of every month—Mother's Day, the day the Aid-to-Dependent-Children checks are received.

When the sharp cost of ghetto credit is added to the cost of goods that is already out of line, the final price tag can be staggering, often twice the retail price of the item. Those who make half as much are thus expected to pay a 200 per cent mark-up. In East Harlem, most stores maintain a "multi-price policy." The price of an individual item is determined by the shopkeeper's assessment of the shopper: Is he a poor risk? Is he naive? Was he referred here by another merchant who must be paid a commission?

One Saturday a reporter and I worked out a scheme whereby I would get some firsthand information about ghetto store practices and his newspaper would print an article on the experience. I put on some old clothes and walked in and out of Washington's Seventh Street stores, stores known for shoddy goods and sharp prices. Before entering a store, I looked at the merchandise in the window and in three instances hungry shopkeepers all but dragged me inside. The first thing I was asked was whether I worked for the Federal Government. At first, I assumed the shopkeepers wanted Federal employees as customers because they were good credit risks, but I later realized that they wanted nothing to do with government workers because government wages couldn't be garnished. And they didn't want customers who were good credit risks. They wanted people who weren't, people who would buy far more than they could afford.

I discovered another sharp practice which such merchants openly engage in. They sell a customer an item—a refrigerator, for instance. When payment on the refrigerator is almost completed, they encourage the same person to purchase a diningroom table and near the end of that payment, convince him to buy a couch and so on. All purchases overlap. If at any time the customer defaults on a payment, a truck backs up to his door, a driver shoves some fine print in front of his face and takes back *all* of the merchandise, despite the fact that the first two or three or four items had been paid for many times over in terms of dollars.

Profit-seeking in its most malevolent form takes place in a well-known ghetto institution, the pawn shop. The enterprise can prosper only as its clients despair. Its business improves as the plight of its customers worsens. The pawn shop dealer encourages theft, for he will buy hot merchandise, no questions asked, and thus rewards the robber. Yet, caged-in pawn shops dot all ghettos, the compelling testimony of a plagued population. Pawn shops exist because there is a need for them. And there is a need for them in the ghetto, not because of the people who live there, but because of the set of circumstances faced by and imposed upon the people who live there. Pawn shops are a last resort, and they thrive in the ghetto precisely because people are so desperate that they will try anything—even a last resort.

The numbers racket is popular for similar reasons. People who don't have anything want to get something for nothing. The only way to beat the system is to turn two cents into five dollars, fifty cents into a thousand dollars. The few cents can't buy anything anyway, and operating within the system is possible for others, not for them.

The ghetto dweller is further victimized by the very services which the city should provide to serve and protect him. The police departments, for one. In some major cities, a larger percentage of the police force operates in the ghetto than in other areas of the community. Yet the presence of the police does not represent police protection, as any ghetto dweller is quick to point out. When I lived in Canton, Ohio, a lady ran into the Urban League Office one day and excitedly asked me to call the police because there was a disturbance in the neighborhood. I called, and while reporting the details, the voice at the other end boomed: "Those are just niggers down there. They're always fighting!" With that he hung up. . . .

Anti-black feelings are strong in most police departments. According to the Reiss report, a study made for the National Crime Committee, 75 per cent of the white policemen who work in the predominantly black areas of Washington, Chicago, and Boston have "markedly prejudiced" attitudes toward Negroes. Only 1 per cent expressed attitudes sympathetic toward them. Data from the same study suggest that in a city like Washington, D.C., with close to three thousand policemen, there are thousands of cases of physical abuse to Negroes every year and tens of thousands of cases of verbal abuse.

Consequently, many ghetto youths are saying more and more that they don't want police protection any longer. They want protection from the police. Ghetto residents are tired of being looted en route to police stations. They have been manhandled enough. Their cries for help have too long gone unheeded. The white cop is their enemy and they mean to run him out of their land. As a thirty-three-year-old Harlem resident put it:

The white cops, they have a damn sadistic nature. They are really a sadistic type of people and we, I mean me, myself, we don't need them here in Harlem. They don't do the neighborhood any good. . . . They start more violence than any other people start. They start violence, that's right.

Yet many a policeman thinks he is accepted in the ghetto. He mistakes surface politeness for sincere concern and trust and fails to see the real emotions his uniform and his manners evoke. I sometimes ride with the police late at night in an attempt to see the problems they face and the way they handle them. One night I rode with a precinct captain and one of Washington's ex-commissioners. We stopped at a crowded fish-fry place and as we walked to the counter, the captain stopped at a few tables, fingering the shoulders of some of the customers, patting others on the back. He had enough smiles for all. "Hi, Mary; hello, Sue; how ya' doing, John? Don't choke on the fish!" Later we barged into a few area houses for no apparent reason, and watched the captain walk in and out of rooms. Residents had no advance warning of the "search"; the captain said he was just checking his beat. Yet no residents dared try to stop the investigation; most just hid their outrage and indignation and forced a smile when the captain called them by their first names.

When I later pointed out to the officer the ill will he creates everywhere by his condescension and by invading the privacy of others, he looked astounded. He saw no reason why routine checks should bother the poor, why his attempts at pleasantries were offensive. . . . How insensitive he was to the people, "his" people. How unprepared he was for ghetto service.

Emergency situations often turn into disasters because of the poor service offered the ghetto. Fire departments are often blamed for answering too late when Harlem or Watts or Hough calls. Firemen are often assailed for providing inadequate ambulance service. Hospitals are frequently too many miles away to make access easy. Watts, for example, is not only without any public hospital, but there is no such facility within ten miles of the area. The ride from Watts to the County General Hospital on public transportation takes approximately two hours.

In Chicago in 1960, there were about 500 beds available to blacks in private hospitals, while the city had a black population of 900,000. There was a half a bed for every thousand blacks, four and a half beds for every thousand whites.

Sanitation departments are notorious for the poor service they provide to areas which are most congested and are, therefore, in need of the greatest service. In Washington, D.C., a youth organization called Pride, Inc., was established to do the job the Sanitation Department left undone. For four weeks in the summer of 1967, 1,080 youths were put to work full-time and 980 youths continued to work throughout the year to clean up the refuse and the rats the Sanitation Department neglected.

Ghetto areas don't get their share of recreational and cultural facilities either. There are no movies in Watts. In Harlem, there is no art gallery, no museum. In 1964, parks and playgrounds constituted only 10 per cent of Harlem's acreage as compared with 16 per cent of all New York City. . . . To make matters worse, blacks are not welcome outside the ghetto, even in public places, and transportation departments often see to it that they don't venture forth.

Space is usually available in the ghetto for that enterprise which is debilitating. Bars are everywhere. There are liquor stores by the hundreds. Fortunetellers' doors are open, offering mystical charm, magical flights. The ghetto dweller needs these dens, for they offer an escape from all that is troublesome—indeed, from life itself. The white invader, too, needs these places for his occasional flights into oblivion and lust. Yet, the black man has to pay the price. It is his family which must daily be exposed to the sordidness lining the streets. . . .

The ghetto resident knows that his life is doomed. His future will resemble the present just as the present is a copy of the past. He can no longer hope. At best he can endure.

Can there be any doubt that two worlds presently exist in America? They are separated, if not by actual walls, then by forces which achieve the same result. In one world, white men move with freedom; in the other, blacks are serving time.

This selection by Ben Bagdikian allows the reader to witness the process by which one black family moves from the rural South to the urban North. Why did Alice Perkins send for her husband and children? What advantages did the Perkins family expect to gain by moving to Chicago? Would your aspirations be different? Did all members of this family improve their "life chances" by moving to Chicago? Is the author justified in using the title "The Black Immigrants"?

These excerpts are from Ben Bagdikian, "The Black Immigrants," *The Saturday Evening Post*, July 15, 1967.

☞ From Here to Chicago—Step by Step

Ben Bagdikian

Alice Perkins took that other mode of the Underground Railroad—the bus. On a Wednesday before the Christmas holidays, Harry Perkins got a letter from Alice in Chicago. He had to quit school in the fifth grade and can't read (Alice went through ninth grade), so he paid a neighbor 50 cents to drive him the two miles to his mother-in-law's house where she read the letter. Tickets for him and the two older children were inside. The next day the children turned in their school books. Saturday morning Harry went to work as usual. That night he got his week's pay, $36 minus $10 taken out toward his debts. By now it was dark. He walked home, pulled out a footlocker he had quietly bought in Clarksdale for $7.95 two weeks ago, put in two bedspreads, one quilt, two sheets, three pairs of pants, two shirts and three hats for the children. He paid the neighbor 50 cents again to drive him and the children to his mother-in-law's, where her son drove them to the 9:30 night bus from Clarksdale.

The children had never been to Clarksdale (population, 21,000), and when they saw it Harry Jr., 6, said "Daddy, is this Chicago?"

On the bus was a man named Willie, brother of a friend, returning after a visit. Willie lived in Chicago and worked in a barrel factory where he thought there was an opening. Three days later Harry Perkins was stacking steel rings for $1.55 an hour, and three days after that he was running an automatic welder. He now makes $2.00 an hour with six or seven hours' overtime for about $100 a week.

Harry Perkins is a boyish, handsome, open-faced man who can't read but knows letters and remembers street signs and bus routes. At Christmas time he used the holiday tape to make letters on the wall over the double bed where he and his wife and their new infant sleep: ALICE.

Both of them insist on an unrelieved list of advantages Chicago has over their old life: Now they eat together at the same table because they have enough dinner plates; they have milk and fresh fruits and meats they never ate before; instead of a cold-water tub and washboard she gets the week's laundry delivered for $9; the school doctor and dentist examine their children regularly; instead of paying a neighbor $1 to take them shopping she can walk to a local market or take the rapid transit for 30 cents downtown; there the children often stayed out of school for lack of clothes but never here; down there Christmas meant at best a piece of simple clothing for each child, but here they have turkey and fur-lined jackets and guitars for the children.

"Look," Harry Perkins said as he sat in his tiny blue-and-pink kitchen, "for the first time in my life I own an innerspring mattress, three of them, a gas oven, a dinette, a TV, a stereo set. They treat me like a grown man. Down there the police killed colored men, two I knew just in the last couple of years we were there."

Alice Perkins shook her head slowly. "There ain't nothing I miss down there."

He nodded, "That goes for me."

Did that mean they would be happy to continue just as they are?

Alice Perkins looked surprised and said, "No, of course not."

And then she and her husband began a new recital that told the story of why families who move hopefully into the big cities then turn bitter and apathetic. Compared to the desperate poverty and endemic violence of the rural South, the city is obviously better in pay, in food, in material goods. But as the years go by, it becomes plain that the city makes demands the family never before had to meet: more education to get ahead, better clothes to enter the better world, participation in the vague and remote territory outside the ghetto in order to succeed. Food and a tight roof are no longer the focus of life. Simple survival is no longer enough; they must meet the requirements of highspeed urban life. Typically, the families enter eager and striving and then in three or four years get stalled. The Perkinses were still ambitious.

Now, the children want a bicycle, a piano, some new clothes like the ones they see on TV in *American Bandstand*. Harry Perkins would like to get a car. Mrs. Perkins has fallen in love with sectional couches. But she then described what they want more than anything else. With her husband's solemn nod of approval, she said softly, "A better house with no rats, in a better neighborhood, you know, some space for the kids to play in their own yard, with some grass in the back and in the front."

A nice house in a nice neighborhood is the conventional American family dream, but it has a special meaning in the ghetto, where most families are enclosed in a triple prison. The first is their own home.

Slum-tenement doors are locked. The knock is answered, if at all, by a voice, "Who's there? What you want?" Unless the voice is familiar and the message safe, that may be the last communication from the other side. Young children are forbidden to go out alone, and hundreds of thousands of them spend all their time, except for a few hours a week, locked inside their rooms often with the harshest discipline to quell their restlessness. Only when they go to school is there freedom. When the three Perkins schoolchildren go, they run like rabbits released from cages. The fear is real, for outside there is the second prison: the neighborhood.

The range of movement of most slum dwellers is measured in yards and, at most, a few blocks. The density is enormous, the possibilities for play and relaxation almost nil. A 50-by-100-foot playground operated by the Marillac settlement house near the Perkinses' flat is the only one available to 4,000 children. One result of this merciless compaction is the teen-age gang, which follows a territorial imperative that includes murder of teen-agers who intrude from other neighborhoods. For all of them are trapped in the larger prison, the ghetto itself.

In Chicago the ghetto is divided in two territories, the West Side, with more than 300,000 Negroes, and the South Side, with more than 600,000. Each is a vast black island surrounded by whites. In 1950 there were only 500,000 Negroes in the city, in about five smaller islands interspersed among white neighborhoods. But now the spaces between the islands have been abandoned by whites who moved to the suburbs. So now the West Side is almost 9 square miles of black territory, the South Side, 30 square miles. On the South Side there remain a few white belligerent, and some middle- and even upper-income blocks. But the mass is black and poor, the former rows of white homes partitioned and bringing in as much as 200 per cent of their old rents. In 1950 it was possible in any given ghetto to walk five blocks to a white neighborhood; now on the South Side a man can walk ten miles almost in a straight line, and never pass a home occupied by whites.

Inside the ghetto the schools are wretched, the unemployment rate three times the outside rate, the municipal services minimal, the landscape demoralizing. The uneducated parents get stalled in their climb up the work ladder, trapped in their ghetto. They produce new generations of the defeated.

So Alice Perkins, her large brown eyes longing, says, "I want a house of my own. Out in the suburbs. Like Maywood. A friend of mine drove me out there once and, oh, I want to move to a place like Maywood."

Maywood is about nine miles out on the expressway that goes by the Perkinses' flat, an "industrial suburb" in the metropolitan sprawl. It has its own character, a pleasant place of 27,000 working-class people with small one-family houses with small lawns front and back, children on swings in the yard or skipping rope on the side walks. There are 5,000

Negroes in Maywood, and they average $1,500 a year more than Negroes in the central city.

What are the odds of the Perkinses, or any ghetto family, making it out to Maywood? About 1-in-11. In 1960 Chicago had 813,000 Negroes in its central city, the ghetto, and only 77,000 in the suburbs. In 1950 the ratio was about the same.

Chapter
20: The American Dream in the 1960's

◖ PETER J. FREDERICK

Throughout American history the concept of the "American dream" has been used to describe the aspirations of individuals, as well as the over-all mission and purpose of the United States. There are, of course, as many American dreams as there are American dreamers. Nonetheless, there is essentially a twofold thrust to the American dream. The first thrust, the dream of freedom, promises to fulfill the historic ideals expressed in such documents as the Declaration of Independence, the Bill of Rights and Reconstruction Amendments to the Constitution, and Lincoln's Gettysburg Address. Briefly stated, all men are entitled to the rights of life, liberty, and the pursuit of happiness; civil liberties and equal protection of the laws are guaranteed to all citizens; and government is understood to be of, by, and for the people. The emphasis of this dream is on the fulfillment of human values through political freedom for all citizens. The dream is idealistic, universal, and promissory.

The second thrust, the dream of success, derives from the first. This side of the dream is individual rather than universal, realistic rather than idealistic, and stresses material rather than human values. The individual dream is embodied best in the self-help examples of Franklin and Carnegie, and in the log cabin to white house tradition of Jackson and Lincoln. Emphasis is placed on the rags to riches novels of Horatio Alger and the hard work ethic of the McGuffey Readers. Success is achieved by pursuit of one's self-interest, which is equated most often with monetary, material interests. In theory, pursuit of personal success represents the means to fulfillment of idealistic ends. In reality, however, the emphasis on success has often become an end in itself.

These two sides of the American dream, therefore, are in constant tension, creating a dilemma between idealistic political promises on the one hand and selfish economic expectations on the other. Often the two sides are compatible, as in the material benefits and increased opportunities afforded to millions of Americans as a result of the selfish energies of industrial statesmen, or as in the various extensions of the suffrage by those in power. Just as often, however, the two sides are in conflict, as when one man's self-interested desires have been achieved only at the expense of another's, or when property values are deemed more precious than human or spiritual ones. The pursuit of property at the expense of people has given rise to slaveholders, robber barons, suffrage discrimination, restrictive covenants, and slumlords. Throughout American history, therefore, many personal dreams of success have been fulfilled only by impeding or negating the dream of freedom.

The inherent tension in the American dream is as old as American history. The Puritans of colonial Massachusetts began their settlement as a Holy Commonwealth, "a Citty vpon a Hill." They sought to regenerate the sinful Church of England by their example of Christian perfection. The Puritans aspired both to personal sainthood and to a community of saints. Charged by God with "a speciall Commission," they could do no less. The demands of God and a hostile wilderness, however, required them to pursue both missionary idealism and economic realism. Despite John Winthrop's plea for sharing, generosity, and sacrifice "in some speciall seruice for the Churche," it was not long before the need to tame the wilderness caused many Puritans to turn their eyes away from heaven toward the riches of the sea and the land. John Cotton exhorted his parishioners to work hard in their calling, but warned them not to "labor too much in pursuit of worldly gain." The narrow path between service to the community and service to self was precarious and difficult to follow. At last one Puritan professed: "my ancestors came here for religion; I came here for fish." By the end of the seventeenth century the basis for franchise privileges became property holdings rather than evidence of sainthood. Piety gave way to property, spiritual values to material ones.

The conflict between the idealistic dream and the personal dream persisted in the differing orientations of the two dominant intellectual figures of the mid-eighteenth century. As a leader of the Great Awakening in the 1730's and 1740's, Jonathan Edwards sought to inspire men to spiritual freedom and perfect holiness through a belief in the absolute sovereignty of God. While Edwards was exhorting sinners to seek heavenly salvation, his contemporary, Benjamin Franklin, was offering practical advice on the ways to health, wealth, and earthly success. "The way to wealth . . . is as plain as the way to market. It depends chiefly on two words, industry and frugality; that is, waste neither time nor money, but make the best use of both." Franklin's own story of success, as described in his *Autobiography*, was clearly an example of the earthly rewards of a life of virtue.

The Founding Fathers reaffirmed America's idealistic mission, but defined it as political rather than religious. Nevertheless, the "catch-penny opportunism" illustrated by the Franklin example prevailed throughout the nineteenth century. Many individuals achieved success by exploiting slaves, immigrants, small farmers, and unorganized laborers. The dichotomous American dream was illustrated most sharply by the existence of slavery in the land which had dedicated itself to human freedom. In the last half of the century the self-help success ethic was given both scientific and religious justification by the doctrines of social Darwinism and the gospel of wealth. The prophet of wealth, Andrew Carnegie, wrote that "there is no use whatever trying to help people who do not help themselves. You cannot push anyone up a ladder unless he be willing to climb himself." Monetary success was evidence of superior virtuous living while poverty was proof of defective moral character. This "bootstraps" ethic permeated the spirit of the age. Fourth of July orators droned on about the promises of the Declaration of Independence and the Reconstruction Amendments while the few amassed fortunes and built economic empires and the many suffered in poverty. Mark Twain, himself infected by the get-rich-quick spirit, commented on the Gilded Age: "America has dethroned God and set up a shekel in His place. O the dreams of our youth,—how refreshing! and how perishable!"

What of the dreams of America's youth in the 1960's? Have they perished? To what extent have they been fulfilled? The reform movements of the twentieth century—populism, progressivism, trade unionism, and the New Deal—have fulfilled to a large extent the dreams of small businessmen, farmers, organized workers, and most European immigrants. Political freedom and economic success have gone hand in hand for these groups. But twentieth-century reforms have failed to improve the quality of life for the neglected groups of the "other America": migrant farm workers, the aged, Indians and Mexican-Americans of the Southwest, Appalachian poor whites and, most notably, black Americans of the rural South and northern ghettos. The sixties was a decade marked paradoxically by both a renewed commitment to the idealistic promises of the American dream for these groups and by a revolt against the perversion of the values found on both sides of the dream. The assault on the perversion of American values and institutions came mostly—but not exclusively—from the younger generation: black militants, hippies, and students.

Several years before the sit-ins, marches, and urban disorders of the sixties the black poet, Langston Hughes, predicted that when a dream is promised and deferred, it may explode. In the 1950's the civil-rights movement emerged, the result of years of promises made and broken. In part because the dream had long been deferred and festering for black Americans, the civil-rights movement was born. More specifically, the movement was caused by a series of Supreme Court decisions ordering desegregation of schools, by President Truman's Executive Order integrating the armed services, by the success of the Montgomery bus boycott in 1956, by the increasing migration of blacks to northern cities, by the cold war conflict with the Soviet Union, and by the emergence of a Third World bloc in the United Nations.

The focus of the civil-rights movement in the early sixties was on the fulfillment of constitutional guarantees. The movement defined its goals in acceptable American terms: equal opportunity, judicial due process, freedom and equal protection of the laws for all citizens, and the elimination of artificial racial barriers which prevented black people from enjoying their rights as "first-class" citizens and from sharing in the material accomplishments of an increasingly affluent society. The methods of the civil-rights movement, as led by Dr. Martin Luther King's Southern Christian Leadership Conference (SCLC), the Congress of Racial Equality (CORE), and the Student Nonviolent Coordinating Committee (SNCC), were also in the acceptable tradition of American reform. Nonviolent tactics and peaceful demonstrations were designed to cause a "creative tension" which would force negotiations at the local level and awaken an apathetic populace nation-wide. By forcing confrontations, King reasoned, awareness of injustices would lead to national legislation eradicating discrimination and opening the doors to equal opportunity.

To some extent the civil-rights movement succeeded. King's methods shamed northern liberals and broke down many of the barriers of segregation in the South. The Civil Rights Act of 1964, which desegregated public accommodations, was passed in response to the Birmingham demonstrations in the spring of 1963 and the March on Washington in August of that year. The Voting Rights Act of 1965, which protected the rights of southern Negroes to register to vote, was passed in response to Mississippi voter registration drives during the summer of 1964 and to demonstrations in Selma, Alabama, early in 1965. These acts, however, were difficult to enforce, and full implementation was slow. Many southern sheriffs and governors openly resisted the civil-rights movement by standing in schoolhouse doors to stop integration, by refusing to protect peaceful demonstrators and civil-rights workers from mob reprisals, and by exercising an excessive use of police power in order to intimidate them. Many civil-rights workers, black and white, were martyred, including King himself.

If King's approach succeeded only partially in the South, it succeeded hardly at all in the North, where the barriers to equal justice and opportunity were less visible and more subtle, but just as dehumanizing. It was one thing to confront Sheriff Jim Clark or Governor George Wallace in moral conflict on nation-wide television; it was quite another thing to break down the labyrinth of economic deprivation and political powerlessness in northern ghettos. For many black people, especially those living in northern cities, the response of the federal government to the civil-rights movement was insufficient legislation, token enforcement, and more deliberateness than speed. The dream was crusted over with syrupy sweet promises of fulfillment that had little application to an unemployed black man caught in the cycle of poverty in Chicago or Newark. Many blacks began to question the dream itself. A SNCC Position Paper in 1966 proclaimed that "we reject the American Dream as defined by white people and must work to construct an American reality defined by Afro-Americans."

And in the mid-sixties, as Langston Hughes had prophesied, the dream exploded. It erupted in the burning, looting, and violence in Watts, Harlem, Cleveland, Detroit, and other northern cities. The mood, tactics, and even the ends of the black movement shifted dramatically. The solemn vow that "we shall overcome" was replaced by the angry slogan of "black power." "Freedom now" became "power to the people." The tactic of nonviolence was replaced by the threat of "by any means necessary." Increasing numbers of black youths preferred the more militant rhetoric of Malcolm X and Stokely Carmichael to the lofty eloquence of Dr. King. SNCC shifted its goal from integration into the white community to self-determination and the autonomy of black communities, and excluded whites from the organization. By 1967 the civil-rights movement had evolved into the "revolution for black liberation."

Despite disagreements in the domestic struggle, both major expressions of the black protest movement were agreed in their opposition to the escalating war in Vietnam. King argued that peace and freedom were inextricably related, and that the vast expenditure of funds in Southeast Asia drained resources needed for rehabilitation of America's urban centers. Carmichael, increasingly following Malcolm X's concept of the unity of Third World peoples, declared that "no Vietnamese ever called me nigger" in an effort to discourage young blacks from participating in the war against their colored brothers. The Black Panther Party boldly stated that blacks should be exempt from military service.

In the mid-sixties the civil disorders in the cities and the increasing militancy of the black and anti-war movements were accompanied by a full-scale revolt by youth against traditional American values. The revolt followed two paths: intense political activism and the flowering of the hippie sub-culture. The political activists focused their assaults on the war in Vietnam, the selective service system, racism, and higher education. They repudiated conventional democratic processes, integration, and American militarism; instead, they advocated "participatory democracy," black separatism, and a form of neo-isolationism. The hippies, many of whom were disenchanted activists, rejected outright what they thought to be a sterile middle-class ethic of work, productivity, success, and acquisitiveness. They "dropped out" to communities like the Haight-Ashbury in San Francisco, embraced voluntary poverty, and "turned on" to various forms of self-expression. Their assault on conventional values was manifested in unorthodox styles of dress and personal appearance, sexual freedom, new art forms, and experimentation with mind-expanding drugs.

The hippies achieved some success in maintaining their new life styles in the midst of a disapproving American public. The impatient young blacks and whites in revolt against institutional manifestations of racism and militarism, however, were consistently thwarted in their more ambitious efforts. They sought to eradicate racism from American life and institutions; racism continued. The conclusion of the National Advisory Commission on Civil Disorders that white racism was the fundamental cause of urban riots gave official sanction to what blacks had always known. The activists sought to end the war and the draft; the war and the draft went on, despite bloody confrontations at the Pentagon in October, 1967, the Democratic National Convention in Chicago in August, 1968, and at various induction centers. The failure of Senator Eugene McCarthy's campaign to win the Democratic Party nomination for President in 1968 only confirmed the young people's belief that conventional democratic processes were an inadequate means to achieve the reconstruction of American society.

Frustrated by losing confrontations with the "power structure," and encouraged by liberal rhetoric from academics, the students shifted their attentions from the Pentagon, realtors, convention delegates, and legislators to their own colleges and universities. The student revolt at Columbia University in the spring of 1968 heralded an increasing tendency to direct action and violent disruption on college campuses. The revolts at Columbia, San Francisco State, Berkeley, Cornell, Harvard, and scores of other colleges in 1968 and 1969 all followed a familiar pattern, whether led by white radical members of the Students for a Democratic Society (SDS) or by black militant members of Black Student Unions. This pattern included the issuing of angry manifestoes and "non-negotiable" demands, the disruption of classes, the seizures and "liberation" of campus buildings, violent confrontations between students and police, and often the calling out of the national guard to restore order. The students focused on the two issues which symbolized the larger concerns of the sixties: first, institutional racism, as manifested by admissions policies, faculty hiring, white-oriented curricula, and university expansion into the surrounding, usually black community; and second, American militarism, as manifested by university participation in the war through defense contracts and R.O.T.C. As campus revolts increased, an aroused and irate public demanded legislative action in quelling the dissident students.

To those calling for a renewed respect for order and decency, the most disturbing aspect of the hippie and student revolts was that disenchantment with traditional American values and institutions was not confined to a few revolutionaries but was widespread among young people. By the end of the sixties American citizens were polarized not along socioeconomic or regional lines, as they had been throughout most of their history, but into black and white, young and old, voiceless poor and bureaucrat, and "hippie" and "straight." In a nation which had achieved widespread but by no means universal affluence and a steady rate of economic growth, passions were aroused and divisions created less by economic differences than by differences in attitudes, values, and life styles. Increasing numbers of citizens questioned historical definitions of the American dream, the persistent preference for material over human values, and the viability of democratic political institutions. They advocated alternative value systems, often claiming that they were inherent in the American tradition. Other Americans, usually white and older, reaffirmed the conventional American dream and traditional values, and pointed to the achievements of the sixties in narrowing the gap between promises and fulfillment of the dream. They promised further progress in extending the benefits of America's economic growth to all citizens, but only according to orderly and acceptable methods of change.

The documents that follow, all of them written in the middle and late sixties, represent a variety of statements about American ideals and values. Each document reflects the fundamental dilemma in the American dream between human and material values. In some cases the material values of American life are seen to interfere with the achievement of human dignity; in other cases material accomplishment is seen as the means to human fulfillment. Each document raises questions, moreover, about the health of the society and the ability of America to fulfill its traditional promises. All of these documents can be viewed as statements by American dreamers as well as statements about the American dream. Each author describes the dream as he understands it, and each reflects a fundamental commitment to a system of values he believes is uniquely American. The kind of response one makes to these documents depends in large measure on one's own understanding of the American dream and on the kind of dreamer he imagines himself to be.

It has long been argued that the pursuit of profits and material satisfaction serves human happiness for the greatest numbers of citizens. As Calvin Coolidge put it, "the business of America is business." Richard Cornuelle was a writer-editor for various businessmen's associations and a founder of the Center for Independent Action, an agency for meeting social needs through nongovernment action; in 1966 he joined the National Association of Manufacturers as an executive vice-president. He argued in the mid-sixties that the abandonment of corporate and private philanthropy in favor of a centralized welfare state had thwarted the historical thrust toward fulfillment of human needs and had created "a cut-rate version of the American dream." Cornuelle's book, *Reclaiming the American Dream* (New York: Vintage Books, 1968), was a richly documented defense of the "independent sector" (as opposed to the public and private sectors, government and commerce) as a vital force in remedying social problems. Excerpts from *Reclaiming the American Dream* are reprinted by permission of Random House, Inc. Copyright © 1965 by Richard Cornuelle. As is shown in the following excerpt from his book (pages 107–08, 111–15), the independent sector is largely indistinguishable from private business and its allied foundations. Were the American businessmen Cornuelle describes manifesting altruistic concerns for the social rehabilitation of society, or were they retaining their own motives and thus reaffirming enduring American material values? Can a private corporation generate both profits and public services? Which serves which: is material success a means to human fulfillment, or does meeting human needs serve material goals?

⊂Ξ   The Dream of Material Success

RICHARD CORNUELLE

A restless spirit moves among businessmen. They employ a clumsy language about "corporate citizenship," "company responsibility to the community," and even "stewardship." Such talk is, of course, not new, but it is gaining a fierce and significant intensity, more in private than in public. Some businessmen worry over an apparent conflict of values. Proud of a tough-minded approach to profits and aware that they cannot be social workers with shareholder money, they are on the prowl for an underlying idea that is missing.

What causes this concern? The businessman's desire for meaningful service, I believe, is pushing against inadequate machinery through which to function. He has the will but does not see the way. In this uneasy mood, the U.S. business community is the group most likely to trigger a renaissance of the independent sector.

Many reach instinctively in this direction. In city after city, when you look carefully, you find businessmen leading a strong resurgence of private charities. They have led most of the successful urban renewal efforts since Pittsburgh's Golden Triangle. But few sense the effectiveness of their own efforts. The traditional rhetoric of "private charity" reminds them that they are not John D. Rockefellers; they fail to see that with proper organization and tactics, they have far greater resources than businessmen had in the days when a few financial giants dominated the economy. Today's businessmen don't really know their own strength. So, even while working to prevent it, most are resigned to an ever greater government monopoly on public service.

They hear urgent warnings. In an echo of Tocqueville, Donald David, as an officer of the Ford Foundation, said, "I am convinced that if private enterprise philanthropy were to abdicate to government, private business would follow not too far behind."

But businessmen are not sure they can respond to the warnings. More than any other group, they are victimized by the "public-private" division of all U.S. life. It traps them. So long as we view society as a two-part system, business is exposed to a direct, losing battle with government. The profit discipline becomes a fatal handicap rather than an essential strength. Only when you understand the important array of institutions that are neither commercial nor governmental, but provide a buffer between the two, do you understand how the American dream once combined the ideals of freedom and welfare. Since the decline of this decisive force, business has paid a high price in regulation, taxes and public ill will. And as of 1965, the future of the commercial sector depends upon the reemergence of a vital independent sector. . . .

Business is itself a welfare system. As the prime producer of goods and services, it provides abundantly for the general welfare. It has lifted the American standard of living to embarrassing heights compared to socialized nations, and it provides public services that dwarf government's contribution. From baseball to good books, from toys to ranch houses, the necessities and luxuries we take for granted are produced by private companies.

Let me illustrate. In September, 1964, a group of ten investor-owned utilities announced a $10.5-billion project to expand electric power in the nine Western states. It was a wholly commercial undertaking with no government financing involved. The project, when completed in 1986, will produce thirty-four thousand new jobs, $200 million in new payroll, $75 million in new tax revenue, and $75.2 million in new retail sales. This project was given scant notice in the press. Yet it will produce three times the power output of the Tennessee Valley Authority, which has, after a generation of sustained public attention, become a subject on which almost any citizen considers himself an expert advocate or critic.

The human "welfare" generated by these projects is surely the same, except the private project will be measurably more productive than TVA. Yet TVA was hailed as a great innovation, the other accorded about as much attention as the air we breathe. . . .

Commerce manages a lot of "public" enterprises skillfully. The Bell Telephone System is the best example. Travelers tell me that we have the world's best telephone service and the Western world's worst mail service. One is run by business; the other by government. In England, where the telephone is a subsidiary of the post office, the phones often work like Alexander Graham Bell's first models, and expansion-minded businesses often have to wait months for desperately needed service. One economic analyst is convinced that the failure of government-supplied communications is the main bottleneck to more rapid expansion of the European economy.

One hundred and forty-five million Americans have some form of commercial health insurance—up from forty-two million in 1946. Forty-three million workers are privately insured against disability. Ten million people age sixty-five and over—three out of five—have private medical insurance. Businesses build and lease college dormitories. Private developers renew cities. Jim Walter, the flamboyant shell-house pioneer, has put more low-income people in decent houses on a business basis than has any government project. When business operates "public" facilities—parking lots, parks—the costs are almost always lower and the service better; most important, the facility constantly renews itself to serve changing wants and demands.

A most dramatic example of commercial welfare came across my desk the other day. The foundation I direct had for several months been planning to develop a national chain of low-cost nursing homes. We studied in particular the methods of Holiday Inns, the very successful motel franchise, thinking that if nonprofit organizations could imitate their methods, we could provide nursing-home care at very low cost.

Then one day last March, I read in the *Wall Street Journal* that Holiday Inns had formed a subsidiary to "operate a nation-wide system of franchised nursing homes, patterned somewhat after the motel chain." Their studies show that "reasonably priced, well-designed and economically built homes, under properly trained personnel, can render the service . . . at money-making prices." We had hoped, with our "welfare" project, to get the price-per-resident down to a rock-bottom $250 a month. Holiday Inn's probable price: $250 a month. For the old folks, which is welfare and which is not? The commercial entry into this badly needed public service reduced our role to a fraction of what I had expected it to be. One of my associates went to Holiday Inn executives to see if we could borrow their know-how to create a nonprofit system of homes for areas that would not be commercially profitable to them.

The nursing homes are no exception to the general rule. Businessmen constantly hunt for new markets by identifying a special need and then finding ways to meet it at lower cost than anybody else. In such effort, the profit motive often serves as an instrument rather than an original cause. This fact is hard to explain, because it contradicts the standard clichés. J. Irwin Miller, chairman of Cummins Engine Company, operates a highly profitable bank, the Irwin-Union Trust Company, in his home town of Columbus, Indiana. His bank outgrows any other in its Federal Reserve District because it constantly hunts for new financial services needed by people and institutions (especially churches) in its market area. "If you try to run a bank with the primary goal of making the biggest profit possible, you won't," says Miller. "But if you approach the operation of a bank from the point of view of how best it can serve the community, then the profits will follow."

To cynics, in and out of business, such remarks sound fatuous. But they may be nearer the truth than the rhetoric of profits as normally used. Time and again, the most successful businessmen are those who seek first to provide the best service and then work on the arithmetic of profit. Florida's George Jenkins, who has transformed his Publix Supermarkets into an expansive chain of pleasure domes for shoppers, broods about the competitors he has faced over the years. "If a man wants to be a good grocer, he can generally make a profit," muses Jenkins. "But these get-rich-quick fellows tend to lose their shirts."

Other businessmen, among them Chicago banker Gaylord A. Freeman, Jr., have developed a line of thought about the difference between short-term and long-term profits. If a professional manager tried to look good in each year's annual report by showing a dramatic profit, Freeman argues, he might be working against the interest of the shareholders. Their equity gains or loses value on the prospect for future profits, not just in the current annual report. So a real concern for the shareholder, says Freeman, could even justify a corporation investment in improving the society in ways that will provide a favorable climate for profits in the long run.

For Martin Luther King the efforts of the independent sector had not been enough; indeed, he regarded "business as usual" a serious obstacle to the fulfillment of the idealistic dream of freedom and human dignity for black people. From 1956, when as a young minister he organized and led the bus boycott in Montgomery, Alabama, until his assassination in 1968 while rallying striking garbage collectors in Memphis, Dr. King eloquently inspired black and white Americans alike with his passionate commitment to a free and just society. On August 28, 1963, the "drum major for justice," as he preferred to be remembered, delivered his "I have a dream" address before some 250,000 civil-rights marchers from the steps of the Lincoln Memorial in Washington, D.C. In what ways does King's oration reflect traditional definitions of the American dream? Is King's method—here stated implicitly—in the acceptable tradition of reform, and how effective do you think his method was? Is he optimistic or pessimistic about the ability of American society to fulfill its promises? To what extent is the United States today closer to or farther from the fulfillment of Dr. King's dream of freedom? King's address—reprinted here in its entirety—can be found in the SCLC *Newsletter*, I (September, 1963), pp. 5, 8.

⊂⊇ The Dream of Freedom

MARTIN LUTHER KING, JR.

Five score years ago, a great American, in whose symbolic shadow we stand, signed the Emancipation Proclamation. This momentous decree came as a great beacon light of hope to millions of Negro slaves who had been seared in the flames of withering injustice. It came as a joyous daybreak to end the long night of captivity.

But one hundred years later, we must face the tragic fact that the Negro is still not free. One hundred years later, the life of the Negro is still sadly crippled by the manacles of segregation and the chains of discrimination. One hundred years later, the Negro lives on a lonely island of poverty in the midst of a vast ocean of material prosperity. One hundred years later the Negro is still languished in the corners of American society and finds himself an exile in his own land. So we have come here today to dramatize an appalling condition.

In a sense we have come to our nation's Capital to cash a check. When the architects of our republic wrote the magnificent words of the Constitution and the Declaration of Independence, they were signing a promissory note to which every American was to fall heir. This note was a promise that all men would be guaranteed the inalienable rights of life, liberty, and the pursuit of happiness.

It is obvious today that America has defaulted on this promissory note insofar as her citizens of color are concerned. Instead of honoring this sacred obligation, America has given the Negro people a bad check; a check which has come back marked "insufficient funds." But we refuse to believe that the bank of justice is bankrupt. We refuse to believe that there are insufficient funds in the great vaults of opportunity of this nation. So we have come to cash this check—a check that will give us upon demand the riches of freedom and the security of justice. We have also come to this hallowed spot to remind America of the fierce urgency of *now*. This is no time to engage in the luxury of cooling off or to take the tranquilizing drug of gradualism. *Now* is the time to make real the promises of Democracy. *Now* is the time to rise from the dark and desolate valley of segregation to the sunlit path of racial justice. *Now* is the time to open the doors of opportunity to all of God's children. *Now* is the time to lift our nation from the quicksands of racial injustice to the solid rock of brotherhood.

It would be fatal for the nation to overlook the urgency of the moment and to underestimate the determination of the Negro. This sweltering summer of the Negro's legitimate discontent will not pass until there is an invigorating autumn of freedom and equality. 1963 is not an end, but a beginning. Those who hope that the Negro needed to blow off steam and will now be content will have a rude awakening if the Nation returns to business as usual. There will be neither rest nor tranquility in America until the Negro is granted his citizenship rights. The whirlwinds of revolt will continue to shake the foundations of our Nation until the bright day of justice emerges.

But there is something that I must say to my people who stand on the warm threshold which leads into the palace of justice. In the process of gaining our rightful place we must not be guilty of wrongful deeds. Let us not seek to satisfy our thirst for freedom by drinking from the cup of bitterness and hatred. We must forever conduct our struggle on the high plane of dignity and discipline. We must not allow our creative protest to degenerate into physical violence. Again and again we must rise to the majestic heights of meeting physical force with soul force. The marvelous new militancy which has engulfed the Negro community must not lead us to a distrust of all white people, for many of our white brothers, as evidenced by their presence here today, have come to realize that their destiny is tied up with our destiny and their freedom is inextricably bound to our freedom. We cannot walk alone.

And as we walk, we must make the pledge that we shall march ahead. We cannot turn back. There are those who are asking the devotees of civil rights, "When will you be satisfied?" We can never be satisfied as long as the Negro is the victim of unspeakable horrors of police brutality. We can never be satisfied as long as our bodies, heavy with the fatigue of travel, cannot gain lodging in the motels of the highways and the hotels of the cities. We cannot be satisfied as long as the Negro's basic mobility is from a smaller ghetto to a larger one. We can never be satisfied as long as a Negro in Mississippi cannot vote and a Negro in New York believes he has nothing for which to vote. No, no we are not satisfied, and we will not be satisfied until justice rolls down like waters and righteousness like a mighty stream.

I am not unmindful that some of you have come here out of great trials and tribulations. Some of you have come fresh from narrow jail cells. Some of you have come from areas where your quest for freedom left you battered by the storms of persecution and staggered by the winds of police brutality. You have been the veterans of creative suffering. Continue to work with the faith that unearned suffering is redemptive.

Go back to Mississippi, go back to Alabama, go back to South Carolina, go back to Georgia, go back to Louisiana, go back to the slums and ghettos of our modern cities, knowing that somehow this situation can and will be changed. Let us not wallow in the valley of despair.

I say to you today, my friends, that in spite of the difficulties and frustrations of the moment I still have a dream. It is a dream deeply rooted in the American dream.

I have a dream that one day this nation will rise up and live out the true meaning of its creed: "We hold these truths to be self-evident; that all men are created equal."

I have a dream that one day on the red hills of Georgia the sons of former slaves and the sons of former slaveowners will be able to sit down together at the table of brotherhood.

I have a dream that one day even the state of Mississippi, a desert state sweltering with the heat of injustice and oppression, will be transformed into an oasis of freedom and justice.

I have a dream that my four little children will one day live in a nation where they will not be judged by the color of their skin but by the content of their character.

I have a dream today.

I have a dream that one day the state of Alabama, whose governor's lips are presently dripping with the words of interposition and nullification, will be transformed into a situation where little black boys and black girls will be able to join hands with little white boys and white girls and walk together as sisters and brothers.

I have a dream today.

I have a dream that one day every valley shall be exalted, every hill and mountain shall be made low, the rough places will be made plains, and the crooked places will be made straight, and the glory of the Lord shall be revealed, and all flesh shall see it together.

This is our hope. This is the faith with which I return to the South.

With this faith we will be able to hew out of the mountain of despair a stone of hope. With this faith we will be able to transform the jangling discords of our nation into a beautiful symphony of brotherhood. With this faith we will be able to work together, to pray together, to struggle together, to go to jail together, to stand up for freedom together, knowing that we will be free one day.

This will be the day when all of God's children will be able to sing with new meaning "My Country 'tis of thee, sweet land of liberty, of thee I sing. Land where my fathers died, land of the pilgrim's pride, from every mountainside, let freedom ring."

And if America is to be a great nation this must become true. So let freedom ring from the prodigious hilltops of New Hampshire. Let freedom ring from the mighty mountains of New York. Let freedom ring from the heightening Alleghenies of Pennsylvania!

Let freedom ring from the snowcapped Rockies of Colorado!

Let freedom ring from the curvacious peaks of California!

But not only that; let freedom ring from Stone Mountain of Georgia!

Let freedom ring from Lookout Mountain of Tennessee!

Let freedom ring from every hill and mole hill of Mississippi. From every mountain side, let freedom ring.

When we let freedom ring, when we let it ring from every village and every hamlet, from every state and every city, we will be able to speed up that day when all of God's children, black men and white men, Jews and Gentiles, Protestants and Catholics, will be able to join hands and sing in the words of the old Negro spiritual, "Free at last! free at last! thank God almighty, we are free at last!"

By the mid-sixties increasing numbers of young black men and women were disillusioned with Dr. King's non-violent methods and integrationist goals. They urged instead, under the slogan of "black power," an emphasis on black cultural consciousness and on black economic and political control of black communities. Mrs. Jean Smith, a recent Phi Beta Kappa graduate of Howard University, went south to work for SNCC's voter registration drives in 1964 and for the "War on Poverty" Head Start program in Mississippi in 1965. She described her frustrating experiences and consequent evolving "black consciousness" in the article, "I Learned to Feel Black," reprinted here from *Redbook* magazine (August, 1967), pages 64, 128–31. Copyright © 1967 McCall Corporation. To what extent does her "American image" and program for black Americans differ from that of Martin Luther King? Why did she change? Has Mrs. Smith defined here an "American dream" or a uniquely "*black* American dream?" By the late sixties she and her husband, whom she met while working for SNCC, had settled in Greenville, Mississippi, where they operated a janitorial supplies and household goods store and ran vocational training and literacy programs. What does this commitment suggest about the changing direction and emphases of the black revolution?

The Dream of "Black Consciousness"

JEAN SMITH

I think that once you knew me. It was a time not long past, about four years ago. I was the bright, well-mannered girl who lived down the street from you. My grandmother was always stopping you on your way to the grocery store; she would call you to the door to show you, proudly, college-newspaper clippings about her granddaughter's winning a scholarship or achieving a place on the dean's list.

Or possibly you remember me from church. I was the girl who helped sustain the small, overambitious choir by appearing faithfully every Sunday to sing the praises of the Lord in songs that often were too difficult or out of my range. Sometimes you would stop and offer me a few words of encouragement because you said, you liked my spirit.

Or you may remember me as the girl in the neighborhood who went off to join the civil rights movement or the Peace Corps. You might even have been among those who tried to persuade me not to waste my talents on those other people when there was so much work to be done at home. I could build a fine professional career, you told me; I could make a starting salary of $7,000.

I'm sure you knew me once. At least you knew a something in me, something that continued to grasp at the reality of the American image of the full person, blessed by our society with the resources and opportunities to be whatever he wants to be. I kept trying to be that full person, to use the talents I had toward widening opportunities for other people so that they also could make the most of their lives.

And so I tried to know everything and to be the best at everything I tried. I wanted to learn all about science, art, music, Greek mythology, Oriental philosophy. I wanted to learn the newest theories, study the most difficult courses and sing the hardest songs. It all would be useful in the refinement of this society where every man could be his best.

Thus I studied chemistry at college and planned to go to medical school, because I felt that I could be most useful in this way. And I had to join the civil rights movement because I saw in it a basic method of making our society stand completely behind its image of the full person and of every man's right to be a full person. I felt sure that once the country was made aware that some of its Negro citizens were being deprived of very basic rights and was brought face to face with the contradiction between its image and what was happening to the Negro people, then our society would necessarily correct the oppressed condition of the Negro people.

Yes, I'm certain that you knew, if only superficially, that *something* in me which reached toward the American image.

What was the source of my belief? It was based on my assurance that in this country there was room for everybody, that for every man there was, or soon would be, some place where he could be free to explore and employ the creative potential within him. So that my job was simply to develop the skills I possessed and then to fit my abilities into the massive machinery that, I trusted, was working day and night to create for every person a place of comfort and freedom. In short, I believed in guaranteeing everyone freedom, equality and democracy as the means of living full lives, and I thought that the rest of the country believed in these things too.

I had good reason to believe all this. My family was sort of upper lower class. There were just four of us, my mother, my two sisters and I. (My father, a pilot in the Army Air Force, was killed in World War II.) My mother worked as a practical nurse in Detroit, Michigan, when we were young, and she managed to get two of us through college. She herself graduated from college at the age of 40 and has just embarked on a new career, teaching deaf children. My youngest sister is in college now. All of us have or can get any *thing* we really want (a house, a car, a trip to Europe).

Thus my early personal experiences suggested that there was room for everybody. After all, I was nobody special and yet I was doing quite well.

In fact, it was a long time before I became conscious that being a Negro made me different. I thought I was like everybody else.

It was in the context of my belief in our society's potential for making good on its promise of full men through freedom and democracy that I responded to the urgings of some of my classmates at Howard University. They were members of the Students' Nonviolent Coordinating Committee (or SNCC, pronounced "Snick") and I joined the Movement. I truly felt, and I think that many SNCC workers then felt similarly, that most Americans believed in these principles, and that when confronted with our documentation that they were being violated in the South, Americans would move to support the rights of Negro citizens.

When I left Washington, D.C., in 1963 to go South with SNCC, you knew me. Now, four years later, I am a different person.

Essentially the difference is that I became consciously black. I came to understand that there wasn't room enough in the society for the mass of black people, that the majority of Americans are acting either in unbearably bad faith or in tragic ignorance when they project to their children the image of an American society where all men are free and equal.

Since, in a way, I was once a friend of yours, perhaps you'll invest a little time and emotional energy in trying to understand what happened.

I went South after the sit-ins that were aimed at desegregating eating places. In the summer of '63 I went to Georgia and then to Mississippi as a SNCC field worker. The focus of SNCC's activity in the Deep South then was voter registration. The logic of it seemed very clear to me. Negroes had a right to vote, to participate in our democracy. In fact, our society wanted everyone's participation. Because of some curious isolation from the rest of the country, the white Southerners had managed to deprive Negroes of this right. But the South was still part of the United States. What we had to do was to show the rest of the United States that democratic participation was being denied our people. Then the rest of the country would insist that the South allow Negroes to vote.

I saw the relationship between political representation and economic and social development: If Negroes could get the vote, then we could use it to attack the poverty and misery which plagued the Negro community. If we could vote, we would be well on our way to full economic and social participation in the larger society. And so I worked with the other SNCC staff people to show the rest of the country that Negroes in the South wanted to vote and couldn't.

We got our people to go down to the courthouse to try to register to vote. After they were turned away from the courthouse or were not allowed to "pass" the test of eligibility for voting or were intimidated by threats of violence from whites, we appealed to the Justice Department, documenting carefully the instances of refusal and intimidation. Next we organized picket lines and marches to the courthouse to demonstrate to the rest of the country that Negroes *did* want to vote. The marches often ended in mass arrests and in violence, but they were reported in the newspapers and on television and the Movement's case was made clear to the public. After there had been much marching and many protests, Congress passed the 1965 Voting Rights Act, which assured Negroes the right to vote.

It would seem that this was a great victory. It was certainly a goal into whose attainment I had put my heart. I worked every available minute at reaching it. I used to walk through the whole town every day, canvassing neighborhoods to tell people about voting. I canvassed until evening; I took part in the mass meetings that were held every two or three nights. Then I went back to the office to work until one or two o'clock in the morning to establish files on potential voters and help organize our new library.

When finally I went home it was to a deep, satisfying sleep. I would be ready to go again at six the next morning, awakened by my eagerness to start a new day of efforts to secure the right of my people to vote and be represented. We all worked so hard. And Negroes did get the right to vote.

We found it was a shallow victory. After the earlier sit-ins, the civil rights movement had had to stop and ask: "What have we gained by winning the right to a cup of coffee downtown?" In the same way, we who had worked for voting rights now had to ask ourselves what we had gained. In both cases the answer was the same: Negroes were in fact not basically better off with this new right than they had been before; they were still poor and without the power to direct their own lives.

It is a subtle problem to acknowledge that there was some value in having achieved these rights and yet to understand that there was no basic gain. The value was in the way Negroes could feel like real men and women as they broke old traditions about "staying in their place" and went up to the courthouse to vote. The value was in the solidification of the Negro community, in our recognition of the possibility that we could work together to build decent lives. But you must see that there was no basic change. I personally resisted seeing this for a long time. I had invested so much of myself in the fight that I didn't want to admit that it came to so little.

The best way to understand is to look at what the Negro people who cast their lot with the Movement believed. They believed, I think, that their participation in the drive for voting rights would ultimately result in the relief of their poverty and hopelessness. They thought that with the right to vote they could end the exploitation of their labor by the plantation owners. They thought they could get better schools for their children; they could get sewers dug and sidewalks paved. They thought they could get adequate public-health facilities for their communities. And of course they got none of these.

The crux of the matter is that they believed there was a link between representation in government and making that government work for you. What they—and I—discovered was that for some people this link does not exist. For most black people, voting has not much more benefit than the exercise of walking to the polls. Why is this the case? Because the link between voting and partaking of the benefits of society exists at the pleasure of society. The society must be willing to respond to the legitimate needs of the people; only then can the channels for the expression of these needs, such channels as voting, be meaningfully employed. . . .

The loss of my belief was damaging to me as an individual. I had been stripped of a principle around which my life had been organized. No more could I seriously think that I was helping to build this country by making it stand behind its promises to all its people. I could no longer work at helping to build a society of full, free men. The image of that society was a joke. When considered in this light my work became meaningless. In existentialist terms, I was reduced to absurdity.

For me and many other black people the only allowable conclusion from these experiences has been that Negroes must turn away from the preachings, assertions and principles of the larger white society and must turn inward to find the means whereby black people can lead full, meaningful lives. We must become conscious that our blackness calls for another set of principles, principles on whose validity we can depend because they come from our own experiences.

We have to build a broad-based black consciousness so that we can begin to depend on one another for economic, political and social support. We have to build our own businesses to put money into the development of the Negro community, businesses to establish foundations to support our own new educational and social ventures. We have to make our politicians responsible to us so that either they improve our communities or they go. Living, growing communities must be built to replace our strife-ridden ghettos. The problems of illiteracy and the inability to communicate must be tackled.

Can we do all this by ourselves? Probably not. Obviously we need access to the capital and to the intellectual resources of the larger society. We need to know how to build lathes and how to market products. We need to learn the ins and outs of prevailing political forms and to have access to the body of scientific knowledge and cultural tradition. We need those few white people who are genuinely interested in helping.

It's not that we have to do it by ourselves. Rather it is that we have to reorient our efforts and to train ourselves, black people, to build for us. Our immediate objective must be the strengthening of the black community instead of the apparently unattainable goal of diffusion of all black people into the main stream of American life. We have to become strong so that we can depend on one another to meet our needs and so that we'll be able to deal with white people as we choose to, not as we are obliged to.

I realize that we are only ten per cent of the population and that in the end we may well need the large-scale assistance of the larger society. But I also realize that except on the level of tokenism, we can't win the fight for meaningful integration any time soon. (Soon, for me, means in my lifetime.)

I think the fight for integration must continue because we derive some benefits from it. It means better living conditions for a few of us, a few more low-cost housing units, a few more yearly incomes above the poverty level. It means that we can feel more like men and women because we've insisted on the rights that society says are ours. And we gain valuable knowledge and experience by being the only Negro architect in the firm or by being one of three Negro judges in the city or by being the agency's only black model.

Clearly there's much to be learned in the outside world. But basically I think we must have before us the objective of building strong black communities on which we and our children can depend and in which we can lead full, rich lives. I think that after the black community has become strong enough, the rules of the game may change; society may decide that it can live with us on equal terms. It may even decide to join hands with us to build a country where all of us, white and black, can live.

The call for black consciousness is at first painfully hard to answer. It's hard to start all over again and establish new principles and modes of operation. For we have struggled vainly for so long, trying to approximate white culture! Our artists, our scientists, our leaders, have been respected by us only after they have been "legitimatized" by the white world. For so long, events have not occurred unless they were recorded in the white press; world issues have not existed unless the President made a speech about them. The extent of our reality has been the width of our TV screens. We face a prodigious task. We've danced to the tune so long; and now it becomes necessary to stop and gather our senses, to stop and listen to the tune and decide which of its elements warrant our response.

Sometimes I am nostalgic for the days when you knew me. Sometimes I miss the clarity of those days, the assurance that what I was doing was right because it was helping to make a better country and, in turn, a better world. The black self that I am now has a difficult time, having to start all over again and discover the best ways to work in this new, black world. And yet, after a searching and painful evaluation of the last years' experiences, it is the only self that I can honestly allow.

Both King and Mrs. Smith emphasized community and collectivism. For many Americans in the sixties, it was precisely the increase in enforced collective behavior by mass society and the welfare state that had violated traditional American values of individualism, self-help, local initiative, and freedom of expression. Curiously, two extremely different groups, conservatives and hippies, argued this point and asserted a dream of renewed individualism. Although they shared an intense hostility to each other, libertarian conservatives and anarchist hippies were agreed that the price of centralized power and increased security was the loss of individual freedom. The following are two brief excerpts which portray the conservative and hippie positions. James J. Kilpatrick is a highly respected syndicated columnist and editor of the Richmond, Virginia, *News Leader;* in editorials and books he has long defended the rights of the states against the encroachments of centralized power. This excerpt is from an article, "The New Right: What Does It Seek?" (*Saturday Review*, October 8, 1966). Copyright 1966 Saturday Review, Inc. Kilpatrick, in his article, castigated contemporary liberalism for manifesting itself "in aggrandizement of the central state, and . . . in a benevolent contempt for the individual man." The second excerpt is from "The Social History of the Hippies" (*Ramparts*, March, 1967), by Warren Hinckle, then the editor of *Ramparts.* Copyright Ramparts Magazine, Inc., 1967. By Permission of the Editors. Hinckle, a not altogether sympathetic observer, described a meeting of hippie leaders to discuss their political future. Does his account reveal any inner inconsistencies in the political philosophy and vision of the hippies? How would you compare the conservative and hippie dreams? Would Kilpatrick's call for "experimenting with new forms of government" include what Hinckle calls the "wholly cooperative subculture" of the Diggers? What has happened to the hippie and conservative dreams since the mid-sixties?

The Dream of Individualism

James J. Kilpatrick and Warren Hinckle

By James J. Kilpatrick:

The false values of today's liberalism, rooted in a secular materialism, do not admit any other approach to the needs of the people. Money is seen as the great mustard plaster, sucking the ill humors forth. Are they rioting tonight in Harlem? Then pay the savages not to riot. Are libraries undernourished? Let us buy socially enriched books to fill them. . . . Are poorly skilled workers underpaid? A higher minimum wage will put more 50-cent dollars in their pockets. This folly applies abroad as well as at home: If the United States cannot command respect, or win it, or earn it, the United States will buy it by the billions in foreign aid.

In this kindly and loving and profligate fashion, today's liberals advance along their munificent way, oozing rectitude from every pore. They *know* that fluoride is good for our teeth; so they would compel all men to drink it. They *know* that supplementary vitamins are unnecessary; so they would make it inconvenient to buy them. They *know* that racial integration is a good thing, right down to the semi-private hospital room; so they will swing the crowbar. They *know* that local building codes are obsolete; so they will compel the codes' revision, willy-nilly, to meet their own ideas of what is best. They *know* that the mountain people of Appalachia are unhappy, so they will impose a program to make them happy even if it makes them miserable. . . .

The American conservative holds fast to the conviction that there is something better than all this.

If our cities are to be made genuinely beautiful, and not merely plastered over, the beauty must come from within. It must be achieved primarily by the cities themselves—by the people who dwell within them, exerting their own leadership, pursuing their own dreams, acting within their own inheritance. The wounds of our cities cannot be healed by busy little federal surgeons operating with great whacks of their carving knives, and leaving a Band-Aid of rent supplements behind.

If the problems of the Negro people are ever to be solved, these, too, must be solved primarily by the Negro people themselves, and on their own terms, in their own way. . . . When the white power structure attempts to impose its solutions upon the colored community, as [James] Farmer says, the Negro resents it to the depth of his soul.

It is a false approach. The conservative would hope to provide genuine opportunities for the Negro, to make training available to those with gumption enough to struggle up, and then to leave integration to find its own natural level. And the conservative, in opposing the unfair provisions of "fair housing" laws, would insist that two equal and very human rights are involved in the right of free contract—the right to buy, and the right not to sell.

The conservative would insist that the principles of a wise and constructive federalism be returned from the liberals' attic. There still is a great role for the states and cities to play in creating and experimenting with new forms of government and new areas of local responsibility. The conservative would urge that the old doctrine of separation of powers also be revived, and propped up in bed, and given a transfusion, toward the end that the regulatory powers of the executive agencies be kept strictly within the surveillance of the legislative branch.

In every applicable policy of government, the conservative would seek to preserve the individual's right to be left alone—to buy potato chips as he pleases, to take vitamin pills as he pleases, to enjoy his private property as he pleases, so long as he causes no harm to his neighbor. . . . In a nation that is beginning to ache for a return to law and order, for a renewed respect for property rights, and for a greater measure of personal freedom, the time for these ideas moves steadily toward the striking hour.

By Warren Hinckle:

. . . Hippies are many things, but most prominently the bearded and beaded inhabitants of the Haight-Ashbury, a little psychedelic city-state edging Golden Gate Park. There, in a daily street-fair atmosphere, upwards of 15,000 unbonded girls and boys interact in a tribal, love-seeking, free-swinging, acid-based type of society where, if you are a hippie and you have a dime, you can put it in a parking meter and lie down in the street for an hour's suntan (30 minutes for a nickel) and most drivers will be careful not to run you over.

Speaking, sometimes all at once, inside the Sierra cabin were many voices of conscience and vision of the Haight-Ashbury—belonging to men who, except for their Raggedy Andy hair, paisley shirts and pre-mod western levi jackets, sounded for all the world like Young Republicans.

They talked about reducing governmental controls, the sanctity of the individual, the need for equality among men. They talked, very seriously, about the kind of society they wanted to live in, and the fact that if they wanted an ideal world they would have to go out and make it for themselves, because nobody, least of all the government, was going to do it for them.

The utopian sentiments of these hippies were not to be put down lightly. Hippies have a clear vision of the ideal community—a psychedelic community, to be sure—where everyone is turned on and beautiful and loving and happy and floating free. But it is a vision that, despite the Alice in Wonderland phraseology hippies usually breathlessly employ to describe it, necessarily embodies a radical political philosophy: communal life, drastic restriction of private property, rejection of violence, creativity before consumption, freedom before authority, de-emphasis of government and traditional forms of leadership.

Despite a disturbing tendency to quietism, all hippies *ipso facto* have a political posture—one of unremitting opposition to the Establishment which insists on branding them criminals because they take LSD and marijuana, and hating them, anyway, because they enjoy sleeping nine in a room and three to a bed, seem to have free sex and guiltless minds, and can raise healthy children in dirty clothes.

The hippie choice of weapons is to love the Establishment to death

rather than protest it or blow it up (hippies possess a confounding dis-
concern about traditional political methods or issues). But they are
decidedly and forever outside the Consensus on which this society places
such a premium, and since the hippie scene is so much the scene of those
people under 25 that Time magazine warns will soon constitute half our
population, this is a significant political fact.

This is all very solemn talk about people who like to skip rope and
wear bright colors, but after spending some time with these fun and fey
individuals you realize that, in a very unexpected way, they are as serious
about what they're doing as the John Birch Society or the Junior League.
It is not improbable, after a few more mountain seminars by those
purposeful young men wearing beads, that the Haight-Ashbury may
spawn the first utopian collectivist community since Brook Farm.

That this society finds it so difficult to take such rascally looking types
seriously is no doubt the indication of a deep-rooted hang-up. But to
comprehend the psychosis of America in the computer age, you have to
know what's with the hippies.

Except for the obvious fact that he wasn't covered with fur, you would
have said to yourself that for sure there was old Frodo Baggins, crossing
Haight Street. Frodo Baggins is the hero of the English antiquarian
J. R. R. Tolkien's classic trilogy, *Lord of the Rings*, absolutely the favorite
book of every hippie, about a race of little people called Hobbits who live
somewhere in pre-history in a place called Middle Earth. Hobbits are
hedonistic, happy little fellows who love beauty and pretty colors. Hobbits
have their own scene and resent intrusion, pass the time eating three or
four meals a day and smoke burning leaves of herb in pipes of clay. You
can see why hippies would like Hobbits.

The hustling, heroic-looking fellow with the mistaken identity was
Emmett Grogan, kingpin of The Diggers and the closest thing the hippies
in the Haight-Ashbury have to a real live hero. Grogan, 23, with blond,
unruly hair and a fair, freckled Irish face, has the aquiline nose of a
leader, but he would prefer to say that he "just presents alternatives."
He is in and out of jail 17 times a week, sometimes busted for smashing
a cop in the nose (Grogan has a very intolerant attitude toward policemen), sometimes bailing out a friend, and sometimes, like Monopoly,
just visiting. The alternatives he presents are rather disturbing to the
hippie bourgeoisie, since he thinks they have no business charging hippies
money for their daily needs and should have the decency to give things
away free, like The Diggers do, or at least charge the squares and help
out the hippies.

Grogan has a very clear view of what freedom means in society
("Why can't I stand on the corner and wait for nobody? Why can't everyone?") and an even clearer view of the social position of the hippie
merchants ("They just want to expand their sales, they don't care what

happens to people here; they're nothing but goddamn shopkeepers with beards.")

Everyone is a little afraid of Grogan in the Haight-Ashbury, including the cops. A one-man crusade for purity of purpose, he is the conscience of the hippie community. He is also a bit of a daredevil and a madman, and could easily pass for McMurphy, the roguish hero in Kesey's novel set in an insane asylum. There is a bit of J. P. Donleavy's *Ginger Man* in him, too.

A few weeks ago, out collecting supplies for The Diggers' daily free feed, Grogan went into a San Francisco wholesale butcher and asked for soup bones and meat scraps. "No free food here, we work for what we eat," said the head butcher, a tattooed Bulgar named Louie, who was in the icebox flanked by his seven assistant butchers. "You're a fascist pig and a coward," replied Grogan, whom Louie immediately smashed in the skull with the blunt side of a carving knife. That turned out to be a mistake, because the seven assistant butchers didn't like Louie much, and all jumped him. While all those white coats were grunting and rolling in the sawdust, a bleeding Grogan crawled out with four cardboard boxes full of meat. . . .

Every Bohemian community has its inevitable coterie of visionaries who claim to know what it is all about. But The Diggers are, somehow, different. They are bent on creating a wholly cooperative subculture and, so far, they are not just hallucinating, they are doing it.

Free clothes (used) are there for whomever wants them. Free meals are served every day. Next, Grogan plans to open a smart mod clothing store on Haight Street and give the clothes away free, too (the hippie merchants accused him of "trying to undercut our prices"). He wants to start Digger farms where participants will raise their own produce. He wants to give away free acid, to eliminate junky stuff and end profiteering. He wants cooperative living to forestall inevitable rent exploitation when the Haight-Ashbury becomes chic.

Not since Brook Farm, not since the Catholic Workers, has any group in this dreadfully co-optive, consumer society been so serious about a utopian community.

If Grogan succeeds or fails in the Haight-Ashbury it will not be as important as the fact that he has tried. For he is, at least, providing the real possibility of what he calls "alternatives" in the down-the-rabbit-hole-culture of the hippies.

Grogan is very hung up on freedom. "Do your thing, be what you are, and nothing will ever bother you," he says. His heroes are the Mad Bomber of New York who blissfully blew up all kinds of things around Manhattan over 30 years because he just liked to blow things up, and poet Gary Snyder, whom he considers the "most important person in the Haight-Ashbury" because instead of sitting around sniffing incense and talking about it, he went off to Japan and became a Zen master. "He did it, man."

This is an interesting activist ethic, but it remains doubtful just what the hippies will do. Not that many, certainly, will join Grogan's utopia, because utopias, after all, have a size limit.

The New Left has been flirting with the hippies lately, even to the extent of singing "The Yellow Submarine" at a Berkeley protest rally, but it looks from here like a largely unrequited love.

The hip merchants will, of course, go on making money.

And the youngsters will continue to come to the Haight-Ashbury and do—what?

That was the question put to the hippie leaders at their Summit Meeting. They resolved their goals, but not the means, and the loud noise you heard from outside was probably Emmett Grogan pounding the table with his shoe.

The crisis of the happy hippy ethic is precisely this: it is all right to turn on, but it is not enough to drop out. Grogan sees the issue in the gap "between the radical political philosophy of Jerry Rubin and Mario Savio and psychedelic love philosophy." He, himself, is not interested in the war in Vietnam, but on the other hand he does not want to spend his days like Ferdinand sniffing pretty flowers.

This is why he is so furious at the hip merchants. "They created the myth of this utopia; now they aren't going to do anything about it." Grogan takes the evils of society very personally, and he gets very angry, almost physically sick, when a pregnant 15-year-old hippie's baby starves in her stomach, a disaster which is not untypical in the Haight-Ashbury, and which Grogan sees being repeated ten-fold this summer when upwards of 200,000 migrant teenagers and college kids come, as a psychedelic "Grapes of Wrath," to utopia in search of the heralded turn-on.

The danger in the hippie movement is more than overcrowded streets and possible hunger riots this summer. If more and more youngsters begin to share the hippie political posture of unrelenting quietism, the future of activist, serious politics is bound to be affected. The hippies have shown that it can be pleasant to drop out of the arduous task of attempting to steer a difficult, unrewarding society. But when that is done, you leave the driving to the Hell's Angels.

By 1968 discontent in America grew more serious than chiding liberals for their follies and playfully exploring communal utopias. Radical students, shunning "the hippie political posture of unrelenting quietism," adopted instead direct action and violence in expressing their hatred for the values and institutions of their society. At Columbia University, militant students protested against the university's intention to build a gymnasium in nearby Harlem's Morningside Park and against Columbia's affiliation with the Institute for Defense Analysis (IDA). The revolt began on April 22, 1968, with an open letter from Mark Rudd, the chairman of the local chapter of SDS, to Grayson Kirk, president of Columbia University. Rudd's letter, printed in the Columbia *Daily Spectator*, was a response to a charge by Kirk, with which Rudd prefaced his letter, that "our young people, in disturbing numbers . . . have taken refuge in a turbulent and inchoate nihilism whose sole objectives are destruction." Does Rudd's letter confirm or refute Kirk's charge? In what ways are Rudd's dream and methods similar to and different from those of the other dreamers in this chapter? The letter was later published in a history of the Columbia crisis, titled *Up Against the Ivy Wall* by Jerry Avorn, Robert Friedman, and members of the staff of the *Columbia Spectator*. Copyright © 1968 by Members of the Board Associates. The letter is here reprinted in its entirety by permission of Atheneum Publishers and *Columbia Spectator*.

☭ The Dream of Revolt

MARK RUDD

Dear Grayson,

Your charge of nihilism is indeed ominous; for if it were true, our nihilism would bring the whole civilized world, from Columbia to Rockefeller Center, crashing down upon all our heads. Though it is not true, your charge does represent something: you call it the generation gap. I see it as a real conflict between those who run things now—you, Grayson Kirk—and those who feel oppressed by, and disgusted with, the society you rule—we, the young people.

You might want to know what is wrong with this society, since, after all, you live in a very tight self-created dream world. We can point to the war in Vietnam as an example of the unimaginable wars of aggression you are prepared to fight to maintain your control over your empire (now you've been beaten by the Vietnamese, so you call for a tactical retreat). We can point to your using us as cannon fodder to fight your war. We can point out your mansion window to the ghetto below you've helped to create through your racist University expansion policies, through your unfair labor practices, through your city government and your police. We can point to this University, your University, which trains us to be lawyers and engineers, and managers for your IBM, your Socony Mobil, your IDA, your Con Edison (or else to be scholars and teachers in more universities like this one). We can point, in short, to our own meaningless studies, our identity crises, and our revulsion with being cogs in your corporate machines as a product of and reaction to a basically sick society.

Your cry of "nihilism" represents your inability to understand our positive values. If you were ever to go into a freshman CC [Contemporary Civilization] class you would see that we are seeking a rational basis for society. We do have a vision of the way things could be: how the tremendous resources of our economy could be used to eliminate want, how people in other countries could be free from your domination, how a university could produce knowledge for progress, not waste consumption and destruction (IDA), how men could be free to keep what they produce, to enjoy peaceful lives, to create. These are positive values, but since they mean the destruction of your order, you call them "nihilism." In the movement we are beginning to call this vision "socialism." It is a fine and honorable name, one which implies absolute opposition to your corporate capitalism and your government; it will soon be caught up by other young people who want to exert control over their own lives and their society.

You are quite right in feeling that the situation is "potentially danger-ous." For if we win, we will take control of your world, your corporation, your University and attempt to mold a world in which we and other people can live as human beings. Your power is directly threatened, since we will have to destroy that power before we take over. We begin by fighting you about your support of the war in Vietnam and American imperialism—IDA and the School of International Affairs. We will fight you about your control of black people in Morningside Heights, Harlem, and the campus itself. And we will fight you about the type of mis-education you are trying to channel us through. We will have to destroy at times, even violently, in order to end your power and your system—but that is a far cry from nihilism.

Grayson, I doubt if you will understand any of this, since your fantasies have shut out the world as it really is from your thinking. Vice President [David B.] Truman [of Columbia] says the society is basically sound; you say the war in Vietnam was a well-intentioned accident. We, the young people, whom you so rightly fear, say that the society is sick and you and your capitalism are the sickness.

You call for order and respect for authority; we call for justice, freedom, and socialism.

There is only one thing left to say. It may sound nihilistic to you, since it is the opening shot in a war of liberation. I'll use the words of LeRoi Jones, whom I'm sure you don't like a whole lot: "Up against the wall, motherfucker, this is a stick-up."

Yours for freedom,
Mark [Rudd]

Many young people shared most of Mark Rudd's criticisms and dreams but repudiated his militant language and tactics. Despite tactical disagreements, however, the challenge of youth was serious enough to prompt older Americans to reexamine the positive values and accomplishments of the American experience. Eric Sevareid, political analyst for CBS television news, has been for many years an astute observer of America. His judgment enjoys the perspective of one who has lived through and analyzed two world wars, the Cold War, the depression, and the social crises of the sixties. In an article on "The American Dream" in *Look* (July 9, 1968), Sevareid took an optimistic look at America. The article was copyrighted in 1968 by Eric Sevareid and reprinted by permission of the Harold Matson Company, Inc. Significantly, his article included eight pages of photographs depicting quiet, idyllic scenes of midwestern America "beyond the cities," Sevareid's own background. What is the basis of his confidence in America, and do you think his optimism is justified? Do you agree with Sevareid's convictions that laws will eradicate racism and that the end of the war in Vietnam will represent "a victory in our own soul"? What views, if any, are shared by Sevareid and the other authors in this chapter?

The Dream Lives On

ERIC SEVAREID

There are those who say the dream is dead or dying, poisoned by self-interest, rotted by surfeit and indifference, maimed by violence. The great aspiration is ended, they tell us, and America is now only another crowded nation, not even able to maintain order; a Power, but not a society, not a culture. We have gone, almost directly, they would have us believe, from primitiveness to decadence, a far poorer record than that of Rome.

The fireworks of this July 4—which may well illuminate the scene, again, of whole urban blocks consumed by flames, from the Molotov cocktail, not the holiday sparkler—will give further force to this cry of the Cassandras.

But the cry is as old as the nation. It was sounded in Jefferson's time, when the states seemed ready to drift apart; in Lincoln's time, when they split apart; in Roosevelt's time, when, by the millions, husbands shuffled in soup lines; in Truman's time, when the Russians and Chinese were supposedly reordering the earth and Communist traitors were supposedly infesting the Government.

But this is not It—this is not our Armageddon, not the great day of judgment on America. For America is change, and the changes have come, often enough, in convulsive spasms. This country is the vast experimental laboratory in human relations for the twentieth century; it is, in a sense, defining and creating the twentieth century for much of the world.

Unless it is seen in this light, America cannot be understood at all. If many of our contemporary intellectuals, especially those communing with one another in New York City, almost a separate nation in spirit, do not understand it, this is partly because they do not understand themselves. As they attest in innumerable books, they do not know who they are. It may be news to them that the overwhelming majority of Americans *do* know who they are, do *not* feel alienated from their country or their generation. . . .

Why, then, are we in such a state of uproar in this year of Our Lord, and why is much of the world upset about the America of today? Because, as a philosopher once said, "nothing that is vast enters into the life of mortals without a curse," and America is struggling to rid itself of one old curse and one new one. The old curse is the Negro slavery Europeans fastened upon this land long ago, which continues in a hundred psychological, social and economic, if not legal, forms. The Negro Passion of today is a revolution within the continuing American revolution, and the one absolute certainty about it is that it is going to succeed, however long and distracting the agony for everyone. It will succeed not only because it has justice with it (justice has been suppressed before) but because there is a deep evangelical streak in the American people, a true collective conscience, and it has been aroused.

Racism exists in almost all societies on this globe, virulently so, incidentally, in Black Africa. It may be that race prejudice—the psychologists' "stranger hatred"—is an instinct tracing from our animal origins, and therefore ineradicable. Yet man is the only animal *aware* of his instincts; the only animal, therefore, capable of controlling, if not eliminating, his instincts. New law, enforced, compels new behavior. Behavior repeated daily comes to seem normal, and attitudes change. Illusions tend to vanish. The idea that a difference in skin color is an essential difference is an illusion. I am struck by an observation of

McGeorge Bundy of the Ford Foundation. He said discrimination will end, partly because this college generation regards racial equality as natural, whereas the older generation regards it only as logical.

The twentieth-century war over racial injustice is now in its virulent stage. The nineteenth-century war in its virulent stage lasted four years. This one will last much longer because it is fought on a thousand narrow fronts, like guerrilla war, and because no grand climacteric is possible. But it is not going to "tear this country apart" or "burn America down" or anything of the sort. A tiny percentage of extremists among only 12 percent of the American population can do much, but they cannot do that.

The new curse has come with America's new military power. A form of Parkinson's Law operates here. The greater the power, the more the men who associate with it, extoll it and find needs, real or sophistical, for its use. The use of available, flexible force becomes easier than hard thought; and the worst aspect of the curse is the gradual, almost unconscious identification of power with virtue. . . .

We have fallen into this trap with the Vietnam intervention. For the first time, we have misused our power on a massive scale. But it does not mean that we are a "Fascist" or aggressive people, any more than the racial mess means that we are a hating or oppressive people. Vietnam is not typical; it is a mistake, now recognized as such by most serious thinkers in this country. If millions of people in Europe (every province of which is soaked in blood) stand aghast at what we have done and reproach us bitterly, one unarticulated reason is that they *expect* the United States to act with humaneness and common sense. They do not shout advice to Russia and China, whatever their misdeeds, for the same reason that the crowd in the bullring does not shout advice to the bull but to the bullfighter.

The reassuring thing is not merely that we will get out of this trap and undo the damage as best we can but that we will do so because our own people demand it, not because the enemy is too strong, not because of foreign criticism. We could, if we would, lay North Vietnam totally waste. The American conscience will not permit it. We may not win a military victory in Vietnam, but we will win a victory in our own soul.

No—the humaneness of the American people is still here. The new problems have piled up too rapidly for our brains and our institutions to cope with at anything like the same rate, but the will for justice is as strong as ever—stronger, in my own belief, because thought and expression are freer today than ever before. This is why the Negro revolution has come now—not because conditions of life became worse, save for some, but because of a climate of free expression. In just such periods of great intellectual freedom have nearly all revolutions been generated.

It is a remarkable fact that great numbers of very ordinary people in distant lands understand all this about America better than some of our own intellectuals. If, by some magic, all barriers to emigration and immigration around the world were lifted tomorrow, by far the single biggest human caravan would start moving in one direction—our way.

One day recently, I asked a Cuban refugee why most Cubans like himself want to come to the United States rather than go to Latin American countries with the same language and the same general culture. Was it just the thought of greater economic opportunity?

"No," he said, "many of us would have an easier time, economically, in a Latin country. It's just that we feel better here. We can feel like a human being. There seems to be something universal about this country."

This is living testimony, not abstract argument, from men who know the meaning of America in their bones and marrow. Of course, it is the truth. Of course, the dream lives on.

Let those who wish compare America with Rome. Rome lasted around a thousand years.

The sixties ended as they began, with renewed affirmation of the promises and expected fulfillment of the American dream. On August 8, 1968, one month after the publication of Sevareid's article and four months after the assassination of Martin Luther King, Richard Nixon delivered his speech accepting the Republican party nomination for President. A small portion from the end of his address is reprinted below. What similarities exist in the speeches by both Nixon and King? To what extent does this short excerpt reveal the essential dilemma in the American dream between collective idealistic promises and personal achievements of success? Mr. Nixon, of course, did succeed; he rose from obscurity and defeat to become President of the United States. How successful has he been in securing the help he sought in order to make the "impossible dream" come true for others? Which of the dreamers in this chapter comes closest to uttering your own dreams?

⊂⊒ The President's Dream

RICHARD M. NIXON

Tonight I see the face of a child. He lives in a great city. He's black or he's white, he's Mexican, Italian, Polish—none of that matters. What matters is he's an American child. That child in that great city is more important than any politician's promise. He is America. He is a poet; he's a scientist; he's a great teacher; he's a proud craftsman. He's everything we ever hoped to be and everything we dare to dream to be. He sleeps the sleep of childhood and he dreams the dreams of a child.

And yet, when he awakens, he awakens to a living nightmare of poverty and neglect and despair. He fails in school; he ends up on welfare. For him the American system is one that feeds his stomach and starves his soul. It breaks his heart. And in the end it may take his life on some distant battlefield. To millions of children in this rich land, this is their prospect for the future.

But this is only part of what I see in America. I see another child tonight. He hears the train go by at night, and he dreams of faraway places where he'd like to go. It seems like an impossible dream. But he is helped on his journey through life. A father who had to go to work before he finished the sixth grade sacrificed everything he had so that his sons could go to college. A gentle Quaker mother with a passionate concern for peace quietly wept when he went to war, but she understood why he had to go. A great teacher, a remarkable football coach, an inspirational minister encouraged him on his way. A courageous wife and loyal children stood by him in victory and also in defeat. And in his chosen profession of politics, first there were scores, then hundreds, then thousands, and finally millions who worked for his success. And tonight he stands before you nominated for President of the United States of America.

You can see why I believe so deeply in the American dream. For most of us the American Revolution has been won, the American dream has come true. And what I ask you to do tonight is to help me make that dream come true for millions to whom it's an impossible dream today.